William Greaves

William Greaves

FILMMAKING AS MISSION

Edited by
Scott MacDonald and
Jacqueline Najuma Stewart

Columbia University Press

New York

Columbia University Press
Publishers Since 1893
New York   Chichester, West Sussex
cup.columbia.edu

Copyright © 2021 Columbia University Press
All rights reserved

Library of Congress Cataloging-in-Publication Data
Names: MacDonald, Scott, 1942– editor. | Stewart, Jacqueline Najuma, 1970– editor.
Title: William Greaves : filmmaking as mission / edited by Scott MacDonald and Jacqueline Najuma Stewart.
Description: New York : Columbia University Press, [2021] | Includes bibliographical references, filmography, and index.
Identifiers: LCCN 2020047650 (print) | LCCN 2020047651 (ebook) |
ISBN 9780231199582 (hardback) | ISBN 9780231199599 (trade paperback) |
ISBN 9780231553193 (ebook)
Subjects: LCSH: Greaves, William—Criticism and interpretation. | Documentary films—United States—History and criticism. | Experimental films—United States—History and criticism. | Documentary television programs—United States—History and criticism. | African American motion picture producers and directors—Biography. | African American television producers and directors—Biography.
Classification: LCC PN1998.3.G7265 W55 2021 (print) | LCC PN1998.3.G7265 (ebook) |
DDC 791.4302/33092 [B]--dc23
LC record available at https://lccn.loc.gov/2020047650
LC ebook record available at https://lccn.loc.gov/2020047

Cover image: William Greaves during the shooting of *Symbiopsychotaxiplasm: Take One* in 1968. Courtesy Louise Archambault Greaves.

For Louise Archambault Greaves

Contents

Acknowledgments xiii

Preface. William Greaves: Renaissance Man and Race Man
JACQUELINE NAJUMA STEWART AND SCOTT MacDONALD *xvii*

Note on Style xxxi

1. William Greaves, Documentary Filmmaking, and the African-American Experience
   Adam Knee and Charles Musser 1

2. Meta-interview with William Greaves (an Audiobiography)
   Scott MacDonald 17

3. Interview with Louise Archambault Greaves
   Scott MacDonald 96

4. Interview with David Greaves
   Scott MacDonald 107

5. The Efficacy of Acting
   Katherine Kinney 114

6. POEM/1965
William Greaves 137

7. The First World Festival of Negro Arts:
An Afro-American View
William Greaves 139

8. Views Across the Atlantic: An American Vision
of the First World Festival of Negro Arts
Joseph L. Underwood 148

9. Sisters Inside *Still a Brother: Inside the Negro Middle Class*:
Black Women Through the Lens of William Greaves
Jacqueline Najuma Stewart 161

10. The Documentary as Sociodrama: William Greaves's
In the Company of Men (1969) and *The Deep North* (1988)
J. J. Murphy 187

11. Pugilism and Performance: William Greaves, Muhammad Ali,
and the Making of *The Fight*
Alexander Johnston 206

12. *Black Journal*: A Few Notes from the Executive Producer
William Greaves 226

13. 100 Madison Avenues Will Be of No Help
William Greaves 233

14. *Black Journal*: A Personal Look Backward
St. Clair Bourne 239

15. "By, For and About": *Black Journal* and the Rise of Multicultural Documentary in New York City, 1968–1975
Charles Musser   246

16. William Greaves, *Black Journal*, and the Long Roots of Black Internationalism
Celeste Day Moore   271

17. Government-Sponsored Film and *Latinidad*: *Voice of La Raza* (1971)
Laura Isabel Serna   285

18. Afterthoughts on the Black American Film Festival
William Greaves   299

19. *Ida B. Wells: A Passion for Justice*: Personal Production Notes
Michelle Duster   303

Dossier on the *Symbiopsychotaxiplasm* Films   309

20. Proposal: *Theatrical Short Subject*
William Greaves   311

21. *Symbiopsychotaxiplasm: Take One* Rediscovered: A Conversation with Dara Meyers-Kingsley
Scott MacDonald   315

22. The Country in the City: Central Park as Metaphor in Jonas Mekas's *Walden* and William Greaves's *Symbiopsychotaxiplasm: Take One*
Scott MacDonald   319

23. "Just Another Word for Jazz":
The Signifying Auteur in William Greaves's
Symbiopsychotaxiplasm: Take One (Excerpt)
Akiva Gottlieb   336

24. Symbiopsychotaxiplasm: Take 2
William Greaves   341

25. Some Concepts and Logistics in Shooting
the Two Excerpts of Take 2½
William Greaves   344

26. The Symbiopsychotaxiplasm Effect
on Filmmaking Dynamics: An Editor's Examination of the Power
of Corruption on Expectations in Filmmaking
William Greaves   346

27. The Symbio Cinematic Environment:
An Aesthetic yet Scientific Theory for the Film
William Greaves   348

28. The Daring, Original, *and* Overlooked:
Symbiopsychotaxiplasm: Take One
Richard Brody   350

29. Still No Answers
Amy Taubin   356

30. "We're Not Raping Bill": Race and Gender Politics in
Symbiopsychotaxiplasm: Take One and *Take 2½*
Joan Hawkins   362

31. Symbiopsychotaxiplasticity: Some Takes on William Greaves
    Franklin Cason, Jr., and Tsitsi Jaji   374

32. A Guy Who Could Think Around the Corner:
    Ralph Bunche: An American Odyssey
    Patricia R. Zimmermann   395

33. Revealing Greaves: Unhiding His Archive
    Shola Lynch   413

Filmography   421
Bibliography   431
Contributors   437
Index   443

Acknowledgments

Many people and several organizations have provided various forms of support over the years for what has become *William Greaves: Filmmaking as Mission*. From the beginning, we had the enthusiasm and continuous assistance of Louise Archambault Greaves, William Greaves's widow, whose commitment to her partner's mission and work remains fierce. Of course, Louise Greaves's own labors, both domestic and over the years increasingly professional, were crucial for William and the many films and television shows he produced, wrote, directed, and filmed. We could not have done this book without Louise, and we have dedicated it to her.

In addition to her personal support of our project, Louise Greaves made her photographic archive available to us. Jennifer Friede assisted the three of us in working through the photographs to begin finding those that seemed most relevant to our project, and Louise, Muriel Peters, Kent Garrett, and Artemis Willis helped us identify people in the photographs.

Louise Greaves also kindly agreed to our publishing, for the first time, several of William Greaves's writings related to the *Symbiopsychotaxiplasm* films, including "Proposal: *Theatrical Short Subject*"; "Symbiopsychotaxiplasm: Take 2"; "Some Concepts and Logistics in Shooting the Two Excerpts of Take 2½"; "The Symbiopsychotaxiplasm Effect on Filming Dynamics"; and "The Symbio Cinematic Environment: An Aesthetic Yet Scientific Theory for the Film"; as well as "100 Madison Avenues Will Be of No Help," reprinted from the *New York Times*, August 9, 1970; and "POEM/1965."

In the summer of 2018 we hosted a workshop on our Greaves project as part of the Visible Evidence conference, held that year at Indiana University in Bloomington. Our panel included Terri Francis (Indiana University, Black Film

Center/Archive), Joan Hawkins (Indiana University, Bloomington), Irina Leimbacher (Keene State University), Louis Massiah (Scribe Video Center, Philadelphia), J. J. Murphy (emeritus professor, University of Wisconsin-Madison), Charles Musser (Yale University), Patricia Zimmermann (Ithaca College), and Louise Archambault Greaves, whose enthusiasm and support confirmed our efforts. Many of the conference participants attended the session and demonstrated their interest in and excitement about Greaves and his work. Janice Frisch, then acquisitions editor at Indiana University Press, was present for the workshop, recognized the significance of a William Greaves book, and enthusiastically confirmed our belief that our project would be a significant contribution to film scholarship.

Out of respect for William and Louise Greaves and their work, two indefatigable individuals went out of their way to be friends of this project at crucial moments. During the spring of 2020 the historian/filmmaker Paul Cronin (who has often included *Symbiopsychotaxiplasm: Take One* in his courses at the School of Visual Arts in New York City) offered to support this project in any way he could and, with the assistance of Ryan Bojanovic, was invaluable in preparing many of the photographs for publication.

In late spring 2020 Su Friedrich, independent filmmaker and filmmaking professor at Princeton University, helped us make contact with Michelle Duster and then joined in the effort to finish this book, providing assistance and support in various ways. Friedrich has made her own significant contribution to William Greaves studies by working with Louise Archambault Greaves to update and expand the Greaves website, www.williamgreaves.com.

During the several years we have worked on this project, both of us have had institutional support from our home institutions. In 2018 Margaret Gentry, then dean of the faculty at Hamilton College, provided a subvention that made possible our access to and use of Louise Greaves's collection of photographs, and during the spring of 2019 she granted Scott MacDonald a course reduction that allowed him to devote much of his time to the project. Digital media technology specialist Benjamin Salzman assisted MacDonald when digital challenges arose.

At the University of Chicago, the Division of the Humanities provided Jacqueline Stewart with research funding that paid for our reprinting the Laura Isabel Serna essay, "Government-Sponsored Film and *Latinidad*: *Voice of La Raza* (1971)"; many thanks to Duke University Press. Stewart's research funding also provided a subvention to Columbia University Press and paid for the index. Stewart's colleague, graduate student Aurore Spiers, was invaluable in constructing as complete a filmography of Greaves's career as has been possible so far and an extensive bibliography of writings about Greaves and his films. Spiers continued this work, begun by Nicole Morse, to make these materials available to the book's contributors throughout the process of researching and writing.

In the wake of the development of the Covid-19 pandemic during the spring of 2020, the Academy of Motion Picture Arts and Sciences, specifically the FilmWatch program, made it possible for us to redirect a portion of a grant it had awarded to Hamilton College for a film series devoted to Greaves's work to *William Greaves: Filmmaking as Mission* instead (which will function as a catalog for the film series when it is offered). We are grateful to Shawn Guthrie, in particular, for his support. At Hamilton, Krista Campbell first alerted Scott MacDonald to the FilmWatch program, then helped with the application for funding and with the redirection of some of the funds to this book.

Our thanks also go to Jane Gaines (Columbia University), who made clear to us that Columbia University Press was the obvious choice to take on the Greaves project, since Greaves was a lifelong New Yorker who grew up in Harlem and had had many contacts with Columbia over the years. We are especially grateful to Philip Leventhal, senior editor at Columbia University Press, who quickly recognized that a William Greaves book was long overdue and has been consistently supportive of our efforts.

Many thanks to our families—especially Maiya and Noble Austen, and Patricia Reichgott O'Connor and Ian MacDonald—for the ongoing love, support, and patience that sustain any scholarly project, particularly one completed during a period of singularly intense household and social stresses.

We are also grateful to be able to reprint several significant essays by Greaves and a number of seminal contributions to earlier Greaves scholarship. The Greaves essays include "The First World Festival of Negro Arts: An Afro-American View," reprinted from *The Crisis* 73, no. 6 (June–July 1966): 309–14, 332; "*Black Journal*: A Few Notes from the Executive Producer," reprinted from *Television Quarterly* 8, no. 4 (Fall 1969): 66–72; and "Afterthoughts on the Black American Film Festival," reprinted from *Black American Literature Forum* (now *African American Review*) 25, no. 2 (summer 1991): 433–36.

During 2018–2019 we worked with the many scholars who have contributed to this project by allowing us to reprint crucial early contributions to Greaves scholarship and/or by writing original essays. Reprinted essays by scholars, some of them with corrections and modifications since the original publication, include Adam Knee and Charles Musser's "William Greaves, Documentary Filmmaking, and the African-American Experience," reprinted from *Film Quarterly* 45, no. 3 (Spring 1992): 13–25; St. Clair Bourne's "*Black Journal*: A Personal Look Backward," originally published as an online feature, dated April 1, 1989, of the Spring/Summer 1989 issue of *Documentary*; Laura Isabel Serna's

"Government-Sponsored Film and *Latinidad: Voice of La Raza* (1971)," which originally appeared in *Screening Race in American Nontheatrical Film*, edited by Allyson Nadia Field and Marsha Gordon (Duke University Press, 2019); Scott MacDonald's, "The Country in the City: Central Park as Metaphor in Jonas Mekas's *Walden* and William Greaves's *Symbiopsychotaxiplasm: Take One*," *Journal of American Studies* 31, no. 3 (December 1997): 337–60, then, revised, as chapter 7 in *The Garden in the Machine* (University of California Press, 2001); an excerpt from Akiva Gottlieb's "'Just Another Word for Jazz': The Signifying Auteur in William Greaves's *Symbiopsychotaxiplasm: Take One*," originally published in *Black Camera* 5, no.1 (Fall 2013); Richard Brody's "The Daring, Original, *and* Overlooked: *Symbiopsychotaxiplasm: Take One*," which appeared in the *New Yorker*, February 5, 2015; Amy Taubin's "Still No Answers," reprinted from the booklet accompanying the Criterion DVD release in 2006 of *Symbiopsychotaxiplasm: Take One* and *Symbiopsychotaxiplasm: Take 2½* (thanks too to Liz Helfgott at Criterion for allowing us to use Taubin's essay); and Franklin Cason, Jr., and Tsitsi Jaji's "Symbiopsychotaxiplasticity: Some Takes on William Greaves," reprinted from *Cultural Studies* 28, no. 4 (March 2014): 574–93.

Preface

William Greaves: Renaissance Man and Race Man

JACQUELINE NAJUMA STEWART AND SCOTT MacDONALD

The complex career of William Greaves remains among the most productive and diverse in the annals of American cultural history. Growing up in a working-class family in Harlem in the apartheid American society of the 1930s–1940s, Greaves, from a young age, seemed able to defy whatever limitations he faced by taking full advantage of the opportunities that Harlem made available to him. He was born in 1926 during the heyday of the Harlem Renaissance, and by the 1940s he was a successful songwriter whose songs were being recorded by major recording artists, a dancer performing with Pearl Primus at Carnegie Hall, and an actor in Broadway productions. A member of the Actors Studio from 1948, Greaves had featured roles in several of the last independent Black-cast "race movies"—*The Fight Never Ends* (Joseph Lerner, 1948), *Miracle in Harlem* (Jack Kemp, 1948), and *Souls of Sin* (Powell Lindsay, 1949)—and in the Hollywood "problem picture," *Lost Boundaries* (Alfred L. Werker, 1949), and he would continue to teach acting for many years. Against all odds, he would become one of the most prolific filmmakers of his era and the most prolific African-American documentary filmmaker of all time.

From the beginning, Greaves saw filmmaking, and documentary filmmaking in particular, as a way of channeling his artistic impulse, so evident throughout his youth and young adulthood, into a creative practice that might contribute to a more humane understanding of the realities of American and world history. He hoped to use his artistic gifts not only to help expand the possibilities of documentary filmmaking itself, but to dignify the ways in which modern people, of whatever ethnicity and from whatever background, thought about themselves and others. Greaves was the ultimate humanist, both spiritually directed and politically aware. For many years he was a devotee of the work of Indian philosopher, poet, and guru Sri Aurobindo. The trajectory of Greaves's filmmaking life, which is echoed by the structure of this book, demonstrates his fundamental commitment to a deepening recognition of immediate political realities and to an expansive and expanding global awareness.

During the late 1940s Greaves became interested in directing films and in documentary filmmaking. Since he could find no opportunities for documentary film training for African Americans in the United States, he moved to Canada to apprentice at the National Film Board, first in Ottawa and then, when the NFB moved to Montreal in 1956, in Montreal, where he honed his filmmaking craft by working in one crew capacity or another on any production he could join. In Canada, Greaves became a member of the first cinéma-vérité documentary unit in North America, while also instigating and teaching acting workshops modeled on the Actors Studio in Montreal, Ottawa, and Toronto.

Though there were considerable opportunities for Greaves at the NFB, as there had been on Broadway, by the early 1960s he had come to understand that his mission as filmmaker was to use filmmaking as part of the American Civil Rights Movement. He had become committed to documentary filmmaking because he believed in its potential for transforming how European Americans understood African-American life, history, and struggle, and for rehabilitating African Americans' senses of identity and pride. In 1959 he married his lifelong partner, Louise Archambault Greaves. They moved to the United States in 1963 and went to work raising a family and producing often award-winning films, first for the United Nations, then for the United States Information Agency. William and Louise established their own production company, William Greaves Productions, in 1964.

Many of the Greaves films explored crucial events, situations, and personalities relating to African-American history, culture, and politics. And when it became clear, in the wake of the National Advisory Commission on Civil Disorders (the Kerner Commission) report of 1968, that there was a need for a nationally broadcast television news show focused on African-American issues, Greaves became the executive producer and cohost of the Emmy Award–winning *Black Journal*, while continuing to produce and distribute his own films.

From the outset, Greaves was less interested in becoming a filmmaker than in using filmmaking to create change, and particularly to correct falsehoods and misunderstandings regarding the contributions that African Americans had made to the United States and to the world. As he would say later, "I'd rejected the idea of going out to Hollywood. It felt like working out there would be like working on a plantation: you had to answer to the Man for everything you did.

We had a different mission." And while his documentaries won many awards and were recognized for their artistry and technical excellence, Greaves was not as interested in becoming known as an auteur or being identified with a particular approach or style as he was in using whatever cinematic options that presented themselves for making the most effectively informational and consciousness-raising films he could.

It is likely that Greaves's refusal to wed himself to a specific filmmaking mode has played a role in keeping many of his films from receiving the serious attention they deserve. Greaves's return to the United States coincided with the flowering of cinéma-vérité documentary; that is, sync-sound shooting from within events as they develop. This included both the French approach exemplified by Jean Rouch in *Chronique d'un été—Paris 1960* (1961), where shooting was used to provoke revelations about individuals and the world, and what Erik Barnouw called "direct cinema," where filmmakers like the Maysles brothers and Frederick Wiseman (and Greaves, in *Emergency Ward* [1959]) worked to be "flies on the wall," recording events, insofar as feasible, without interfering with what they recorded. Whereas the cinéma-vérité filmmakers had a preferred method and found topics this method could effectively explore, Greaves decided on what situation or topic needed to be illuminated by a film, then adapted his production process in whatever ways were best suited for that project.

COMMITTED TO EXPERIMENTATION

Given the dearth of documentary films about the history, realities, and complexities of African-American life in the United States when Greaves began making films, the very decision to make a film about one or another aspect of the African-American experience could be considered an experiment. The rare exceptions—for example, *All My Babies: A Midwife's Own Story* (George Stoney, 1953) and *The Quiet One* (Sidney Meyers, in collaboration with James Agee, Helen Levitt, and Janice Loeb, 1948)—were essentially acts of courage. For Greaves to document a Black psychiatrist and a White psychodramatist exploring how to build bridges between White factory managers and "hard-core unemployed" Black workers in Georgia for *In the Company of Men* (1969), or to face the challenge, on his own, of documenting the first national Black political convention for what became *Nationtime—Gary* (1973), involved a determination to try things that had never been done before: that is, to experiment and see what filmmaking could discover and communicate.

Over the decades, Greaves worked in a wide variety of ways, many of them unusual and experimental, sometimes even when, to modern audiences, aspects of what he did can now seem conventional—in some instances, for example, their use of "voice-of-god" narrators. But even when he used documentary conventions, Greaves often combined them with unusual approaches. In *From These Roots* (1974), he celebrates the accomplishments and impact of the Harlem Renaissance entirely in still photographs, accompanied by actor Brock Peters's narration and an original score by Eubie Blake. In his documentation of the buildup to the first heavyweight fight between Muhammad Ali and Joe Frazier, direct cinema seemed the best option, but an innovative multicamera setup allowed the fight itself to be seen in an entirely new way. For *Still a Brother: Inside the Negro Middle Class* (1968), Greaves chose a combination of interviews, narration (by Ossie Davis), on-the-street footage, editorializing music, and even a campy dramatization lampooning Black elitism to illustrate the economic and cultural complexities of middle-class African-American life during the emergence of Black Power consciousness.

During his time with *Black Journal*, Greaves brought a Pan-African sensibility to American television that was entirely novel, producing episodes of the show that dignified the complex history of African peoples and their many contributions to world culture. And for his project on Nobel Peace Prize laureate and diplomat Ralph Bunche, a feature documentary on the diplomat's epic career, *Ralph Bunche: An American Odyssey* (2001), was later accompanied by a multifaceted set of video modules designed for classroom use, along with an elaborate website and study guide.

Though he was always more interested in education than in cine-entertainment, Greaves was not afraid to test the waters of the film industry when he thought it might be open to films that served his fundamental goals. He was executive producer for Universal Pictures' *Bustin' Loose* (1981), starring Richard Pryor—an experience that, in the end, returned him to documentary. Greaves's mission to be, insofar as possible, a changemaker came first, and throughout his career he remained committed to a fierce independence in getting his work done. On most of his films, he was his own producer and director, usually his own writer and cameraperson, and (with Louise Archambault Greaves) his own publicity person and distributor.

It is perhaps the central irony of Greaves's long, productive career that his experiment in cine-metaphysics, *Symbiopsychotaxiplasm: Take One*, seemingly a cine-vacation from more serious documentary filmmaking, has become his best-known film, at least among cineastes and film scholars. For the film (shot in 1968; first edited version, 1971), Greaves employed a virtually unprecedented way of filming a film being made and constructed a feature docu-entertainment that is simultaneously reflective and critical of American culture and implicitly utopic. Misunderstood and ignored when Greaves attempted to find a distributor and shelved for decades, *Symbiopsychotaxiplasm: Take One* was rediscovered in 1991 and has since become canonical and widely recognized as one of film history's most engaging films about filmmaking. In recent decades it has drawn new attention to Greaves's other work, and its growing reputation instigated *Symbiopsychotaxiplasm: Take 2½* (2005), made with the support of Steve Buscemi and Steven Soderbergh.

Despite the fact that during the years when Greaves's films were being produced they regularly won awards and were fixtures in public and academic 16mm film libraries across the country, most of his many accomplishments remain under the current cultural and film-historical radar. In some measure, this is a function of the fact that, throughout his career, Greaves believed that whatever experiments he was willing to attempt needed to be accessible to general audiences who would see his films not in commercial theaters or on television, or as part of the New York "underground" where experimental or "avant-garde" film was the order of the day, but in college classrooms, public libraries, community centers, churches, or union gatherings; that is, in circumstances where general audiences could expect culturally and historically informational films to be presented in a relatively predictable manner that was understandable and useful to them. Above all, Greaves was an educator, in the best sense: he was devoted to providing information and broadening the understanding of those who might see his films.

It seems likely that the long-standing lack of scholarly and critical attention to the history of what traditionally have been called "educational films" as well as other forms of "nontheatrical" cinema has worked against Greaves receiving the recognition he deserves. In recent years scholars and archivists have been paying increasing attention to nontheatrical film, as part of the recovery of "orphan" media histories. As more scholars explore the histories of educational and sponsored filmmaking, Greaves seems sure to have a prominent place.

BLACK MEDIA PIONEER

Greaves's focus on nontheatrical spheres for much of his career likely accounts for the lack of attention to his work in histories of African-American filmmaking, focused as they have been on identifying the stereotypical depictions of

African Americans in American commercial media and on recovering and highlighting Black cinematic auteurs. And yet, as Phyllis Klotman observes, Greaves is a crucial bridge between the era of "race movies" and the boom of Black independent filmmaking in the 1980s and 1990s. Reflecting on his work in the 1940s with Black independent feature and newsreel producer William Alexander, Greaves argued that the early Black pioneers (Alexander, Oscar Micheaux, Spencer Williams) were important forefathers of all American independent filmmakers, creating maverick stylistic and business strategies that could operate outside of the dominant film industry. Under the banner "William Greaves Productions," Greaves created a structure for his filmmaking that endured for decades, generating films that took ever-fresh approaches to Black subject matter and could be circulated in the comparatively evergreen nontheatrical market. The Williams Greaves Productions website (www.williamgreaves.com) functions now as catalog of his productivity, as testimony of his (and Louise's) business acumen, and as evidence of their early adoption of online tools for distribution.

On *Black Journal*, Greaves mentored a next generation of Black filmmakers. He directly affected the Black independent film scene on the East coast, including such accomplished figures as St. Clair Bourne, Madeline Anderson, and Kathleen Collins. More indirectly, his approach to filmmaking for social change is evident in the West Coast works of the LA Rebellion, filmmakers training at UCLA between the late 1960s and early 1980s with a mandate to speak of, for, and to the marginalized communities from which they came. We see nods to Greaves's vérité approach to Black life in the realist approaches we find in the fiction films of Charles Burnett, Haile Gerima, and Billy Woodberry shot in South Central Los Angeles. While these filmmakers received international cinephile and festival attention, closer to home they routinely screened their films in community centers, schools, libraries, and other sites where they, like Greaves, would find their intended communities. It is important to note that these and other LA Rebellion filmmakers have also made documentaries. Indeed, the turn to documentary that is routinely made by major Black filmmakers like Spike Lee and Ava DuVernay suggests the importance of tracing the relationships between Greaves's foundational documentary practice and the styles and circulation of "Black filmmaking" writ large.

Another important lesson Greaves's career teaches us is to reexamine tendencies to separate theatrical film productions from nontheatrical and television work. While scholars have downplayed works for television made by celebrated Black filmmakers like Burnett and Julie Dash, the contemporary "prestige" television landscape has been a productive space for serious filmmakers of all sorts, including African-American directors like Lee and DuVernay. Taking in the full scope of Black media making requires a deeper and more comprehensive understanding of the realms of television, documentary, sponsored film, and the avant-garde—domains Greaves identified and explored in compelling ways across his career. The stylistic radicalism we see in moving image works by a wide range of contemporary Black artists, including Arthur Jafa, Cauleen Smith, Martine Syms, Kevin Jerome Everson, Ytasha Womack, and Ja'Tovia Gary, picks up on threads Greaves laid out over decades of work: exploring multiple Black temporalities, recording testimonies of everyday Black subjects, detailing intimate dimensions of Black spaces and gestures, turning to Black music as a source of wisdom, reflection, and power.

Later in life, Greaves remembered that he had seen Oscar Micheaux in the flesh, walking down the street in Harlem with film reels under his arm. For Greaves, this childhood memory served to connect him to the wellspring of creative, socially engaged filmmaking and film business practices that Micheaux forged in the crucible of American racial segregation. All in all, Greaves's long career was itself an ongoing experiment in attempting to use filmmaking to make a measurable difference in a troubled society. What might an African-American filmmaker, committed to progressive social change, be able to accomplish in a lifetime?

WILLIAM GREAVES: FILMMAKING AS MISSION

William Greaves: Filmmaking as Mission is the first comprehensive attempt to come to terms with Greaves's career and to provide scholars with a foundational context for exploring his many films. The book's structure and design have been conceived in the hope of evoking both the multifaceted nature of his accomplishments and some of the many angles from which these accomplishments can be assessed. We hope to provide a substantial foundation for future scholarship, a "take one" of Greaves's achievements, in the expectation that other scholars will more easily follow our lead. This volume offers a panorama of approaches that deal in a variety of ways with general and specific elements of Greaves's life and career, including interviews; writings by Greaves himself; reminiscences and reviews; reprints of crucial early attempts by scholars to examine the many levels and layers of his career; a range of new explorations by critics and scholars from across the country; an update on the current state and plans for the Greaves archive at the New York Public Library's Schomburg Center for Research in

Black Culture; and the most detailed Greaves filmography and bibliography to date.

This preface is followed by "William Greaves, Documentary Filmmaking, and the African-American Experience" by Adam Knee and Charles Musser, a reprint of Greaves's favorite essay about his career and a useful introductory overview. Further context is created by the three interviews that follow. Chapter 2 is a meta-interview with Greaves, constructed by Scott MacDonald from edited versions of a broad range of interviews conducted in various ways by individuals and institutions at nodal points during Greaves's career. In lieu of a biography or an autobiography, the meta-interview is designed to provide readers with a sense of Greaves's childhood and maturation, and a record of his thinking during several eras of his film and media production. The meta-interview is followed by interviews with Louise Archambault Greaves (chapter 3) and with David Greaves (chapter 4), his son and sometimes collaborator.

The writings that form the body of the volume, by Greaves himself and by critics and scholars, are arranged as a rough chronological record of his activities. Greaves's own writings include "POEM/1965" (chapter 6), an unpublished poem that is heard as the final voice-over in his film *Wealth of a Nation*; and "The First World Festival of Negro Arts" (chapter 7), a review of a gathering of artists, musicians, and scholars in Dakar, Senegal, in April 1966, written for *The Crisis* and contextualized by Joseph L. Underwood's "Views Across the Atlantic: An American Vision of the First World Festival of Negro Arts" (chapter 8). Greaves's two essays on his experiences and accomplishments as executive producer for *Black Journal* include a report on the successes and challenges of the program during his tenure (chapter 12) and a polemical assessment of the situation of African Americans vis-à-vis television (chapter 13), written for the *New York Times* soon after Greaves left *Black Journal*. These are supplemented by St. Clair Bourne's "*Black Journal*: A Personal Look Backward" (chapter 14).

Greaves's review of his experiences (along with Donald Bogle, Ruby Dee, Ivan Dixon, Michelle Parkerson, and Cicely Tyson) at the twelfth annual International Film Festival (1989) in New Delhi, chapter 18, was written for *Black American Literature Forum* (now *African American Review*). Also offered are several previously unpublished writings about the *Symbiopsychotaxiplasm* films, including Greaves's original proposal for what became *Symbiopsychotaxiplasm: Take One* (chapter 20), written on March 9, 1967, and mailed to himself, apparently as a way of documenting and protecting his original concept. Several of the writings were produced during the preparation for and production of what would become *Symbiopsychotaxiplasm: Take 2½*.

The scholarly essays are wide ranging. Two focus on interests that played key roles in various Greaves films: his expertise as an actor and teacher of actors (Katherine Kinney's "The Efficacy of Acting," chapter 5) and his fascination with psychodrama (J. J. Murphy's "The Documentary as Sociodrama: William Greaves's *In the Company of Men* and *The Deep North*," chapter 10).

Other essays center on particular films or aspects of particular films: the depiction of women in *Still a Brother* (Jacqueline Stewart, "Sisters Inside *Still a Brother: Inside the Negro Middle Class*—Black Women Through the Lens of William Greaves," chapter 9); Greaves's film about Muhammad Ali, in several versions with various titles (Alexander Johnston, "Pugilism and Performance: William Greaves, Muhammad Ali, and the Making of *The Fight*," chapter 11); and Greaves's complex exploration of Latinx life in *Voice of La Raza* (Laura Isabel Serna, "Government-Sponsored Film and *Latinidad*: *Voice of La Raza*," chapter 17).

Two scholars focus on the significance of Greaves's years with *Black Journal*. Charles Musser's " 'By, For and About': *Black Journal* and the Rise of Multicultural Documentary in New York City, 1968–1975" (chapter 15) is followed by Celeste Day Moore's "William Greaves, *Black Journal*, and the Long Roots of Black Internationalism" (chapter 16).

Coverage of two other projects completes our foray into Greaves's oeuvre. First, we have assembled a dossier on the two *Symbiopsychotaxiplasm* films (1971, 2005), Greaves's two-pronged, microcosmic exploration of the psycho-philosophical dimensions of the filmmaking process and his most radical critique of the hierarchical organization of commercial filmmaking and its dedication to the financial bottom line. His own writings about the *Symbio* projects are supplemented by an interview with Dara Meyers-Kingsley (chapter 21), who discovered *Symbiopsychotaxiplasm: Take One* in a closet while curating a breakthrough retrospective of Greaves's career for the Brooklyn Museum (at the time, Missy Sullivan was manager of public programs and media).

The dossier offers a panorama of critical and scholarly approaches to the *Symbiopsychotaxiplasm* films. Scott MacDonald's "The Country in the City: Central Park as Metaphor in Jonas Mekas's *Walden* and William Greaves's *Symbiopsychotaxiplasm: Take One*" (chapter 22) explores the implications of Greaves's love and knowledge of Central Park, near to which he spent much of his life, within the immigrant context of Mekas's sense of the park as an urban Walden. Akiva Gottlieb, in an excerpt from his " 'Just Another Word for Jazz': The Signifying Auteur in William Greaves's *Symbiopsychotaxiplasm: Take One*" (chapter 23), details, among other things, the doubt of one of Greaves's collaborators, Bob Rosen, that Greaves knew what he was doing as he directed the film.

Richard Brody's *New Yorker* review, "The Daring, Original, *and* Overlooked: *Symbiopsychotaxiplasm: Take One*" (chapter 28), expresses the astonishment so many of us have felt when first seeing the film. Brody's critique was written in the wake of a screening of the film as part of "Tell It Like It Is: Black Independents in New York, 1968–1986," presented at Lincoln Center in February 2015 and followed by a discussion of the film with Brody, Su Friedrich, and Shola Lynch at the Brooklyn Historical Society. Amy Taubin's essay, "Still No Answers" (chapter 29), was written for the Criterion release of the two *Symbio* films. (The Criterion DVD, produced by Debra McClutchy, includes the film *Discovering William Greaves*.) In "'We're Not Raping Bill': Race and Gender Politics in *Symbiopsychotaxiplasm: Take One* and *Take 2½*" (chapter 30), Joan Hawkins sees a comment by Bob Rosen at a secret meeting of the crew during the filming of *Symbio* as a punctum for thinking about the political complexity of the *Symbio* films. And in "Symbiopsychotaxiplasticity: Some Takes on William Greaves" (chapter 31), Franklin Cason, Jr., and Tsitsi Jaji make a case for the two *Symbio* films to be understood as a single, ongoing project.

The scholarly essays conclude with "A Guy Who Could Think Around the Corner: *Ralph Bunche: An American Odyssey*" (chapter 32), Patricia R. Zimmermann's exploration of Greaves's Ralph Bunche project, the final major undertaking Greaves was able to complete. *Ralph Bunche* and its various satellite videos represent a macrocosmic commitment to the development of a fuller global awareness of racism and colonialism. Greaves understood the project not as an informative and inspiring stand-alone film but as a catalyst for an elaborate, ongoing educational process. From our perspective, nearly two decades later, we can understand the Bunche project as an early attempt at using a transmedia approach to effect change in the world.

The final essay, "Revealing Greaves: Unhiding His Archive," is by Shola Lynch, curator of the Moving Image & Recorded Sound Division at the Schomburg Center for Research in Black Culture (a division of the New York Public Library). Lynch describes her adventure in tracking down the Greaves films and papers housed at the Schomburg and elsewhere, and working to make Greaves's archive available to scholars and others committed to a broader awareness of African-American contributions to modern culture. The volume concludes with the most complete filmography of Greaves's work possible at this time, plus a bibliography of writings about his work, both assembled by Aurore Spiers.

In organizing *William Greaves: Filmmaking as Mission*, we have attempted to provide a sense of both the evolution of Greaves's career and the various kinds of personal, critical, and scholarly commentary that his work has attracted so far. In a number of instances, noteworthy attempts to assess Greaves's work have not been included here, or not included completely, because we wanted to avoid repetition. Our apologies for excerpting Akiva Gottlieb's essay and for not including both St. Clair Bourne's eloquent overview of Greaves's career, "An Independent for All Seasons," written in the wake of Greaves's career achievement award from the International Documentary Association (and published in the January 2005 issue of *International Documentary*), and Noelle Griffis's "'This Film Is a Rebellion': Filmmaker, Actor, *Black Journal* Producer and Political Activist William Greaves (1926–2014)," which appeared in the Spring 2015 issue of *Black Journal*.

TAKE ONE

The essays included in this collection reference many elements of Greaves's career, place his work within a wide range of contexts, and provide insight into crucial films. But it will be obvious to those already familiar with Greaves's accomplishments that there are significant gaps in our coverage. For example, there is barely a mention of Greaves's early successes as a songwriter. How did his involvement in songwriting affect other aspects of his career? Did he meet the musicians (Percy Faith, Al Hibler, Donna Hightower, Eartha Kitt, Arthur Prysock, and so on) who recorded his songs?

Many of Greaves's accomplished films are not discussed at length in this volume. His involvement in several of the final "race films" is fertile territory for further exploration, as are the many films he worked on, in various capacities, at the National Film Board of Canada. Greaves's evocation of the Harlem Renaissance, *From These Roots* (1974), which won many awards, deserves attention, as do the dozens of sponsored projects he produced.

Nationtime—Gary, originally considered too militant for television broadcast and now available in a 4K restoration, is the only substantive report on the National Black Political Convention held in Gary, Indiana, in 1972. We hope the premiere of the IndieCollect restoration of the long-lost full-length version of the film (funded by Jane Fonda and the Hollywood Foreign Press Association), which premiered at MoMA in New York City on January 22, 2020, will instigate further interest in a historic event that gathered Black voices from across the political spectrum (Jesse Jackson, Dick Gregory, Coretta Scott King, Richard Hatcher, Amiri Baraka, Charles Diggs, and H. Carl McCall, among others) for a collaborative imagining of the future of Black America.

FIGURE 0.1 Cover of sheet music for "African Lullaby," composed by William Greaves (copyright 1951). Courtesy Louise Greaves.

Greaves's explorations of crucial contributors to African-American history—*Booker T. Washington: The Life and Legacy* (1983), *Frederick Douglass: An American Life* (1985), *Ida B. Wells: A Passion for Justice* (1989), *A Tribute to Jackie Robinson* (1990), and "Resurrections: Paul Robeson" (1990)—a project for Black Entertainment Television that was researched but never produced—each worthy of attention, are represented here by a single essay: "*Ida B. Wells: A Passion for Justice*: Personal Production Notes" (chapter 19), Michelle Duster's reminiscence of her work as a production assistant on Greaves's film about her great-grandmother.

There are also Greaves's personal/professional relationships with other major contributors to African-American film history, from Spencer Williams, Sidney Poitier, and Harry Belafonte to Melvin Van Peebles, Kathleen Collins, Julie Dash, Stanley Nelson, and Spike Lee: How did his efforts contribute to their work and vice versa? And what about the wider world of filmmaking? What were Greaves's contacts with and thoughts about American commercial filmmakers and about directors from other cinematic traditions? How does his never-distributed fiction feature *The Marijuana Affair* (1976), produced for Film Jamaica Productions, fit within his career? There is so much to study, so much still to learn.

This book was inspired by and is to some extent modeled on *Oscar Micheaux and His Circle* (Indiana University Press, 2001), edited by Pearl Bowser, Jane Gaines, and Charles Musser—among the finest and most crucial books in the

FIGURE 0.2 Greaves, with Elia Kazan and Satyajit Ray, at a "Film India" event, circa 1983, sponsored by New York's Asia Society, the MoMA film department, and the Indo US Subcommission (probably at the opening of the Satyajit Ray retrospective, according to Muriel Peters, director of New York's Asia Society at the time). Photographer unknown. Courtesy Louise Greaves.

field. We hope our book will be understood as a worthy successor to that volume. William Greaves often thought of himself as a filmmaker who had taken the baton from Oscar Micheaux, and, like his predecessor, he was both immensely productive and widely influential. *William Greaves: Filmmaking as Mission* only begins to reveal the remarkable networks of filmmakers, television producers, critics, scholars, actors, writers, musicians, activists, and other interlocutors Greaves collaborated with and inspired over the decades. Of course, our dearest hope is that, as was true of *Oscar Micheaux and His Circle*, our efforts will bring the attention to his work that it has always deserved. We have already begun making plans, with the help of the Academy of Motion Picture Arts and Sciences (the FilmWatch initiative), for more than one series of events honoring Greaves's immense oeuvre.

Note on Style

Contributors to this volume have used varied capitalizations of racial identifiers (e.g., Black/White, black/white, Black/white). Greaves himself uses a different format depending on context: it is "I am furious Black" in "100 Madison Avenues Will Be of No Help" (*New York Times*); and "black" and "white" in "*Black Journal*: Notes from the Executive Producer," in *Television Quarterly*. We are adhering to the format chosen by the individual writers anthologized here.

William Greaves

I

William Greaves, Documentary Filmmaking, and the African-American Experience

ADAM KNEE AND CHARLES MUSSER

The reputations of many documentary filmmakers rest on their production of one or two groundbreaking pictures. But there are some, such as William Greaves, whose real achievements only become apparent when we look at the full accumulation of their work. In Greaves's case, this was made possible by a recent retrospective of his films at the Brooklyn Museum. It included a screening of his never-released, unconventional, cinémavérité-ish feature film *Symbiopsychotaxiplasm: Take One* (1968/1971), which is now being screened at festivals, art houses, and museums. Moreover, Greaves is still making innovative, rigorous films—as demonstrated by his documentary *Ida B. Wells: A Passion for Justice* (1989), a historical biography of the black feminist civil rights leader Ida Wells that recently aired on PBS's *The American Experience* and that has won numerous prizes on the festival circuit.

Black independent filmmaker Bill Greaves has played a significant if not always fully appreciated role in the creation of a new post-1968 era in U.S. documentary cinema—one that is characterized by greater cultural diversity among those making films. During the nineteen-fifties and early nineteen-sixties Greaves endured a protracted struggle to establish himself as a documentary filmmaker of artistic integrity. By the mid-nineteen-sixties he finally began to produce films on subjects of particular importance to African Americans. In 1968, while continuing to further develop his own still limited filmmaking opportunities, Greaves began to assist a new generation of young black documentarians through the initial stages of their professional careers—filmmakers such as Kent Garrett, Madeline Anderson, and St. Clair Bourne. Greaves was not only a harbinger of a new era of multicultural filmmaking but a pivotal figure in the history of African-American cinema.

Greaves, in addition to being an important historical force, has produced an impressive and surprisingly diverse body of work, both in approach and in subject matter. This testifies, on one hand, to his inventiveness and broad range of interests and, on the other, to the numerous practical exigencies he has faced over several decades. Greaves has received much recognition for his work as executive producer and cohost of public television's *Black Journal*, an Emmy-winning public-affairs series, and for his direction of such groundbreaking films as the historical documentary *From These Roots* (1974), which looks at Harlem during its cultural renaissance in the twenties and early thirties. However, the broader course of Greaves's career and the substantial contribution he has made to African-American film production—from acting in black-cast films during the nineteen-forties to serving as executive producer on Richard Pryor's 1981 hit, *Bustin' Loose*—are only now starting to receive adequate attention.

Even aside from the scores of films and television programs that Greaves has produced, directed, edited, photographed, written, and/or appeared in, his career itself deserves attention for the way it traces many aspects of African-American involvement in (and exclusion from) motion picture, television, and related industries. He was born and raised in Harlem and educated at Stuyvesant High School. While enrolled as an engineering student at City College of New York during the early forties, Greaves used his skills as a social dancer to become a performer in African dance troupes. From there he moved into acting at the American Negro Theatre (ANT) and was soon working in radio, television, and film. Among the films he was featured in (and sometimes sang in) at this time were the whodunit *Miracle in Harlem* (1947), one of the most technically polished of black-cast films, and the Louis de Rochemont–produced *Lost Boundaries* (1948), a popular film based on a true story about a black doctor who set up a practice in a New England town while "passing" for white.[1] The doctor and his family are played by white actors (in keeping with Hollywood conventions of the day), while Greaves portrays a debonair black college student who is completely comfortable with his African-American identity as he interacts with his white counterparts. It was an image seldom if ever seen in American films prior to that date. Greaves's role here clearly prefigured many of those played by Sidney Poitier in the next decade, and one is apt to wonder whether Greaves would have become one of the crossover stars of the fifties had he remained in screen acting.[2]

GREAVES ON *LOST BOUNDARIES*

You have to decide when you make a movie—and it's a tough decision—how authentic, how pure, how faithful you must be to reality while at the same time making this product so that people will go to see it. This is an extremely tricky, difficult challenge for a filmmaker. And in the climate of an extremely racist society, this was a marketing problem. Now *Lost Boundaries* turned out to be a massive hit. It ran for six months on Broadway, which was practically unheard of. It played at the Astor Theater and won awards and one thing or another. Mel Ferrer, the star, did a very fine piece of work. It was a very moving film. You say, Jesus, why didn't they have some light-skinned blacks in those roles? You can ask that question very aggressively today, but at the time you had to take into account the very cold temperature of the country.[3]

Greaves himself moved easily between the white and black worlds. After acting in such ANT productions as Owen Dodson's *Garden of Time* and *Henri Christophe*, he appeared in the musical *Finian's Rainbow,* which began a two-year run on Broadway in January 1947. As the show came to a close, Greaves joined the Actors Studio, becoming a member alongside Marlon Brando, Shelley Winters, Eli Wallach, and others. Despite this illustrious affiliation, Greaves was increasingly frustrated with the demeaning roles available to him (and blacks more generally) in theater and film. A decisive moment came in 1950, when he was slated to appear in the Broadway revival of Ben Hecht and Charles McArthur's *Twentieth Century*, starring Gloria Swanson and José Ferrer (who also directed and produced).[4] Upon reporting to the theater, Greaves discovered that he was to play a stereotypical bumbling porter and quit on the spot.

GREAVES ON *TWENTIETH CENTURY*

All I knew was that I had built up a little reputation and my agent said, "You have a part." So I reported to the theater. And then I saw this goddamn dialogue which they put in my hand and Ferrer said, "You're going to be this Uncle Tom type." I just walked out. Whenever that kind of role came up I would never play it, because it was just too demeaning. Actually that was the final straw. That was the thing that made me realize I have to get on the other side of the camera because they were messing with the image of black people with impunity.

Deciding he had to move into film production, Greaves enrolled in filmmaking courses at City College. With the exception of de Rochemont, who allowed him into the studio as an apprentice, no one seemed prepared to provide him the needed opportunities to achieve his goals. Like Melvin Van Peebles and many other African-American artists during the fifties, Greaves finally had to leave the country to practice his craft. In 1952, fed up with McCarthyism and the exclusionary practices of motion picture unions, Greaves moved to Canada.

GREAVES ON HIS MOVE TO CANADA

> It became obvious to me that either I would stay in America and allow myself to be made a fool of, or become a very neurotic person, or be destroyed. Or leave. So I left, which was fortunate because I had a very good opportunity in Canada. The Canadians were much more liberal than Americans. Race didn't have that much meaning to them. And I was fortunate to be taken onto the production staff of the National Film Board of Canada, set up by John Grierson.
>
> I had been reading Grierson on documentary and was very taken by his discussion of the social uses of film. He proposed ways in which film could be a social force, an educational tool, and this interested me.

Greaves worked his way up over the next six years at the National Film Board through various editing jobs to directorial work. His tenure there culminated with his directing and editing of *Emergency Ward* (1958), a production for the Canadian government that documents the events of a typical Sunday night at a Montreal hospital emergency room.

Stylistically, *Emergency Ward* falls somewhere between the "Free Cinema" of Lindsay Anderson's *Every Day Except Christmas* (1957), with its carefully prepared setups and tripod-dependent shooting style, and the cinéma-vérité style of *Lonely Boy* (1961), by Roman Kreiter and Wolf Koenig. (Not uncoincidentally, Koenig served as Greaves's cameraman on the film.) *Emergency Ward* was shot over the course of many nights and exposes us to the range of people admitted to the hospital: accident victims, people with imagined illness, people abandoned by their families, and others who are just plain lonely. Grierson's influence on Greaves is evident in this film: Greaves humanizes his subjects and reassures the viewer that the emergency ward at this institution is run as responsibly and as well as the post office in *Night Mail* (1936). The doctors know their jobs and care; orderlies and nurses are ennobled. At the same time, this film might be seen as a forerunner of Frederick Wiseman's *Hospital* (1968), for instance in its visual sensitivity to character quirks, although it ultimately lacks Wiseman's aggressiveness and sense of style. While Greaves found the subject matter fascinating, it offered little for him to grab hold of, given his reasons for moving behind the camera. In the all-white world of a Montreal hospital, black racial identity was not a pressing issue. Greaves learned his craft and escaped the humiliations of American racism in Canada, but it was not a place where he could readily develop the kind of distinctive voice he had displayed as an actor.

Greaves was perfectly positioned to participate in the cinéma-vérité revolution of the early sixties—until new senior management at the Film Board decided to place him in charge of its unit making science films. Sensing a dead end, Greaves left to create and direct with a Canadian acting troupe. In 1960 he joined the International Civil Aviation Organization (ICAO), an agency of the United Nations, as a public information officer. This, in turn, led to his making a one-hour television documentary about a round-the-world flight of a major airliner (*Cleared for Takeoff*, 1963; featuring Alistair Cooke). The UN job eventually required Greaves to move back to New York.

Greaves was by this time eager to return to the United States, as race relations were rapidly changing: the Civil Rights movement was gaining momentum, and Kennedy's New Frontier was seeking to respond to its demands. New York filmmaker Shirley Clarke had seen *Emergency Ward* and was impressed. She told George Stevens, Jr., who was head of the United States Information Agency's film division, about Greaves, and Stevens, looking for a black director, soon contracted with him to do a documentary on dissent in America. The topic quickly proved too controversial for the agency, especially when it learned that Greaves planned to include people like professed atheist Madalyn E. Murray, the "no prayers in the school" leader, in the film. USIA subsequently decided to change the film's focus to freedom of expression. Essentially, the resulting *Wealth of a Nation* (1964) maintains that America is great in part because its citizens are allowed "to do their own thing." In this context, Martin Luther King, Jr.'s, "I have a dream" speech at the Lincoln Memorial takes on unexpected meaning, suggesting a purely personal vision rather than the expression of a larger political movement. Featuring footage of various artists and visionary architects at work, the film relies on a heavy narration to assert the potential social usefulness of individual creative expression. It ultimately becomes an essayistic paean to American myths.

Wealth of a Nation, nevertheless, established Greaves as an independent producer, and with his next USIA production he finally won the opportunity to focus on black culture from behind the camera. The African-American filmmaker was originally dispatched to Dakar, Senegal, to shoot a historic gathering of black artists and intellectuals from throughout the African diaspora. The USIA wanted a five-minute news clip. Upon arriving, however, Greaves immediately realized the value of a longer piece. After he, his cameraman, and his driver shot as much footage as possible, largely without synchronous sound, Greaves utilized those editing skills acquired at the NFB to put together an effective and comprehensive record of the event. This record, *The First World Festival of Negro Arts* (1966), features performances by dancers from throughout the black world and appearances by Duke Ellington, Katherine Dunham, Langston Hughes (whose poetry frames the film), and many others. Greaves's juxtapositions explore and affirm the links between African and African-American culture. It was Africans, however, rather than African Americans, who were given the opportunity to appreciate these links: while *First World Festival* proved the most popular USIA film in Africa for the following decade, USIA films were prohibited at the time (and until recently) from distribution in the United States.[5] Although such links could have been radicalizing for African Americans, this affirmation was more likely to serve a conservative agenda when presented to Africans—in suggesting greater identity with the United States and, by implication, with its Vietnam-era policies. If the film is considered in terms of the politics of production, however, it represents an important achievement.

GREAVES ON *THE FIRST WORLD FESTIVAL OF NEGRO ARTS*

> You have to realize that the reason why I went into motion pictures was to make films like *The First World Festival of Negro Arts*. It was the first opportunity I had to make films that expressed a black perspective on reality. Until then I had not had access to financing which would permit that.

The First World Festival of Negro Arts was quickly followed by another breakthrough film for Greaves, *Still a Brother: Inside the Negro Middle Class*, a ninety-minute television documentary made in collaboration with William Branch for National Educational Television (NET). By the summer of 1967 the nation's inner cities were in turmoil. Television news featured rioting blacks, creating a perception among many whites that African Americans were burning down the country. As envisioned by NET, *Still a Brother* was to focus on a group of "good negroes" as a way to challenge negative stereotypes held by whites and to encourage poorer blacks to see that the system was working and creating new economic opportunities. *Still a Brother*, completed in 1967, proved more controversial than NET had expected—ultimately focusing as it does on the rise of contemporary black-pride movements. Although the film's interviews with a number of successful blacks at times suggest a preoccupation with material gains—most pointedly in the opening interview, where a man describes his version of the American dream as owning a yacht and wearing a Brooks Brothers suit—they also bespeak the extreme barriers to achieving such gains, and their great fragility once achieved. Many interviewees agree that the loss of a well-paying job often means instant loss of middle-class status to African Americans. In its emphasis on the concerns of an emerging African American middle class, the project was an especially personal one for Greaves.

Still a Brother looks at the danger of passive wholesale acceptance of white middle-class values by blacks—a phenomenon which Greaves has referred to as mental enslavement. The film's main contention, however, is that in the turbulent sixties, economically successful blacks were undergoing a mental revolution. Again and again, those interviewed reveal a growing understanding that the oppression of lower-income African Americans is their oppression as well. The perspective of the film, which supports black pride while stopping far short of advocating separatist politics, is one that continues to emerge in Greaves's work. It is better described as liberal than radical, but it is always questioning of liberal assumptions and sympathetic to radical goals.

GREAVES ON *STILL A BROTHER*

We had difficulties once *Still a Brother* was finished because NET had not expected that kind of film. They had expected an Ebony magazine kind of film, but we brought them this documentary that talked about mental revolution and showed increasing militancy in the black experience. People are talking about black is beautiful, the African heritage, militancy, and championing Rap Brown and Stokely Carmichael. So when NET executives saw the film they sort of blinked because they didn't know whether or not they really wanted to put it into the system. They weren't clear whether or not it would be acceptable. There was a great deal of anxiety because these executives were looking at their mortgages and didn't know whether they would be tossed out of their jobs. They didn't tell me that but it was obvious that they were really under pressure.

But I must say that they rose to the occasion, which speaks well of them, and of course the film eventually received an Emmy nomination and a Blue Ribbon at the American Film Festival.

Still a Brother was finally shown by NET on April 29, 1968, less than three weeks after the death of Martin Luther King, Jr. The newest round of riots, sparked by King's assassination, reemphasized the urgency of the Kerner Report and its call for increased media coverage by minorities in the face of a growing separation between blacks and whites. Meanwhile, NET began to develop a national monthly magazine format "by, for and about" black Americans. Called *Black Journal*, it had a predominantly black staff that included Lou Potter as "editor," Sheila Smith as researcher, Madeline Anderson as film editor, and Charles Hobson, Kent Garrett, St. Clair Bourne, and Horace Jenkins as associate or full producers. From the many who auditioned to fill the roles of cohosts, Lou House (who later changed his name to Wali Sadiq) and Bill Greaves were selected. Alvin H. Perlmutter, who is currently known for producing various Bill Moyers specials and *Adam Smith's Money World* (1984–1997), was at the top of the pyramid, acting as executive producer.

The series debuted in June and was broadcast during prime time by many public television stations (Wednesdays at 9:00 P.M. in New York City). The first program displayed remarkable promise. It begins with Coretta Scott King, the widow of Martin Luther King, Jr., giving a commencement speech at Harvard and concludes with a brief, reasonably sympathetic portrait of the Black Panthers. Not only is the spectrum of black political opinion surveyed, but there is an historical segment on the black press. Even the portrait of the only black jockey in the United States is given a historical context, reminding viewers that jockeys of African descent had once been common in horse racing.

After the third program had been aired, certain contradictions within the production of *Black Journal* had crystallized. Although the series was being sold as "by, for, and of the black community," the white Perlmutter was firmly in charge, and the programming was often dominated by white-produced segments. In mid-August there was a palace revolt. Eleven of the twelve black staff members resigned in protest. NET was ready to rescind the "by, for, and of" claims as deceptive. The staff members, in contrast, demanded a black executive producer—suggesting Lou Potter. NET maintained that Potter lacked adequate experience.[6] The staff then suggested the two producers of *Still a Brother*, William Greaves and William Branch. Both were, NET claimed, unavailable. Greaves, in fact, was vacationing on Cape Cod, and a quick phone call ascertained that he would take the position while retaining his role as cohost. Perlmutter became a consultant to the series, and black representation on the staff was increased.

Program No. 5 for *Black Journal* (October 1968) shows the series in full stride. In some respects, the format and aspirations of the series have changed little. Most obviously, Greaves now wears a dashiki instead of a sports coat and turtleneck, and Lou House begins and ends the program with greetings to "brothers and sisters" and a few words of Swahili. More substantively, the staff investigates controversial issues, such as the crisis surrounding the Community School Board in Oceanhill-Brownsville, in a polished and insightful manner. The producers emphasize those ways in which community control can provide better schooling that will result, for example, in dramatically improved reading scores. Black members of the school board make the case for community control, while the efforts of the United Federation of Teachers and its president, Albert Shanker, to subvert such an administrative structure are convincingly documented.

While offering a multiplicity of voices from within the African-American community, *Black Journal* presents forthright editorial comments without feeling the need to give "equal time" to extremely conservative blacks or to white spokespeople. In Program No. 5's short panel discussion, Professor Charles Hamilton, coauthor with Stokely Carmichael of *Black Power*, simply states that there can be no peace in the nation until the United States gets out of Vietnam; ending the war is thus a key priority for African Americans. The program condemns the expulsion of protesting "black power" medal winners from the American Olympic team as excessive and insensitive to past racial injustices. It then documents the longstanding devaluation of African-American history and scholarship by profiling Professor William Leo Hansberry, a prominent scholar who was once denied a PhD by Harvard University because no one at that institution was qualified to supervise his dissertation on African-American history.

Black Journal clearly deserved the Emmy it received in 1969. In a manner unique to magazine-format programming, the events of the present are situated in the context of unfolding African-American history, giving them deeper meaning and resonance.[7] Black identity is powerfully constructed. *Black Journal* consistently shows representatives of the African-American community to be reasonable, articulate, and authoritative. These spokespeople are often in the position of judging the antisocial behavior of hysterical, unreasonable whites such as Albert Shanker, presidential candidate George Wallace, or the Oakland police chief who condemns the Black Panthers in vitriolic terms. Traditional codings of authority by race are inverted; the nature of mainstream television representations stands exposed. As the experienced Greaves told his young staff, never again were they likely to find a production situation that was so protective of their views and offered them so much freedom.

GREAVES ON *BLACK JOURNAL*

Periodically there was a little anxiety at NET, for instance when we decided to do a show on the Black Muslims, or Paul Robeson, or Malcolm X; but quite interestingly we had a great deal of freedom on that show. That is to say I was not bugged by the management of NET for several good reasons. First, they were basically people of good will. But more importantly, perhaps, was the fact that we had developed a lot of political clout. I had purposely cultivated the black press, so they were very much behind us; I cultivated the people in the Congressional Black Caucus.

And, of course, there were all these riots and demonstrations going on, so they knew if they in a sense touched us, they might get burned. I'm overdramatizing this, but the situation in the sixties was so volatile and tense that it would have made no sense whatsoever for them to have this heavy hand on a show that had been put together specifically for the purposes of expressing the concerns of the black community. That was the point made by the Kerner Commission on Civil Disorder and the Carnegie Endowment. They would have been violating the mandate of the show.

While serving as executive producer on *Black Journal*, Greaves continued to operate his own production company, William Greaves Productions, which he had set up in 1964. In 1967 he applied his long-standing interest in acting and dramatic processes to a highly innovative feature film, eventually titled *Symbiopsychotaxiplasm: Take One*. This picture eluded traditional generic categories, being an often humorous cinéma-vérité-style documentary about the filming of a screen test for a larger dramatic work—and ultimately about its own making as well. In its freewheeling camera style, its playful editing and jump cutting, its use of direct camera address and improvisation, its self-aware, tongue-in-cheek humor, and its foregrounding of the filmmaking process and the medium's materiality, *Symbiopsychotaxiplasm* shows affinities with the contemporaneous French New Wave, American avant-garde cinema, and cinéma-vérité documentary. In many respects, Greaves's work predates the wave of American features that were to make use of such techniques over the next few years, from Haskell Wexler's *Medium Cool* (1969), which mixes documentary and fiction about events coinciding with the 1968 Chicago Democratic Convention, to Rick King's *Off the Wall* (1976), in which a counterculture youth steals a camera from the documentary crew that is filming his life and begins to make his own record of life on the lam. One of the most distinctive aspects of *Symbiopsychotaxiplasm: Take One* is its emphasis on both filmmaking and acting as creative, improvisational processes. The actors do not merely play out the drama-within-the-film in New York's Central Park, they are actively involved in shaping it; the director attempts to put the rehearsing performers into a framework of tension and confrontation with each other and with himself—and then records the results. These planned dramatic conflicts sometimes spill out beyond the realm of fictional drama into actual tantrums and frustrations. The affinity between this approach and psychodrama therapy, in which patients act out their anxieties and conflicts, is hardly coincidental. Greaves has had a long-standing interest in psychodrama, seeing it as closely allied with the techniques of method acting.[8] He focused on psychodrama sessions in two later documentaries—*In the Company of Men* (1969) and *The Deep North* (1988).

As Greaves has explained his approach, "Everything that happens in the *Take One* environment interrelates and affects the psychology of the people and indeed of the creative process itself." Greaves's shooting methods—the simultaneous use of numerous cameras to cover both the drama and the filming context—are designed to best capture this total interactive "environment." Wary of Greaves's approach, the production crew film their own meeting, a kind of mini-"revolt," over the shape (or lack of one) that the film appears to be taking. Within the film's frustrated diegesis, Greaves plays the role of a rather inept director trying to make a film tentatively entitled "Over the Cliff." Yet through his own audacity and directorial vision, Greaves the filmmaker comically upends the demeaning stereotypes of black ineptitude that haunt American cinema. The racially mixed film crew of men and women (a makeup that was then quite unusual in filmmaking) is itself refreshingly open and committed in its ardent questioning of creative processes, conventional aesthetic forms, and, ultimately, attitudes toward sexuality (albeit in some terms that today one may find off-putting). It is a film that continued Greaves's interest in issues beyond the immediate ones of African-American politics and identity—and yet the film's failure to win critical affirmation and a commercial release discouraged him from pursuing further work along these lines.

GREAVES ON *SYMBIOPSYCHOTAXIPLASM: TAKE ONE*

Symbiopsychotaxiplasm is neither a documentary nor a traditional feature. At least I don't feel that it is. It is more of a happening. Instead of being a form of conventional art, it is a piece of abstract art. Abstract in the sense that it does not obey the language of convention. It obeys the mind, the heart, the intuition, the subconscious. These are the determinants, rather than the Aristotelian approach to drama—the traditional dramatic form of Sophocles or Ibsen or whomever. You're going for—let's call it divine action, another level of insight into the human condition, using cinema.

The fact is that we could take this event—this scene, this screen test—and throw it into a community of actors and cinema technicians, and no matter how it fell, it would be a film. Before we knew it, we were dealing with some of the basic points of drama, which is conflict and development, progression, a rising conflict into some kind of crisis, climax and some resolution. It may not happen as we would like it, but some variant of that theme will occur. The problem for the filmmaker is to find what the variant is and how to put it together in the editing room with the materials you have.

Ultimately Greaves recognized that he had to either become a full-time television executive or retain his independence as a filmmaker and devote greater energies to independent production. In 1970 he left *Black Journal*. The following year he made the feature-length "docutainment movie" *Ali, the Fighter*, about Muhammad Ali's first, unsuccessful effort to reclaim his heavyweight crown from Joe Frazier. (Ali had been stripped of his crown because of his radical politics and opposition to the Vietnam War.) Greaves deftly interweaves exchanges between fighters and their fans with scenes of press conferences, training sessions, and business discussions—then ends with the fight itself. The film's behind-the-scenes images often pertain to the economic politics—and more implicitly the racial politics—involved in the promotion of the fight.

While *Ali, the Fighter* received national distribution in commercial theaters, Greaves was not so fortunate with *Nationtime—Gary*, his film of the historic first National Black Political Convention in Gary, Indiana. Attended by about ten thousand people, this 1972 gathering included representatives from the full range of African-American culture and politics, from Amiri Baraka (LeRoi Jones) to Jesse Jackson and Coretta Scott King. The film covers the efforts of participants to create a platform acceptable to the numerous constituencies within the black community. Jackson steals the show with a rousing and uncompromising speech calling for black political unity in the face of white-dominated party politics. The subject matter was considered too militant by commercial broadcasters, and the film never aired.

GREAVES ON *NATIONTIME—GARY*

There was a guy who came into my office and said to me, "The Gary convention is going to be the greatest event in the history of black America, and you've got to take some cameras there. I can get you some money to make this film, and then after you make it you can sell it to television." He talked like that. "Money is no object." To make a long story short, we went down there and ended up paying our own fares because I was interested in the event anyway. We took some raw stock and filmed this event. Our company paid for that film entirely. So it practically bankrupted us (as have several other films). But we put the film together and I got Sidney Poitier and Harry Belafonte to do the narration. And I thought that with the two of them we wouldn't have any problem getting it onto the networks. But the networks and local stations wouldn't touch it. They thought the whole event was too militant and that the film was as well. Don't misunderstand me.

There were some technical problems with it that we couldn't afford to fix. But essentially it was a major, major event. How can you say you don't want to show material of the crucifixion because it is out of focus? I'm not saying it was of that magnitude but it was a very important historical moment.

At this same time, Greaves relied for much of his income on films made for the Equal Employment Opportunity Commission (*The Voice of La Raza*, 1972), the Civil Service Commission (*On Merit*, 1972), NASA (*Where Dreams Come True*, 1979), and other government agencies; but he also began to produce important historical documentaries, beginning with *From These Roots* (1974), a look at the Harlem Renaissance of the nineteen-twenties. Among other things, the film was a return to Greaves's own roots growing up in Harlem. This pioneering effort treated the major contributors to that Renaissance with much greater sympathy and insight than the then standard book on the subject—Nathan Huggins's *The Harlem Renaissance*. With little stock footage of Harlem and its intellectuals available, Greaves decided to construct a film composed exclusively of photographs. What emerged was a compelling portrait of a community made strong by relative freedom and opportunity. Within the larger context of documentary practice, the film helped to inaugurate a cycle of city neighborhood films that focused on local communities. One of the best known, William Miles's *I Remember Harlem* (1980), owed much to Greaves's earlier effort.

Greaves went on to direct a number of biographical portraits of significant figures in African-American history. Two efforts from the early 1980s were *Booker T. Washington: The Life and Legacy* (1983) and *Frederick Douglass: An American Life* (1985), both for the National Park Service. *Booker T. Washington* is notable for the way it seeks to understand the historical pragmatics of Washington's accommodationist politics, while also continuing to question them through critical responses from a committed W. E. B. Du Bois and a "reporter" (played by Gil Noble) covering his life. These two half-hour films are basically dramatizations, but they also incorporate the limited number of available archival illustrations. (The paucity of visual documentation on important figures in black history is something with which Greaves and other filmmakers must frequently struggle, as did Jackie Shearer with her documentary, *The Massachusetts 54th Colored Regiment* [1991].) At times *Booker T. Washington* and *Frederick Douglass* bear the trappings of their educational purpose quite heavily. Yet they, along with the numerous other government-sponsored films on a broad range of topics, enabled Greaves to keep working and producing films on important African-American subjects—no mean achievement during a period in which projects concerned with African-American culture were receiving little national attention or funding.

Greaves's most recent work in the area of biography is the documentary *Ida B. Wells: A Passion for Justice*, coproduced with his wife, Louise Archambault Greaves. A reporter who developed her craft in Memphis, Tennessee, Wells became an important black leader who knew how to use both the black and mainstream press to support the struggle against racism—particularly lynchings—and to fight for women's suffrage. She realized that newspapers could mobilize citizens to boycott either specific businesses or whole towns that failed to acknowledge their patronage with appropriate services and legal due process. Again Greaves encountered a paucity of visual documentation: fewer than fifteen photographs of this courageous, militant woman survive, and almost all are formal portraits. Yet the filmmaker succeeds in shaping these limited materials into a masterful film. Toni Morrison reads movingly from Ida Wells's autobiography, which functions not unlike a protracted interview with Wells herself. In all these biographical documentaries, Greaves explores the possibilities and responsibilities of leadership within the black community. He investigates the parameters within which these individuals operated and the social and economic forces to which they were attuned and which they mobilized. Biography is used as a way of presenting African-American history to both a general audience and, more specifically, the black community.

These historical portraits are balanced by such documentaries as *Black Power in America: Myth or Reality?* (1986), which profiles a group of successful African Americans working in professions not traditionally associated with black leadership. The hour-long program includes Franklin Thomas, head of the Ford Foundation; June Jackson Christmas, psychiatrist; Clifton Wharton, chancellor of the SUNY system; Charles Hamilton, political scientist; and Richard Hatcher, mayor of Gary, Indiana. Yet just as the critic is ready to suspect that Greaves has been overwhelmingly preoccupied with the black elite, a film like *Just Doin' It* (1976), an informal cinéma-vérité look at two neighborhood barbershops in Atlanta, defeats any such easy conclusion.⁹

Greaves has constantly struggled against being stereotyped in his work—as an actor and as a filmmaker. His work has always displayed diversity: he has balanced his numerous documentaries with repeated forays back into fiction filmmaking, such as *Bustin' Loose* (as executive producer, 1981) and the never-released, hurriedly made black exploitation feature *The Marijuana Affair* (1974). Furthermore, Greaves has alternated films on contemporary subjects and issues with historical treatments. Films focusing on African-American concerns are countered by numerous films preoccupied with other issues (e.g., *Symbiopsychotaxiplasm: Take One*). According to Greaves, roughly half his films have addressed topics other than the black experience. Industrials and government-sponsored films that operate within circumscribed parameters are offset by films in which Greaves took large artistic or financial risks.

In many respects Greaves has adapted what is most positive and progressive in Grierson's writings regarding the possibilities of and need for nonfiction films that can inform and educate the public. His approach has differed from that of many leftist or art-oriented documentarians—Barbara Kopple being one example of the former and Errol Morris an instance of the latter—in that his conception of filmmaking avoids fetishizing the individual work and instead looks to each work as one instance in a larger struggle. It takes a pragmatic rather than a romantic approach, one that has its roots in the black filmmaking experience—in the race films of Oscar Micheaux, Spencer Williams, and William Alexander, which were typically made under considerable financial constraints. Like those leaders that are the subject of some of his films, Greaves has had insight into the changing realities of his time, has persisted, and, often enough, has triumphed.

An examination of the career of William Greaves suggests that we need to rethink our conception and periodization of documentary film practice, which has typically been divided into two eras—the one before the cinéma-vérité revolution of 1960 (e.g., *Primary*, *Chronicle of a Summer*) and the one after. There are other turning points of equal or perhaps even greater importance, not all having to do with technology. The year 1968 can be seen as a watershed, a moment when access to the means of production and distribution began to be more open; not only *Black Journal* but *Inside Bedford Stuyvesant* and *Like It Is* also began to air in that year. These and other initiatives—such as Newsreel, Third World Newsreel, and New Day Films—began to chip away at white male hegemony in documentary filmmaking. Today, documentarians come from much more diverse backgrounds in terms of race, gender, and publicly acknowledged sexual orientation. Although problems of discrimination and social democracy have not been fully overcome even in this limited area, the manner in which these substantial changes have occurred needs to be better understood. Such historical reconsiderations are particularly urgent at a moment when many ideologues have launched gross polemics against multiculturalism, "political correctness," and arts funding—seemingly to taint if not obliterate our memory of these achievements.

NOTES

This chapter is reprinted with permission from *Film Quarterly* 45, no. 3 (Spring 1992): 13–25.

1. Like many black-cast films, *Miracle in Harlem* had a white director (Jack Kemp)—as did *Lost Boundaries* (Alfred L. Werker).
2. In fact, Greaves was seriously considered for the part in *No Way Out* (1950) that launched Poitier to stardom. Greaves's association with renegade Louis de Rochemont, however, may have hurt his chances of being selected for the role.
3. This and subsequent quotations come from the authors' interviews with William Greaves in April and May 1991.
4. Both stars were hot properties, boasting Oscar nominations for that year: Gloria Swanson as Best Actress, for *Sunset Boulevard* (1950); and José Ferrer, who went on to win the Oscar, as Best Actor, for *Cyrano de Bergerac* (1950).
5. Greaves succeeded in acquiring the distribution rights to this film through his own company.
6. "11 Negro Staff Members Quit N.E.T. 'Black Journal' Program," *New York Times*, August 21, 1968, 91.
7. Because the shows work effectively as unified wholes, the screening of excerpted segments was possibly the only disappointment of the Brooklyn retrospective.
8. Greaves had taught method acting for Lee Strasberg over an eleven-year period and occasionally substituted for him at the Actors Studio when Strasberg was unavailable.
9. Interestingly, Greaves's *Just Doin' It* predates Spike Lee's fictionalized portrait of a neighborhood barbershop, *Joe's Bed-Stuy Barbershop: We Cut Heads* (1982), by six years.

2

Meta-interview with William Greaves (an Audiobiography)

SCOTT MACDONALD

Throughout his filmmaking career, William Greaves was far too committed to making films that could serve the African-American community, his country, and the world, and to getting the films seen, to make a sustained effort to tell his own personal story. From time to time, however, he made himself available to interviewers, and, at least for now, his responses to their questions will have to serve as the primary record of his memories and his thinking.

To construct the following meta-interview, I combined the most substantive interviews I could find (along with one conference presentation), hoping to provide something like an overview of Greaves's understanding of his life and filmmaking through the decades. Not surprisingly, given the longevity and complexity of his career, Greaves was interviewed for a considerable range of written and audio publications, some easily available, others more obscure. The overview presented here developed through accretion: each new interview I discovered necessitated an expansion and a new set of modifications to the meta-interview.

In some cases, multiple interviewers talked with Greaves about some of the same events and films, and Greaves responded in more or less the same way. In those instances, I usually privileged the interview that provided the most thorough commentary. Of course, many Greaves films have not instigated formal interviews, but I hope that what is here not only will be useful to those finding their way into the particular films discussed but will tempt readers to explore this remarkable and prolific career more fully.

Once I had found what seemed to be all the substantive interviews (others came to my attention too late to be included), I worked to provide a coherent, consistent, and readable sense of Greaves as filmmaker and thinker. In some instances, the texts I worked with were not-fully-corrected transcriptions of audio and video recordings, rather than carefully edited interviews; in those instances, I played particularly fast and loose with the transcriptions in order to maximize clarity and efficiency—but in all instances, I took liberties with the original transcriptions or edited texts, hoping to minimize confusion and maximize information.

To facilitate access to what is a long piece, I've divided the meta-interview into ten distinct sections, arranged chronologically according to the period of work addressed in the interviews. Each section engages a particular moment in Greaves's career, but individual sections also reveal his thinking about different dimensions of his life and work: the opening section focuses on his memories of his childhood and youth; "Hollywood Circa 1979–1983" articulates his understanding of how race has played and continues to play a role in what films get made; the section on *Just Doin' It* (1976) explores his approach to cinéma-vérité shooting, and so forth.

While the primary focus of this meta-interview is, of course, Greaves's memories and thoughts, I've consistently indicated which particular interviewer originally asked a question or raised an issue, using the interviewer's full name in the first instance and subsequently the interviewer's initials.

I am grateful to the Center for the Study of Popular Television (specifically the Steven H. Scheuer Television History Collection), housed in the S. I. Newhouse School of Public Communications at Syracuse University, for making available to me a copy of a 1998 video interview of Greaves conducted by Morton Silverstein (MS), as well as LaShanda Q. Brown's transcription of that interview.

In 1990 James Hatch (JH) interviewed Greaves for the journal *Artist and Influence: The Journal of Black American Cultural History*. I found my way to this interview after I had processed the Silverstein interview and after I'd found the other interviews I've worked with here. My edit of segments of the Hatch interview (made available to me by the Stuart A. Rose Manuscript, Archives, & Rare Book Library at Emory University) contributes to discussions throughout the meta-interview.

I was fortunate to attend the 1991 Robert Flaherty Film Seminar (programmed by Coco Fusco and Steve Gallagher), where Greaves presented *Symbiopsychotaxiplasm: Take One* to an astonished group of seminarians. The Flaherty Seminar was kind enough to make a recording of the postscreening discussion available to me. I transcribed and edited that discussion, which is included in Scott MacDonald and Patricia R. Zimmermann's *The Flaherty: Decades in the Cause of Independent Cinema* (Indiana University Press, 2017). I have included identifications for Flaherty seminarians who spoke during the Greaves discussion (that is, who the speakers were at the time of the discussion). Then, during the months following the seminar, I interviewed Greaves myself, combining our conversation with the Flaherty discussion; the result was published in my *A Critical Cinema 3* (University of California Press, 1998). My six Greaves tapes are in Special Collections at the Margaret Herrick Library of the Academy of Motion Picture Arts and Sciences ("Scott MacDonald Interviews").

Greaves spoke about his adventures in Hollywood with St. Clair Bourne (SCB) for *Chamba Notes* in the spring of 1979; then with Peter Castaldi (PC) in June 1992, during a short video interview for ABC-TV in Sydney, Australia; and again on July 4, 1993, during a conference in Munich, Germany, focusing on Black creativity. As is true throughout this meta-interview, I excerpted, edited, and combined Greaves's comments into a single conversation.

In May 1995 Sonja Bahn-Coblans and Arno Heller (SB/AH) interviewed Greaves as part of an in-depth project, *William Greaves:* Just Doin' It *(1976): An Analysis* (Wissenschaftlicher Verlag Trier, 1997), the seventh in a series of studies on American documentary film. The Bahn-Coblans/Heller interview concentrates on a single short film, *Just Doin' It*, but Greaves's comments reveal a good deal about his approach to cinéma-vérité filmmaking.

On December 23, 1989, Greaves was on a panel at Howard University as part of the National Conference on the Status of African Americans, where he spoke about the African-American community's addiction to media, the potential of video cassettes, and *Ida B. Wells: A Passion for Justice*, then scheduled to be aired on public television. A video recording of Greaves's talk is available at https://www.c-span.org/video/?c4787086/user-clip-william-greaves-natl-conferencer-status-african-americans-howard-university; a transcription is included here.

In 2001 Freda Warren (FW) and Greaves talked about *Ralph Bunche: An American Odyssey* for *Cineaste* (vol. 26, no. 2); and in 2003 George Alexander (GA) conducted a wide-ranging interview with Greaves for *Why We Make Movies: Black Filmmakers Talk About the Magic of Cinema* (Harlem Moon, 2003). I've incorporated questions and answers about Greaves's *Ralph Bunche*, and other matters as well, from both interviews.

Also in 2003, on April 17, the HistoryMakers project in Chicago recorded a three-hour video interview with Greaves, conducted by Larry Crowe (LC). My meta-interview begins with an edited version of the early section of the HistoryMakers interview where Greaves provides information about his and his parents' backgrounds and history. In several instances later on, I quote from this interview to expand on issues raised by other interviewers.

CHILDHOOD AND YOUTH

LARRY CROWE: Could you please state your name.

WILLIAM GREAVES: My name is William Garfield Greaves.

LC: Your date of birth?

WG: I'm not going to tell you my date of birth because in the film industry we filmmakers don't reveal our age! Let's say that I'm a bit over thirty-five. [Greaves was born on October 8, 1926.]

LC: Your place of birth?

WG: Flower Hospital in Manhattan, New York City. You're looking at a Harlem boy.

LC: How far back can you trace your family?

WG: On my father's side, back to Benin, which in colonial times was called Dahomey. On my mother's side, my family can be traced to Sri Lanka to some degree and to Jamaica. My grandmother on my mother's side was a Maroon. The Jamaican Maroons were a militant people who did not tolerate colonialism or slavery. They escaped from slavery and formed what amounted to a small country of their own in the mountains of Jamaica. Also, on my father's side, I think we have an infamous character, "Red Legs" Greaves, a Scottish pirate and slave trader who cut a swath through the Caribbean and up the Mississippi River—there are Greaves all along the Mississippi.

LC: Tell us about your father.

WG: My father was Garfield Gilbert Hannibal Greaves [in the Hatch interview, Greaves calls his father Hannibal Gilbert Garfield Wilburforce Greaves]. He was born in 1890 in St. Lucy Parish in Barbados. My father used to play the guitar but, unhappily, having not obeyed *his* father, he came home late one night strumming the guitar. When he arrived at the doorstep of his house, he was met by my grandfather, who promptly took the guitar from him and smashed it over his knee. My grandfather was a very strict West Indian gentleman who brooked no indiscipline.

My father was very interested in the Bible and was a part-time minister at a Pentecostal church in Harlem. He also drove a taxi that he owned. He had a feeling for literature, for words, for quotations from the Bible. He was a very hard-working, religious man.

LC: Did he tell you why he left Barbados?

WG: My father was interested in coming to America, like so many people from various parts of the world, in his time and ours. I guess he heard from some of his friends that if you worked on the Panama Canal you could go to America. So, after he finished working on the construction of the canal under General

Goethals, he went to Boston, then came down to New York and joined the Mount Calvary Pentecostal Church (I think that was the name)—on 12 West 131st Street.

He arrived in Harlem just at the beginning of the Harlem Renaissance, on the wave of the Marcus Garvey movement as it was developing during 1917–1918–1919. To my knowledge he was not a member of the UNIA [Universal Negro Improvement Association], but I guess practically every black person in America was either an official member of the UNIA or believed in it—except for W. E. B. Du Bois and the "talented tenth," who had a somewhat separate orientation.

LC: Tell us about your mother.

WG: My mother, Phyllis Emily Muir [in the Hatch interview she is Emily Phyllis Muir], was born in Kingston, Jamaica, in 1898. She came to America in her teens. She loved poetry. She used to take us to museums. And she read information about black history—Frederick Douglass, Booker T. Washington—to us. She was a very cultured woman and very religious. In her later years, she became an evangelist and preached at various black, white, and Puerto Rican churches.

She was a very interesting woman.

LC: Did your parents have a story about how they met?

WG: They met at the Pentecostal church, I believe.

LC: Did you know your grandparents?

WG: No. The closest I came to knowing my grandfather—he was ninety-four when he passed—was when my father went down to Barbados to see him, after thirty or forty years, and came back with stories.

LC: Do you have siblings?

WG: Oh yes. I have four sisters (two of whom have passed away) and two brothers. I was the middle child: three sisters were older than me, and the two brothers and one sister were younger.

MORTON SILVERSTEIN: Tell us about your growing up days, your early epiphanies.

WG: I had occasion recently to describe one very early epiphany at the Apollo Theater in Harlem. Turner Broadcasting was sponsoring a series of race movies: black feature films that were produced by black producers beginning in the 1910s and continuing into the 1940s, including, from 1919 on, Oscar Micheaux. My epiphany centers on my first exposure to Oscar Micheaux and his work, as a young kid growing up.

We used to hang out on the stoop of the building in which I lived at 203 West 135th Street, between Frederick Douglass Boulevard and Lenox Avenue (now Malcolm X Boulevard). On late summer afternoons around dusk, we would see, across the street, a man carrying what seemed to be a heavy suitcase in one hand and something that looked like flat cans under his other arm. Whenever we saw this man appear from his building, at 200 West 135th Street, we knew that he was going to set up his projector and show some movies at the Big Apple Bar & Grille, which was across the street from where he apparently had his offices. We couldn't go into the bar & grille, but we could climb onto the railings outside and peek through the windows to see the images moving on the screen. We were only seven or eight years old, but it was enough for us just to see that motion on the screen, because for us it was something new and different.

Just ten or fifteen years ago, in doing some research, I learned that this was Oscar Micheaux. For me this experience is a metaphor for what my life became and certainly what the life of the black filmmaker has to be in America, particularly when one thinks of America in the early part of the twentieth century, when it was truly an apartheid society for black people and people of color in general, as well as for other minorities for whom the American Dream had not yet begun to manifest itself.

In remembering this experience and sharing it with the audience at the Apollo Theater, I was pointing to the position that the black filmmaker has had in the constellation of American media. I guess you could say that the black filmmaker has been the precursor of the independent filmmaker, black, white, and all colors in between. From the beginning, the black filmmaker has had to be part of a parallel, separate cinema. That's the track I've been on as a filmmaker.

Of course, you, Mort, were part of that parallel track when we worked together on *Black Journal*.

MS: What kind of activities were you involved in as a young person?

WG: I remember reciting some poems in grammar school, at P.S. 89. During those years I did a lot of artwork. I was named one of the seventy-five best child artists in New York State and got a scholarship to the Little Red School House, where I used to go on Saturday mornings to paint. And also, I went to the Harlem YMCA and was involved in wonderful after-school art courses there.

JAMES HATCH: I've heard that you began to draw at the age of four.

WG: Yes, I drew continuously and obsessively from the age of four until I was sixteen or seventeen, then left it behind and went into other things.

JH: In your elementary school days, do you remember any teachers who were important in shaping your life?

FIGURE 2.1 William Greaves (*second row, far left, kneeling*), age eleven, and others after a school play at P.S. 89 in New York City. Courtesy Louise Greaves.

WG: Oh yes. There was a music teacher at Frederick Douglass Junior High School in Harlem: Mr. Dixon. He and his wife were very supportive. Brock Peters and I were in the glee club together at Frederick Douglass, and Mr. Dixon used to invite us to his house. His wife would serve us tea and crumpets.

In junior high school Mr. Dixon put me in a play, apparently because I spoke Spanish pretty well at that time—I'd won the school medal in Spanish. I don't remember the plot of the play, but someone had cheated somebody out of something. This was the graduation play, and at the end, here comes the curtain line, my line, and I began, "Banderas! Eso es...," then couldn't remember the rest. What I said sounded like "SOS," and all the Spanish-speaking students roared! I was so ashamed. I don't think I acted after that in school.

My art teacher, Mr. Sherwood, was also very supportive. When I was about fourteen, he brought me to a WPA Federal Art Project on Lenox Avenue. This WPA project was headed by a wonderful woman, Augusta Savage, who had done a famous sculpture that was shown at the 1939 World's Fair [*Lift Every Voice and Sing*, also known as *The Harp*].

I studied painting with a now-famous artist, Ernest Crichlow, and sculpture with William Artis, another famous black artist. As a matter of fact, William Artis decided I was talented enough to be in his adult class at the federal project, which was on 116th Street and Lexington Avenue.

It was in that adult class where I saw my first naked woman! I was only fourteen years old, the only kid in this class of adults, so when I saw this woman coming into the room with a kimono on, I didn't know what was happening. I was at my workstation, kneading clay, getting things set up to do some sculpting, when Artis said, "Ladies and gentlemen, this will be our model for tonight." Then, to my absolute amazement, this woman took off her kimono and she was nude. I almost went through the floor!

Bill Artis saw that I was ready to take flight, grabbed me by the arm, and sort of half-nelsoned me up to the podium where this woman was reclining. He said, "Now, Bill, have you noticed how her arm is lying on the surface? And pay attention to this other arm, the way her body is...." He was talking to me in very technical terms, while I was trying not to look at what I thought was this embarrassed lady—because *I* certainly was embarrassed.

I think if my father and mother had seen me in that WPA art school—financed by the American government if you please—with this naked lady, they'd have taken me to the woodshed and given me a thorough spanking. They had no interest in art or in dancing; to them this was the work of the devil. And because they didn't approve of what I was doing, I naturally rebelled against their disapproval.

As a fourteen-, fifteen-year-old kid, I studied African and Afro-American history with my best friend, Mark Desgraves, who was from Haiti. His father was Professor Desgraves, who used to teach Haitian history on Saturday mornings. I learned all about Toussaint l'Ouverture, Henri Christophe, Jean-Jacques Dessalines, Pétion, and the others who were connected with the Haitian Revolution.

The Haitians were the first to defeat Napoleon (in 1804). As a matter of fact, the Haitian Revolution gave a lot of support to the American Revolution. It's ironic that today some Americans begrudge whatever America does in the way of helping Haiti.

Later I went on to Frederick Douglass Junior High School, where I acted in a couple of school plays (the poet Countee Cullen was one of my teachers). Then I attended Stuyvesant High School, and it was while I was at Stuyvesant that I became interested in African dancing. I studied it and eventually danced with Pearl Primus as part of her professional company for a couple of years. I went from there into the theater.

Also, I used to go to the Harlem YMCA where I played basketball and belonged to a team called the Panthers—not, of course, the legendary Black Panthers of the sixties, just a little basketball club. We won a couple of awards. I used to box and won some awards doing that too. And I ran track.

MS: You became an engineering student at City College in the 1940s?

WG: Yes, but I need to go back a bit. As I've said, when I was at the YMCA and the WPA school, I wanted to be an artist. My father liked the idea of my being an artist, until it was time for high school. He was a very stern, no-nonsense man—quite the realist. We were in the middle of the Great Depression, and my father felt that there was no sense in me painting pictures. Even *white* painters weren't making any money, so black artists in America in the 1930s were *definitely* not going to make money. He felt that I should learn a trade.

I didn't want to learn a trade, and fortunately, I was one of the top students in my class, so I was able to take the entrance examinations to Stuyvesant High School. I'd really wanted to go to Music & Art High School, but my father turned thumbs down on that. So we negotiated my going to Stuyvesant High School because it was a science high school: he could relate to "science" and "technology."

I passed the examinations for Stuyvesant and seemed on the way to becoming a mechanical engineer—music to my father's ears. Actually, Stuyvesant was a great experience for me. I found out not long ago that I graduated in the top 10 percent of my class. Long after I graduated, Stuyvesant honored me as one of its distinguished graduates.

When I graduated, I entered City College with a view to becoming a mechanical engineer, but that was where I was smitten by the theater bug. At the time, Mark Desgraves and his sister Cleante were dancing for a West Indian dancer called Belle Rosette. I used to attend the rehearsals and watch them. Both Mark and I were pretty good social dancers. I was a great lindy-hopper at the Savoy, the Renaissance Ballroom, and the Golden Gate in Harlem, and at the YMCA on Friday and Saturday nights after basketball games.

So I used to attend these rehearsals and was very taken by what I was seeing. Then Mark and I joined a dance group headed by Asadata Dafora, of Sierra Leone, who had introduced African dancing to the black community in Harlem in the 1940s. Asadata Dafora's group was part of the African Academy of Arts and Research, an organization set up by African students that would organize and present cultural events. We had the honor of studying with him and dancing in his group at Carnegie Hall, at Town Hall, and at the old Roxy Theater—a very big theater, second in size only to the Radio City Music Hall—on 7th Avenue and 50th Street. The Roxy presented a combination of stage performances and motion pictures.

Then Pearl Primus became aware of my work as a dancer and auditioned me for *her* group and I danced professionally with her at the Roxy and at Town Hall. Pearl's forte was not only modern dance but also African dance. Our dance performance took place in a mock-up African village. At the Roxy, the actor Gordon Heath narrated events that were supposed to be happening in Africa. I still remember that the motion picture that was showing when I was dancing at the Roxy with Pearl was *Laura* [Otto Preminger, 1944], with Dana Andrews and Gene Tierney. And I remember that Mildred Bailey was singing on that bill, as was Bill Baird, the puppeteer—I used to chat with Bill backstage.

THE THEATER

JH: *Garden of Time* [Owen Dodson, 1945] was not only the first time you performed with the American Negro Theatre [ANT]; it was the first time you ever acted professionally on stage.

WG: Yes. Gordon Heath had suggested that I audition for a role in a play that a talented guest director from Howard University, Owen Dodson, had written. Owen was holding auditions at the ANT. I told Gordon, "I'm not an actor," and he said, "But you're a very good *type*." So I agreed to audition. I remember going into what felt like a big room, with all these actors sitting around in a circle. I read and got the role of Blues Boy.

Garden of Time is an interracial play, sort of a parody of Medea and Jason. Jason is white and Medea, black. The play begins in ancient times with Jason and the Golden Fleece, then shifts to modern times. As Blues Boy I was supposed to be singing and playing the guitar. I couldn't play guitar, but Gordon could, so he sat backstage and played, while I mimed playing.

There were reviews in the *New York Times*, the *Christian Science Monitor*, and the *Nation*. The play was very well received, and I think I got the best notices of all the actors. The critics said that if I kept going, I'd have a brilliant career. In fact, someone said, I'd "out-Cotton Joseph Cotton"!—because on stage I was this very unaffected, natural persona, which apparently was appealing to the critics.

JH: What did you know about the ANT before joining?

FIGURE 2.2 Production photo: Greaves as Blues Boy in *Garden of Time* (Owen Dodson), performed by the American Negro Theatre in 1945. Courtesy Louise Greaves.

WG: As a kid, I used to go down into the basement of the library in Harlem and watch some of the plays that the ANT put on. When I was about fifteen, I sneaked in and saw *On Strivers Row* [Abram Hill, 1940] by Abe Hill—and thought it was very funny. It captured the archetypes and the stereotypes that characterized black culture and the black community at that time. The play included elements of highbrow culture and of what W. E. B. Du Bois had called the "talented tenth," as well as underclass street characters.

JH: Would you say that the audiences for the American Negro Theatre were more from the blue-collar end of the culture clash of Harlem or more from the upper-class end?

WG: They were more upper class, but there were blue-collar people as well.

JH: Were the audiences able to laugh at themselves?

WG: Oh, yes, definitely.

JH: How would you describe the social atmosphere of the American Negro Theatre itself?

WG: It was quite congenial; there was a lot of camaraderie.

JH: Abram Hill mentioned once that *Garden of Time* had created a bit of a division within the company because so many artists, like yourself, were brought in from the outside. Do you remember anything about that?

WG: Now that you mention it, there were a few people who seemed cold and distant. But I guess I was having too great a time to notice.

The ANT had invited Owen Dodson to put on his play. He came on the condition that he could cast anyone he felt was right for the part. Dodson brought in Sadie Browne to play the female lead. There may have been people who thought that they were the right type for my role, so why bring me in?

JH: You came to the ANT very soon after their enormous Broadway success with *Anna Lucasta* [Abram Hill and Philip Yordan, 1944]. Had that experience changed the group? Were there people hoping to get back to Broadway?

WG: Yes. The hope was that there would be a succession of plays going from the ANT to Broadway. A war had just been fought and won against the fascists/racists in Germany, and a new day had been born with the United Nations and Ralph Bunche winning the Nobel Peace Prize in 1950. America was in an optimistic mood. But, unfortunately, racism was still very much entrenched on Broadway, and that continued to affect programming.

JH: What were your initial impressions of *Garden of Time*?

WG: I thought it was interesting to set part of the play in ancient times, and it helped to stimulate my interest in ancient African history.

Through *Garden of Time* I met a wonderful African scholar named Austin Briggs-Hall. Later he played Toussant L'Ouverture in Dan Hammerman's *Henri Christophe* [1945]. Austin took me under his wing and schooled me in the history of Ethiopia, Ghana, Zimbabwe, and other ancient civilizations. I ended up attending classes at the Ethiopian Library in Harlem [later renamed the Charles C. Seifert Library] and also got great exposure to that history from Professor William Leo Hansberry, the uncle of Lorraine Hansberry, who came up from Howard University on the weekends to lecture at the Ethiopian Library. In that class were some people whose names you may know; I can't call them "classmates" because I was just a young kid, the mascot of the group, which included John Henrik Clarke; Jean Blackwell Hutson, who was the head of the Schomburg from 1948 to 1980; the historian J. A. Rogers, and George Haynes, Richard B. Moore—all people much involved with the retrieval of our lost history.

JH: *Garden of Time* was so different from anything else that the ANT had produced. How did audiences accept it?

WG: Owen Dodson was well known to the cultural elite of Harlem, many of whom had gone to Howard University or Lincoln University or other black colleges. *Garden of Time* may not have had the wide appeal of *On Strivers Row* or *Anna Lucasta*, because for one thing it was not a comedy. But Langston Hughes came to see it, and Alain Locke too, and other intellectuals. I suspect Ralph Bunche, who was very interested in theater and had been Owen's colleague at Howard, must have come to see it.

The stage was one of the few platforms for serious theatrical performance for black people in the 1940s. *Walk Hard* [Abram Hill, 1944] and then *Garden of Time*, then *Henri Christophe*, were serious, as was *Freight* [written by Kenneth White, 1949] a few years later.

After *Garden of Time*, I had a role in *Henri Christophe*. Joe Newton Hill, a professor from Fisk University, was the director. Fred O'Neal played Henri Christophe, and I played the young Black-Nationalist, fire-eating rebel, Jean-Jacques Dessalines.

I thought *Henri Christophe* was an important play, because in racist America, the idea of revolt against racist domination was attractive, particularly to young teenagers in Harlem like myself. I was delighted to play this rabid nationalist.

The play opened, but nothing else happened with it. The only thing I remember was that I gave a very hammy, artificial performance. I'd assumed that the critics had made a mistake in thinking that my performance in *Garden of Time* was the best I could do. I thought, wait until they see me when I'm *really* acting! But I was terrible as Jean-Jacques Dessalines, and the critics lambasted me, said that I was chewing up the scenery. [Laughter]

Gradually, I realized that maybe I'd made a mistake in thinking that good acting was overacting—and I began *studying* acting.

JH: Did it matter to you or anyone else at the ANT what the race of the playwrights was? Owen Dodson was black, but Dan Hammerman was white.

WG: I don't think we were psychiatrically deficient in that way. The content was what mattered. If anything, many of us were pleased, even flattered that there existed white people who could be sufficiently interested in the African and Afro-American experiences to write about them.

I did one more play at the ANT: *Freight*. John O'Shaughnessy was the director. When *Freight* went to Broadway, Sidney Poitier played my role. After *Freight* I didn't have very much to do with the American Negro Theatre. By that time, I had a role in the original production of *Finian's Rainbow*, which starred Ella Logan and Albert Sharp.

I got the lead in *A Young American* by winning a prize at the John Golden auditions, which were held every year by producers and casting agents at a large Broadway theater. Then I costarred with Ruby Dee in the all-black version of Norman Krasna's *John Loves Mary*. Also, I was featured with Todd Duncan in Maxwell Anderson and Kurt Weill's *Lost in the Stars*, which was based on Alan Paton's *Cry, the Beloved Country*. The play was directed by Rouben Mamoulian.

While I was doing theater, I was also writing popular songs.

JH: Did you have any musical training?

WG: My uncle gave me a saxophone, which I think my father pawned during the middle of the Depression. My uncle played the trumpet, and he let me play his trumpet. Later, I began studying trumpet and have the distinction of

FIGURE 2.3 Cast rehearsing *Lost in the Stars* for Sunday, October 30, 1949, opening at the Music Box Theatre. *Left to right*: Van Prince, Mable Hart, Sheila Guyse, Julian Mayfield, Greaves (*sitting*), director Rouben Mamoulian, and La Verne French. Photographer George Karger. Courtesy Schomburg Center for Research in Black Culture.

studying with the same teacher as Miles Davis: Charles Colin. In the end I found playing the trumpet uncomfortable and decided that I'd just as soon write music as play it. That's how I got into song writing.

JH: You wrote a hundred songs?

WG: Between the ages of seventeen and twenty-five, I wrote a lot of songs, maybe as many as a hundred. Buddy Johnson, Percy Faith, Arthur Prysok, Al Hibler, Donna Hightower, and others recorded my songs. At one point I really wanted to be a songwriter, but I got so involved with acting that I left that behind after 1952, when I think I wrote my last song, "African Lullaby," which Eartha Kitt recorded. My wife Louise told me she'd heard it up in Canada, before we met. It was on the other side of "Ce Si Bon." It sold a million records. [Percy Faith also recorded "African Lullaby"; Prysok recorded "Baby, You Had Better Change Your Ways," as did Al Hibler and Donna Hightower.]

MS: How many parts were there for African-American actors in those days?

WG: Not many.

MS: Even the U.S. Army was segregated.

WG: All the military services were. As a matter of fact, I'd hoped to do officer training in the navy, but they rejected me. They said I showed "unfixedness of purpose," a euphemism, I think—I'd passed the officers' training tests for both the air force and the army. And because I'd taken and passed those other two tests, and *then* took the naval test, they said I didn't know whether I wanted to be in the army, an air force pilot, or an ensign in the navy, which apparently made me unsuitable.

MS: You didn't "know your place"?

WG: Didn't know my place, right. Because at that time blacks in the navy were relegated to being stewards. Of course, the army was the same thing—by and large, blacks did service work—until toward the very end of the war, when the army began to change. Of course, there were the Tuskegee airmen.

Anyway, eventually I said, "The hell with all this! I'm not going to enlist."

EARLY FILM ROLES

SCOTT MACDONALD: Your first film roles were in "race films."

WG: I have the honor of being featured in the last two black-cast films of that era: *Miracle in Harlem* [Jack Kemp, 1948] and *Souls of Sin* [Powell Lindsay, 1949]. It's a curious experience to have been present at the tail end of that history. I feel like a relay racer, having taken the baton from William Alexander and the others. I did two films that William produced, *The Fight Never Ends* [1948], with Joe Louis, and *Souls of Sin*.

Actually, I had worked on a number of films before that but in smaller parts. Fritz Pollard, a close friend of Paul Robeson—both were football players [Pollard and Bobby Marshall were the first black NFL players, and Pollard, the first black NFL coach]—had a casting agency called Suntan Studios, which used to supply extras to the various black films that were being made. I was sent to some of these companies and became involved in various productions. I don't remember what the productions were. All I knew was that I was on a set under the lights.

William Alexander was an important producer at that time. Unlike Oscar Micheaux, Bill did both features and newsreels: *All-American News, By-Line Newsreel*. He also was doing musical shorts, what today we'd call music videos, as well as long-form documentaries. Bill was the quintessential independent movie producer, an unstoppable wheeler-dealer, not in any way intimidated by the notion that he was black and "couldn't" make movies because of his blackness.

The Fight Never Ends was my first real film role. Joseph Lerner was the director and Bill the producer. We got along very well. Lerner was a good director, I thought, and a savvy guy. He was smart enough to keep me relaxed. In those days film directors must have felt there was no sense trying to push me out of joint.

At the time, *Miracle in Harlem* was considered a prestigious film, the first independent black-cast film done to so-called Hollywood standards. The Goldberg brothers, who produced the film, had a company called Herald Pictures. *Miracle* was done with the support of the NAACP, who were very concerned with the image of black people at that time.

I played the romantic lead in *Miracle in Harlem*, which has a very confused plot. I do have a memory of the leading actress in the film, Hilda Offley, who played Aunt Hattie. Aunt Hattie made believe she was dying: she had this coffin laid out and got into the coffin in order to thwart a robber who was trying to steal the business. *Miracle* was playing in New York at the same time as *Lost Boundaries* [1949] and *Lost in the Stars* [1949]. I think I have the distinction of being the first black actor to be featured in three different productions concurrently.

Stepin Fetchit was wonderful in *Miracle*. When you saw him in the context of black society, you said, "Gee! This is one good actor!" It's too bad that he'd had to be isolated, that Hollywood could reach into the black community and extract one stereotype to the exclusion of all other possibilities—so that you got a terribly distorted view of black America and of Stepin Fetchit,

FIGURE 2.4 Advertisement for *Miracle in Harlem* (1948, directed by Jack Kemp); Greaves is in the middle between the arguing couple, *bottom right*. Courtesy Louise Greaves.

FIGURE 2.5 Poster for Powell Lindsay and William Alexander's *Souls of Sin* (1949); Greaves on right with guitar. Courtesy Louise Greaves. Thanks to Su Friedrich.

who in his real habitat was wonderful. He was a nice guy, very simple, dignified, and clearly a wonderful actor who had been exploited and misused by the fascists in Hollywood.

SM: *Souls of Sin* seems barely directed. The acting isn't bad, but cinematically it doesn't work at all.

WG: Well, Powell Lindsay was a stage director; he didn't have a sense of the cinematic the way Jack Kemp did.

Powell Lindsay wrote the script of *Souls of Sin*, which is about two characters: "Dollar Bill," a young black man in Harlem trying desperately to get to the top of the world through crime, and "Alabam," a country bumpkin who plays the guitar and ends up becoming a big star. I played Alabam. From the acting point of view, it was a nice challenge.

Shooting *Souls of Sin* was an interesting experience. Bill was adept at shooting on a shoestring. That film played throughout the black film circuit, which was something like 1,200 theaters at the time. When I first saw the finished film, I almost crawled underneath my chair! Seeing myself acting on screen was a shock. We all have these idealized images of ourselves, and neurotic notions about how we perform.

Bill Alexander was a role model. I saw him functioning effectively in what was an entirely fascist state. What a horrendous period.

SM: Even on the most mundane levels! In my junior high school, there were regulations about exactly how close to the floor girls' skirts needed to be. And of course, no one was allowed to wear jeans.

WG: You know, Brando and I were at the Actors Studio together, and he always used to wear jeans. At that time, we all thought, me included, that if we didn't wear suits and ties, God would strike us dead. Everyone knew that if you went on a casting call, you showed up with suit and tie—cleaned and pressed—and you were deferential to the producer or the director or the casting agent. You grinned from ear to ear and did all the things that Uncle Toms do, whether you were black or white.

And here comes Brando, sauntering into the producer's office in his jeans, and if he didn't like the producer, he wouldn't shake his hand. Marlon had this marvelous instinctual radar that decoded phonies. He wanted to be himself, and he worked hard at it. He realized the polluting effect that American society had on consciousness, so he was very defensive of himself, which everyone decided was his being an asshole—not realizing that the man was in a very nurturing state with respect to his talent and his consciousness. All this was part of the fascism of that period: the hemline, the demands of authority in the theater business—and yet it came to pass that Brando became the preeminent actor of that era.

SM: Who else did you meet at the Actors Studio?

WG: I'd auditioned for the Actors Studio in 1948. In my class—fifty or sixty altogether—were Brando, Anthony Quinn, Arthur Kennedy, Dorothy Maguire, Richard Boone, Rod Steiger, Maureen Stapleton, Julie Harris, Peggy Ann Garner, Kim Stanley; Peggy Feury, Ann Jackson, Eli Wallach, Frank Silvera, Lou Peterson.

SM: Strasberg?

WG: Kazan, Lee Strasberg, Daniel Mann, and David Pressman were my teachers at the Actors Studio. Actually, Strasberg didn't come in initially.

Robert Lewis, Kazan, and Cheryl Crawford formed the Actors Studio. They'd come out of the 1930s Group Theater, which had been formed by Harold Clurman, Strasberg, and Cheryl Crawford. Lewis and Kazan were actors in that company. When the Group Theater folded, they formed the Actors Studio. Lee Strasberg came in a year or two later.

I'm on the board of directors of the Actors Studio now [2003] and part of their auditioning committee. I was one of the people Lee Strasberg chose to substitute for him when he was out of town, like when he left to work on *The Godfather* [1972]. I taught for Lee for twelve years at his private institute.

MS: Did your dad see you in any of the films or stage productions you were in?

WG: Never saw me in anything. But, every now and again, as he was driving his cab, someone would look at his picture and his name, "Garfield Greaves," and say, "Do you happen to know William Greaves, the actor?" And he would have to say that I was his son. There I was, doing work for the devil!

He'd expected that I was going to become a Harlem hoodlum. I probably disappointed him [laughter].

MS: Did he ever come to terms with it?

WG: He mellowed in later years. By the end of his life I think he was pleased with what I had done with myself. He realized that the advice he had given me had been correct, because filmmaking *is* a trade, a special trade that can have an impact on how people think.

SM: How do you understand the demise of the all-black cinema? There had been some production, even during the 1930s, when nobody had two pennies to rub together. And then at the end of the 1940s, when you would think there might be a market, it disappeared.

WG: It collapsed for several reasons. American apartheid, as it had been practiced, was collapsing. The black film industry was a creature of that apartheid system. Black people did not want to be discriminated against in the white theaters downtown any longer. They hadn't been able to get into some of the theaters, and when they did get into them, they'd had to sit in the balcony. Very dehumanizing. So they went to the black independent films.

But change was happening. All the post–World War II rhetoric about democracy and the New World and the United Nations was having some impact on white America, which was relaxing some of its neurotic need to oppress black people. The horrors of Nazism, Hitler, the Holocaust—what a racist propensity on the part of a large population can lead to—was having an effect on the American psyche.

And don't forget, Jews were major players in Hollywood. The Jewish community had come out of this horrific experience and had, at that particular time, a great sensitivity to humanity and a strong empathy with oppressed people. Recently, much of the Jewish community has become increasingly conservative. But at that time, I remember distinctly that most of the progressive white people I knew were Jewish. Sure, there were conservative Jews, but there was a progressive group in Hollywood and they had an impact.

I'm thinking of Dalton Trumbo and the people who were active in writing *Back to Bataan* [written by Ben Barzman and Richard H. Landau; directed by Edward Dmytryk, 1945], *Gentleman's Agreement* [written by Moss Hart and Elia Kazan; directed by Elia Kazan, 1947], and *Pinky* [written by Philip Dunne, Elia Kazan, Dudley Nichols, and Jane White; directed by Elia Kazan, 1949], and in bringing Sidney Poitier to the fore. As a matter of fact, both Sidney and I were up for the role in *No Way Out* [Joseph L. Mankiewicz, 1950]. I didn't get it, maybe because I'd done *Lost Boundaries* [directed by Alfred L. Werker; produced by Louis de Rochemont, 1949]: Darryl Zanuck didn't want to use anybody from one of Louis de Rochemont's films; he was feuding with de Rochemont at the time.

Anyway, to get back to the original question, these new Hollywood films began to attract black audiences, and the segregation began to break down. *Brown v. the Board of Education* was decided in 1954. There was an attenuation, or a dilution, whatever you want to call it, of racism. Finally, black people could go to any theater they wanted, and they were looking at lots of films not made by blacks. There were a few black-cast films made, but the bulk of the films we were looking at were white films coming out of Hollywood.

SM: At the point when you were in *Souls of Sin* and *Miracle in Harlem*, were you conscious of a history of that kind of work? The last few years or so have seen the reconstruction of the history of African-American underground filmmaking since Oscar Micheaux.

WG: No, I didn't know that history. I was a young actor gratifying my ego by seeing myself on the screen. It wasn't until I was eighteen or nineteen that I started becoming aware of the processes of history. And I didn't think about *film* history, just history in the larger sense. So I was part of it, but didn't even know about it!

MS: Were you ever in touch with Spencer Williams?

WG: At that time, I didn't know that much about Spencer Williams, didn't even know he made movies.

SM: *Lost Boundaries* was one of a half a dozen Hollywood films of the late 1940s and early 1950s that broke through in terms of dealing with race. Did the cast and crew feel as if they were involved in a breakthrough production?

WG: Oh, very much so! We felt we were involved in something important. Hollywood was still doing all these horrible Uncle Tom things—Mantan Moreland and the rest. This film was different: there were classy black people in it....

SM: And a lot of variety, too: wealthy blacks, working-class blacks, black doctors, black cops....

FIGURE 2.6 Greaves, as Arthur Cooper, playing piano with Howard Carter (Richard Hylton), in *Lost Boundaries* (1949), produced by Louis de Rochemont; directed by Alfred L. Werker. Production still, courtesy Schomburg Center for Research in Black Culture.

WG: De Rochemont had done *March of Time*, then went into feature film production. He produced *The House on 92nd Street* [Henry Hathaway, 1945], *Boomerang* [Elia Kazan, 1947], then *Lost Boundaries*, which was a hit that ran for six months in New York.

SM: You shot on location for *Lost Boundaries*?

WG: Yes, in Keene and Portsmouth, New Hampshire.

SM: Both *Lost Boundaries* and *Intruder in the Dust* [Clarence Brown, 1949] were shot on location about events which took place locally. In the case of *Lost Boundaries*, the events had actually occurred. What was the public surround of the shooting?

WG: Keene was very New England WASPy, but I didn't find the people inhospitable at all. They were cool, as New England types often are, but I don't remember feeling any racial pressures. Of course, you have to understand that by then I was an actor and so full of myself that I didn't have time for racism. I didn't like it when it revealed itself and could be very angry, but I had no problems in Keene.

A few years ago, we had a big reunion in Keene. Larry Benequist, head of the film department at Keene State University, thought it would be a good idea to bring the cast and crew, and the townspeople who had been involved, together for a fortieth reunion. It was a very emotional coming together, a wonderful evening.

SM: I assume you met the actual family who had passed for white?

WG: Oh yes.

SM: There's a photograph of the Johnston family in Donald Bogle's *Blacks in American Film and Television* [(New York: Fireside, 1989), 139]....

WG: The actual family wasn't that white!

SM: It seems remarkable now that they could pass.

WG: According to some of the townspeople, the family had deluded themselves into thinking they had passed. To some people they may have, but not to others. It was just that some of the white people didn't think it was important enough to make a fuss about. They just took the guy the way he was. Johnston himself was apparently very uptight about the whole thing. Of course, the kids would think of themselves as white because up there in Keene they didn't have anything to do with black kids.

In going to de Rochemont's place during the *Lost Boundaries* period, I began to chat with Lou Applebaum, the composer for *Lost Boundaries* and the principal composer for the National Film Board of Canada. Lou was delighted that I was interested in the NFB. After *Lost Boundaries*, de Rochemont, who was a great guy, allowed me to become an apprentice in his studio. As a matter of fact, Mike Roemer (who would go on to make *Nothing but a Man* [1964] with Bob Young) and I were like two little kids in de Rochemont's studio. But even he didn't have any black people working there—and anyway, there were no black people with the necessary skills for the work.

The unions were entirely racist. Even Bill Alexander hired white cameramen and technicians. The McCarthy thing was happening, and I was having some trouble getting work, not because I was a member of this or that, but because the whole climate of the industry had begun to change. America was locked up.

MS: After *Lost Boundaries* you were going to read for *Twentieth Century*, the revival of the Ben Hecht, Charles MacArthur play?

WG: Yes. The revival was going to star Gloria Swanson. José Ferrer was the director. My agent, Max Rosenbaum, had arranged for me to have a part in this play. He hadn't seen the script, nor had I, but when I showed up for the first day of rehearsal, I was told I would play a Pullman porter. I said, "All right,

I'll play the Pullman porter, but I'll play him with some dignity. I won't do an Uncle Tom, Stepin-Fetchit-type depiction."

And wouldn't you know it? That's exactly what José Ferrer and the rest of them were expecting from me! They wanted me to do "Yassa massa" and all that foolishness. I'd become aware of ancient African civilizations and how the information about them had been suppressed because Western civilization needed a philosophical basis for the oppression of people of color. You couldn't legitimately oppress a people who had a long and important history stretching back thousands of years. How were you going to rationalize the oppression? You had to say they're a bunch of silly natives running around in the jungle, waiting to be civilized by white European Christians.

The kind of work I was doing with Strasberg and Danny Mann and the others at the Actors Studio didn't call for the kind of racially embarrassing characterization Ferrer wanted me to do in *Twentieth Century*, because Strasberg and Mann and Martin Ritt—who was another of my teachers—were progressive, liberal people. They would have disowned me if they'd seen me on the stage doing that kind of thing. But I wouldn't have done it anyway.

I quit the production after the second day of rehearsal and decided, once and for all, that I needed to get behind the camera and start *making* movies, documentaries that spoke to the needs and interests of the black community and to the dignity of our history.

NATIONAL FILM BOARD OF CANADA

WG: I realized that I needed to find some way to get into filmmaking. I learned that there were only two major film schools in the country—the film institute at City College of New York and the other, at UCLA. Each had fifty students. That was the ballgame for the whole of America at that time. Of course, today there are fifty–sixty thousand students studying film.

I began studying filmmaking at City College in the evenings (while studying acting at the Actors Studio during the day). Hans Richter was head of the film institute at City College. I studied with Rohama Lee, Louis Jacobs, Arthur Knight, Leo Seltzer, Jack Knapp, and Jean Lennard. For a time, I also studied at the New Institute for Film & Television out in Brooklyn, which was headed by Don Winkler and his wife.

While I was studying at City College, I was living near Gramercy Park. A friend of mine had this big brownstone. There was a painter living there,

Samuel Countee, who mentored me and became a good friend. Also, in that same house was a wonderful actor named Frank Silvera, who, a few years later, would play General Huerta in *Viva Zapata* [1952].

I had a girlfriend who was friends with a fellow she said was a budding filmmaker. Believe it or not, this budding filmmaker was Stanley Kubrick!

Actually, at that time he hadn't even made a film; he was working in his father's camera shop and taking photographs [in fact, Kubrick's father was a doctor; from a young age, with his father's support, Kubrick had taken still photographs], but he apparently wanted to make a movie. Since I was studying filmmaking, my girlfriend introduced us.

I'd read John Grierson's *Grierson on Documentary* [originally published 1946], which became one of the inspirations for my work as a filmmaker, and began counseling this young guy on how he might begin a filmmaking career. So here I am advising Stanley Kubrick on how he should go about getting into the business! I don't know if Stanley remembers this experience, but I can see him so clearly, sitting in the kitchen with me telling him, "You know, Stanley, you really should start studying filmmaking. Why don't you come up to the film institute? They've got some great teachers up there. Hans Richter is a very interesting man from Germany."

MS: Did you meet Kubrick later on?

WG: No, never saw him again. Later on, Frank Silvera had a role in Kubrick's *Killer's Kiss* [1955].

I remember that when I told Sidney Poitier and Harry Belafonte that I was studying filmmaking, both said, "How are *you* going to produce movies in this country? Impossible! It can't happen."

One of the incentives for my going to Canada was [Joseph] McCarthy. I didn't get a role in one of the feature films I was up for, because they said that, somehow or other, I'd gotten onto somebody's list as being too interested in the Bill of Rights, too interested in the American Constitution and the Declaration of Independence. Anathema to the truly loyal, patriotic Americans! I thought, "I'm out of here."

Reading *Grierson on Documentary*, I'd realized that documentary was the way I wanted to go, and it was obvious that the documentary path would be the easiest path for me since for documentaries you didn't need big budgets. And documentary spoke to the issue of vindicating the history of the African-American people in a very direct way, as opposed to what was possible in fictional Hollywood films. I thought that maybe I could learn to make films in Canada, which led me to talk with Lou Applebaum.

Lou and I had become great friends. He'd been around the de Rochemont studio, developing the musical score for *Lost Boundaries*. I'd read about the National Film Board of Canada in the Grierson book, and it seemed a wonderful place to be an apprentice. I talked to Lou about it, and he said, "Sure! I know the guy who's in charge. I do music for them all the time."

I'd heard that the John Hay Whitney Foundation was making grants to black artists, dancers, and actors. I proposed that they finance me for a period of apprenticeship in Ottawa so that I could learn how to generate images that would be mass-produced and disseminated throughout the world. They thought I was crazy and turned me down. I decided to go up to Canada anyway—because by that time I'd been in touch, through Lou, with Donald Mulholland, the head of production at the Film Board, who encouraged me to come as an apprentice.

For three months I lived on water and sugar because I didn't have much money. I'd go into a restaurant, eat a few sugar cubes, and drink some water, and that would be my meal for the evening. When the waiter arrived and asked, "What would you like?" I'd say, "Sorry, I've changed my mind" and leave. Finally, I got a couple part-time jobs—scrubbing floors, washing windows—and for three or four months was able to eke out a living. After a while I guess Don Mulholland, Norman McLaren, and Guy Glover decided, "This guy is serious," and Mulholland gave me a job working at the Film Board.

At first, I worked as a gofer, then I became an assistant editor, then a sound editor for two or three years—a pretty good one, I must say. Then I became an editor and then a chief editor in the fabled Unit B. Norman McLaren, Roman Kroiter, Colin Low, Wolf Koenig, and Terry Filgate [Terence Macartney-Filgate] were my colleagues. It was a wonderfully creative environment. Tom Daly was the mother hen of the whole group, the executive producer.

JH: Were there other black filmmakers at the Film Board at that time?

WG: Yes. Ron Alexander, a Canadian, was a laboratory technician who became a sound recordist.

When the Film Board moved to Montreal in 1956, we all worked there. A lot of British filmmakers came over to work at the Board, and I worked with Ken Healy-Ray, the master sound editor who did the sound on *Odd Man Out* [Carol Reed, 1947], and Fergus McDonald, who cut *Odd Man Out*. It was a stimulating environment, and gradually I rose up the ladder to become a writer and director.

MS: Was Grierson still alive?

WG: Oh, yes. I remember a time when Grierson came by and we threw a big party for him. All the Grierson disciples—the acolytes and the sycophants—were gathered around the feet of the master. He was holding forth, giving his views on film and society, and rhapsodizing about the truth: "And what we are trying to do is get the truth out. The truth is like Louis Armstrong hitting high Cs. It's Joe DiMaggio hitting a home run."

I asked him, "Why are you so interested in truth?" Well, he freaked out and excoriated me: "If that isn't the goddamnedest stupid question." Apparently, I'd touched a nerve. I don't know what led me to ask him that. Maybe it was some kind of divine prodding! But that's my Grierson story. Actually, he was a wonderful guy, and very supportive of us.

MS: Did you have later conversations with him?

WG: Just once or twice in passing. I didn't get to know him the way that some of the others did. But he was a very nurturing man, as was Tom Daly, who was one of his people.

MS: How long were you at the NFB?

WG: About eight years.

MS: Was *Emergency Ward* [1958] your first film?

WG: No, the first film I directed (and wrote and edited) was *Smoke and Weather* [1958], which was about forest fires. Then I directed and edited a film called *Putting It Straight* [1957], which is about orthodontia. It had to do with the formation of teeth in young children. Then I worked on *The Magic Mineral* [1959; at the NFB site, Greaves is not listed in the credits of this film] and *High Arctic* [1959; Greaves is credited with script and editing].

The mandate of the National Film Board was to make documentaries for the various government departments and agencies. They also did films for television. I worked on a series called *On the Spot* [none of the films in this series, produced from 1953 to 1955, credit Greaves].

The NFB also produced films that were, for one reason or another, considered more artistic, including *Emergency Ward* and *Neighbors* [Normal McLaren, 1952], *Universe* [Roman Kroiter and Colin Low, 1960], *Lonely Boy* [Wolf Koenig and Roman Kroitor, 1961], and *Blood and Fire* [Terence Macartney-Filgate, 1958].

MS: Tell me about *Emergency Ward*.

WG: Unit B was a very aggressive, artistic, creative group. We became very interested in what had come to be called cinéma vérité. As a matter of fact, we were into cinéma vérité in 1957–1958—before Leacock and Pennebaker and the other Americans. Pennebaker used to come up to the Film Board to have a look at what we were doing and to show us what he was doing.

One of our influences was, of course, Jean Rouch. Also, the work of Henri Cartier-Bresson interested us. Of course, as an actor and acting teacher, I was very involved with the Method, the Stanislavski system, Strasberg and Kazan—so the improvisational dynamic of the Method and the cinéma-vérité dynamic coalesced in my mind. For *Emergency Ward* I was working with a life-and-death situation in which people would be so absorbed in what they were confronted with that they would have no time to think about the intrusive nature of a camera. We lit up the emergency ward of a hospital and positioned three cameras—cameras were very heavy at the time, nothing like the handheld cameras of today—and we spent a month in the emergency ward. I think we went on weekends: Thursday, Friday, Saturday, and Sunday nights.

MS: The same ward every time?

WG: Yes.

MS: Trauma cases, whatever was coming in?

WG: Whatever was coming in. *Emergency Ward* was considered one of my best films and one of Unit B's best films.

MS: It's one of Bill Sloan's favorites [Sloan (1928–2017) was for years head of the New York Public Library film collection and later curator of independent film at MoMA].

WG: That's right.

MS: Did *City of Gold* [1958] come out of Unit B?

WG: Yes. It was directed by Colin Low and Wolf Koenig; Roman Kroiter did the screenplay.

MS: That was an early instance of the use of still photography in documentary.

WG: That's right. When I came back to the States, I did several films using that technique. *From These Roots* [1974], a film about the Harlem Renaissance, was done entirely with still photographs.

MS: Was George Stoney part of the National Film Board when you were there?

WG: No, he came later [Stoney (1916–2012) directed the *Challenge for Change* project at the NFB from 1968 to 1970]. We knew of George and his *All My Babies* [1953], which we saw at the Film Board in Ottawa.

MS: Your years in Canada seem to have been open and creative.

WG: Yes, wonderful!

I had continued to act, and to teach acting, from the time I first arrived at the Film Board in 1953. In those days no one was teaching the Method in Canada. Some of the people at the Board wanted training as actors for their work as directors. Then I expanded into the larger Ottawa community. When the Film Board moved to Montreal, I started a group there.

FIGURE 2.7 Greaves with George Stoney during Stoney's ninetieth birthday party at Betty and Dennis Puleston's home in Brookhaven, N.Y. Photographer unknown. Courtesy Louise Greaves.

A number of the French actors who were in my group, the Canadian Drama Studio, went on to become big stars. Monique Mercure was one of our actor-students, along with Luce Guilbeault and Marcel Sabourin. The American actor Michael Sarrazin joined us.

For a time I shuttled back and forth between Montreal and Ottawa to do this work. Then some people in Toronto heard about what I was doing and wanted to start a branch of the Canadian Drama Studio there. So I was shuttling back and forth between three cities.

MS: Are you multilingual?

WG: I wish I were. My wife, Louise Archambault, is French Canadian. I know a few words in French, but I regret to say I'm parochial in my linguistic propensities.

MS: Were you doing any acting at the Canadian Drama Studio?

WG: No, I taught the actors and directed: we put on plays. It was an exciting experience. We did some improvisational stuff that went on television.

MS: Original works?

WG: Yes. I'd have actors come up from the Actors Studio. Alfred Ryder came up and Peggy Feury. They taught for us whenever I had work to do at the Film Board or somewhere else. And Johnny Randolph, Kevin McCarthy, John Styx, John Strasberg, and Ellen Gerber. Whenever I was too involved with production work, I'd have them substitute for me.

MS: When did you leave the NFB?

WG: In 1960. I felt I had pretty well come to the end of the line in terms of the kinds of training and information about filmmaking that I needed in order to continue my work liberating the minds of Americans—black Americans in particular—from the socially negative conditions that were operating in American society.

The thing that enabled me to come back was the changing political climate: the Selma, Alabama, events; the civil rights marches and sit-ins; Malcolm X and Martin Luther King, and James Farmer and CORE [Congress of Racial Equality]. Baldwin was on television, doing interviews with Sidney Poitier and Harry Belafonte.

I also left the Film Board because the head of production at that time, Grant McLean, wanted me to become head of the science film unit. While I liked science very much, I felt that this was going to take me off track, making me a government filmmaker doing films on microbes or radioactive isotopes. I remember thinking, "Wait a minute! I got into filmmaking because I saw it as a weapon for social action, political change." I was committed to revealing the true history of a people.

I'd gotten an opportunity to become a public information officer for a UN agency in Montreal, the International Civil Aviation Organization (ICAO). I'd made some films for them, including *Roads in the Sky* [available at https://www.youtube.com/watch?v=ZDLA5ft9IJI]. I also produced radio programs for them, and once I edited their magazine.

Quite coincidentally, the United Nations in New York needed a film on the flight of an airliner around the world; air-navigational services and air-traffic-control procedures needed to be made compatible. Whether you were from one country or another, there had to be a lingua franca as your plane flew through the airspace of another country—with no common language, air safety could be jeopardized. Because of my work with the ICAO, I was a logical person to head up this project, but I was in Montreal.

They requested that I come to New York.

FILMMAKING (AND TELEVISION) IN THE UNITED STATES

WG: Louise and I moved down to New York, and I made *Cleared for Take-Off* [1963], about the flight of an airliner around the world. I shot it in a more or less cinéma-vérité format; it's a nice film. Alistair Cooke wrote and performed the narration. He was a great raconteur and a wonderful person to fly around the world with. Of course, I was not the only person who thought so. Our executive producer, George Movshon—I was producer/director—was an Alistair Cooke groupie. I couldn't stop him from coming, so George went around the world with us.

We shot all over the place: Hawaii, Fiji, Bangkok, Singapore. When we got to Calcutta, George said, "Why don't we go down to the railroad station and get some local-color footage. We can film Alistair against the railroad station and the hurly-burly of the crowds there. It'll be wonderful!" Alistair said, "Sure, fine, George, we'll go." Naively I said, "Okay."

At the time, I didn't know that India, having just gotten rid of the British, was very active in decolonization. I took the crew down to the railroad station and there we are filming Alistair Cooke saying, with his velvet voice, "I am now in the center of Calcutta, this teeming city of millions. Everywhere you can see the wonderful colors of the people, the saris of the beautiful ladies...." As he's rhapsodizing, a scrawny little Indian student comes up to us and says to me, "What are you doing?" I say, "We're making a film." "What is the film about?" "It's about the flight of an airliner around the world." He says, "Wait a minute. Let me understand you. You're making a film about the flight of an airliner around the world? The airport is thirty kilometers away. This is the railroad station, where there are a lot of very poor, starving people. *That's* where *you* are. Why are you shooting *here*?"

This guy is kind of hostile, so I say, "We're doing the film for the United Nations." I thought he would say, "Oh, hosanna! Hooray! God bless!" But he says, "You're making the film about the flight of an airliner around the world, for the United Nations. And you're filming it here with these poor people. Clearly, your purpose is to show India at its worst. Is that not so?" I said, "No, no, we're just trying to create a sense of the whole region in which we're functioning."

Then George Movshon says, "Bill, I think I can handle this"—because now this kid is getting angry. You've got to picture George Movshon: a heavy-set, blonde, blue-eyed, South African, with a South African accent. He walks up to this emaciated Indian student, who was probably in one of the militant groups in Calcutta, and starts poking him in the chest and saying, "Now see here, my good man, we're doing this."

That moment when he started poking the kid in the chest was the first time I saw levitation in India. This kid literally rose up off the ground and landed on the hood of a car and started shouting at the top of his lungs: "These people are here to disgrace us! They want to show us at our worst! They want to put our images on the screens of the world! These are not friends!"

Alistair was terrified. I said, "Let's get out of here," and got the crew into the cars. George was still determined to argue his point with this kid, but Alistair and I stuffed him into the car and started moving very slowly, because by this time crowds of people are beginning to converge on the car. They're pounding on the windshield and on the back of the car, ready to turn it over. By the time we got to the hotel, all of us were shaking.

MS: You didn't do any more films with George?

WG: No. I left the United Nations television department to do films independently for the United States Information Agency [USIA].

MS: When did you meet Shirley Clarke?

WG: Canada Lee and I were good friends, and Canada Lee's son, Carl Canegata [Carl Lee], was also a good friend of mine. So once I was back in New York, Carl looked me up and we revived our friendship. Carl was going out with Shirley and brought her by the house for dinner with Louise and me. Shirley was absolutely wonderful.

Shirley was interested in the fact that I'd worked at the NFB and wanted to see some of the films. So I showed her *Emergency Ward* and she freaked out! I think she told Bill Sloan and Willard Van Dyke and George Stevens about me, because I remember her telling me, "Bill, when George heard about you and saw your film, he absolutely *shit*!" Apparently, Stevens liked the movie: he gave me a contract with the USIA to do a film about dissent in America.

MS: *Wealth of a Nation* [1964]?

WG: Yes. We danced around the maypole a lot with that project. *Wealth of a Nation* started out as "A Nation of Dissenters." The USIA wanted to do a film showing, in Cold War terms, that America was friendly to dissent, a free society where people could speak their minds. I filmed Madalyn Murray, Saul Alinsky, Lawrence Lipton (he wrote *The Holy Barbarians* [published in 1959]), and various other people I had researched—but when the USIA realized who I was focusing on, they decided they didn't want *that* much dissent!

Finally, George and McKinney Russell, the wonderful policy guy for the USIA, decided it would be a film dealing with "freedom of individual expression." Martin Luther King was in the film and a lot of artists.

MS: What footage did you have of Dr. King?

WG: The march on Washington. And we filmed Lee Montague, a wonderful artist, and William Catabalis and the architect Paolo Soleri, and various soapbox orators.

When I was in Arizona filming Soleri at Arcosanti, I visited a town called Jerome, where I was almost lynched by some "minutemen." Here I am on location, doing this film about the right of individuals to speak freely, no matter what their persuasion, and these bastards are seriously considering lynching me (and the architect with me who was a refugee from the Third Reich and his eight-year-old son). We'd been sightseeing and went to have some malted milks. Somehow these guys found out that I was making a film for the government and must have thought maybe this black guy and this German Jew were doing some kind of undercover work, spying on them.

When we left the restaurant, the bastards chased us. We finally eluded them, but they called ahead and another car picked us up. It was a hair-raising experience getting out of the hills of Arizona and back into Phoenix. The kid was in hysterics, because his father and I were arguing back and forth: should we take this road or that road? We didn't know where the hell we were going. And it was late at night. We finally solved the problem by going into a place where there were a lot of cars. When we saw a car coming that didn't have anything to do with these guys, we followed that car and we were able to elude them.

MS: I trust that your filming *The First World Festival of Negro Arts* in Dakar was less hair-raising.

WG: That was an epiphany, a *great* experience! The first time I had gone to Africa. There was a huge turnout for the event: to Dakar came two thousand people from thirty countries, celebrating negritude, the liberation of the African spirit, the renaissance of Black talent and creativity and genius. Emperor Haile Selassie was there, and Leopold Senghor, who was the president of Senegal; Aime Cesaire, Langston Hughes, Duke Ellington, Katherine Dunham, Alvin Ailey and his dance company, Alioune Diop—intellectuals and artists from all over the African diaspora.

The Russians were there with a twenty-person crew; the Belgians were there with their crew, the Italians, the French, the British. The USIA had given me a contract to do a story for *Today*, the screen magazine they published monthly, but as soon as I got to Dakar and had a sense of the scope of the event, I told them, "This seems big. Are you sure all you want is a little story for your screen magazine?"

So here's our puny USIA team, me and my cameraman—though I was operating the camera, too. I trained our chauffeur to do sound. We made our film using guerrilla tactics. The Russians would light the stage and the dancers and we'd sneak around getting shots. We filmed the outdoor events cinéma vérité. I was fortunate in getting Langston Hughes to visit a fishing village called Rufisque, where I filmed him against the sea with the fishermen, then later paraphrased his poem, "The Negro Speaks of Rivers," for context. We see him later on with Duke Ellington.

It all worked out. The film became the USIA's most popular film in Africa for at least ten years. Langston came to our studio when we'd finished the film. When he saw what I'd done with the footage, he loved it. Sad to say, he died shortly thereafter.

I'd known Langston when I was an actor; he showed up at the American Negro Theatre all the time. There are a lot of fond memories—Langston and I and the poet Yevgeny Yevtushenko riding around in Yevtushenko's limousine, where bottles of vodka were stashed! Usually I managed to retain some semblance of sobriety, but they got plastered. We had a lot of fun.

First World Festival still holds up.

FIGURES 2.8 Frame grab of Langston Hughes on the beach in Dakar, Senegal, filmed by Greaves for *First World Festival of Negro Arts*. Thanks to Paul Cronin for assistance.

MS: I understand that working with the USIA was the first opportunity you had to make films that expressed a black perspective on reality—until then, you'd not had access to financing that would permit that.

WG: That's right. The United States government was on the cutting edge, as far as the African American was concerned, with altering the body politic—creating access to various professions, for example. It's a product of the military. The military was the first area where massive desegregation took place.

Without United States government financing, my career in this country would have been zilch. From 1964 through the late 1970s I did scores of films for the government, and was able to develop my craft and work productively as a film producer. This support sustained our company. And in fact, we did have a lot of freedom of expression—more than people might think.

I'd set up my own production company in 1964. I'd rejected the idea of going out to Hollywood. It felt like working out there would be like working on a plantation: you had to answer to the Man for everything you did. We had a different mission.

I'd come back from Canada because the country had begun to change. You can see that in *Black Journal*, the very first show of its kind. The idea of black people producing a network show, let alone a series, had been unthinkable.

MS: Let's talk about NET [National Educational Television]. How did you come to work at 10 Columbus Circle?

WG: Don Dixon was the head of public affairs at NET (not to be confused with WNET, which came later). Don had seen *Cleared for Take-Off* and liked it. He'd told me, "I'll certainly keep you in mind for something." Then Bill Branch brought a film project to Don, who told him, "You don't have experience as a film producer on a project of this magnitude. Why don't you associate yourself with someone who has?" He suggested me.

Bill and I worked together to produce *Still a Brother: Inside the Negro Middle Class* [1968]. He was the writer, and I photographed, directed, and edited. It worked out nicely. *Still a Brother* was about the black middle class and its relationship to the civil rights revolution. What was their status as a group in American society? What were the tensions between the black middle class and the larger white society, as well as the tensions within the black community itself—the problems of identification and the mental revolution that the black middle class was going through, given the rising militancy? The black middle class had been brainwashed by white society, and now they were having to brainwash themselves to get in synchronization with the new developments that were taking place.

Then, of course, came *Black Journal*. The National Advisory Commission on Civil Disorders—the Kerner Commission—came into being in the wake of the riots that had been taking place—150 riots in different cities in one year. The assassinations of Martin Luther King and Malcolm X led to a Kerner Commission finding that American society had not given the African-American community an opportunity to express its needs, interests, grievances, et cetera. The African-American community had become pretty pissed off with this situation and had finally said, "Enough! We're going to have this freedom that you keep talking about in America, or there's not going to *be* an America." It was as simple as that.

The black community offered two alternatives: the nonviolent alternative, as enunciated and shepherded by Martin Luther King and people like James Farmer and CORE, and the more militant alternative: Stokely Carmichael and Malcolm X. Within this equation, of course, was Ralph Bunche, who attempted to clarify and explain the dynamics of the situation to the American elite. Although it was not well-known, Bunche had the ears of the Establishment and could interpret these two dynamics to the leaders of American society. In fact, he played no small role in creating an international climate for human rights and self-determination, all those principles that found their way into the United Nations.

The African and Third World countries that became part of the United Nations exerted a very heavy pressure, as did European nations who were more liberal than America. All this combined with the internal dissent and ferment and the protests and agitation by both the black community and white people of good will who were sick and tired of the duplicity and hypocrisy of America. It was a wonderful period in American history, in many ways a watershed period, quite similar in its impact to the Emancipation Proclamation itself.

Having said that, we're still waiting for another watershed period that will eliminate this curious racial pathology that seems endemic to this country. The average white American simply cannot get his/her head around this problem of race. Nor can the black American. It's a sick, enervating sociological dance that drains everybody's energy. When we should be coming to grips with the problems of nuclear disarmament and ecology and the elderly and of the cities and of education, half of our energies are deployed to deal with this craziness.

Frankly, I've grown sick and tired of having to make films dealing with the racial issue when I know there are other films about important issues that need to be made. But if I don't do these films, and if others feel that they shouldn't bother to do them, there's a problem. This festering sore of racism is eventually going to pull the whole thing down. It will be the Trojan Horse of America.

The Kerner Commission said African Americans needed to have access to the media. There was a lot of anger among blacks at not seeing ourselves on screen, and whenever we *were* seen, we were maligned: stereotypically depicted with no sense of the realities of African-American life. The Ford Foundation and the Carnegie Endowment—I think, Rockefeller was also somehow involved—got together and put up the money for *Black Journal*, which NET developed for public television. I was chosen to be a cohost, along with Lou House (who later became known as Wali Sadiq). Al Perlmutter was to be executive producer, and you, Mort, were one of the producers.

After the first two installments of *Black Journal* there was a palace revolt by the black staff, led by Kent Garrett, Charles Hobson, St. Clair Bourne, and others who felt that the show should be black controlled. They all agreed that I should be the one to take over as executive producer because of my experience in film production in Canada, and with work on more than eighty films under my belt.

We began a series of monthly shows and were nominated for an Emmy as the best public affairs show on television after our first year, and won the Emmy our second year.

MS: As I recall, the original plan of the non-African-Americans—Al and myself, several other producers—was just to lend support at the beginning, then to phase ourselves out.

Black Journal was a groundbreaking show in many respects.

WG: Absolutely. We were lucky to have very talented people on our staff: St. Clair Bourne, Madeline Anderson, Horace B. Jenkins.... And for a while we had money to work with. I sent a crew to Vietnam to look at the war from a black perspective. We had a crew go to Ethiopia. We sent a crew down South to look at a southern farm collective run by black people. We did shows with Malcolm X and Amiri Baraka. It was an independent-thinking show.

LC: In 1972 you covered the Gary convention [the first National Black Political Convention, held in Gary, Indiana].

WG: Yeah, we covered that. But I lost a lot of money producing *Nationtime—Gary* [1973]! I'd seen this as a momentous event and assumed all the networks would say, "Hallelujah, we'll air your film!" But none of the networks wanted it. Fortunately, we distribute our films ourselves.

About two years ago [here, Greaves is speaking in 2003], Peter Jennings or someone he worked with decided they wanted to do something on the Gary event. They wanted to cannibalize our footage. I went through a long, deep soul searching: in the end I decided we'd let them have bits and pieces, which they sprinkled through their show.

Black Journal used a magazine format. I'd have meetings with the staff every week to determine what the content of the next show was going to be. As I've said many times, one of the ways in which I arrived at my decision for a particular program was to make sure that the content of whatever we did would be acceptable to the black community. I did this by way of the black barbershop, where you hear a lot about the issues that concern the black community. After the producers would present their ideas, I'd say, "Now, will this fly in a black barbershop? If it does, it gets the green light; if doesn't, off with its head!"

MS: It was a terrific beginning.

WG: *Black Journal* was the flagship for all the black programs that subsequently came into being throughout America. Localities across the country began to think seriously about having their own shows. Within a couple of years, there were two or three hundred—so many that we formed the National Association of Black Media Producers.

JH: When did you leave *Black Journal*?

WG: In 1970.

SM: A number of filmmakers were mentored at *Black Journal*.

WG: Yes, Stan Lathan, St. Clair Bourne, Kent Garrett, Madeline Anderson, Horace Jenkins, Jimmy MacDonald, William Gaddis, Leroy McLucas, Osborn Smith, Angela Fontanez, Hazel Bright....

SYMBIOPSYCHOTAXIPLASM: TAKE ONE

SM: How were you able to finance *Symbiopsychotaxiplasm: Take One* [1971], a feature-length film experiment?

WG: I'd taught actors in Canada, and one of my actors there was extremely adroit at business ventures and had become very successful. He wanted me to make a feature: "Anything you want to make, just tell me." I began to realize I could put a feature together using some of the actors I knew, and so I went ahead [see the Louise Archambault Greaves interview for details on the financing of *Take One*].

JACKIE TSHAKA (coordinator, National Black Programming Consortium): I understand that *Symbiopsychotaxiplasm: Take One* was not shown much, at least at first.

WG: The film was never released. We shot *Symbio* in 1968 and then had difficulty getting anybody to finance finishing it. We finally got the money for a blow-up in 1971 but then had the problem of getting the film launched. I thought I could get it into the Cannes Film Festival and flew over to France. The problem was that Louis Marcorelles, the influential critic, went to a pre-screening of the film where the projectionist got the reels all fouled up. *Take One* is already chaotic. It's so fragile that if you mix it up even a little, you lose the film. Marcorelles and I had dinner after the screening, and he said, "I couldn't understand what the film was about!" I was surprised at his reaction and later, too late, discovered that his projectionist had screened the reels out of order.

I like to think of that incident as divine intervention: it kept this film buried for almost twenty-five years.

BILL SLOAN (chief, Circulating Film and Video Program, MoMA): I saw *Symbiopsychotaxiplasm* back in the sixties, when it was still in a rough cut, and I couldn't believe what I was seeing! What did you have in mind at the time?

WG: I had a whole range of concerns. The term "symbiopsychotaxiplasm" is a takeoff on "symbiotaxiplasm," a concept developed by philosopher/social scientist Arthur Bentley in his book *Inquiry Into Inquiries* [Beacon Press, 1954] as part of his study of the processes of social-scientific inquiry. Bentley explored how various social scientists went about the business of approaching "civilization" and "society."

"Symbiotaxiplasm" refers to all those events that transpire in any given environment a human being impacts. Of course, the most elaborate symbiotaxiplasm would be a city like New York. I had the audacity to insert "psycho" into the middle of Bentley's term. I felt the longer term more appropriate to my idea, which was to explore the psychology of a group of creative people who would function as an entity in the process of making a film.

I called it *Symbiopsychotaxiplasm: Take One* because the plan was to make five "Takes." But we couldn't even get the first one off the ground and didn't develop the others.

SM: The thing that used to be said about the generation of experimental filmmakers making films in the late sixties and early seventies is that they taught you how to watch the film as you were watching it. *Symbiopsychotaxiplasm: Take One* does that, in an unusual way: you have your surrogates on screen reacting the way that the audience is reacting.

WG: Well, the function of that first scene, when all hell breaks loose and you're suddenly seeing three separate images on the split-screen and all the ambivalent craziness that surrounds this kind of location shooting, was to push the audience into a state of annoyance.

When people in the crew appear on screen and say, "This is not the way you make a movie!" and "What the hell is this all about?," the audience begins to relax and say, "That's right!" They find themselves looking for an on-screen clue that articulates what they've been experiencing. The crew says, "This is a piece of shit. He doesn't know what he's doing. I read the script; it doesn't mean anything. It's just bad writing." And the audience thinks, "Yes, it *is* bad writing."

SM: Did you write the basic scene?

WG: Yes. Of course, the actors will suddenly take hold and sometimes have a moment of truth, which takes what is purportedly bad writing and moves it to another level. The nature of acting is that you can put Shakespeare into the mouth of a horrible actor and it's a disaster, but with a superb actor, Shakespeare takes off. And you can take very neutral dialogue and, by varying the basic circumstances of the dialogue, entirely change its impact. For example: "Hello. How are you?" "What's new?" "Nothing too much." "Have you seen so and so?" "No, I haven't" means almost nothing. But if one person is a killer and the person he's talking to is a potential victim, the same dialogue is entirely different. Suddenly, the person coming away from the piece says, "Gee, that was well written!" It's in the configuration of motivations and basic circumstances that the full reality of the scene emerges.

Anyway, in the film you find yourself moving back and forth among all those kinds of realizations. One minute the thing is lousy, the next minute it's interesting.

SM: And the different levels are often mutually referential. What the man and woman are saying to each other within their story can be interpreted as reflecting our feelings about the film, but even the struggle they're having getting along is analogous to our struggle as audience with what's on the screen.

WG: Also, for a variety of reasons I felt it was necessary to factor into the equation of the film the whole issue of sexuality. I was certainly mindful of the fact that sex/love makes the world go round and makes Hollywood go round.

It's the easiest way to capture the attention of the average American audience. Failure to address the issue of sexuality has dire implications in terms of the marketplace.

During the opening credits we see the maturation of the child in a series of Family-of-Man-type images. And then at the end of that sequence, you're focused on the butt of the black girl with the bike; the cycle is starting all over again. After that, the film focuses in on a couple in a relationship opposite to what has been projected as the normal cosmic cycle: two people getting together and procreating. This relationship threatens that possibility.

Also, in *Symbiopsychotaxiplasm* the sexual issue has more than one level of meaning. It has to do with birth and life versus nonbirth and nonlife, abortion. In 1966 the abortion issue was (for me) a metaphor for the Vietnam War, where many babies were killed. I also felt that the discussion of sex—especially homosexuality, which many considered unorthodox or unconventional at that time—would be controversial and would elicit audience attention and interest. Using sex as the focal point of the scene, I could then orbit the rest of my concerns around it.

SM: Abortion is still rarely dealt with so directly in films.

WG: Abortion was an issue moving up on the wheel of time. It's interesting that in my film Alice wants a child, Freddy does not, whereas in *Roe v. Wade*, it's more an issue of a woman having the right to say she doesn't want this new life. What I like about the scene today is that it prevents the film from seeming like advocacy for a particular issue. It creates an interesting tension.

SM: At one point, I thought you were indirectly using homosexuality and abortion as metaphors for the idea that this particular film is not what Hollywood would consider a creation, that the industry would consider *Symbiopsychotaxiplasm* an "abortion," a "perversion."

WG: For me, the homosexuality was more involved with the simple fact that people change, people become homosexual, and people become heterosexual. People have the right to change direction.

SM: So it fits with this film as a production process, as an open system?

WG: Sure.

SM: I assume that on one level, the choice of Central Park as the location was just the practical availability of having a space in New York City that you could control in certain ways. But there's also an Edenesque quality to the landscape you use. . . .

WG: Oh, absolutely! I mean we could have shot the scene inside an apartment. Central Park was an absolutely pregnant Eden. The park was appropriate for the traditional Family-of-Man cycle, and it had opportunities for uncontrollable events taking place, like the policeman coming in and asking, "What are you doing?" And in the wider social environment of Central Park, there were so many opportunities for an interaction between our creative nucleus, the cast and the crew, and the public surround.

SM: If we think of the layout of New York City, from 14th Street north, Manhattan is arranged as a grid for efficiency in doing business (at least in theory). It's all about doing things in rigorously structured ways to make money. Central Park is one of the few public places in the city that creates a sense that you can escape (even if that escape is an illusion). It's interesting that this film, which rebels against all the standard assumptions of the movie business, was made in this particular space. You evoke the whole tradition of the park as a form of therapy.

WG: Absolutely.

SM: Did you shoot material for all five *Symbiopsychotaxiplasm* "Takes" and just edit one?

WG: Yes.

SM: The original plan was to have each Take center on a different couple?

WG: *Take One* was going to be an omnibus version, a kaleidoscope of the couples. Then Takes Two, Three, Four, and Five would have focused on individual couples. We decided to abandon the omnibus version during the original editing; it was going to be too much.

SM: Did you decide to start with the Don Fellows/Pat Gilbert Take because their performances were the strongest?

WG: No. Originally, we were going to start with the interracial couple you see at the very end of *Take One*. But it didn't matter where we started; we were going to make all five films anyway, so we decided to go with what was available financially and get started. It was a pragmatic decision, but I felt comfortable with Pat and Don, who had done fascinating work.

Each pair dealt with the scenario in a different way. For the interracial couple, we drew on the works of J. L. Moreno, a student of Freud, who conceived psychodrama as a psychotherapeutic tool—a way of accessing and objectifying the subconscious—and brought it to this country. We had a psychodramatist, someone who had been trained by Moreno, come onto the set and work with the actors.

SM: So there's the version that's the focus of *Take One*; there's the version with elements of a musical. . . .

WG: Yes, where Susan Anspach and the young man who played opposite her would sing some of their lines. And then there are two other straight-ahead efforts by actors not as experienced as Pat and Don.

SM: Is there a lot more material of the crew meeting among themselves and responding to the project?

WG: Oh yes, but not as much as I originally thought I would get. I had thought the crew would challenge me on camera and that this conflict would be central to the drama of the film. My thinking was that if I made the crew sufficiently angry by certain types of redundancies and repetitions, they would begin saying, "What the hell's going on? Why are you doing this? What's this all about?" They'd rebel. But they didn't do that, and it was a source of grief, frustration, and depression for me during the course of the shooting.

Similarly, I thought that the actors would periodically have trouble with their lines or with me and that we'd get into debates over the relative merits of this or that passage of dialogue, of this particular psychological adjustment versus that motivation—that kind of thing. But the actors and the crew were so professional that they couldn't cross that boundary; they were too accustomed to situations where the director is god.

SM: There's a difference though. The crew sneaks away to have their own discussion about you and then presents you with the results, while the actors seem to assume that if something is going wrong it's because they're not good enough.

WG: Well, actors tend to be like that.

SM: I assume it's also because they knew you and your reputation as a teacher of actors.

WG: That may have had something to do with it, but typically actors are an oppressed community, a desperate community. They have so few opportunities to work that the last thing an actor wants to do is get a reputation for confronting directors.

So I didn't get what I wanted, except for that moment near the end where I say, "Cut!" and Pat says, "This is not working out," and I say, "Yes, it is," and she yells, "It's *not* and *you know it*!" I thought, "Oh boy, here she comes," because Pat was an intelligent, talented, sensitive actress with a volatile personality. She had radar about when something was truthful and when it wasn't. I figured that once she decided to confront me, she'd pull out all the stops. And I assumed that the crew would catch the whole thing. Of course, by that time the crew were so pissed off with me that they'd become sloppy in their camera reloading and, wouldn't you know, just at that moment they didn't have any film in the fucking camera! So when I walked across the bridge after Pat, they didn't follow. And then once the cameras were loaded, they felt it was too private a moment to interrupt. They fell back into the conventions.

FIGURE 2.9 Alice (Patricia Ree Gilbert) and Freddie (Don Fellows) in *Symbiopsychotaxiplasm: Take One* (1971). Courtesy Louise Greaves.

SM: Was this Pat Gilbert's first film? Don Fellows mentions acting in advertisements.

WG: I think it was her first film.

SM: Because there's that added dimension of thinking you may be screwing up because the process of doing takes over and over wastes film. Fellows talks about that.

WG: Don was not accustomed to cinéma vérité as a methodology for filming. When you do a commercial, you've got a slate, a scene number, a script clerk. Everything is all set up. Of course, cinéma vérité doesn't adhere to that, and even in the moments when we were filming in a more or less structured and conventional way, Don was surprised that we would do so many takes and that we would do improvisations.

Up to that point there really weren't many incidences of improvisation being done in feature films. Cassavetes, but not much else.

LAZAR STOJANOVIĆ (director of *Plastic Jesus* [1971]): In 1970 a Yugoslavian writer came back from the United States and told me about Bill Greaves and this film. He knew that I was interested in what I call self-analytical movies, movies that consider the medium. I couldn't get a clear picture of Bill's film, only that it was related to some of Godard's work. Now that I have finally seen *Symbiopsychotaxiplasm*, I think it's a milestone in the history of the sixties.

MICHELLE MATERRE (writer/producer for Blackside Productions): You must have had your ego in a great place to be able to allow the crew to think about you the way they did.

WG: It was a calculated risk. In general, my livelihood turns on people's perceiving me as a director, and yet, for this particular film to work, a flawed, vulnerable persona was essential. I must say I feel very good about my relationship with the crew. Even when they spoke about me at their meeting, they didn't speak in anger. They were six characters in search of an author.

MARIA DELUCA (director of *Green Streets* [1990]): I have a mundane question about the sequence of the crew at their private meeting. Did I miss something? It's one thing for them to say, "Let's get together and have a conference," but film stock is expensive. How did it happen that they were shooting film?

WG: We were well endowed with raw stock. They saw I was burning it up with these three cameras rolling at once, and I guess they figured I wouldn't miss two or three thousand feet!

RICHARD HERSKOWITZ (director of Cornell Cinema): Did you think of *Symbiopsychotaxiplasm* as a satire of cinéma vérité in particular?

WG: At the National Film Board of Canada, Terry Filgate, who was part of the crew, and I were together in what was called Unit B. We worked on *Lonely Boy* [Wolf Koenig and Roman Kroitor, 1962]. The process of learning to do that kind of shooting made me very attuned to the spontaneous capturing of reality and certainly laid the groundwork for this film.

But I should tell you some of the other thinking that I had in mind while making *Symbiopsychotaxiplasm*. I went to a science high school in New York City and was pointed in the direction of science; I broke that off after high school, but I continued to be interested in various scientific theories. The Heisenberg Principle of Uncertainty, in particular, fascinated me. Heisenberg asserts that we'll never really know the basis of the cosmos, because the means of perceiving it alters the reality. The electron microscope sends out a beam of electrons that knocks the electrons of the atoms being observed out of their orbits.

I began to think of the movie camera as an analog to the electron microscope. In this case, the reality to be observed is the human soul, the psyche. Of course, as the camera investigates that part of the cosmos, the individual psyches being observed recoil. Behavior becomes structured in a way other than it would have been had it been unperceived—a psychological version of the Heisenberg Principle. In this sense, my film was an environment in which movie cameras were set up to catch the process of human response.

I was also interested in the Second Law of Thermodynamics, which describes the distribution of energy in a system. In *Symbiopsychotaxiplasm* the cameras were to track the flow of energy in the system I had devised. If the cameras looked at one person and the level of spontaneous reality began to recede as a result of their being observed, that energy would show up somewhere else, behind the cameras in the crew, for example. The cameras were set up to track the flow of energy from in front of the cameras to behind them and back to the front.

ALAN ROSENTHAL (documentary filmmaker): Did you look at the rushes in between the filming, or did you just continue shooting?

WG: We had to look at the rushes to see whether we were getting things on film, but I didn't see the rushes of the crew at their secret meeting until after the shooting was over. Bob Rosen came to me and said, "Bill, we have a little present for you."

PATRICIA ZIMMERMANN (professor, Ithaca College): In documentary and in certain narrative forms, there's a long history of self-reflexive filmmaking as a political intervention to disengage the traditional power of the director. It's evident at least as early as Dziga Vertov. In the sixties, self-reflexivity became an international movement: Godard, Dusan Makavejev, Lazar Stojanović, many American and European avant-garde filmmakers, you....

In all these instances, self-reflexivity functioned as a way of disengaging from certain authoritarian power relations to make way for more utopian ways of working in the world. The scene where you're sitting with your multiracial, multinational, mixed-gender crew seems to encapsulate this. And you're an African-American director. Could you situate your method within the politics of the time?

WG: Clearly, we were working in a context of the urban disorders of the sixties and the rage of the African-American community against the tyranny and racism of the American body politic. Plus, there were more specific struggles: the civil rights marches and the other strategies that were being employed by the African-American community. And there was the whole Vietnam problem and the growing dissent over the war. There was the emerging feminist movement. And Woodstock. There was an unhappiness of massive dimensions over the way in which society had been run and about the covert authoritarianism that was evident everywhere. True, America was no dictatorship, but there certainly were mores, local and federal laws, social structures in place that inhibited the flowering of the human spirit.

Symbio was an attempt to look at the impulses and inspirations of a group of creative people who, during the making of the film, were being "pushed to the wall" by the process I as director had instigated. The scene that I had written was fixed, and I was in charge. I was insisting that this scene be filmed by cast and crew, even though it was making them very unhappy. The question was, "When will they revolt?" When would they question the validity, the wisdom, of doing the scene in the first place? In this sense, it really was a reflection of the politics of the time.

MARIA AGUI CARTER (independent filmmaker): The issue this film raises for me is individual power versus collective power. At one point in the film, you say, "I represent the establishment." I find that when I'm directing a mixed crew, particularly a gender-mixed crew, I have power relationship problems because of my gender and race. When you as an African-American director said, "I represent the establishment," how did your crew respond?

WG: You have to think in terms of the sixties, when there was a breaking out of a lot of ossified thinking. The people who worked on *Symbiopsychotaxiplasm* were Age-of-Aquarius-type people, in many respects shorn of the encumbrances that many white Americans are burdened with. If you investigated the psychology of these people, you wouldn't discover racism or prejudice. They had a very collaborationist approach.

JOHN COLUMBUS (director, Black Maria Film Festival): Did you expect a counterculture audience for the film? Or did you hope for distribution through commercial theaters?

WG: When we first had a blow-up, we did show it to a couple of distributors, and their eyeballs went around in their sockets. They couldn't figure out how to categorize and package it. One of the critics from *Time* magazine had come by my studio in the sixties and said, "Gee, this thing is not going to be acceptable for twenty years."

The audience here at the Flaherty Seminar represents a high level of appreciation. You're all cinema people: filmmakers, cinema scholars, and so on, and that's always an unusual situation. I think that the film will make its way into art theaters and through the college circuit and to whatever film societies are out there. But it will probably get wider consumption in the twenty-first century because of its increasing archival value: there were few films made in the sixties that so effectively tracked the psychological and emotional mechanisms of young people. From a sociological or anthropological perspective, it will have some utility.

STEVE GALLAGHER (programmer, The Kitchen): What was the reaction of the cast and the crew when they saw the film?

WG: To date, only three or four of them have seen it. Bob Rosen saw it, and he was amazed. I don't think he anticipated the film that he saw. I think (I hope) he was surprised in a pleasant way.

JACK CHURCHILL (filmmaker): Did you always know what you were doing while you were shooting?

WG: There were certain constants that I tried to predetermine as much as possible, and then I released the human consciousness into this field of determinants. It was similar to the way we come into this room. We've all agreed to be here to talk about the film, but what happens takes its own direction.

The interesting thing to me is that if you take a filmmaker, or any artist or writer, and throw them into any milieu, any situation, they will probably land feet first—if they've had enough experience. If you sit a pianist at a piano, even though that person has no music in front of him, even though he may not even decide to play any particular piece, he can still improvise. I used Miles Davis music [from *In a Silent Way*] in *Symbiopsychotaxiplasm* as a metaphor for the film, which is a form of audiovisual jazz. It was improvisational within a certain structure.

SM: One of the things I noticed when I looked carefully at *Take One* is that while it has this feeling of informality and spontaneity, it's very rigorously composed.

WG: Well, the finished film did not develop overnight. There was a lot of agony in the editing room—a lot! I had sixty or seventy hours of film. I can't tell you how many editors I burned out. The film had to be chaos, but chaos of a very special character: *intelligible* chaos. It had to hold your attention, even when it seemed to be a lousy film.

SM: From the opening minutes it's evident that the film is precise in what it does. During the preface, we no sooner start to get engaged in this argument about abortion than you flip us out of it by switching to a split-screen image of two different angles on the two characters. And the moment we're starting to become accustomed to the split-screen, you flip us out of that and into candid shots of bystanders observing the shoot. The switch from one level to another in the preface sets up the overall rhythm of the film.

And the opening credit sequence reconfirms the film's precision. Often credits are little more than throwaways, but as you've said, you move through a whole cycle of life, while a sound that was identified as an error during the final moments of the preface gets louder and louder so that we know that even if it was an error then, it sure as hell is conscious now. The film is loaded.

WG: It *is* loaded, and that took a lot of time. It flows very easily now, but obviously there was a time when nothing flowed. In a way it comes out of my own background as a filmmaker. I began as an editor, editing maybe sixty or seventy films as a sound editor, as a picture editor, and as chief editor. I was counseled at the NFB to understand that the editing room was the best possible place to get a good grounding in filmmaking, and for that I will always be grateful.

SM: One last question about the film's subtlety. The first time we see you in the film, you're listening to the sound and saying, "This is terrible, this is terrible," but you don't look like you feel it's terrible; you look amused. It's a kind of foreshadowing, as is your statement a moment later, "Don't take me seriously."

WG: I was very happy with the fact that there was error and confusion. If you notice me with Victor, the homeless guy at the end, I have the same kind of private smile. That emotion reflects the fact that the thing was going my way: there was confusion and conflict and an unpremeditated development that was important for the life and success of the film. That's on one level.

Now on the second level, there's a paradox. I wanted to harness the paradox of doing failure, of *using* failure and error and confusion and chaos and unhappiness and conflict! The film is a tour de force. You are drawn inexorably through this cosmic flux. At the end you say, "Wait a minute, what was that about and why was I so transfixed by it?" Well, life is like that; life keeps you totally absorbed from moment to moment to moment, and yet oftentimes you can't tell what it's "about." I like that paradox. My filmmaking always goes for paradoxes, ironies, contradictions.

It's like Zen: here we are on this Earth, this ball suspended out in space; we're all tied in with the gravitational forces of the sun, and yet we're speeding and trying to go off in another direction. Cosmically, we're caught in an equilibrium of paradoxical forces.

JC: Today some people might be a little troubled by the way you handle the homeless man, Victor. Did you have mixed feelings then, or do you now, about that scene?

WG: We were confronted with that individual, and we said, "Do we want to let this survive as a sequence or not?" I made a determination at the time that we were going to go with it, because though he was intrusive, this was reality—and reality was what the film was all about. I decided to stay open to it, and I'm so glad I did. As you see in the film, I did take the precaution of getting the guy to sign a release.

There's a mystical element to *Symbio*. We certainly recognized that Victor was drunk and homeless, but in his confrontational nature, he articulated what I was trying to get at in the film. During the years between the shooting and finishing *Take One*, Victor was in different sections of the film, but he works best at the very end: you can't go beyond *that* level of truth. Even though we were all being very spontaneous up to a point (I was probably the least spontaneous of anyone), he was even more spontaneous. And that's the nature of film truth: the closer you come to it, the less permissive it is of artificiality following it.

SM: How many versions of *Symbiopsychotaxiplasm* have there been?

WG: We went through many permutations of the material until we arrived at what we had at the Flaherty in 1991. After he saw the film that day, Steve Gallagher (he was one of the programmers) asked me if I'd cut something out of the film since he'd seen it a short time before. The answer was yes. Over the years, every time I've looked at the film, I've thought, "Shit," and have fiddled with this and that.

SM: I understand that you did *Take One and a Half* and a *Take Two*. What did you have in mind?

WG: I decided to do a *Take One and a Half* because we were caught in a logjam at a festival in Austria. They were supposed to send *Take One* to France for another event, and they didn't do it, so we had to scrounge around and pull together all the answer prints of *Take One* and assemble a film. In the process of making this emergency film for the Amiens Festival, we used a few things we liked that weren't in *Take One*, so you can call that version "Take One and an Eighth." It was the same as *Take One*, with a few additions.

Take One and a Half used sequences of couples who were left out of *Take One*: the interracial couple and Susan Anspach and her partner. I'm not quite sure how we'll weave their storylines into the larger situation, though I did sketch out one outline we might follow. *Take One and a Half* will probably be about ninety minutes, as opposed to the seventy minutes of *Take One*. [What Greaves calls *Take One and a Half* is, I believe, the version of *Symbiopsychotaxiplasm: Take One* now available on a Criterion DVD/BluRay.]

SM: You've mentioned a *Take Two*.

WG: It occurred to me, when I was in Germany recently, that since the actress [Audrey Henningham] I'd originally planned to use in *Take Two* has lived in Germany for almost twenty years, and since the people at the Munich Film Festival like *Take One* so much, it might be interesting to have a look at some of the concerns in *Take One* within the context of that lapse of time.

The actor who plays her partner in the original shooting [Frank (now Shannon) Baker] is still in New York at the Actors Studio, and his craft has developed. So they would interact on several different levels: on the level of the basic screen test (the argument between them) and on a psycho-dramatic level (they did have a relationship with each other in real life); and on a third level, in terms of their here-and-now professional and personal realities and whatever has happened to them in the interim.

I'd like to bring the actress's German reality into the film—especially the Munich beer halls. I love the energy there, which is kind of ironic because Dachau is only a few miles away. It's hard to conceive of those horrors. For me, it only underscores the idea that, as an old professor of mine used to say, "Genius and gentility, stupidity and savagery are not the private preserve of any one group or race of people."

We would have *Take Two* unfolding in Central Park in the original footage, and then there'd be this abrupt cut into this new recent material. Or we could start off in Germany and intercut between present and past. Those are some of the thoughts I've been playing around with. How much of that I'll be able to get to, I don't know. [What Greaves describes as *Take Two* became *Symbiopsychotaxiplasm: Take 2½*, also available on the Criterion DVD/BluRay.]

SM: Which of your other films do you see as particularly experimental?

WG: *The First World Festival of Negro Arts* is experimental in the sense that it uses poetry in conjunction with cinéma-vérité shooting in an unusual formulation. *From These Roots* is all still photographs. To make a documentary that was dramatic in its impact with only still photographs and sound was still experimental then. Today you have Ken Burns's *The Civil War* [1990] and so on. *Ida B. Wells, A Passion for Justice*, which also came out before *The Civil War*, combined sound effects, still photographs, and interviews overlaid with graphics. I think that film was innovative.

And *Ali, the Fighter* was experimental in the sense that it was shot cinéma-vérité but has a progressive, dramatic story line [see Alexander Johnston's essay in chapter 11 for details on the various versions of what Greaves here calls *Ali, the Fighter*]. Certainly, the chronology of the event itself was helpful—using two camera crews, we shot the events at the training camps and so on, leading up to and including the first fight between Ali and Joe Frazier. On the night of the fight we deployed something like twelve cameras in Madison Square Garden to capture many different angles.

But apart from the shooting, there was character delineation and a development of dramatic themes. Up to that point in American filmmaking, I don't know if there were many films that used cinéma vérité in such a dramatic way. I could be wrong, of course; I'm looking at this through my own tunnel vision.

We had a mountain of material that we edited down first to a two-hour film, then to ninety minutes. It was released into something like thirty theaters in the New York area, and subsequently nationwide. It was on one of the networks—ABC, I think. Howard Cosell showed it several times. I'm proud of that film.

You know, *Ali, the Fighter* was an experiment that went on to become conventional. Our film became the basis for *Rocky* [1976]. If you analyze *Rocky*, you'll know that Rocky is a white Joe Frazier, who was in my apartment about four months ago, saying, "Goddammit, they ripped me off!" They used his public persona as the basis for Rocky and Muhammad Ali as the basis for Apollo Creed. They even purchased sequences from our film to use as crowd reactions during the fight. The *Raging Bull* [1980] people also studied our film. There are echoes of our way of shooting in both films.

LC: How did the fighters feel about the film?

WG: Well, Ali didn't want us filming him, because we weren't paying him anything. But the contract he'd signed with the fight promoters stipulated that films could be made about the events leading up to the fight and the fight itself. He didn't cooperate during the first half of the shooting, but he did cooperate later on.

Ali called me up four or five years later and said, "Hey, I want to see the film you made!" We made arrangements for him to come to the studio. He was delighted with the film. "How did you get this shot!" "How did you get *that* shot!" We became friends after he saw the film.

JUST DOIN' IT AND CINÉMA VÉRITÉ

SONJA BAHN-COBLANS/ARNO HELLER: What motivated you to make *Just Doin' It*?

WG: *Just Doin' It* was to be part of a series of films that we were going to do for the Public Broadcasting System on different areas of black life: the black church, the black barbershop, the black newspaper.... The series was conceived with Lou Potter. We decided that doing a film about the black barbershop would be a good beginning. *Just Doin' It* was to be the pilot program.

SB/AH: What approach did you have in mind?

WG: It seemed to us that the cinéma-vérité approach, the candid-camera technique, was the wisest way to film the black barbershop.

SB/AH: Did you have an overall theme in mind before you started filming?

WG: Not really—but having grown up around black barbershops, I knew that filming there would be a fantastic experience. I knew it would be funny, that there'd be interesting things going on, and that there would be socially critical, politically sophisticated insights enunciated. I knew it would be a rich vein to mine.

SB/AH: Does that apply to all black barbershops, regardless of social stratification?

WG: Well, it seems to me that it doesn't matter how upscale the barbershop is or how down in the so-called ghetto it is. While the articulations may not be the same, they will certainly give you all of what I've just mentioned.

SB/AH: When you conceived the film, were you thinking of a white and/or a black audience?

WG: While I assumed that these films would be seen by white audiences, the central concern was to raise the consciousness of the black community and also to express that community's concerns to the larger, white American audience.

SB/AH: Did you choose these two barbershops to create a contrast?

WG: I'm trying to remember why we chose two. We probably felt that we would get a better sampling of the subject matter. The crowd that went in to one of the barbershops was younger than the crowd that went to the other.

SB/AH: Where were the barbershops located?

WG: Three or four miles apart in different sections of Atlanta, Georgia.

SB/AH: Did the barbershops give you complete freedom to do what you liked?

WG: Yes. That's the power of the media. If you film in their barbershops, you elevate their status in some way. Also, implicit in appearing in a film is the promise of immortality—your image will live after you've gone—and people tend to be very positive about this.

Of course, in 1978, America in general, and certainly the black community, was still relatively unsophisticated about documentary film. The black community had not been exposed to the film process, or to cinéma-vérité filmmaking. Today, of course, they are very familiar—and might not agree to be filmed.

SB/AH: Did you pay the people you filmed in *Just Doin' It*?

WG: We may have paid the minister, and we may have paid $200–$300 to film in the barbershops.

SB/AH: Did the people in the film ever see *Just Doin' It*?

WG: Not to my knowledge.

SB/AH: Did you tell them what they should talk about?

WG: No. You don't violate the truth. When I'm shooting, I avoid tampering with reality, and part of the reason for this goes back to my early experiences as a filmmaker. I began in the editing room and know the power of editing. My manipulation of reality comes during the editing, not during the shooting, because for this type of film, I don't care what the subjects do: I will find a way to use whatever they do. I don't feel obliged to try to manage what is manifestly a candid-camera situation.

If I'm working with actors, then I'm all over them. I'm directing them; I'm saying, "Well, you could do this." "Would you make this adjustment to that emotion?" "Could you think about this motivation?" But with a documentary, particularly a cinéma-vérité documentary, you do it as little as possible.

SB/AH: How long did you film?

WG: Something like five days in one place and three days in the other.

SB/AH: How many cameras did you have?

WG: Just two. I operated one of them; David Greaves, my son, the other.

SB/AH: Did you have any problems with the sound?

WG: You always have problems when you're shooting in a candid-camera situation, both with sound and image. You don't have the time to avoid problems because the events are taking place too quickly: you have to anticipate, be intuitive, and realize when something is getting ready to happen, so that you can catch the moment. As a result, your soundtrack and your visual imagery are oftentimes defective. They don't have the careful composition, the stability, the color and lighting values that you would have if you had the time to structure what will be seen and heard.

In the editing you do the best you can. The finished film will be made of bits and pieces of sound and image from all over the place, but with luck it can look like it's one continuous event.

SB/AH: Did you repeat takes of particular sequences?

WG: No. You can't do that.

SB/AH: No outside interference? No rehearsing?

WG: No. We just set up the camera and waited. If we saw someone who looked interesting come through the door, we said, "Let's roll it."

SB/AH: Did the patrons ever object?

WG: No, they just looked at us and said, "What's all this? What's going on?" We'd say, "Don't worry about us. Just go on with what you're doing; be yourself."

SB/AH: So you didn't have a story; you didn't have a script.

WG: No, but I researched these barbershops, taking still pictures there to acclimatize the patrons and the barbers to having a camera present. By the time we came in with the motion picture cameras, which were also hand-held, the patrons and barbers were not as intimidated as if we had come in straightaway with motion picture cameras. We never used tripods, just shoulder-mounted cameras, and there may have been one or two lights at most.

SB/AH: Was it difficult shooting with all the mirrors?

WG: There were moments when we were seen in the mirrors, but we cut them out during the editing. Also, because we didn't want you to see our reflections, we shot at a low angle.

SB/AH: We thought that was an aesthetic decision.

WG: The reality of what you're filming mandates your aesthetic decisions. If you surrender to the truth, cosmic reality takes over: it's a philosophical, mystical kind of thing. One has to surrender to the divine, to the subconscious, to the reality of the cosmos; you've got to let go. You must not try to manage the brilliant piece of creation that is the human experience. There's nothing you can do to augment it. One of the wonderful things about cinéma-vérité filmmaking is that you can catch absolutely breathtaking moments of human behavior that you could never preconceive or get an actor to replicate.

SB/AH: *Just Doin' It* certainly follows cinéma-vérité principles, but would you say that in the course of the editing the sequences fall into place to create a story?

WG: Editing permits you to arrive at a thematic line. Looking at the material, you begin to discern that there are certain basic thematic points or premises around which the film can orbit, and then you decide that you're going to make your film about one of them. The themes are developed as part of a permutation and combination process.

SB/AH: Would you compare this to chaos theory?

WG: Or you can call it "cosmic theory," which is what we pursued and played with in *Symbiopsychotaxiplasm: Take One*. You're juggling realities and discovering that sometimes there are connections that you never realized were in the material.

For example, take the barber in *Just Doin' It*, who says, "I'm very old, you know. I'm older than the rocks; I'm older than midnight." In the editing you realize this is a metaphor for who he really is, a man of the Bible.

SB/AH: Did you know beforehand that he was a preacher?

WG: No. We found that out after we'd started shooting. And that's how we decided to go into the black church at the end of the film. We assumed the black church would be our next port of call for the series, and that during the shows that followed we would wander through the black community in that way. In the black church we might find a lawyer who would say or do something that would cause us to say, "Wouldn't it be interesting to follow a black lawyer?"

SB/AH: But by putting the church scene at the end you also created a kind of story reaching from the beginning of the film to the end.

WG: Well, this is part of chaos theory. You wander into the barbershop and start listening to people and seeing the things that they're concerned with. You find that they're concerned with issues connected to civil rights—because we're coming out of the civil rights era. So an organizing principle might be the theme of civil rights, or human rights, or justice.

And yet, everything that you saw in *Just Doin' It* happened by chance. The nephew of Martin Luther King just happened to wander in! But to answer your question about the story: it develops out of the organizing principle of the film, which, let's say, is justice.

SB/AH: But that was not your organizing principle going in?

WG: No. Surfers swim around until they see a wave that they want to ride, then they surf into shore. The same thing happens with a film of this kind: you're looking for a wave to ride. It could be a wave of love or a wave of fear; it could be a wave of justice. Having opened yourself up as a cinéma-vérité filmmaker to "whatever happens is going to happen without my tampering with it," you film all those things that seem to be electrifying, exciting, interesting. Oftentimes you'll find yourself gravitating toward one or another kind of wave to surf. And you may see three, four, or five different waves, not just one—but there will probably be one tidal wave that will carry everything, including the subsidiary waves, into shore toward the climax of the film.

SB/AH: So you did not consciously create an underlying dramatic structure in advance?

WG: No. An underlying dramatic structure comes out of the tension between the social reality of America and the aspiration and struggle of the people criticizing this social reality.

What I'm trying to say is that, for a filmmaker, everything in life is absolutely perfect! This moment that we're in, right here, is perfect! It needs no further management by anybody. A camera could be present, filming our discussion, and this conversation would be just fine. The artist has got to have that kind of trust in order to make this kind of film.

Now, once you've gotten the "perfect moments" to the editing room, then you get to work and, as you explore these moments, you decide, okay, *this* is the dramatic structure; *here's* my theme. This is my point of attack for the drama; this is the conflict; this is the crisis and this is the climax; this is the resolution. These are the crucial characters; this is the orchestration of these characters; this is the environment in which they will function; and they will delineate their personalities through these particular lines and actions.

If you're writing a dramatic film, you set this all up when you're writing the screenplay, but when you use the vérité approach, you must be willing to take dictation from life.

This doesn't mean that you can't go into a situation that demands social criticism. You can do that by choosing certain kinds of events to abandon yourself to during the shooting.

SB/AH: But despite your cinéma-vérité approach, we clearly see subliminal associative symbolic devices in the film. To what extent did you consciously plan them? For example, when there's the talk about Vietnam, we see the little boy playing with a toy airplane; and when the nephew of Martin Luther King talks about himself, you zoom in on King's picture on the wall.

WG: Yes. This is what I mean by surrendering. If you come into this reality, you leave yourself open to it. I didn't know the little boy was going to be there with a plane; I didn't tell him, "When this fellow talks about Vietnam, you start playing with your plane." No. It's just that in the process of shooting, I tried to be conscious of whatever was inside that field of vision. Either while I was shooting or later, when I was editing, I saw the connection, the metaphor, the symbiosis, the sympathetic vibrations between that toy plane and the Vietnam story.

SB/AH: Your process seems like a mixture of calculation and intuition.

WG: That's right. It's the intersection of the scientific method with art.

SB/AH: How did you decide on the transitions between the alternating barbershop scenes?

WG: The changes were totally arbitrary in the sense that I wanted to avoid an obvious, mechanical pace and predictable alternations. Sometimes a particular transition had to do with artistic rhythm or texture. If one barbershop was getting profound and I thought we'd dealt with that long enough, we'd change over to the other. Sometimes there was a subtle resonance between what you were seeing in one barbershop and what you were seeing in the other. In some cases, there was a continuation of a particular line of thought.

The thing you always want to do is to try and keep a variety of transition devices operating, rather than staying solely with one. You need to leave yourself open to a variety of ways to get from A to B to C to D.

SB/AH: You seem to approach reality in almost a postmodern way, in the sense that you refuse rigid structuring. You seem to have a much more exploratory attitude.

WG: Yes. We're exploring and discovering while we're filming and while we're editing too.

SB/AH: How much footage did you shoot, and how much did you use? It's a short film [thirty minutes].

WG: The ratio was probably on the order of about 30 to 1. We probably shot 30,000 or 40,000 feet of film.

SB/AH: It would be interesting to study the footage to see what you left out. Our students have seen the film, and one question that cropped up again and again is its possible "message." Would you say you had a particular message?

WG: I'd say *Just Doin' It* is a bitter indictment of America, an indictment of modern civilization; it's a plea for a higher level of consciousness and sensibility. It's an attempt to get people to think of black people as human beings with a variety of strengths and weaknesses and foibles, and also, I guess, to enjoy the experience that I always enjoyed in a black barbershop.

SB/AH: The overall atmosphere of that film is not at all negative. We have this strong feeling of an intact community, of people criticizing a lot of things, but being alive in a functioning community. That, in itself, is a kind of consolation.

WG: Absolutely! And a kind of dignity. The whole issue for me is the dignity of the black community.

SB/AH: There is secular black community in those two barbershops, but at the end you have the church community. What is the relationship between the barbershop communities and the church community?

WG: Well, on the one hand, there *is* a philosophical relationship; there's a progression within the film from the mundane to the spiritual. The world of the barbershop moves progressively during thirty minutes to a higher and higher level of thought and meaning. *Just Doin' It* starts off mundane, randomized, then becomes more sociological, then philosophical, and finally spiritual and religious.

You've taken the discourse from one level to the next, until the minister/barber and the salesman are talking about whether an idea is tangible and can be manifested in three or four dimensions. And, of course, manifestation is a spiritual issue, a religious issue: religion is the manifestation of the godhead on Earth, through nature. And you're hearing conversation about Martin Luther King, about how old the Earth is—all that.

SB/AH: In our interpretation of the film, we saw parallels between certain biblical or liturgical acts and what goes on in the barbershops. In the final analysis, we thought that the barbershops could be called secular churches that act out some of the essential symbolic procedures of the church liturgy, from foot-washing (shoe-shining) to anointing (grooming) to spreading the word.

WG: I love it! That's great! I'd never thought of the situation of Christ washing the feet of his disciples when I was shooting and editing, and yet you're absolutely correct.

This is exactly what I was trying to communicate before. There's a certain genius operating in the world. I don't want to get too mystical, but the fact is that whatever is happening *is* truly miraculous! And practically everything that happens is *correct*, worthy of being shot. In doing your work, you're trusting that correctness.

SB/AH: At the end of the film the barber/minister's movements and his language become fully ritualized.

WG: The black community is notorious for its involvement with the spirit and spiritual matters. Whether you go to a place in Harlem or to Brazil or to Africa, there's an inordinate absorption with the metaphysical. That's certainly an element of the film.

SB/AH: The final scene allows us to look backward and reinterpret what went before. The strong church scene at the end puts the other scenes into a new perspective.

WG: For me, seeing the barber/minister in church was a thing of wonder. We thought we knew this man, but then we began to realize that we didn't really know him. When he says, "I'm older than midnight," the film becomes metaphysical: are you watching a barber or some extraterrestrial being?

SB/AH: He's very different from that other minister.

WG: Oh, that wonderful other minister is a total reprobate, an awful man. We absolutely loved him, because he was such a great contrast to the barber/minister.

SB/AH: We wondered which of the two ministers you were siding with, so to speak. At the end it becomes clear.

WG: Sure. And yet the other minister is in the background at the church.

SB/AH: Do you think the film creates an authentic picture of black life? Is it dated or still valid?

WG: I think it's still a valid representation of the black community. In the black community, you still find people like the two ministers and the others.

SB/AH: When we presented our discussion of the film, a German colleague said that we missed one of its most crucial aspects. To him *Just Doin' It* was basically a close analysis of American black speech patterns.

WG: You do get black dialect in the film, but because this is a candid-camera look at this situation with no tampering on our part (other than in the editing room), it's a repository, a distillation, of *many* different aspects of black life, including black English.

SB/AH: Why did you call the film "Just Doin' It"?

WG: "Just doin' it" is a vernacular expression. "How you doing, man?" "Oh man, I'm just doin' it." On one level, "just doin' it" means "everything is okay." But it also means that you're doing the best you can under the circumstances, in the face of whatever the adversities of life are for you. "Just doin' it" is a way of enjoying whatever is going on.

It's just enjoying *being*.

The African American has been under assault for hundreds of years. Today the assault is not as vicious physically as it has been, but psychological assaults are still taking place. There have been so many assaults that it's almost a miracle that African Americans have survived, and the fact that we have survived what we've survived is part of "just doin' it." But the phrase is not a political statement as such. It's a human statement, a triumph-of-the-human-spirit statement that flows out of the racial genius of the African, who has been on the planet for thousands of years, who has gone through innumerable permutations and combinations of adversity of one kind or another and has survived. It's in that sense that "just doin' it" has its deepest meaning.

SB/AH: Do you think this film should be discussed at European schools and universities?

WG: Yes, particularly if it's put in context. *Just Doin' It* gives you a good sense of a certain area of black American life in the mid-1970s; it's a good look at some of the concerns of black people, whether of the 1970s or the 1990s. I think it would be very educational for students.

SB/AH: Could you recommend any complementary material or maybe other films?

WG: Well, my personal feeling is that you could use a film like *Booker T. Washington: The Life and Legacy* [1983] or *From These Roots* [1974], or *The Deep North* [1988], or *Still a Brother: Inside the Negro Middle Class* [1968], or *Black Power in America... Myth or Reality?* [1986]—the various films that we've made are, in one way or another, vantage points from which you can look at the black experience.

SB/AH: The reason we have chosen *Just Doin' It* for our analysis and discussion is that it is not a film just *about* black life; it *is* black life. We also like that the film is short, like a poem. You meditate on it, and after a while you realize it has all these levels. To us this is more valuable than a film with a clear-cut "message."

WG: Well, we like to make films with many dimensions. I rely heavily on metaphor because with metaphor you can say so many different things simultaneously.

SB/AH: Even the colors of the two barbershops contribute to the experience.

WG: Yes, very much so. You go from the garish and young first one to the serenity of the second.

SB/AH: Do you think *Just Doin' It* is one of your artistically more important films?

WG: I think it's a good film that has not been fully appreciated. And I'm absolutely delighted that you appreciate it. The film has never been broadcast; it was a pilot and the larger project was killed.

We distribute the film to schools and colleges for educational purposes, and the film was shown at the 1991 Brooklyn Museum retrospective. It did win an award: first prize at the first Black International Film Festival in New York.

SB/AH: The films you're making right now are more structured. You haven't shot cinéma vérité recently.

WG: No, not all films lend themselves to that approach.

SB/AH: What might you focus on if we offered you the chance to do a film?

WG: I would probably focus on something within a black, middle-class environment, maybe something about the Congressional Black Caucus.

I might also do a film on African history. As a matter of fact, I went to the Egyptian and Ethiopian museum here in Munich and looked at the *Denkmäler* of Karl Richard Lepsius, a thirteen-volume work on Ethiopia and Egypt. The world is crawling with European history, French history, Italian history, Greek history, Jewish history. But Black history does not enjoy the same degree of attention. People think that the Africans are only the Hutus and Tutsis—crazy tribes slaughtering each other—and that the Europeans had to develop colonialism to keep these crazy tribes in line.

But at one time, Africa was an advanced part of the world. Christianity is only a two-thousand-year-old exercise. African history goes back ten to fifteen thousand years.

HOLLYWOOD, CIRCA 1979–2003

ST. CLAIR BOURNE: What are you involved with these days [1979]?

WG: I'm in the middle of a development deal with Universal. I'm reading a lot of books and a lot of scripts, and talking to writers—hoping to arrive at a property or two or three that Universal and I would consider marketable. Once we come up with these properties and go into production, I'll function in some instances as a producer, in others as an executive producer. The deal I have with Universal doesn't necessarily prevent me from directing, though my directing isn't currently contemplated.

SCB: Did this deal grow out of your relationship with Universal/MESBIC [Minority Enterprise Small Business Investment Company, a program created by the U.S. government in 1958 to assist disadvantaged entrepreneurs]?

WG: It did and didn't. This deal is a result of the relationship I had with Universal when I was working with Norbert Simmons on the MCA/MESBIC's financing of "Heaven Is a Playground." Once that project went down the tubes, Universal offered me this development deal.

SCB: Why didn't the MCA/MESBIC deal happen?

WG: MESBIC is in a state of development and growth. Norbert Simmons is in a state of development and growth. Where MESBIC is in terms of the hard realities of Hollywood, given all of the traditional resistances with regard to the black product, I don't know.

The distributors are complaining that black films don't sell; exhibitors are complaining that black audiences deface the theaters; and the black leadership complains about the quality of the films that are being done.

Hollywood is a very big pot of gold, and as is always the case with a big pot of gold, those who have the pot don't really want to share it.

Hollywood controls both the financing and the distribution of films, so that a person who sets up an independent production company has a difficult time trying to move his product inside or even outside of the traditional Hollywood circuit. He can do it, but he's at the mercy of the independent distributors across the country.

SCB: You yourself have had a lot of difficulties with that.

WG: We've tried to get distribution deals outside of Hollywood, and it's been very hard. The difficulty is raised to the nth power by the fact that we're black: there's a track record of resistance to black incursions into moviemaking. I think this is a mixture of a number of factors.

The psyche of the American theatergoing and television-watching public is under tremendous financial pressures, from taxes, the rising cost of living, inflation, the recession. And this is a public that lost a war in Southeast Asia, a public that's been watching the emergence of African nation-states, a public that's confronting the recognition of Communist China, a public that generally feels very intimidated, perhaps even isolated—and blacks are still the number one scapegoat.

A lot of the resistance is the result of the subconscious mindset of the white American viewer, who may now be more resistant to black product than he might have been just a few years back.

SCB: Your feature *The Marijuana Affair* [1976] is a commercial action film. Why hasn't it been distributed?

WG: After about fifty approaches and attempts, we finally came up with a distributor for *The Marijuana Affair*, but, unfortunately, the deal fell through. I'd spent so much time and energy trying to put that deal together that in the end I lost interest. I couldn't afford to spend more time on it.

Since then, I've completely stopped all work in distribution; I have people who do that for me. My focus is on producing and directing films. Currently I'm doing a film for NASA on minorities and women in science and space careers: black and female astronauts. I have a grant from the National Endowment of the Arts to do a film on African art, and other government contracts as well. And on the feature-film side, there's this opportunity with Universal, which I'm trying to pull together.

SCB: Recently I've heard, both on the East Coast and on the West Coast, that my contemporaries—people in their mid-thirties—don't see anyone coming up behind them, like you saw me coming up behind you.

WG: On the one hand, I feel very depressed at how little work there is for black filmmakers, but I'm also aware that when I started out, there were no opportunities at all. In 1950, when I first knew I wanted to make films, William Alexander was the only black filmmaker I knew. And Bill left the country and went to England to set up Blue Nile Productions. Then I left and spent years in Canada.

My point is that I'm delighted that the situation is so much better today than it was then. But my delight can only be seen in relative terms: in objective terms, the situation today is still horrible.

SCB: I had opportunities because of the time and the exposure I had on *Black Journal*. Maybe my generation got too much too soon.

WG: I don't think you got too much too soon. Everything that you and Stan Lathan and Kent Garrett and the others got, you were fully entitled to. What happened was that American society regressed in its commitment to equal opportunity. The riots cooled out and the pressure was off—suddenly we weren't the top priority. And we aren't today.

And also, unfortunately, black people have gone to sleep. The media has lulled us to sleep. There have been enough crumbs falling from the table to make much of the black middle class comfortable. And we simply haven't grasped the nature of the problem that confronts us in the media.

We're in danger of losing our identity. We're being told by others who we are.

When I see young black kids coming out of the theaters downtown, it freaks me out! These were the kids that I was making films for, but they don't seem to care about anything that I care about. Somehow or other I need to become mature enough to recognize that fact, and figure out how to help them care about what I believe to be the important things.

SCB: Do you see this as a part of a cycle? Will we be in this period for a while?

WG: I think that in time it will become politically expedient for blacks to be the American bridges to the larger world. In geopolitical terms, America's international credibility will increasingly hinge upon its treatment of its nonwhite population. By way of the UN and other international organizations, the larger world will begin investigating the human rights problems within America. It's at that point that there will be a new wave of "equal opportunity." I don't see this happening as a result of anything going on internally in America now.

Of course, that doesn't preclude internal things occurring, like this Universal deal. But regardless of what happens with Universal, it behooves us to make sure that we have alternative circuits of distribution, alternative circuits of financing. We shouldn't turn our backs on Hollywood, but black filmmakers should work to expand their options.

SCB: Do you think they can expand their options without weakening their commitment to making political films?

WG: I don't think black filmmakers should make themselves captive solely to black-oriented productions. A black filmmaker should be willing to do films that relate to the entire marketplace. A film could still be a "black film" even if it were about whites. If you think only in terms of the black filmmaker trying to get financing for productions that are specifically targeted to black survival in America, you're going to find financing very hard to come by.

SCB: You don't think it's possible for a black survivalist film to appeal to a general audience?

WG: It's *possible*, but the probability of getting it financed domestically, and once having gotten it financed, of getting it distributed nationally... look, I did *Nationtime—Gary*, which was narrated by Harry Belafonte and Sidney Poitier. It had Dick Gregory, Richard Hatcher, Jesse Jackson, Isaac Hayes, a whole array of well-known black figures speaking militantly about the liberation of black America and the Afro world in general. I approached all the major networks with that film, put $45,000 of my personal dollars into it, and *Nationtime—Gary* never saw the light of day.

SCB: If you'd put it out on the nontheatrical circuit, do you think it would have earned that money back?

WG: The complication is that the white body politic doesn't want to look at black militancy, and that wipes out large sectors of the collegiate market and the collegiate film-library market. Then if we turn to the black community as film consumers, we don't find sufficient interest in or sophistication about documentary film.

We've not said anything here about what a black filmmaker *can* do, right now, to develop a career. For example, the government's Small Business Administration program offers a possible way for a filmmaker to stay alive. There are grant programs offered by state councils for the arts. There's a potpourri of sources for risk capital. Real estate speculators are a good source for tax shelters; it's good for people to get to know accountants, because they know where the money is.

People who have money in countries like the Philippines or the West Indies, where the currency is captive to that country, can be sources of financing. If filmmakers can find just one-tenth of the money needed for a film in American dollars, they can liberate money from those countries by shooting there. They can use the American money to pay the expenses of the key personnel; then the bulk of the film is financed in that country. At the end of the shooting, the film negative leaves the country and the film is edited, and as the finished film circulates around the world and earns money, the backers in country X get some of their money back.

This is why I said that black filmmakers should widen the kinds of films they do, because if they only do films that relate to the black experience in America, they're not going to get Filipinos to put up money for those films.

PETER CASTALDI: Your one major motion picture credit is for *Bustin' Loose* [1981]. Why only one?

WG: Hollywood is a tough nut to crack! It's a highly competitive, nepotistic, in-group type of environment, and it tends not to open itself to the independent filmmaking community in general or to the black filmmaker in particular. Of course, that situation has been changing as of late, so hopefully I'll find more opportunities to work with Hollywood. But my not working with them more often is not my doing; it's theirs.

GEORGE ALEXANDER: How did you get involved with the *Bustin' Loose* project?

WG: I was one of several black producers approached by MCA New Ventures, a subsidiary of MCA, a sister company to Universal Pictures. They were supposed to be helping black productions, so they asked my company to take on a project called "Heaven Is a Playground." We developed it but never got the financing for the film. The management team at Universal, especially Ned Tanen, who was the president, were impressed with the way I'd conducted the project and offered me *Bustin' Loose* to executive-produce.

They also wanted me to come on staff there, which I turned down, because by then I had my own company and my own freedom of action to do the films I was interested in making.

Most of the films one makes in Hollywood have a short shelf life; they're a big deal for a few months, then they're gone and usually provide no lasting, nourishing psychological or social impact. On the other hand, our films are practically indestructible. *From These Roots* was done in 1974, *First World Festival* in 1966, but they are constantly being used by academic and special-interest communities.

My feeling is that a film that's an educational tool can do the work of a major advocacy organization if the film is strong enough. Ironically, you see this very starkly with *The Birth of a Nation* [1915], which was able to mobilize public thinking with respect to the African American in a very significant way for decades.

GA: Would you like to do more feature film work?

WG: I'd love to do more, but it's difficult. For about seven years Paul Robeson, Jr., and I tried to get the money to make a film about his father's life. And I tried very hard to get money to adapt Langston Hughes's "Sweet Flypaper of Life," a wonderful story written by Langston and Roy DeCarava . . .

GA: . . . the great photographer.

WG: Right. They got together and did a book, which I got hold of (through Liska March at the Actors Studio) and turned into a screenplay. Langston read the screenplay and was very excited about it, and Roy was too. I took it to the Sundance Lab and worked on it with Robert Redford, Paul Newman, Karl Malden, James Brooks, and they were all excited to do the film—but I couldn't raise the money. The Hollywood studios wouldn't back it. "Sweet Flypaper of Life" deals with the rehabilitation of a young black man in Harlem by his grandmother. That didn't seem important to the Hollywood moguls.

PC: Are people like Spike Lee, John Singleton, and the Hudlin Brothers, who have had commercial success, breaking down the barriers for African-American filmmakers, or is there something else going on as well?

WG: Hollywood will always find ways to make money. If they decide to have Asian filmmakers make some films, they can make money with Asian films. It's the preferences and the prejudices and the predilections that operate in Hollywood that determine what films will and won't be made.

Thousands of screenplays are submitted to Hollywood every year, maybe 10,000–15,000 screenplays; and of that number, I'd guess no more than 500 make it to the screen. Over the years, Hollywood has developed a number of formulas that can help a film to be a hit, whether it's directed by the Hudlin Brothers or Spike Lee or Martin Scorsese. If they want films to be successful, the producers can make sure these formulas are part of the films they produce.

Having said that, of course you *do* need talent. The intersection of talent with some of those formulas can result in films being hits.

PC: You've spoken with admiration about Spike Lee and other African-American filmmakers—do you also look upon them with a bit of envy?

WG: No, I don't envy them. Their time has come. Listen, I've done a lot of films; we've gotten a lot of attention, and we've won lots of awards. I'm not as rich as Spike Lee or John Singleton—I do envy their wealth and what it makes possible. But my focus is on my own work.

Some progress has been made, but, unfortunately, Hollywood (and it's really not *Hollywood*; it's greed, corruption, the lust for power) continues to make decisions that are hostile to black filmmakers—these days in a much more moderated, subtle, and devious form. If you go to see a Hollywood film now, you won't see a Mantan Moreland or a Stepin Fetchit, but in most any film that includes African Americans, you can still see moments of castration. You see them in the Eddie Murphy films and in some of the Whoopi Goldberg films. It's subtle, but it's there.

When I was executive producer of *Bustin' Loose*, I was constantly barraged by one of the chief executives at Universal who wanted Richard Pryor to say more "muthafuckas." If you know anything about Richard, you *know* he's going to curse. I didn't need to *ask* Richard to curse; it'd be like asking the pope to pray! So I would say, "Why does he need to curse any more than he would automatically?" "Well, you know, the kids like it." Asking a black actor to say more "muthafuckas" isn't creative; it's a subtle way of obscuring the complexity of our lives.

Of course, Hollywood does occasionally do films that are more positive, films like *Glory* [Edward Zwick, 1989] or *To Sleep with Anger* [Charles Burnett, 1990]. But the overwhelming center of gravity is made up of films geared simply and solely toward instant gratification.

The challenge is to liberate oneself in one's films, whether they're documentary or fiction films. Once one achieves some degree of liberation, some degree of empowerment, *then* one can really talk about creativity and aesthetics, because up to this point, most black films have had at best a reactive aesthetic. Of course, many of the great works of art all through history have been done in response to one or another form of oppression, but ideally one should be able to express oneself either in reaction to adversity or in the excitement of playing with a new idea, an idea not necessarily tied to the issue of racism.

One of my missions as a black filmmaker has been to use filmmaking to assist audiences, black and white, to understand the complexity of the African-American experience and of African history. But, like other black filmmakers, I don't want to be ghettoized inside the "black experience." There's a whole range of concerns that don't necessarily speak to the issue of race but are crucial parts of human experience and the cosmos that surrounds us, concerns we want to explore. This was the context for *Symbiopsychotaxiplasm*, which was an aggressive attempt to break out of the conventions of Hollywood and the conventions of most independent film.

What *is* an independent filmmaker or an independent black filmmaker? If the individual is working in a major studio—someone like Spike Lee or John Singleton—there are certain restraints that the corporate structure imposes on him. *Do the Right Thing* has an independent thrust. It's independent of a lot of what has gone on in Hollywood before it, but it still has a dialogue with conventional Hollywood values.

On the other hand, Haile Gerima's *Ashes and Embers* [1982], made entirely outside the Hollywood system, is shorn of any obligation to industry power structures. In a sense, Gerima wasn't concerned with the kind of marketing that would be implicit in a Hollywood production, including one like *Do the Right Thing*. He was entirely focused on articulating the subject matter of the black experience in America (and on paying his respects to the African roots of the black experience). But, of course, this limited his audience.

These are two different senses of "independent" film production. They offer different challenges.

MEDIA ADDICTION, VIDEO CASSETTES, AND IDA B. WELLS: GREAVES AT THE NATIONAL CONFERENCE ON THE STATUS OF AFRICAN AMERICANS, HOWARD UNIVERSITY, DECEMBER 23, 1989

WG: We blacks are becoming a race of drug addicts—of a special kind. I don't mean chemical drugs; I'm speaking of spiritual, psychological, and intellectual drugs. The constant bombardment of our consciousness by television, by the mass print media, by the motion picture industry with images that are not friendly to us is destructive of our self-esteem, of our sense of who we are and of what we can do with our lives.

The major studios put out films like *Star Wars* [1977], *The Exorcist* [1973], and *Jaws* [1975] that in no way take into account our existence in the world—and yet we flock to the theaters to see these films. The Hollywood studios boycott *us*. I'm a black producer and I can tell you that they also boycott our products.

But *we* don't boycott *them*. They know that we don't discriminate against them and that they can make vicious, hostile products that assault our consciousness and the consciousness of our children with impunity.

Now, this is a very serious problem because as this massive control of information takes more and more root, our consciousness as a people will be fully decimated unless we take remedial steps. It's important for us to take control of our images, but it's also important for us to have control of our minds. If we look at the consciousness of Black America over the past 100 or 150 years, we can see that during the abolitionist period, the slaveholder, the slaveocracy, mounted a vilification campaign against us as a people, to show that we were inferior. They took some sections of Darwin's thesis and the writings of various others and roundly financed negative stereotypical projections of who we are as a people, in order to provide a philosophical basis for our economic, social, and political oppression.

That legacy of vilification is still with us today. It's become very sophisticated, but we still have minstrels operating under various electronic guises. A study found that an inordinately large number of black performers on television are in one way or another connected with comedy. This is not an accident. Similarly, those black performers who can be taken seriously don't appear with the same frequency. I used to be an actor many years ago—as a matter of fact, a film that I acted in, *Lost Boundaries* [1949], showed here [Howard University] recently. As an actor, I was very interested in projecting a very different image of the black American—people like Paul Robeson and Canada Lee and Gordon Heath were wonderful role models for me.

Also, I had the good fortune of studying African history with one of the most illustrious professors that you've had at this university, Dr. William Leo Hansberry, who used to come up to Harlem every weekend. I was privileged to learn how we come from a very distinguished series of major civilizations in Ethiopia and Egypt, civilizations that predate Greece, that predate the European renaissance. Our presence in northern Africa and in southern Europe during the Moorish period was very significant and contributed to the development of the European renaissance. Here we are in an African-American university and I don't know that you're pursuing that kind of information, which can nourish our consciousness as a people.

I quit acting because there was a constant tendency to ask me to produce characterizations that were stereotypical—deleterious characters like Stepin Fetchit and Mantan Moreland—and I realized that I had to get behind the camera. But I when I tried to get into the American motion picture industry back in 1950, 1952, what we had in the industry was a form of apartheid that completely excluded people of color. I went to Canada and worked on eighty films up there, then came back in 1963 during the Civil Rights revolution. I set up my own company, and we've been producing films that in one way or another address our needs and interests as a community.

My company did a film on the first black national political convention [*Nationtime—Gary*]. That film cost us $100,000 of hard-earned cash. When we took the film to the networks—no one else was seriously covering this event—they didn't want any part of it, despite the fact that Sidney Poitier was a narrator, that Harry Belafonte was a narrator, that Jesse Jackson gave a brilliant speech, and that Dick Gregory was in it, and Richard Hatcher, Mrs. Martin Luther King, Betty Shabazz (Mrs. Malcolm X).

Nationtime—Gary was chock full of theatrical and informational value, but the networks didn't want any part of it because they really aren't interested in our empowering ourselves in any way, and this is a major tragedy *for us*. Unless we perceive this in an immediate, ongoing, moment-to-moment fashion, we're in serious trouble. Stuff that ignores us is coming at us at an incredible rate; unless you're aware of it, you're swimming against the current. You can drown.

Up until now, the Hollywood studios and the television networks have maintained a stranglehold on the information that goes into black homes, until, god-bless-them, the Japanese marketed the video cassette recorder. Today, there are something like sixty million video cassette recorders in this country. In many ways the video cassette recorder, along with cable television, can help us retrieve our dignity as a people. But we have to be aware of how to use this mechanism for the dissemination of information. We have to understand how to set up, throughout this country, a multiplicity of distribution outlets for video cassettes, a multiplicity of video clubs, of video special interest groups that target those products that in one way or another address our needs and interests.

As media consumers, we, the black community, are currently spending something like a billion, or a billion and a half, maybe two billion dollars on video cassettes. The value that we get back from that expenditure, from the standpoint of serving *our* needs and interests, is miniscule, maybe fifty or a hundred million dollars. Ludicrous!

We talk about the Jews; we talk about the Japanese and the Koreans, but I think that instead of criticizing, it's incumbent upon us to study them. How do they go about this business of collaborating and cooperating and working with each other and producing things that in the final analysis result in their financial, social, political, and spiritual empowerment?

I don't want to continue rambling, but I want to give you my perspective as a film producer, a filmmaker, on how we might relate to this issue. Right now, my company is making a film on a woman who fully understood what I'm talking about. Her name was Ida B. Wells. She understood the necessity for economic self-reliance, economic nationalism. She understood the necessity for the use of the media in raising mass consciousness, and she pursued it vigorously and successfully until she ran up against some of the negative forces that were railed against her. Public television will air *Ida B. Wells: A Passion for Justice* [1989] on December 19.

Wells is a wonderful role model for all of us to really take our minds in hand, shall we say, and start to resist the tendency in our community of not being, if you'll excuse the expression, discriminatory, of not discriminating between those sources of product that are hostile to our interests and those that can develop our appreciation for opportunities to collaborate and support Black Entertainment Television or Third World Press. Whenever black companies are moving into the public arena, we should *flock* to them and support their products. Other ethnic, racial groups do it. White America does it.

We have been the victims of a continuing and massive psychological warfare campaign and we are survivors, but our problem now is to escape media tyranny and oppression, no matter what façade it uses. Thank you.

GLOBAL PERSPECTIVE

JH: In 1989 you were the head of a delegation of Americans who went to the International Film Festival in New Delhi—and you later went to China [see chapter 18, Greaves's essay, "Afterthoughts on the Black American Film Festival"].

WG: Yes, our contribution to the film festival was called "Black American Cinema" and was composed of twenty films: ten documentaries and ten features. The delegation was invited to India by the government of India and the Indo-U.S. Subcommission on Education and Culture. I was asked by these two entities to choose the films and the people who would come with me to the festival. I chose Cicely Tyson, Ruby Dee, Ivan Dixon, Michelle Parkerson, and film scholar Donald Bogle.

We showed our films at the festival and did television appearances and interviews. After the festival was over in New Delhi, the Indian government sent us to Bombay, Calcutta, and Thiruvananthapuram. The Indians enjoyed having us, and we enjoyed being there. Cicely and Ruby handled themselves wonderfully with the media.

After the tour, I was asked to do a workshop at the Film Institute in Puna, which I did—and after that I went to China, where Louise joined me. The United States Information Agency had asked me to do a lecture tour in China on filmmaking in America and to show some of the films my company had made. We stayed in China for about a month—a great experience. We went to five major studios, saw films, and I conducted an acting workshop in Beijing with talented young people.

FIGURE 2.10 *Left to right*: Film scholar Donald Bogle, Cicely Tyson, and Ruby Dee in India with Greaves. Photographer unknown. Courtesy Louise Greaves.

The Chinese know a lot about us, but, ironically, we don't know much about them. The people in the American Embassy in Beijing told us that by the year 2020 China would be one of the top three or four countries in the world. There's a tremendous explosion of business and building going on there; I never saw so many construction cranes in my life!

FREDA WARREN: What brought about your interest in doing a film about Ralph Bunche?

WG: Several things. As a young actor in New York, I had a featured role in a Broadway production of *Lost in the Stars*, the musical based on *Cry, the Beloved Country*. Todd Duncan was the star. After the show, Bunche came backstage with Jawaharlal Nehru, Krishna Menon, and other world leaders. I was impressed that he wanted to share the black experience with these famous people.

Later, I worked as a producer/director at the UN's film and television section here in New York, and I became much more aware of Bunche. By this time, although he was an international civil servant working very productively at the United Nations, a lot of black people wondered whether he was just another Uncle Tom. They bought into the criticism leveled at Bunche by sixties radicals who thought he was too busy hanging out with mainstream white people.

My own belief was somewhat similar until I finally realized what Bunche's covert agenda was. He was busy working for the uplift of humanity—from inside the powerful elite. He knew that the Soviets and the Chinese were beating the drum for the liberation of Third World peoples and the destruction of the European colonial empires, and that unless the United States got into the decolonization game at the UN, it would leave an open field for Cold War rivals. So he helped draft those sections of the UN Charter that were instrumental in speeding up the decolonization of the world.

Working closely with his good friend Eleanor Roosevelt, Bunche helped bring attention to humanitarian and human rights issues worldwide. These kinds of activities brought international pressure to bear on the American body politic and were one of the main reasons why the American establishment embraced the Civil Rights Movement. Bunche played an important role in making it possible for these forces to have positive impact on domestic policy in America.

He also appreciated the "good side" of America, the fact that Americans think of themselves as decent, democratic people who want to live up to the ideals expressed in the Declaration of Independence and the Bill of Rights. I take nothing away from the important work of Martin Luther King,

Malcolm X, and the other civil rights leaders, but for my money, Bunche is an equal and perhaps more important figure in the struggle for civil and human rights. Marching, singing "We Shall Overcome," and holding hands is wonderful, but it's not the same as putting in place, worldwide, structural and legal principles for self-determination, conflict resolution, and global human rights, which is what Bunche was involved with.

Human rights is now established as a criterion for judging nations throughout the world, including the United States. Bunche was critical to the Universal Declaration of Human Rights being endorsed by the UN General Assembly in Oslo and Paris in 1948.

So Bunche is hot stuff, the consummate insider global activist. He most resembles the men who put together the American Constitution, most of whom were libertarian, at least in the John Stuart Mill sense. Of course, the Constitution itself was hardly ideal; it took people like George Mason to lead the struggle for the Bill of Rights.

I could go on and on about Ralph Bunche! He was an intellectual athlete, the Michael Jordan of international affairs.

SM: Is the Ralph Bunche project the biggest you've taken on?

WG: Well, yes and no. *Bustin' Loose* was a twelve- to thirteen-million-dollar production. But an executive producer is a glorified babysitter. You just hover while the film is being shot, trying to keep harmony on the set and stay within the budget.

In terms of real hands-on direction, the Bunche project is the most expensive film I've done.

I'm pleased with the Bunche film. We worked very hard on it. Originally it was going to be a six-part series, but we couldn't get it into the PBS system at that length, so we cut it down to four parts, then to three parts, and finally to a two-hour special. We got help from the Ford Foundation, the MacArthur Foundation, the Cosbys, and various other foundations: the National Black Programming Consortium, the National Endowment for the Humanities, and the Corporation for Public Broadcasting.

Now [2003], we're at work on fourteen teaching modules, thirty minutes each, on various facets of Bunche's life—most of which didn't make it into the two-hour film [in the end, twelve modules were completed]. We hope these mini-productions will be useful for teachers in universities and colleges. Sidney Poitier will be narrating.

The Bunche project has been an arduous, difficult, painful, frustrating experience. Unless you have the commitment—the psychological, psycho-spiritual commitment—to the subject matter you're working on, filmmaking can be destructive to your health and everything else. I've been around for a long time, but my psycho-spiritual center is not involved with making some executive in Hollywood happy. I'm focused on the psychospiritual liberation of people of color and of the white community as well.

Mind you, I love money, but I like to make money doing what I want to do, what I feel needs to be done, rather than what someone else wants me to do.

GA: Was it challenging to adapt the Bunche documentary from Sir Brian Urquhart's book [*Ralph Bunche: An American Odyssey* (Norton, 1998)]?

WG: No, in fact the book was very helpful. Without Urquhart's book, the film would not have had the basis in scholarship that it has. Of course, there were twelve scholars working with us too, but Brian Urquhart was Bunche's closest friend and colleague, and his replacement as undersecretary-general of the United Nations.

When I showed the finished film to Kofi Annan [UN secretary-general from January 1997 to December 2006], he and his staff freaked out. Annan said, "This is a film on one of our heroes. It's got to be seen by everyone in the UN system and beyond." We gave the UN 117 prints of the film, and it also traveled around the United States to roughly twenty-five cities, under the umbrella of the Human Rights Watch Festival. My company continues to distribute *Ralph Bunche* to schools, colleges, universities, libraries, and special-interest groups.

MS: What were the special challenges in the Ralph Bunche project, other than the financing and the issue of how long the film would be?

WG: It was a daunting project, the toughest film I've made. Bunche's life spans a great deal of time and a wide range of issues: decolonization, peacekeeping, mediation, scholarship, civil rights, diplomacy, the whole thrust of the Human Rights Convention that he developed with Eleanor Roosevelt. He set up the International Atomic Energy Agency of the United Nations. His life and accomplishments were all over the place.

And there's Bunche's relationship to his children and his wife, his problems with his own physical well-being caused by the sacrifice of his body for the success of the United Nations—he had a series of illnesses that could not deter him from his UN work. Eventually, he succumbed to the effects of those illnesses.

It was a complicated story. We found that if we just followed the chronology of his life, we weren't developing a very exciting narrative, so we tried to surf various thematic lines of inquiry, giving lip service to chronology wherever possible.

MS: You've said that this film has been your toughest. But aren't all of them tough?

WG: I suppose so.

MS: Shouldn't they be challenging? Otherwise, we don't have much fun.

WG: If you call agony, pain, and suffering "fun"!

On the other side of the coin, it *was* exciting to make a film about Ralph Bunche. We knew this could be the only time this story would have a chance to be told so comprehensively—which filled Louise and me with anxiety. We'd go from the mountain peak of elation over how well things were going to the nadir of depression over how difficult this was. It was a roller coaster.

GA: The subjects of your films have honor and courage, and you're able to bring this out in the films, whether it be Ralph Bunche or Booker T. Washington. Given the power of film and the fact that, as technology advances, more African Americans are able to make films, why don't we see more people using film to honor those who have made important contributions in effecting social change?

WG: Well, I think it has to do with society as a whole. It's not only black people; it's white people, all people in modern society—and particularly as modern society is being promoted in America. There's a tendency in America to denigrate intellectual development and education and to gravitate towards instant gratification through violence, sex, and comedy. It's Roman circus time. When you're involved in the circus, you don't have time for intellectual, political, sociological, and cultural development. All communities in America are in the grip of a media epidemic that creates diseases of the mind of all kinds—and most people are not even aware of it.

This media pathology can be very dangerous. To create a society that is silly, immature, and dysfunctional is to create a national security problem. Such a society can be vulnerable to all kinds of destruction both from within and without.

I was thinking recently about the American ethos and how Hollywood sets up the guidelines for our expectations and responses. We see hundreds of hours of film and TV, and we may, at some point, see one or two films that work in a different way in order to actually deal with our issues as a nation. There's a related development in Europe. At least a couple generations of Europeans were largely raised on their own films, films from their cultures about what concerns *them*. Then here comes the American film invasion, wiping their screen culture—and as a result, their actual culture—off the map.

I've been to France, Italy, Spain, and Sweden recently, and to me, Europeans look less and less like Europeans and more and more like Americans. And

European films are mimicking American action films. The American motion picture and television industry and print media are the engine that's driving the cultural transformation of the world.

At the Goethe Institute recently, I saw a German action film with lots of blood and guns and all these phony film conventions, the stock-in-trade of a Hollywood product.

Europeans figure if they make these films, they'll be able to access the American market. At least some of them think that. Another group makes these films in the hope of recapturing their own marketplace—not to preserve their spiritual or cultural integrity, but for business reasons. As I understand it, in Germany right now [1995], 12 percent of the market is controlled by the Germans; 85 percent, by Americans; and 3 or 4 percent, by people from other parts of the world.

As a juror at the San Sebastian Film Festival, I saw a lot of films from different countries: all clones of American films and not as good. I mean we do our films very well; they're what we *do*. Not long ago I was back in China and, to my utter amazement, when I'd talk to Chinese filmmakers about the aesthetics of film, about cinema language, they'd ask, "Where do you get the money? How do you make a deal?" Unhappily, the world seems progressively oriented to the bottom line, and the impact on cinema is devastating. It sure plays havoc with *my* truth. When you've got x hundred thousand dollars of debt to pay off, you have to watch what you say. Unfortunately, I don't know any way around it.

When I was starting out, I couldn't get my films distributed—because of the racism and apartheid nature of this country. I said, "Well, screw those folks; I'll do the distributing myself." I guess I have racism to thank, because it's made me much more self-reliant—in the Booker T. Washington tradition. With the help of my wife, Louise, who took charge of our distribution, we've been able to get our films out.

The path I've taken to do my filmmaking has been to develop a multiple front: to have three or four projects I'm interested in, while keeping myself available for other kinds of production work that might interest me. I've always tended to turn down commercials and industrials, but education interests me. I've done educational films for the U.S. government, for the American Cancer Society, for Exxon (a film having to do with minority businesses)—all with interesting subject matter.

This work has provided enough money to put my children through school and to have something resembling a decent life, although at times it's been stressful financially. When you commit yourself to independent filmmaking, no matter what level you're at, you've taken a vow of poverty. You keep putting your money into your films because you need to enhance the quality of what you're doing. That's why you *are* independent, because you want to do something that's pristine, something that's precisely the way you want it to be. But it's a burden.

On the plus side, that kind of reinvestment does result in a qualitative improvement of your product, which then makes it more viable and attractive. *From These Roots* [1974] is considered a high-quality film. It won twenty-two awards. But *From These Roots* practically bankrupted us, at least in terms of the energy and time we put into making what we felt would be an interesting cinematic experience.

GA: You've covered so many wonderful aspects of African-American history, but we seem to live in a society that doesn't value history. Does it concern you that audiences, especially young audiences who could benefit the most from your films, may not appreciate them?

WG: One of my most depressing experiences occurred when we showed the Ralph Bunche film to an audience of high school seniors in Westchester County. The town where we showed the film is largely white, and the school felt that they ought to bring in black students from other communities. It was interesting to me that some of those black kids took to the film, but others were asleep by the end of the screening. None of the white kids were asleep, which tells you the degree to which we have been, and are being, mentally enslaved by not getting our kids to focus on the whole range of past history, events that, whether they realize it or not, have to do with their present and future, with the nature of their families and communities and their own minds.

Fade out, fade in: I'm down at Spelman College in front of an audience of young black female students, and after the film, students come up, complimenting me. One girl pushes her way through the crowd to say, "Mr. Greaves, I enjoyed your film very much. It meant a lot to me and I learned a great deal that I didn't know. Dr. Bunche was a very important man, and I want you to remember me, because I'm going to be president of the United States someday." I looked at her and said, "Fantastic! Right on, sister!"

At Morehouse I had an audience of about six hundred black male students. They were quiet as mice, just vacuuming up the information in the film. It was marvelous. I thought, "*This* is why I make movies!"

FW: Your work is often shown during Black History Month and events of that kind. Do you think this may have the effect of keeping black films segregated from American film studies and other related areas?

WG: My films have strong elements of black pride, which are a reaction to white racism—but they are ultimately pointed in the direction of the humanity and dignity of *all* people. I think there's been entirely too much emphasis placed on black or white identity. If we allow ourselves to be continually divided in that way, we can't get to the essential humanity that joins us. Either a person is going to be a member of the human race or they are going to be "black" or "white." Unless a sense of common humanity and dignity becomes dominant, we're in for a lot of trouble in the twenty-first century.

One of the unhappy features of American society has been a tendency to "ghettoize" the black achiever by featuring his race. He or she is described as the finest black person that has come down the pike in some field, rather than the finest person, or a fine person, in the field. That is one of the problems we confronted with Ralph Bunche. He'd been constantly presented as a black this or a black that, which underestimated his importance. He was also a citizen of the world and wanted to be seen as that.

I get invited to many campuses for all kinds of events. I speak about a variety of the subjects that I address in my films—black consciousness, the quality of American life, the various techniques and styles of filmmaking, the problems of working with actors and nonactors. *All* these are areas that concern and interest me. I tend not to categorize myself, and I hope that's a statement in itself.

LC: How would you like to be remembered?

WG: I'd like to be remembered for the films I've done, maybe especially for the films I've coproduced in the last twenty–thirty years with my wife, Louise Archambault Greaves.

But let me tell you about something I'm involved with now [2003]: I would like to do a film about Sri Aurobindo, an Indian World humanist who led the self-determination movement in India at the beginning of the twentieth century and who later became a mystic. The Aurobindo people are telling me that if I will do a film, they will back it. That project will keep me energized for quite a while.

3

Interview with Louise Archambault Greaves

SCOTT MACDONALD

SCOTT MACDONALD: When did you meet Bill?

LOUISE ARCHAMBAULT GREAVES: We met back in 1957, in Montreal. At the time Bill was working at the National Film Board of Canada, but he also conducted a workshop for actors based on the Method.

SM: You met him at that workshop?

LAG: That's the embarrassing truth.

SM: Why would it be embarrassing?

LAG: Well, you know, it's the age-old issue of a teacher-student relationship....

SM: How old were you?

LAG: I've always said I was old enough to know better, but I would have been twenty-three or twenty-four.

SM: So you were an adult.

LAG: True! And Bill was just six years older, but from my perspective at that time, he might just as well have come from another planet. I did not realize it then, but looking back, it's pretty obvious that the workshop was an opportunity for Bill to explore the creative process, using the Stanislavsky acting technique that Lee Strasberg had developed at the Actors Studio. It was a process that fascinated him throughout his life. Witness *Symbiopsychotaxiplasm*! For me, it was a mind-expanding experience.

SM: Were you planning to be an actress?

LAG: My plans—such as they were—were pretty vague. I think basically what I had in mind was just to learn how to express myself in public situations with greater confidence than my convent background had allowed. Need I say that Method acting turned out to be more than I had bargained for?

FIGURE 3.1 Greaves teaching acting in Canada. Photographer unknown. Courtesy Louise Greaves.

SM: Your "convent background"?

LAG: Yes!

SM: You went to Catholic school?

LAG: A girls' boarding school—in Quebec in the 1940s. The Catholic Church was very much in charge.

SM: Do you still have relatives in Canada?

LAG: Except for a niece, no immediate family. I didn't keep in touch with my extended family or friends, which I now regret. But it was complicated.

SM: Because Bill was American or because he was African American?

LAG: Oh, American might even have been a plus. Canadians like to talk about Americans as being brash, but underneath it, they secretly admire them. As far as Bill being African American, that was more of a problem. At the time, even in Canada, the social stigma was very real. This is prior to the Civil Rights Movement of the sixties.

But I have to say that my family genuinely liked and admired Bill—how could they not? Ultimately, they not only accepted our marriage but were very supportive of us.

SM: So, you guys get married in 1959 and you come back to New York in 1963. What made Bill decide to come back to the States?

LAG: Bill had always planned to come back. He never considered himself an expatriate—unlike many who left the States during the McCarthy period. Bill left because, as an African American, he was unable to gain the work experience he needed to be a documentary filmmaker. Even the unions were closed.

Initially he had thought of producing dramatic feature films about the African-American experience modeled on the post–World War II Italian Neorealist films that he greatly admired. He thought that approach was ideally suited to tell the African-American story. That proved impractical for him, and, upon discovering John Grierson, Bill realized that it might be possible to accomplish much the same goal as a documentary filmmaker.

His plan in coming to Canada and the National Film Board was to learn everything about documentary filmmaking from the ground up so he could function independently when he got back. He wouldn't have to rely on anyone. If necessary, he could do it all by himself. He figured this might take him a year.

The reality proved a bit more complicated. It wasn't until the sixties when the Civil Rights Movement was picking up steam that he could seriously contemplate returning. Fortunately, a job offer from United Nations Television made the move to New York possible, but I don't think that at that point anything could have stopped him from returning.

SM: How was it for you coming to the States, to New York City?

LAG: It felt absolutely right—almost preordained. I felt confident that everything was going to work out for us, and for the country.

SM: So you arrived here in 1963.

LAG: Yes, right in the midst of the Civil Rights movement. Over the years a lot has changed, but recently there's a new consciousness of the social and economic ramifications of racism. Especially on the part of the younger generation, as well as the media. It's absolutely amazing. Not sure what is prompting this, but I think we've reached a turning point. The groundwork done during the Civil Rights era is beginning to have an impact. Many young African Americans are now coming out of colleges and universities and moving into so many areas of American life and culture. I don't think White Backlash has the power it once had.

Bill believed that humanity had the potential to change. For him the question was, where do you exert what force you have to get the most effect? Film was just one way to go about it, but it was his way.

SM: I assume that when you first came to New York, you two were involved with building a family as well as with Bill's career as a filmmaker.

LAG: Very much so. Not that we had a whole bunch of kids, but somehow it was taken for granted that it would be possible to both have a family and make films. A bit unrealistic perhaps.

Finding an apartment for an interracial family (our first child, Taiyi, was two years old when we arrived) was a major challenge. The city was segregated in terms of housing. I'd respond to ads for apartments in the paper and when I'd show up with Taiyi (I had no babysitter), the apartment had always been rented. I always arrived "too late." At first, I didn't get it. In retrospect I can see what the problem was.

We were holed up for six months in a two-room residential hotel on 23rd Street. If it had not been for a Mitchell-Lama housing project opening up in Washington Heights, I'm not sure where we would have ended up. Our second child, Maiya, arrived in 1965, and at that point, Bill's son from a previous relationship, David, was about to graduate from high school and go off to college. There was no slush fund to rely on. It was a balancing act.

SM: At what point did you first take part in the production of films?

LAG: Production came later—but I was involved in other ways from the start, largely in an administrative capacity which allowed for greater flexibility, time-wise. Film production is not a 9:00 to 5:00 job. Frankly, my goal in life did not center on becoming a producer. In any case, I had my hands full, managing the business and the family. Bill was the filmmaker and breadwinner, but we were both running very hard. There was never a boring moment; we were both under a lot of pressure.

SM: In more recent years Bill often referred to you as a producer.

LAG: I became more directly involved in production as time went by and the children left home. It was almost inevitable! Another part of the operation that I should point out is that even as far back as 1968–69 we were distributing Bill's films. I dealt with the bookkeeping and managed the distribution. We had to have prints made at the labs and shipped to exhibitors. And the exhibitors had to be billed for the rentals.

It wasn't only rentals. In those days a lot of schools, libraries, and not-for-profit organizations would buy prints. This was a big part of my job. I had a degree in business administration, which may have helped.

Bill always said, "I'm not making films just because I like to make movies! I make them to be seen and hopefully to have an impact of some kind. I don't want them to end up sitting on a shelf in a basement somewhere!" At that time, distributors were not particularly interested in Black films.

SM: Was it always just the two of you, keeping the business running?

LAG: Hardly. But there were times between productions when we really were on our own. Bill was not just a producer or a director or a writer. He actually *made* films—shot and edited them, and then helped with promotion and distribution as well. There were always a number of projects in the works, but when each might actually "land" depended on a number of factors over which we had little or no control.

That was the way it was. For better or worse.

Bill was committed to making the best and most compelling films he possibly could. It was not just a matter of presenting the facts or putting them together in a formulaic sense. Each film presented its own set of challenges. I recall him saying that no matter how many films he had made, when he started a new project, and began looking at the footage, it was as if he had never made a film before.

SM: By the time *Symbiopsychotaxiplasm* was shot in 1968, you were already involved in the business. This was a different, even a strange project for him, almost a lark. The irony is that *Symbiopsychotaxiplasm: Take One* has become canonical and perhaps his best-known film.

Bill would always say that he had angel financing for the *Symbio* project. I asked him one time who the angel was, and he said it was Patricia Ree Gilbert, Alice in *Take One*.

LAG: Well, in part—but the major investment did not come from her.

SM: Can you tell me where it came from?

LAG: Well...

SM: Why is it a secret?

LAG: Because...well, it *isn't* a secret....

SM: That angel should go down in history as having been part of a remarkable experiment.

LAG: You're absolutely right. And Bill would agree. It was one of Bill's students from Montreal, who at the time was doing quite well in real estate. Manny Melamed. He appears in *Symbio*, briefly.

SM: Where do we see him?

LAG: At one point the film cuts away to various couples; he's in one of those couples. And in the opening credits Manny is listed as coproducer.

The money that came through Patricia Ree Gilbert was needed for the blow-up to 35mm for a theatrical release and the finishing of the film in the lab. I should point out that while Bill always thought of *Symbio* as an experiment, it was hardly "a lark." He was deeply interested in exploring the creative process. He had a theory about conflict as a source of energy and he thought of creativity as something that arose spontaneously out of conflict. For him this was a serious matter, and he wanted to see if he could capture the process on film. He considered the film worthy of a theatrical release. Manny also had a theatrical release in mind, but he had given Bill total freedom: "Do whatever you want!"

SM: Do you remember particular highs and lows during your long career making films?

LAG: There were a lot of both! But Bill thought of problems as challenges, even as opportunities. Sometimes they turned out to be detours, but he accepted the fact that he wasn't in charge of the timing of events. So we're going in *that* direction, okay—but we're going *here* for the moment because we have to survive in order to get to where we are ultimately going. He just kept moving forward.

When things got tough, he sought help from friends and supporters as well as spiritual guidance from the writings of the Indian mystic, poet, journalist, and early anticolonial activist, Aurobindo. In going through Bill's papers and books after he passed away, I came across at least a dozen of Aurobindo's books, the margins all scrawled with Bill's notes.

Bill read a lot and had a large, eclectic collection of books. He never met Aurobindo, who died in 1971, but he did have the opportunity to meet and was profoundly influenced by the ideas of people like Lee Strasberg, William Leo Hansberry, J. L. Moreno, John Grierson, Tom Daly (the chief editor of Unit B at the National Film Board of Canada), the pioneering film producer William Alexander, and many other leaders in various fields. He was the product of many influences and encounters, including, I should add, those with his West Indian immigrant family.

SM: I remember Bill talking about going to an ashram in India from time to time. Did you go with him?

LAG: Yes, I had the opportunity to join him there on two or three occasions. Once when he was filming in Goa and in the tribal area of Dadra Nagar Haveli. We had extraordinary access to people and to little known areas of Indian life and society. Another time I accompanied Bill when he was on the jury of the International Film Festival of Kerala.

For the most part, however, when Bill traveled abroad it was under the auspices of the State Department, or in the case of India specifically, as a member of the Indo-US Subcommission on Education and Culture. His travel involved presenting his films, giving talks, or conducting workshops at the Film Institute in Puna, on either filmmaking or acting.

On one occasion he took a delegation of African-American filmmakers to the International Film Festival in Bombay (now Mumbai). They traveled extensively throughout India, meeting with their Indian counterparts.

But to get back to your question, Bill would always try to spend a few days at the Aurobindo ashram in Pondicherry. It was a very special place; Bill had some wonderful friends there as well as in Auroville. I think it's interesting that Bill refers to Aurobindo, as well as to Arthur Bentley, in connection with *Symbiopsychotaxiplasm*.

SM: Looking back from this point, which films are memorable as particularly difficult struggles?

LAG: Without a doubt that would be the Ralph Bunche film.

SM: A big undertaking.

LAG: Huge! Bill spent a good part of a decade working on the project, which evolved over time. It went from 16mm, to video, to digital.

It started out as a PBS prime-time special, but the more Bill worked on the Bunche material, the more he realized how important the content was, and he came to feel that it deserved to be a miniseries—PBS was doing miniseries at that time—in which case, it would have to edited in a nonlinear system.

Bill had never used a computer—I'm not sure that he'd ever used a typewriter! But he took a course in digital editing at NYU. At one point he must have realized that he would need help, so he talked his teacher, Stephen Perrotta, into coming onboard and working with him on the Bunche project. After a few weeks, Stephen said to Bill, after we'd just spent thousands of dollars on an Avid, "You don't *need* an Avid, Bill; you've got an Avid in your head!" [Laughter]. But it was true: Bill could remember how a word or an image on that little snippet of film or mag track would work with such and such image later in the film. He edited in his head.

SM: These past years, you've been dealing with the mountain of material Bill left behind. I'm amazed you've survived.

LAG: So far! It's been more than I'd bargained for, but I'm very grateful to have had this opportunity to dig deeper into my husband's work. It's been a learning experience. I've been going through his papers, including his notes, and better understanding where he was coming from.

Bill was extremely resourceful. Even as a child. At a very young age, he was shining shoes at Penn Station, delivering newspapers in his Harlem neighborhood, even scrubbing floors and cleaning the office of a lawyer who had an office on the ground floor of the building where the family lived on 135th Street between Lenox Avenue and what is now Frederick Douglass Boulevard, next to the Schomburg.

INTERVIEW WITH LOUISE ARCHAMBAULT GREAVES

FIGURE 3.2 William and Louise together. Photographer unknown. Courtesy Louise Greaves.

SM: He never talked about this, at least when I've seen him talk (or in the interviews I've read).

LAG: It was the Depression, and an allowance of any kind was out of the question, but Bill seems to have gotten a lot of support from the community. He told me that one of his grade school teachers would give him money to buy lunch for him and allow Bill to keep the change.

He was also blessed in having parents who were proud of their African heritage and encouraged Bill's creativity. They wanted him to succeed—although in those days that did not include making movies. His father supported the family of seven kids as a cab driver and part-time minister. His mother was an evangelist.

SM: Bill's illness came on so fast and was so devastating in terms of his ability to function that there wasn't even much of a transitional period where he could help you figure out what to do.

LAG: Bill was very clear about the fact that he wanted his films to continue to be available. He had made arrangements for his work, including the outtakes, to be held by the Schomburg Center and wanted his papers to be a part of the collection. Bill felt that they were important and could be of value in the future. He'd already started organizing them before he took sick.

FIGURE 3.3 Su Friedrich (*left*) and Louise Greaves on an excursion to visit one of the sites where Greaves materials are stored, part of their work on the Greaves website, on May 19, 2020, during the Covid-19 period (Louise had survived a Covid-19 infection). Photograph by unknown passerby. Courtesy Su Friedrich

SM: Was there a name for his illness?

LAG: It was a rare form of parkinsonism. They referred to it as "progressive supranuclear palsy." In terms of symptoms, he became less and less able to move, even to speak.

SM: I learned about the illness, soon after he'd become ill, at a fundraising event at the Schomburg. You walked up to me and said, "God is a sadist."

LAG: Did I say that?

SM: You did.

LAG: [laughter] I can't *imagine* saying that. But I'm finding stuff in the archives that I said and did, and thinking, "Really?! *I* did *that*?"

SM: I don't think people would imagine how small the enterprise was that produced all the films. When people think of filmmaking, they think there's a floor of a building and a connection to a studio.

LAG: Not many independents can boast of that. Of course, with the new digital technology there is less need for physical space, but that certainly wasn't the case when we were working in 16mm. We rented office space as the need arose and moved around a lot. We became pretty expert at moving out and moving in. In those cases, I called what I did "picking up the pieces."

The question you raised in the subtitle of the preface [in an early draft, the preface to *William Greaves: Filmmaking as Mission* was subtitled "Why a William Greaves Book?"] has prompted me—has actually forced me—to think more deeply about Bill's contribution to film and perhaps to American society. What has he done that would justify a book entirely devoted to his work? Is he just another African-American filmmaker who happened to be in the right place at the right time? In what way could/should he be considered *exceptional*? Frankly, I am embarrassed that it has taken me this long to deal with these basic questions.

I hadn't really thought about what set him apart from other filmmakers of his era. It's not the sheer volume of his work or the awards that he won. It's really a matter of *how* he used his talent! Making movies was Bill's way to contribute to society, a form of social activism. He used his talent, his hard-won expertise, and his extraordinary energy not only to enlighten the citizens of this country but to help *all* of us rise above the country's horrendous past and live up to our ideals as a just and equitable society.

He was *very* conscious of what he was doing. He refused to give up on the human race. This was a challenge he faced every day of his life, an ongoing struggle that he dealt with in every film that he made—no matter what the subject or the budget. He *felt obligated* to do so. Perhaps the alternative was not something he could deal with and remain sane; he would have ended up a broken man, crushed physically or spiritually.

Instead, he dedicated himself to making films that were as powerful and as engaging as his talent and resources would allow. I am just beginning to appreciate what he meant when he said that he made films to "raise consciousness." Thanks to the book, his work may be recognized more broadly. His impact continues to be felt today not only in his own work but in the work of other people. Bill was, and is, a national treasure; Steve Buscemi's words—not mine!

Unfortunately, Bill was not able to finish the project he was working on when his health started to deteriorate. He wanted to explore the contributions that African-American artists have made to American and world culture. The new film would have incorporated some of the extraordinary archival footage that he had shot back in 1972 when he was working on *From*

These Roots [1974]. I tried to keep the production going, but eventually we ran out of funds and Bill needed my full-time attention. I'd like to see what could be done with some of the footage that he'd started to edit. It's unique historic material and should be available to the public. I have a concept in mind that would involve presenting it to the public as an installation. It would commemorate the centenary decade of the Harlem Renaissance.

SM: You've become the person everybody interested in Bill's work contacts....

LAG: Well, for the moment, Scott. I love what I'm doing. It's challenging but it gives my life meaning. However, I am hardly alone! There's a growing appreciation of the contribution Bill has made to the art of the documentary and more importantly, a growing appreciation of the power of film to create a more just and equitable world.

4

Interview with David Greaves

SCOTT MACDONALD

SCOTT MACDONALD: David, could you talk about how you came to be working with Bill Greaves on his early 1970s films?

DAVID GREAVES: I was a student at Syracuse University and was looking to attend UCLA graduate school for psychology when I spent a school holiday in Dad's editing room rolling film outs for the *First World Festival of Negro Arts* [1966] to send to Washington.

I remember thinking that instead of spending two or four more years in a library, I'd rather work with my father, who I'd not met until I was twelve years old.

I applied to the Columbia University film department to do an MFA in film. I know that Dad's friendship with then department chair, Arthur Barron, smoothed that entry. I attended Columbia while working at WGP, William Greaves Productions.

SM: In general, what was it like working with your father?

DG: It was a lot of interesting, unusual, and good times and also stressful and nonstop. It was educational in terms of doing whatever it took to make things work. In the editing room, where sometimes thirty thousand feet of film had to be cut down to thirty minutes, Dad would explain his choices of segues, some based on movement, others based on ideas—sometimes referring to Sergei Eisenstein or Sri Aurobindo as reference points.

At WGP I learned many elements of film production and performed mostly as a sort of Jack-of-all-trades.

SM: What do you remember about working on *Voice of La Raza* [1972] and *From These Roots* [1974]?

DG: *Voice of La Raza* was produced for the EEOC [Equal Employment Opportunity Commission].

The big thing about *La Raza* was Anthony Quinn. Dad had hoped to have Quinn do the narration, and one mission I had while we were in Los Angeles was to get the script to him. Quinn's home was within a gated community, past walls of anonymous high hedges. It was dark when I found the driveway and drove up, Quinn came out, his arm in a sling, shouting, "Who's there?" I told him who I was, gave him the script, and got the hell out.

I remember Dad was excited the next day after speaking with Quinn, who had told him he loved the project. He didn't just want to do the narration; he wanted *to be in the film*. And as you can imagine, when Anthony Quinn insists he wants to be in your documentary, that changes everything.

Our project manager for the EEOC was Olivia Stanford, and she very much liked the idea of including Mr. Quinn and yes, please change the script as required. We were scheduled to film in Hawaii and I was sent on my own, armed with an Arri-S to do B-roll shooting while Dad stayed in LA, working on script and location changes with Quinn.

What I remember most was kneeling on broken glass in a vacant lot in El Barrio, holding a Sennheiser 805 microphone pointed up at Quinn and the young questioners who surrounded him. As usual, Bill was on camera.

Anthony Quinn had a sense of humor. We were in his office, sitting on a sofa made from the very nice hide of some animal, and among the things he spoke about, and imitated, was how when Hollywood slicksters would glide into his office to pitch a project, he would stand in front of his mantle with an Oscar on each side of him. I can't do justice to the way he described the scene, but we were roaring with laughter.

SM: *From These Roots* was a very different film.

DG: *From These Roots* was originally to be a film with live action as well as historical photographs. We used an apartment at 444 Central Park West as the main location for recording a series of interviews with extraordinary people: artist Aaron Douglas, for example, and poet Arna Bontemps; actor Leigh Whipper, who recited a speech of Haitian revolutionary Henri Christophe—or was it Dessalines? Singer Noble Sissle sang "If You've Never Been Vamped by a Brownskin," from Sissle and Blake's 1921 *Shuffle Along*. Legendary Harlem activist and owner of the Frederick Douglass Book Center, Richard B. Moore, spoke of poet Claude McKay, and when Dad asked if he remembered McKay's "If We Must Die," he said, "Of course!" "Can you recite it for us?" Mr. Moore took a moment, then began, "If we must die. . . ."

Artist and writer Bruce Nugent was interviewed at another location, and he spoke about luminaries and the ambience of the period. He described seeing actress Rose McClendon in a scene where "she came down the stairs with such elegance and grace," and then he saw her in another production where she played an old, haggard woman. He remembered that when a question arose as to her makeup, she said, "Oh I never use makeup, I just think it." He spoke also about his friendship with Langston Hughes, and how "I'd walk him home and he'd walk me home," back and forth all night in Harlem.

And author and social commentator George Schuyler was interviewed, and Mrs. Countee Cullen, and others I cannot call to mind right now. I've always felt that those interviews of firsthand recollections will prove important to anyone studying the Harlem Renaissance.

The live action culminated at a party Dad had arranged to be held at Ruth Ellington's home at 333 Riverside Drive. I was one of three cameramen filming these folks from another era, folks who hadn't seen each other in decades.

After the live shooting, I began putting still images on film. An Oxberry animation stand was not in the budget, so I used our Éclair NPR camera with the 12–120 Angenieux lens, augmented with series of macro lenses and a motorized zoom mounted on a liquid-head tripod.

Along with filming in the office, there were several trips to see the translucent walls of the Beinecke Rare Books and Manuscript Library at Yale University. Here we had what I thought was unusual access to do the filming. I was given a room and shown downstairs where the trays of photos in the James Weldon Johnson and Carl Van Vechten collections were. I had permission to take entire trays up to my room, film them, and return the trays. No supervision needed. When I told my father about the situation, he said, "It was Exxon who asked permission"—Exxon had financed the film.

Putting *From These Roots* together was a problem.

Dad was editing and I was assisting, and try as he might, he could not get the live action to go with the stills. It had to be one way or the other and he decided that to tell the story of the Harlem Renaissance we had to go with the stills.

The most notable event during the editing happened the night before the people from Exxon were flying in from Texas to see what we had. At 3:00 A.M. that Sunday morning, we had *nothing*. Just a jumble. Dad said, "Let's go get something to eat."

New York may be the only place in the world where at 3:00 A.M. on a Sunday morning there are three or four places you can go and have a hot apple pie a la mode with melted cheese and a coffee. Our choice was the Howard Johnson's on Eighth Avenue and 50th Street, almost around the corner from our 54th Street office.

When we got back to the office, my father sat at the machine and then it was, "Put this behind that," "Tail sync this to that," "This section goes...," me furiously writing on my ever-present yellow pad. Finally, he said that was it; he was going to lie down until they came, which would be in a couple of hours.

I took to the editing bench. Today, the work could be done in a café on a laptop, but this was still the analog world of trim bins, synchronizers, splicers, rewinds, and split reels. I spent a couple of frantic and exhilarating hours, watching order being brought out of chaos.

I was still working when the receptionist we shared with others on that floor called to say our guests had arrived. I told Dad and went out and greeted them as though we were happy to see them right on time. I escorted them back to my father's office, and I took and delivered a coffee order from our coffee machine, before racing back to the editing room.

As my father was explaining how the concept for the film had changed to all stills with narration, he would periodically buzz on the intercom to ask nonchalantly, "How's it coming?" I would tell him and he'd translate my response as "A few more moments." Finally, they came into the editing room, saw the film, and despite that it was not what they'd expected, they liked it.

That was the high point. The low point was when the fine cut was taken to Texas for preview. They liked the film except for one shot. When I was filming the stills, I'd found one of a grinning blonde girl, perhaps ten years old, standing next to the burned corpse of a Black man. As I zoomed in to her face, you heard Claude McKay's, "And little lads, lynchers that were to be, / Danced round the dreadful thing in fiendish glee." My zoom into the girl was a bridge too far for the Exxon execs. In the finished film, the poem is in, but the zoom is into a sculpture.

SM: You also had a role in *Nationtime—Gary* [1973]. Were you present at the convention during the shoot?

DG: I did the budget, acted as production manager, and was the second cameraman and assistant editor.

The film began with a visit to the office from Amiri Baraka, asking if we could film the convention he was pulling together in Gary, Indiana. Today, a couple of filmmakers could get on a plane with their cell phones and record and edit the event. At that time, however, film needed to be bought, developed, and printed. Then the physical editing and synching of tracks, followed by the mixing studio, negative cutting, printing, color correction, and then final prints.

When I told my father what the film would cost, he said, "It's not going to cost that much." What he meant was that it did not matter what the calculations said, we were doing the film anyway. He paid for it all.

At the convention, Dad had the floor camera and I had the high camera, and a very smooth Doug Harris was filming near the podium. It was a week of little sleep and constant activity. One day our production assistant was driving Dad and me to film Mayor Richard Hatcher. As we're approaching a railroad crossing, the bells begin to ring, signaling the approach of what looks like a mile-long freight train. When the assistant quite properly begins to stop the car, both my father and I erupt, "What are you doing!" and in unison (me pounding on the seat back and him on the dashboard), we yell, "GO! GO! GO!" She floors the pedal and races across the tracks as the crossing arms are coming down. My father and I were both manic at that point and thought it was hilarious. The assistant was hunched over the steering wheel, holding tightly with both hands, saying, "Ya'll are crazy! Ya'll are crazy!"

Back in the editing room after the shoot, I faced one of those invisible challenges an assistant editor faces: we had no synch sound. The sound was drifting and had to be corrected. But in the end, all that was needed for each shot was reading lips and matching to sound for a start synch, the same for a tail synch, some high school math to determine the percentage of change, a speed controller for the Nagra IV, and a 16mm mag transfer machine in the editing room for immediate transfers.

In synching the footage, I came to the Jessie Jackson speech. This was when Jackson was at the height of his oratorical powers, and when he finished his speech, no more work could be done, as the conventioneers, unable to contain the emotion and energy that Jackson had brought, jumped from their seats. The music was up and everybody was dancing. In my camera I could see my father, overhead, panning, focusing, zooming, but later I could not find those shots anywhere in the footage. Of course, this is why assistant editors sleep on editing room floors!

When we were viewing the footage and came to the point where we should see the overhead shot of him shooting, I told Dad I'd looked at every roll of film we had but couldn't find that one. Dad said I wouldn't find it: "There was no film in the camera." "Then what were you doing?" He responded wistfully, "It was such a great shot; I didn't want to miss it."

SM: You were also the production manager on the Ali-Frazier film, which has been in a kind of cine-limbo for years. This seems strange, given what the audience could be expected to be for the film, even now.

DG: That project began when I answered a telephone call from Robin French, Jerry Perenchio's assistant with GUTS, Inc. They wanted to know if we could film the upcoming Ali-Frazier fight—only the biggest thing in the world at that time! I told him Mr. Greaves was not in, but I would give him the message as soon as he returned.

When Dad got to the office, I told him what had happened, and within a day or two, Jerry Perenchio and his wife were in the office to discuss the project and take us to dinner, where the waiters hovered and Perenchio purchased a box of cigars.

I believe it was after that, or maybe before, that Dad, Louise, and I had a production meeting at the now extinct Ye Olde Triple Inn on the southwest corner at 54th and Eighth. The question before us was, is this a project we can take on, given the work we already have? At the time, we were already editing one or two films and committed to another. I said, "You *know* we're going to do the fight; the question is how?" We had to submit a budget immediately.

Dad set up an alternate universe for the filming that I mostly watched from afar. It involved three crews, one traveling with the business partners Perenchio and French; another, with Ali; and a third, with Frazier—for thirty days. The budget, which had to be done immediately, also included the cost for a twelve-camera shoot on fight night on Monday, and the contract stipulated the delivery of a 35mm blow-up to be available in theaters the following Friday.

Fight week was 120-hours of adrenaline, including my attempt to explain the negative cutting process to Robin French, who couldn't give a shit. "*Where is it*!?" was all he wanted to know. Maybe we slept four hours that week.

With the negative locked, I was at the elevator, finally going home, when the doors opened and my father got off holding a reel of mag track. "Where are *you* going?" "Home." "Oh no, my boy, you have to edit this." It was the narration that Don Dunphy had done. "Why me?" "Because *you* will hear the inflections"—the racial undertones of the different takes. Dad felt that sometimes Mr. Dunphy took a certain glee when Frazier landed a blow.

I went through the tape, selected what from our point of view were the best takes, and delivered them to a bleary-eyed Louis de Rochemont, Jr., at Magno Sound, where everyone was gathered for the mix. I spied an empty patch of dirty carpet by the sound booth wall, stretched out on the floor, and went to sleep.

There were too many other moments in the making of the fight film to go into now. The film is approaching its fiftieth anniversary, and I'd love to see a restoration of the three-hour version.

Note: When the GUTS auditors came to the office after the fight, went through the files, and questioned me, they found that the budget I had put together in a mad rush was off by only a negligible amount.

SM: Bill's ultimate experiment, or certainly one of them, was *Symbiopsychotaxiplasm: Take One*. How long were you involved with the project?

DG: For *Take One*, I came onboard as the synching was being completed. I was just out of college, so this would have been the summer of 1969.

Dad had seen some of the footage, but it was after we moved from the penthouse to the eighth floor at 254 West 54th Street, which we shared with Depicto Films, that we began screening all of what had been shot, filling two racks eight feet high and four feet across. At that time, we were working on the state-of-the-art KEM editing table with three screens that were interchangeable with sound modules.

Mike Wadleigh had purchased what I understood to be the first KEM table in the country to do *Woodstock* [1970], and Dad had the next two editing tables to do the multicamera *Symbio*.

In the editing room, *Symbio* was a process of constantly falling in and out of love with scenes and favorite moments. "Do you miss that?" "No, I don't miss it."

The regret Dad kept coming back to was that there was no record of his first reaction to seeing the criticism session the crew recorded on their own, when they were trying to figure out what was going on in front of and behind the cameras.

SM: How closely did you stay in contact with your father's work after the 1970s?

DG: I had burnt out and left the company for several years, when Dad asked me to come back and work on what was then called "Movers and Shakers," a look at major figures in Black America. This was a dream project; it became *Black Power in American: Myth or Reality* [1986]. We had the opportunity to travel all over the country, interviewing leaders such as Clifton Wharton, Jr., then chancellor at the SUNY [State University of New York] system; and following the Jesse Jackson campaign; filming activists in North Carolina....

SM: For more than twenty years you've been publishing *Our Time Press*, a neighborhood newspaper that serves twenty thousand readers in Brooklyn, and in particular the Bed-Stuy area. This seems the quintessential *local* activity, whereas your father's films usually tended toward the global. Looking back, do you think your work with your father had an impact on your publishing *Our Time Press*?

DG: The two similarities between making documentaries and publishing a newspaper are that you are constantly learning new and fascinating things and that you feel your work has an effect on society. Putting the paper together is a lot like making a film: you find an interesting story and record it in a way that is both instructive and entertaining.

5

The Efficacy of Acting

KATHERINE KINNEY

In 1954 the Ottawa Film Society announced a screening of *Lost Boundaries* with "brief comments on film acting by William Greaves of the National Film Board who appears in Lost Boundaries." The text of those comments survives: seven carefully typed pages on onionskin paper with revisions in pen tracing the history of naturalism in acting. The talk ends with a description of Method acting, without naming it as such, and innovations in cinema "designed to bring the audience into greater intimacy with the actor's performance."

Throughout his career, William Greaves was deeply invested in the theory and practice of acting. His development as a director of documentaries was paralleled by his success directing acting workshops, at first in Ottawa and then in Montreal, Toronto, and New York. These workshops were more than a source of income. As Greaves said in an interview, "The improvisational dynamic of the Method and the cinéma-vérité dynamic coalesced in my mind," a fusion brilliantly realized in *Symbiopsychotaxiplasm: Take One*.[1]

In this essay, I want to make a first attempt to define Greaves's complex understanding of the efficacy of acting and his commitment to the acting workshop as a space of collaboration and discovery. Louise Archambault Greaves generously shared with me files related to the acting studio Greaves directed in Canada as well as his work with the Actors Studio in New York. These papers show a deep and continuing interest in the power of actor training to heighten sensory perception and responsiveness, which Greaves understood as agents of creativity and truth.[2] He returns to these ideas again and again, in formal talks, press interviews, workshop commentaries, and notes apparently jotted to himself on whatever was at hand—the backs of envelopes or a blank check, for example. I trace Greaves's fascination with the craft of acting in his early professional career from Harlem's American Negro Theatre to Broadway, and through his work at the Actors Studio and his creation of the Canadian Acting Studio. Acting was far more than a series of roles for Greaves. This excess challenges a number of contemporary critical assumptions about the nature of acting, the significance of Method acting, and the opportunities available to black actors in the postwar period.

For Greaves, the acting workshop offered a richly generative experimental model of creative practice. The scenario of *Symbiopsychotaxiplasm: Take One*, for example, shares many characteristics of an acting workshop. A short scene is performed by different pairs of acting partners. The scene offers a communal experiment in dramatic trial and error, repetition and improvisation, rather than developing fully realized characters bound within a dramatic structure. I have transcribed approximately 5,600 words of Greaves's handwritten notes about acting, which include accounts of sessions from both his studio and the Actors Studio, as well as more essay-like discussions and informal notes. Based on this narrow if rich body of evidence, my argument is speculative and necessarily open to future revision. It offers one possible answer to the question of how and why apparently disparate or even opposed practices, Stanislavskian actor training and documentary filmmaking, could simultaneously feed Greaves's intellectual curiosity and artistic vision.

Greaves's career as an actor began at Harlem's American Negro Theatre (ANT) in 1945. He was nineteen years old and already immersed in African-based dance performance, working first with Asadata Dafora, "who had introduced African dancing to the black community in Harlem in the 1940s," and then Pearl Primus, whose choreography combined modern and African forms.[3] In 1944 the Primus ensemble performed her "African Ceremonial" at the midtown Roxy Theater, one of the prestige movie palaces that featured various acts between movie screenings. Set in an African village, the dance was accompanied by Gordon Heath's contextual narration about African culture.[4] Heath recruited Greaves for ANT's March 1945 production of *Garden of Time* during the booking at the Roxy. Heath was personally and professionally close to Owen Dodson, who had written the experimental and lyrical play as his MFA thesis at Yale. *Garden of Time* retells the classical story of Medea, with the first act preserving the ancient Greek setting with a black Medea betrayed by a white Jason and the second act continuing the story in the Deep South during slavery.[5] Greaves was

FIGURE 5.1 Production photo: Greaves as Blues Boy in *Garden of Time* (Owen Dodson), performed by the American Negro Theatre in 1945. Courtesy Louise Greaves.

cast as Beles/Blues Boy, a musician from Medea's homeland and friend to Jason. He had no training as an actor at that point and had to mime playing the guitar as Heath played off stage in the wings. Nonetheless, Greaves received the best reviews of any cast member, a fact Heath recalls ruefully.[6] Heath had told Greaves that he was the right "type" for the part; it did not matter that he knew nothing about acting. Even so, the role of Beles/Blues Boy played to Greaves's performative strengths. If acting is the art of dramatic embodiment, Greaves was grounded in traditions of African and African-American movement, which likely shaped his stage presence as the itinerant musician.

In interviews, Greaves attributes the success of that first stage performance to a naïve naturalism, which would be undone in a too self-consciously actorly performance in the next ANT production, the less well received *Henri Christophe*, written by Dan Hammerman and directed by Abram Hill (June 1945). Greaves was "delighted" to play the young Haitian revolutionary, Jean-Jacques

Dessalines: "The whole idea of revolt against the racist domination was very attractive, particularly to young teenagers in Harlem like myself."[7] Dessalines was apparently scripted as the antagonist if not the villain of the play. "Abe would give me all the inflections that I was supposed to use and all the movements that would help me create a mean-spirited character as far as white people were concerned because he hated the oppression of black people." The resulting "bizarre histrionics" earned terrible reviews, and that failure would drive Greaves to actively study acting.[8]

I have yet to find any description of Greaves's earliest training as an actor, but ANT was a very actor-centered institution with an acting program led by Osceola Archer, whose commanding presence is memorably described by Sidney Poitier in his autobiography.[9] Certainly, the people Greaves met through ANT were central to his development as an actor. In the summer of 1945 Greaves played a "touching adolescent Laertes" in a black-cast summer stock production of *Hamlet* directed by Dodson and starring Heath. According to Heath, "Owen's direction was two-thirds coaching and teaching as he went along."[10] In the fall of 1945 Gordon Heath would open on Broadway in *Deep Are the Roots* (written by Arnaud d'Usseau and James Gow), directed by Elia Kazan, which ran for over a year.[11] Heath starred as a decorated black soldier who returns home to the South and the uncomfortable patronage of the white senator's family his mother serves as a domestic. Greaves played the role in summer stock in 1949, a credit long carried on his resume.

Greaves describes his move into acting as an accident. But in those key postwar years, a web of sustaining institutions and relationships existed in Harlem that nurtured an extraordinary generation of black actors. Greaves benefited from the overlapping friendships and working relationships between Primas, Heath, Dodson, and Abram Hill, who cofounded ANT with actor Frederick O'Neal, which offered resources for creative collaboration and models of ambition for the generation ten or more years younger. Greaves was a year older than Poitier and Harry Belafonte, who also began their acting careers at ANT; they, too, describe their initiations at ANT as accidental.[12] Scholars have debated how well ANT fulfilled W. E. B. Du Bois's call for a Negro Theater of, for, by, and near the black community, but the repetition of this tale of accidentally encountering the stage and acting suggests one transformative effect of ANT's existence from 1940 to 1949.[13] Greaves is particularly eloquent about the importance of his early friendships with Sidney Poitier, whom he met at ANT, and another young actor, Julian Mayfield. "We were a very good group of young people, I think, in that we stimulated each other. We really challenged each other's intelligence in one way or another. I think that out of it came a consensus of

FIGURE 5.2 Publicity shot of Greaves as a young actor, circa 1950. Courtesy Louise Greaves.

how we might relate to the media and to America, but also a kind of individuation where each of us realized more and more how individually viable we were."[14]

In early 1946 Greaves seemed on the verge of major breakthrough. Undeterred by bad reviews and a poor performance in *Henri Christophe*, he entered the John Golden Auditions, an acting competition in which thirty finalists culled from more than a thousand auditions competed for prizes by performing scenes at the Shubert Theater. That competition led producer Lee Shubert to cast Greaves in the lead role of the Broadway-bound production of *A Young American* by Edwin Bonner, a white New York music and drama critic. The play centers on the complications that result when a white conductor invites a young composer to stay at his home to work on an excellent score he has written, unaware that the younger man is African American. The original off-Broadway production received very good reviews with Louis Peterson, Jr., as the composer, and Broadway producer Lee Shubert "picked up the play and arranged for a pre-Broadway tryout in Chicago" with Greaves in the lead.[15] In late February 1946 the new production opened to mixed reviews and never made the transition to Broadway. Even so, Greaves's theatrical ambitions continued to grow. That summer he organized an integrated summer stock company with Savannah Churchill and Steven Scheuer, performing at the Crest Theater in Wildwood Crest, New Jersey. For years after, Greaves's professional résumé carried the credit: "co-produced, co-directed, stage managed, and acted" at the Crest, testimony to how early Greaves embraced a holistic ambition to create theater.

Greaves's Broadway debut came in January 1947, just eighteen months after his appearance in *Garden of Time*, in a small but noteworthy comic role in the original Broadway cast of the musical *Finian's Rainbow*. The play ran for 725 performances, nearly two years, offering the young actor an invaluable education in contemporary theater. Greaves called it "the ideal role for a curious 20-year-old at least. I was on stage for seven minutes and got the biggest laugh of the evening" as "the college student who ever so slowly brought a Bromoseltzer to the ailing Southern Senator."[16] The play's comic repudiation of racial prejudice may have stayed safely within middlebrow sensibilities, but the opportunities the play afforded Greaves were not limited to the role. After his scene was finished, Greaves "was free to see the second and third acts of everything in town."[17] Greaves's scene was featured in the 1948 ANTA Album, an "all-star review" of current Broadway shows benefiting the American National Theatre and Academy (ANTA). Greaves described working on the ANTA Album in idealistic terms: "I sat in on everybody else's rehearsals. It was incredible seeing all the titans of the theater doing the best scenes of their most famous roles.... There was a communality in the effort, a shared interest; you felt it was born out of the love and tremendous élan of the performers in their art."[18] While appearing in *Finian*, Greaves starred with Ruby Dee in a single-night, black-cast performance of the Norman Krasna comedy *John Loves Mary*, which was in the midst of a very successful run at the Music Box Theater. The Greaves-Dee performance was a fundraiser for the Urban League, directed by ANT's Abram Hill.

In retrospect, the range of roles Greaves played between 1945 and 1948 evidences overly familiar casting practices: black-cast productions of white-originated plays; comic support or the singular black lead; and an ambitious, underfunded black theater. But Greaves also entered Broadway at a transformational moment in American theater. *Finian* opened a month after Tennessee Williams's *A Streetcar Named Desire*, starring Marlon Brando and Jessica Tandy, began its revolutionary run. All the more surprising that Greaves singles out David Wayne's performance as the leprechaun Og in *Finian's Rainbow* as "thoroughly worked out and constantly inspired. It was the best performance on Broadway at the time, and I should know I saw them all."[19] Greaves does not acknowledge any tension between his admiration of Wayne as a "sensitive artist—introspective and thoughtful" and the investment of that talent in playing a leprechaun in danger of becoming human. His judgment attests to acting as art and craft rather than representation, an approach too often elided in critical readings focused primarily on scripted roles and social realist assumptions about type, character, and plot. Greaves's stage roles suggest his early range and ambition, but also the ways in which breaching segregation seemed, in that moment, of a piece with the transformation of American theater.

It was in this context that Greaves auditioned for the Actors Studio in 1948. He was in the second group of actors accepted, joining the impressive initial cohort that included David Wayne and African-American actor Frank Silvera, as well Marlon Brando. In the first year, actors had been invited by the individual teacher, with open auditions beginning in 1948. According to David Garfield, "Between the fall of 1948 and the spring of 1951, over two thousand performers auditioned. Of these, thirty or so were accepted." The experience of black actors in the Actors Studio has not, to my knowledge, been studied. Sidney Poitier and Roscoe Lee Browne were among the small number of actors "voted directly into membership by the Studio's directorate or by Strasberg himself."[20] Al Freeman, Jr., Diana Sands, Raymond St. Jacques, and Richard Ward were all members by the 1960s, if not before. Freeman and Greaves would appear together in an Actors Studio special performance in 1966.

There is much about Greaves's acting career I have yet to learn. He appeared in one of the final ANT productions, *Freight* (1949). Résumés from the period include unspecified credits at the Equity Library Theater and Bar Harbor Playhouse, as well as extensive listings for radio and television appearances by station or network rather than title and date. A set of unidentified publicity stills show Greaves and Sheila Guyse, who played the female lead in *Lost in the Stars*, in a CBS drama (the camera is visible in one picture) playing newlyweds. The Actors Studio produced a television series for two seasons beginning in the fall of 1948.

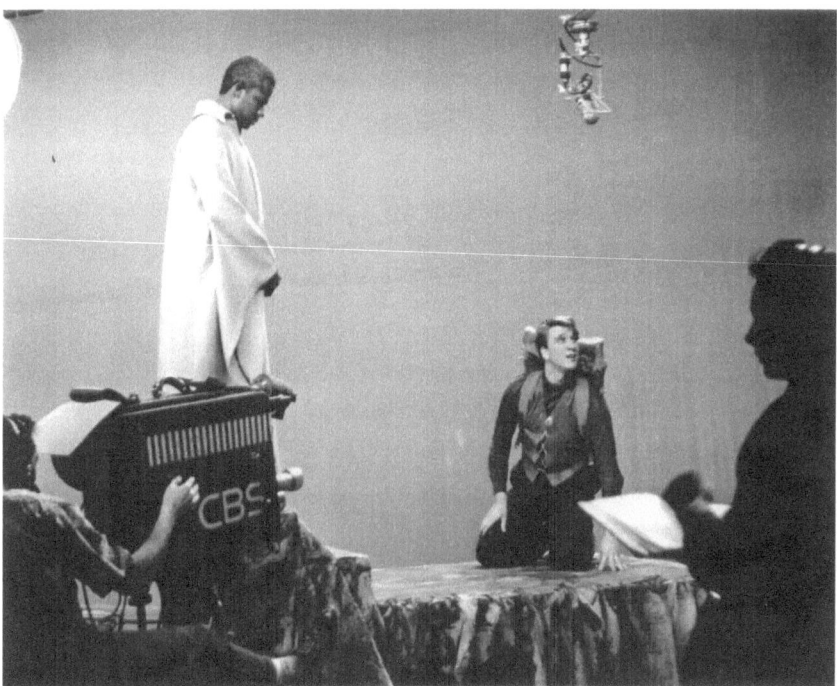

FIGURE 5.3 Production still of Greaves during shooting of the CBS series *Lamp Unto My Feet*. Photographer unknown. Courtesy Louise Greaves.

CBS broadcast the second season, Greaves's second year in the Actors Studio, a possible source for this production. Another set of stills shows Greaves in military uniform on what appears to be a New York street, also likely a television appearance. A third set, marked c. 1949, shows Greaves appearing in the television series *Lamp Unto My Feet*, a religious series that ran from 1948 to 1979.

The ambition that Greaves shared with Poitier and Mayfield coalesced in the 1949 Broadway production of *Lost in the Stars*, a musical adaptation of Alan Paton's *Cry the Beloved Country* by Maxwell Anderson and Kurt Weill. Poitier had been cast in the play but turned it down to make his first film, *No Way Out* (1950). The part went to Mayfield, with Greaves in a featured role and as understudy to Mayfield. "We toured around the country, and as young actors the world was stretching out in front of us and we thought we were going to become major stars and all," Greaves recalls.[21] Greaves had also made a number of films by this point. *Lost Boundaries* (1949) opened during the run of *Lost in the Stars*, as did *Souls of Sin* (1949); three marquee roles running simultaneously would be any young New York actor's dream. Greaves saved a photograph of himself

FIGURE 5.4 Greaves and Leslie Nielson on the CBS series *Lamp Unto My Feet* (c. 1949). Photographer unknown. Courtesy Louise Greaves.

standing before the poster for *Lost in the Stars* in front of the Music Box Theater along with another photograph, apparently taken at the same time, of the poster announcing the prestige run of *Lost Boundaries*. The shared optimism of the young actors was also grounded in signs of a new "more democratic" moment in the United States, which was "moving out of its apartheid state," and the larger world. "We were focusing on the positives that were in place in America at that time, but at the same time we were being frustrated by this negative, oppressive, morbid absorption by white America with the need to retain us in second class citizenship status. That was the America that Julian, myself, and Sidney were facing and we were dialoguing with each other on all these paradoxes. I think that we all benefitted from each other."[22]

Those paradoxes came to a head for Greaves in 1950 when he walked away from a supporting role as a porter in José Ferrer's Broadway revival of the romantic comedy *Twentieth Century* when it became clear he was expected to do a "Stepin Fetchit"–style performance.[23] "They wanted me to do 'Yassa massa' and all that foolishness.... I quit the production after the second day of rehearsal and decided, once and for all, that I needed to get behind the camera and start *making* movies, documentaries that spoke to the needs and interests of the black community and to the dignity of our history." What Greaves describes as the decisive moment of dedicating himself to filmmaking on behalf of black people was not a turn away from acting per se. As he explains, "The kind of work I was doing with Strasberg and Danny Mann and the others at the Actors Studio didn't call for the kind of racially embarrassing characterization Ferrer wanted me to do in *Twentieth Century*, because Strasberg and Mann and Martin Ritt—who was another of my teachers—were progressive, liberal people. They would have disowned me if they'd seen me on the stage doing that kind of thing. But I wouldn't have done it anyway."[24] Greaves's comment about being "disowned" by liberal progressive white teachers seems, to say the least, out of character. Most discussions of the Actors Studio tend to be star-struck. In interviews, Greaves is almost always asked about who he knew at the studio, never about the work he did there. Viewed within the longer perspective of Greaves's active engagement with the Actors Studio as an institution and Stanislavskian actor training as theory and practice, I would argue that "the work I was doing" is the essential part of that statement. "Doing the work" was the creed of the Actors Studio, and Greaves would continue that work as he began taking classes on filmmaking at City College and the Institute for New Film. He attended classes at the studio whenever possible after moving to Canada to pursue work with the National Film Board (NFB).[25]

The Actors Studio was more precarious in the early years than its outsized later reputation suggests. Founded in 1948, for its first eight years "the Studio lived a gypsy existence, moving from location to location," until securing a permanent home on West 44th Street.[26] There were internal disagreements and Richard Lewis, one of the original teachers along with Elia Kazan, left the studio abruptly in August 1948. Kazan was increasingly drawn away by directing work on Broadway and in Hollywood. A series of interim teachers, including Joshua Logan, David Pressman, Daniel Mann, Lee Strasberg, and Martin Ritt, carried the studio until Strasberg was appointed artistic director in the fall of 1951. David Garfield's account of these years, while largely anecdotal, suggests how rich the work was during this period of flux, offering actors a heady immersion in improvisational study and the opportunity to try out roles that seemed outside their previous or likely casting; comedians, for example, reveled in working on Chekhov.[27] Garfield is silent on the possibilities this approach offered in relation to race, casting and opportunity. He mentions Greaves only as a member of the first class entering through audition. Given Greaves's decades-long work with the Actors Studio, this is a shocking and yet also typical elision that reflects the persistent erasure of African-American actors from histories of New York theater as well as the star focus of most accounts of the institution.

The Actors Studio was not immune to the pressure of racism and the deep segregation of American society, media, theater, and imagination. Greaves kept a typed draft, with revisions in pen, of a letter he wrote to Strasberg not long after his resignation from the National Film Board in 1960.[28] Greaves warns Strasberg at the outset that it will be a long letter and it is—three single-spaced typed pages. The letter offers a remarkable account of the reality he faced as an African American and the conflict it posed for the work the studio required. Greaves begins with two things he knew with certainty: "When I left for Canada, I was an extremely tense actor. I found it extremely difficult to do scenes in class because they were accompanied by profuse perspiration and general constriction of my muscles and emotional faculties." Second, at that time he was "preoccupied" with the "problem of discrimination." "Outraged by the second-class status of the Negro" and the ignorance of "the colored man's contributions to civilization," he determined to fight both "through the agency of the motion picture."

Over his time in Canada, however, he began to understand a more complex relationship between his work in the studio and the antiracist struggle.

> As a Negro I, like 20 million others in 1949, had the feeling of being in an essentially hostile white community.... I had this difficulty, I must confess, even within the Studio, which I consider decidedly progressive and humanistic. Only with a few did I genuinely feel emotionally secure. So there I was being asked by you, Gadge [Elia Kazan] and Stanislavsky to reveal and share my most personal feelings with what I felt to be a largely hostile and negatively critical white community. I was being asked to allow members of this community to enter the secret recesses of my heart, risking rejection at every turn. I think you can see, as perhaps you did, the kind of conflict this produced.

The gap between Greaves's deepening consciousness of racism and the self-revelation required by his studio classes made him withdraw from the work required: "I did fewer scenes. When I did act, I felt my work was very bad because of the increasing tension."

An ironic realization motivates the letter. By 1960 Greaves has come to understand that "the sense and emotional memory work" he learned at the studio, but practiced more freely at home, "was making me more and more aware of my psychic reality." He was more distrustful and withdrawn in 1951 than when he began in 1948 because he had become a more sensitive person. His apparent failure to master techniques of the Method (e.g., relaxation) was in fact a sign of success.

> Even though on the surface it seemed to me that I was becoming a worse and worse actor, in point of fact I was becoming a more sensitive person capable of responding to stimuli and capable of revealing the feelings they generated. Because my inner feelings were often hostile, they came out as tension and perspiration. Actually, I was responding quite well to what I was feeling, and this was considerable fear and consequence [*sic*] hostility to my audience. I was making progress and I thought I was regressing.

The letter to Strasberg belies any notion of acting as transcending race or racism and simultaneously offers one of the fullest expressions of Greaves's belief in the efficacy of acting. The use of sense and emotional memory work to realize a psychic reality defines Method acting for Greaves. He came to believe these practices were capable of revealing the structure of individual social experience. That he continued to attend Actors Studio classes whenever he could after leaving New York testifies to his ongoing faith in the process.

In a note from his files on the Canadian Acting Studio, Greaves writes, "Acting is really so simple that most of us cannot see the forest for the trees." On another small, blank piece of paper, he typed (ellipses in original):

> on acting. . . .
> subjective belief in the sensory reality of past and present given circumstance and sharing this belief with others. . . . . . .
> responding to selected stimuli, real or imagined, within the disciplines of a dramatic form. . . . . .

This succinct definition distills the American approach to Stanislavsky's methods of training and preparation, balancing "subjective belief" and "given circumstances." In this context, acting is not defined by playing a role; the role is a set of given circumstances, as is the nature of the audience, as are social structures shaping character and performance.[29] The techniques of actor training cultivate a recognition of human behavior and its unconscious as well as conscious intentions and the manifestation of those intentions in body and voice. Sensory exploration opens the imagination to yet unrecognized possibilities for response and action. On the back of a blank check, turned lengthwise, Greaves wrote: "Human experience is the vehicle of theater. Thru the agency of human experience messages of the author are conveyed. If no human experience then no

FIGURE 5.5 Greaves directing an acting workshop in Canada. Photographer unknown. Courtesy Louise Greaves.

need for theater. Why not issue a pamphlet with the message on it." The check has also been reversed, with practical realities addressed on the other end in green ink: "Deposited 100 from Chase/ Phone 25.00/ Marian 40.00."

Greaves's work with his own studio in Canada was no doubt key to the realizations he shared with Strasberg. His hasty notes on the back of the check capture both his deep intellectual engagement with acting and more pragmatic motivations for teaching. This work began with informal sessions on Method acting for interested colleagues at the NFB. Greaves describes first offering acting workshops as a "hobby" without student fees. More formal instruction likely began in April 1954, when the monthly newspaper of the Ottawa Civil Service Recreational Association (RA) featured a banner headline announcing, "NEW RA DRAMA GROUP: Ex-Broadway Actor to Conduct Course in Acting Technique." A production still from *Lost Boundaries* accompanied the news that the RA had "acquired the services" of New York actor William Greaves to conduct the new "Experimental Drama Group" with approximately twenty members and following a "method of work" similar to the Actors Studio. The goal was to cultivate actors for various theatrical groups across Ottawa. It is not clear how long Greaves led the workshop under the auspices of the RA.

By 1956, when the NFB headquarters relocated from Ottawa to Montreal, Greaves was directing the Experimental Studio Group, an independent organization supported by student fees. Home was now the Monument Nationale on St. Lawrence Boulevard, Montreal's oldest theater, long unused and located in a working-class, largely immigrant neighborhood of small businesses. Louise Archambault Greaves recalls students being led by Greaves up the stately marble staircases, passing by the balconies, and then climbing narrow, painted wood stairs to the attic. Huge skylights wrapped one side of the dusty room in which large plaster casts of classical French sculptures were stored. St. Lawrence Boulevard ran east/west, dividing working-class French and middle-class English parts of the city. The workshop enrolled a number of professional Québécois actors and mostly amateur English ones, a cross-cultural collaboration and dialogue rare in that period. In a note, Greaves comments on the difficulty of cultivating Canadian actors since their starting point is either English or French. A magazine story from 1961 describes the members of one class as including a boy from Greece, a middle-aged man, an English girl, a boy with a Czech accent, and two others, reflecting the larger diversity of the city and neighborhood.[30] A surviving dues record for February–March 1959 lists forty-one current members, including Michael Sarrazin (*They Shoot Horses Don't They*, 1969) and Louise Archambault, with four others "absent for period due to rehearsals." Fee income for the month amounted to $564.50, with $284 outstanding.

By 1960 the name had been changed to "The Canadian Acting Studio," and Greaves reported forty-five students in three cities: Montreal, Ottawa, and Toronto, with an enrollment goal of seventy-five. Greaves brought in members of the Actors Studio, including Kevin McCarthy and Margaret Feury, to offer summer evening sessions. In 1961 an advertisement in Harlem's *Amsterdam News* announced: "Special Weekend sessions in Acting with William Garfield Greaves, James Weldon Johnson Community Center, Lexington near 112th." This expansion coincided with Greaves's decision to leave the NFB.

Greaves's ambitious plans for the studio were of a piece with his desire for creative and financial independence. Press coverage in Canada was both interested and admiring. The *Toronto Star Weekly*, for example, carried a three-page story on September 9, 1961; "One Man's Three-City Drama Circuit" includes pictures of Greaves leading a class in Montreal, his "Mad Dash" to catch a plane from Montreal to Toronto, and "Same Rush" at the Ottawa train station.[31] Another paper featured the headline, "Method Actor on the Move."[32] The press applauded Greaves for offering Method-based workshops, although some of the more common stereotypes come into play as well. "No Slob, He," reads a subheading in a 1961 article, describing Greaves as "the living denial that a method actor must be a mumbling, snuffling youth in torn T-shirt and blue jeans. Nattily attired in gray business suit with black tie and carrying a big, somber briefcase (his only concession to 'art' may be his neat, black beret), he speaks eloquently and with excellent diction."[33]

When Greaves moved back to New York in 1962, he turned the Canadian Acting Studio over to one of his students. He continued giving occasional acting workshops and attending classes at the Actors Studio.[34] He became one of a handful of studio members trusted to sit in for Strasberg when he was away and later taught film acting at the Lee Strasberg Institute. His engagement with the Actors Studio was long and varied, serving on the members board and judging auditions among other service roles.

In film studies scholarship, the Actors Studio has long been viewed with suspicion. In his still influential 1988 account of film acting, James Naremore offers a representative if harsh critique of Lee Strasberg's influence as "feeding the star system, promoting conventional realism at the expense of the avant-garde, and giving American drama a less forceful social purpose."[35] Greaves's career so obviously repudiates this agenda that it seems impossible to understand why he would work so long and so closely with both Strasberg and the studio. The capaciousness of Greaves's intellectual interests offers perhaps the best answer to this question. Stanislavsky and Strasberg defined one rich vein, but not the only or dominant one. For example, Greaves lists "*Influences*, concepts and aesthetics" in his production notes for *Symbiopsychotaxiplasm: Take Two* as "Jazz, J. L. Moreno's psychodrama theory, Eisenstein film theory, 2nd Law of Thermodynamics, Arthur Bentley's 'An Inquiry into Inquiries,' Heisenberg theory of Uncertainty, Aurobindo on mysticism, Strasberg on acting, Stanislavsky on theater and acting."[36] Greaves studied Stanislavsky and Strasberg's methods closely and fitted their ideas and practices to his own ends.

An enduring "cardinal principle" defined in the early years of the Actors Studio captures, I believe, its deep attraction for Greaves: "The work at the Studio was exploratory, experimental, process work and not preconceived, audition like 'performing.'"[37] Greaves's notes detailing studio sessions offer insight into the nature of improvisation and the interconnected values of spontaneity and truth in acting. The notes primarily cover sessions held at both Greaves's studio and the Actors Studio in 1957–1958 and feature analyses of actors performing in short scenes and the direction given by himself or Strasberg. In his sessions, Greaves describes specific instructions he gives the actors, which he is careful to define as suggestions. At one point he crosses out "made" and writes "encouraged." In the bar scene from *Death of Salesman*, for example, the actors "were very emotional and persuasive," so he asks them to do it again but "to suppress their emotions. They were told not to raise their voices and not to let their emotions be revealed." As a result, "the scene had an added interesting dynamic." In a third try, he had them use "relax, suppression and release," a technique focused on releasing muscle tension. This time the scene "lacked spontaneity because they were not feeding their minds with changing basis for their emotion and impulses."

Greaves's analyses are largely objective. He will comment on an actor with obvious talent or the brief achievement of a "piece of charming theater," but his focus rests primarily on experimentation in which failure is as interesting as success. I want to look in detail at a set of notes on the "bandage scene" from Anton Chekhov's *The Seagull* because it most fully expresses the "science" of this experimentation and Greaves's ongoing personal investment in studio work.[38]

> I suggested an interesting problem to Rene who played Arcadina. [The character is an actress.] That she is to be in the middle of rehearsing a scene from Trigorin's newest and most promising work which is to be put on in Moscow in the fall. Her anticipation of the applause on key moments is a *solid incentive* to keep her engrossed and preoccupied with *her private rehearsal*
> (THIS WAS THE SECRET OF STANISLAVSKI)
> It is at this time that Treplyov, her son, interrupts and asks her to bandage his wound.

The actor playing Treplyov is asked to "activate" all his experiences: his need for his mother's love and his resentment of her "private world," as well as the actual circumstances of the scene. Rather than evaluate the quality of the resulting performances, however, Greaves makes broader comments beginning with dramatic form: "*It is now clear*, there is an inverse relationship between the development of character and the development of plot in the writing of the script," a thesis which he then revises as "superficial" because "good and clear character development can be best viewed through the agency of a changing dynamic environment within and outside the play which would cause [in Treplyov] a feeling of deep all-pervading hunger for love." The "secret of Stanislavsky" lies in the recognition of the dynamic relationship between inner ("her private rehearsal") and outer realities (her son's request), which can be accessed through techniques of actor preparation. The experimentation required to achieve this level performance generates a deeper understanding of scene, character, play, and the nature of drama.

Greaves's notes on this session end with an excited insight into the nature of directing:

> The thing which I found curious and which fascinated me was the richness of my suggestions which came spontaneously as the scene unfolded and when it was over it made clear to me that all people are brilliant containing information within them, it only needs to be STIMULATED GO TO THE STIMULUS for creative thought. Finally, like the performing artists the director's best work is when he is spontaneous.

As I quoted earlier, Greaves defines acting as "responding to selected stimuli, real or imaginary, within the disciplines of a dramatic form." The director is most deeply invested in creating the stimulus; the actor, in creating the response. Each focus seeks spontaneity. The endless fascination of the workshop lies in cultivating techniques that open the imagination to the immediate moment of creativity.[39] Improvisation was central to this cultivation, and it defined the "the work" to be done.[40] If "all people are brilliant" and acting is more than realizing a role determined by author and script, the scope of dramatic form expands. Greaves was not "antitext"; he wrote a long cogent set of notes on the comic genius of Chekhov, which he believed Stanislavsky, in his class-bound empathy for the characters, had failed to understand. In the acting workshop, the script could be studied but also set aside; paraphrasing the text, for example, is a Method technique. The search for spontaneous revelation in which a scene comes to life is collective and expansive.

This dynamic creative practice served Greaves well as a filmmaker. The notes on *The Seagull* scene date from May 1957, the period when he began directing documentaries at the National Film Board. When asked about *Emergency Ward* (1958), Greaves begins with his work on acting:

> I was very involved with the Method, the Stanislavsky system, Strasberg and Kazan—so the improvisational dynamic of the Method and the cinéma-vérité dynamic coalesced in my mind. For *Emergency Ward* I was working with a life-and-death situation in which people would be so absorbed in what they were confronted with that they would have no time to think about the intrusive nature of a camera. We lit up the emergency ward of a hospital and positioned three cameras—cameras were very heavy at the time, nothing like the handheld cameras of today—and we spent a month in the emergency ward.[41]

The Method and cinéma vérité share a vocabulary in which "improvisation" and "truth" loom large. In his comments to the Ottawa Film Society, which I invoked at the beginning of this essay, Greaves outlines four technical reasons for the "rise and preeminence of naturalistic realism in acting" (e.g., "physical conditions and limitations of the medium in which the acting performance occurs"). He added a fifth reason in ink to the typescript: "the search for truth." The Method provides actors and directors with a common language for that search and a collective space in which to experiment and innovate. Greaves's interest in a life-and-death situation offers a heightened structure for the stimulus and response essential to acting. Camera placements define the "dramatic form," but a form that more closely resembles the workshop than the staged performance of a play. In workshop, the director's best work, like that of the actors, occurs when he or she is spontaneous. The value of such spontaneity is especially acute in live documentary filmmaking, in which the director must immediately engage with the evolving scene of performance.

One scene in *Symbiopsychotaxiplasm: Take One* exemplifies Greaves's expansive engagement with the experimental possibilities of the acting workshop. A new Alice and Freddy, played by Susan Anspach and Johnny Diamond, sit on a bench next to the lake in Central Park and sing lines of dialogue that the audience has heard over and over by this point in the film. After a few lines the actors pause and laugh awkwardly. Greaves reassures them and encourages them to go on: "Try to go into the situation as you sing." "Yes," Diamond responds earnestly. Two lines later, Greaves interrupts, "Oh I can't take that," and steps in front of the camera. He begins to talk to the actors, and Bob Rosen interrupts, laughing: "Is that really what they do at the Actors Studio all the time?" "Silence, boy," Greaves comically intones and then more softly demurs, "No, that's not what they do." As Greaves quietly encourages the actors once again to enter the situation, Jonathan Gordon interrupts, sounding impatient: "Why do you want them to sing?" Greaves shrugs the question off. "I don't know, just an idea." When pressed, Greaves says he wants "to know if the scene can play in song," an experiment that elicits critique, interruption, and commentary, but also a touching seriousness from the actors following his direction. For the restive crew, having the actors sing is an eccentric whim, associated with perceived excesses of the Actors Studio. Actress Susan Anspach (a studio member) defends the acting exercise in which you "sing and therefore bring other elements that your imagination wouldn't have normally have gone to, that's the value." But she also sees a line being crossed from exercise to performance: "But to sing a duet, you know, it's like we should have an orchestra." Greaves signals the end of the experiment by saying, "I think we can use this. I think it will add an interesting texture." When no one responds, he encourages them. "Doesn't anyone think so?" The camera pans over the embarrassed-looking crew. The singing experiment is an obvious failure; the scene does not "play in song." The crew's questions and emotional responses register the value of that failure, which they are unable to recognize. In the earlier "palace revolt" scenes, the crew eloquently debates the meaning, or the lack thereof, of what they are doing. In response, Greaves invites them to accept the challenge they have identified: "Now your problem is to come up with creative solutions that make this a better production than we now have." They remain constrained in many ways by their own professionalism.

"There's no sense of reality in it. Who goes around singing to each other?," one crew member says at the close of the scene. The apprehension of reality remains an open question in the film. The actors understand the nonrepresentational process that leads to such apprehension. They share with Greaves an understanding of improvisation and truth, although they stay perhaps too faithful to the given circumstances of the script. Greaves makes room for both actors and their fictive roles at the center of the film, foregrounding elements often viewed as antithetical to reality when judged against the nature of documentary filmmaking or the inherited terms of an older antitheatrical bias. This highly experimental moment offers one the most vivid insights into Greaves's conception of a good director as "a person who gets his ego *out of* his own way, he is at best a collaborator and servant of nature ... but who, paradoxically, *firmly* controls the conditions of spontaneity, theatricality, and drama."[42] By acting the role of a less-than-authoritarian director, Greaves achieves precisely that, suppressing his ego and stimulating embodied response and creative thought throughout the cast and crew.

For William Greaves, acting became a lifelong frame for study and experimentation that extended far beyond the Stanislavskian ideal of "living the part." The efficacy of acting lay in its skilled development of sensory response, imaginative engagement, and access to psychic reality. It offered a path to personal development grounded in a profoundly communal practice, evident in the twenty-two-year-old Greaves's idealistic response to observing the "titans of the theater" in rehearsal: "There was a communality in the effort, a shared interest; you felt it was born out of the love and tremendous élan of the performers in their art."[43] In the late 1940s Greaves was part of another, equally important communality as one of a generation of actors from Harlem staking ambitious careers on stage, in film, and in television. His career as an actor in New York was short, rich, and stymied by an intractable racism. His continued dedication to acting as student and teacher became a repudiation of racism, feeding in various and unexpected ways his determination to "get behind the camera and start *making* movies, documentaries that spoke to the needs and interests of the black community and to the dignity of our history."

NOTES

1. Scott MacDonald, "Meta-interview with William Greaves: An Audiobiography," chapter 2 of this volume.
2. Unless otherwise noted, information about Greaves's career is drawn from these files and my conversations with Louise Archambault Greaves, without whom this essay could never have been written.
3. MacDonald, "Meta-interview."
4. Gordon Heath, *Deep Are the Roots: Memoirs of a Black Expatriate* (Boston: University of Massachusetts Press, 1992), 60–61.
5. As Kevin Wetmore has demonstrated, Medea has proven a compelling dramatic figure for black playwrights. Wetmore's collection focuses on six versions of the play in African and diasporic contexts written between 1968 and 2003. See Wetmore, *Black Medea: Adaptations for Modern Plays* (Amherst, N.Y.: Cambria, 2013).
6. Heath, *Deep Are the Roots*, 76–77. Heath offers a rich account of the postwar theater world from the perspective of a black actor. See also Lewis Nichols's review: "William Greaves, as a wandering singer, is excellent in both parts of his ancient and modern role." Nichols, "Uptown Jason," *New York Times*, March 10, 1945.
7. Jonathan Shandell, *The American Negro Theatre and the Long Civil Rights Era* (Iowa City: University of Iowa Press, 2018), 35.
8. James Hatch, "William Greaves: Filmmaker," *Artist and Influence* 9 (1989): 58.
9. Sidney Poitier, *This Life* (New York: Knopf, 1980), 90–91.

10. Heath, *Deep Are the Roots*, 74.
11. Play credits are drawn from the Broadway (IBDB.com) and Off-Broadway (lortel.org) internet databases.
12. Poitier, *This Life*, 84; Harry Belafonte, *My Song*, with Michael Shnayerson (New York: Knopf, 2011), 57–60.
13. On debates regarding the American Negro Theatre in light of DuBois's blueprint, see Shandell, *The American Negro Theatre*, 4–12.
14. Hatch, "William Greaves: Filmmaker," 71. In the interview, Hatch asks Greaves directly about his relationship to Mayfield and Poitier. The circle of black actors from Harlem coming up together and finding success in theater, television, and film was certainly broader than this. In another context, Greaves mentions Brock Peters as a lifelong friend. They were the same age and sang in the glee club together at Harlem's Frederick Douglass Junior High School (Hatch, 55). Peters made his stage debut in the Broadway production of *Porgy and Bess* in 1943 at the age of fifteen. On Peters's career, see Mel Watkins, "Brock Peters of 'To Kill a Mockingbird' Is Dead at 78," *New York Times*, August 24, 2005.
15. Matthew Powell, *God Off-Broadway: The Blackfriars Theater of New York* (Lanham, Md.: Scarecrow Press, 1998), 55.
16. Fred Fehl and William Stott with Jane Stott, *On Broadway* (Austin: University of Texas Press, 1978), 100.
17. Fehl and Stott, 100.
18. Fehl and Stott, 139.
19. Fehl and Stott, 100.
20. David Garfield, *A Player's Place: The Story of the Actor's Studio* (New York: Macmillan, 1980), 90, 93.
21. Brock Peters starred in the 1972 Broadway production of *Lost in the Stars* and received an Emmy nomination for Best Actor in a Musical. He reprised the role in the 1974 film version, directed by Daniel Mann, one of Greaves's early teachers at the Actors Studio.
22. Hatch, "William Greaves: Filmmaker," 71–72.
23. Greaves worked with Lincoln "Stepin Fetchit" Perry in *Miracle in Harlem* (1948). As he told James Hatch, "He was a nice guy, very simple, dignified, and clearly a wonderful actor who had been exploited and misused by those fascists in Hollywood" (61).
24. MacDonald, "Meta-interview."
25. Hatch, "William Greaves: Filmmaker," 63.
26. Garfield, *A Player's Place*, 5.
27. Garfield, 57–63.
28. The copy of the letter I saw is clearly a draft, with edits and a paragraph crossed out. I have not found direct evidence that the letter was sent. That draft was kept along with two other letters to Strasberg from the same period, one a query about the directing class that had begun and the Actors Studio, and the other asking for recommendations of other members who could lead some of Greaves's workshops as he expanded the studio. There is a file of correspondence from Greaves in the Strasberg papers at the National Archives, but that material concerns plans

for a multipart television series Greaves wanted to make about Strasberg in the 1970s.
29. On given circumstances, see Sharon Marie Carnicke, *Stanislavsky in Focus: An Acting Master for the Twenty-First Century*, 2nd ed. (New York: Routledge, 2009), 218.
30. Anne MacDermott, "One Man's Three-City Drama Circuit," *Star Weekly*, Toronto, September 9, 1961.
31. MacDermott, 28–31.
32. A clipping of this article was in Greaves's files but did not include the date or the newspaper's name. Film advertisements on the same page suggest it was Toronto 1961.
33. See note 32.
34. Greaves may have been attending directing as well as acting sessions at the Actors Studio.
35. James Naremore, *Acting in the Cinema* (Berkeley: University of California Press, 1988), 199. In "I Hate Strasberg: Method Bashing in the Academy," David Krasner rebuts the denigration of American Method acting, and Strasberg as its major proponent, common in scholarship. See David Krasner, ed., *Method Acting Reconsidered: Theory, Practice and Future* (New York: Palgrave, 2000), 3–41. Recent work in film studies has moved away from ideological readings of the Method to more practice-based considerations. See Cynthia Baron and Sharon Marie Carnicke, *Reframing Screen Performance* (Ann Arbor: University of Michigan Press, 2008), 24–32.
36. William Greaves, "Production Notes," ed. Scott MacDonald, booklet, *Symbiopsychotaxiplasm: Two Takes* (Criterion Collection, 2006), DVD.
37. Garfield, *A Players Place*, 99.
38. In the talk for the Ottawa Film Society, Greaves cites "available scientific information on the reasons for and the characteristics of the phenomena of human behavior" and "a method of acting that integrates this scientific knowledge into the actor's instrument" as conditions for the emergence of realistic naturalism in acting. In *The Player's Passion: Studies in the Science of Acting*, Joseph R. Roach traces the long history of this scientific approach. See especially his last chapter on Stanislavsky, "The *Paradoxe* as Paradigm: The Structure of a Russian Revolution" (Ann Arbor: University of Michigan Press, 1993), 195–217.
39. Daniel Belgrad has argued that "a will to explore and record the spontaneous creative act characterized the most significant developments in American art and literature after World War II." Belgrad does not discuss Method acting or cinéma vérité, but both belong to this intellectual and artistic gestalt. Belgrad, *The Culture of Spontaneity: Improvisation and the Arts in Postwar America* (Chicago: University of Chicago Press, 1998), 1.
40. Greaves's investment in "doing the work" is evident in his condemnation of established Canadian actors, including Jean Gascon (1921–1988), a founding member of the Montreal theater company Théâtre du Nouveau Monde. In his extended notes on Chekhov, Greaves imagines the actors themselves as Chekhovian characters, who "speak in philosophical jargon and 'serious' ways but are not really conscious of the utter mediocrity of their lives. They are not sure of the fact that they do not

mean what they say." Such characters pose a technical problem for performance. "Certainly, they wear the most ostentatious and misleading mental clothing which hides an inner reality that has nothing in common with the outer-garments. One thing is certain, they refuse to look at their nakedness. The nature of this nakedness is [?], inadequacy, and mediocrity. This [?] and mediocrity is a distinct unwillingness to think because of the energy this requires. *These people are basically anti-work*. And the humour of them is that they want all those things which only work brings. They want something for nothing and *This is a scream, a riot, a farce!!*" [Emphasis added.]

41. MacDonald, "Meta-interview."
42. Greaves, "Production Notes."
43. Fehl and Stott, *On Broadway*, 131.

6
POEM/1965

WILLIAM GREAVES

Editor's Note: This poem was used as the concluding narration of the documentary *Wealth of a Nation* (1964).

POEM/1965

In summertime
in quiet wood
and friendly shade
from secret regions of myself
my soul screams the question
ancient as man
and older than the sound of human song

Must we die so soon?
Must we sicken and suffer
and cry for comfort?
Must great men and infants
be plucked from our midst
well before their time
by the thousand awful plagues
that steal inside us?

If we can build a nation
out of virgin land,

can split the smallest atom
and climb beyond the stars
must we die from trifling plagues?

What madness is here
that we, like bleating sheep,
accept so short a life
on earth?

And yet, should some day we conquer death,
Or win a momentary truce in time,
multiplying our earthly journey
by a thousand fold,

never must we forget
our hard-won victory
over yet another kind of death
that all too quickly claims the human spirit
when it breathes no more the air of freedom

For the treasured prize of our survival
is the joy of self-expression
in all those unique thoughts and actions
that each person has to tell himself
and all the world

"I live."

NOTE

Wealth of a Nation was produced, written, and directed by Greaves for the Motion Picture and Television Service of the United States Information Service in 1964.

7

The First World Festival of Negro Arts

An Afro-American View

WILLIAM GREAVES

I have had the good fortune to attend the First World Festival of Negro Arts, which took place in Dakar, Senegal, from April 4 to April 24, 1966. It was truly an historic occasion. Approximately 2,000 black artists from all over the world met in that West African city. They came to get acquainted, to be inspired, to return to their origins, but mainly to help reveal the important contributions the black man has made, and is making, to world civilization. The event, which was covered by the mass media of a number of countries, received worldwide recognition.

From the outset, the idea of such a festival raised some searching questions. Why a Negro Arts Festival? What is "Negritude"? Is there such a thing as a black man's art? How will the festival be received by the Western World? Will it be tinged with racism? And so on. In order to see a World Negro Arts Festival in its proper perspective, one must first consider the historical background against which it appears,

For the past several hundred years the white people of Europe and America, in quest of a better life for themselves, engaged in the business of nation and empire building. This required large reservoirs of manual labor. In that pre-industrial period, the type of man best suited for working impossibly long hours performing backbreaking chores was the slave—black or white. The black slave eventually won out as the "Joe boy" of the Western World. After all he was a "foreigner," different in color, and worshipped divine power in strange ways. Tired, in the twilight of their decaying cultures, the Africans were easy victims for the younger, more industrialized, more aggressive Europeans who used them to hew wood and draw water.

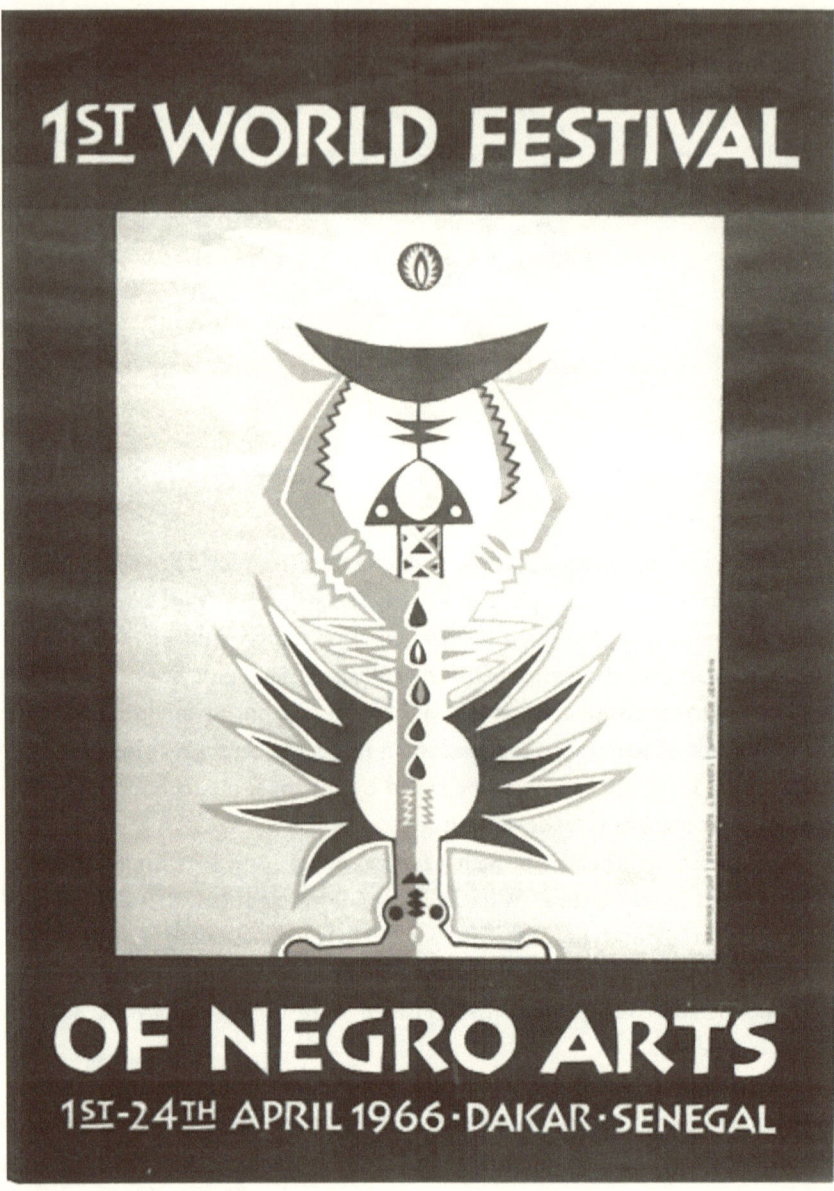

FIGURE 7.1 Poster for First World Festival of Negro Arts, held in Dakar, Senegal, in 1966.

There were, however, complications. The movement towards humanitarianism and liberty which was sweeping Europe and America made the problem of securing and maintaining slave labor very difficult, particularly from the standpoint of conscience. This "problem" was overcome largely through special efforts of the press. A campaign of vilification was unleashed to so downgrade the intelligence, humanity, and spiritual qualifications of the black man that he would in the eyes of white society be rendered a savage, a near-animal whose heathen ways completely disqualified him from sharing in the liberty and justice of the newly emerging modern world. It followed that, if he were a near-animal, it was quite all right to exploit his labor and take away his land. The legacy of these distortions is still with us.

Under the influence of international realities and domestic pressures, a new attitude toward black people is developing in this country. Attempts are being made to correct the false notions about the Negro. And one of the most important challenges facing our country as well as the rest of the Western World will be that of setting the record straight. An indication of just how distorted the picture is can be seen from the following statement by the late William Leo Hansberry, widely recognized authority on African history: "Most people are unaware that more stone age cultural artifacts have been found in Africa in the past 50 years than have been found in all of Europe during the past 2,000 years."

Seen in this light, the emergence of a Negro Arts Festival becomes a rational and necessary development. It seeks to close the enormous information gap regarding the cultural achievements of the black peoples—a gap which has caused much suffering and tragedy, for men both black and white.

Can this gap be closed? And will it affect the status of the black man? One might argue that the Jewish people, particularly since World War II, have been most adept at publicizing their cultural prowess, and still they suffer. Why bother where the Jews have failed? But have they failed? I think not. I think there is less anti-Semitism in the Western World today largely because the West is now more aware of the Jewish contribution to the arts of peace. I don't think there is any need for anxiety or guilt concerning the production of a Negro Arts Festival for it simply serves the highest purpose of education—to enlighten and enliven the human spirit. The First Festival of the Negro Arts was a big step in the attainment of that objective.

The subject of Negritude dominated the discussions and debates which took place at the Colloquium, a two-week-long conference of intellectuals. As I understand it, however, this controversial concept, as propounded by President Leopold Senghor of Senegal, asserts that the black artist has a special and important contribution to make to world culture, that he should be proud of that contribution, and that the non-black world has much to gain from a fuller recognition of it.

Negritude had given rise to anxiety among some white people who feared that it represented a return to the racism which they themselves are trying to eliminate from Western civilization. Some American Negroes fear it because they feel that, at a time when the American Negro is striving for full equality, Negritude might antagonize whites and delay the full integration they seek in American society. If Negritude is a negative concept with negative purposes, if it is a return to the racism of the past, then it is a concept both useless and dangerous to the modern world. Yet, viewed through the lens of history, it is an inevitable development. And when defined in President Senghor's terms, it is obvious that Negritude is a positive response to negative historical events. It is an attempt at cultural survival in what has been, until recent times, a predominately hostile world.

Always, there will be those, black and white, who seek to exploit any negative racial aspect of the situation. These people are the agents of death; there were very few at the festival. Its overriding mood was that of interracial harmony. It was a pleasure to see audiences, which were sometimes two-thirds white, enthusiastically enjoying the fruits of "Negritude." This is as it should be; the white world has long thrilled to such meagre fruits of Negritude as were available. Indeed, one can now visualize a day when there will no longer be a dearth of information on the contribution of the Negro to world culture. Once this gap is closed, the feelings of racial superiority and inferiority which afflict both black and white communities will die more easily. For if Negritude can serve the purpose of correcting the widespread notion that the black man is a cultural Johnny-come-lately, it will provide a firm basis for racial respect, an important prerequisite for the equality the black man is seeking.

Thus, the festival took on a special significance, a significance which to the African mind transcended all other arguments which some American Negroes gave for not attending the festival. Why did not more show up in Dakar? Some probably didn't know the festival was taking place; some simply didn't have the money. Some may not have wanted to antagonize those members of the white community who feared or disliked the idea of such a festival. Some didn't go because the United States State Department had a hand in the American participation at the festival; some didn't go because a white woman was put in charge of the U.S. Committee for the festival. Some did not approve of some of the international policies of President Senghor's government; and some didn't go because of their disapproval of the war in Vietnam. Some artists didn't go or enter their work because they felt they should be paid to participate in the festival. Some didn't go because they don't believe there is any such thing as a "Negro artist."

And finally, some Negroes didn't go because they dislike Negroes and Africans. The Africans with whom I spoke felt that these arguments were irrelevant, that except in cases of financial difficulty, at this turning point in history American Negroes should have come—were a "green" woman in charge of the U.S Committee. It is the hope of many Africans that, at the next festival, more of the "big guns" in Afro-American arts and letters will, despite their grievances, be on hand to celebrate the black man's contribution to world culture.

As for the festival itself, much has been written elsewhere extolling the sheer theatricality and brilliance of the Sierra Leone, Mali, Ivory Coast companies. Full tribute has been paid to the vastly impressive exhibit of ancient African art. The contemporary art exhibit would have watered the mouths of most American art gallery owners had they had the foresight to attend. The Ethiopian participation was majestic. And the Republic of Chad's performance was a cosmic experience of the first order. Most of the performances were essentially symbolic in character. They illustrated the African view of art, which is utilitarian. To the African, art is a bridge linking the soul of man with cosmic experience, an instrument enabling man to vibrate with existence itself. It is not an end in itself, but a means to a greater end.

Despite the absence of many big names, the American participation was one of the highlights of the festival. Langston Hughes, the De Paur Chorus, and Duke Ellington were outstanding; Marion Williams and her gospel singers were absolutely electrifying. The Alvin Ailey Company was a roaring smash hit, and this is particularly interesting because in outer form there was little in their performance reminiscent of the dance of Africa or even American Jazz. They relied on modern dance forms, on excellent, but Westernized, choreography to convey their "Negritude." In terms of style, at least they proved that the concept of

Negritude is valid only when one considers it in an historical, anthropological, and geographical context, and that its classic example is African art. In other words, Negritude has neither more nor less validity than European or Chinese influence in art. In form it is most evident in African art. It is least obvious in some of the art of the American and French Negro, which often relies on European models of expression.

The Ailey Company, working with non-African styles, demonstrated that Negritude does not necessarily rely on external form to reveal itself, that it can be a state of consciousness which reflects itself in many ways. Some Afro-Americans call that state "soul." While there was often variety of style, that which was common to most contributions to the festival was "soul"—in delightful, unusually great quantities. The Ailey Company was successful partly because of their skill, but also because "soul" veritably cascaded from them out over the footlights.

There is a tendency among some Negro intellectuals to view soul as the private property of the black man—a ludicrous notion. Soul is the necessary ingredient of all great art—white, yellow, brown, or black. Without it, great art does not exist. It is interesting, however, to view this phenomenon in a "Negro" context in that it occurred with such profusion at the festival. It is often said that an artist, to be great, must have suffered, must have struggled for survival, physical or psychic. The Negro eminently qualifies by these criteria. I would guess that the Negro, suffering through the centuries, has become very aware of human emotions, of sadness, of joy, of pain, of pleasure, and he has, through his art, expressed this awareness.

It is a fact that most works exhibited at the festival contained tremendous emotional vitality. Perhaps this vitality is one of the major contributions of African creativity to the world of the arts. It certainly was one of the primary reasons for the festival's great success.

Dakar is a beautiful city; the Senegalese are a beautiful people. It is delightful to see a Senegalese woman walking, tall and elegant, with her long dress, or "gran bou-bou," billowing after her in a dance of color. The food is fine, the beaches are magnificent. And yet one soon becomes aware of an undercurrent, an undercurrent of tension between the French and Senegalese.

The French are in full economic control of this African nation; they seem also to exert considerable political influence. And one has only to walk down the streets of Dakar, to look at her restaurants, beaches, and private clubs, to get the message that this is a country whose real independence is yet to come. I was often amused (perhaps this is the wrong word) by some of my French friends' continual rationalizations, continual insistence that the Senegalese are "like children," "stupid," that "they don't think," "they don't want responsibility," etc.

I am fully aware of the racial prejudice and discrimination so evident in America. From my own experience I know that there are many people in America, both black and white, who actually believe that the black man has made no significant contribution to world culture, but I was somewhat unprepared for the variations on the theme I encountered in Senegal.

There seemed to have been considerable ambivalence among some of the French in Dakar in regard to the success of the festival. It was even rumored that one or two members of the French community associated with the management of the festival sought to subvert, subtly to be sure, the efficient functioning of the event in order to demonstrate the Africans' inability to properly manage their own affairs. I was told that France has spent considerable time and money persuading the Senegalese that France was the "mother" country, that culturally they should be Frenchmen. And here was a festival which might culturally alienate the Africans by persuading them that they should be Africans more than Frenchmen, that they should cherish their own cultures as well as those of others.

As I moved around the city listening, talking with, and observing the Senegalese in their neocolonialist relationship with the French, a passage from French literature continually passed through my mind. It was written in the eighteenth century by Count Volney, a French nobleman, who was a brilliant philosopher and political figure. His book, *Ruins of Empires*, contains the following statement: "There, a people, now forgotten, discovered, while others were yet barbarians, the elements of the arts and sciences. A race of men now rejected from society for their sable skin and frizzled hair, founded on the study of the laws of nature, those civil and religious systems which still govern the universe."

This statement coming from a present-day African or Afro-American would immediately be interpreted by some as racist in character. But Count Volney was a respected figure in French political affairs, and his views on the Africans were not uncommon in the Europe of his day. Yes, some Frenchmen now seem to hold the view that the newly independent Senegalese are constitutionally unable to run a modern state by themselves, and they have undertaken to unburden them, indirectly, of the awesome responsibilities of nation building. No doubt the Senegalese have heard these suggestions so often that some may behave in such terms. But I also met many Senegalese who were hell bent on the idea of building a healthy nation for themselves.

To be sure, the sentiments expressed by Volney pertained to ancient Ethiopia (which formerly included the Sudan and much of East Africa), whose history he had studied. In recent years, however, there has been a steady build-up of information on Africa, which now suggests that the arts of peace flourished not only in Ethiopia but in other parts of that vast continent as well. Today there is growing talk of Benin, Ife, Songhay, Mali, Monmatapa, Zinbabwe. All of these are now regarded as outstanding examples of human endeavor in civilization. It is in this context that a World Festival of Negro Arts takes on special significance, for in displaying the cultural artifacts of those civilizations, it provided a proper antidote for French, European, and white American chauvinism toward the black man. It is more than unfortunate that knowledge of early African civilizations, so widespread in the Europe of Volney, does not have wider currency in the modern Western world, for I am certain that if more people knew that the black peoples of the world are the possessors of a rich cultural history, much of the foundation upon which racial discrimination is built would crumble.

Unfortunately, ignorance still prevails in this regard, and we Negroes have been faced with the arduous task of gaining political, economic, and social equality without the special advantages which a wider familiarity of such facts might afford us. The Europeans have been quite skillful at the business of disseminating information about their culture and civilization; so skillful that, during the past 200 years, it was seemingly thought that they were the only custodians of civilization, that the endeavors of other cultures were of trifling value. As I see it, the overall purpose of the festival was to help correct this tragic misconception.

Personally, I look forward to the day when there will be no need for a Negro Arts Festival to counteract ignorance and malicious propaganda, when black and white will be fully apprised and appreciative of the black man's contribution to world culture. I look forward to the day when we, like the Europeans, can sit back and relax—secure in the knowledge that we are studied, respected, and appreciated. Paradoxically, it is largely the white world which will tell the black world when there is no longer a need to stage a festival based on the theme of

Negritude. But let us also hope that when that day arrives there will be festivals not only in Africa, but everywhere, which celebrate the human spirit with all of the fire and soul generated at the First World Festival of Negro Arts.

NOTE

Reprinted from *The Crisis* 73, no. 6 (June–July 1966): 309–14, 332.

8

Views Across the Atlantic

An American Vision of the First World Festival of Negro Arts

JOSEPH L. UNDERWOOD

"Let us meet often.... Remember what has happened here in Dakar." William Greaves's textured voice and even tone conclude *The First World Festival of Negro Arts* (1966) as he narrates these two imperative statements for the viewer. The final visuals that accompany these cautionary words record a cohort of African-American visitors, ranging from Alvin Ailey to Duke Ellington, as they board planes to depart Senegal. As they shuffle from the airport tarmac onto the planes, bespectacled with oversized sunglasses, we observe how their arms are laden with briefcases, carved objects, and newly acquired books. Greaves foregrounds the material accumulation by the festival visitors as an allusion to the weight of the intellectual, spiritual, and emotional souvenirs that would long outlive the three-week celebration of historical and modern Black culture. With the aspiration of meeting often, the voices and visions of Blackness on either side of the Atlantic would resonate and build on one another. Indeed, in situating his film between mounting U.S.–U.S.S.R. Cold War tensions, competing African-American agendas, and opposing African philosophies for the continent's future, Greaves crafted a personal vision that affirmed the significance of this festival as a nexus for exchange. This equilibrium between individual and collective identities played out among those visiting Dakar and those onlooking from afar: "For the artists participating in the festival, as well as those who merely followed the event through news reports, it was an occasion to reassess their own relationships to Africa."[1] As the only film Greaves produced on the African continent, *First World Festival* stands unique in his oeuvre as it champions this landmark 1966 African-sponsored cultural event. For Greaves, the festival's ideological accomplishments should not be forgotten, and its effect would be the inspiration of further reunions.

Formally titled the Festival Mondial des Arts Nègres (FESMAN), the popular English translation would serve as the title of Greaves's forty-minute film. One of the most significant and expensive cultural manifestations to take place in the Global South, FESMAN was a landmark achievement for the newly independent nation of Senegal. By all accounts it was a feat that the young nation managed to mount such an elaborate infrastructure and robust schedule of events. Spanning three weeks in April 1966, approximately two thousand musicians, dancers, artists, singers, poets, playwrights, and intellectuals participated in some aspect of the festival before an international audience that comprised representatives from Africa, the Caribbean, Latin America, North America, Europe, and Asia. Most of the main attractions of the festival receive some screen time in Greaves's film: an exhibition of classical African art (*art nègre*) culled from premier national and royal collections; a second exhibition of modern and contemporary artwork that represented the experimental, genre-bending art being developed throughout Africa and its Diaspora; a dynamic performance schedule that filled several spaces throughout the capital and featured all styles of singing, dance, and theatrical productions; and a rigorous colloquium that gathered premier philosophers, authors, and cultural critics whose writing sought to define Blackness. The festival as a whole, as well as these individual components, has come to be regarded as a major touchstone for fields of inquiry ranging from network building in the Global South, to debates on Pan-African philosophy, to culture as soft power during the Cold War.

As with historical World Fairs or Expositions Universelles, these enormous national exhibitions with international participation are so multifaceted that it is daunting to attempt a succinct summary of the sights, experiences, and statements that shape them. Amid the constellation of news reports, personal accounts, and historic photographs, Greaves's film remains one of very few audiovisual records of this important world event. And while other films were produced by Soviet, Italian, and Romanian crews of various sizes and skills, *The First World Festival of Negro Arts* became the most distributed version because of the reach of its commissioning body (the United States Information Agency, or USIA). Although it has been critiqued as a "somewhat partial vision of the event," this is the nature of any record of an event of this magnitude.[2] To that end, this essay blends an analysis of the film with new interviews from Greaves's family and USIA colleagues to emphasize how this project walks the line between the storytelling of a consummate filmmaker and the nostalgia of an African American visiting the continent for the first time.

FIGURE 8.1 Crowd at First World Festival of Negro Arts event. *Left to right*: George H. H. Lascelles (Earl of Harewood), Colette Senghor, President Leopold Senghor, Vashti Smith (wife of U.S. ambassador to Senegal Mercer Cook), and Léon Boissier-Palun (president of Senegal's Economic and Social Council). They are at one of the festival's opening performances (likely by Duke Ellington) at the new stadium. Possibly photographed by William Greaves. Courtesy Louise Greaves.

FIGURE 8.2 Greaves standing behind Senegal's president Leopold Senghor during the First World Festival of Negro Arts. Photographer unknown. Courtesy Louise Greaves.

DEFINING THE VISION

U.S. participation in the festival was anticipated to be one of the larger showings of Black excellence from the Diaspora. From being allotted twice the exhibition space in the modern art exhibition to American performers being given prime concert venues, a significant investment was made to welcome the U.S. delegation. Greaves even conveyed this aggrandizing nationalist sentiment himself:

"Despite the absence of many big names, the American participation was one of the highlights of the festival."[3] Originally enthusiastic about the project, Romare Bearden, Hale Woodruff, and other artists ultimately withheld their work from traveling to Dakar owing to underfunding for visual artists and organizational contention over the definition of contemporary African-American art. Author and critic Hoyt Fuller, among others, later decried the American contingent at FESMAN as a carefully manicured vision of Blackness, stripped of the politics that animated many African-American writers, artists, and thinkers.[4] Indeed, in the years to come, a complex relationship between the American Society of African Culture (AMSAC, the group who organized American representation at the festival with a budget of $150,000) and the CIA became public—even Greaves was implicated in this as his sponsoring institution, the USIA, was essentially the propaganda arm of the Foreign Service.

Historians like Jody Blake and Anthony Ratcliff have addressed the role that cultural events like FESMAN could play as liminal spaces during the Cold War: semineutral grounds where adverse parties might briefly share the space of a colloquium, musical performance, poetry reading, or art exhibition.[5] It was in the midst of these nuanced politics that William Greaves and a threadbare film crew were tasked with creating a short reportage of this festival for a larger newsreel about U.S. activities abroad. Boarding a plane chartered by AMSAC for the American delegation, Greaves took to the skies toward what would be the first contact with African soil for him and many others on the flight. Harold Weaver later recounted how joyous the flight of two hundred–plus passengers was, and the spirit of celebration that the group carried from the airport to their hotel.[6]

Greaves was welcomed to Dakar by William Stott, a junior officer who had been in training with USIA for a year. It was only a month prior to the beginning of the festival that the USIA had realized the urgency of filming the event. Through Ted Tanen, director of the American Cultural Center in Senegal since 1961, USIA wrote to the festival organizers asking for permission to send news reporters, photographers, and two videographers—the latter they recognized being "the most prickly" request.[7] The letter states that USIA would be employing M. Georges Bracher and a second cameraman to record a thirty- to sixty-minute video of the American artists interacting with their Senegalese counterparts, the events and exhibitions of the festival, and the city at large. Concerned at the lack of response, Tanen wrote to the organizers again only nine days later, simplifying his request for filming permission to the American delegation and their interactions within the city—but no longer at official ceremonies or performances. He listed William Greaves as the second cameraman for the project, having just received the name from Washington.[8]

In fact, Greaves's partnership with USIA had begun a few years earlier when the head of film was looking for a Black director to make a film on dissent in America.⁹ Given the difficulty of obtaining permission, and noting how many requests to film were denied by festival organizers, the limited film records of FES-MAN become all the more important. It seems that Greaves meshed well with Bracher, a French videographer who had moved to Africa with his wife, Maya, in the 1950s. The couple had worked in Senegal for over a decade, collaborating with photographer Eliot Elisofon, naturalist Theodore Monod, and Senegalese filmmakers like Ousmane Sembène, Djibril Diop Mambéty, and Ben Diogaye Bèye.[10] Between the guidance of Stott and the local expertise of Bracher, Greaves was well positioned to create a savvy film, rooted to the space in a way that the other film crews were not, even as he was experiencing the continent for the first time.

Inspired by the prefestival atmosphere, Greaves requested additional rolls of film, and Stott was given permission to secure more black-and-white 16mm film. Stott, Greaves, Bracher, and their Senegalese driver toured the city, recording Dakar's coasts, the rehearsals of the performers, and the quotidian life of Senegalese denizens. At the rehearsal of the Alvin Ailey dance company, Greaves noted the scope of the Soviet film crew—their equipment was not the newest, but between cameramen and the light and sound technicians, they numbered over twenty. Recruiting his driver—who was actually a writer for *Actualité Africaine*—to run sound for the barebones production, Greaves had his team follow the Soviet crew to various venues in order to capture the scenes under their lighting equipment. With this guerilla style of filming, the American team was able to deliver a cinéma-vérité lens on the faces and events of FESMAN. The footage from the piecemeal team alternates between light-hearted travelogue and austere reportage, all of which would be compiled and edited back in the United States during postproduction. It is for this reason that almost all the film's audio was postsynchronous music clips and authorial narration. A stark contrast to the polished full-color production by the Soviets entitled *African Rhythms*, Greaves's film is monochromatic, light-footed, and inescapably personal. Or, as characterized by Tsitsi Jaji, Greaves's intention was to "capture the historic nature of an event which his film already laced with nostalgia."[11]

A SEA OF FACES

In just under forty minutes, *The First World Festival of Negro Arts* spans the full breadth of the festival, regaling the viewer with recognizable Black performers and introducing countless others from the continent and its Diaspora.[12] Josephine Baker, Duke Ellington, Ben Enwonwu, Langston Hughes, Keorapetse Kgositsile, Katherine Dunham, James Porter, Wole Soyinka, and Alvin Ailey are just some of the luminaries who attended. Greaves took the opportunity to emphasize the coming together of Black culture-makers across not only geographic expanses but also epochs and eras.

The introductory scene meanders with Langston Hughes's steps, traversing a beach in the Rufisque neighborhood of Dakar. His silhouette contrasts with the teams of Senegalese men pulling their pirogues out of the ocean, a leitmotif of the traditional meeting the modern that permeates the film. The scene unfurls as Greaves himself narrates a reading of Hughes's poem "The Negro Speaks of Rivers" (1920)—his voice, speaking as Africa personified, becomes the element that unifies the diverse subjects and abrupt cuts. In the next scene he asks, on behalf of the continent, "Who am I?" as he cuts from artifact to artifact in the museum display. A collapsing of time and space, his contemporary narration juxtaposes with these ancient objects from the civilizations of Nok, Ife, and other seminal African societies. The layers further collapse and commingle as the viewer realizes the waxing melody of the instruments is a modern jazz riff. Do the brassy tones of the saxophone modernize these historic sculptures? Or does the stately carving and ancient materiality of the art objects imbue the jazz melody with an archaic gravitas?

Only moments later, as Duke Ellington pivots back and forth beside the bass player, Greaves drives home this point of his film—that FESMAN was an opportunity to uncover universal qualities of the Black experience. For a history marked by great expanses of space, forced relocation, and modern displacement; for the diversity of cultures, historic kingdoms, and newly independent nations, the experience of Black culture-making would be accessible in one defined locale for these three weeks. Referring to Ellington, Greaves's voice declares, "3,000 miles and 400 years separate you from Africa... yet here you are to tell the world who I am." This visual is, in fact, a looped clip. Though Greaves may have looped this clip in order to keep Ellington visually centered while discussing his spatial and temporal distance from Africa, it is also conceivable that Greaves employed this technique as a metaphor for return. Just as the musician advances and returns with each loop, so the festival witnessed the physical return of members from the African Diaspora and their departure. With Greaves's vision of the festival programming, FESMAN offered a cotemporal event wherein canyons of divide could be bridged, and an era of displacement could achieve reunion.

One of the more novel interpretations of FESMAN's significance is Tobias Wofford's alignment of the festival with the jet age.[13] Seeing the new possibility for international travel, he posits that African Americans and others in the Diaspora could more readily enact the return to the continent their ancestors had envisioned for centuries. FESMAN capitalized on the nostalgia for a motherland and offered a convenient locus for the voyage. Greaves's film seems to emphasize the assembly of festival-goers as a response to this historic scattering. With multiple shots of the city from an aerial vantage point, and returning to shots of airplanes taxiing into Dakar, Greaves acknowledges great technological advances. But, again, the phrasing of his narration evinces a dichotomy of history and modernity that is simultaneously complementary and divisive: "Once upon a time, all Africa south of the Sahara was called Ethiopia by the Ancient Greeks who sometimes journeyed here. To them, Ethiopia meant 'the land of the sunburnt faces.'" This statement reifies the alterity of Blackness even as it recounts a premodern example of Africa as a gathering place, a destination for many travelers.

Ethiopia's participation in FESMAN signals a significant Pan-African spirit since many postcolonial African countries looked to the nation for its impressive legacy of autonomy. And since Emperor Haile Selassie was the only African head of state to attend, besides Senegal's own Leopold Senghor, it is natural that Greaves would follow the emperor's arrival from the airport, through the processional across Dakar, and into the performance venues. Again, Wofford emphasizes this "Ethiopianism" wherein "Pan-Africanist discourses of racial progress and self-determinism were often associated with Ethiopia"—a sentiment embodied by simultaneously referring to Ethiopia's presence in the ancient world and to its modernity via air travel and nation building.[14] For the populations gathered at FESMAN, the festival offered the possibility of return, reunion, and revalorization. FESMAN's ability to connect an international network of Diaspora creators makes it not only a landmark cultural event but also one of the first platforms through which artists could autonomously create networks of exchange in the postcolonial period.

As Greaves considered the two major art exhibitions on display—*L'Art nègre*, featuring six hundred masterworks and artifacts from eighty-eight collections around the world, and *Tendances et Confrontations*, an assortment of modern and contemporary art from living African artists—his lens constantly gravitated toward faces. Focusing on various sculptures, paintings, and drawings, he abruptly zoomed in on the expressive face before cutting to the next object. The work of artists from the United States is given extra screen time. From the large metal sculptures of Barbara Chase-Riboud to the massive charcoal drawing by Charles White, Greaves captures patrons of diverse skin tones, ethnicities, and garment styles, analyzing the contemporary concerns offered up by the

African-American artists. For example, White's *Birmingham Totem* conveys the chaotic aftermath of the bomb that killed four children at an African-American church in Birmingham, Alabama, in 1963. A young boy, covered in a disaster relief blanket, sits atop the mound of wooden debris. With no time for mourning the loss of these lives and this sacred communal space, he sifts through the rubble to salvage a future. While the majority of American art had veered into abstraction—evidenced even by some exhibiting at FESMAN—there was a strong trend of socially engaged messages from African-American artists. Indeed, White's drawing and Greaves's film fit into a much larger constellation of forces aimed at shaping a certain vision of American society to the world that had gathered in Dakar.

The conservative African-American contingent of artists and performers that AMSAC chose to represent the United States was a carefully curated effort to portray a positive image of the country—even as the Civil Rights Movement waged its battles across the ocean.[15] Similar to the covert CIA funding of abstract expressionism as soft power against the Soviets in the 1950s, the CIA promoted a generally positive image of Black life and a spirit of celebration for the African American's heritage on the continent. These were evidenced by the singers, performers, and artworks chosen by AMSAC, and they also echoed through Greaves's film. In fact, by USIA policy, USIA-produced films were prohibited from distribution in the United States until the agency folded in the late 1990s. However, *The First World Festival of Negro Arts* circulated widely in Africa and remained one of the most-requested USIA films for nearly ten years. If the events of the festival and Greaves's film could only be experienced outside of American soil, for whom was this vision of solidarity between Black Americans and the African continent, between the modern masters of music, dance, and fine art and the genius progenitors of ancient kingdoms, literature, and spirituality?

The depth of Cold War politics at play in the festival and this film is evidenced just as much by what is left off of the film reel. When Greaves was not at work with Bracher, he spent an extensive amount of time with Langston Hughes and his entourage. Yevgeny Yevtushenko was a well-known Soviet poet who orbited Hughes throughout the festival, as he was being featured in the Soviet film production.[16] Yevtushenko engaged a wide variety of attendees socially, from Tanen and other Americans from the embassy to President Senghor himself—though Senghor asked him to refrain from public readings for the duration of the festival so as not to pull focus from the Black creators and performers.

The fact that the Soviets were represented at all at FESMAN is somewhat bizarre given their lack of Black citizens. Yet for all the influence they exerted through cultural actors and cruise liners, which served as additional lodging for visitors, the only evidence of the Russian presence in Greaves's film comes whenever one of the Russian cameramen was caught in one of his shots. The Soviet mission of building fraternity with African nations by highlighting their lack of participation in the slave trade and formal colonization foregrounds the use of "culture" as a form of soft power during the Cold War. Just as the United States organized a polished veneer of race conscientiousness, Soviet actors were actively wooing Africa's political and cultural spheres. It is somewhat ironic that during a USIA-funded assignment, and on his first trip to the African continent, Greaves built connections with parties on both sides of the Iron Curtain—even though the final film evinced a fairly patriotic, nostalgic vision of Blackness and Africa.

TRANSATLANTIC EXCHANGES

Welcoming nations from five continents, FESMAN served as a meeting ground that had been hallowed with a spirit of fertile exchange. It may have been, however, more effective on a one-to-one register than on a governmental one. Duke Ellington recounted his conversations with the audience members who dashed backstage at the end of each concert, describing how the Africans' "acceptance at the highest level" inspired a "once in a lifetime feeling of having truly broken through to our brothers."[17] This sense of intimacy comes through in Greaves's organization of the film, which makes liberal use of wide establishing shots, followed by many distinct cuts to individuals: U.S. ambassador Mercer Cook at the reception he hosted; a painting by Nigerian artist Uche Okeke at *Tendances et Confrontations*; American actress Marpessa Dawn of *Black Orpheus* (1959) fame as she gazes on Amharic texts, etc. The festival was, for Greaves, a personal affair and an impactful professional experience.

Shortly after his return from Senegal, Greaves published a short account of his experience at FESMAN in the 1966 summer issue of *The Crisis* (chapter 7 in this volume). Since this was written in the midst of editing his film, we are afforded a candid perspective on how Greaves was processing the significance of the event and its impact for African Americans more broadly. He echoes the goals that President Senghor expressed in organizing the festival: "[The Black Diaspora] came to get acquainted, to be inspired, to return to their origins, but mainly to help reveal the important contributions the black man has made, and is making, to world civilization." Though Greaves's text reveals a learned colonial bias about African autonomy ("Tired, in the twilight of their decaying cultures, the Africans were easy victims for the younger, more industrialized, more aggressive Europeans"), he astutely conveyed the breadth of Black cultural force to the African-American readers of *The Crisis*:

> It was a pleasure to see audiences, which were sometimes two-thirds white, enthusiastically enjoying the fruits of "Negritude." This is as it should be; the white world has long thrilled to such meagre fruits of Negritude as were available. Indeed, one can now visualize a day when there will no longer be a dearth of information on the contribution of the Negro to world culture. Once this gap is closed, the feelings of racial superiority and inferiority which afflict both black and white communities will die more easily.

For Greaves, the status quo was maintained because of a lack of accessible knowledge, that the fruits of Negritude—the cultural contributions of Black makers and thinkers to the universal mission of civilization—were sparse and scarce. Inspired by the philosophy of Sri Aurobindo and the wonders of ancient Africa from the writings of William Leo Hansberry, Greaves felt a sense of melancholy for the African masterpieces: the Dan mask, the Dahomean lion, the Tsoede bronze figure, and Ethiopian manuscripts that represented a bygone golden age. FESMAN, however, marked a turning point, a nexus for exchange. Dozens of dancers, from Haiti to Burundi to Togo, are reunited on a single stage. As festival-goers wander through a book fair, Greaves narrates, "Continue the dialogue which has begun. The floodgates are being opened. Words are flowing freely here, washing away misunderstanding and misconception, uncovering the mystery that has been Africa." The camera again zooms in to focus on titles that represent the full breadth of literature from Africa and the Diaspora: *Balles d'or* by Guy Tirolien, *Aube Africaine* by Kéita Fodéba, *Let My People Go* by Albert Luthuli, *Névralgies* by Léon-Gontran Damas, *Nobody Knows My Name* by James Baldwin, *My Lord What a Morning* by Marian Anderson, and many other legible titles.

Ironically, it was Greaves's article in *The Crisis*—not his film—that represented his vision of FESMAN and Africa to his fellow Americans. His unheard call to African Americans to "Remember what has happened here in Dakar" demonstrates how FESMAN's attempt to foster exchanges "was mediated by powerful forces that a post-imperial world would struggle to overturn."[18] It was only after obtaining distribution rights to his film in the early 1990s that Greaves could redress this withholding. While he would later convey a sense of incompleteness, that the film represented merely what could be made with the limited resources at hand, the finished product remains the most thorough audiovisual record of the historic 1966 festival made by a Black visitor.[19] Though some have overstated the patriotism of Greaves's film, characterizing its coverage of festival events as if "they were Olympic medal contests," it is still a departure from the heavy-handed nature of earlier USIA films.[20] Having already completed commissions for the USIA, Greaves remembered *The First World Festival of Negro Arts* as "the first opportunity [he] had to make films that expressed a Black perspective on reality."[21] And some modern scholars read enough subversion in Greaves's film to call it a "snub to the manicured representation of the United States" and a definitive "departure from didactic messages."[22]

It is a talented filmmaker who can condense a sprawling, ephemeral event into a coherent narrative that engages the viewer on the levels of self, race, and nation. Even more so when he is navigating a continent with which he is simultaneously intertwined and at arm's length. The sole film that Greaves produced in Africa during his long career, *The First World Festival of Negro Arts* captured the optimism for burgeoning transatlantic relationships, both between the United States and the young countries of independent Africa, and between Black populations in the Americas and their modern counterparts across the ocean.

NOTES

1. Tobias Wofford, "Exhibiting a Global Blackness: The First World Festival of Negro Arts," in *New World Coming*, ed. Karen Dubinsky, Catherine Krull, Susan Lord, Sean Mills, and Scott Rutherford (Toronto: Between the Lines, 2009), 180.
2. David Murphy, *The First World Festival of Negro Arts, Dakar 1966* (Liverpool: Liverpool University Press, 2016), 8.
3. William Greaves, "The First World Festival of Negro Arts: An Afro-American View," *The Crisis* (published by the NAACP) 73, no. 6 (June–July 1966): 312 (chap. 7 in this volume).
4. Hoyt Fuller, *Journey to Africa* (Chicago: Third World Press, 1971), 92.
5. Jody Blake, "Cold War Diplomacy and Civil Rights Activism at the World Festival of Negro Arts," in *Romare Bearden, American Modernist*, ed. Ruth Fine and Jacqueline Francis (Washington, D.C.: National Gallery of Art, 2011), 43–58; Anthony J. Ratcliff, "When Négritude Was in Vogue: Critical Reflections of the First World Festival of Negro Arts and Culture in 1966," *Journal of Pan African Studies* 6, no. 7 (February 2014): 167–86.
6. Dominique Malaquais, interview with Harold Weaver, PANAFEST Archives, November 4, 2013 (Paris, France).
7. Letter from Ted Tanen to Malick Sidibé, March 4, 1966, Folder no. 9, National Archives of Senegal.

8. Letter from Ted Tanen to Malick Sidibé, March 15, 1966, Folder no. 37, National Archives of Senegal.
9. Penny Von Eschen, "Soul Call: The First World Festival of Negro Arts at a Pivot of Black Modernities," *Nka: Journal of Contemporary African Art*, nos. 42–43 (November 2018): 132.
10. Raoul Granqvist, *Photography and American Coloniality: Eliot Elisofon in Africa, 1942–1972* (East Lansing: Michigan State University Press, 2017), 192, n. 38.
11. Tsitsi Jaji, "Negritude Musicology: Poetry, Performance, and Statecraft in Senegal," in *Africa in Stereo: Modernism, Music, and Pan-African Solidarity* (Oxford: Oxford University Press, 2014), 93.
12. Of all the festival events, the notable absence from Greaves's film is the *son et lumière* spectacle on Gorée Island, which Louise Archambault Greaves remembers him describing upon his return. I would speculate that it would be difficult to film since the event took place outdoors at night or, possibly, that Greaves and the USIA were hesitant to refer to the Translatlantic Slave Trade, which was integrally tied into this island, the performance staged for FESMAN, and a problematic aspect of U.S. history.
13. Tobais Wofford, "Diasporic Returns in the Jet Age: The First World Festival of Negro Arts and the Promise of Air Travel," *Interventions: International Journal of Postcolonial Studies* 20, no. 7 (2018): 952–64.
14. Wofford, 961.
15. In fact, only one year after the festival, American ambassador to Senegal Mercer Cook would lament that "the greatest cause of [America's] unfavorable 'image' in Africa is the racial situation. This is ironical because the riots in Watts and elsewhere, the police dogs in Birmingham...loom larger in African eyes than all the history-making progress in recent years." Mercer Cook (c. 1967), as cited in Blake, "Cold War Diplomacy," 51.
16. Arnold Rampersad, *The Life of Langston Hughes: Volume II: 1941–1967: I Dream a World* (Oxford: Oxford University Press, 2002), 401.
17. As cited in Jaji, "Negritude Musicology," 102.
18. Murphy, *The First World Festival of Negro Arts*, 31.
19. Interview with film historian Bouna N'Diaye (May 8, 2018, in Dakar), who spoke with Greaves at the Nasher Museum of Art in 2006.
20. Blake, "Cold War Diplomacy," 50.
21. Adam Knee and Charles Musser, "William Greaves, Documentary Film-Making, and the African-American Experience," *Film Quarterly* 45, no. 3 (Spring 1992): 17 (chap. 1 in this volume).
22. Text panel for Greaves's film in the exhibition *Dakar 66: Chronicles of a Pan-African Festival*, Musée Quai Branly, 2016. Original French: "Mais le film est aussi un pied de nez à cette représentation lissée des Etats-Unis." Von Eschen, "Soul Call," 134.

9
Sisters Inside *Still a Brother: Inside the Negro Middle Class*

Black Women Through the Lens of William Greaves

JACQUELINE NAJUMA STEWART

A brown-skinned woman, perhaps in her thirties, stands on a verdant golf course with a serene demeanor. She wears a dark V-neck sweater, half-dollar-sized gold hoop earrings, and a long, thin gold necklace. Her straight, shoulder-length hair blows in the breeze, her pastel lipstick catches the sunlight. A group of white golfers crosses at a distance behind her. Her steady medium close-up appears between panning and zooming shots of Black men golfing, screen direction implying that she is watching them play.[1]

The early shot in *Still a Brother: Inside the Negro Middle Class* (1968) that I describe above encapsulates the film's general approach to Black women.[2] Seen, but not heard. Admired visually, but on the sidelines of the central topic. The film, written by William Branch and photographed, directed, and edited by William Greaves, is a ninety-minute tour de force exploration of the external and internal pressures that the Negro middle class faces at a watershed moment in American political history. Using extensive location shooting, archival footage, a bit of dramatization, and interviews with more than two dozen subjects, *Still a Brother* demonstrates how persistent racism negates the Negro's increasing educational and professional advances, dashing their hopes for a "truly equalitarian multiracial America." At the same time, the middle-class Negro struggles psychologically with a normative white middle-class value system, particularly as that system is challenged by rising Black militancy and "Soul" aesthetics among Black youth and lower classes. As the film's

FIGURE 9.1 William Greaves and William B. Branch working on *Still a Brother: Inside the Negro Middle Class* (1968). Louise Greaves: "Branch is credited as writer and co-producer with Bill, but the film was produced by William Greaves Productions. If ever a film was made in the editing room, it was *Still a Brother*" (email to editors, May 2, 2020). Courtesy Louise Greaves.

title signals, *Still a Brother* explores what it means to be a Negro middle-class subject primarily from Negro male perspectives. In keeping with prevailing norms of racial discourse, "The Negro" is consistently masculinized in the text of Branch's script, in Ossie Davis's voice as narrator, and in the preponderance of male interviewees.

The woman on the golf course is part of an opening montage that reveals a Negro middle-class world largely invisible to the predominantly white National Educational Television (NET) audience for whom the film was commissioned. She may read as an ornamental feature of a story about race and class. But her appearance also signals the host of subterranean stories about women that live inside this inside look at Negro identity in transition. Across the film, Greaves's camera registers issues about Black women that Branch/Davis's narration does not speak, in ways that I detail below: How do Black women experience their class status in relation to Black men, white norms, and other Black women across social and economic scales? What shapes their political views and activities? How do they respond to the personal and political declaration that "Black Is Beautiful"?

> *A young woman in a formal white gown and long white gloves, a tiara atop her loosely curled hair, walks across a stage in a large ballroom. She curtseys deeply as her name is called, to the applause of a large audience of Black people in white-tie. She is followed by another debutante, who is presented and then guided off the stage by two young Black men in tuxedos.*

Greaves brings to *Still a Brother* some of the incisive cinéma-vérité strategies he developed during his training at the National Film Board of Canada in the late 1950s and early 1960s. He enters real-life activities in progress—at the golf course and the cotillion, for example—and captures the action with a handheld camera, mostly without "directing" or interfering. But in his observational footage, Greaves does not attempt to disappear entirely. Rather, he exhibits a participant-observer shooting style, one that evokes the sense that the film is speaking in a collective and credible Black voice. At a time when, as the Kerner Commission would observe in its report, there were few Black people working in film and television, it means something that Greaves is holding the camera, enlisting the trust or at least the comfort of his Black subjects in documenting this crucial moment in Black American history, politics, and culture.[3] He combines his own presence and perspective behind the camera with the actions and commentaries of the Black people observed and interviewed, and with the script written and narrated by fellow, socially conscious Black artists William Branch and Ossie Davis (both of whom, like Greaves, were actors and writers, with careers spanning theater, film and television).[4] As a gifted cameraman and editor committed to racial justice, Greaves sees an abundance of possibilities in each "film situation," and he is deeply mindful of the strategies he uses to convey "the Black reality" within those situations.[5] Committed to using film as a tool for racial re-education and Black liberation, Greaves photographs Black people in ways that were groundbreaking in their detailed appreciation of Black daily activities, environments, and styles of dress, speech, and gesture. These are hallmarks of Greaves's long career of corrective and affirming Black image-making, and they are revolutionary in picturing Black women on screen.

And yet, with the exceptions of his powerful documentary *Ida B. Wells: A Passion for Justice* (1989) and his study of an interracial couple of characters/actors in *Symbiopsychotaxiplasm: Take 2½* (2005), Greaves's films rarely present Black women as narrators of their own experiences, or as analysts of the

FIGURE 9.2 Greaves during the shooting of *Still a Brother*. Photographer unknown. Courtesy Louise Greaves.

intersecting forces that shape their life possibilities, their histories, and the multiple hierarchical structures that perpetuate social inequities.[6] It is this tension that makes *Still a Brother* such a rich text for intersectional analysis. When we are attentive to the interlocking dynamics of gender, race, and class in the film, we recognize the patriarchal terms in which its prescient profile of "the Negro" is elaborated. We track the appearances of Black women: how Greaves shoots and edits them, and how they present themselves (e.g., their hair and clothes, movements and facial expressions, and, in a few cases, how and what they speak). The experiences and perspectives of Sisters inside *Still a Brother* are not simply minimized. Rather, they are implicit. That is, Greaves shoots and edits their mostly brief and unidentified appearances in ways that point us to latent meanings that he and Branch did not, and maybe could not, examine directly. *Still a Brother* contains within its patriarchal frame a myriad of portraits that suggest the distinct ways that Black women and girls experience racism and sexism and class oppression, how they occupy public and private spaces, and how they have figured into thinking about Black futures.

Greaves and Branch expanded the purview of *Still a Brother* substantially beyond the "*Ebony* magazine kind of film" on Negro middle-class lifestyles that NET executives anticipated.[7] Greaves shot the film in 1967 in an extensive array of Black milieus (streets, residences, offices, and places of learning, meeting, and recreation). As a result, the film captures Black women playing a striking variety of social roles. We see them as wives, workers, ladies, activists, and intellectuals. Greaves presents some Black women in ways that focus on them as sexual beings, and he includes shots of Black girls (the debutantes, for example)—women of the future. *Still a Brother* does not explicitly explore the ways in which these roles are shaped by "interlocking oppressions" that constrain Black women's lives. There is no discussion of the particular forms of racism or economic precarity they experience as women, or the sexism they experience with Black men. NET commissioned Branch and Greaves, two credible Black male filmmakers, to tell a story about "the Negro" to a predominantly white audience, a male-dominated interracial production framework that renders intraracial gender issues tangential at best. Moreover, the film aired in late April 1968, shortly after the assassination of Martin Luther King, Jr., as increasing civil unrest across the nation heightened the sense of racial crisis in ways that subsumed questions of gender oppression within the Black community and in American society more broadly. But while the film does not include gender in its political analysis, Greaves's culturally astute, contextually proficient camerawork records ample visual evidence of how deeply embedded Black women are in the stories of Black class mobility and identity formation.

Greaves and Branch mobilized the issues of Black consciousness and militancy to pack more into *Still a Brother* than they were initially authorized to include. We can today, in turn, use a Black feminist approach to unpack the film's images of women, to examine the multiple oppressions that, when left unaddressed, render any efforts toward Black liberation inequitable and incomplete. Implicitly, the Sisters pictured in *Still a Brother* grapple with the predicament described unequivocally by the Combahee River Collective of Black feminists a decade later: "We struggle together with Black men against racism, while we also struggle with Black men about sexism."[8]

> Marlene Jones, sporting a pixie haircut, sleeveless white dress, and large sunglasses, sits smiling and holding her daughter next to her husband, Bobby, who pilots their yacht. A distant shot of the speeding boat dissolves to a shot of the interior of the Joneses' midcentury modern, open-plan suburban home in the Hudson Valley. Marlene wears a floral print housedress. She and Bobby kiss, then she and their son wave goodbye from the doorway as Bobby walks past her small car in the driveway and enters his vehicle for his morning commute.

Women are a key feature of the observational footage Greaves shot for *Still a Brother* in the New York, Chicago, and Atlanta metropolitan areas, and in the vacation spots of Martha's Vineyard and Sag Harbor. Marlene Jones and several other women in the film (arguably including the woman on the golf course) are presented under the rubric of Wife, a prized position within heteronormative structures, and a key feature of Black bids for respectability dating back to slavery.[9] The Black wives we see in *Still a Brother* display styles of dress, homemaking, child-rearing, and entertaining that function as supportive analogues to their husbands' professional attainments and mirror those of their white middle-class counterparts. Marlene Jones and other Black middle-class wives (seen waving from the porch of a summer home or sliding into the passenger seat of a fancy car ushered by her husband) can normalize the presentation of Black families in the eyes of white viewers. They serve as rejoinders to the narrative of Black pathology associated with fatherless, female-headed households infamously propagated by the Moynihan Report.[10] When we view Marlene Jones's performance of the role of wife for Greaves's camera within this Black historical context, we can appreciate the heightened stakes of her chic physical appearance, her tasteful home décor, her well-groomed children.

Importantly, Marlene and the other Black wives who join their husbands at swank parties and house-hunting outings in *Still a Brother* do not simply affirm the normativity and respectability of their families. They also signal the layers of protection and security that marriage promises to women, psychological and social shields against the discrimination Black women face in a society that does not extend to them the patriarchal protections offered to white women. Of course, marriage hardly guarantees safety for women. We are reminded of this fact, in an alarmingly nonchalant way, in a scenario that sociologist St. Clair Drake describes during one of his multiple, lengthy interviews in *Still a Brother*. To make the point that middle-class identity is shaped more by behavior than by income, he animatedly compares the contexts in which two hypothetical Black Chicago stockyard workers engage in domestic violence. Though they make the same salary, one openly drinks and physically fights with his wife after work while the other, temperate worker "pulls down the shades to make sure the neighbors don't see" him beat his wife before they decide together how they will invest his income (tithing, children's education). If Black wives lend Black husbands measures of authority denied to them in a racist society, Drake's story suggests that marriage can also authorize abusive male behavior, across class lines. More specifically, marriage provides a cover for domestic violence in middle-class homes. For Drake, this is merely a descriptive detail and does not constitute a particular form of Black oppression to be analyzed.[11] The film offers no intimations of domestic violence among its subjects. But Drake's story points to the importance of positive public appearance in Black middle-class behavior, and how such appearances—like the one Marlene Jones performs for Greaves's camera—depend on concealing women's oppression behind closed doors.

> *A brown-skinned woman in her twenties, wearing a short natural (or afro) hairstyle and vibrant print dress, cowry shells dangling from her ears, staffs a registration desk at a "job opportunity center" event in a large hotel conference room crowded with Black candidates. With a smile, and pen in hand, she reviews information on a piece of paper with a Black male registrant in a suit, tie, and glasses, possibly directing him to the rooms where his job interviews will take place.*

For some Black women, middle-class lives, as wives, offer freedom from generations of obligatory work outside of their homes to support their families—notably as domestic workers in white households. Marlene Jones, for example, appears not to have a morning commute, her house dress suggesting that her daily labors are focused on/in her own home. Other Black women, however, have sought mobility into the middle class through professional training and opportunities—as teachers, beauticians, nurses.[12] One of the most striking features of *Still a Brother* is the number of Black women it depicts working in white-collar jobs. The woman working at the job fair sits alongside other women who are also working to facilitate the entrance of Black women and men into the workforce. We see other Black working women, including Bobby Jones's secretary at the New York Housing and Redevelopment Board and John H.

Johnson's staffers at the Johnson Publishing Company in Chicago. Indeed, we see rooms filled with Black women at the JPC headquarters, working at typewriters and keypunch machines, and constituting almost half of a jovial, all-staff going-away party for a male colleague.

The film focuses on the significant rise in Negro salaries and describes ongoing disparities compared to white salaries. But the narration does not address the different kinds of work opportunities available to Black men and women, or any differentials in their incomes, or any differences in the experiences they have on the job. As the camera follows a Black male applicant into what is apparently a hotel room where a prospective white employer greets him, we must wonder if the Black women candidates at the job fair are interviewed in the same settings. How would the Black women seen milling about somewhat nervously in the registration area navigate the prospects of sexual harassment and assault? How do Black women deal with such threats when they enter white- and male-dominated workplaces?[13] Writing about her entry into the television industry in the late 1960s, Sheila Smith Hobson describes the scope of women's work in the corporate arena: "PA's forever. What a thrill! Typing, fetching, or making coffee, delivery girl, office girl, and sexpot all rolled into one."[14] Black women with college degrees were routinely deemed underqualified for even these menial and exploitative tasks.

This generation of Black women entering the white-collar workforce are largely without the benefit of sympathetic supervisors, mentors, or role models, making them particularly vulnerable as they move into corporate and other professional settings. We are told that the job fair organizer, Richard Clarke, boasts of his capacity to create "instant middle-class Negroes," indicating the modest salaries and backgrounds of the candidates he places. But he observes that despite his successful placements, middle-class status is "a very precarious thing" for Black people in economic terms, because it depends entirely on the continuity of the higher-paying job rather than accumulated wealth. This precarity continues to characterize the Black middle class today. There is a particular edge, then, to the moment when Clarke boasts that his gathering of Black people looking for gainful employment is the antithesis of the rioting and looting that white people associate with masses of Negroes, while we see several conservatively dressed young Black women job seekers rather timidly enter the registration hall. We recognize that many, if not most, of these women, though college graduates, are likely at a small remove from Black "masses" in the streets pictured in news coverage of the ghetto. They have no safety net as they attempt the climb into corporate America.

> *Two fair-skinned, middle-aged Black women wearing pale skirt suits sit against cushions on an oversized sofa. Behind them a huge window is draped in elaborate curtains. A massive white lamp sits on a table to their right, near a chandelier wall sconce. The lamp table and the round mahogany coffee table in front of them hold several small metal and porcelain serving dishes. As the camera zooms in, light glistens from the wedding ring worn by the woman sitting couch right. The woman couch left pets a large black dog. These women are interview subjects. They describe the racial segregation of their social lives. In close-up, one observes that she has "a lot of white friends" with whom she works and meets "on certain bases." "But," she states, "I don't think they want to particularly invite me to their homes to their parties, which is perfectly alright with me." The woman on the right chimes in, "and you wouldn't want to go."*

The first section of *Still a Brother* offers a general overview of the economic features of the Black middle class, flagging inequities that people entering this bracket face in salaries, housing, and business opportunities, compared to their white counterparts. At the same time, it focuses on certain subjects, lifestyles, and attitudes in ways that come across as critical of the Black middle class as a whole. The film opens with an interview of an unnamed, light-skinned Black man with wavy hair in a seersucker suit who itemizes his list of desired material possessions and states his unwillingness to identify with the race: "I don't think of myself as a Negro." From there, the film displays signs of Black affluence and aspiration that suggest widespread disconnect from the majority of the race, and the lengths to which some members of the Black middle class have gone to create their own, insulated social sphere patterned on white models. The critical tone increases in pitch in the segment featuring the film's first women interview subjects.

Greaves frames these women with his camera and his editing in ways that emphasize their performance as Ladies. Elegantly appointed, refined in their taste and manners, they illustrate St. Clair Drake's point about class status as behavioral: whether or not these women have significant incomes or wealth, they make social and consumer choices that showcase an elite status. They are initially framed in a long shot, showing them from well-dressed head to toe, within a sizable portion of a well-decorated living room. In this tasteful space, they describe the work of The Girl Friends, the social club that stages an opulent debutante ball, created in response to the racially exclusionary practices of the white Junior League. Their high-society activities correspond with the view articulated by John H. Johnson: "I don't think we ought to be content just to be in the middle class; I think just as we have whites in the upper class, we've got to have Negroes in the upper class."

But it becomes clear that for Black women, this aim is not only a matter of racial equity. It is also a struggle to occupy a category of revered and protected womanhood that has been fiercely reserved for white women. Greaves moves to close-ups as they profess their lack of interest in socializing with white women who would shun them, and we can see in their expressions and hear in their tone more than a little resentment at the prospect of being snubbed. At the center of their short interview, one of the women voices a telling contradiction: with icy eyes and jaw clenched in a tense smile, she first speculates coolly that she and these white women "probably wouldn't have anything in common," but she then adds quickly with a loud biting tone, "and we probably *would*!" Greaves captures a jumble of desires here: the woman seeks to steel herself against racist rejection as an inferior by taking on an air of superiority, while at the same time suggesting that there is likely common ground, an equal "lady" status to be found across racial lines. Her reiteration at the end of the interview of the same point she made at the start—"I don't expect to be invited to their parties, and I'm sure they wouldn't enjoy coming to mine"—exposes the uneasy emotional loop within which these Black ladies are caught with regard to their class aspirations.

In his editing, Greaves places these Black ladies within a cluster of shots, as well as a group of scenes, that destabilize Black performances of refinement. As Ladies, these women do not roll their necks or suck their teeth. But they display an unmistakable edge of Black women's attitude as they reflect, with strained nonchalance, on the racism of white women. Greaves may do a bit of coaxing to get this attitude on film. The couch-left woman's repetition of her point almost verbatim, and the inclusion of separate close-up shots of the other woman agreeing, with indignant expressions, suggest that Greaves stayed on this topic for a while during their interview. The women appear between two other scenes that point to the artificiality of Black elite posturing, and raise pointed questions about the cultural, political, and psychic costs of elite class aspiration. We first hear them in voice-over with shots of the debutante ball, where nervous Black girls in stiff white formalwear wait awkwardly in a receiving line. And their interview is followed by shots of "An Evening of Elegance," an exceedingly formal charity event where Black and white couples sip champagne on the lawn of "Mrs. Sidney Poitier's Westchester estate," apparently unaffected by the fact that, we are told, it proceeded within days of the excessively violent police siege on Black residents in Newark in July 1967. Notably, the first woman interviewee in the film identified by name also appears in this segment. Cathy Aldridge, women's editor at the New York *Amsterdam News*, on location at the "Evening of Elegance," confirms that "there is a 'Black society.'" *Still a Brother* features its most concentrated group of Black women's voices when Greaves and Branch are critiquing the elite Black stratum for its artificiality, materialism, and disconnection from the Black "masses."

> An older black woman wearing glasses and a mix of textures—dark cardigan sweater half-buttoned over a butterfly-print blouse and a pleated white skirt, translucent below the knees—crosses a Harlem street, then stands on the corner in front of a trash receptacle. Behind her, tattered advertising posters cover the side of a brick building, and several Black folks enter and exit shops. She clutches keys and possibly a handkerchief in one hand. The camera zooms in to catch her rather fatigued expression, as she rubs her forehead and scratches her slightly disheveled gray hair.

Based on her expertise as editor of the society pages for the New York *Amsterdam News*, Cathy Aldridge explains in her interview that "Black society" consists of those who interface regularly with affluent whites via "advisory boards and benefit committees" and contribute resources to "those less fortunate than they." But their philanthropic motivations and social impact are rendered questionable, if not negated altogether, when the supercilious organizer of "An Evening of Elegance," Vassal Thomas, states in his interview that so much of the money donated by attendees is spent on the lavishness of the event that "there isn't *too* much going to the particular charity that has been chosen." This might seem like a comically embarrassing revelation, except that it also functions to assuage any concern that his donors (or the film's viewers) might have that his event supports controversial (i.e., empowering) efforts among an increasingly militant Black population. Thomas speaks with an effeminate, exaggerated aristocratic affect, which the film seizes on to amplify its representation of wide gaps (political, cultural) between the Negro elites and masses. Greaves further emphasizes this disjuncture by cutting directly from Thomas in his white tuxedo at the Poitiers' Tudor estate gala in Westchester to shots of tenements and street life of Harlem, where "less fortunate brothers" sit on stoops and gather on street corners.

Among these "less fortunate brothers" are "less fortunate" sisters, women and girls traversing the streets, including an older woman Greaves captures as she apparently waits for a traffic light to change. Roughly twenty-five seconds in length, this shot is one of the longest in Greaves's observational sequences. We can take in the details of her inexpensive clothing and her arms-back, rocking gait. She is a stark counterpoint to the well-dressed, middle-class Black women we have seen earlier in the film, not least because they behave as if they know they are being looked at, if not by Greaves's camera, then by the private or public audiences around them. Greaves zooms in on the Harlem woman's face. Her eyes scan her surroundings. She appears slightly fatigued, her gaze seemingly focusing on nothing in particular. This visual study of the Harlem woman invokes sympathy—not simply in an effort to inform the film's viewers about Black poverty but, more important, as part of the film's consideration of how the Black middle class has been "negligent," as Ralph Featherstone of the Student Nonviolent Coordinating Committee (SNCC) puts it, in its response to "the struggles of the masses of Black people in this country." Greaves's camera looks at her to consider how and why the Black middle class has failed to really look at her in the past, and to consider what would happen if they studied her face and condition now. The film details how a "mental revolution" is taking place among some members of the Black middle class, and Greaves uses the Harlem footage, and particularly the shot of this woman, to illustrate this coming to racial consciousness. He brings back for a longer interview the snobby Black man in the seersucker suit who opens the film, and we hear the man's voice over her image as he says that he has become aware of the plight of the Black masses and now knows that he "should help" by picketing, protesting, and speaking out to his "white counterpart about the injustices that have occurred to my people." We continue to see this woman on a Harlem street corner as he says that in younger days, he "behaved like it [racial inequity] didn't exist." Her image accompanies his closing observation: "Now I'm thinking as a Negro; and I think more people in my group are thinking as Negroes."

We must imagine that this woman has always thought as a Negro, living in the conditions of poverty and segregation that the man in the seersucker suit was unaware of in his middle-class upbringing in another part of town. We cannot know what she is thinking at the moment Greaves shoots her. But the duration of his shot, and the zoom in to her face, capture her thinking something. This shot calls to mind images of Black women in acts of contemplation that we find in later Black independent films, notably those made by the group dubbed the LA Rebellion, such as Haile Gerima's *Bush Mama* (1975), Billy Woodberry's *Bless Their Little Hearts* (1984), and Julie Dash's *Daughters of the Dust* (1991).[15] Greaves does not just render this woman in terms of the physical ghetto conditions in which she lives but also attempts to register that she navigates these conditions psychologically. Here *Still a Brother* displays its masterful double voice, making a case to the Black viewers inside of the predominantly white National Educational Television audience. She becomes a bridge across the class divide that can enable Black middle-class people to feel not simply guilt but a shared consciousness and, by extension, a shared destiny.

> *A group of state troopers with batons and gas masks charge, beat, and trample a predominantly Black group of protesters. Cut to more troopers advancing on horseback. Cut to two Black protesters struggling to lift the slumping body of an injured Black woman wearing a light-colored coat from the ground, a white trooper standing close behind.*

We have seen this footage of "Bloody Sunday" many times, when the first of three attempts by civil rights activists to march from Selma, Alabama, to the state capital of Montgomery in March 1965 was met with brutal state opposition. The image of wounded activist Amelia Boynton circulated worldwide. But as is the case with many Black women activists and organizers during the Civil Rights Movement (and before, and after), her role as a leader in Selma's voter rights campaign has not been widely known.[16] Greaves uses the Selma footage to illustrate Branch's point about how the promise of racial equality felt so keenly at the March on Washington in 1963 was not fulfilled and in fact eroded as the 1960s rolled along. Here the film takes a serious turn from its profile of middle-class lifestyles into the political strife that binds all Black people in their histories and their fates. *Still a Brother* uses the gut-wrenching image of injured Amelia Boynton as it is nearly always used: as documentation of Black victimization and white racist brutality, meted out equally to Black men and women. Black women are visibly denied any special consideration by white power to be treated as "ladies."

The horrific treatment of Amelia Boynton, like the slaying of four girls at the 16th Street Baptist Church bombing in Birmingham and countless other acts of violence against Black women and girls, has also served to highlight crises of Black masculinity. When Black women and girls are characterized as defenseless, patriarchal logics are activated in which Black men feel compelled to protect the weaker sex, their dependents, their property. This posture is of course complicated by the disempowered position Black men occupy in American society, the lack of structural supports for Black patriarchal authority, which compromises their ability to prevent harm to "defenseless" women and girls. One effect of Black investments in normative gender hierarchies that situate Black men as the rightful, primary responders to racist oppression is the downplaying of the fundamental roles that women like Amelia Boynton have played throughout the Black liberation struggle as brave and self-conscious agents of change for themselves and the race as a whole.[17] Accounts of women in the Movement, from the Montgomery bus boycott to the March on Washington, from the Southern Christian Leadership Conference (SCLC) to the Black Panther Party, consistently describe the rampant sexism they faced even as their labor was deemed essential to the cause.

> *Three young Black women walking in a business district are approached by two young men in crisp white shirts. Cut to a close up of the CORE (Congress of Racial Equality) logo on fliers one of the men is holding, then a wider shot of them in conversation.*

Other archival footage of the Movement featured in *Still a Brother* shows men up front and out-front. We see Martin Luther King, Jr., A. Phillip Randolph, Roy Wilkins, and Whitney M. Young walking in the front row of the March on Washington. We see Maulana Karenga, H. Rap Brown, Ralph Featherstone, and Dick Gregory at the Black Power Conference in Newark in 1967. But some of this footage shows Black women as participants in the Movement over the years—faces in the crowd at the March on Washington, and at the National Urban League Community Action Assembly in 1964 as Lyndon B. Johnson outlines the recently passed Civil Rights Bill. The newsfilm archive of the Civil Rights Movement does not give Branch and Greaves (or any of us) sufficient documentation of Black women's broad-based, tireless, infrastructure-building activism, from the thousands working in the rank and file to key organizers. Late in *Still a Brother*, in one of Greaves's street scenes, we get a moment that suggests the importance of Black women's participation in the present and future direction of the Movement. Two young men work the street with CORE materials at a moment when the organization was shifting from its longstanding and influential philosophy of nonviolence to a Black Power platform. The recruiters stand in front of a women's clothing and wig shop.

> *A middle-aged woman with a conservatively rounded bob haircut, identified as "Mrs. Millicent F. Jordan, Spelman College, Atlanta," speaks about Negro feelings of shame in a society that valorizes "Nordic standards of beauty." She speaks rhythmically, with precise pronunciation and passionate authority. The camera moves between extreme and medium close-ups of her face, so that we can see a bit of her long, beaded necklace, her small, flat white earrings, her pale, sleeveless white dress, and the African sculpture behind her.*

Of the twenty-nine interviewees featured in *Still a Brother*, six are women, and two of these are identified by name: Cathy Aldridge from the *Amsterdam News* and Millicent F. Jordan, a faculty member at Spelman College. The other four women interviewees are shown in pairs (all the men are interviewed individually) and speak as unidentified types (two ladies on the couch discussed earlier; two beauticians quoted below). The film distinguishes Aldridge and Jordan from these unidentified women by tapping expertise beyond their personal experiences: Aldridge provides an account of the existence of a "Negro society," and Jordan discusses the causes and impact of low Black self-esteem. While other interviewees in the film's impressive roster of "spokesmen"—including learned figures like sociologists St. Clair Drake and Nathan Hare, minister and scholar Nathan Wright, and chemist Percy Julian—sometimes describe personal experiences, these are shared in service of the broader insights and analyses they articulate.[18] This is one of the most significant aspects of *Still a Brother*: its demonstration of the wide range of expertise that exists within the race, men (and a couple of women) who can speak with authority and eloquence about race matters. Even the spokesmen who speak most animatedly (Bayard Rustin, Nathan Wright, and the fiery Pan-Africanist bookstore owner Richard B. Moore, who gets quite loud) demonstrate keen insights into Black social, psychological, and political issues, such that their deeply personal, passionate stake in these questions does not invalidate their status as analysts.

Clearly a skilled orator, Millicent Jordan speaks with a modulated passion. One of the ways she displays her analytical skills is in her use of masculine pronouns when describing the problem of low self-esteem: "I suppose every Negro, sometimes in his life, has been ashamed of being a Negro." Jordan's exclusive use of "he" and "his" in her interview reflects conventions of speaking about a people as a whole. But it also has the effect of depersonalizing the dynamics she is describing, and doing so to a greater degree than many of the "spokesmen" in the film. She appears just after Julian Bond (then a Georgia state representative) describes an experience from his high school days of feeling shame about his race, then extrapolates it to consider how his affirming participation in "the Movement" is relevant to others: "I think people who don't have that struggle, that participation in struggle, have more difficulty overcoming that shame and that fear that living in America I think forces on you." In contrast, when Millicent Jordan wonders about the Negro struggling with shame, asking, "Can he overcome it?," her language of inquiry as a scholar distances her observations from the sense that she speaks from personal insight. Jordan hails from an academically distinguished family.[19] Still, her manner of speaking responds to her vulnerable status as an intellectual in a society that would underestimate her expertise and capacity for objective reasoning both as a Negro and as a woman. Jordan is adhering to scholarly norms that held even for a Black woman scholar teaching at Spelman, a historically Black college for women.[20] Even in Black academic contexts, women scholars like Jordan would be under some pressure to demonstrate their ability to speak beyond the realms of the personal and the emotional, areas that Black feminism and women's studies would soon mine in their transformative work within the academy.

Jordan speaks at a moment when rising student protests would shortly lead to the establishment of Black studies and women's studies programs on college campuses.[21] Black women found themselves torn between, and marginalized within, both of these fields.[22] Women's studies excluded women of color and, as Jordan's own language suggests, Black studies marginalized women. Greaves shoots footage at Howard and Columbia Universities, where we hear the concerns that fueled the Black studies movement, and see its gender dynamics. Two Black male students talk about their frustrations with the conservatism of their respective administrations: Howard's leadership fears losing white funding if the school appears too militant; Columbia refuses to address racial biases in its curriculum. These two male students serve as the film's primary representatives of the next generation of Black intellectuals, those who agitate for institutional reform. At Howard, a group of male students listens to young professor Nathan Hare (whom we are told was recently fired from Howard because of his militancy) as he castigates the university for being complicit in an unequal educational system that underfunds Black colleges while giving huge grants to white universities to do "research on the Negro." He jokes that "they've been studying the wrong man." Who, we might ask, is studying the Negro woman? In many ways, *Still a Brother* exemplifies the logics of Black studies as that field was being founded, sublimating gender in the study of race.

What are Black women studying? We see Black women in Greaves's campus shots, but because he shoots exteriors we primarily see students socializing. The film's representation of Howard focuses on how this storied Negro middle-class institution has been transformed by the "Black is Beautiful" ethos. In place of its long-practiced "strict pseudo-Victorian" elitism and colorism, we see that Howard is now pulsating with Black pride: brown-skinned cheerleaders high step at a homecoming game, fraternities dance with abandon to the beat of African drums, women students sport natural hairstyles. The scenes at Columbia are mellower: we see a gathering of Black women and men of the campus Afro-American Society; a few white students join the conversation. One Black woman holds a publication featuring portraits of W. E. B. Du Bois and Malcolm X. In its representations of both Black and white college environments, *Still a Brother* shows Black men as the primary agents and subjects of (what was being formalized as) Black studies. Black women's scholarly pursuits and activism have been framed not only by expectations to focus on race ahead of gender but also by the ways in which intelligence in Black women has been stigmatized. The Combahee River Collective of Black feminists wrote in their landmark statement that "we discovered that all of us, because we were 'smart,' had also been considered 'ugly,' i.e., 'smart-ugly.' 'Smart-ugly' crystallized the way in which most of us had been forced to develop our intellects at great cost to our "social lives."[23] The women Greaves shoots at Howard and Columbia are navigating both the academic and the social dimensions of campus life. And in doing so, they face a web of challenges that Black men do not share, including the sexist judgments of male faculty and students, white and Black, inside and outside of the classroom.

Still a Brother features a few other scenes that suggest the challenges Black women face as scholars and thinkers in a range of contexts. *Jet* magazine editor Bob Johnson brags about his preteen daughter Janet's award-winning science fair project on Dr. Charles Drew and Dr. Daniel Hale Williams, while she smiles shyly, holding a tennis racket.[24] Johnson goes on to talk about how he helped his other daughter research famous Negroes born in February: Langston Hughes, Todd Duncan, Richard Allen, W. E. B. Du Bois, Frederick Douglass. He takes great pride in his daughters' scholarly acumen, and it goes unremarked that their studies focus on Black men. Men dominate not only scholarly subject matter but also the settings in which Black intellectual exchange takes place. In a scene showing the kind of "serious debate" that "is commonplace at Negro middle-class gatherings today," a woman struggles to get a word in edgewise as Richard Moore shouts his support for Black militants and their "revolt for manhood status."

On the other hand, at a meeting of the mostly male board of the DuSable Museum of African American History in Chicago, museum founder Margaret Burroughs sternly pressures members of the group to come up with needed funds, tapping the table as she says, "We should not leave this meeting unless we see that $53,000, you know, even if various people have to go to their credit unions and borrow some of it." As she speaks, Greaves brings up the nondiegetic sound of African drumming, emphasizing the work that Burroughs and her colleagues are performing as "keepers of the flame" of Black cultural heritage.[25] Both Margaret Burroughs and Millicent Jordan are surrounded by their collections of African art. This surely resonated with Greaves, who was a longtime student of African history and cultures and believed, like Burroughs and Jordan, that Black people in the United States suffered greatly from their forced alienation from their African heritage. When he brings up drums behind Burroughs's words, Greaves recognizes the museum's proud African consciousness (we learn it has recently replaced "Negro" with "African American" in its name). And perhaps more than he intended, the drums evoke the militancy of Burroughs's cultural and institutional leadership in particular.[26] In the company of (mostly) men, Burroughs breaks from expectations of female subservience, bringing the full range and intensity of her intellect.

> *A group of young professional men, four white, one Black, sit smoking outside of an office building, looking left toward where the Black man points. Cut to two young Black women walking across a bustling street from left to right, one in a floral dress and natural hairstyle, the other with straightened hair in a sleeveless, dark top. The women's eyes catch the camera, and one maintains her look into the camera for several beats, smiling. Cut to a close-up of another Black woman on a busy street, wearing a short afro, dangling earrings, and a soft, high-collar white coat. Cut to a medium shot of two Black men in suits, looking left. Cut back to a closer shot of the woman in white. Cut back to the two men in suits, smiling and talking. Cut to a white woman with brown hair passing the first group of men on their smoking break, their eyes following her as she passes.*

A key feature of the film's discussion of the "mental revolution" taking place among some members of the Black middle class is a discussion of self-image and beauty standards. We hear from several interviewees—including Millicent Jordan, psychiatrist J. Denis Jackson, and Bayard Rustin—about the denigration of Black skin and kinky hair, leading to generations of self-hatred. The slogan "Black is Beautiful" is developed as an antidote, meant to repair damaged Black psyches, a mantra to facilitate coming to political consciousness. Greaves shoots a Black woman model with a "natural" hairstyle posing for a photographer, an *Ebony* magazine spread featuring women with "The Natural Look," as well as an *Ebony* cover featuring Black male celebrities wearing naturals—Sidney Poitier, Harry Belafonte, Lew Alcindor (soon to be known as Kareem Abdul Jabbar), and even Sammy Davis, Jr. *Ebony* publisher John H. Johnson describes the newfound, healthy pride in African heritage expressed by the natural. Greaves captures a variety of men and women in the streets wearing naturals, within a landscape of many Black women who continue to straighten their hair. It is during this period that haircare entrepreneurs George and Joan Johnson develop their pioneering Afro Sheen line of products, supporting an emerging style choice that was not yet served by the hair care industry. Two Black beauticians, one with an asymmetrical bob and the other in a blonde wig, say that while "our girls wear it very well," naturals are "bad for business." But Johnson authorizes the "trend" in his influential magazine and in his remark that, while still in the minority, "there are a growing number of Negro men and women who are wearing their hair in a natural form and I think quite attractively."

Greaves captures street scenes to illustrate the embrace of "Black is Beautiful," with a telling emphasis on the ways in which that phrase evokes sexual attraction. More specifically, his sequence on the natural hair trend is organized primarily in terms of Black women's physical appearance and the attention they attract from men. This is the only section of the film that explores Black sexuality, a topic addressed in minimal and oblique terms in Branch's script but amply by Greaves's camera. The sequence begins and ends with men engaged in the pastime of women watching in a central urban district (maybe Midtown Manhattan). Editing suggests that the women are objects of their gaze, and that these natural-wearing women invite and enjoy these looks. As one woman holds her look at the camera, there appears to be mutual delight in the exchange.[27] The second part of the sequence is more conventional in its sexualized look at women. Greaves introduces the woman in white via shots of two men looking, but she does not return their gaze or the gaze of the camera (the men look left, and she also looks left). All the men in this sequence wear naturals too. But they are aligned with Greaves's camera, and presented by his editing, as the lookers, not the looked at. For many Black women, the decision to go natural was heavily shaped by concerns about the approval of Black men as prospective romantic partners.[28] This, along with the responses of family members, employers, and colleagues (particularly white ones), raised the stakes of redefining attractiveness for Black women.

This segment is also notable for the ways in which the presence of white people points to the legacy and consequences of interracial sexual relationships. The white woman at the end, ogled by an interracial group of men, illustrates the hegemony of white beauty standards discussed by some of the interviewees, but with the visual addition of Black male sexual attraction to white women. Shot during the summer that the Supreme Court struck down laws banning interracial marriage (*Loving v. Virginia*, June 1967), this profile of the Black middle class leaves the volatile topic of interracial sexual relationships, of major consternation to Black and white people, mostly unspoken.[29] No doubt this topic would have been prohibited by NET executives who were already stretching beyond the boundaries they expected from the program. It is an unavoidable but conspicuous omission in a film that advocates for increased interracial interaction and explores the histories of Black wealth and anti-Black violence in the United States. In the 1890s journalist Ida B. Wells exposed how white lynch mobs targeted Black entrepreneurs and systematically murdered Black men on false charges of raping white women, using "lynch law" to intimidate Black communities as they were becoming more economically and politically independent. She also suggested, at great personal risk, that white women and Black men engaged in consensual sexual relationships.[30]

Greaves and Branch are fully aware of these issues but can only hint at them. For example, the long, deeply repressed history of interracial sexual relationships is indirectly referenced a bit earlier in *Still a Brother*. Drawing on E. Franklin Frazier's damning 1955 study of the "Black bourgeoisie,"[31] the film traces the source of white identification among Black people back to slavery, particularly the fealty of "house Negroes" who were "often the illegitimate offspring of the slave master himself." Telegraphed here is the systematic rape of enslaved Black women, a practice that continued, alongside lynching, as a form of racial terrorism. It does not seem, though, that Greaves and Branch connect this traumatic history of assumptions about Black women's sexual availability and consent to the contemporary street scenes celebrating Black women's attractiveness, even though editing suggests that white men are also looking at Black women on the street with a sexualized gaze. The sequence is focused instead on demonstrating that Black men and women have newfound, culturally affirming space in the public sphere to engage in heterosexual mating rituals. And that Black and white male colleagues can more openly bond in acts of shared interest.

The film moves from this exploration of Black pride and sexual attraction into a rather ethnographic sequence that discusses the rise of "Soul" aesthetics, an embrace of "indigenous Negro music and dance" and "traditional lower-class Negro food favorites." This is a strikingly sensual segment of the film, in which Black couples grooving flirtatiously in a nightclub (with close-ups on shaking booties) and eating in soul-food restaurants (with close-ups of biting and chewing) signal how Black people, including those in middle class, are feeling less repressed by a disapproving white gaze—external or internalized. Significantly, "soul brothers and soul sisters" display a cultural comfort, even audacity, via expressions of healthy heterosexuality. This stands in stark contrast to an earlier scene parodying the excesses and depravity of the Black bourgeoisie. Greaves dramatizes a garden party, which he shoots with a distorting fish-eye lens, making the characters appear grotesque. As we hear a passage from Frazier's *Black Bourgeoisie* castigating Black elites for their self-delusion, we see an older Black woman in a blonde wig enter a party of comically overdressed Black characters with overdramatic flair. She greets a clergyman and young polo player with inappropriately extended kisses, then inserts herself into a man-on-man polo lesson. This garden party scene functions as a rather direct commentary on the real-life "Evening of Elegance" portrayed earlier in the film, a scene that also (as discussed earlier) links Black elite aspiration to an unnatural (i.e., white-identified) femininity and to queerness. The film's celebration of Soul as expression of a "new and healthier self-image" prominently features Black women, admiring them within the framework of a "natural" heterosexuality.

> *A girl, perhaps in her early teens, stands on a football field with her father and three brothers. She wears glasses, a dark coat, knee-length skirt, and white high-top shoes. Her shoulder-length bob is topped with a dark beret. The camera's pan catches her very briefly as it follows the others tossing a football around. She stands stock still, arms clenched up against her chest.*

The title *Still a Brother* comes from a lengthy and moving interview with Horace Morris, associate director of the Washington, D.C., branch of the Urban League. With astonishing composure, Morris recounts the harrowing story of being fired on for ten minutes by Newark police officers as he and other innocent bystanders, including his close relatives, stood outside of a residential building. Morris's stepfather was "mortally wounded" in the siege in front of his home, and his brother was severely wounded. Morris visited Newark after attending an Urban League conference in New York, signaling the alarming disjuncture between the gradual, policy-focused approach fostered by interracial organizations like the Urban League and the anti-Black violence practiced on the ground by white police officers. In Newark and other cities, Black citizens armed themselves to resist ongoing subjugation, escalating the level of police violence that claimed Morris's unarmed relatives and that he narrowly escaped alive. Morris notes that despite the credentials he has amassed across his life (two degrees, football player for Syracuse University, principal of an integrated elementary school, work with white people at Urban League, white friends), he's "still a brother" in the eyes of a racist, authoritarian state.

Morris invokes his seventeen-year-old son as representative of the more militant Black youth, paraphrasing how he and his friends view the racial situation: "You can have that Urban League approach. I'm ready to be a man in America now.... I want full equality with no holds barred, and if I can't have it, no one can have it." Greaves cuts to shots of Morris and his son tossing a football, ingeniously rendering the differences between their philosophies, as well as Morris's respect for his son's position. We don't see them in one shot that frames them together, but rather in three separate shots that cut between son-father-son seen tossing, anticipating, and catching the ball. The sequence evokes the rhythms of intergenerational dialogue and presents the son first and last; he raises the challenge and his generation is the one that will run with the ball. Greaves nicely captures the back-and-forth between philosophies that Black individuals, families, and communities were debating. Moreover, as Horace Morris, the former Syracuse player-turned-civil rights administrator, tosses the ball with his letter-jacket-wearing son, the film's predominantly white audience is invited to read Black militancy not simply as a ghetto phenomenon but in light of one of the film's central observations: as St. Clair Drake puts it, the Negro middle class is "like [the white middle class] in every respect except for the color of their skin."

Greaves returns to Morris and his progeny at the film's conclusion. We return to the football field and see Morris go out for a pass, tracking the ball in flight as Ossie Davis concludes: "Hanging in the air therefore is the ominous question: How much longer can America evade honoring its most basic and pressing commitment? Will the younger and more militant be forced to continue losing faith in the promise of a truly equalitarian, multiracial America? If so, then the troubles we've recently seen could be but a prelude to national disaster." Branch's powerful and prescient script challenges viewers in 1968 to examine the toll that unchecked racial discrimination, structural inequality, and anti-Black violence will take on American democracy writ large. Greaves couples these concluding remarks with images of the Morris family, and we now see more children: his seventeen-year-old son as well as two younger boys, and a daughter who appears to be the second oldest in the group.

Morris's daughter is filmed in the background of the father-son imagery that the film uses to promote urgently needed dialogue on its central questions of race and the nation's future. Like the appearances of other girls across the film—the debutantes, girls in a group of children watching negating white images on a TV, girls giggling shyly while vacationing on Martha's Vineyard, girls exiting a Harlem storefront, Janet Johnson presented by her father as winner of the science fair, the daughter in Marlene Jones's lap on the family yacht—this brief appearance by Horace Morris's daughter raises questions about where Black women figure into the futures the film encourages us to imagine. In the positive vision of the future, racial inequities are addressed effectively and Black people "share unhindered in the great American Dream." In the dystopic one, "the Dream itself [is] jeopardized for all." Without directly addressing gender, *Still a Brother* does not articulate any particularities in the ways Black women would benefit or suffer in these possible futures. However, the rich archive of images of Black women and girls that Greaves assembles in *Still a Brother* provides us with material to imagine these and other Black trajectories, ones that extend from the underexplored histories and contemporary experiences these women and girls from across the class spectrum call to our attention.

We should not simply write off the marginalization of women and gender analysis in *Still a Brother* as an unfortunate effect of the times in which it was made. We should read it as further evidence that systems of oppression are interlocking. And we should excavate, from the film's Black patriarchal discourse, material we can use now to develop political and representational strategies that are consciously inclusive. St. Clair Bourne recalls that when Greaves was executive producer of the NET public affairs series *Black Journal* between 1968 and 1971, "Greaves knew what we younger staff members didn't: this filmmaking opportunity would not last but the films would." When we focus on the ways *Still a Brother* represents Sisters, with close attention to the film's formal and cultural logics, we see that it provides—in its content and structure—what Greaves felt Black documentary ought to offer contemporary and future viewers: a "teaching tool on how Black people could work to resolve common problems."[32]

NOTES

1. The focus on scenes of women in this essay is inspired by the brilliant scholarly and political insights shared by Daphne A. Brooks and Kara Keeling, particularly during our 2017–2018 collaboration on the multimedia lecture/performance project "Combahee River Collective Mixtape: Black Feminist Sonic Dissent Then and Now," which we presented at venues across the country. I wish to thank a group of wise and generous Black elders who watched and dissected *Still a Brother* with me at a small screening in Chicago in March 2019: Timuel Black, Carol House, Zenobia Johnson-Black, Deborah Minor Harvey, Masequa Myers, Pemon Rami, Christopher Reed, and Kamau Tyehimba. Thanks to Sabrina Craig and Avery LaFlamme for coordinating and recording that gathering.
2. All the women I point to in the block descriptions in this essay are Black. I use the term "Black" here, in my title, and in most of my general references to the film's subjects and subject matter because it is in general usage today and was used at the time the film was shot. In the late 1960s the term was coming into wider, positive use by people who had long been described, and described themselves, as "Negroes." The title of the film under discussion uses the term "Negro," and that is the racial descriptor used in most of the film's script and by most interviewees (notably, one older, elite woman interviewee goes back in her lexicon to the term "colored"). However, the more militant commentators in the film, including Ralph Featherstone (SNCC), Nathan Wright (organizer of the 1967 Black Power Conference), an anonymous Columbia University student activist, and Richard B. Moore (owner of the nationalist Fredrick Douglass Book Center), use "Black." (Moore also uses the

term "Afro-American," and we learn in the film that Chicago's DuSable museum has recently adopted the term "African American," but these were not yet widely adopted.) By the end of *Still a Brother*, the narration uses "Black" with more frequency. In my discussion of subjects in the film, I attempt to reflect the self-description, the language, and in some cases the implied or stated political consciousness of the subjects themselves. Thus in my references to the race as a whole, I move between "Negro" and "Black" and sometimes use quotation marks, as the context would seem to dictate. And sometimes I leave these terms out altogether in hopes the reader gets my drift. These variations in my descriptions are not presented casually, and they feel quite awkward at many moments. I believe these variations appropriately reflect the politicized tensions of racial identity so powerfully captured by this film. I acknowledge that I do not know what term most of the women I describe in visual detail would have used to describe themselves. I call them "Black women" as I reach back to them from now, reading in their presence some of the political and representational possibilities that Greaves's camera intimates.

I refer at times to the skin color of the subjects under discussion, where it seems that is an important detail for points the film is making with regard to Negro/Black class politics. This sometimes proves a challenge in Greaves's black-and-white cinematography.

3. *Report of the National Advisory Commission on Civil Disorders*, intro. by Tom Wicker (New York: Dutton, 1968).
4. Nathaniel G. Nesmith, "William B. Branch, Playwright of the Black Experience, Dies at 92," *New York Times*, November 6, 2019.
5. St. Clair Bourne, "*Black Journal*: A Personal Look Backward," *Documentary Magazine* (Spring/Summer 1989), https://www.documentary.org/magazine/springsummer-1989 (reprinted in chap. 14 of this volume); Jonathan Scott Holloway, "The Black Body as Archive of Memory," in *Jim Crow Wisdom: Memory and Identity in Black America Since 1940* (Chapel Hill: University of North Carolina Press, 2013), 93.
6. For the Ida B. Wells documentary, Greaves features Toni Morrison reading passages from Wells's writings and includes historians Paula Giddings and Rosalyn Terborg-Penn prominently among its experts. In *Symbiopsychotaxiplasm: Take 2½* (2005), the central tension involves the willingness of a Black woman (Audrey Henningham) to reconcile with her estranged white lover via mentoring his beloved Black female protégée (Ndeye Ade Sokhna).
7. Adam Knee and Charles Musser, "William Greaves, Documentary Film-making, and the African-American Experience," *Film Quarterly* 45, no. 3 (Spring 1992): 17 (reprinted as chapter 1 in this volume).
8. Combahee River Collective Statement, 1977, reprinted in Keeanga-Yamahtta Taylor, *How We Get Free: Black Feminism and the Combahee River Collective* (Chicago: Haymarket Books, 2017), 19.
9. Tera W. Hunter, *Bound in Wedlock: Slave and Free Black Marriage in the Nineteenth Century* (Cambridge, Mass.: Harvard University Press, 2017); Anastasia C. Curwood, *Stormy Weather: Middle-Class African American Marriages Between the Two World Wars* (Chapel Hill: University of North Carolina Press, 2010).

10. Daniel P. Moynihan, *The Negro Family: The Case for National Action* (Washington, D.C.: Office of Policy Planning and Research, U.S. Department of Labor, 1965), https://www.dol.gov/general/aboutdol/history/webid-moynihan.
11. For a study of Black women's experiences with domestic violence, see Hillary Potter, *Battle Cries: Black Women and Intimate Partner Abuse* (New York: NYU Press, 2008).
12. Jacqueline Jones, *Labor of Love, Labor of Sorrow: Black Women, Work and the Family from Slavery to the Present* (New York: Basic Books, 2009).
13. Catherine McKinnon, *Sexual Harassment of Working Women* (New Haven, Conn.: Yale University Press, 1979); Carrie N. Baker, *The Women's Movement Against Sexual Harassment* (Cambridge: Cambridge University Press, 2007).
14. Sheila Smith Hobson, "Women and Television," in *Sisterhood Is Powerful: An Anthology of Writings from the Women's Liberation Movement*, ed. Robin Morgan (New York: Vintage, 1970), 78. Hobson describes her experience working on NET's *Black Journal* in extremely negative terms, though she does not mention any specifics about Greaves (who became executive producer). Charles Musser describes the limited roles for Black women on *Black Journal* (Smith, Peggy Pinn, Madeline Anderson) in chapter 15 of this volume, "'By, For and About': *Black Journal* and the Rise of Multicultural Documentary in New York City, 1968–1975."
15. Allyson Nadia Field, Jan-Christopher Horak, and Jacqueline Najuma Stewart, eds., *L.A. Rebellion: Creating a New Black Cinema* (Berkeley: University of California Press, 2015).
16. Belinda Robnett, *How Long? How Long? African-American Women in the Struggle for Civil Rights* (Oxford: Oxford University Press, 2000).
17. Janet Dewart Bell, *Lighting the Fires of Freedom: African American Women in the Civil Rights Movement* (New York: New Press, 2018); V. P. Franklin and Bettye Collier-Thomas, eds., *Sisters in the Struggle: African American Women in the Civil Rights–Black Power Movements* (New York: NYU Press, 2001).
18. The term "spokesmen" is used in the NET promotion of the film. "NET Journal; Still a Brother: Inside the Negro Middle Class," April 29, 1968, American Archive of Public Broadcasting (WGBH and the Library of Congress), Boston and Washington, D.C., http://americanarchive.org/catalog/cpb-aacip-516-kd1qf8kh4s.
19. Amber L. Moore, "John Wesley Dobbs Family Papers: The Six Dobbs Daughters," *Amistad Research Center*, May 9, 2011, amistadresearch.wordpress.com/category/millicent-jordan/.
20. In 1976 Jordan would participate in what was "perhaps the most aggressive [protest] in the history of Spelman" when students and faculty confronted the university's trustees for failing to appoint a Black woman president. "Held as Hostages, Trustees Yield to Angry Spelmanites," *Jet*, May 13, 1976, 22–23.
21. Martha Biondi, *The Black Revolution on Campus* (Berkeley: University of California Press, 2012).
22. Barbara Christian, "But Who Do You Really Belong to—Black Studies or Women's Studies?," *Women's Studies* 17, nos. 1–2 (1989): 17–23; Frances Smith Foster, Beverly Guy-Sheftall, and Stanlie M. James, eds., *Still Brave: The Evolution of Black Women's Studies* (New York: Feminist Press, 2009). For an exhaustive

compendium of publications charting the development of the field, see Stephanie Y. Evans, *The Black Women's Studies Booklist: Emergent Themes in Critical Race and Gender Research*, https://bwstbooklist.net/.
23. Combahee River Collective Statement, in Taylor, *How We Get Free*, 20–21.
24. "Attorney Janet Johnson Grant, Daughter of Late Jet Associate Publisher Robert E. Johnson, Dies in Chicago Building Fire," *Jet*, November 3, 2003, 54–55.
25. Mary Ann Cain, *South Side Venus: The Legacy of Margaret Burroughs* (Evanston, Ill.: Northwestern University Press, 2018).
26. Celeste Day Moore describes how Greaves's framings of Pan-African thought and Black internationalism "were frequently predicated on masculinity" in chapter 16 of this volume, "William Greaves, *Black Journal*, and the Long Roots of Black Internationalism."
27. Shortly after this scene, another Black woman with a natural preens playfully for Greaves's camera as he shoots on the street. Greaves displays a visual admiration for the visual beauty of Black women in his earlier film, *The First World Festival of Negro Arts* (1966); as he puts it (and his camerawork reflects), "the Senegalese are a beautiful people. It is delightful to see a Senegalese woman walking, tall and elegant, with her long dress, or 'gran bou-bou,' billowing after her in a dance of color" (William Greaves, "The First World Festival of Negro Arts: An Afro-American View" *The Crisis* 73, no. 6 [June–July 1966], reprinted in chap. 7 of this volume). In his *Symbiopsychotaxiplasm* project, Greaves concludes *Take One* (1968) with a freeze-frame of Black actress Audrey Henningham. *Symbiopsychotaxiplasm: Take 2½* features Henningham more centrally, not just in the film's contemporary storyline but also in footage from the 1968 shoot, where in one lengthy shot Greaves (acting as director and acting coach) sits next to her, studying her face, and removes something from her hair.
28. Noliwe M. Rooks, *Hair Raising: Beauty, Culture and African American Women* (New Brunswick, N.J.: Rutgers University Press, 1996); Maxine Leeds Craig, *Ain't I a Beauty Queen? Black Women, Beauty, and the Politics of Race* (Oxford: Oxford University Press, 2002).
29. Werner Sollors, *Interracialism: Black-White Intermarriage in American History, Literature, and Law* (Oxford: Oxford University Press, 2000).
30. Jacqueline Jones Royster, ed., *Southern Horrors and Other Writings: The Anti-Lynching Campaign of Ida B. Wells, 1892–1900* (Boston: Bedford/St. Martins, 1997).
31. E. Franklin Frazier, *Black Bourgeoisie: The Rise of a New Middle Class* (New York: Free Press, 1957).
32. Bourne, "*Black Journal*: A Personal Look Backward."

10
The Documentary as Sociodrama

William Greaves's In the Company of Men *(1969) and* The Deep North *(1988)*

J. J. MURPHY

In *Symbiopsychotaxiplasm: Take One* (shot in 1968; first edited version, 1971), William Greaves employed a psychodramatist from the Moreno Institute, Marcia Karp, to work with an interracial couple who appear as the Freddie and Alice characters toward the end of the film. Neither Karp's presence nor her role in the production was evident to viewers when the film was released in 1971. This became apparent only when Greaves was able to obtain financing to complete *Symbiopsychotaxiplasm Take 2½* (2005), the revisiting of what originally had been conceived to be a series of five films. Shot in 2003, the film follows the same couple (Shannon Baker and Audrey Henningham) thirty-five years later. Yet Greaves made two other films that drew heavily on techniques developed by J. L. Moreno. The corporate-sponsored documentary *In the Company of Men* (1969) also used a psychodramatist in examining racial friction between white management and chronically underemployed black workers in a southern auto plant. Greaves's later documentary, *The Deep North* (1988), adopted a similar approach in exploring the continuing problem of racism in the New York City area. Both films provide evidence of the importance of the issue of race for Greaves, as well as the impact that Moreno's theatrical and therapeutic work exerted on his filmmaking.

On the recommendation of noted documentary filmmaker Willard Van Dyke, who served as director of the film department at the Museum of Modern Art (MoMA) at the time, *Newsweek* offered Greaves a commission to make a documentary. When the subject turned out to be about the problems of hard-core unemployed African Americans, Greaves was initially skeptical about accepting the assignment because he doubted that he would be given free rein to make the kind of film he believed was needed on the subject. After all, within the context of the politically turbulent late 1960s, he considered *Newsweek* to be a news organization heavily allied with the "establishment." Greaves, however, relented after Denny Crimmins, the project supervisor at *Newsweek*, assured him that the only condition was that the film needed to focus on the issue of communication between management and workers.[1]

As the executive producer of the noted TV show *Black Journal*, Greaves understood too well that the problem of the hard-core unemployed workers stemmed from a larger culture of institutionalized racism. Neither the middle-class manager nor the working-class hard-core man relished having to interact with each other within the workplace. Their interaction involved a radical clash of different cultures that was fueled by issues of both race and social class. The conflict between the white foremen and African-American workers was further exacerbated by the fact that the white foreman faced constant pressure to increase productivity, at the same time that companies were being pressured by the federal government to hire minority workers. As a result, Greaves observed that the foreman winds up "trapped between top management and the hardcore man, and he doesn't like it one bit."[2]

The hard-core unemployed also brought their own set of problems to the workplace. Due to prior traumatic experiences that resulted from a culture of racism, a black employee had no expectations that the work experience would prove any different. As Greaves explains, "He sees the white supervisor as a symbol of rejection, of authoritarian racist America, intent on inflicting pain, and he wants no part of this." As a consequence, according to Greaves, "He will come late and leave early to avoid contact with his foreman. He will take long coffee breaks, and he will argue trivialities. He will unconsciously foul up the job in a wish to be fired, i.e., set free from the supervisor." Greaves articulated the problem that the film attempts to tackle in the article he wrote for *Film Library Quarterly*:

> Here we have a classic dramatic situation: Two characters, who want no part of one another, must relate to each other if each is to survive. In a way, it is a not-too-inaccurate image of black and white America as we move into the next decade. Is it possible for America to survive? Is it possible to get the mental and emotional mechanisms of these two groups to gear into one another and develop a productive relationship? If it is possible, then how in the hell is it done?[3]

In approaching the film, Greaves devised two strategies. He would use techniques that he had learned from attending numerous psychodrama sessions at the Moreno Institute in New York City. In addition, he would shoot the documentary without a written script, using a cinéma-vérité style.

J. L. MORENO AND THE ROOTS OF PSYCHODRAMA

The Romanian-born psychiatrist J. L. Moreno (1889–1974) came to prominence in Vienna, Austria, in the early 1920s. He is credited with creating, in 1922, the first professional theater group devoted to theatrical plays based on improvisation rather than a written script, which he called "Stegreiftheater."[4] Several early experiences in Moreno's life contributed to the development of his ideas. In 1908 he became fascinated by the spontaneity of children playing in the Augarten, the public park surrounding the royal palace. Dressed in a green cloak, he began to tell stories to them and was amazed at their uninhibited ability to fantasize and role-play. There was a subversive aspect to Moreno's storytelling. Many of his stories to the children encouraged them to challenge authority, such as renaming themselves based on personal attributes, which caused their parents to become alarmed.[5]

While at the University of Vienna, with four college friends, Moreno established a House of Encounter, which provided food and shelter to recent immigrants to the city and became a meeting place for people to engage with one another interpersonally. John Nolte indicates that Moreno's idea of "encounter" represented a much deeper form of interaction: "Each party to an encounter has a profound impact upon the other and both will be changed as a result of the meeting."[6] Moreno later began to work with a group of prostitutes in Vienna's red-light district. He held support sessions with the sex workers a couple of times a week in order to understand their problems and help defend their rights. His social activism served to convince him of the inherent power of group interaction. After he became a medical doctor, Moreno joined a local adult theater group in order to put some of his theoretical ideas into action.

In 1921 Moreno rented a theatrical space. Dressed as a court jester and using a series of props—a throne, a crown, and a purple mantle—he invited audience members onto the stage to participate in an improvised and interactive theater piece that dealt with the nature of social power in Austria. According to René Marineau, "Moreno introduced himself and told the audience that he was looking for the king. He was looking for the kind of person who does not crown himself, but emerges naturally from the crowd and whose wisdom makes him a natural choice as leader. He then invited people to come up on the stage, talk about their ideas of a leader, and to sit on the throne if they wished."[7]

Although Moreno's initial improvised attempt proved unsuccessful, the following year Moreno again rented a theater and had a group of actors perform spontaneous plays based on suggestions from the audience, the daily newspaper, and themes that he suggested. Marineau notes, "Peter Lorre performed in an act of his own, soon to become a favourite of the audiences—'How to catch a Louse.'" This sketch, in addition to allowing Peter Lorre to poke fun of people in the audience, may have had a direct relationship to his original name, Ladis*laus* Löwenstein."[8] Moreno's "theatre of spontaneity" received favorable reviews in the press and soon began to draw large audiences. Those who attended were intrigued by Moreno's emphasis on "audience participation," in which they played an active rather than passive role in the improvised theatrical pieces.

Moreno published a short, polemical book, entitled *Das Stegreiftheater*, or *The Theatre of Spontaneity* (as it was later translated), in 1924, in which he elaborated on his views about the subject. In the foreword to the enlarged 1973 edition, he explains the radical motivation for his spontaneous theatrical experiments. Moreno indicates that he was attempting to change conventional theater in four major ways: (1) elimination of the playwright and the written play; (2) audience participation; (3) complete improvisation; and (4) the creation of an open stage, which included "life itself." Moreno's notion of spontaneous improvisation was meant to be inclusive: "Everything is improvised, the play, the action, the motive, the words, the encounter and the resolution of the conflicts." In discussing Stanislavsky's *An Actor Prepares*, Moreno was critical of the Stanislavsky method because, like the work of Freud, it is rooted in the past rather than the present moment. Moreno explains, "Once we permitted the actor a full spontaneity of his own, his full private world, his personal problem, his own conflicts, his own defeats and dreams came to the fore."[9]

In 1925 Moreno fortuitously discovered what we recognize today as psychodrama. When the husband of one of his spontaneous actors complained about marital difficulties, Moreno had the couple role-play on stage, which led to marked improvement in their relationship. He quickly realized the therapeutic value of improvising theater pieces based on the personal lives of performers. Moreno was intent on moving away from scripted theater. He wanted not only to focus on spontaneous behavior and interactions of the performers but to base the productions on their own lives. This emphasis caused some of the actors who had greater professional ambitions, such as Peter Lorre, to leave and join more traditional theater groups. Essentially Moreno's interest in spontaneous acting appealed to those performers who were interested in personal growth and change. According to Marineau, "Therapeutic theatre as Moreno begins to develop it here is also different from psychoanalysis in that it is action-oriented, public, and rooted in immediate reality. It brings the group into the picture as an essential part of therapy."[10]

Moreno moved to the United States in 1925 and later experimented with what became known as Impromptu Theatre. His new group, however, met with limited success. In 1936 he built his own specially designed stage at the Beacon Hill Sanitarium, in Beacon, New York, and began having the patients enact psychodramas. The theater in Beacon Hill became the working laboratory for Moreno's ideas and concepts, which included such techniques as doubling, role reversal, mirroring, chorus, and soliloquy. What Moreno created in Beacon was much more than a theater—it became the locus of an entire therapeutic community. Marineau describes its utopian aspects: "In the theatre patients were encouraged to act out their past and present lives, and fantasies about the future. It was the place where the whole community met to explore each other's ideas and ideals about living. There were no spectators since everybody was involved in one way or another."[11] Psychodrama recognizes that all human beings engage in social roles in their everyday lives but that past experiences can inhibit the spontaneity of their current behavior. Through theatrical role-playing, Moreno sought to bridge the inner and outer reality of his patients.

As Moreno's fame as a group therapist grew, he began to perform public psychodramas in New York City beginning in 1942. He also performed psychodramas in various institutions, such as prisons and mental hospitals. In a set of four DVDs, *Moreno Movies*, the third video, entitled *Psychodrama in Action (in the 1960's)*, was filmed in a California mental hospital.[12] The psychodrama session Moreno conducted there was broadcast to other patients within the institution. In the film, he employs psychodrama to determine whether one of the patients is ready to be released back into the community.

For his case study, Moreno selected a twenty-year-old man from Los Angeles named Gary. Through the use of psychodramatic techniques—most notably, auxiliary egos and role reversal—Moreno has Gary interact with his parents, employer, and girlfriend (who is also now in a mental hospital), as well as enact a dream. In the encounter involving his girlfriend, played by an auxiliary ego (a surrogate for the person), Gary suddenly breaks down and sobs uncontrollably. The conclusion reached by both Moreno and the live audience in attendance is that Gary is not sufficiently ready to leave the institutional setting. Moreno ends the program by discussing the cost-effectiveness of mass psychotherapy. He declares that psychodrama is entering a new era and that being able to see it on television will contribute to national mental health.

FROM PSYCHODRAMA TO SOCIODRAMA

In the 1950s and 1960s Moreno's public psychodramas grew in popularity and drew performers and directors from film and theater, who were interested in creating more authentic dramas and performances. William Greaves was only one of a number of well-known artists—from Arthur Miller to Dustin Hoffman—to attend these public sessions. Indeed, Walter Klavun (1906–1984), the psychodramatist who appears in Greaves's documentary *In the Company of Men*, was an accomplished stage and screen actor who was trained by Moreno. Klavun appeared on Broadway, in films, and on TV, where he played Judge Santini in the series *The Defenders* (1961–1964).

What were the techniques derived from psychodrama that Greaves employed in *In the Company of Men*? Greaves specifically mentions role-playing and sensitivity training in relation to Moreno. A syllabus or study brochure that accompanied the film goes into more explicit detail: "Psychodrama, in training the imagination to perceive other points of view and to see one's self in another perspective, overcomes the differences which hinder communication between the sexes, between the races, between the generations, between the classes in society. Thus it serves to develop insights, reshape values, remove prejudices."[13] Moreno became interested in racial issues early in his career when he worked at the New York State Training School for Girls in Hudson, New York, in the 1930s.[14]

Moreno understood that human beings were not simply individuals but also members of social groups, which shaped their personal values and their perspectives on how they viewed the world. Moreno developed a method of analysis of social networks, which he called "sociometry," in an attempt to understand the dynamic within social groups. His work in sociometry began in the early 1930s when he developed social scientific techniques to measure and understand the behavior of prisoners incarcerated at the Sing Sing Correctional Facility at Ossining, New York. He developed a measurement quotient, which could be used as part of the rehabilitation process and as a tool for "transforming the prison into a better social community."[15] He used similar techniques when he was invited to conduct research at the New York State Training School for Girls in Hudson, New York, where he collaborated with Helen Jennings. Moreno, however, went much further than sociometry by using role-playing and psychodramatic techniques in an effort to "retrain" the young women's behavior through group psychotherapy.

Moreno also developed what he termed "sociodrama" as a means to understand conflict within and between groups. Indeed, along with his Living

Newspaper experiments, it is possible, as Moreno himself maintained, to view his very first improvised theatrical event as a sociodrama. According to Marineau:

> In this actual sociodrama, Moreno attempted to find new organizational alternatives for Austrian people and to give power to every voice within the political and social spectrum. He failed, either because there was no will on the part of people to really look at everyone else's suggestions (meaning there was no will or readiness for role reversal), or because the neophyte sociodramatist, Moreno, overlooked the difficulty of leading such a big and heterogeneous crowd.[16]

Moreno nevertheless continued to develop strategies and approaches to increase the efficacy of sociodrama. Although Moreno might have been interested in using improvised theater as a form of sociodrama from the start, he had yet to discover psychodrama as a therapeutic technique.

Sociodrama focuses on the group rather than on the individual and involves role-playing in order to get people to understand the perspectives of others. The goal is for members of disparate groups to become more empathetic and, hence, achieve better integration. According to Peter Felix Kellermann, "Sociodrama may be simply defined as a group method in which common experiences are shared in action. It is the application of psychodrama techniques to social situations in the community."[17] Patricia Sternberg and Antonina Garcia explain the difference between psychodrama and sociodrama: "Moreno devised two modalities to facilitate exploration of role: sociodrama for collective components and psychodrama for private components. Sociodrama, then, concerns itself with the collective role aspects."[18]

Racial tensions in the United States became exacerbated during the Second World War, which led to race riots occurring in a number of U.S. cities. Following the Harlem Riot of 1943 that left six people dead and hundreds injured, Moreno's interest in racial conflict intensified.[19] One sociodrama he conducted in response dealt with two young African-American women who were denied jobs due to their race.[20] A. Paul Hare and June Rabson Hare summarize a sociodrama about race relations that Moreno conducted in 1945. It involves an African-American couple, Richard and Margaret Cowley, who are studying at a university. Richard tells of meeting a white person who is critical of African-American soldiers as combatants during the Second World War. The couple's own version of the event is to understand that the black soldiers had morale problems due to the racial attitudes of the white officers who were in command. After a session in which Moreno discusses the various incidents with the audience, he ends the session by suggesting that these events need to be understood not only intellectually but also psychodramatically.[21] The sociodrama involving the Cowleys and their response to white people's perception of African-American combatants turns out to be very similar to the power dynamic that Greaves tackled in *In the Company of Men*.

RACIAL CONFLICT ON THE ASSEMBLY LINE IN A SOUTHERN AUTO PLANT

The *Newsweek* syllabus or study guide that accompanies *In the Company of Men* mentions a variety of group psychotherapy techniques in relation to the film, such as T-groups, encounter groups, and the Managerial Grid. Greaves's idea was to use a Moreno-trained psychodramatist to create a sociodrama to deal with racial conflict within the workplace. His approach proved to be novel for a sponsored film. Instead of relying on a written script, Greaves chose to structure the film around a series of improvised situations consisting of the two conflicting sides within the workplace: the white foremen and black hard-core unemployed workers. Each group had deeply held prejudices against the other. In the film, Greaves was not interested in simply presenting the issue of racial conflict within the workplace. Instead, he wanted the film to enact meaningful change between the white foremen and the alienated African-American workers at the auto plant.

Greaves believed very strongly that media had an obligation to deal with what he considered the pathological effects of racism. In 1970, a year after he made *In the Company of Men*, Greaves wrote a scathing op-ed in the *New York Times* that began, "I am furious Black." He suggested that the amount of money spent on entertainment as opposed to educational programing needed to be completely inverted. As an African-American producer, Greaves also strongly advocated for "encounter television" as a way to get different social groups to confront each other on an interpersonal level. He writes: "The case for 'encounter television' can be made easily by the following analogy: When two people, particularly if they are hostile to each other, are brought together for a psychodramatic encounter, there is great distrust, more so when they are dependent upon each other, as in the case of man and wife. What is needed is the willingness of both to encounter each other psychologically." Greaves argues for a model developed by Moreno as a measure to combat social diseases, such as racism, by placing "the rednecks of Alabama in a direct encounter with the Black militants of Harlem, either on public or closed-circuit television."²²

In the Company of Men can be viewed as an encounter film. It begins with the white psychodramatist Walter Klavun playing the role of a black worker in an argument with a white manager over a parking space. He then engages in role-playing with a black worker, before the two of them reverse roles. The switching of roles represents an attempt to understand the position of the other person in the conflict. Greaves cuts to a group of African-American men. They discuss the need for militant change, especially for their young black brothers, in standing up to some "cracker who pulls out a gun" by suggesting that the person will need to have a lot of ammunition. The scene cuts to a white manager, who asks, "How do you reach these people if they're so headstrong that they don't want anything to do with us or with any of the establishment? How do you reach the people?" Klavun argues with a black worker while role-playing, as a voiceover narration explains the basic conflict at issue and the government's efforts to ameliorate the situation through such programs as job training.

After the film's title, Klavun has the white foremen arrange office chairs in order to form an assembly line. The voiceover explains the purpose of sensitivity training and role-playing: "It's a way to put yourself in the other guy's shoes." The voiceover clarifies that these men are not actors but rather foremen in an actual factory. After the managers, who are all dressed in white shirts and ties, simulate an assembly line by pushing chairs containing salt-and-pepper shakers into a circle, Klavun attempts to put the managers in the position of the workers. He gets the white foremen to open up about their experiences with the hard-core unemployed black workers they have encountered. Two of them discuss their surprise that some of these workers actually don't miss work. Once Klavun suggests, however, that the workers in this job program cannot be fired, he immediately gets pushback. One of the white managers strenuously objects and defends his right to fire any worker who, for whatever reason, is incapable of performing the job.

The film introduces a case study in the form of a skilled, young black worker named Charles Darby, who has the problem of being chronically late to work. In two role-playing sessions with Klavun, set six months apart, Darby explains that he was hired as a shipping clerk but has spent his entire time on the job working as a packer. The young man feels deeply offended as well as betrayed by the work experience. In re-creating a scene where he complains to his boss, the fact that he is enacting a traumatic experience from his own life causes Darby to become so upset that tears well up in his eyes. What deeply perturbs him is the sense that he was duped into taking the job under false pretenses. Darby feels degraded by the low status and pay, and he is especially upset about being called "boy." When Klavun, playing the role of his white supervisor, concludes that it is obvious that Darby is unhappy working there, he fires him and begins to write him a severance check. Darby suddenly explodes in anger and quits.

In a session with the white managers, Klavun plays the role of a black worker who not only arrived late to work but parked in an unauthorized space. He defends himself, especially against being called "boy." He queries one of the managers, "Would you like to be called 'boy' all the time?" The white foreman claims he has been called "boy" by the same person but admits afterward that he fabricated this detail while role-playing. In another session with a group of more militant black workers, one of them claims that he was cheated out of a pay raise by "whitey." Instead of getting the extra quarter per hour he was promised, he was only given a dime per hour. The black worker indicates that he accepted the lesser raise but no longer performed the same quality work.

In a session with an African-American psychiatrist, Dr. Denis Jackson, the black workers open up and role-play about their experiences in the workplace. One of them found himself in in a managerial position. When a conflict arose, however, a white worker refused to listen to him, and his white boss refused to support him. Another worker, who has six kids, complains that he has only eight cents in his pocket, while the government spends money on foreign aid and the space program. Klavun role-plays with the black workers in order to discover how they perceive the white managers. When he directs a racial slur to one of them, the worker indicates that his response would be to strike him in retaliation.

Klavun explains that he has no idea what will happen in the next session. He has role-played with the black workers separately under the supervision of Dr. Jackson, as well as separately with the white foremen. Now, however, the white managers are slated to interact with the group of black workers. As the two groups come together and assemble in a circle, Klavun introduces Dr. Jackson, a psychiatrist from Atlanta, who explains that these workers have reacted against what they perceive to be institutionalized white racism. From their perspective, they would rather be unemployed and hanging out on the street corner than working within what they perceive to be an unfair, unjust, and degrading system. One man describes an experience of being chewed out by the manager after three hours on the job. When one of the white managers experiences difficulty playing the role, the men reverse roles so the black worker can demonstrate the part for him. Although one of the white supervisors claims that no manager at the plant would ever pressure a worker after only three hours on the job, one of the African-American men tells of being harassed after only a half hour. He also lets it be known that the offending white manager is present in the room, which adds an element of tension.

After the two men involved role-play the situation, the black worker claims that what just transpired was not an accurate portrayal of what actually happened. He explains that being made to walk the assembly line as a punishment by the white foreman affects his sense of masculinity. The black worker claims that he has a choice in this situation, which is either to "pack my balls up and put them in my back pocket" or "be a man and knock his teeth out." Either one, he argues, is a losing proposition. As a white manager responds to the group, he initially refers to the black workers as "fellas," but he quickly changes it to "men." Laughter suddenly erupts among the black workers, who have noticed the switch in words by the white foreman as a result of the sensitivity training sessions. This causes an immediate change in the atmosphere of the room. The film repeats the scene for emphasis. Afterward, the two groups have an interchange, where they begin to communicate with one another as equals. A rapport starts to develop between the two sides, as the black workers begin to talk more freely and personally with the white foremen, and vice versa.

As a white foreman discusses his personal experience of how he rose within the company, a voiceover talks about black workers' sense of rejection by white managers who are often "too busy, biased, or too careless" to understand the feelings of the black workers. This dialogue represents a first step in the process of achieving empathy for what it is like to be the other person. One of the black workers, Al Judge, an ex-sergeant, discusses the skills it takes to lead men on the battlefield. The film comments that he could easily become a supervisor, but he is at risk of becoming part of the hard-core unemployed. A voiceover explains that supervisors need to understand that the black worker faces incredible odds in achieving success, and that both sides have to show a sensitivity and willingness to communicate "face to face in the company of men."

The dynamic shown in the film was apparently manifest in the production of the film itself. According to Greaves, the composition of his crew, as well as his dress and demeanor, played a pivotal role. For the section on the hard-core unemployed black workers, who were found in the Kirkwood area of Atlanta, Greaves used an all-black crew, which proved inspirational to the black participants. In the session with the white foremen from General Motors, Greaves used an all-white crew in order to ease the foremen's resistance to the idea of an African-American producer, writer, and director. Greaves explains how he dealt with the situation. He dressed conservatively in a white shirt, tie, and suit; he spoke like an educated, middle-class person; and, finally, he deliberately played a secondary role to Klavun in his interactions with the foremen "in order to reduce their anxieties, their feelings of being threatened by a dominating northern black."[23]

Greaves admits, however, that he made a blunder in not telling Dr. Jackson and the black workers that he would be shooting their group interaction with the white foremen with an all-white crew. He writes, "The first thing they did on seeing me was to give me a tonguelashing for my 'duplicity.' They really tore me apart in a sequence which I filmed and hoped to use subsequently. I was actually delighted by their hostility to me, as it improved the possibility of the white foremen loosening up, based on the fact that the Kirkwood men were hard on middle class types, white or black." Greaves was confident that the black workers would be uninhibited in their responses while role-playing, but he was less certain about the white foremen. As he puts it, "So my crucifixion was functionally useful in solving that particular problem."[24]

In the Company of Men was released a year after Greaves shot his now legendary feature film *Symbiopsychotaxiplasm: Take One* in 1968. Both films are sociodramas that employed Moreno-trained psychodramatists as part of the production. Yet the intent behind *Symbiopsychotaxiplasm: Take One*—an interrogation of the hierarchical structure of a film production—was not obvious to the cast and crew members while the film was being shot. Greaves secretly tried to incite rebellion among them through his deliberately inept direction. The clandestine filmed meetings by the rebellious crew, however, became known only after a crew member slipped the secret crew sessions to Greaves, who later decided to include their critique as part of the final film. Thus *Take One* can be viewed as a covert sociodrama.

On the other hand, as a sponsored documentary, *In the Company of Men* was an overt sociodrama, which had a clearly defined educational and social mission. In discussing his use of a cinéma-vérité style of filmmaking, Greaves indicates that it places a burden on the director, writer, and cameraperson because the person needs to be able to distinguish between "what is dramatic and what is not" while an event is unfolding. He also observes that the participants in front of the camera, the real-life performers, "are unwitting co-writers and co-directors of the project." As he did with *Take One*, Greaves invokes Heisenberg's Uncertainty Principle in asserting that the camera crew using a cinéma-vérité style of filming "by their mere ego-assaulting presence, stifle and kill the spontaneous impulses of live, everyday people."[25]

As a result, Greaves argues for the need to minimize the size of both the camera and crew. He writes, "The smaller the camera, the better; the further away they are from the subjects, the better; the more powerful the microphone and lenses, the better; the less ego and personality presence of director and crew members, the better; the more the crew dissolves into the background scenery, the better." Greaves's critique of the effect that cameras have on documentary events and his invoking of Heisenberg's Uncertainty Principle relate to Moreno's goal for psychodrama. Most telling is Greaves's deliberate use of the word "spontaneous" in discussing the filmmaker's ability "to apprehend and perceive the spontaneous life before them."[26]

In *The Theatre of Spontaneity*, Moreno emphasizes that his ultimate objective is for a person to be able to achieve a "spontaneously creative self." For him, spontaneity and creativity are inextricably linked or twin concepts, but they are by no means identical in the sense that you could have one without the other. Yet spontaneity is key to creative behavior, or, in Moreno's words, "The first character of the creative act is its spontaneity; the second character is a feeling of surprise, of the unexpected." According to Moreno, the self has various dimensions—social, sexual, biological, and cosmic—but he contends that it goes far beyond these. He writes, "My thesis is, the locus of self is spontaneity."[27] He defined "spontaneity" as being "challenged to respond with some degree of adequacy to a new situation or with some degree of novelty to an old situation."[28] Moreno believed that various individuals exhibited different degrees of spontaneity and creativity (a "spontaneity quotient," which he attempted to measure), but someone with a fully developed self has the ability to live in the present moment and experience a full range of human emotions.

The key scene in *In the Company of Men* occurs in the brief moment when the white foreman suddenly corrects himself and uses the word "men" to refer the African-American workers who were not used to being accorded respect. In making the film the way Greaves did, there was an element of extreme risk. There was no guarantee that his deployment of the technique of sociodrama would prove successful. In fact, it turns out to hinge on a single moment that manages to transform the antagonism between the two groups into meaningful dialogue and enables the two sides to be able to empathize with one another. In his article about the film, Greaves discusses the importance of editing in cinéma-vérité filmmaking: "If what the producers have to say is not very important to life, *cinéma vérité* turns upon itself, losing its credibility, and committing suicide in full view of producer and sponsor. Both Jack Godler (*Newsweek* project supervisor and co-writer with me on the commentary) and I found out how easily this kind of tragedy could occur."[29]

Greaves's last comment raises questions. Did the sponsors insist on certain edits? Did they perhaps not want to include the footage of Greaves being verbally attacked by the black workers for shooting with an all-white crew? Greaves does go on to say that he found the response of the participants to the finished film to be "gratifying." Yet he nevertheless concludes the article by writing: "*In the Company of Men* is now history, but I must now deal in the here and now of my forthcoming feature, *Symbiopsychotaxiplasm: Take One*."[30] Not surprisingly, Greaves's remark can be viewed as textbook Moreno. For Greaves, the sponsored film that he's been discussing is already an event that occurred in the past. In wanting to live in the moment—the primary goal of psychodrama—he indicates that he is more engaged with his current project, which turned out to be his groundbreaking, reflexive feature, *Symbiopsychotaxiplasm: Take One*.

RACISM AND RACIAL CONFLICT IN THE URBAN NORTH

As Martin Luther King, Jr., found out when he came to Chicago to organize the Civil Rights Movement in 1966, racism in the North proved to be just as virulent as it was in the South. In *The Deep North*, which Greaves made for CBS with support of the Anti-Defamation League of B'nai B'rith, he turned his attention to the issue of deep-seated racism that existed in the New York City area. In the film he uses two different psychodramatists connected to the Moreno Institute—Zerka Moreno and Robert Siroka (a third, Jaqueline Dubbs Siroka, is also credited)—to work with a racially and ethnically mixed group of subjects who discuss their own experiences and views concerning issues about race.

In the first workshop, conducted by Zerka Moreno (the wife of J. L. Moreno), a short white man named Howard volunteers to stand up in front of the group. He talks about a childhood experience in which a black kid continually harassed him on the way home from school. The kid hit him in the back of the head, knocked his books out of his hand, and threw him to the ground. After this occurred several times, Howard finally became fed up and retaliated. He admits, however, that the experience had a big impact on him because when he now sees a black kid, his first instinct is to feel physically threatened.

When Moreno asks whether he would like to address the black kid about the incident, Howard responds, "Why do I want to talk to him?" Moreno answers, "It's not for him; it's for you—he's gone." The perpetrator might be gone, the psychodramatist explains, but these past experiences negatively imprint themselves on us, and confronting them might give some emotional release. After Howard finally agrees, a middle-aged African-American woman, who has defended her race to the group and identified herself as working as a court reporter for twenty-five years, volunteers to play the role of the black kid from his past. Howard eventually tells her to leave him alone. He contends, however, that she is not a good representative of that type of person from his past because she is obviously very accomplished. The woman argues that when most people see her, all they see is "her whole race," and they have no idea of her accomplishments.

Greaves provides a capsule history of racial conflict in the 1960s—from Selma, Alabama, to the riots that occurred in 160 cities throughout the United States, to the establishment of the Kerner Commission in 1968. The Kerner Report found that the country was racially divided to the point where the United States appeared to consist of two separate nations. Greaves jumps ahead in time to show footage from the then recent racial incident in Howard Beach, Queens. The notorious incident, which occurred in December 1986, resulted in the murder of a young black man, Michael Griffith, who was chased by a mob of white teenagers onto a busy highway, where he was struck by a car and killed and another black man was mercilessly beaten. Howard Beach became evidence of bitter and entrenched racial conflict that existed in New York City.

Robert Siroka, another Moreno-trained psychodramatist, then leads a larger group to discuss the current problems surrounding race. One woman from the South explains that, at least there, racism was out in the open and not hidden like it is in the North. Siroka asks if anyone in the group is aware of their own prejudice and how it operates in their life. He gives them a situation of walking alone at night and seeing a black person. One heavyset white man explains that, as a white New Yorker, his gut instinct would be to be afraid.

A blonde-haired white woman confesses that when she walks down the street and sees five black men, she feels more worried than if she sees five white men. The woman tells Siroka that in such a situation she is very aware of what she's doing—that her reactions are based on a person's color. Siroka asks her to come up and stand before the group. He asks her to create a "monodrama," as she's walking down the street, in which she role-plays the conflicting internal voices inside her head in such a situation. Her first monologue is a rational explanation for why she shouldn't feel fearful based solely on someone's race. In the second short monologue, the woman admits to herself that even though she knows better and understands that her reaction is prejudicial, she asks, "What are you going to do about it? You haven't learned to deal with it." The woman is upset with herself for not living up to what she actually believes.

Greaves follows this with an interview with an African-American psychiatrist, Dr. Hugh F. Butts, who defines racism as "the number one mental health or public health problem in our country, and in other countries as well." He defines racism as "prowhite, antiblack paranoia." One group—the one in power—feels entitled, while the other group feels unentitled and unable to achieve their goals. Butts describes racism as "a shared mental disturbance" that is based on projection. He concludes that both groups—the entitled and the disparaged parties—become engaged in a fixed way of relating, so that both groups "share in the delusion."

A black minister, Dr. Benjamin F. Chavis, Jr., discusses the dynamics of racism in the United States. He notes that whites cannot continue to dominate racial and ethnic people. He argues, "If I had to choose or state what is the single most pressing domestic problem in the United States of America today in the late 1980s, it would still be the problem of racism and, in particular, the institutionalization of racism." He observes that compared to the 1960s, racism is "not as overt; it's more covert, more institutionalized, which makes it more dangerous, which makes it more hard to tackle, more hard to define, more hard to put your finger on, and say, hey, this is racism."

After presenting statistical information about the effect of racism on blacks and Hispanics, Greaves returns to Zerka Moreno leading a group workshop. An Italian woman blames minorities for their plight. When she praises the hard work of immigrant Asians, an Asian woman accuses Moreno of diverting attention from racism against Asian Americans. She complains that the group has spent seven hours discussing black issues as well as prejudice involving Hispanics, but she argues that Asian Americans experience a type of racism that is far more subtle. A man of Sicilian descent complains that the Puerto Ricans in his building on the Upper West Side of Manhattan are intimidating the other residents. An articulate Puerto Rican man objects to such stereotyping. A young woman chimes in that even though she at times faces the same threats from minorities, she doesn't blame them based on their race or ethnicity. Instead of talking about three Puerto Ricans, she passionately tells him, you should be talking about "three son of a bitches [sic]."

The film fades and cuts to the onscreen narrator, who suggests that the full impact of what happened in the workshops may not be apparent, but hopefully progress has been made. He insists that more efforts will need to be made if we are to eliminate these divisions so that we can become "one nation, indivisible, with liberty and justice for all." The film cuts back to a workshop, as one of the group sessions ends. We hear someone ask, "What is psychodrama?" Robert Siroka laughs and answers, "Ah . . . a good question . . . a good question."

As a sociodrama, *The Deep North* is less successful than *In the Company of Men*. What accounts for the difference? For one thing, *In the Company of Men* had a clearer and more specific focus. It deals with strife between two distinct groups: the white managers and the hard-core unemployed black workers in a southern auto plant. *The Deep North*, on the other hand, tackles a much broader issue: the many forms of racism and prejudice that exist in the New York City area, post–Howard Beach. Although there are two highly experienced pyschodramatists running the workshops, it is not clear how participants were chosen for the sessions. As the final question to Siroka suggests, some participants appear unfamiliar with how psychodrama actually works. It also might be safe to assume that many of the people attending the workshop sessions might not be fully open to the demands of the process.

During *In the Company of Men*, Charles Darby becomes very emotional in role-playing because he is enacting a traumatic workplace situation that caused him significant personal pain. We might compare him to Howard, the white man in *The Deep North* who was harassed by a black kid as a child. Howard is initially reluctant to confront an auxiliary ego in the role of the black kid, and even less so when the role is played by an articulate and middle-aged black female court reporter. Howard fails to get in touch with his real anger over the trauma he experienced as a child, which he still carries around with him as an adult. The obvious question is: Why? For one thing, he might be unwilling to show such vulnerability in public, especially in a film that is going to be aired on television. If he did, it most likely would have led to a powerful dramatic explosion, much like what eventually occurs when Shannon Baker and Audrey Henningham interact with Marcia Karp in *Symbiopsychotaxiplasm: Take 2½*.

There is another possible reason why the use of psychodrama proves less successful in *The Deep North*. Robert Siroka has indicated that the psychodramatists had a very limited opportunity to work with participants in the workshop. According to Siroka, there was not enough time set aside for the process of warming up to do psychodrama.[31] John Nolte emphasizes how crucial this first stage is for participants in a psychodrama. He writes:

> A group warms up to engaging in a psychodrama or another activity. A chosen member warms up to the role of protagonist and then to a relationship, a feeling, a mental state, or an event to be explored on the psychodrama stage. Directors and auxiliary egos also must warm up to their respective roles. We talk about warming up to roles both within and outside psychodrama. We warm up to emotional states. We also warm up to the spontaneity state.[32]

The lack of warmup time is not necessarily William Greaves's fault. In all likelihood, it had more to do with the exigencies and time restraints involved in producing a sponsored documentary for major broadcast television.

Greaves's two early documentaries that involved psychodrama, *In the Company of Men* and *The Deep North*, shed light on his interest in the pathology of racism that plagued, and plagues, the United States. In addition, they also highlight his considerable interest in the efficacy of psychodrama as a force to combat it. Yet the use of psychodrama as a technique involves a high degree of risk because the actual outcome always remains in question. In such terms, *In the Company of Men* proved more successful than *The Deep North*. Nevertheless, both *In the Company of Men* and *The Deep North* provide a fruitful context for viewing Greaves's best-known films, *Symbiopsychotaxiplasm: Take One* and *Symbiopsychotaxiplasm: Take 2½*. The two documentaries also aid in our understanding how J. L. Moreno's concepts of psychodrama and sociodrama served to influence Greaves's thinking and filmmaking during this critical phase of his career.

NOTES

1. For details about the genesis of the production, see William Greaves, "Log: *In the Company of Men*," *Film Library Quarterly* 3, no. 1 (Winter 1969–70): 29.
2. Greaves, 30.
3. Greaves, 30.
4. See R. Keith Sawyer, *Improvised Dialogues: Emergence and Creativity in Conversation* (Westport, Conn.: Ablex, 2003), 17.
5. René F. Marineau, "The Birth and Development of Sociometry: The Work and Legacy of Jacob Moreno (1889–1974)," *Social Psychology Quarterly* 70, no. 4 (2007): 322.
6. John Nolte, *The Philosophy, Theory and Methods of J. L. Moreno: The Man Who Tried to Become God* (London: Routledge, 2014), 20.
7. René F. Marineau, *Jacob Levy Moreno 1889–1974: Father of Psychodrama, Sociometry, and Group Psychotherapy* (London: Tavistock Routledge, 1989), 71.
8. Marineau, 72.
9. J. L. Moreno, *The Theatre of Spontaneity* (Beacon, N.Y.: Beacon House, 1973), a, 101, 102.
10. Marineau, *Jacob Levy Moreno*, 76–77.
11. Marineau, 133.
12. *Psychodrama in Action (in the 1960's)*, Moreno Movies Disc 3 (Mill Valley, Calif.: psychotherapy.net, 2007), DVD.
13. John McAllister, *Syllabus: Accompanying In the Company of Men* (New York: Newsweek Magazine, n.d.), 6.
14. Jonathan D. Moreno, *Impromptu Man: J. L. Moreno and the Origins of Psychodrama, Encounter Culture, and the Social Network* (New York: Bellevue Literary Press, 2014), 129.

15. Marineau *Jacob Levy Moreno*, 112.
16. Marineau, 71.
17. Peter Felix Kellermann, *Sociodrama and Collective Trauma* (London: Jessica Kingsley, 2007), 15.
18. Patricia Sternberg and Antonina Garcia, *Sociodrama: Who's in Your Shoes?* (New York: Praeger, 1989), 5.
19. Nat Brandt, *Harlem at War: The Black Experience in WWII* (Syracuse, N.Y.: Syracuse University Press, 1996), 207.
20. Nolte, *Philosophy, Theory and Methods*, 205–6.
21. A. Paul Hare and June Rabson Hare, *J. L. Moreno* (London: Sage, 1996), 59–62.
22. William Greaves, "100 Madison Avenues Will Be of No Help," *New York Times*, August 9, 1970 (reprinted in chap. 13 of this volume).
23. Greaves, "Log," 33.
24. Greaves, 33.
25. Greaves, 34.
26. Greaves, 34.
27. Moreno, *Theatre of Spontaneity*, 5, 42, 8.
28. Moreno, *Psychodrama: First Volume*, 4th ed. (Beacon, N.Y.: Beacon House, 1972), xii.
29. Greaves, "Log," 34.
30. Greaves, 34.
31. Robert Siroka, conversation with the author.
32. Nolte, *Philosophy, Theory and Methods*, 85.

11
Pugilism and Performance

William Greaves, Muhammad Ali, and the Making of The Fight

ALEXANDER JOHNSTON

THE FIGHT GAME

"You're as good with that camera, as I am with my fists." So says Muhammad Ali, mid-sit-up, to the filmmaker William Greaves. The image we see is not shot by Greaves but one in which the filmmaker appears, in the act of filming. An upside-down, over-the-shoulder shot, it is taken from Ali's perspective, meaning Greaves's camera is trained on both the boxer and the other cameraperson. The image and the snatch of dialogue come midway through the first half of Greaves's film *The Fight*, which documents the "Fight of the Century," a famed 1971 boxing match between Ali and Joe Frazier at New York's Madison Square Garden. It is the most explicitly self-reflexive moment in the film, signaling the deep sense of connection that Greaves felt with Ali, a fellow "furious Black" intent on disrupting the racist status quo that defined (and continues to define) the fight game, the film industry, and the nation as a whole.[1]

If you purchased a copy of the 2005 DVD release of the documentary that Greaves made about the Ali-Frazier fight, you would not find this scene. Nor would you find the sequence where a middle-aged white man calls Ali "a disgrace to the nation," or one where Greaves makes legible the carefully constructed artifice of promotional sports media. Examining the DVD case, you might notice that it actually bears the name *Ali, The Fighter*, not *The Fight*. Similarly, you might notice that the title at the beginning of the film is also not *The Fight* but *The Fighters*.

To write about William Greaves's documentary depicting the "Fight of the Century" is to reckon with a confusing and convoluted postproduction,

FIGURE 11.1 Poster for first Ali/Frazier fight.

distribution, and exhibition process, notable for its inconstancy and multiplicity. To begin with, one has to deal with the fact that one is not technically writing about a single, discrete work but rather three variations of a film bearing three different (but confusingly similar) names: *The Fighters* (1972),[2] *Ali, the Fighter* (1975), and the unreleased *The Fight*.[3] Of these variations, the only one that is widely accessible is the DVD release of *The Fighters*. This low-quality DVD transfer started life as a bootlegged, unlicensed version of the film, before the distributing company, Anchor Bay, negotiated a licensing deal with Chartwell Artists, the agency founded by the bout's promoter, Jerry Perenchio.[4] *Ali, the Fighter* has not been available for viewing since its original 1975 release, when it was screened as one part of an Ali diptych alongside Rick Baxter's film *Ali, the Man*.[5] The third film, *The Fight*, was Greaves's preferred take on Ali, but it was unseen in its day and continues to lack any wide distribution. However, *The Fight* was screened as part of the seminal Brooklyn Museum Greaves retrospective in 1991, which brought renewed interest to the filmmaker's work, and it has since come to be seen as the definitive version of the film.

In this essay, I seek to unravel the confusing and convoluted history of Greaves's Ali-Frazier project. I do so through an analysis of the two variations of the film that are known to exist in the present day, *The Fight* and *The Fighters*. I detail the production process and offer a comparative close reading of each film, including an analysis of what was cut from *The Fight* for the theatrical release of *The Fighters*. Alongside this is a consideration of Greaves's interest in making a film about Ali. I argue that this interest was rooted in a sense of identification that the filmmaker felt with the fighter, not only as a successful, prominent, and politically outspoken African-American public figure but as a media artist engaging in a kind of performative deconstruction of mass media forms.[6]

Driving my analysis is an argument for the significance of *The Fight* as a masterpiece of social documentary. While the film constitutes a hybrid work within Greaves's oeuvre, I assert that it benefits from this formal and thematic liminality. As the first feature made by Greaves following the completion of his more famous (and, in recent years, less neglected) masterpiece, *Symbiopsychotaxiplasm: Take One*, *The Fight* engages aspects of the formal experimentation and deconstruction of media tropes that characterize that film. In fact, Ali's performance as "himself" can be understood as a continuation of Greaves's performance of "himself" in the earlier film. *The Fight*, however, also enlists some of the more traditional formal strategies Greaves would utilize during his run on *Black Journal* and shares thematic concerns that explicitly mobilize many of his pre- and post-*Symbio* productions, including explorations of black leadership and representation in the media, and a rigorous analysis of the intersection of race and class in American society.⁷ The result is a daring yet accessible film, a melding of Greaves's camera and Ali's fists that lays bare the brutality of the fight game, both inside and outside of the ring.

"SOME TRICK BAG!"

In early 1971 William Greaves was approached by the talent agent Jerry Perenchio and his partner, Robin French, to produce a feature film about the Ali-Frazier fight. In his own words, Greaves "leapt at the chance," having "always wanted to do a fight film." What's more, as Ali's first title fight since the reinstatement of his boxing license, this "was not only a contest of physical strength and valor between two very different kinds of men but . . . a contest drenched in controversy."⁸ On Perenchio's part, the details and reasoning behind hiring Greaves are not known. By this time, however, Greaves had established himself as an African-American filmmaker producing insightful and complex media works about the contemporary "black experience," in his role as executive producer of the television newsmagazine *Black Journal*, and as the director of the feature documentary *Still a Brother* (1968). He was a seasoned documentarian, having cut his teeth during a multi-year run at the Canadian National Film Board, followed by a position making documentaries for an agency of the United Nations. Returning to the United States in the early 1960s, Greaves made two films for the United States Information Agency (USIA), including a 1966 documentary about a seminal Pan-African arts and music festival in Dakar, Senegal, *The First World Festival of Negro Arts*.⁹ Taken together, the director's extensive professional experience and demonstrated track record of producing thoughtful media about contemporary race issues likely made him an appealing choice to produce a documentary about the racially charged spectacle of the Ali-Frazier bout.

Jerry Perenchio was the fight's primary promoter, but most of the bout's five-million-dollar purse was put up by the businessman Jack Kent Cooke, then owner of two Southern California sports franchises, the NBA's Los Angeles Lakers and the NHL's Los Angeles Kings. Both men end up figuring prominently in Greaves's depiction of the event. Interestingly, despite being the fight's driving force, Perenchio was not himself a boxing fan, with the printed fight program describing his "knowledge of the ring world" as "cursory." Yet Perenchio believed—and was able to convince Cooke—that the closed-circuit market for the fight would be a cash cow.¹⁰ Rather than being shown live on television, the fight was to be broadcast via closed circuit to movie theaters around the country. Ticket prices for the live screening averaged $20 (roughly equivalent to $125 per ticket today). This was a prohibitive sum for many in 1971, and the issue became a focal point for civil rights groups protesting the lack of accessibility to the fight and lack of financial benefit to African-American communities.

On top of filming the fight, Perenchio hired a film crew to produce a series of staged vignettes in the weeks before the bout, depicting the fighters at their respective training camps, and trading barbs during press conferences and contrived encounters with each other.[11] Burt Lancaster, who was an avid boxing fan and close friend of Perenchio, served as a kind of host for these sequences, and as a color commentator for the fight. This production process ran parallel to, and apart from, Greaves's own, yet it offered him a unique opportunity to repeat a key strategy from *Symbiopsychotaxiplasm: Take One*; namely, making the media production process a central focus of the film itself. In addition, the protests surrounding ticket prices for the fight broadcast gave the filmmaker a framework for exploring the racial politics surrounding the event.

Unlike the closed-circuit crew, Greaves's task was to produce a film for a later theatrical release, documenting not only the match but the promotion, reception, deal-making, logistics, media coverage, and general spectacle that surrounded it. Beyond producing a round-by-round depiction of the fight, it is unknown what specific guidelines Perenchio gave Greaves, but the promoter seems to have been ambitious regarding the scope of the production. Greaves was provided with extensive access to the major players involved in the fight and to prime viewing angles for filming the fight itself, and he was tasked with shooting throughout the country and abroad.[12] He describes the elaborate production process in his 1978 essay "Two Fighters on Film":

> Within a week of signing the contract we had camera crews shuttling about the country and in Europe covering all the pre-fight events: the business and closed-circuit communications arrangements, the promotion, the training camps, the people on the street.... It was no small job just to keep on top of the incredible pace set by Jerry Perenchio.... The fight itself was covered by twelve camera crews using twelve 16mm Éclair cameras, strategically located to make certain we obtained a good view of every move the fighters made. Not even the judges could have seen the fight the way the cameras did. (135)

The "Fight of the Century" lived up to its hyperbolic billing, both in and out of the ring. A brutal and bloody affair, the fight went all fifteen rounds,

FIGURE 11.2 William Greaves at Madison Square Garden, preparing to shoot the Ali/Frazier fight in 1971. Photographed by David Greaves? Courtesy Louise Greaves.

culminating in a victory by decision for Frazier. With his twelve cameras, Greaves was able to produce comprehensive coverage of the entire bout. And with multiple film crews at his disposal, he was able to produce similarly comprehensive coverage of the spectacle surrounding the event. This included not only the prefight press conferences and glamorous A-list celebrities in attendance at Madison Square Garden, but also the immense outlay of labor, logistical efforts, and economic negotiations (and machinations) required to pull off an event of this scale.[13]

Distilling this massive array of footage into a coherent feature film required an innovative approach to structure and form. Both *The Fighters* and *The Fight* reflect a unique amalgamation of genres: the first half of each film is an observational documentary examining the production and promotion of the fight. The second half focuses on the fight itself, shown in its entirety, without titles or nondiegetic sound, including play-by-play announcing or color commentary.[14] This unusual bifurcated structure is what is most likely to jump out at contemporary viewers, yet as Scott MacDonald asserts, the film's original novelty lay in Greaves's attempt to turn "a documentary about Muhammad Ali . . . into a kind of story," an approach that has since become commonplace, "but at the time... was still a relatively new idea."[15] Greaves himself concurred, writing that his film constituted a "new form," which he dubbed a "docudrama," because "it catches people in actual dialogue in real life, in highly dramatic situations."[16]

While Greaves's assessment perhaps reflects some degree of self-aggrandizement, the first halves of *The Fighters* and *The Fight* certainly offer a dramatic depiction of the lead-up to the match. In both films, the filmmaker pinballs around a dizzying array of players and entities instrumental to the event (the Ali and Frazier camps, the broadcasters and journalists, the protesters, promoters and money men, etc.), his cinéma-vérité approach propelled by a judiciously used hard-funk score. As with his depiction of the fight, Greaves eschews the use of subtitles or voiceover to provide context for the proceedings or identify the figures on screen. The decision seems compelled by his interest in supplanting the didacticism of traditional documentary tropes with a more dramatic and immersive diegesis. However, it also has the effect (whether intended or not) of leaving the viewer constantly playing catch-up, which further heightens the drama and feeling of frantic action surrounding the execution of such a massive event.[17]

Greaves publicly described the project as an "in-depth study of the two fighters as well as a blow-by-blow record of the fight itself," yet his vision for the film was actually much loftier. As described by Louise Archambault Greaves, William Greaves's widow, the director was "fascinated with the power structure of society... and he thought the fight symbolized American society." Central to Greaves's position was an analysis of the intersectional nature of race and class, and its ugly (but symbolically potent) articulation through the event of the fight: "Here you see two black guys knocking each other's brains out to make a buck. While white folks are covering the story, or cheering them on. And the money is coming from another source. The money is creating this."[18]

Louise Greaves's expression of her husband's position is corroborated in a typed-up series of production notes, documenting discussions that Greaves and his crew were having about the raw footage and its potential inclusion in the film.[19] For instance, in notes on a sequence filmed on a bus, the driver is quoted as saying: "Joe Frazier and Ali have hustled the system... they've put the white man into a trick bag." This quote is followed by a sharply worded suggestion for its inclusion in the film, typed in all capital letters: "PUT THIS LINE IN COUNTERPOINT OF FRAZIER AND ALI BEATING SHIT OUT OF EACH OTHER... Some trick bag!"[20]

It is difficult to imagine that Perenchio, as the fight's primary promoter and one of its primary financial beneficiaries, envisioned bankrolling a film with this as its central message.²¹ And indeed, when compared to the unreleased *The Fight*, *The Fighters* is more subtle in conveying its politics. A half-hour shorter than Greaves's preferred version, the theatrical release cuts some of the material that explicitly deals with the racial politics surrounding the fight, as well as a key scene depicting the production of one of the prefight closed-circuit sequences.²² For all that—and despite a choppy jaggedness that likely resulted from the need to obtain a shorter run time—Greaves was still able to insert into the film a sense of his larger social concerns. While *The Fight* is in most ways a superior work, analyzing the two versions together offers an object lesson in Greaves's mastery of the observational documentary as a form for exploring social issues, regardless of editorial and commercial constraints.

TWO FIGHT FILMS

Greaves's "docudrama" approach, his desire to tell a story, in no way diminishes the observational rigor he brings to bear on the social and economic forces structuring the event. "Who's got power? Who's pulling the strings?"²³ These were the questions underlying the project, according to Louise Greaves. There are numerous examples in both films of the director articulating the racial dynamics inherent to these questions. Given the nature of the event ("two black guys knocking each other's brains out" for the amusement and benefit of whites), these dynamics are often shown playing out through the simultaneous spectacularization and dehumanization of black athletic bodies. In scenes depicting training sessions for instance, Greaves regularly cuts away from the action in the ring to shots of older white men "assessing" the boxers' bodies as they spar. Similarly, during a press conference with Jack Kent Cooke, the wily, unctuous money man refers to the bout as a "primitive contest" between the two African-American fighters.

A key scene that appears in both films exemplifies Greaves's intersectional analysis of the power hierarchy structuring the event. The scene depicts the civil rights protests against the fight, which centered on two specific issues. The first was the exorbitant ticket prices for the closed-circuit broadcast, making viewing the fight inaccessible to many African Americans. The second issue was that the bout was being funded and promoted by two white men, Perenchio and Cooke, and that none of the substantial profits from the event would be going to African-American communities.²⁴ The scene opens with establishing shots of picketers outside of Frazier's training gym. The mostly African-American crowd marches back and forth on the sidewalk, wearing signs that read "Lower Ali-Frazier Ticket Prices." Greaves then cuts to the gym's interior, where we see one of the protesters from the street confronting Frazier's trainer and manager, Yancey ("Yank") Durham. As the representative for the reigning heavyweight champion, Durham was the person responsible for accepting Perenchio and Cooke's bid to bankroll and promote the fight.

The protester chides Durham: "Outside the money that your fighter and Ali are gonna get, none of that money will go into the black community, or the poor community." Durham, a pugnacious, middle-aged African-American man, responds, "What do I care how much money go here, how much money go there? . . . I'm doing the right thing that I think is right for this fighter I'm working with." He explains that he solicited bids from both black and white investment groups, and that Perenchio and Cooke were the first with the money. This leads to a forceful diatribe in which Durham rationalizes his decision for accepting the bid by reflecting on his own economic precarity: "Nobody has ever given me anything. The white group has never given me nothing. The black group has never given me nothing. I've worked for everything I've gotten. I worked on the railroad. I worked as a stevedore. I've worked with fighters. . . . This is the only fighter I've had that's been successful. And in return, I ain't giving up nothing!"

Durham's justification comes off less as prideful individualism than as a frank articulation of his social location. Despite hitting it big with Frazier, he harbors no illusions about his place in the social and economic hierarchy, as a middle-aged, working-class black man. He doesn't see altruism or racial solidarity as a choice afforded to him. Acknowledging this reality, the protester says they will turn their attention to Perenchio and Cooke: "We can still deal with these Hollywood boys." Durham's response to this concretizes for the viewer his sense of precarity and lack of power: "I don't have no rights. I have to live where they tell me to live at. . . . I don't want to go to New York, but Cooke is saying 'you go to New York.'"

Durham's encounter with the protester is perhaps the most explicit illustration of "who's got power" and "who's pulling the strings." However, Greaves's desire to produce a systemic and structural critique of the fight-game-writ-large—rather than a specific and discrete exploration of this single event—means that the form and structure of both films reflects this overarching analysis. In his use of editing and sequencing to further illuminate the hierarchies of power determining the event, and to show how racially coded narratives are actually used to promote it, we can see Greaves's mastery of the social documentary form. This is on display in two sets of sequences, appearing (with variations) in both films. The first juxtaposes scenes of Ali and Perenchio, and the second complicates dominant narratives about Frazier.

The opening credits of *The Fighters* play over a sequence of Ali holding court on a city street, drumming up business for the fight. A lively and compelling performance, it is, as Richard Brody describes it, an example of Ali's "aesthetic outside the ring, a jovially boisterous and boastful encounter with a New York City bus and its passengers that displays his thrilling real-life performance art."[25] Opening the film in this way, Greaves—who called Ali "a whole drama in himself"—displays an understanding of the power of the boxers' charismatic performances, their aesthetic appeal.[26]

The director, however, is also executing a kind of bait and switch. Following brief shots of a press conference between Ali and Frazier, and of a group of black men debating the fight on a street corner, Greaves cuts to the interior of an expensive town car. Sitting in the backseat is Jerry Perenchio, a well-coiffed, middle-aged white man wearing a heavy winter coat. The film's score comes in for the first time—a hypnotic and funky flute vamp backed by a roll of conga drums—as Perenchio gazes out the window of the town car, regally surveying the streets of Manhattan. We now cut to a handheld shot from outside of the car, which is stopped in front of a skyscraper. The camera tracks the driver, wearing a chauffeur's uniform, as he exits and walks briskly around the car, opening the door for Perenchio and another man, who proceed to walk into the building. After they do so, the camera pans up to reveal the imposing scale of the building, its roof barely visible against a dull gray sky.

With this opening scene, Greaves suggests the power dynamics between Ali the performer and the fight's sponsors and overlords, which will be made explicit in the sequence with Durham. Ali may own the streets, he may be the "people's champ," Greaves seems to be telling us, but this white man, conducting his business up in the sky, owns the city.[27] It is a perspective that echoes the filmmaker's own experiences as a black man confronting what he called a "wall of racism in the motion picture industry."[28] Greaves himself makes this connection explicit in his previously cited article for the *Black American Literature Forum*, "Two Fighters on Film." Ostensibly about the making of *The Fighters*, the "two fighters" of the title has a double meaning, referencing Ali and Frazier, as well as Ali and Greaves himself. While offering insight on the production process of the film, the bulk of the article chronicles Greaves's struggles to establish himself as an African-American director, whose "goal was not only to direct and produce films, but to change the direction of films" (137). In Ali he identifies a kindred spirit in audacity, someone willing to challenge the status quo despite the overwhelming structural forces arrayed against him.

As Greaves details, he got his start as an actor but was "revolted" by the types of roles he was offered, which were "not only unacceptable but insulting." The racist archetypes that dominated available roles for actors of color compelled his move behind the camera, where, he writes, "I could control what appeared on the screen" (136). In both *The Fighters* and *The Fight*, we see Greaves's sensitivity to this issue, and his directorial control, in the subtle way he problematizes the racial stereotypes that structure the bout's dominant narrative, the contrasting styles and personas of Ali and Frazier. As with the opening section, he achieves this through a juxtaposition of sequences: a description of the boxers by the film's "fight film consultant," Jim Jacobs, and a scene chronicling Frazier's visit to a black church.

The first sequence begins with Jacobs, encircled by a phalanx of observers, discussing Ali's famed speed as a puncher. He details an experiment he conducted using a film synchronizer, comparing Ali's jab with that of the legendary (and legendarily fast) middleweight boxer Sugar Ray Robinson, concluding "Clay is the fastest human I have ever seen."[29] Jacobs gets to his feet now and begins shadowboxing, illustrating the "tools of Muhammad Ali's trade." Ali "throws punches, bing, bing," he explains, but when he does so, "he doesn't have bad intentions." In contrast, Jacobs asserts, "When Frazier throws punches, they're not the tools of his trade. When he throws a punch at you, he wants to kill you."

Jacobs characterizes the lighter-skinned Ali, despite his controversial standing, as playful and good-natured, and the taciturn and darker-skinned Frazier as brutish, unskilled, and violent. It is a neat, legible, racially determined narrative, which Greaves promptly dismantles, enlisting the same bait-and-switch strategy as in the previous example. He cuts from Jacobs to a close-up of Frazier's stony face, looking sufficiently brutish and violent. This image is followed by a wide shot showing the boxer sitting on a church pew, listening to the choir sing. We see the choir, then other parishioners, then cut back to the wide shot of Frazier, and finally back to the same close-up on his face. This time however, Frazier bobs his head to the beat as the music starts working on him. He begins to sing and, as he does so, breaks out into a massive joyful grin. Now the camera zooms out to catch the fighter, unable to contain himself, rising to his feet as he sings and claps his hands.[30]

It is a masterful juxtaposition of narrative and reality. Greaves identifies the racial stereotype inherent in Jacobs's characterization of Frazier and quietly but pointedly discredits it. Frazier's beaming face, however, is not simply a repudiation of Jacobs, who was a respected boxing mind with fairly progressive racial politics. It is also part of Greaves's broader deconstruction of the modern athletic spectacle and its grand narratives, which hail audiences at the same time that they obscure the unequal distribution of power, often along racial lines. He is not only trying, then, as he purports, to "change the direction of films." Rather, Greaves is using his skills as a filmmaker to make the audience cognizant of the hegemonic representational regimes that maintain and perpetuate entrenched power structures.

"FILM PEOPLE" AND "FIGHT PEOPLE"

Describing Greaves's editing process, Louise Greaves makes a basic distinction between the project's "film people" (Greaves and his crew) and the "fight people" (Perenchio, Cooke, and their associates): "Bill was told, 'Oh, you cut this, cut that, cut that,' and that was it. 'You know, we can't sell it otherwise.' They weren't interested in the film; they were interested in the fight. And the money that they could make from the fight."[31] In both *The Fighters* and *The Fight*, Greaves produced a nuanced exploration of the social and economic forces at play in the modern athletic spectacle, offering the viewer a sustained articulation of Stuart Hall's pithy observation that "race is the modality through which class is experienced."[32] However, in the significant differences that do exist between the two films, we can clearly discern the effect of the "fight people" on determining what was suitable for a theatrical release.

Louise Greaves asserts that the push for a shorter run time was likely motivated by a desire to program additional screenings of the film during its theatrical run, thus increasing the box office take. This may well be true. What was actually cut from the film, however, tends to minimize the film's most explicit social critiques and Greaves's deconstructionist tendencies. This includes moments depicting the ugly antagonism directed toward Ali by white boxing fans and a scene depicting the closed-circuit production process.

The opening sequences of *The Fight* present a similar juxtaposition of Ali and Perenchio as described earlier. In this iteration of the film, however, that dichotomy is superseded by a new trichotomy. Like *The Fighters*, *The Fight* opens with Ali in the streets. Yet now a loud, off-screen exhortation of "Right on brother!" dominates the sound mix, giving the viewer an immediate sense of the filmmaker's solidarity with Ali. The ensuing sequence of black men debating the fight on a street corner ends with a hard cut to a middle-aged white man explaining why he has "no interest" in the fight: "This fella they call Clay or Muhammad Ali or whatever he wants to call himself is a disgrace to the nation. When I have to see young kids run up to Canada to avoid the draft and that bum flounced along, is running around loose, and people admire him? This champion fight is a farce."

From here, Greaves cuts to an image of Muhammad Ali, in shirt and tie, giving a speech in what appears to be a hotel ballroom. Shot from a low angle, with a single condenser mic in front of him, Ali looks both suave and authoritative. He proceeds to lay out the myriad reasons why people are rooting against him in the upcoming fight: "A lot of them want me whipped because of the draft! A lot of them want me whipped because of religion! A lot of 'em want me whipped because I'm black!" Now Greaves cuts to Perenchio in the town car as the funk score comes in.

The insertion of "Right on brother," the antagonistic white man, and Ali's speech results in a more confrontational opening than in *The Fighters*. The articulation of the event's power structures remains intact, but it is now complemented by a much more explicit illustration of the racial dynamics at play. A trichotomy is formed, first between the black men on the street corner and the vitriolic white man, and then between the white man and Ali himself. Instead of a subtle critique of the intersectional nature of race and class in determining the power dynamics and hierarchies of the fight game (and the nation at large), we have a more explicit one about xenophobic perceptions of Ali as un-American. As with the later Jacobs/Frazier sequence, Greaves gives us the perception versus reality between the white man's assessment of Ali and who Ali actually is.

This sequence echoes a key representational strategy the filmmaker uses during his run as producer of the seminal Afrocentric newsmagazine *Black Journal*. Through casting decisions and a canny use of sequencing, Greaves would invert dominant racial stereotypes, presenting whites as zealots and blacks as respectable and articulate. As Adam Knee and Charles Musser observe, *Black Journal* regularly put "reasonable, articulate, and authoritative" black voices "in the position of judging the antisocial behavior of hysterical, unreasonable whites." In this way, the authors argue, "traditional codings of authority by race were inverted." The implications of such an inversion had particular importance in the realm of popular media, in that "the nature of mainstream television representations stands exposed."[33] Having seen the effectiveness of this approach on *Black Journal*, Greaves enlisted it again in *The Fight*.

While *The Fight* foregrounds a critique of racial representation, a key scene showing the filming of a telephone conversation between Ali and Frazier for the closed-circuit broadcast gives viewers a glimpse behind the curtain of the nuts-and-bolts of mass media production more generally. The scene opens on a medium shot of two closed-circuit cameras. Greaves's camera pans left, past a boom pole operator, to a man talking on a pay phone. Burt Lancaster suddenly walks into the frame and asks someone off camera: "What do you want me to do? Pick the phone up?" The man on the phone explains to Lancaster, while gesturing to the handset: "This is the open line now, we're gonna have to keep it open." He then points to the rotary dial of the phone and mimes the act of dialing, telling Lancaster, "So you'll have to fake this."

Greaves cuts to Ali now, postworkout, lying face down on a bench in his bathrobe. He is surrounded by a large closed-circuit production crew being given orders by a technocratic director in a cream-colored leisure suit. The director bends down to Ali, asks him to sit up and remove his robe, hands him the phone, and tells him that Lancaster is on the other end. As the production crew scurries around setting up the shot, Ali waits patiently, phone at his ear. Greaves's camera is positioned behind Ali, the boxer framed in a wide shot. While Ali waits, the director zooms in on one of the closed-circuit camera monitors, revealing a close up of the boxer's face.

Having established two different locations, Greaves now intercuts between Lancaster and Ali, and then Frazier (to whom Lancaster has passed the phone) and Ali. The boxers attempt to engage in the usual prefight trash talk but are immediately interrupted by the director, who doesn't like the look of a pile of towels sitting beside Ali and halts the proceedings so he can move them. As he does so, Ali talks quietly into the phone to Frazier, explaining the delay. When they are finally given the green light to proceed, the two men are out of sync—perhaps due to the delay and a poor connection—and keep stepping on each other's words. This plays most awkwardly for Ali, who is twice interrupted while trying to deliver one of his trademark rhymes: "I'm glad you can sing and have a band for hire because after the ... hey Joe, listen to this." He finally and halfheartedly delivers the full rhyme on his third attempt, "I'm glad you can sing and have a band for hire, because after this fight you must retire."

The scene offers a complex picture of the interwoven layers of reality and unreality in the fight promotion and production process. It does not undermine the truth claim of Greaves's documentation of the event, but it reminds us that despite the very real boxing match at its center, and the very real financial stakes involved, the film's subject is defined by artifice and fakery. While the behind-the-scenes machinations of the event are depicted throughout both *The Fight* and *The Fighters*, this is the clearest picture we get of the mass media apparatus at work, troubling the ideology of "liveness" that defined the hegemony of televisual media during this period.[34]

In a 2016 article about the film, Richard Brody claims that *The Fight* shows Ali's superior charisma and performative abilities as compared to Frazier.[35]

Throughout much of the film his claim rings true. Yet in this scene, Ali's stiltedness and inability to shift gears from his usual shtick make him appear both stiff and flustered. Frazier by contrast, is measured and nonplussed. Ali does not "break character" per se, but through Greaves's inclusion of these closed-circuit "outtakes," the filmmaker shows the artifice and craft that go into making Muhammad Ali "Muhammad Ali." By showing what was not meant to be seen, Greaves undercuts the mythmaking apparatus surrounding Ali. By extension, he also undercuts the racialized juxtaposition of the two boxers, as articulated by Jacobs and others. The scene offers viewers a crucial reminder of the substantial differences between narrative and reality, and the central role of the media in collapsing and erasing those differences.

"TWO FIGHTERS ON FILM"

While documenting the Ali-Frazier bout, Greaves was also editing his previous film, *Symbiopsychotaxiplasm: Take One*. We can see a clear through-line from that film's meta-textual formal approach and philosophical exploration of media reality to Greaves's depiction of the closed-circuit production process. As with Ali and Frazier's phone call in *The Fight*, *Symbiopsychotaxiplasm: Take One* constitutes an elaborately choreographed but intentionally messy object lesson on the conflation of reality and performance. Greaves plays "himself" in the earlier film, as an incompetent director holding auditions in Central Park for a scene depicting an argument between a couple. The rest of the cast and crew, however, are seemingly kept in the dark about the fact of Greaves's performance, believing they are actually partaking in the audition process and its documentation. Their response to his seeming incompetence and boorishness, which ultimately results in a mutiny on the set, is captured by multiple film crews tasked with filming the production of the production.[36] The film-within-a-film-within-a-film structure reveals the underlying power dynamics inherent in the production process and shows how the act of performance extends into the ostensible reality behind the camera.

If Greaves needed to create the conditions for the production of this illuminating meta-context in *Symbiopsychotaxiplasm: Take One*, the presence of the closed-circuit crew allowed him to enact a kind of ready-made iteration in *The Fight*. Similarly, in Muhammad Ali he had an on-screen proxy, muse, and compatriot. Greaves identified Ali as a kindred spirit, a black man who rejected the unbearable compromises of assimilation into his chosen field. Yet in addition to

Ali's audacity, the filmmaker was also likely drawn to the boxer's sophisticated deconstruction of popular media forms through his on-screen performances. Both the exaggerated nature of Greaves's performance in *Symbiopsychotaxiplasm: Take One* and the fact that his crew is largely ignorant that he is performing at all echo Ali's own memorable media performances. Perhaps the most famous example is Ali's performance at the weigh-in before the first Ali-Liston bout, the fight that resulted in his first world heavyweight title. His behavior during that event was so outré, and his performance so believable, that the physician for the Miami Boxing Commission described him as "emotionally unbalanced, scared to death, and liable to crack up before he enters the ring."[37]

Apart from the closed-circuit scene—which was excluded from the theatrically released *The Fighters*—Greaves's Ali-Frazier project mostly eschews the destabilizing formal experimentation and explicit self-reflexiveness of *Symbiopsychotaxiplasm: Take One*. The presence of Ali, however, allowed the director to do some of the same critical work of that earlier film, despite its more traditional approach. We see an example of this in a sequence immediately following the closed-circuit scene, in which Ali draws attention to the media's role in narrativizing the event. Shot at Ali's training camp before a sparring session open to journalists and the public, the scene shows the boxer clothed in a white bathrobe, pacing around the ring and pontificating. The journalists are seated on one side of the ring, the spectators on the other. Ali playfully mocks the former, calling them "bigshots" who receive "free steak dinners" and always "know the news first." He tells them he will circumvent them when giving his prediction for the fight, instead offering it directly to the public. In so doing, he burnishes his populist credentials while at the same time asserting his independence from, and power over, an often-critical press corps, a number of whom still refuse to call him Ali. On a more fundamental level, he is making the audience (both us as viewers of Greaves's film and those at ringside) aware of the central role of the media in the production of the spectacle. Being a master showman, Ali is also both calling attention to and at the same time exploiting the fabricated and performative nature of the prediction ritual. While there is no doubt that he will predict victory, he teasingly waves around an envelope in which he has recorded his prognostication. Written on the outside of the envelope: "THE SECRET OF MUHAMMAD ALI."

"You're as good with that camera, as I am with my fists." So says Muhammad Ali to William Greaves, game respecting game. The result of their pugilistic "collaboration" is *The Fight*, a restless and kaleidoscopic film that is unified by a comprehensive and clear-eyed interrogation of the intersections of race and class that structure the fight game, mass media, American society, and life under capitalism. Greaves's formidable skills as a filmmaker and social documentarian are on full display, providing the viewer an immersive fly-on-the-wall experience that doubles as an incisive and comprehensive social critique. Akiva Gottlieb asserts that Greaves's oeuvre reflects a political worldview that "oscillated between radicalism and liberalism."[38] *The Fight* most assuredly falls in the former category. It does not pull its punches.

In our current historical moment, the Overton Window that frames acceptable political discourse in the United States is in flux. The election of Donald Trump as president in 2016 opened the floodgates for protofascist, racist, and xenophobic rhetoric to enter mainstream media discourse. We have seen, however, a corresponding rise of voices of radical resistance on the Left, many of which are explicitly (and intersectionally) anticapitalist. Within that context, *The Fight* has renewed resonance and a place in contemporary public discourse. It offers viewers a lively but pointed analysis of the hegemonic functions of mass media spectacles and is a masterful example of the social documentary form, with much to teach the current generation of filmmakers.

And yet the film is almost entirely unavailable to contemporary viewers. Louise Greaves states that her husband gave the original negative of *The Fight* back to Chartwell Artists, but it has since been lost. The version in her possession is a time-stamped digital transfer from VHS. Shortly before Jerry Perenchio died—and shortly after Greaves and Ali passed away—Louise Greaves called Perenchio to discuss the possibility of finally releasing *The Fight*. He claimed he was in the process of negotiating a sale of the rights to the film to a cable network. He died before the deal was consummated.[39] Hopefully, between growing interest in the work of William Greaves by scholars and filmgoers and seemingly never-ending interest in Muhammad Ali, this is neither the end of the story nor of *The Fight*.

NOTES

1. "Furious Black" is a term used in William Greaves, "100 Madison Avenues Will Be of No Help," *New York Times*, August 9, 1970 (reprinted in chap. 13 of this volume).
2. The date 1974 is often incorrectly cited (including on Greaves's IMDb page) as the year *The Fighters* was originally theatrically released. This is perhaps due to a review of the film published in the *New York Times* on January 5, 1974, which references a

run of *The Fighters* at Harlem's Apollo Theater, beginning the prior day. However, newspaper advertisements from the period date the actual release of the film to the spring of 1972.
3. Greaves's widow, Louise Greaves, provided me with a DVD transfer of *The Fight*.
4. Louise Greaves, interview with author, November 14, 2018.
5. This is the film that confusingly gives its name to the mistitled DVD of *The Fighters*.
6. As indicated by the quote that begins this essay, Ali had in turn identified with Greaves.
7. I say "explicitly" here because, while these concerns are also at the forefront of *Symbiopsychotaxiplasm: Take One*, their articulation is intentionally muted. As Akiva Gottlieb argues: "One gets the sense that for Greaves, any overt introduction of the race question would be, in Barthesian terms, a way of imposing a limit upon the text." Gottlieb, "'Just Another Word for Jazz': The Signifying Auteur in William Greaves's *Symbiopsychotaxiplasm: Take One*," *Black Camera* 5, no. 1 (Fall 2013): 172. (An excerpt of Gottlieb's essay is reprinted as chap. 23 of this volume.)
8. William Greaves, "Two Fighters on Film," *Black American Literature Forum* 12, no. 4 (Winter 1978): 135.
9. See Adam Knee and Charles Musser, "William Greaves, Documentary Filmmaking, and the African-American Experience," chap. 1 in this volume.
10. "Anatomy of a Deal" fight program.
11. The exact intended purpose of shooting these sequences is unclear, though the most likely explanation is that they would have played in movie theaters as a lead-in to the live closed-circuit broadcast of the fight.
12. Ironically, the person that Greaves initially had the hardest time getting access to was Ali himself. According to Louise Greaves, Ali had not read the clause in his contract that required his participation in the documentary and was annoyed when Perenchio notified him of the production. While Ali would eventually come to respect Greaves, his frustration is playfully apparent in an early sequence of the film, which depicts a car chase between the director and the boxer in Miami. Louise Greaves, interview with author.
13. Attendees captured by Greaves's cameras included Diana Ross, Mia Farrow and Woody Allen, Robert Goulet, Miles Davis, and Frank Sinatra, who had been "hired" by *Life* magazine to photograph the fight.
14. The only parts of the fight shortened through editing are the breaks between rounds.
15. Debra McClutchy, *Discovering William Greaves* DVD, Disc 1, *Symbiopsychotaxiplasm: Two Takes by William Greaves* (Irvington, N.Y.: Criterion Collection, 2006).
16. Greaves, "Two Fighters on Film," 135. Writing in 1978, Greaves may not have been familiar with what was then becoming the primary definition of the term "docudrama" as a film form usually classified as either an adjacent genre or a subgenre of documentary. That usage seems to have entered into common parlance in the 1970s, to describe dramatized reenactments of real events, particularly in television movies and miniseries of the period. Famous docudramas produced in the United

States during this period include *Brian's Song* (1971) and *Roots* (1977). Greaves's films, which contain no reenactments, do not seem consistent with this definition.

However, Çiçek Coşkun identifies an earlier description of the term that does seem closer to Greaves's usage. In an unpublished paper on docudrama, "Docudrama: The Real (Hi)story," Coşkun cites the work of Edgar E. Willis, who in his book *Foundations in Broadcasting: Radio and Television* (1951) defines the docudrama as "a program presenting information or exploring an issue in a dramatic fashion, with story emphasis usually on the social significance of the problem." Perhaps it is this broader definition, centered on a work's dramatic presentation instead of the act of reenactment, that Greaves was thinking about when he called his film a docudrama.

17. This dynamic is likely even more pronounced for a contemporary viewer, as details of the event and the figures depicted are increasingly obscured by the passage of time.
18. Louise Greaves, interview with author.
19. "William Greaves Production Notes Typescript," original manuscript, 1971, in private collection of Louise Greaves.
20. This sequence did not appear in either available version of the film. While Greaves ultimately went with the bifurcated structure (separating the fight itself from the rest of the event), the meaty, thudding, brutal soundscape of the fight, sans narrativization through Greaves's editing or the inclusion of play-by-play announcing, viscerally drives home the point.
21. This is not to say that Perenchio necessarily disagreed with Greaves's assessment of the fight game as a brutal metaphor for racial and economic injustice in America. Rather, I am arguing that Perenchio might have regarded a film that explicitly articulates this viewpoint as unpalatable—and thus unprofitable—to a wider audience.
22. *The Fighters* has a run time of 93 minutes, and *The Fight* runs 126 minutes.
23. Louise Greaves, interview with author.
24. The fighters (and their respective camps) split a $5 million purse, but all profits went to Perenchio and Cooke.
25. Richard Brody, "The Muhammad Ali Documentary That Gets to the Existential Heart of Boxing," *New Yorker*, June 13, 2016, https://www.newyorker.com/culture/richard-brody-the-muhammad-ali-documentary-that-gets-to-the-existential-heart-of-boxing.
26. Greaves, "Two Fighters on Film," 137.
27. A variation of this hierarchical delineation as the point of entry into the film is discussed in the unpublished production notes, lending credence to this interpretation of the opening. In a section with the heading, "How do you begin the film," Greaves and his crew consider beginning "the film with the little guys and moving up to the top . . . like to Jack Kent Cooke." While the director ultimately settled on the juxtaposition between Ali and Perenchio, this alternative opening to the film would have similarly served to foreground the power dynamics determining the event as the film's focus. Greaves production notes typescript.
28. Greaves, "Two Fighters on Film," 137. It is important to note that Greaves is the only African-American filmmaker to produce a major work on Ali. A troubling

29. reflection of the very marginalization of filmmakers of color that Greaves rails against, this fact may also inform the project's more sophisticated treatment of racial politics as compared to other documentaries about the boxer.
29. Robinson, Jacobs explains, threw his jab in eight and a half frames; Ali, in six and a half.
30. As with the opening sequences, the intention to reframe the perception of Frazier is addressed in the unpublished production notes, with Greaves and his crew discussing "turn[ing] the corner with Frazier's personality... from dumb ape and slugger to a man with dignity." Greaves production notes typescript.
31. Louise Greaves, interview with author.
32. Stuart Hall, Chas Critcher, Tony Jefferson, John N. Clarke, and Brian Roberts, *Policing the Crisis: Mugging, the State, and Law and Order* (New York: Holmes & Meier, 1978), 394.
33. See chapter 1 of this volume.
34. Although the fight was screened in movie theaters and was afforded the pomp of a cinematic premiere, it bore many hallmarks of the televisual culture of the period. Not only was it a live event, but it featured an unpredictable personality in Ali, who was closely identified with the Civil Rights Movement. As Sasha Torres argues, television's rise as a mass medium can be credited in part to the simultaneous (and symbiotic) ascendance of the Civil Rights Movement. Torres, *Black, White and In Color: Television and Black Civil Rights* (Princeton, N.J.: Princeton University Press, 2003).
35. Brody, "The Muhammad Ali Documentary."
36. In all, Greaves gave the film crew three jobs. The first was to film the actors' auditions; the second, to document the filming of the auditions; and the third, to roam around, filming the larger environment. Finally, Greaves himself also periodically shot footage.
37. Thomas Hauser, *Muhammad Ali: His Life and Times* (New York: Simon & Schuster, 1991), 71.
38. Gottlieb, "Just Another Word for Jazz," 171. Tellingly, a similar observation can be made about Muhammad Ali's politics.
39. Louise Greaves, interview with author.

12

Black Journal

A Few Notes from the Executive Producer

WILLIAM GREAVES

When the urban riots of 1965–1966 erupted in all their fury, it slowly dawned on the leaders of this society that high among basic causes stood this stark fact: the black communities of America had no important public platforms of expression. In particular, the television screens of America were notoriously lacking in black faces and black thinking. On those few occasions when blacks were shown, we were usually slandered or put down in some chauvinistic way. Only on occasion does one see a black or brown face even today; and of course there are few Indians, Chinese, and other peoples in TV's racist image of America. From this state of affairs, it is easy to see how rage and anger might develop in the minds of all black people, whether on the block hanging out or in an office hanging in.

The rage stems also from the *lack of a mass media communication mechanism* to adequately *protest* the outrages perpetuated against the black man in housing, employment, education, politics—in all those areas crucial to his existence. Most important, he doesn't gain from the one-eyed monster *constructive information about himself* and his people, information that will enable us to survive in a generally, though often subtly, hostile white environment. We are *prevented from communicating among ourselves over the airwaves*, a privilege lavished on White America.

It is in the context of a racist society that *Black Journal* has meaning and relevance.

An hour-long TV news magazine airing once a month, *Black Journal* is the first network television series of its kind in the United States. On June 12, 1968, it was introduced over 141 National Educational Television–affiliated stations, and now it appears on roughly 180 such stations. Its purpose: to focus on Afro

America. A production staff composed of blacks and whites created the new series in the first major attempt to implement recommendations of the President's Advisory Commission on Civil Disorders, which had called on the communications media to "expand and intensify coverage of the Negro community... to recognize the existence of Negroes as a group within the community."

Black Journal provides blacks and whites a continuing view of life in Black America. It explores problems and contributions of Afro Americans and delineates the obstacles to black fulfillment and better race relations. Its emphasis is on news and cultural developments in the Afro-American community, ranging from politics to business, from education to the arts, from hard news to humor.

A prime objective in creating *Black Journal* was to train and develop black television reporters, editors, producers, and technical personnel—again in keeping with the recommendations of the President's Commission that cited the urgent need for more black people in broadcasting. This series is specifically geared to serve as a *training workshop* through which Afro Americans can develop the skills and experience to build careers in broadcasting.

Needless to say, *Black Journal* is no more than the proverbial drop in the bucket. But, judging by the feedback that we get from the black and white community, it would seem that our efforts are meeting with unusually high levels of appreciative response. We are convinced that it is not only the artistic quality of *Black Journal* that people are responding to, but the fact that so far as candor and relevance are concerned, *Black Journal* is, in network terms, an oasis in a very large desert.

Almost two years after the Kerner Report, *Black Journal* remains the only network program of its kind. This gives us some idea of how slowly television is moving in this regard. As a matter of fact, out of the 1,800 hours a month of television network programming across the country, *only one hour, Black Journal*, is black controlled! This glaring statistic, in our opinion, graphically illustrates the extent to which white racism permeates the airwaves of America.

During our production meetings at *Black Journal*, we find mounting up on the desk in front of us a wide variety of subject matter that should go on the show. As a result, there is tremendous competition for air time. One hour a month makes it obviously impossible to cover the multitude of subjects relating to the black community.

Our production meetings are filled with endless frustration. We want to talk about the black man in prison, about the problems of our young men who have come out of prison. We want to talk about the black man in the labor movement; the problems of black senior citizens, the lack of old-age homes; birth control and genocide; air pollution and sanitation; the lack of proper health facilities in the North as well as the South.

We want to discuss the government's poverty programs and model cities: who runs them, who plans them, who benefits from them. We want to investigate and expose violations by federal and state laws of the American Constitution; we want to correct distortions of Afro-American and African history and give honest reporting of current events. Yes, we even want to examine the black "silent majority."

A film segment on our fourth show dealt with the Southern Louisiana Consumer Co-op and produced exciting, widespread response from people around the country. Inspired by it, these viewers wanted to adapt some of the measures developed by the Louisiana Co-op to their own communities. This is just one example of the lasting positive benefits that can emerge from *Black Journal* programming—that is, we are putting before the Afro-American public the many problems the black community faces, and ways that can lead to some type of solution. As a matter of fact, more and more *Black Journal* is concentrating on programming *that assists the black community in its problem-solving efforts*, whether in the fields of politics, labor, or business.

AUDIENCE REACTIONS

Unlike most television programming, *Black Journal* is not targeted to middle-class viewers since the number of Afro Americans who are middle class is inordinately small. Rather, its target audiences are lower-class and leadership groups within the black community.

Some white reviewers complain, we are told, that *Black Journal* is not for them—that it is not interested in a dialogue with the white community. Yet, curiously, they continue to watch us. We are fascinated by such reports. While *Black Journal*'s primary target *is* the black community, its second major target is the white community—*especially* those within the white community who feel that it is *not for them*, who are often surprised and irritated by the content of our shows.

There are those who find *Black Journal* "too militant, too nationalistic" and think of us as "uppity niggers." We can assure them that *Black Journal* is a mirror image of the thoughts and feelings of the black community *when* it has the chance to freely express itself. That these people respond emotionally gives us on *Black Journal* considerable satisfaction. The fact that month in and month out, they continue to watch without turning us off—and that when they do turn us off, they continue to think about what has been said and shown—also gives us satisfaction. These responses indicate to us that *Black Journal* is fulfilling the primary task of all educational programming: sensitizing the general public to the issues and problems with which our world is faced.

One of the objectives of Black Journal *is to sensitize white Americans to those mechanisms of prejudice and discrimination by which they consciously and unconsciously oppress the black community.* Black Journal *is, after all, merely an answer to the thousand "White Journals" that proliferate from American television screens. The need for* Black Journal *and more of the same will cease when, and only when, White America stops making White Journals.*

The white community has felt an ongoing need to learn what goes on at the back of the black man's mind. Paradoxically, the same people who wish to know what is at the back of the black man's mind also wish to block information from that region. We hope that for these people *Black Journal*, in its own way, is serving to answer their ongoing need rather than to indulge their escapist wishes.

Some people within the white and black communities view a program like *Black Journal* as one of the national safety valves—to release the pressure increasingly building up within the black community as a result of the pressure *it* faces in turn from the white community. In that we do serve as an outlet through which legitimate grievances can be aired in a democratic society, perhaps our program *does* constitute a safety valve. While this safety valve school of thought may be simply another tactic in riot control, our primary task at *Black Journal* remains the more constructive business of providing the black community with those facts from which dignity and enlightened community action flows.

As would be expected, the whole character of television industry staffing, commercial and non-commercial, has in the past reflected the racially discriminatory hiring practices of most job sectors of American life. Now, with the stated commitment toward integration of Afro Americans into the industry, the search is on for potential black television filmmakers and other personnel.

From various corners, the constant complaint is the difficulty of finding interested and qualified black personnel. These complaints do not include the larger fact that, until recently, the idea of black people working in the film and television industry on a professional level was met with a pervasive hostility. No machinery, no procedures existed through which an aspiring black person might crack the walls of discrimination. (As a matter of fact, I was obliged to spend eleven long years outside of America in film and television production, due to these practices of the industry in America.)

Very early in the life of *Black Journal*, the black members of the staff rebelled against white control of the show. Walking off their jobs on the *Journal*, the staffers insisted on a black executive producer heading the show. Conceding the fact that the show should be black controlled, NET management approached me to become executive producer. There was no question about my qualifications on all levels of production since I had worked on close to 100 productions at the National Film Board of Canada and also now operate my own film production company. But as NET found out, the number of black people in the United States who can point to that kind of track record can be counted on one hand.

TRAINING PROGRAMS

Today, thanks to the existence of *Black Journal* and the relatively few local programs across the country, so serious is the interest of black people in film and television production that National Educational Television has set up the *Black Journal* Training School to develop aspiring black talent. Ably headed by our associate producer, Peggy Pinn, the training school is considerably oversubscribed.

The classes now total 65 with a waiting list of close to 100. The twelve-week intensified course, covering still photography, cinematography, sound recording, and editing, includes some on-location filming. The students choose their locations; write the script; direct, photograph, and edit the film under expert supervision. At present the school is hanging by a thread as it seeks funding to continue through the year.

Black Journal and other production units are now hiring some of the training school's graduates. *Black Journal* has thus served as a vehicle for the further development of black filmmakers who heretofore have not had the opportunity to participate in a major network television series.

Our staff is quite an expert one, and we are indeed pleased with the work of people like Kent Garrett, Stan Lathan, St. Clair Bourne, Phil Burton, Tony Batten, and Bob Wagoner. These men are hard-working full-time producers capable of holding their own in any production situation. We have a very able host in the person of Lou House, and I am co-host.

The growth and development of the black members of the staff is illustrated in the ever-increasing professionalism of the program. The *New York Times* TV critic, Jack Gould, gave the following review of the show:

By the acid test of professional and perceptive journalism, *Black Journal* has earned its rightful niche as a continuing and absorbing feature of television's out-put.... By any color standard the program is rendering a thoroughly worthwhile journalistic contribution, one deserving to be judged on merit alone. Mr. Greaves is simply covering the story that should be covered and covering it with distinction. White journalists could well share his pride of craft.

In last night's repeat, involving too many gifted people to enumerate, *Black Journal* reminded the viewer of its accomplishments in the first year over National Educational Television and reminded him, too, that at least on TV a black editorial staff can detect and obtain stories that may escape its white counterpart.

Despite this level of critical reaction, some local stations have made sporadic attempts to take the show off the air because of its "militance." Most such attempts have failed because of the strong viewer support the show enjoys in the black community.

Budget has constituted one of the major problems that have plagued *Black Journal* since its inception. The costs per show have undergone considerable change since its beginning, starting at roughly $100,000 per show and now standing at $50,000. We have tried to stay within the confines of our latest grants; but it is virtually impossible to produce a major hour show each month (that covers the black community throughout the country, and now internationally) without exceeding these budgetary limitations. From $100,000 to $50,000 per show constitutes a 50 percent reduction, and puts considerable pressure on the staff to maintain the quality of *Black Journal*. Despite this fact, the quality of the show is still going up. However, in light of projected cuts for the summer period, we may not be able to maintain past standards.

Each year it seems we must struggle to stay on the air because of the lack of funds. It is incredible that this *should* be so for the single black-controlled show in all of television. How this tenuous state of affairs might reflect the workings of American society at large and the industry in particular is, of course, an interesting question.

As long as government involvement in public broadcasting does not mean or imply government control or censorship, we of the *Black Journal* staff are not at all hostile to the idea. Thus far, our relations with the Public Broadcasting Corporation have not involved any editorial strings on the monies received from them. It is to be expected that, through our political representatives, the black community will strive to make certain that public broadcasting in the future will more accurately reflect the multiracial character and realities of this country.

This kind of pressure we regard as positive in a situation manifestly negative as far as black people are concerned. We would hope that with the coming of the public broadcasting system, *Black Journal* will thrive. We hope, in fact, that there will be more *Black Journals*, Black and White journals, Black, Brown, Yellow, and White Journals—and fewer White Journals. We would also hope that, with the emergence of the Public Broadcasting Corporation, the integration of technical, production, and management personnel of all stations will accelerate.

NOTE

Reprinted from *Television Quarterly* 8, no. 4 (Fall 1969): 66–72.

13

100 Madison Avenues Will Be of No Help

WILLIAM GREAVES

I am furious Black. Over the last year, in Harlem alone, over 100 teenagers died from overdoses of drugs. I also learned with horror that roughly four-fifths of a major American city's white population voted for a white candidate whose underworld connections are thought to be extensive, rather than see an honorable Black man attain that office. Thor Heyerdahl reports that during his Egyptian-style crossing of the Atlantic, he encountered on the ocean the filth and garbage of what we are told is an advanced civilization. Tens of thousands of dollars are being paid individual American farmers not to produce surpluses that would feed starving people in America and the rest of the world. The summer riots are in gear, with promises that the nation's campuses will throw up more violence in the fall. After their second trip into space, a couple of astronauts have reported detecting a progressive deterioration, due to pollution, of the earth's atmosphere. Oh, hell, the list is endless.

America is obviously sliding into an abyss of tragedy at an accelerating speed. The supreme tragedy is that she may not go into the abyss alone, but will probably take half, if not the whole, world with her. The paranoia and other mental illnesses of the society continue unabated and unattended. It seems it all started with the "discovery" of the first Indian "sniper" in America, almost 500 years ago, and comes down to the present fiasco involving hundreds of thousands of Vietnamese "snipers" in Southeast Asia.

In these grotesque circumstances, the rational response would be to throw all of society's energies and resources into crash programs in an attempt to sharply turn this whole thing around. Instead, rational men do little more than watch with disbelief. And how does television, the most powerful medium of communication ever devised by man, react to all this? *Truth or Consequences, Peyton*

Place, *Leave It to Beaver*, and endless ball games. In other words, business as usual in one of history's most irrational societies.

As an Afro-American film and TV producer, I, for one, haven't time to be either entertained or entertaining. And I won't take advantage of this opportunity to be "nice" and "positive" and talk about "progress now taking place...," which might make us feel good, while the woods are burning. Maybe television can't solve all the world's problems, but I think it could, at the very least, give it a good college try. For a start, why not invert the ratio of monies spent on educational, as opposed to entertainment, television? Who knows, a couple of billion dollars, instead of the present few million spent for public service programing, just might give America a fighting chance. This is a fast turnaround, but this is the kind of thing that is necessary to help avoid the crash.

I'm not at all suggesting that all existing program formats be abandoned for plodding documentaries. Some of the old formats could lend themselves just as easily to relevant programming as they do to irrelevant programming. Surely, it's not beyond American ingenuity to place relevant themes and subject matter in *Bewitched*, *That Girl*, et al. The point is that programming should be built around priorities that foster civilization rather than the fast buck; that foster life rather than death.

But criticism of the one-eyed monster has appeared on these pages before. The question now is what constructive suggestions can a Black producer offer the irrelevant frightened media establishment, that has been too frightened to speak the truth, and was certainly irrelevant long before the vice president ever raised his voice.

From a Black producer's point of view, it's just plain silly to discuss programing for America without taking into account the social, historical realities that surround our society today. If, and it seems more and more likely, the racists of America carry out their sick, misguided plans of oppression, or attempt to halt the progress of the Afro-American community, the United States will accelerate the process of discrediting itself in the world community. Unlike South Africa, which enjoys the protective umbrella thrown up over her by the United States and Britain to ward off world pressures, the United States herself has no such protector.

As revulsion to American racism spreads into all sectors of America's international relations, all our uptight conservatives, ultraconservatives, reactionaries, and just plain silent majority types will be crying in their suburban beers over America's loss of trade and influence in world affairs. Some of them, perhaps a little more thoughtful than our governor friend in Alabama and his more subtle allies across the country, are already learning that repression and military power alone cannot positively influence the feelings of large masses of the earth's peoples. On the contrary, such repression is the midwife of militancy. The second lesson they are to learn is that racism is equally subversive and counterproductive in terms of America's other short-term and long-term interests. They will learn that they will have destroyed America's capacity to communicate with the rest of the world, which is overwhelmingly nonwhite, and one hundred Madison Avenues will not be able to help her. Only through nonwhite America will this country be able to communicate with the world.

In other words, contrary to their deepest yearnings, white racists all the way from uptight southern governors to phony northern "liberals" will have played no small part in helping Black and other nonwhite people in America into the very leadership roles they covet for themselves. Actually, it doesn't matter whether they oppose or support Black aspirations. We are a dynamic people who will thrive one way or another. Interestingly, the emergence of the Afro-Americans as a leader group in American society will probably not come as a result of any military-style revolution, but largely by the default of a mentally sick predatory white culture.

Black and other minority people have suffered more, are more sensitive to social problems and injustices. Our leadership of America will come just as easily and naturally as has our leadership in American music. We know more about pollution, dope, abuses of power, not to mention white disregard for law and order. Consequently, we and other minorities in America are truly sensitized to the moral, spiritual, political, social, and economic problems which would concern the leadership of a country. Our sensitivity not only develops from our recent history, but from our ancient history, which, despite present scholastic hypocrisy, goes back over ten thousand years. And despite the cold winter winds of slavery and depression that have blown across our race, we still have not lost our faith in humanity and ourselves.

As Count Volney, a high official in Napoleon's government, wrote of the Africans at the beginning of the nineteenth century, "There a people, now forgotten, discovered, while others were yet barbarians, the elements of the arts and sciences. This race of men, now rejected from society for their sable skin and frizzled hair, founded on the study of the laws of nature those civil and religious systems which still govern the universe." Because we brought them science and culture in centuries long past, the ancient Egyptians referred to us as the "blameless Ethiopians." We were blameless because to them we had a high degree of awareness of what real civilization was all about, and did not abuse the immense power we held in their country.

What has all this to do with the thinking of Black producers? Everything. Besides the immediate problems of community control of television, the Black pride and productivity of Black and other minority producers, as well as white American youth, must develop programming which prepares the minority community for assuming the responsibilities of leadership a sick society is forcing upon them. As Black producers, our task will be to encourage mental health among the Black, Brown, and Red people, to help still adaptable white people to be healthy, so that the transition from rule by racial paranoia to rule by racial harmony can be as painless as possible. Thus, the wide circulation of history will appear to close in on itself though rising to a new plane of human consciousness.

Just as our music has set the pace of American music, at home and abroad, our contribution to American film and TV will be of a similar order. Just as black people are giving America a "soul" of its own, as well as excellence in sports, and innovations in language, so, too, will we contribute to America in the field of television. Like it or not, we will play the Greeks to America's Rome, the Ethiopians to Americas Egypt. Let's face it, virtually all the older white producers and programmers have been either ineffectual, derelict, or even hostile in regard to nurturing film and television productions which help to reconstruct our society and its self-destructive attitudes. Even today, most white producers and directors still indulge in racist casting, white writers still turn in racist scripts, and most white directors neurotically call for Aryan typecasting. As an ex-actor, I know only too well from where I speak. Black producers must re-define Blacks to Blacks and Blacks to whites. We must re-define whites to whites, and not in the sick way some white producers have defined Blacks to Blacks.

In years to come, the Afro-American producer will concern himself with an ever- widening range of issues that will spring from the material, social, and spiritual climate of America. Having encouraged the cultural, psychological, political, and economic development of the Black community, we will also concern ourselves with methods by which an obstinate, ethnocentric white society can be more sensitized to the social and physical world in which it lives.

For example: there's been a lot of talk about violence in our society today. This violence has not come about in a vacuum. It is the end result of the intolerable frustrations Black people have experienced during the long winter of arrogance and insensitivity in which we have lived. Violence comes when white youths become aware of the self-destructive nature of this arrogance and insensitivity. It comes when the establishment itself becomes so alienated from the rest of society that its alienation begins to dwarf all other alienations within the society. Opposing groups, be they Black and white, youth and police, doves and hawks, radicals and establishment, militant and reactionary, seek through the primitive agency of violence to transmit information and thus influence each other's behavior.

Instead of these confrontations occurring in the four dimensions of hard physical reality, the violent energies could conceivably be channeled through the electronic circuit that serves a two-dimensional television screen. What we have here is "psychodramatic and sociodramatic encounter television." By putting members of each group before a set of television cameras, and geographically removing them from each other, we introduce the safety factor. Under these "sanitized" conditions, it would be possible for such groups to go after each other hammer and tongs, no holds barred! They can call each other all kinds of dirty names without the danger of actually doing violence to each other.

The theatrical, not to mention the mental health dividends that would accrue from such encounters on television would be incalculable. The paradox is that while these groups might not meet in private to discuss their grievances without violence, they would meet on television because it offers precisely the public they wish to influence. Obviously, there are those who would use the opportunity for strictly propaganda purposes, but the logic and the techniques of psychodramatic encounter are such that these purposes would be quickly eroded and what would be left would be men and women communicating.

The case for encounter television can be made easily by the following analogy: when two people, particularly if they are hostile to each other, are brought together for a psychodramatic encounter, there is great distrust, more so when they are dependent upon each other, as in the case of man and wife. What is needed is the willingness of both to encounter each other psychologically.

America is caught in the grip of myriad neurotic and psychotic trends. Call these trends racism, sexism, chauvinism, militarism, sadism, what you will. The fact remains that it is virtually impossible to develop the necessary number of psychiatrists, psychologists, analysts, therapists, and the like to cope with America's emotionally disturbed population. The concept of television group encounter, patterned after the interpersonal encounters which take place at such organizations as the Moreno Institute, headed by Dr. J. L. Moreno, the pioneer of psychodrama, offer a stopgap mechanism to arrest the deteriorating social diseases which are presently eating away at American society. Using the techniques of twentieth-century communications, we are now in a position to put the rednecks of Alabama in a direct encounter with the Black militants of Harlem, either on public or closed-circuit television. This is but one way to help America achieve mental health. Spending money on escapist crash programs in outer space will not solve the problem. Of course, the big question is, can this kind of programming surface from the present flood of video trivia, or will it have to wait upon the courage of some forward-thinking programmer in 1994?

In short, the search for candor, for honesty, and truth—rather than hypocrisy and self-delusion—must become a basic component of television programing. On such a foundation, other kinds of programing can easily be built. On such a foundation the Black producer of today and tomorrow will most likely build his programing. For him, the mass media will be an agency for improving mass mental health and social reform, will be a catharsis, a means of purifying the emotional and spiritual life of this country. In other words, for the Black producer, television will be just another word for jazz. And jazz for the Afro-American has been a means of liberating the human spirit.

NOTE

Reprinted from the *New York Times*, August 9, 1970.

14
Black Journal

A Personal Look Backward

ST. CLAIR BOURNE

Let me begin by stating the obvious: images in U.S. media—not just images of Blacks, but all images—are highly influenced by the political conditions of the times. Moreover, Black images have not been and still are not controlled by Black producers, and, therefore, these images were created to serve the psychic purposes of those that do control them. Because Europeans originally brought Africans here as slaves to provide service and labor and nothing more, the representations of these slaves were used to rationalize and reinforce their intended place in society. Thus, racial stereotypes came to symbolize the mental restructuring of the African presence in America.

My own beginning in filmmaking as a member of the production staff of the *Black Journal* public television series in 1968 is due as much to the social conditions of the times as to my own energy. During those days, there was general active unrest among the African-American population, due to discrimination and treatment as second-class citizens. The Civil Rights Movement, based on the principles of nonviolence and petitions to larger society for justice, was beginning to run its course as the marchers and activists were thwarted by violent resistance and government inaction. In addition, the energy and frustration with the slow rate of fundamental change moved from the rural towns of the South to the inner cities of the major urban centers in the North. Thus, planned and spontaneous rebellions, usually sparked by a symbolic incident but also caused by a long list of unjust conditions, erupted in the cities where there were large Black populations like Detroit, Newark, and the Watts section of Los Angeles.

In addition to being subjected to discrimination, Black people especially resented the lack of acknowledged participation in and contributions to U.S.

society. A specific complaint was the lack of presence in the electronic media and the negative distortion that took place when we were represented. Therefore, programs, funds, and positions were made available to provide media access for Black images so that Black issues could be addressed. It should be noted that these changes, welcomed by African Americans because of their belief in the power of the media, were not made out of charity, benevolence, or goodwill, but rather were the result of pressure by the revolutionary potential of the Black protest movement, pressure from the people in the streets who disrupted the normal flow of business and demanded in one form or another—some with bricks, others with pencils—a share in social processes as they perceived them.

It was from these conditions [that] the *Black Journal* series was created within the tax-supported public television sector. Alvin Perlmutter, a white staff producer at National Educational Television (the pre–Public Broadcasting Service public TV system), conceived of the series idea in April 1968 following the murder of Dr. Martin Luther King, Jr. The idea was enthusiastically approved as an overdue response to both the Kerner Commission report on U.S. race relations, which called for the media to "expand and intensify coverage of the Negro community," and to the growing mood for self-determination in Black communities around the country. Perlmutter and Black producer/writer Lou Potter were assigned to develop a format and to secure a staff.

After extensive meetings with both leaders and ordinary folks in Black communities around the country, a public-affairs-oriented, magazine-format program was decided upon. Then a staff composed of both NET personnel and others hired specifically for *Black Journal* was assembled. I was a graduate film student at Columbia University at the time but had been recently suspended due to my involvement in the 1968 Columbia University student takeover. Fresh from the barricades and a night in jail, I was interviewed and hired by NET as an associate producer. At this point, there emerged a basic contradiction that came back to traumatize this effort. The NET public relations department heralded the series in their press releases as programs "by, for, and about Black people," but, although two Black on-camera hosts—independent filmmaker William Greaves and former Chicago radio news reporter Lou House (who later changed his "slave" name to an African name, Wali Sadiq)—were hired, the staff ended up with twelve Blacks out of a staff of twenty. More important, Perlmutter, who was white, became the executive producer with editorial control for the series.

This series went into active production in May, had its premiere broadcast in June 1968, and was greeted by both critical acclaim and unprecedented (for public television) viewer response. The first show's segments consisted of an interview from an Oakland prison with Huey Newton on the future of the Black Panthers, a report on the Poor People's Campaign in Washington, D.C., a satirical skit about the use of Blacks in advertisements, an essay on the view of the future by graduating Black college seniors, a profile of a Harlem-based manufacturer of African-style clothing, a portrait of a Black jockey, and coverage of a Coretta King address at Harvard University.

Despite the immediate public success of this series, certain questions still had to be addressed: Who was the primary audience? Did this decision affect the content of the program and how? Was the use of largely white film crews a contradiction to the stated goals of *Black Journal*? Little by little, questions of assignments and editorial points of view became points of dispute among the staff. For example, when a breakdown of the percentage of white-produced shows to Black-produced shows was done, it was discovered that the former far outnumbered the latter. Disagreements over editorial politics emerged as well. When a white producer wrote a news piece introduction stating that the Black community supported Israel and disavowed Arab protests over the seizure of land, an argument broke out in the studio during the taping and was quelled only after the narration was rewritten.

The issue came to a head when eleven Black members of the production staff demanded that the white executive producer be replaced by a Black executive producer, citing the NET press statement that *Black Journal* was produced "by, for, and about Black people." When the NET management refused to appoint Lou Potter, the series' managing editor, as the executive producer, the eleven went out on strike in protest and made the incident public in a press conference.

In an article printed in *Variety*, NET's management claimed that its intention was "to promote from within the unit and to increase the black composition of the unit as quickly as staff members were ready for advancement." Wire services, trade papers, and mainstream media columnists wrote extensively about the strike, and within a week NET agreed to the demands. Greaves, the show's host, became the new executive producer. Perlmutter became a consultant with no editorial power. Potter was given the new position of executive editor and the option of working on other NET projects, and most of the other white producers were phased out to return to other NET commitments. (Phil Burton remained as the sole white producer and did several excellent pieces.)

After this traumatic experience, several changes took place. The spirit of the *Black Journal* staff took on an added commitment to "the people," but also, because of the well-publicized struggle around the control of the show, we regained support from leaders of the national Black community. Furthermore, we gained a sizable white audience who wanted to see what all the noise had been about. Interestingly, the overall white reaction was not as antagonistic as we expected, primarily because we didn't use our airtime denouncing white racism (that it existed was given) but rather documenting, exploring, and articulating African-American political, economic, and cultural issues. With only one hour per month of *Black Journal* programming competing with the infinite hours of "White Journals," we thought that we shouldn't waste time ranting against whites, because our mission was to supply Black people with valuable information and analysis. Another important change that occurred after the strike was staff editor Madeline Anderson's promotion to producer, the staff's first Black woman producer. Although there had been a white female producer and Black women had served as production assistants, editors, and researchers, there had never been a Black female producer at NET.

In our editorial meetings, executive producer Greaves laid out the editorial guidelines that came to distinguish and unify our content. *Black Journal*, he stated, should: (1) define the Black reality of any potential film situation, (2) identify the causes of any problems in that situation, and (3) document attempts to resolve those problems, whether successful or not. In this way, Greaves believed, each short documentary would be a teaching tool on how Black people could work to resolve common problems. Films about important cultural, political, and educational figures should document their existence within a society whose history almost always excluded them. Greaves knew what we younger staff members didn't: this filmmaking opportunity would not last but the films would.

Because of the unique national position of *Black Journal* within the media landscape during 1968 to 1971, we undertook several projects to improve so-called minority (what we called Third World) participation.

Even our own producers on the series relied on largely white crews because there were extremely few Third World freelance technicians, due to the difficulty of finding work regularly and thus gaining experience and skill. The *Black Journal* Film Workshop was created to fill this void. Word soon got around that a ten-week crash course in basic film production was being offered and that accomplished graduates could possibly get camera crew assignments. The instructors were both Black and white technicians who volunteered their time to teach the new recruits. This created a pool of Third World technicians who began to work on not only *Black Journal* documentaries but, armed with sample reels, began to get work on other productions as well. Ultimately, Peggy Pinn, staff production coordinator, quit that post, raised money for staff and equipment, and managed the Film Workshop for five years, training hundreds of

Third World technicians, many of whom still work in the film and television industries.

Film critic and historian Clyde Taylor has written extensively about contemporary independent filmmaking and the influence of the style of *Black Journal* on the editorial tone and the documentary images used to define Black issues. Previously, television would rarely, if ever, present material from the Black participant's point of view. A white commentator always interpreted for the audience "what those people want," through either narration or an on-camera appearance. This was standard television news procedure. At *Black Journal* we insisted that the people in our films speak for themselves as much as possible and, if narration was used, that the narrator assume a tone of advocacy. There was also a strong cultural identification with Africa, which was a part of the reassertion of the movement's African roots and cultural values: for example, the show's hosts often wore African dress, and African drumming was used as intro music.

At that time—again, because of the political clime—a constituency was created for this new Black programming or, as it began to be called, "minority programming." As we saw it, the purpose of "minority programming" in the public affairs sector of television news was clear—to provide the so-called minorities with an opportunity to address each other on issues that they considered important. In addition to *Black Journal*, there was a series called *Soul!*, an entertainment program that provided a forum for performers who had virtually been ignored by mainstream television. It's hard to imagine in this era of Bill Cosby, but there was a time when one could look long and hard without seeing a Black face on any TV program. Then came *Black Journal* and an explosion of local public affairs shows aimed at the so-called minority audience.

Both of these pioneering programs performed a necessary function quite effectively but were created as a response to an admitted deficiency: to serve an audience that had never been adequately addressed directly before. The programs and their imitators could be called "the first generation of minority programming." If there was a flaw in this first effort, it was a narrowness of vision that could not be avoided at that time. By addressing Blacks about Blacks only, for example, a large part of the viewing audience was excluded, but more importantly, the role of so-called minorities within the total framework of U.S. society and culture was ignored.

The second generation of "minority" programming—based on the premise that in the beginning it had been necessary to affirm our culture—attempted to correct some of these unavoidable limitations. An example of this corrective programming was a PBS program called *Interface*, which showed the interaction of various cultures in the U.S. by tackling topics based in everyday life. Developed by Black producer/writer Ardie Ivie and hosted by *Black Journal* graduate Tony Batten, *Interface* concentrated on ethnic group interactions but also limited itself to a certain aspect of life in United States, namely, cultural (in the anthropological sense) interaction. At the same time, another program, *Black Perspective on the News*, took a "hard news" approach and opened its list of guests to all the races, with the understanding that all people in this country can be affected by a variety of newsmakers of all skin colors. However, the news format prevented the viewer from receiving a multidimensional understanding of the issues covered. In short, we still spoke to Blacks but about non-Black issues as well as Black issues.

The next step which should have been taken would have featured Blacks as participants in U.S. society talking about any issue, that is, a view and interpretation of issues based in the so-called minority experience but treating issues, trends, and phenomena not necessarily connected to "minority" life. This would bring an unjaded eye to not only institutions of special interest to "minorities" but also to those institutions that affect everyone as well, for it must be understood that all things in the United States affect all people in the United States in some way. However, this phase never developed fully, primarily because of the political resurgence of right-wing conservatives, calculated attacks by the Nixon and Reagan administrations to stop and, in fact, roll back the social advances that people have struggled to achieve, and, most important, the lack of Black participation in decision-making within the political and economic process.

The life of *Black Journal* was closely allied to the Black movement that gave birth to it. And so, as money for social programs began to be cut back in the early seventies, *Black Journal*'s production budget was reduced from $100,000 a program to $50,000 a program by the NET management. To compensate, on-location documentaries were cut back, more in-studio production was done, and summer reruns were instituted. Appeals were made to foundations, corporations, and community organizations for production funds, but the change in the political agenda affected the ability and/or willingness to contribute to a television series that advocated social change.

As the production funds decreased, it became more difficult to maintain the high standard with which we started, so, little by little, the staff began seeking other avenues for their ideas and talent. Greaves, who had his own production company before he joined the *Black Journal* staff, resigned. Other producers applied for and got jobs at network news departments. I left in April 1971 to pursue more personal and more stylized film projects. Several months later, Tony Brown became the new executive producer and began experimenting with formats that would attract financial underwriting. After several format changes ranging from a game show to a Carson-type talk show to a variety entertainment show, Brown changed the name of the series to *Tony Brown's Journal*; he continues as executive producer/host to this day. As one of six staff producers for the series, I spent almost three years traveling around the United States making documentaries about various aspects and issues of Black America. It is a lesson I have never forgotten—that as a filmmaker or film artist, my source comes from the audience that I hope to serve. Of course, my understanding of what this means became more complicated as time went on.

The political swing to the right and the deterioration of the economic system that occurred in the past decade and a half affected Black filmmakers more than their white counterparts. In the Black independent production sector, an area that has always been difficult to sustain, alternative sources like public television, foundation grants, and other special programs have decreased. Furthermore, the dominance of the right wing has reduced the range of "producible subjects" and acceptable images. This, in turn, has created a wave of escapist images and stories that distort and/or reinterpret any creative elements that might seriously challenge the worldview of those who control the principal resources. Despite these major obstacles—obstacles that affect all independent producers, not just Black filmmakers—Black history in this country has proven that we have been strong in our cultural expression, and, after all, film and television are indeed that. The social movement that engendered the *Black Journal* series did achieve some of its aims in terms of racial identity and recognition of the need for economic and political self-determination. Overall, we are no longer obliged to prove our worth or validity on either the small or large screen. Self-determination is an act of liberation and, in the end, a healthy process. Everyone should have the right and opportunity to see themselves reflected in the cultural expressions and the reporting of current events of the land in which they live. Mainstream television has proven that, up to now at least, it is incapable or unwilling to do that, so it is up to us, the independents, to fill that vacuum.

NOTE

Originally published as an online feature, dated April 1, 1989, in the Spring/Summer 1989 issue of *Documentary Magazine* (formerly *International Documentary*), the journal of the International Documentary Association, a nonprofit media arts organization based in Los Angeles. Special thanks to Judith L. Bourne for making this essay available to us.

15
"By, For and About"

Black Journal *and the Rise of Multicultural Documentary in New York City, 1968–1975*

CHARLES MUSSER

For many years, film scholars generally saw documentary as falling into two historical periods: one that preceded the cinéma-vérité revolution circa 1960 and another that followed it.[1] Today, given the transformations made possible by the introduction of video and digital media, our sense of periodization is doubtlessly more complex. Yet if we decline to foreground technological innovation in our schema, we can see how the period around 1968 entailed another kind of profound transformation—particularly when focused on American documentary film. It was a moment when marginalized groups of people (racial, ethnic, gendered, and so forth) began to win access to "the media" in significant numbers and change the politics of production, representation, and addressed audience—however imperfectly and incompletely. These were films and programs that were "by, for, and about."

The year 1968 began with the Tet offensive in Vietnam and included the assassinations of Martin Luther King, Jr., and Robert Kennedy, renewed rioting in major U.S. cities, the bloody Chicago Democratic Convention, the rise of the Black Panthers, the Kerner Report, student protests and the occupation of Columbia University (as well as May '68 in Europe), Richard Nixon's election as president of the United States, and three teachers' strikes over the issue of community control in New York City. This destabilization created an environment in which change, whether reformist or revolutionary, seemed not only possible but inevitable. Yet if we are to understand how this affected documentary at large, we must go beyond looking at documentary film per se and consider a wide range of media, including broadcast television and radio.

For pragmatic purposes, this current investigation is focusing on New York City, a preeminent center for the production and distribution of nonfiction

FIGURE 15.1 Greaves on the street, shooting for *Black Journal*. Photographer unknown. Courtesy Louise Greaves.

programming in a wide range of media forms. One organization that is well-known to those in film studies is Newsreel.[2] Formed in December 1967, Newsreel was highly visible by 1968 as it produced films such as *Columbia Revolt*, *Summer of '68*, *Black Panthers*, and *Community Control*. Nevertheless, initial breakthroughs toward the creation of multicultural media through the production of programs "by, for, and about" marginalized groups happened less in alternative or oppositional cinemas, whether documentary or experimental, than in television programs such as *Inside Bedford-Stuyvesant*, *Black Journal*, and *Like It Is*, which were all started in the spring and summer of 1968. (They would soon be followed by *Soul!*, the innovative weekly black variety and talk show that appeared on NET for four years, beginning in mid-September 1968).[3]

The landscape for independent documentary filmmakers was radically different in the 1960s when compared to later decades. Television series such as *NBC White Paper* were in-house, network productions. The Drew Unit in New York City, funded through the Time-Life Broadcast, a Division of Time, Inc., and David Wolper Productions in Los Angeles had difficulties getting their work onto major TV channels.[4] Cable would not become a factor until well into the 1970s. Although the National Endowment for the Arts had been launched in

1965, media funding was limited to arts programming. State arts councils in New York and elsewhere were in an embryonic state. There was neither a Haymarket Peoples Fund (established in 1974) nor a Paul Robeson Fund for Independent Media. Most documentary filmmakers gained funding from a variety of miscellaneous sources, notably by making documentaries sponsored by industry as well as federal and state institutions such as the United States Information Agency. The National Educational Network (NET), which would be replaced by Public Broadcasting Service (PBS) in 1969, was a notable exception. Owned essentially by the Ford Foundation, it provided some funding for documentaries taking on important social issues.[5] Opportunities for minorities and women were further constrained by such factors as the "old boy" network and unions' exclusionary policies. Television production staffs remained almost lily white, particularly in the area of news and documentary. A few particularly determined African Americans such as William Greaves, Melvin Van Peebles, and Ellis Haizlip left the United States in the 1950s and found work in Europe and Canada.

One important catalyst for change was the National Advisory Commission on Civil Disorders, which was set up by President Lyndon Johnson in July 1967. Formed in response to another summer of rioting (U.S. cities experienced over 150 race riots that summer), this group was composed of moderate and liberal Democrats and Republicans.[6] Otto Kerner, Jr., governor of Illinois, was chair, and John V. Lindsay, mayor of New York City, was vice chair. Senator Edward W. Brooke of Massachusetts and Roy Wilkens of the NAACP were its two black members. The resulting Kerner Report proved far reaching in its conclusions: "What white Americans have never fully understood—but what the Negro can never forget—is that white society is deeply implicated in the ghetto. White institutions created it, white institutions maintain it, and white society condones it." The Kerner Report went on to castigate the news media in several areas. Newspapers and television had "failed to report adequately on the causes and consequences of civil disorders and on the underlying problems of race relations. They have not communicated to the majority of their audience—which is white—a sense of the degradation, misery and hopelessness of life in the ghetto."[7] Because African Americans saw their presence in the news systematically distorted and marginalized, they expressed a corresponding skepticism and hostility toward the white press and to a considerable extent television.

Among its many recommendations, the Kerner Report urged that these institutions "recruit more Negroes into journalism and broadcasting and promote those who are qualified to positions of significant responsibility." "News organizations must employ enough Negroes in positions of significant responsibility to establish an effective link to Negro actions and ideas and to meet legitimate employment expectations," it argued.[8] Or, as William Greaves would subsequently articulate the problem, the black man "doesn't gain from the one-eyed monster *constructive information about himself* and his people, information that will enable us to survive in a generally, though often subtly, hostile white environment. We are *prevented from communicating among ourselves over the airwaves*, a privilege lavished on White America."[9] Almost immediately after the Kerner Commission published its results in late February 1968, television stations responded by putting a half-dozen black-oriented series and multipart programs into preproduction.[10] In New York City, these included three television programs of particular interest: *Inside Bedford-Stuyvesant*, *Black Journal*, and *Like It Is*.

INSIDE BEDFORD-STUYVESANT AT METROMEDIA

Metromedia, Channel 5 or WNEW, offered *Inside Bedford-Stuyvesant*, a half-hour, semiweekly local program that "is produced by Negroes, tells what Negroes are doing and most significantly is aimed at Negro viewers themselves."[11] *Inside Bedford-Stuyvesant* was initiated by the Brooklyn-based Bedford Stuyvesant Restoration Corporation, whose president, Franklin A. Thomas, subsequently headed the Ford Foundation. The show maintained a base at the organization's offices as well as at Metromedia in Manhattan. Robert Kennedy had strong ties with the Bedford Stuyvesant Restoration Corporation, which he had helped to establish in the mid-1960s while attorney general.[12] As a U.S. senator from New York who was running for president, Kennedy and his associates facilitated the program's rapid fruition.

Inside Bedford-Stuyvesant had six weeks of preproduction before going on the air.[13] It debuted on April 8, 1968, four days after the assassination of Martin Luther King, Jr. The show was done on a shoestring: start-up funding of $45,000 for thirteen programs came from Consolidated Edison, New York Telephone, and First National City Bank. Elizabeth Morris "Lally" Graham Weymouth, the daughter of *Washington Post* publisher Katharine Graham, worked on the program, as did Leo O'Farrell, a staff director at Channel 5: both were white. However, producer Joseph A. Dennis, associate producer Marian Etoile, writer Charles Hobson, and program hosts Jim Lowry and Roxie Roker were black. Dennis was an actor who worked with one of the Kennedy children in sensitizing white corporate America to racial issues.[14] Lowry was a twenty-eight-year-old Peace Corps teacher employed by the Bedford Stuyvesant Restoration Corporation. Roxy Roker, an ex-drama student who was coordinator of public service announcements for NBC, would later go on to play an important role in *The Jeffersons* television series.

Charles Hobson, who was hired as staff writer two weeks into preproduction, deserves particular attention because he worked on all three television programs that are the focus of this essay. Hobson was born on June 23, 1936, in Brooklyn, New York, and spent much of his youth in Bedford-Stuyvesant. Graduating from Brooklyn College in 1960, he later wrote articles on jazz while he made his living selling oriental rugs on 42nd Street. After he wrote a letter to WBAI protesting its shoddy programming of Black gospel music, the radio station offered Hobson an unpaid job producing a weekly music show, late Friday nights. He became WBAI's first black producer. The show gained a wide following, and in 1964 he was hired full-time as production director. During this period he instituted a program featuring news from the black press that went unreported by mainstream newspapers. He also produced a series of radio programs featuring the speeches of Malcolm X. In addition, television programmers hired him on occasion to interview black nationalists who refused to talk to white reporters. For Hobson, working on *Inside Bedford-Stuyvesant* was just one more responsibility.[15]

Inside Bedford-Stuyvesant programs were restored from Ampex 2-inch helical scan videotape in the early 1990s and are archived at the Brooklyn Historical Society, the Schomburg Center in Harlem, and the UCLA Film and Television Archives.[16] Programs were typically televised from one location, which varied from week to week. Often this was an outdoor locale such as Fulton Park (tape 1353), but when weather was inclement, a program could be televised from a very minimal studio (tape 2468). *Inside Bedford-Stuyvesant* was basically a talk show. After some preliminary banter followed by commercials, cohosts Jim Lowry and Roxie Roker would introduce the first set of guests. Another station break would provide the bridge to the next segment. A final television break was usually followed by a closing exchange between Lowry and Roker.

Truly this was community television. At least in the early segments that I have viewed, there is a wide diversity of participants, most of whom are pitching something—in the style of the *Today Show*. A typology of guests would include performing artists, usually local musicians: The Channels 4, a Motown-style quartet; Lord Superior, a singer-songwriter with backup vocalist; and the cast from *To Be Young, Gifted and Black*, a show running at the Cherry Lane Theater in Manhattan, based on the life and writing of Lorraine Hansberry, who wrote *A Raisin in the Sun*.[17] Another guest was an old and then forgotten musician—Eubie Blake. A second grouping centered on community activists: a woman on welfare who was seeking to organize people to oppose major funding cuts; or parents and a school administrator who were urging people to find ways to reopen their schools during the United Federation of Teachers strikes. Programs sometimes featured a "community sound-off" in which people from various political persuasions expressed their views—from supporting the teaching of African-American history in the schools to opposing the Vietnam War. A third grouping involved local black entrepreneurs: J. T. Freeman, whose Ebbets Field Dodge was one of six or seven black-owned car dealerships in the country; and two brothers who were bringing jazz back to Brooklyn, opening a jazz club in Bedford-Stuyvesant, the Blue Coronet.[18]

Inside Bedford-Stuyvesant helped to forge a sense of community in an area that did not have the well-publicized cultural heritage of Harlem. It allowed the community to see itself on the screen in a new way. Here was not a "ghetto" filled with enraged protesters and rioters. Here were people struggling to live their lives with dignity, grace, and ambition. This was hardly news to people living in Bedford-Stuyvesant, but it articulated, enriched, and extended these perceptions, which had previously been denied any kind of official recognition. As cohost Jim Lowry explained, "Our goal was to instill pride in our community."[19] For those not from Bedford Stuyvesant—and there were apparently many viewers from the affluent suburbs of Westchester, Fairfield, Suffolk, and Nassau Counties—the series provided a kind of revelation that Bed-Stuy was "far from an impoverished, crime-ridden and hopeless area."[20] This fresh perspective provided a new truth as these largely white audiences developed a sense of the community's immense diversity and its unexpected similarities to their own neighborhoods.

On the other hand, it would be a mistake to ignore the real limitations of *Inside Bedford-Stuyvesant*. Much of its charm comes from its semiprofessional look. As *Variety* remarked after its debut: "To be sure, it's a series worth rooting for. But it clearly needs some hard think on format and point of view—even if it's to dent only the Negro community hereabouts."[21] The *Variety* reviewer may have wanted the series to be more than what it was—something closer to the declared ambitions of its promoters and those hoping for a fundamental shift in TV programming. It was, rather, a well-intentioned change at the margins: *Inside Bedford-Stuyvesant* was broadcast in black-and-white at a marginal time on a somewhat marginal local station and was of marginal interest to potential viewers outside the community. It was community programming in the days before Public Access Television.

BLACK JOURNAL AT NATIONAL EDUCATIONAL NETWORK

Black Journal was much more ambitious. Produced in New York at Channel 13, WNDT, for the National Educational Network, this monthly show with its magazine format was for a national audience, both black and white. A typical program included a number of short documentary segments, interludes of video graphics with commentary by one of the cohosts, and perhaps a panel discussion. Alvin H. Perlmutter—who produced *NET Journal*, Bill Moyers specials, and *Adam Smith's Money World*—was at the top of the pyramid in the role of executive producer. Perlmutter's idea, according to Hobson, was to create a collaboration between experienced white producers and young black talent. This would provide the training to the black members of the production staff and ensure pertinent programming. Its senior producers were white, with the exception of Charles Hobson and Horace B. Jenkins. Jenkins had studied at the Sorbonne Institute of Film in Paris and worked there for a dubbing company. He later returned to the United States, where he was an associate producer on the NET science series *Spectrum*.[22] While still retaining his ties with *Inside Bedford-Stuyvesant*, Hobson was hired away from WBAI as a full producer.

Black Journal could nonetheless boast a predominantly black staff, which included Lou Potter as "editor." Potter's brief experience in documentary had included work on the NET-produced *Color Us Black!*, which looked at how and why African-American students shut down Howard University in March 1968.[23] Kent Garrett and St. Clair Bourne were associate producers.[24] Before joining *Black Journal*, Garrett had worked at Ted Bates Advertising in New York as an account executive and then went to Grey Advertising, where he became a television commercial producer.[25] Bourne had joined the Peace Corps and was sent to Peru, where he helped publish a Spanish newspaper, *El Comeno*. After returning to the United States, he completed his undergraduate degree at Syracuse University, where he majored in journalism and political science. According to his *Boston Globe* obituary, "he won a scholarship to Columbia University's Graduate School of the Arts, where his involvement in the radical black student movement led to his expulsion when he was among the students arrested for taking over the administration building in [May] 1968."[26] Among the many who auditioned to fill the roles of cohosts, Lou House (who later changed his name to Wali Sadiq) and William Greaves were selected. House was probably chosen in part because he was an established radio personality in the Midwest, complementing the New York–based Greaves, and giving the program more of a nationwide appeal. He had been news director of radio station WAAF in Chicago for five years and earlier worked as a producer-director for the Minneapolis–St. Paul television station KCTA in 1960–1961.[27]

The African-American women at *Black Journal* held lesser positions: Shelia Smith as researcher, Peggy Pinn as project coordinator, and film editor Madeline Anderson. Pinn had worked for ABC on a four-hour special program on Africa and as an associate producer on a pilot film, also on Africa. Although she was respected by her colleagues and had as much or more experience as many of the male associate producers, Pinn would not be given the title of associate producer at *Black Journal* until 1969.[28] Madeleine Anderson eventually produced one program segment, but that was apparently it. Shelia Smith expressed her frustrations with *Black Journal* in an essay for *Sisterhood Is Powerful* (1970):

> I went over to the big time of educational television, NET. I was working on a "black" (pardon the word) show called "Black Journal." NET set my TV career back three years. I clipped newspapers for the better part of my brief stay with them. My brain was picked—clean. And my womanhood and blackness were constantly insulted. That's not particularly new, but the manner was. Here I was working for the first time in my life with other blacks in television. Black men, too, who for once weren't mail boys. I guess for about one day I thought it was something else. And it was. Something else. Something entirely else.[29]

Smith was working most closely with Hobson, and the fallout from their romantic entanglement may have shaped her characterization of the experience. Nevertheless, *Black Journal* clearly functioned in a prefeminist world.

Produced in living color, *Black Journal* was initially shown nationwide on 141 television stations in different time slots (and at its height on as many as 180 different channels).[30] In New York it was broadcast Wednesdays at 9:00 p.m.—prime time. The first program premiered on June 12 and displayed remarkable promise. It began with Coretta King, Martin Luther King, Jr.'s, widow, giving a commencement speech at Harvard and concluded with a brief, reasonably sympathetic portrait of the Black Panthers. Not only is a broad spectrum of black political opinion surveyed, but there is a historical segment on the black press (produced by Hobson utilizing expertise he developed from his radio show). Even the portrait of the only black jockey in the United States is given an historical context, reminding viewers that until relatively recently riders of African descent had been common in horse racing. Black newspapers praised the program: the *Chicago Defender* called it a "sock-it-to-me winner."[31] The white, mainstream press was also generally enthusiastic. Hal Humphrey of the *Los Angeles Times* declared the program to be "packed with interest for all races and nationalities."[32]

After the third program had been aired in August, certain contradictions within the production of *Black Journal* had crystallized. The series was being sold as "by, for, and of the black community." In fact, the programming was dominated by white-produced segments—five out of six for that third program. This produced a "palace revolt" in mid-August. Eleven of the twelve black staff members resigned in protest. Only Horace Jenkins and Lou Potter (who was not considered "staff") stayed. At a news conference on August 20, held at Kent Garrett's apartment at 118 West 21st Street, Sheila Smith read a prepared statement noting that on May 28,

> we held a meeting with N.E.T. on this matter (before the first show). That meeting addressed itself to the discrepancy of the by, for and of phrase and to the imbalance of white versus black produced segments on the first show. It was said by N.E.T. at that time that the 'by, for and of' phrase would be rectified as far as further releases and advertisements were concerned. As for the question of black versus white production segment goes, nothing has been changed. Therefore, we, not only as black professionals but also mainly because we are black people, feel that N.E.T. has been hypocritical in its presentation of "Black Journal" to the viewing public, especially to the black viewing public.[33]

St. Clair Bourne remarked that "what was involved was not 'tokenism' but 'frontism,'" since black staff members felt they were being used as a front to create the illusion that Negroes controlled the program. Hobson was the most senior staff member to resign. If he had stayed, as NET executives expected, the strikers would have been in a far weaker position. Hobson was thus seen by many as the ringleader.[34]

In response to the strike, NET offered to rescind the "by, for, and of" claims as deceptive. The staff members, in contrast, wanted them to become a reality and demanded a black executive producer—suggesting Lou Potter. NET maintained that Potter lacked adequate experience. They then suggested William Greaves or William Branch, who had recently produced Greaves's *Still a Brother: Inside the Negro Middle Class* for NET. Both, NET claimed, were unavailable.[35] Although Greaves was vacationing on Cape Cod, a quick phone call ascertained that he was prepared to assume the position. By August 23, he had been hired as executive producer for at least one program.[36] Perlmutter became a consultant to the series, and several white producers departed for other programs, while black staff members were promoted and black representation on the staff increased.

William Greaves emerged as the key figure in *Black Journal* for the next year and a half (August 1968–April 1970), serving as both cohost and executive producer. Greaves's history as an actor and filmmaker has been detailed elsewhere in this collection. His experience in a wide range of media forms—theater, film, television, and radio—both as a performer and behind the camera—gave Greaves a wide range of experience. Much of this training was in Canada, where he worked for roughly a decade before returning to New York City, where he made films for the United Nations and USIA.[37] In 1967 he had produced, directed, and photographed *Still a Brother* with writer-producer William B. Branch for *NET Journal*. Branch was an award-winning playwright and Greaves a veteran director.

Still a Brother includes several scenes of performative role-playing, giving the documentary a distinct aesthetic at a moment when cinéma-vérité had achieved a certain hegemony. Its politics were even more unexpected. Initially meant to reassure black viewers that there were opportunities for upward mobility and to remind white audiences that not all African Americans were rioters living in the inner cities, the film revealed that middle-class blacks were rejecting the models of white middle-class America. There was a new black consciousness, a new affirmation of racial identity within the black middle class. The documentary sat on the shelf for several months until the rapid pace of events—which included the Kerner Commission's recommendations as well as the King assassination—made broadcasting possible.[38] Broadcast Monday, April 29, on Channel 13, it received an admiring review from Robert E. Dallos, who noted, "The program shows that there is still very little communication between whites and blacks. The Negro middle class entertains the Negro middle class. The Negro middle class vacations with the Negro middle class." He also quoted Horace Morris of the Urban League: "No matter how far up the economic ladder you climb, there's still the oppressive prejudice of the white man . . . you're still a brother."[39] The film would go on to win a Blue Ribbon at the American Film Festival and be nominated for an Emmy.[40]

William Greaves had the experience and executive skills to act as a buffer between NET's white senior executives and his young *Black Journal* staff. As the executive producer, he told these Young Turks that never again were they likely to find a situation that was so protected and yet offered them so much freedom. The palace coup did end with the departure of two black staff members—Shelia Smith and Charles Hobson. Hobson had also been working as a producer for *Like It Is*, a local program on WABC with Gil Noble and actor Robert Hooks as cohost, which had begun what would be a forty-four-year run on June 2, 1968. Newspaper attention may have forced him to regularize his employment situation, so he chose to leave *Black Journal* once the transition was resolved. Smith joined *Like It Is* as his assistant.[41] In fact, Hobson and Smith were married before the year was out, though their marriage would last little more than a year.[42] Greaves and Hobson thus had little direct contact, though they played somewhat similar roles at *Black Journal* and *Like It Is*—as buffers between liberal white integrationists and black power advocates.

Black Journal's fifth program (October 1968) shows the series in full stride. In some respects, the format and aspirations of the series changed little. Most obviously, Greaves and Lou House wear dashikis instead of sports coats and turtlenecks, while House begins and ends the program with greetings to "brothers and sisters" and a few words of Swahili. More substantially, the staff investigates controversial issues such as the crisis surrounding the Community School Board in Ocean Hill-Brownsville and the upcoming U.S. presidential election, doing so in a polished and forthright manner. The dominance of white producers was clearly shown to be nonessential; quite the reverse—the series displays a new authority and self-confidence.

While offering a multiplicity of voices within the African-American community, *Black Journal* presented forthright editorial comments without giving equal time to either highly conservative or white spokespeople. In a short panel discussion, Professor Charles Hamilton, coauthor of *Black Power* with Stokely Carmichael, simply states that there could be no peace in the nation until the United States got out of Vietnam. Ending the war was thus a key priority for African Americans. The expulsion of "black power" medal winners from the American Olympic team was condemned as excessive and insensitive to past racial injustices. Later in the same program, the longstanding devaluation of Afro-American history and scholarship was documented by profiling a prominent scholar who had once been denied a Ph.D. degree by Harvard University because no one at the university was qualified to supervise his dissertation on black history!

Black Journal clearly deserved the Emmy it would receive at the end of its second season.[43] In a manner that was unique to magazine-format programming, the events of the present are situated in the context of unfolding Afro-American history in ways that give them deeper meaning and resonance. Black identity is powerfully constructed but not essentialized. Unlike other national news programming then on the airwaves, representatives of the African-American community are consistently shown to be reasonable, eloquent, and authoritative. Indeed, they are often shown judging the antisocial behavior of

FIGURE 15.2 Jimmie MacDonald (associate producer on *Black Journal*), William Greaves (*middle*), and Tony Brown at Emmy ceremony for *Black Journal*. Photographer unknown. Courtesy Louise Greaves.

hysterical, unreasonable whites such as Albert Shanker of the United Federation of Teachers, presidential candidate George Wallace, or the Oakland police chief who condemns the Black Panthers in vitriolic terms. Traditional coding of authority by race was inverted; the nature of mainstream television stood exposed.

Both *Inside Bedford-Stuyvesant* and *Black Journal* shared flexible political stances, their inclusion of conflicting ideological positions being a crucial basis for their success. On one level, they operated within white institutions and were part of an integrationist impulse. In some crucial respects the programs were tokens, initiated in obedience to the Kerner Report. Television executives had to recognize that failure to respond to the commission's recommendations might jeopardize relicensing of their stations. It was, as St. Clair Bourne astutely noted, a kind of "frontism"—like the African-American employee who sat near the front door of a corporate office. Yet black staff members were quick to transform these integrationist initiatives into centers that advocated for a version of black cultural nationalism, which placed emphasis on the development of black culture as a mechanism of black liberation.[44] Their moves conformed to Stokely Carmichael's earlier emphasis on "psychological equality" and "black consciousness." In a 1966 article Carmichael had argued that "only black people can convey the revolutionary idea that black people are able to do things themselves. Only they can help create in the community an aroused and continuing black consciousness that will provide the basis for political strength."[45] These two programs soon became consonant with a Black Power approach:

> Black Power is effective control and self-determination by men of color in their own areas.
> Power is total control of the economic, political, educational and social life of our community from top to bottom.
> The exercise of power at the local level is simply what all other groups in American society have done to acquire their share of total American life.[46]

This concept of Black Power was perhaps more reformist than revolutionary. As Carmichael and *Black Journal* regular Charles V. Hamilton wrote, "The concept of Black Power rests on a fundamental premise: Before a group can enter the open society, it must first close ranks. By this we mean that group solidarity is necessary before a group can operate effectively from a bargaining position of strength in a pluralistic society."[47]

The October 1968 program for *Black Journal* showed the extent to which elections and democracy remained a keystone—as opposed to the revolutionary stance of, for instance, the Black Panthers. Nevertheless, as Sheila Smith Hobson later remarked, "Whether or not *Black Journal* was an example of 'radical journalism' it was, admittedly, Black, therefore radical. (Anytime that Blacks seek to report, interpret and present their own experience that, indeed, in this society is the ultimate of radicalism.) The Black perspective (which many whites still refuse to accept as valid) is, as we all know, radical to those dedicated to a white perspective."[48] Or as Greaves expressed it: "There are those who find *Black Journal* 'too militant, too nationalistic' and think of us as 'uppity niggers.' We can assure them that *Black Journal* is a mirror image of the thoughts and feelings of the black community *when* it has the chance to freely express itself."[49]

With the Nixon administration in power, the funding for *Black Journal* and similar programming on public television became more and more difficult. Greaves left *Black Journal* after the 1969–70 season, refusing to continue when it was reduced from one hour to half an hour of programming per month.[50]

Inside Bedford-Stuyvesant and *Black Journal* can be contrasted to the filmmaking activities of Newsreel, which was in active production by 1968. Newsreel was closely connected to Students for a Democratic Society (SDS), which grew with the burgeoning antiwar movement but increasingly splintered into political factions after the violence surrounding the Democratic National Convention in 1968. Newsreel had a multilayered organization with a central committee consisting of four wealthy white men (three via marriages to trust-fund babies or heiresses), who contributed roughly $10,000 a year to the organization.[51] At least one of the four, Norman Fruchter, was an important figure in SDS and gave the group much of its political direction.[52] They were seeking to provide an alternative to the mass media, to supply the movement with films for informational and organizational purposes. Thus a film like *Columbia Revolt* (1968) was designed to inspire similar political action on other campuses.[53] *Black Panther* (1968/69) not only offers interviews with leaders Huey Newton and Eldridge Cleaver but displays of Panther strength as Bobby Seale recites the Panthers' ten-point program. The film was the product of an alliance between black and white radicals that was being pursued by the Panthers, even as it was being rejected by Black Power activists such as Stokely Carmichael.[54]

Newsreel films were constructed in a dialogic, participatory manner, in association with militant organizations such as the Panthers and the Young Lords (*El Pueblo se Levanta*, 1971). The collaborative approach could lead to difficulties as the client group went through changes in strategy and leadership. Nonetheless, a film such as Newsreel's *Black Panther* was more effective in presenting the Panther program and self-image than the segment appearing in the first program of *Black Journal*. It also could be used more readily by leftists—and by Panthers themselves both internally and as they forged alliances with different radical organizations.

The differences between the representational politics of *Black Journal* and those of Newsreel are evident in a comparison between two pieces that focus on the same issue—the question of decentralization and community control in New York City schools, particularly in the experimental Ocean Hill–Brownsville district. Both pieces support community control as a positive step forward. In both cases, the United Federation of Teachers (UFT), its president Albert Shanker, and the city school system are seen as acting in a racist, self-interested fashion. Nevertheless, from these common starting points, the two pieces quickly diverge.

The *Black Journal* segment, produced by Horace Jenkins, is of a high technical quality, using color film with sync interviews. The interweaving of interviews with news footage of demonstrations and schoolchildren in classrooms is well done. The *Black Journal* filmmakers interviewed exclusively black spokespeople, all of whom were on the Ocean Hill–Brownsville School Board. All are dressed in suits and ties and talk in nonmilitant tones. Their complaints are reasonable; their goals, modest but substantive. Because of a restructuring of the curriculum and the hiring of teachers sensitive to the needs of the children, students who are behind several grades in reading levels are making up lost ground. In contrast, Shanker is shown to be seeking to undermine these achievements. The filmmakers cite an American Civil Liberties Union investigation that concludes: "Our examination convinces us that the chaos was not a result of community control but attempts to undermine community control" by the UFT, which was using due process as a smokescreen to discredit decentralization. The segment concludes with the narrator hailing the benefits of community control: "Most of all, society will have the benefits of these minds which have been freed from the chains of ignorance." A follow-up segment using photo-montage makes clear that decentralization was a success in Harlem at I.S. 201, which had been the site of protests the previous year. The appeal is to a broad audience, black and white. While courses may be made more relevant by including Afro-American history, this was seen as a way to motivate students so they will gain a good education and become productive members of society. Likewise, the police who appear in the cinéma-vérité street scenes are there to preserve order, to ensure that the school stays open.

Newsreel's twenty-eight-minute film *Community Control*, which seems to have incorporated some outtakes from the *Black Journal* segment, differs in many respects. Its representational system, like all Newsreel films from this period, is heavily indebted to the radical Argentine documentary *The Hour of the Furnaces* (*La hora de los hornos*, 1968) and the Cuban documentaries of Santiago Alvarez. The formal tropes and subject matter are Third World even if the filmmakers are not. Two black nationalist leaders from the community are interviewed—Herman B. Ferguson, minister of education for the Republic of New Afrika, and Leslie R. "Les" Campbell, director of the Afro-America Teachers Association.[55] Both wear African-style dress. Both see community control as only a starting point for creating a completely separate school system and for taking over all the other institutions in the community—firefighting, police, and so forth. After some introductory titles, the film begins with a lengthy speech by Herman Ferguson, made without any edits and in fact continuing over the black leader once the film ran out. (The long-take style emphasizes that the film does not selectively extract from, and therefore distort, the speeches of black radicals.) The Community Board members are barely interviewed, and even then they are not identified. Not directly attacked, they are simply ignored (just as the *Black Journal* segment ignores these community-based radicals): if anything, members of the board are considered dupes of the Ford Foundation, which helped to sponsor these community-control experiments and so are almost as much a part of the problem as Shanker and the UFT.

Although the documentary contains a few other sync segments, these are contrasted to extensive sequences in which sound is used nonsynchronously. Crescendos of fast edits, the intercutting of still and motion pictures, and a dynamic, sometimes shaky camera emphasize action, urgency, and confrontation. Police are shown as agents of the oppressive state. This is set up with a classroom lesson on slavery in which a teacher discusses "the breaking-in process"— the instilling of fear in slaves through brutal beatings. The police are then shown to be continuing this role in the present day. Street confrontations between rampaging police and sometimes unsuspecting black students are shown, though the specificity of these incidents is never laid out. Rather, the way that the mass media ignores or covers over these incidents is suggested by footage shot off the TV screen of an NBC news reporter lauding "the diplomacy and cool-headed leadership which prevented an outright explosion."

Despite the militancy of these films, there remained a division between white production staff who performed the work of filmmaking, on one hand, and their Third World subjects-collaborators, on the other. Newsreel's participatory model and its search for a sharp alternative to the mass media had progressive elements, but it does bear a structural resemblance to the situation that existed at *Black Journal* before the palace coup—with one exception: filmmaking knowledge remained much more firmly in white hands.

Both Newsreel and *Black Journal* went through a series of trials and transformations during 1970–1972. Richard Nixon had been elected president on a law-and-order campaign, and his administration had little use for *Black Journal* and similar efforts around the nation. Government support turned hostile. Fundraising from corporations such as Ford and Polaroid was always a challenge. By 1969 the budgets for a one-hour *Black Journal* episode had already fallen from $100,000 to $50,000. By the end of the 1969–1970 season, as he faced further cutbacks, Greaves returned to independent production. In June 1970 Tony Brown, president of the National Association of Black Media Producers, assumed the role of executive producer for *Black Journal*.[56] Greaves penned a *New York Times* article that expressed his deep frustration:

> America is obviously sliding into an abyss of tragedy at an accelerating speed. The supreme tragedy is that she may not go into the abyss alone, but will probably take half, if not the whole, world with her....
>
> As an Afro-American film and TV producer, I, for one, haven't time to be either entertained or entertaining.... Maybe television can't solve all the

world's problems, but I think it could, at the very least, give it a good college try. For a start, why not invert the ratio of monies spent on educational, as opposed to entertainment television?[57]

Public television would continue to be a site of struggle for programming by, for, and about African Americans and people of color more generally. The process, however, would be anything but straightforward.

FROM BIRACIALISM TO MULTICULTURALISM IN DOCUMENTARY

The beginnings of what we might now see as multiculturalism appeared in the late 1960s and focused around a binary black-white spilt. The issue was largely conceived in relation to inner-city neighborhoods and black militancy as a two-term white/black opposition. As Greaves noted in 1969, "Only on occasion does one see a black or brown face even today; and of course, there are few Indians, Chinese, and other peoples in TV's racist image of America." And so he expressed his hope for "more *Black Journals*, Black and White journals, Black, Brown, Yellow, and White Journals—and fewer White Journals."[58]

Given New York City's demographics, Puerto Ricans and other Latinos were the most prominent ethnic group at the margins. Almost completely ignored by the Kerner Commission, they posed a special problem for categorization and analysis. Unlike African Americans, they had not been subject to formal, legalized segregation except to the extent that they might be grouped as black. And yet if most Latinos were not "black," they were people of color. There was also the added problem of language and cultural difference, which made it tempting to treat them like "old ethnics." Puerto Ricans might have their own newspapers and cultural organizations as had other groups before them—Italians, Jews, Germans—but unlike those peoples, who would have to learn English in order to gain the full prerogatives of citizenship, they were already full citizens.

Furthermore, such underlying analogies regarding the relationship of such groups to the media were inadequate in a society where television had become the dominant media form. Broadcasting was still confined to a limited number of channels and was highly regulated, with access to production tightly controlled and very expensive. In a further complication, any resulting programming potentially reached all types of audiences, not just the targeted ones. Language thus posed a particular problem for a form whose practitioners assumed that they catered to mass audiences. Up until 1972 the sole instance of Channel

13 programming about Puerto Ricans throughout its existence, according to José García Torres, had been a one-hour special, for NET Journal: *The World of Piri Thomas* (1968). Gordon Parks directed with García Torres serving as chief photographer, while A. H. Perlmutter was credited as executive producer.[59]

New York–based Puerto Ricans seeking access to audio-visual media could use *Black Journal*, *Soul!*, and similar programming breakthroughs as models; but to achieve programming opportunities at WNET, they had to mobilize community groups. The Puerto Rican Educational and Action Media Council, in particular, applied pressure on the station, ultimately conducting a series of protests during the always crucial fund raising drive.[60] In June 1972 they took over the studio during an evening pledge drive and tried to have Piri Thomas, author of *Down These Mean Streets*, read a statement demanding 20 percent of the airtime since the Puerto Rican/Latino community represented 20 percent of New York City's population. When this was followed by picketing outside WNET, station president Jay Islin found enough money for the local series entitled *Realidades* (Realities).

Previously filmmaker García Torres had made a pilot for *Realidades*: *La Carreta* (The Ox-Cart, 1970?), a free translation/adaptation of the three-act, melodramatic play written by Puerto Rico's renowned author René Marqués. *La Carreta* follows a family as it moves from the Puerto Rican countryside to the slums of San Juan and finally to New York. Driven by economic desperation, they go, as Marqués remarks, "in search of an illusion, a utopia they will never find." Overpowered by economic and cultural alienation, the family gradually disintegrates. Juanita drifts into prostitution, and her brother Luis is killed in an industrial accident. Written in 1951, the play premiered in San Juan and New York in 1953. An English language version was produced Off-Broadway in 1966 and was subsequently performed in the city's parks by the Puerto Rican Traveling Theatre during the summer of 1967. Many of the cast members assumed the same roles in García Torres's film, including Lucy Boscana (Dona Gabriela) and Jamie Sanchez (Luis).[61]

After an opening statement by Marqués himself—filmed in the Puerto Rican countryside, the documentary presents scenes from Act 1 of the play in a filmed-theater style. Act 2 is dropped, and the characters go directly to New York where they are disoriented by the city's indifferences and frenetic pace. Although this section continues in the spirit of the play's third act, García Torres shifted to a documentary mode. The camera crew interviews Puerto Ricans and other Latinos who reveal their frustrated search for a better life. The film forsakes the melodramatic conventions of the Marqués play yet also illuminates them. As Richard Peña has noted, its political militancy and melding of fictional and documentary modes align it with the leftist Latin American cinema of the period.[62] More immediately, NET executives were distressed by both the program's "down" subject matter and the fact that the play and many of the interviews were in Spanish, requiring the documentary to be subtitled in English so that non-Spanish speakers could understand it.

Realidades debuted on Channel 13 on Tuesday, October 31, 1972, at 8:00 p.m. The series presented a series of controversial programs during its three-year run (1972 to 1975) in an effort to deal with dual language hurdles of English and Spanish, radio simulcasts were broadcast over WBNX-AM. According to the *New York Times*, "Puerto Rican activists and the management of WNET are proud of 'Realidades' as the first show dealing with this important part of the population of the metropolitan area, which has until now been all but ignored in television programming."[63] At an early stage it arranged exchanges with KMEX in Los Angeles, first showing Jesus Treviño's *Yo Soy Chicano* (1972). Although the show was funded as a national series in 1974, it closed a year later due to a shortage of funding and other problems. Nevertheless, it was followed by other Latino public affairs programs at commercial stations, including WNBC's *Visiones*, a weekly segment about Hispanic culture, which also airs in Spanish on sister Telemundo station WNJU, and *Imagenes Latinas*, which was broadcast on ABC-owned Channel 50 WWTI in Watertown, New York.[64] Puerto Rican filmmakers also began to make their own films. Carlos de Jesús made *The Devil Is a Condition*, about substandard housing in Spanish Harlem, for German television in 1972. Without forsaking militancy, de Jesús injected a lyrical quality that distinguishes the film from contemporaneous Newsreel productions.

The year 1972 also saw the first public results of significant changes that had been occurring at Newsreel. In this regard, the arrival of Chris Choy in 1971 proved crucial. Choy's appearance coincided with an obviously tardy initiative to recruit Third World peoples into the organization. On her first visit, Choy walked into a rough-cut screening of *Janie's Janie* (1971), for which the principal collaborators were Geri Ashur, Peter Barton, Marilyn Mulford, and Stephanie Palewski, with music by Bev Grant and Laura Liben. Choy remembers that there were fifty people in the audience, and all were white. She criticized the film's lack of evenhandedness: it focused on a white welfare mother while completely ignoring her best friend, who was black—unleashing a tempestuous discussion. The film's feminist perspective was judged insufficient, and ultimately *Janie's Janie* was not distributed by Newsreel.[65]

As a member of Newsreel, Choy helped create a Third World caucus within the group. Soon she was sitting on the central committee.[66] As Bill Nichols has pointed out, there were sharp divisions between white and Third World members, between men and women, between "haves and have-nots"—those from middle-class backgrounds and those from working-class and lumpen backgrounds.[67]

Ultimately its white male central committee members left and several of the groups or caucuses within New York Newsreel disbanded. Newsreel was left with a handful of predominantly Third World members who renamed the organization Third World Newsreel.

As Newsreel was falling apart, Choy and Susan Robeson—granddaughter of Paul Robeson—were able to make *Teach Our Children* (1972). Very much a transitional film, *Teach Our Children* utilizes the repertoire of representational techniques established by the old Newsreel. The documentary examines the uprising at Attica State Prison and its brutal suppression. While the production team offered a promising cross-cultural collaboration (Choy is an Asian immigrant—part Chinese and part Korean), the filmmakers focused on Puerto Rican and African-American prisoners, some of whom had been released from prison and could be interviewed.

With the departure of Newsreel members who took with them their equipment, skills, and financial resources, Third World Newsreel faced an uncertain future. In the early 1970s, however, a new phenomenon began to emerge in the world of independent documentary filmmaking. In 1972–1973, the New York State Council on the Arts was beginning to fund filmmaking projects. Choy and Third World Newsreel received NYSCA funding to make their next several films, including *In the Event Anyone Disappears* (1974), about oppressive living conditions in women's prison, and *Fresh Seeds in the Big Apple* (1975), about the underacknowledged need for daycare—an issue of particular relevance to women. It was only with *From Spikes to Spindles* (1975), about the immigrant Chinese experience and a growing political activism in New York's Chinatown, that Choy began to address issues within her own ethnic community. Moreover, the film was offered in two versions—one for Chinese speakers and an English-language version. Here again the aspiration to make a documentary "by, for, and about" a marginalized community was achieved. Thereafter, much of Choy's work engaged the Asian American community—notably, *Mississippi Triangle* (with Allan Siegel and Worth Long, 1983) and *Who Killed Vincent Chin* (with Renee Tajima, 1989).

PBS was increasingly open to programs by independent documentary filmmakers of color, such as Carlos de Jesus with *The Picnic* (1976) and Bill Miles with *Men of Bronze* (1976), about black soldiers who fought in World War I, and the four-part *I Remember Harlem* (1981). Women filmmakers, particularly white women, made feminist films focused on women, such as Julia Reichert's *Growing Up Female* (with Jim Klein, 1972), *Yudie* (Mirra Bank, 1974), *Chris and Bernie* (Deborah Shaffer and Bonnie Friedman, 1974), and *Joyce at 34* (Claudia Weill, 1974). In 1977 the Mariposa Film Group finally completed *Word Is Out:*

Stories of Some of Our Lives, the first feature-length documentary about lesbian and gay identity made by gay filmmakers. In all these instances, the idea of "by, for, and about" was consciously at play.

William Greaves had a highly productive if not always easy filmmaking career after *Black Journal*. He left *Black Journal* after having won a Blue Ribbon for *In the Company of Men* (1969) and initial presentations of his feature film *Symbiopsychotaxiplasm: Take One*.[68] While involved in the production of low-budget Blaxploitation films, he also made *The Fight* (1971/1974), about the Ali-Frazier heavyweight championship bout, and *From These Roots* (1974), about the Harlem Renaissance. Much more could be said about those who worked with Greaves on *Black Journal*. Kent Garrett worked as a producer for *CBS News* from 1975 to 1986 as part of a thirty-year career in television news. Horace B. Jenkins was based in Ethiopia for a time while working on *Black Journal* but returned to the United States, where he worked on Emmy-winning segments of *Sesame Street*; on *The Advocates*, a weekly television program by KCET in Los Angeles; and on *30 Minutes*, a version of *60 Minutes* for youth. His career culminated with the recently rediscovered *Cane River* (1982) before he died of a heart attack the year of its completion.[69] St. Clair Bourne consistently produced work on black subject matter. He made *Let the Church Say Amen!* in 1973, though his prolific career did not fully take off until the 1980s. Charles Hobson also boasted numerous producer credits in the 1980s, including the nine-part series *The Africans* (1986). Stanley Nelson, who joined Greaves's filmmaking company in 1976, went on to make *Two Dollars and a Dream: The Story of Madam C. J. Walker* (1987) and many other documentaries on the African-American experience.

Black-focused television programs such as *Inside Bedford-Stuyvesant*, *Black Journal*, and *Soul!* were at the forefront of a radical shift in filmmaking practices in the post-1968 era. Amid ongoing struggles, the creation of "of, for, and by" documentaries became more common in the 1970s and eventually almost routine—as the careers of William Greaves and many of his *Black Journal* colleagues demonstrate. Almost routine perhaps, but such endeavors could never be assumed or taken for granted. The mid-1970s through the mid-1980s was to be a decade that challenged the most steadfast.

NOTES

1. This essay revises a presentation I gave many times back in the early 1990s. It overlapped with the Greaves professional biography that I was writing with Adam Knee, and so I put it aside. Thanks to Scott MacDonald and Jacqueline Stewart for

the opportunity to revisit and publish the piece. I am particularly indebted to Charles Hobson, Maren Stange, Chris Choy, Adam Knee, and William Greaves.
2. William J. Nichols, "Newsreel: Film and Revolution," M.A. thesis, University of California, Los Angeles, 1977; Bill Nichols, *Newsreel: Documentary Filmmaking on the American Left* (New York: Arno Press, 1980); William Boddy and Jonathan Buchsbaum, "Cinema in Revolt: Newsreel," *Millennium* 4–5 (Summer/Fall 1979): 43–52; Michael Renov, "Early Newsreel: The Construction of a Political Imaginary for the New Left," in *The Subject of Documentary* (Minneapolis: University of Minnesota Press, 2004), 3–20. More information is now available on the internet. For instance, see Allan Siegel, "Some Notes About Newsreel and Its Origins (for the Yamagata International Documentary Film Festival 2003)," http://www.allansiegel.info/writings/page9/page9.html.
3. Although *Soul!* was an important achievement in the "of, for, and by" movement, it will not be a direct concern of this article. For an excellent examination of *Soul!*, see Gayle Wald, *It's Been Beautiful: Soul! and Black Power Television* (Durham, N.C.: Duke University Press, 2014).
4. Josh Glick, *Los Angeles Documentary and the Production of Public History, 1958–1977* (Berkeley: University of California Press, 2018).
5. Ford Foundation, *Ford Foundation Activities in Noncommercial Broadcasting, 1951–1976*, 1976.
6. Malcolm McLaughlin, *The Long, Hot Summer of 1967: Urban Rebellion in America* (New York: Palgrave Macmillan, 2014).
7. *Report of the National Advisory Commission on Civil Disorders*, intro. by Tom Wicker (New York: Dutton, 1968), 2, 20.
8. *Report*, 21, 385.
9. William Greaves, "*Black Journal*: A Few Notes from the Executive Producer," *Television Quarterly* 8, no. 4 (Fall 1969): 66–72 (reprinted as chapter 12 of this volume).
10. "Of, For and By," *Newsweek*, April 29, 1968, 59.
11. "Of, For and By."
12. Deputy Police Commissioner Franklin A. Thomas was an original board member of the Bedford-Stuyvesant Renewal and Rehabilitation Corporation, which became the Bedford Stuyvesant Restoration Corporation. It was formally established in April 1967, but its immediate antecedents came out of initiatives begun in 1964. See "History," https://restorationplaza.org/about-us/, accessed March 9, 2019.
13. Charles Hobson to Charles Musser, May 15, 1991.
14. Deardra Shuler, "Marian Etoile Watson: Casting Caution to the Wind," *AfroCentric News Network*, http://www.afrocentricnews.com/html/marian_etoile_watson.html, accessed March 24, 2019. Dennis quickly took over from Wadell Gaynor, who was initially announced as the series producer. (George Gent, "TV Series for Bedford Stuyvesant Begins Monday," *New York Times*, April 5, 1968, 93.) Gaynor went to work on other, more established and secure, black-focused nonfiction programs.
15. Hobson to Musser, May 15, 1991; "The Historymakers—Charles Hobson," https://www.thehistorymakers.org/biography/charles-hobson, accessed March 9, 2019.

16. William Cole, "Anomaly TV: *Inside Bed-Stuy*," *Brooklyn Rail* (April–May 2003), https://brooklynrail.org/2003/04/local/anomaly-tv-inside-bed-stuy.
17. See also "Persuasions in Village," *New York Amsterdam News*, July 5, 1969.
18. A fashion designer who appeared in the segment about welfare mothers is another example of a black entrepreneur. This survey is based on an analysis of tapes 1353, 2314, and 2468.
19. "Of, For and By," 59.
20. "Bed-Stuy's New Look," *News of Metromedia* 3, no. 5: 3.
21. "*Inside Bedford-Stuyvesant*," *Variety*, April 10, 1968.
22. "Producer Dies of Heart Attack in New York City," *Norfolk Journal and Guide*, December 22, 1982, 12. Horace B. Jenkins died on December 3, 1982, contributing to the film's failure to find commercial release at that time.
23. NET premiered the documentary on May 6, 1968—a week after Greaves and Branch's *Still a Brother*. "Color Us Black! (Part 1)," https://diva.sfsu.edu/collections/sfbatv/bundles/210745, accessed March 24, 2019.
24. An interesting career overview of Kent Garrett, who graduated from Harvard in 1963, is provided by Sophia Nguyen, "Reel Revolution: A Television Documentarian Looks Back," *Harvard Magazine* (March–April 2017), https://harvardmagazine.com/2017/03/reel-revolution. See also Garrett's website, http://www.kentgarrettproductions.com/about.html, accessed March 9, 2019.
25. Kent Garrett to Charles Musser, email, March 11, 2019.
26. Dennis McClean, "St. Clair Bourne; Captured the Black Experience on Film," *Los Angeles Times*, December 20, 2007.
27. "House Is Host for NET's 'Black Journal,'" *New York Amsterdam News*, July 27, 1968.
28. "Black Woman in Television Is a Real Go, Go, Go, Girl," *New York Amsterdam News*, March 7, 1970. For a brief summary of Peggy Pinn's career, see "Peggy D. Pinn, 65, an Educator in TV," *New York Times*, April 21, 1994.
29. Shelia Smith Hobson, "Women and Television," in *Sisterhood Is Powerful: An Anthology of Writings from the Women's Liberation Movement*, ed. Robin Morgan (New York: Random House, 1970), 72–73.
30. Greaves, "*Black Journal*," 66–72.
31. Bob Hunter, "'Black Journal' Sheds Light on White Hate," *Chicago Defender*, June 15, 1968.
32. Hal Humphrey, "A Black Series for All Races," *Los Angeles Times*, June 14, 1968.
33. Robert E. Dallos, "11 Negro Staff Members Quit N.E.T 'Black Journal' Program," *New York Times*, August 21, 1968, 91.
34. Hobson to Musser, May 15 and 19, 1991. The *New York Times* article mentions that Horace Jenkins also resigned, but Hobson suggests otherwise.
35. Dallos, "11 Negro Staff Members."
36. "9 Negroes Return to Black Journal," *New York Times*, August 24, 1968.
37. For more information on Greaves's early career, see Adam Knee and Charles Musser, "William Greaves: Chronicler of the African American Experience," *Film Quarterly* 45, no. 3 (Spring 1992), reprinted as chapter 1 in this volume.
38. William Greaves to Charles Musser and Adam Knee, April–May 1991.

39. Robert E. Dallos, "Negro Middle Class 'Revolution' Subject of Negro-Made TV Show," *New York Times*, April 26, 1968.
40. "'Still a Brother' Movie Wins 'Emmy' Nomination," *Baltimore African American*, June 7, 1969.
41. Shelia Smith Hobson writes eloquently about some of the achievements of *Like It Is* in "The Rise and Fall of Blacks in Serious Television," *Freedomways* 14, no. 3 (1974): 191–93.
42. Smith and Hobson married in 1968 (marriage license 28853 issued in Manhattan) and collaborated on other projects, such as a joint interview with poet Nikki Giovanni, "The Poet and Black Realities," *Tuesday Magazine* (a supplement to the *Newark Sunday News*), June 4, 1969. Nikki Giovanni, *Conversations with Nikki Giovanni* (Jackson: University of Mississippi Press, 1992), 3; Hobson to Musser, March 24, 2019.
43. "William Greaves Wins Three Film Awards," *Chicago Defender*, May 30, 1970.
44. Robert L. Allen, *Black Awakening in Capitalist America: An Analytic History* (New York: Doubleday, 1969), 139–40.
45. Allen, 46.
46. CORE Resolution, 1966 National Convention, Baltimore, Maryland, cited in Allen, 55.
47. Stokely Carmichael and Charles V. Hamilton, *Black Power: The Politics of Liberation in America* (New York: Random House, 1967), 44.
48. Smith Hobson, "The Rise and Fall of Blacks in Serious Television," 190.
49. Greaves, *"Black Journal."*
50. Greaves, *"Black Journal."*
51. Chris Choy to Charles Musser, May 13, 1991.
52. Norman Fruchter and Robert Machover codirected two documentaries in the mid-1960s about community organizing in black neighborhoods in Newark, New Jersey: *We Got to Live Here* (1965) and *Troublemakers* (1966).
53. I saw *Columbia Revolt* as a freshman at Yale University in the fall of 1969. As viewers, the audience found it instructive and inspirational. Not incidentally, Yale was subsequently shut down for most of the spring 1970 semester. See also Jane Gaines, "Political Mimesis," in *Collecting Visible Evidence*, ed. Jane M. Gaines and Michael Renov (Minneapolis: University of Minnesota Press, 1999), 84–102.
54. Clayborne Carson, *In Struggle: SNCC and the Black Awakening of the 1960s* (Cambridge, Mass.: Harvard University Press, 1981), 282.
55. Herman Ferguson (December 31, 1920–September 25, 2014) fled to Guyana and was in political exile for nineteen years until he voluntarily returned in 1989. Arrested and convicted on his return, he spent three years in prison. See Nayaba Arinde, "Remembering Herman Ferguson," *New York Amsterdam News*, October 2, 2014, http://amsterdamnews.com/news/2014/oct/02/remembering-herman-ferguson/?page=1. Leslie R. Campbell (August 25, 1939–May 22, 2013) later took the name Jitu Weusi and left the New York Department of Education and helped establish a number of black nationalist cultural organizations in Brooklyn (Wikipedia). Lee Ferguson was interviewed for the *Eyes on the Prize* series. A transcription

56. "Brown Succeeds William Greaves," *Sun Reporter*, June 13, 1970, 40.
57. William Greaves, "100 Madison Avenues Will Be of No Help," *New York Times*, August 9, 1970 (reprinted as chapter 13 in this volume).
58. Greaves, "*Black Journal*," 66–72.
59. Beatrice Berg, "Anglos Can Watch, Too," *New York Times*, December 17, 2019.
60. Lillian Jiménez, "From the Margin to the Center: Puerto Rican Cinema in New York," *Centro* 2, no. 8 (1988): 32; "José Garciá Torres and *Realidades*" (Garcia interviewed by Aurora Flores and Lillian Jimenez in 1987), *Centro* 2, no. 8 (1988): 36.
61. Charles Pliditch, "Introduction," in Rene Marqués, *The Oxcart (La Carreta)*, trans. Charles Pliditch (New York: Scribner's, 1969).
62. Richard Peña, talk at New York Historical Society, April 7, 1991.
63. Berg, "Anglos Can Watch, Too."
64. Jiménez, "From the Margin to the Center."
65. *Janie's Janie* was distributed by the Learning Development Center in Newark and Odeon. The film is currently available through Third World Newsreel, http://twn.org/catalog/pages/cpage.aspx?rec=1324, accessed March 12, 2019.
66. Choy to Musser, May 13, 1991.
67. Nichols, *Newsreel*, 30.
68. Alan M. Kriegsman, "Symbiopyschotaxiplasm at the Corcoran," *Washington Post*, June 22, 1970.
69. "Producer Dies of a Heart Attack in New York City," *Norfolk Journal and Guide*, December 22, 1982.

16

William Greaves, *Black Journal*, and the Long Roots of Black Internationalism

CELESTE DAY MOORE

In the first episode of *Black Journal*—which debuted on the National Educational Television (NET) network in June 1968— the African-American actor and comedian Godfrey Cambridge walks on screen dressed in white painter's clothing and holding a can of black paint. He then appears to paint the inside of the screen in black. Peering into the lens as it is brushed into blackness, Cambridge in many ways embodies the program's commitment to transforming the racial identity of public television, which appeared to producers and viewers alike as an especially pressing issue in the wake of a series of rebellions in cities in the summer of 1967. Indeed, the Kerner Commission had—when reporting on this period of urban unrest—pointed specifically to media coverage as a contributing factor. However, while this particular contrivance might have appealed to the white producers at NET, the opening scene in retrospect serves as a potent metaphor for the ways in which *Black Journal* was, at least initially, restricted by the literal and metaphorical frame in which it was imagined to transmit. It was this limited vision, as well as the predominantly white production staff, that prompted the Black staff to strike just a few episodes after the program's debut.[1] They demanded that a program that was said to be made by, for, and about Black people actually meet that promise. While NET's leadership initially claimed that they were unable to find suitably trained Black producers, they agreed in September 1968 to hire the filmmaker William Greaves—who was already an assistant producer on the program—as the new executive producer.[2]

It was in this new capacity that Greaves would transform the ways in which African-American issues were covered on television. Rather than presenting a "blackened" version of the U.S. media perspective, Greaves instead expanded the frame, imbuing the program with a Pan-African sensibility and a vision of Blackness that transcended the borders of the United States. Some of these interventions were more obvious, whether in the sounds of African drumming that were integrated into the theme music; the red, black, and green logo; or its host Lou House (later Wali Sadiq), who was typically dressed in a dashiki and greeted viewers in Swahili, Arabic, and Wolof. It was also manifest in the programming itself: its coverage of African and Pan-African culture, its contextualization of current events, and its Pan-African political perspective. This Black internationalist orientation, I argue, was fundamentally shaped by Greaves's own life and career, in which he had consistently looked outside of the United States to better contextualize the African-American experience and to reject the misrepresentations of Black life that persisted in the media. While Greaves's tenure as executive producer was relatively brief—lasting only twenty-one episodes—his time at the program helped to form a critical link between different generations of Pan-African intellectuals, whose debates and deliberations found in *Black Journal* a new medium of expression. Thus, by focusing on Greaves's early life and career, we not only better understand the kinds of

FIGURE 16.1 Greaves and Wali Sadiq on the set of *Black Journal*. Photographer unknown. Courtesy Louise Greaves.

questions that informed *Black Journal* but also glimpse what Robin D. G. Kelley has termed the long (and intergenerational) "global vision" that has defined Black political thought and culture throughout history.³

Among the most resonant memories that Greaves shared was that of being seven or eight years old and sitting on the stoop of his building on 135th Street between Frederick Douglass Boulevard and Lenox Avenue. On late summer afternoons, just as dusk was falling, he and his friends would often glimpse a man who was carrying "what seemed to be a heavy suitcase in one hand and something that looked like flat cans under his other arm." The suitcase and cans, it turns out, were a projector and films, which the man would then project at the Big Apple Bar & Grille across the street, transforming the well-known jazz club into an ersatz theater. Not permitted to enter the bar, Greaves and his friends would nevertheless climb onto the railings outside to "peek through the windows and see the images moving on the screen."⁴ Years later, Greaves discovered that the man was none other than Oscar Micheaux, who pioneered the Black feature film industry beginning in 1919.⁵ In his retelling, the memory of Micheaux became a potent metaphor for the history of Black cinema. By virtue of the "apartheid society" that persisted in the United States, the Black filmmaker was forced to create a "parallel, separate cinema," which made *Black* filmmaking the precursor to "independent" film precisely because of its alienated position. In glimpsing Micheaux, Greaves redefined the experience of segregation in the United States not simply as an impediment—although it certainly was—but also as a generative space in which Black filmmakers created their own, independent visual framework for understanding the past and present.

This particular perspective, which engaged the Black past to sustain the future, not only was formed on his stoop on 135th street but was in fact rooted in the political culture of interwar Harlem. This neighborhood was by Greaves's birth in 1926 an epicenter of African-American life and letters as well as a central node in the African diaspora, which linked up migrants from the U.S. South with those from the Caribbean.⁶ Indeed, Greaves's own family reflected this diasporic cosmopolitanism. His father, Garfield Gilbert Hannibal Greaves, was born in Barbados but—like many other West Indian men of his generation— had come to the United States after an extended period working on the Panama Canal. As Greaves recalled, his father had arrived in New York not only at the beginning of the Harlem Renaissance but also on the "wave of the Marcus

Garvey movement," which drew its power from the diasporic and transnational dimensions of Black life in this period.⁷ While his father was not to his knowledge a member of Garvey's Universal Negro Improvement Association (UNIA), Greaves guessed that he was so in practice, as "practically every black person in America was either an official member of the UNIA or believed in it." Once in New York, his father began working at a Pentecostal church on 131st Street in Harlem. It was there that he met Greaves's mother, Phyllis Emily Muir, who was born in Kingston, Jamaica, and was herself—in Greaves's retelling—the descendent of Maroons, whom he described as "a militant people who did not tolerate colonialism or slavery."⁸

In addition to claiming a familial legacy of Black militancy, Greaves was also drawn from an early age to African and African diasporic history, and in particular the masculinist narrative that undergirded this intellectual tradition.⁹ One of his early influences was a Haitian friend, Mark Desgraves, whose father would teach him on Saturday mornings about the history of the Haitian Revolution and its heroes, Toussaint l'Ouverture, Henri Christophe, and Jean-Jacques Dessalines.¹⁰ Later, Greaves would join the American Negro Theatre's production of *Henri Christophe*, in which he would depict Dessalines.¹¹ As he recalled, he was "delighted to play this rabid nationalist," reveling in the opportunity to enact revolt against racist domination.¹² He was moreover drawn to the Pan-African organizations that flourished in Harlem in this same period, when scholars and activists alike found ways to "institutionalize" the study of the African past in libraries, associations, and clubs.¹³ At Stuyvesant High School, Greaves became interested in African dance, first with Asadata Dafora, who was associated with the African Academy of Arts and Research, founded in 1943 to educate Americans about African history and culture and to support African independence movements, as well as with Pearl Primus.¹⁴

Greaves's first acting role was in the American Negro Theatre's *Garden of Time*, which, despite its own setting in antiquity, stimulated his interest in ancient African history. It was through the play that he met actor Austin Briggs-Hall, who took Greaves under his wing on set and "schooled him" in the history of Ethiopia, Ghana, and Zimbabwe.¹⁵ In turn, Briggs-Hall introduced Greaves to the "Ethiopian Library," which was founded by Barbadian historian Charles C. Seifert in the 1930s as the Ethiopian School of Research.¹⁶ There, Greaves took classes with Howard professor William Leo Hansberry, who traveled on weekends to lecture on African history. As Greaves recalled, he was the youngest member of these classes, "the mascot of the group," which included an extraordinarily distinguished group of scholars: John Henrik Clarke, a pioneer in Pan-African and Africana studies; Jean Hutson (the only woman, in his recollection), a librarian and curator who eventually headed the Schomburg Center for Research in Black Culture; the Jamaican historian J. A. Rogers, who used public forums to popularize African history; the sociologist George Edmund Haynes, whose research was on South Africa in the 1940s and 1950s; and the Barbadian writer, activist, and bibliophile Richard B. Moore, who would later champion the use of the term "African American" as opposed to "Negro." As Greaves recalled, all these figures were "much involved with the retrieval of our lost history," as well as later anticolonial efforts to reclaim and rebuild African history. While there was one woman in the group, its composition reveals Greaves's own gendered sense of Black internationalism, underscoring the ways in which these claims to dignity, self-sufficiency, and independence were frequently predicated on masculinity.[17]

While Greaves continued to act, he soon found that the majority of roles—both in film and on stage—were far less appealing. When offered a role as a Pullman porter, he first thought that he might be able to "play him with some dignity," thereby rejecting the "Uncle Tom, Stepin Fetchit–type depiction." He soon learned, however, that this particular caricature was precisely what the director desired. Reflecting on this dilemma facing him and other African-American actors of his generation—who were asked to enact racist stereotypes—Greaves invoked his African past. Its dignity and beauty had long been denied, replaced by the vision of a "bunch of silly natives running around in the jungle" to further support claims to Western superiority. Rather than accepting these colonial terms, Greaves decided that the only path forward was to make documentary films that "spoke to the needs and interests of the black community and to the dignity of our history."[18] With this new goal in mind, in 1953 he left the United States, and its "wall of racism and discrimination," for Canada, where he would work for seven years at the National Film Board.[19] Like other artists and filmmakers—including Melvin Van Peebles, whom he would later feature on *Black Journal*—Greaves needed to leave the United States to build his career.

In 1960 Greaves returned to the United States prepared to use documentary film as a tool to liberate "the minds of Americans" and to reveal the "true history of a people."[20] After first making films for the United Nations, he moved to the United States Information Agency (USIA), a Cold War organization whose public diplomacy materials frequently showcased African-American culture.[21] While this perspective limited USIA's understanding of Black culture to its potential as anticommunist propaganda, it nevertheless provided for Greaves—as well as for a range of artists and musicians—an opportunity to create and perform on a global stage, and moreover to gain the technical skills and credentials not otherwise available. This made Greaves, in his own estimation, "the most experienced Black filmmaker in the country."[22] One of his most significant films for the USIA was the documentary of the First World Festival of Negro Arts in Dakar in 1966, where thousands gathered to celebrate the history and future of *négritude*. This was Greaves's first trip to the African continent and would be a critical moment for him in creating a cinematic representation of diasporic connection. The film begins and ends with footage of Langston Hughes, whose poem "The Negro Speaks of Rivers" is narrated by Greaves as Hughes walks along the Atlantic Ocean, underscoring the transatlantic reach of Black memory and culture. This motif continues throughout the film, as Greaves looks for ways to highlight the universal dimensions of Black culture and the diasporic links among Black people.

Building on this experience, and his growing commitment to cultivating Pan-African connections, Greaves arrived at the set of *Black Journal* prepared to transform it. The program constituted, as many scholars have shown, a direct response to the liberal and integrationist aims of the National Advisory Commission on Civil Disorders, or Kerner Commission, which had found that racial disparities in media coverage were a major factor in the rebellions that swept major cities in 1967.[23] The commission found that the media had, in addition to misrepresenting the rebellions, failed to communicate "to the majority of their audience—which is white—a sense of the degradation, misery and hopelessness of life in the ghetto."[24] The commission advised the industry to expand its coverage of the African-American community and to "integrate" Black life into its coverage. By contrast, Greaves sought to change the medium's perspective. In an article published in *Television Quarterly* soon after he took over as executive producer, he critiqued the ways in which the program's first producers replicated the codes and conventions of most public affairs program, with the mere addition of "black or brown faces."[25] Indeed, as producer St. Clair Bourne described, the "image of African Americans" had long served a "specific purpose" in the film industry, which limited them to a stereotypical cast of characters: "toms, coons, mulattoes, mammies."[26]

Instead, Greaves envisioned that the program would be a reflection of "black reality" and a platform through which Black people could communicate "among ourselves over the airwaves" and fight social injustice.[27] In particular, he wanted to create images that reflected the dignity and power of Black history, which would then "be mass-produced and disseminated throughout the world."[28] This perspective spoke to contemporary movements at college campuses, in national politics, and in the media—much of which *Black Journal* was itself documenting—but also suggests that the show itself was oriented around new technologies of mass media. It built on previous forms of media—including libraries, books, journals, and lectures—but by virtue of the television format, *Black Journal* was positioned to institute more radical messages about Black ownership and power through Black-produced mass media. The show would be, in the words of fellow producer Lou Potter, "not just black faces bearing a white message, but black ideals, black achievements—a black world."[29]

That ambition, to define the contours of a Black world, was visible on every level of programming at *Black Journal*. It included the show's iconography and the various permutations of the logo, which was often placed over images of the African continent and then eventually formed inside of it. It is also discernible in its news reporting, which included Greaves and House's programs on the liberation struggle in Mozambique, the civil war in Nigeria, and the anti-apartheid movement in South Africa. These reports connected the experiences of African Americans to Africa, in some cases through direct comparison and in other cases as a means of building connections. In a special episode devoted to conditions for African Americans in the U.S. South, the hosts noted that while the suffering in Biafra got "major play" in the mainstream media, "we might remind white America that there is a Biafra in our own backyard ... what some might call 'Biafra American style.'" In 1969 *Black Journal* devoted an episode to the anti-apartheid struggle in South Africa, which included an older documentary film and an (all-male) roundtable discussion that featured both African and African-American experts. The program ended by noting that while there was a "geographical distance between blacks in South Africa and Afro-Americans, the problems that face black people everywhere and most of Western civilization are essentially the same. We are a colonized people oppressed by racist institutions created by whites ... whether here or in South Africa, black people are struggling toward liberation." As the *Chicago Defender* reported, this was the "first time on national television" that "black Americans will offer their insight into South African apartheid."[30]

Greaves also produced a number of special programs and documentaries intended to deepen his audience's understanding of African and Pan-African histories, including segments on African art and dance, the Haitian Revolution—the "decisive victory in the black man's struggle for emancipation"—and the retentions that existed between African and African-American cultures. Echoing his own persistent frustration with the depiction of Black people, he critiqued the ways in which the richness of African history had been obscured by the mainstream media, which peddled "frightening myths of the primitive savage African" and the "dark forbidding continent." While these myths were created for European exploitation, Greaves used this new media platform to introduce historical research on the "majestic kingdoms" that flourished before the arrival of Europeans and to call attention to the multiple meanings of African art, which provides a sense of "continuity for all Black men from their past, through the present and future."

To help illustrate these connections, Greaves also invited onto the show some of the same people who had influenced him in his youth, including John Henrik Clarke, who appeared on the program in November 1968 to interview the art historian Earl Sweeting about African retentions. In conversation, they described their own attempts to "make something beautiful" that others had said was ugly. In particular, they wanted to illustrate African innovation, civilization, and education, a perspective that still referenced Western civilizationist narratives, yet nevertheless established Black-defined parameters of worldliness, beauty, and value. In February 1969 the program also featured Jean Hutson, who was interviewed at the Schomburg Center, surrounded by books and manuscript materials, to discuss founder Arturo Schomburg's commitment to preserving a Pan-African past.

Just as it made newly relevant an older generation of Pan-Africanism, so too were its gendered dimensions amplified on the program, which focused on the interpretative work male scholars and activists while depicting women primarily as those who either embodied African history or cared for its historical archives. Finally, in the October 1968 episode, the show reported on the annual meeting of the Association for the Study of Negro Life and History, highlighting the challenges posed by a new cohort of historians as well as the elder figures, who were frustrated to learn that the "wealth of material on African history unearthed by the late professor William Leo Hansberry had not found its way into the conference." Greaves lingered on this loss, underscoring the ways in which African-American scholars had been excluded from the academy but also the ways in which "African and Afro-American history" were excluded from mainstream accounts.

While indebted to older generations of Pan-Africanists, Greaves also used the space to cultivate a new generation of Black filmmakers, who were likewise committed to expanding the framework for understanding African-American history, culture, and politics. Indeed, one of the program's most important legacies was its twelve-week training program, which would serve as a "vehicle" for Black filmmakers—whom Greaves and others would term "Third World technicians"—to gain skills and experience for future careers in broadcasting.[31] While Greaves had needed to leave the United States to gain those skills, now he imagined a training program that would serve the Third World. This new generation included Kent Garrett, who traveled in 1969 to Vietnam with a small crew—including sound engineer Andy Ferguson and cameraman Leroy

Lucas—to produce a cinéma-vérité documentary on the Black soldier, linking up the historical experience of Black military service to the experiences of soldiers in Vietnam. It drew connections between the experiences of soldiers in Vietnam and those in the Spanish-American War and World War II, which had been fought in the "name of freedom from tyranny for all men," and expected Black men to once again "make the world safe for others" while it "remained unsafe for themselves." Garrett also traveled to Ethiopia to produce a very different kind of documentary, a lush, highly stylized, and experimental film that documented the architecture, religion, history, and art in Addis Ababa. As Greaves noted in his introduction to the film segment, this documentary took a *Black Journal* "film crew out of this country for the first time to our richly historic mother continent, to Africa." There, the film highlighted the historic role of Ethiopia in fostering African culture but also its potential new role in molding "Africa's hopes and destiny."

This new generation also included Horace Jenkins, whose documentary on the Pan-African festival in Algiers in 1969 highlighted the "common cultural heritage" that connected Black people but also televised the conversations, debates, and at times rancor that defined this festival.[32] As Jenkins reported, the festival attempted to "eliminate the centuries-old rancor between many Arabs and blacks," and the film itself sought to capture this dialogue, documenting one of the first moments in which a "non-Western setting" might provide for an African-American dialogue with Arabs from North Africa as well as "other Africans" and placing the "African-American struggle in an international context."[33] Some of its most powerful footage was of the Afro-American Center, which had been established by the Black Panther Party. At the center, Emory Douglas and Eldridge Cleaver respond to young Africans' queries about Black exclusivity and the kinds of specific claims the Panthers were making with regard to neocolonialism in the United States. It also features an interview with Stokely Carmichael, who discusses whether problems of Africans are the same as those of Afro-Americans. He determines that "our fight is a fight against capitalism and racism" and believes that Pan-Africanism is the only position (and that Black nationalism leads here), but there is a need for a base, and the best place to seize it is in Africa. Just as white Americans are Europeans, he continues, "We are Africans." The program returns several times to the historian Reginald Wilson, who observes the need to re-create "the conscience of our people" and to "re-create what is the common shared experience of black people everywhere." The program ends by claiming that the meaning of *négritude* has expanded since its initial conception and is now part of a much larger liberatory project.

In August 1970, just after Greaves's own departure from the program, Jenkins moved to Addis Ababa to establish a permanent African bureau, so that the show could challenge the dominant images of Africa that were common in media and instead report truthfully on the "social, economic and political developments on the African continent."[34] As was reported later, the programs made there were intended for use by other African countries on their television stations, so as to help create "permanent dialogue between Africans in Africa and Africans in America because of our mutual cultural ties and political needs."[35] Reporting the following month, the *Afro-American* described this as an "event of tremendous significance," for now the African continent would be depicted by Black people. The article continued: "the nation's readers and viewers have been fed over the years ... a less than balanced picture spliced with the drums, spears and tigers." This program, they reported, would do more than "put a different face on the information from Africa" and instead would show how the mass media had neglected African history and politics.[36]

As St. Clair Bourne recalled later, Greaves "knew what we younger staff members didn't: this filmmaking opportunity would not last but the films would."[37] Indeed, conscious of the ephemeral opportunities for Black producers that were created within new media, Greaves made *Black Journal* a means of conservation and cultivation, simultaneously preserving the work of an older generation of activists and intellectuals while creating opportunities for a new cohort of filmmakers. The force that bound these two generations, in addition to their shared commitment to looking outside of the United States to define Black cultural and economic power, was that of William Greaves, who used this new media platform to create continuities and solidarities among Black people. Through his stewardship, *Black Journal* become a new manifestation of the global visions and dreams of Black people, whose lives were in some ways defined by the particular forms of racism that were intrinsic to the United States but could build on broader networks of self and community understanding to fight them.[38]

NOTES

1. St. Clair Bourne wrote later that while there was growing frustration with a number of policies, it was sparked later by a script that indicated that Black people "supported Israel and disavowed Arab protests" over land seizure, which prompted an argument that "broke out in the studio during the taping... quelled only after the

narration was rewritten." St. Clair Bourne, "*Black Journal*: A Personal Look Backward," *Documentary Magazine*, April 1, 1989 (reprinted as chap. 14 in this volume).
2. On this history, see especially Devorah Heitner, *Black Power TV* (Durham, N.C.: Duke University Press, 2013), 83–122.
3. See Robin D. G. Kelley, "But a Local Phase of a World Problem: Black History's Global Vision, 1883–1950," *Journal of American History* 86, no. 3 (1999): 1045–77. On Black internationalism, see especially Keisha Blain, "'For the Rights of Dark People in Every Part of the World': Pearl Sherrod, Black Internationalist Feminism, and Afro-Asian Politics During the 1930s," *Souls* 17, no. 1–2 (2015): 91. On the history of Black internationalism, see especially Michael O. West and William G. Martin, eds., *From Toussaint to Tupac: The Black International Since the Age of Revolution* (Chapel Hill: University of North Carolina Press, 2009); Minkah Makalani, *In the Cause of Freedom: Radical Black Internationalism from Harlem to London, 1917–1939* (Chapel Hill: University of North Carolina Press, 2011); Penny M. Von Eschen, *Race Against Empire: Black Americans and Anticolonialism, 1937–1957* (Ithaca, N.Y.: Cornell University Press, 1997); Carol Anderson, *Eyes Off the Prize: The United Nations and the African American Struggle for Human Rights, 1944–1955* (Cambridge: Cambridge University Press, 2003); Brent Hayes Edwards, *The Practice of Diaspora: Literature, Translation, and the Rise of Black Internationalism* (Cambridge, Mass.: Harvard University Press, 2003); Keisha N. Blain, *Set the World on Fire: Black Nationalist Women and the Global Struggle for Freedom* (Philadelphia: University of Pennsylvania Press, 2018); Keisha Blain and Tiffany Gill, eds., *To Turn the Whole World Over: Black Women and Internationalism* (Urbana: University of Illinois Press, 2019).
4. The Greaves quotes on his early life are from Scott MacDonald's "Meta-interview with William Greaves (An Audiobiography)," chapter 2 in this volume.
5. On this link, see Scott MacDonald *Adventures of Perception: Cinema as Exploration* (Berkeley: University of California Press, 2009), 10–80. On the history of Black filmmaking, see especially Jacqueline Stewart, *Migrating to the Movies: Cinema and Black Urban Modernity* (Berkeley: University of California Press, 2005); Cedric J. Robinson, *Forgeries of Memory and Meaning: Blacks and the Regimes of Race in American Theater and Film Before World War II* (Chapel Hill: University of North Carolina Press, 2007). On Micheaux, see especially Pearl Bowser and Louise Spence, *Writing Himself Into History: Oscar Micheaux, His Silent Films, and His Audiences* (New Brunswick, N.J.: Rutgers University Press, 2000); and Pearl Bowser, Jane Gaines, and Charles Musser, *Oscar Micheaux and His Circle: African-American Filmmaking and Race Cinema of the Silent Era* (Bloomington: Indiana University Press, 2001).
6. On Black internationalism in Harlem, see Makalani, *In the Cause of Freedom*; Lara Putnam, *Radical Moves: Caribbean Migrants and the Politics of Race in the Jazz Age* (Chapel Hill: University of North Carolina Press, 2013); Vanessa Valdés, *Diasporic Blackness: The Life and Times of Arturo Alfonso Schomburg* (Albany: State University of New York Press, 2017); and Clare Corbould, *Becoming African Americans: Black Public Life in Harlem, 1919–1939* (Cambridge, Mass.: Harvard University Press, 2009).

7. "Meta-interview." On circum-Caribbean migrations in this period, see especially Putnam, *Radical Moves*; Jason M. Colby, *The Business of Empire: United Fruit, Race, and U.S. Expansion in Central America*. (Ithaca, N.Y.: Cornell University Press, 2011); Reena N. Goldthree, "'A Greater Enterprise than the Panama Canal': Migrant Labor and Military Recruitment in the World War I-Era Circum-Caribbean," *Labor: Studies in Working-Class History of the Americas* 13, no. 3–4, Special Issue: Labor and Empire in the Americas (2016): 57–82. On Garveyism, see especially Blain, *Set the World on Fire*; Makalani, *In the Cause of Freedom*; Adam Ewing, *The Age of Garvey: How a Jamaican Activist Created a Mass Movement and Changed Global Black Politics* (Princeton, N.J.: Princeton University Press, 2014); and Winston James, *Holding Aloft the Banner of Ethiopia: Caribbean Radicalism in Early Twentieth-Century America* (New York: Verso, 1998).
8. "Meta-interview."
9. On gender and Black internationalism, see Michelle Stephens, *Black Empire: The Masculine Global Imaginary of Caribbean Intellectuals in the United States, 1914–1962* (Durham, N.C.: Duke University Press, 2005); Blain and Gill, *To Turn the Whole World Over*.
10. Interview with Greaves in George Alexander, ed., *Why We Make Movies: Black Filmmakers Talk About the Magic of Cinema* (New York: Harlem Moon, 2003), 30.
11. See Jonathan Shandell, *The American Negro Theatre and the Long Civil Rights Era* (Iowa City: University of Iowa Press, 2018), 20.
12. "Meta-Interview."
13. Corbould, *Becoming African Americans*, 88–128.
14. "Meta-interview." The academy was founded by three African students, Kingsley Mbadiwe, Mbonu Ojike, and A. A. Nwafor Orizu, who were then attending school in the United States. See Sara Diamond, entry on African Academy, in *Organizing Black America: An Encyclopedia of African American Associations*, ed. Nina Mjagki (New York: Garland, 2001). In many ways, the academy was a precursor of cultural and political efforts, including the American Society of African Culture, which was founded in 1957 after the first Congress of Black Writers and Artists in Paris. On African dance and drumming in the United States, see Marcia Heard and Mansa K. Mussa, "African Dance in New York City," in *Dancing Many Drums: Excavations in African American Dance*, ed. Thomas DeFrantz (Madison: University of Wisconsin Press, 2002), 143–67.
15. "Meta-interview."
16. On the Ethiopian Library, see Iris Schmeisser, "'Ethiopia Shall Soon Stretch Forth Her Hands': Ethiopianism, Egytomania, and the Arts in the Harlem Renaissance," *African Diasporas in the New and Old Worlds: Consciousness and Imagination*, ed. Geneviève Fabre and Klaus Benesch (Amsterdam: Rodopi, 2004), 263–86. On Ethiopianism and representations of Africa in the early twentieth century, see especially Jeannette Jones, *In Search of Brightest Africa: Reimagining the Dark Continent in American Culture, 1884–1936* (Athens: University of Georgia Press, 2011).
17. While the history of Black internationalism was fundamentally shaped by women, the historiography and history has been dominated by men and masculinist narratives. On the role of women in this political tradition, see in particular Blain and

Gill, *To Turn the Whole World Over*; Blain, *Set the World on Fire*; Ula Y. Taylor, *The Veiled Garvey: The Life & Times of Amy Jacques Garvey* (Chapel Hill: University of North Carolina Press, 2002).
18. "Meta-interview."
19. "Unions Permit Black Filmmakers," *Jet*, August 20, 1970.
20. "Meta-interview."
21. On the USIA, cultural diplomacy, and African-American culture, see Penny M. Von Eschen, *Satchmo Blows Up the World: Jazz Ambassadors Play the Cold War* (Cambridge, Mass.: Harvard University Press, 2004); Ingrid T. Monson, *Freedom Sounds: Civil Rights Call Out to Jazz and Africa* (New York: Oxford University Press, 2007); Mary L. Dudziak, *Cold War Civil Rights: Race and the Image of American Democracy* (Princeton, N.J.: Princeton University Press, 2000); Hisham Aidi, *Rebel Music: Race, Empire, and the New Muslim Youth Culture* (New York: Pantheon Books, 2014); and Danielle Fosler-Lussier, *Music in America's Cold War Diplomacy* (Berkeley: University of California Press, 2015).
22. Alexander, *Why We Make Movies*, 33.
23. See Heitner, *Black Power TV*; Gayle Wald, *It's Been Beautiful: Soul! And Black Power Television* (Durham, N.C.: Duke University Press, 2015); and Christine Acham, *Revolution Televised: Prime Time and the Struggle for Black Power* (Minneapolis: University of Minnesota Press, 2005).
24. National Advisory Commission on Civil Disorders, *The Kerner Report* (1968; Princeton, N.J.: Princeton University Press, 2016), 21.
25. Greaves, "*Black Journal*: A Few Notes from the Executive Producer," *Television Quarterly* 8, no. 4 (Fall 1969): 66–72 (reprinted as chap. 12 in this volume).
26. St. Clair Bourne, "The African-American Image in American Cinema," *Black Scholar* 21, no. 2 (March–May 1990): 12.
27. Greaves, "*Black Journal*," 67.
28. "Meta-interview."
29. "Black Journal: A Dynamic Show," *Chicago Defender*, January 25, 1969.
30. "Black Americans Offer Views on South Africa," *Chicago Defender*, August 21, 1969.
31. Bourne, "*Black Journal*."
32. Horace Jenkins studied at the Sorbonne Film Institute in Paris and worked in Europe and Saudi Arabia for NBC International before joining *Black Journal* in 1968. He died in 1982. "Horace B. Jenkins, 42; His Films Won Awards," *New York Times*, December 7, 1982.
33. Tommy Lee Lott, "Documenting Social Issues: *Black Journal*, 1968–70," in *Struggles for Representation: African-American Documentary Film and Video*, ed. Phyllis R. Klotman and Janet K. Cutler (Bloomington: Indiana University Press, 1999), 86. On the 1966 festival, see especially Samir Meghelli, "'A Weapon in Our Struggle for Liberation': Black Arts, Black Power, and the 1969 Pan-African Cultural Festival," in *The Global Sixties in Sound and Vision: Media, Counterculture, Revolt*, ed. Brown, Timothy Scott and Andrew Lison (London: Palgrave Macmillan, 2014), 167–84; Olivier Hadouchi, "'African Culture Will Be Revolutionary or Will Not Be': William Klein's Film of the First Pan-African Festival of Algiers

(1969)," *Third Text* 25, no. 1 (2011): 117–28; and Nathan Hare, "Algiers 1969: A Report on the Pan-African Cultural Festival," *Black Scholar* 1, no. 1 (November 1969): 2–10.

34. "African Base Near for 'Black Journal,'" *New York Times*, July 30, 1970; Lawrence Laurent, "'Black Journal' in Ethiopia," *Washington Post*, August 1, 1970.
35. "'Black Journal' Opens Bureau in Addis Ababa," *Baltimore Afro-American*, August 8, 1970. On the Associated Negro Press and Claude Barnett, see Gerald Horne, *The Rise and Fall of the Associated Negro Press: Claude Barnett's Pan-African News and the Jim Crow Paradox* (Urbana: University of Illinois Press, 2017); Adam Green, *Selling the Race: Culture, Community, and Black Chicago, 1940–1955* (Chicago: University of Chicago Press, 2007).
36. "An African Bureau," *Afro-American*, September 5, 1970.
37. Bourne, "*Black Journal*."
38. Robin D. G. Kelley, *Freedom Dreams: The Black Radical Imagination* (Boston: Beacon Press, 2003).

17

Government-Sponsored Film and *Latinidad: Voice of La Raza* (1971)

LAURA ISABEL SERNA

In 1970, the *Albuquerque Journal* announced "Actor [Anthony] Quinn, [producer Lou] Adler May Hoist Banner of Minority Group."[1] *Journal* readers learned that the Oscar-winning actor was filming "a scene" for a "government sponsored study of Mexican-American work opportunities." That "study" was the film *Voice of La Raza* (1971), a sponsored film produced and directed by African American documentary and experimental filmmaker William (Bill) Greaves under the auspices of the Equal Employment Opportunity Commission (EEOC).[2] Quinn, born in Mexico to an Irish father and a Mexican mother and raised in the Mexican immigrant barrio of Boyle Heights in Los Angeles, starred in the film, which Greaves wrote in collaboration with Nuyorican documentary filmmaker José García Torres.[3] Referred to in the press as an example of cinéma vérité, the film combines techniques including direct observation, staged interviews, and dramatizations to educate viewers about the unequal treatment of "Spanish-speaking Americans" (as Latin American immigrants and their children were commonly referred to during this period) in the labor market.

The film premiered in May 1971 at an EEOC celebration honoring Quinn and was then screened at numerous film festivals and on television.[4] It won awards at the Atlanta International Film Festival and the Columbus Film Festival and an Emmy nomination in 1972 after it was screened on public television in the New York City area.[5] The film also circulated in community centers, libraries, union halls, and military bases, initially as part of efforts to increase awareness about labor discrimination and later as part of Hispanic heritage celebrations.[6]

In the context of the EEOC's activities in the late 1960s and early 1970s, *Voice of La Raza* was conceived of as an effective way to educate audiences about labor discrimination. The film mobilizes aesthetic strategies associated with politically committed filmmaking, including shooting on location and showcasing the voices and faces of everyday people in lieu of experts. At the same time, it employs experimental techniques including dramatizations and psychodramatic confrontations that, understood in the context of Greaves's work in the late 1960s, highlight the increasing radicalization of Latinos in the United States and call attention to the need for social change. Thus while some elements of the film align with the federal government's project of constructing an ethnoracial group, Hispanic, whose needs could be addressed by agencies like the EEOC, others draw attention to power relationships between and within racial groups, conflicts within minority groups, and the role of media in effecting social change.

To date, neither this film nor any of the others about Latino issues that Greaves made for the EEOC have been analyzed. Scholarship on documentary treatments of Latino subjects and themes made in the late 1960s and early 1970s focuses primarily on films made by Chicano and Puerto Rican filmmakers. That work, much of which was produced in the context of the broader movement for civil rights, is most frequently discussed as a step toward feature film production.[7] At the same time, *Voice of La Raza* and the other films Greaves made for the EEOC are generally absent from considerations of his career, which focus primarily on his experimental work and documentaries related to African-American history and culture. This chapter situates *Voice of La Raza* at the intersection of African-American documentary, government-sponsored film, and films about the Latino experience.

GOVERNMENT-SPONSORED FILM AND THE EEOC

In the late 1960s U.S. federal agencies charged with addressing discrimination began to use film in their work. Federal agencies had produced films to support programs and policies, train military personnel, and document important events. However, government-sponsored films did not take up race relations and discrimination to a significant extent until the late 1960s.[8] Both the Commission on Civil Rights, formed as part of the Civil Rights Act of 1957, and the EEOC, which was created after the passage of the Civil Rights Act of 1964, saw film as crucial to their missions. The Commission on Civil Rights, which made one film in 1971 and two in 1972, justified the expense by declaring: "Motion pictures present an attractive medium for the dissemination of information about Commission programs. They have the potential to reach a much larger audience than publications, particularly if they can be made suitable for presentation on TV."[9] Reaching a large audience was also crucial to the EEOC, which was established to support legislation forbidding discrimination in employment but lacked any enforcement mechanism for the first six years of its existence.

During this period, film and television constituted an important field of civil rights activism.[10] Activists from African-American, Chicano, and Puerto Rican communities protested the film and television industries that marginalized minority perspectives, traded in stereotypes, or ignored communities of color altogether. This activism led to some changes, especially in public television, where government and foundation support facilitated minority media professionals' participation and subsidized many of the documentaries that became the mainstay of public affairs programs aimed at minority audiences. Some of these media professionals received their training in two important but short-lived university-based programs designed to increase minority participation in film and media production, while others trained on the job.

In this context, William Greaves found opportunities.[11] Throughout the 1960s Greaves made documentaries about African-American culture, public figures, and everyday life. Many of the documentaries he made during this period were government-sponsored projects. As Rick Prelinger notes, in the postwar period sponsored film "production companies and 16mm distribution outlets proliferated," especially in New York, where Greaves was based.[12] In 1964 Greaves founded William Greaves Productions, which promptly received contracts from the United States Information Agency to make a film about freedom of expression in the United States, *Wealth of a Nation* (1964), and document the global gathering of black artists in Dakar, Senegal, *The First World Festival of Negro Arts* (1966).[13] In 1968 Greaves was signed to cohost the national black public affairs program *Black Journal*, where he served as executive director for the final two years he was affiliated with the show. It was in the context of *Black Journal* and public television that Greaves mentored younger filmmakers and likely met José García Torres, who had been a central force in the creation of a New York–based Latino public affairs program, *Realidades*.[14]

Greaves was more than qualified to produce the types of films the EEOC required but also benefited from personal connections and government programs. He came to the attention of the EEOC via Olivia Stanford, the successful Black businesswoman who served as the commission's information specialist from 1967 to 1970 and whom *Jet* magazine credited with being a "leading force" in Greaves landing agency contracts.[15] In addition to Stanford's advocacy, he benefited from a provision of the Small Business Act (originally signed into law in 1954), SBA 8(a), that strove to help businesses owned by women and minorities (like William Greaves Productions) obtain government contracts.[16]

The films Greaves made for the EEOC reflect a documented shift in the federal government's attitude toward Chicano and Puerto Rican communities. Under Lyndon Johnson and then Richard Nixon, the federal government worked to popularize the designation "Hispanic" to signify a broad ethnic group composed of diverse Latino populations. As Cristina Mora explains, the promotion of this term was part of a larger political project: "Fearing the rise of militancy and sensing the opportunity to win more votes both Johnson and Nixon created agencies that would purportedly represent Mexican-American and Puerto Rican needs within the federal government."[17] In this context, the EEOC, which appointed its first Mexican-American commissioner in 1967, began to examine and hold hearings about the question of labor discrimination against Puerto Ricans in New York and Mexican Americans in the Southwest.

The EEOC engaged Greaves's services to help document this work. In fiscal year 1971, the commission reported that it had paid Greaves for four films: *EEOC Story* (1972), a film describing the "machinery of the EEOC and how it serves both the minority community and women," narrated by Ruby Dee; *Power Versus the People* (1973), which consisted of footage from the commission's hearings in Houston, Texas, in 1970; *Struggle for Los Trabajos* (1972), a film depicting the "investigation and conciliation process of a violation of the rights of a Mexican American white collar worker"; and the most expensive of all these productions, *Voice of La Raza* (1971).[18]

VOICE OF LA RAZA

Voice of La Raza cost $87,000 to make and featured the star power of not only Anthony Quinn but also fellow Academy- Award–winner Rita Moreno. Beyond utilizing the exceptional visibility of these two Latino stars, the film appeals, beginning with the term *la raza*, or "the people," in its title, to the spirit of the radical movements that had emerged in Mexican-American and Puerto Rican communities during the late 1960s. Chicano activists had taken up the term as a way of expressing shared experiences of conquest, colonialism, and imperialism amid regional struggles such as land reform in New Mexico or education in Southern California.[19] The title also gestures toward a fundamental strategy for achieving social change that emerged out of this activism: allowing the Chicano community to speak for itself.[20]

Shot in 16mm on the streets of Los Angeles, New York, and Albuquerque, *Voice of La Raza* focuses on everyday people. Descriptions of the film suggest that it emerged organically "out of conversations and questions asked by Quinn in his travels across the country concerning the plight of Spanish-speaking Americans."[21] Characterized as an example of cinéma vérité or direct cinema, the film is structured around a series of interviews with "witness-participants," a strategy that Bill Nichols argues characterizes politically committed films of the 1970s.[22] Significant portions of the film are devoted to sequences of Quinn engaged in conversation with young people on the street. In heavily accented English, street slang, or with traces of regional accents, these men (and one young woman), shown in close-up, recount their experiences of being discriminated against by employers or educators. These interviews take place most frequently on the street but also in other public spaces like a church courtyard or a campus quad, where ambient noise such as traffic, music from a passing band, and other conversations lends an immediacy and authenticity to the scenes. Some people speak timidly, having to be coaxed into speaking by Quinn, while others engage him with confidence.

Though the audience hears the voices of these everyday people, our experience of them is mediated by a series of narrators to whom the film grants varying degrees of authority. The first and most important narrator is Quinn. When the camera focuses on crowds or groups of people on the street, the camera seeks him out and shows him listening intently, head cocked to one side, eyes on whoever is speaking. He reinforces his listening role when he declares, "It doesn't matter if you are in the barrios of Los Angeles or streets of New York, I found there is much to learn if you just listen." At the same time, his mellifluous voice dominates the film, and he is granted interpretive authority as he places his interviewees' comments in broader social and cultural context in the voice-over that follows each interview or in scenes of Quinn himself being interviewed. Phrases such as "I can relate to" and "I have to personalize" and his consistent use of "we" emphasize his connection to the experiences of the people he interviews, even as he seeks to explain them to the film's viewers.

Quinn was well suited to play the role of mediator between the film's informants and audience. An international star, he was well known to the filmgoing public, for whom his Irish surname and a career built playing Mediterranean types obscured his Mexican roots. But Quinn, as the press frequently noted in passing, grew up in Boyle Heights, a barrio of East Los Angeles. Beginning with the Sleepy Lagoon case in the 1940s, he became an increasingly visible advocate for the Mexican-American community. In the early 1970s he lent his name to a range of causes related to education and other issues.[23] He was not, however, considered a radical. As one article phrased it, he was "opposed to nationalism of any sort, but... equally concerned with equality for minority groups."[24] Thus Quinn's politics and public persona were well calibrated to the concerns of the federal government.

Three other voices serve a similar, if secondary, mediating function. A nameless male voice that speaks grammatically correct English with a Spanish accent offers factual commentary in an expository mode at different points in the film. For example, over footage of Spanish Harlem, this voice explains the different Latino groups living in New York and how Puerto Ricans came to constitute a significant ethnic group there. Later, the same narrator explains the work of the EEOC and introduces a brief sequence on filing a complaint. Two other voices belonging to regional commissioners Vicente Jimenez and Tom Robles likewise explain and contextualize. Their white-collar jobs, signaled by office buildings, meeting tables, and desks flanked by American flags, mark them as educated, and they are presented as experts on both the issue of labor discrimination, by virtue of their roles at the commission, and Spanish-speaking populations in the United States, by virtue of their personal backgrounds. Jimenez, the EEOC commissioner in Houston, speaks at length to what the viewer assumes are fellow employees about the degree of alienation Mexican-American children encounter in public schools. Robles, the commissioner in Albuquerque, recounts that when he left the military, he could find work only as a manual laborer, experiencing the problem of discrimination in the workforce firsthand. Like Quinn's, their voices, positioned as native informants and experts, contextualize the experiences of the film's working-class interviewees. While the film eschews the voice of God narration of classical documentary, it offers not the voice of la raza but rather multiple voices that speak from distinct social positions: uneducated, educated, unknown, famous, blue collar, white collar, and so on. Commonalities emerge within this diversity, the most salient being the experience of discrimination in the labor market.

The film uses other formal elements, most notably montage, to construct a shared identity out of historical and regional diversity. Establishing shots of Spanish Harlem, East Los Angeles, and Albuquerque are marked by street signs or other written text to locate sequences at specific geographic coordinates. Montage sequences bind those spaces together. For example, EEOC officer Jimenez's declaration that the nation's ten million Spanish-speaking Americans need to be "treated as a national group in national terms" is accompanied by a montage of workers in various settings: cooks preparing food in hotel kitchens, men clocking in at factory gates and rail yards and pushing carts on urban streets. Another slower and longer montage sequence, with no establishing shot to ground it geographically, shows children, young women, and older people sitting on top of cars, on front porches, at bus stops, or entering their modest homes. Vicente Jimenez, whose voice we hear over the images, invokes Mexican writer Octavio Paz's description of Mexicans in the United States as "beauty in tatters." The Spanish guitar music that accompanies this sequence (and most of the film's transitions) suggests a shared cultural identity regardless of geographic location. Finally, another brief montage sequence composed of a series of photographs of pre-Columbian pyramids and other built structures with paintings of the conquest illustrates Jimenez explaining Latino history and culture to a group of colleagues. This sequence brings to mind the primary visual strategy of Luis Valdez's film adaptation of the important Chicano movement poem by Rudolfo "Corky" Gonzales, *Yo soy Joaquín* (1969), which is composed entirely of filmed still images. In different ways, these montage sequences propose connections across geographical space and historical time, educating viewers—Anglo and Latino alike—about Latinos' shared historical, cultural, and social experiences.

What is more, despite the fact that the film is almost entirely spoken in English, it proposes language as a central axis for a shared ethnic identity.[25] In an extended sequence, Quinn speaks with young children in New Mexico. For the first time in the film, we hear Spanish spoken. The camera moves in closely to their slightly dirty faces, while Quinn asks repeatedly, "Are you Spanish?" They reply that that they do not know or that they are English. A dismayed Quinn asserts, "You have to speak Spanish," a sentiment he reinforces in a voice-over that ties language to identity. These combined strategies—erasing geographical space and proposing a shared history and language as binding forces—offer a cultural rather than political model of ethnic identity. In this way, the film seems to participate in the federal government's project of developing a "bureaucratized category" that could encompass disparate Latino groups in order to "extend and further legitimate, instead of threaten, government policies."[26] While these strategies appear to hold radical politics at bay, Greaves uses experimental techniques to underscore the growing militancy of Chicano and other Latino youth.

THE MESSAGE

Toward the end of *Voice of La Raza*, Tom Robles, the EEOC officer from Albuquerque, declares forthrightly, "The message of this film is you either do it within the law, within the legal system that... we have now. And this is a message to employers. Or else.... Let's get rid of this discrimination bit or you're going to have chaos." His statement raises the specter of civil unrest and recontextualizes the voices we have heard over the course of the film—the dejected young Puerto Rican actor in New York, the frustrated unemployed Chicano in Los Angeles, the Chicano students at the University of New Mexico skeptical about their future employment prospects—as more than expressions of personal experience; their voices are the rumblings of radicalization.

While the film links labor discrimination to racism, primarily through the multiple narrators' explanations and analyses, at key moments in the film Greaves stages conflict to suggest the need for reflection and dialogue. Sociodrama and psychodrama, therapeutic techniques that use role-playing and dramatization to address group or personal issues, had become popular in mental health circles and were being used at the Actors Studio in New York, where Greaves was a director, actor, and teacher.[27] Greaves had used such techniques before. In *Symbiopsychotaxiplasm* [shot in 1968, first edited version, 1971], his now widely hailed experimental documentary, Greaves used the principles of psychodrama to explore the relationship between director, cast, and crew and also to investigate how conflict emerges among members of a group, in this case his crew.[28] His *In the Company of Men* (1969), a management-training film sponsored by *Newsweek*, depicted a sociodramatic encounter between "hard-core unemployed" (as the description of the film on the William Greaves Productions website phrases it) working-class African-American men and white auto industry executives. The film sought to facilitate communication between the two groups and thus to generate understanding and eliminate preconceptions. In 1970 Greaves wrote a *New York Times* editorial in which he hailed "psychodramatic and sociodramatic encounter television" as a means of "improving mass mental health and social reform."[29]

Greaves's commitment to these techniques explains key elements of *Voice of La Raza* that deviate from the film's assumed pedagogical function. The film makes use of both dramatization and sociodramatic techniques to raise awareness of the subjective and social dimensions of race-based labor discrimination. The opening sequence consists of a dramatization in which an Anglo supervisor discourages a Puerto Rican worker from applying for a promotion. In conversation with Quinn after the dramatization ends with José the electrician going back to Puerto Rico, José the actor reflects on his own experiences of labor discrimination in the film and television industry. In the process of playing this role and subsequently reflecting on that process, José and the viewer gain insight into his personal experience and what he might have in common with other Latinos.

This dramatization is mirrored by the penultimate sequence of the film, in which Greaves stages a sociodramatic encounter between a young Chicano and a group of fathers who represent older, middle-class Mexican Americans. Over the course of the film, Greaves establishes the theme of passivity—José the fictional electrician quietly accepts his supervisor's dismissal of his capabilities. A Puerto Rican mail room attendant asked by Quinn if he had hopes of finding a better job replies, "The boss like that I take care of here." The image accompanying his reply shows him literally hemmed in by the walls of his small office, trapped behind the desk where he has worked for fourteen years. Both Quinn and Moreno recall their parents' fears of any government official, a fear Moreno attributes to Puerto Ricans being a "sweet and passive people."

This passivity contrasts sharply with the militancy of the young Chicanos featured in a long sequence shot on the campus of the University of New Mexico. Throughout the sequence, the camera lingers on scenes of Chicano youth engaged in political organizing in a classroom, grilling Quinn about his own politics, and finally in a smaller, mixed-gender group that discusses the failure of agencies like the EEOC to adequately address the issue of labor discrimination. The problem, one young man forcefully declares, is that employers fail to see past race, "what you represent," as he phrases it. He contends that racial thinking contaminates encounters with employers regardless of an applicant's professional or educational qualifications.

The phrase "take away his suit" functions as a sound bridge to a shot of a man with close-cut hair wearing a suit and tie. With this image, the viewer enters a different generational and social space. Jeans and T-shirts have been traded for suits and ties, and the words "Chicano" and "Black" have been replaced by "Spanish" and "Negro." The film's secondary narrator describes this group of parents (fathers actually) seated on sofas in a sterile, institutional room as "willing to work within existing structures." A voice that we learn is that of Greaves asks, off-screen, "Do you have any thoughts on this?" The camera swings left to focus on a young man wearing glasses, a black armband, and a United Farmworkers pin, who had not appeared in the previous shots. He challenges the group of suit-clad men, pointing his finger and raising his voice. The camera captures this conflict, moving back and forth from speaker to speaker. While the fathers assert that things have improved, the young man insists, in ever more heated language, that things are in fact still quite bad. Finally, with an

American flag off to the left of the frame just behind him, he shouts, "If caring about my people makes me a radical, a communist, I am a fucking communist." One of the men stands up, clearly provoked.

At this point Greaves himself appears on screen, breaking the fourth wall and any illusion of objectivity. With his sound tech standing just behind him, Greaves intervenes, urging the man, who accuses him of planning this confrontation, to see the impact the heated exchange will have on the film's future viewers. This encounter visualizes in microcosm two approaches to addressing racial inequality: one gradual and conciliatory and the other militant. While it dramatizes the film's principal message to employers—make change or you will have social unrest—it also throws into high relief tensions within the Latino community and suggests, by modeling such communication, the need for intragroup dialogue.

Setting up and facilitating this encounter also gestures toward the role Greaves imagined for the media in helping communities and individuals navigate the divide between activists and the institutions they sought to do away with or reform, between racial groups, and between militant and more mainstream political orientations within racial groups. The latter was a topic he had explored in his film *Still a Brother: Inside the Negro Middle Class* (1968), made for National Educational Television. As in that film, the question about whether to adopt a radical nationalist stance or take a more accommodationist approach was set against mainstream media's circulation of images of so-called race riots and protests.

While Chicano and Puerto Rican activists received far less media attention than their Black counterparts, when their actions were covered, they were framed in predictably negative ways. As Randy Ontiveros has written, the mainstream media, when it deigned to cover the Chicano movement, "positioned Mexican Americans as radicals while discursively linking the Chicano movement to other perceived threats, including black militancy, war unrest, the youth counter culture, and Latin inflected communism."[30] Similarly, the Young Lords, a radical leftist organization that emerged in Puerto Rican New York and Chicago, was frequently the object of sensational media coverage.[31] These images of militant urban activists hover off-screen in *Voice of La Raza*. Compliance with antidiscrimination legislation, the film suggests, would ensure that violence, protests, and civil unrest stayed off-screen. At the same time, the film pushes less radicalized segments of the Latino community toward an understanding of the motivations of militant young activists.

In 1975 Chicano filmmaker Francisco X. Camplis dismissed *Voice of La Raza* as "little more than an exploration of the problem of job discrimination and unemployment."[32] In part, this dismissal stemmed from his own conviction that only a Chicano filmmaker was qualified to make films about the Chicano experience or the Chicano community. Setting to one side the question Camplis raises about a filmmaker's identity as a prerequisite for representation, a close analysis of *Voice of La Raza* demonstrates that Greaves, even within the confines of sponsorship by a government agency, sought to do more than merely educate or inform his audience about a given topic. Instead he sought to portray the impact of racial discrimination on individuals, carve out a role for middle-class figures (as well as film stars), and model the way that confrontation could generate inter- and intragroup understanding of social issues. While Greaves combines techniques such as montage, direct address, and multilayered narration to construct a shared identity that would fit more readily into the federal government's framework for addressing inequality, he also employs experimental techniques to explore tensions within the Latino community and express the urgency of communication between and within racial groups.

NOTES

1. "Actor Quinn, Adler May Hoist Banner of Minority Group," *Albuquerque Journal*, November 21, 1970.
2. The film's release date has usually been cited as 1972, but the film was finished and had been screened by the spring of 1971. It is available on a number of websites, including Texas Archive of the Moving Image, http://www.texasarchive.org/library/index.php/Voice_of_La_Raza, and is listed as available for purchase on the William Greaves Productions website, http://www.williamgreaves.com/catalog.htm.
3. Surprisingly, García Torres, an active documentarian in the 1960s and 1970s and producer of the WNET public affairs program *Realidades*, has received scant scholarly attention. He is mentioned in overviews of New York–based Puerto Rican filmmakers by Chon Noriega in *Shot in America: Television, the State, and the Rise of Chicano Cinema* (Minneapolis: University of Minnesota Press, 1993), 150–51; and Lillian Jiménez, "From the Margin to the Center: Puerto Rican Cinema in New York," *Centro de Estudios Puertorriqueños Bulletin* 2, no. 8 (Spring 1990): 28–43.
4. "Actor Honored for Battling Discrimination," *Progress-Index* (Petersburg, Va.), May 22, 1971. Television listings in local papers indicate that the film was shown by Los Angeles station KTTV (Channel 11) in the greater Southern California area and subsequently, presumably via cable broadcast of KTTV programming, in

Illinois, Northern California, New Mexico, Arizona, Colorado, and even Pennsylvania. See, for example, *Redlands Daily Facts*, July 22 1972; *Pomona Progress Bulletin*, July 23, 1972; *San Antonio Light*, March 12, 1972; *Oxnard Press Courier*, July 23, 1972; and *Newsday*, August 20, 1972.

5. "Black Producer's Film About Chicanos a Winner," *Los Angeles Sentinel*, July 15, 1971; "Anthony Quinn in Movie," *New York Amsterdam News*, September 25, 1971; and "Greaves Nominated Thrice," *Back Stage*, December 15, 1972.

6. "Awareness Workshop Set in TF," *Times-News* (Twin Falls, Idaho), March 28, 1973; "Hispanic Week" and "Activities Slated for Hispanic Week," *Press-Courier* (Oxnard, Calif.), September 11, 1972; "Cinco de Mayo Films," *Arcadia Tribune* (Arcadia, Calif.), May 5, 1974; and "Hispanic Film Set at Library," *Colorado Springs Gazette Telegraph*, September 13, 1975.

7. See Charles Ramirez Berg, *Latino Images in Film: Stereotypes, Subversion, Resistance* (Austin: University of Texas Press, 2002); Noriega, *Shot in America*; and Rosa Linda Fregoso, *The Bronze Screen: Chicana and Chicano Film Culture* (Minneapolis: University of Minnesota Press, 1993). It is rare to find sustained treatment of specific documentary films from the 1960s and 1970s beyond a handful of key film texts, such as *Requiem 29* (Raul Ruiz and David García, 1971); *Yo soy Joaquín* (Luis Valdez, 1969); and *Chicana* (Sylvia Morales, 1979).

8. In a 1963 catalog of government films available for public use, only one film from 1947 touched on the topic of race relations. That film was listed under three different headings: Discrimination, Minorities, and Race Problems. U.S. Department of Health, Education, and Welfare, Office of Education, *US Government Films for Public Educational Use 1963*, OE-34006–63, Circular No. 742 (Washington, D.C.: Government Printing Office, 1964). Richard Dyer McCann notes only two examples of films with a focus on race in *The People's Films: A Political History of U.S. Government Motion Pictures* (New York: Hastings House, 1973), 55, 192.

9. U.S. Congress, Senate Subcommittee on Departments of State, Justice, Commerce, the Judiciary and Related Agencies, Hearings Before a Subcommittee on Appropriations, 92nd Congress, 1st session, 438.

10. On the Civil Rights Movement and television, see, for example Aniko Bodroghkozy, *Equal Time: Television and the Civil Rights Movement* (Urbana: University of Illinois Press, 2012); Steven Classen, *Watching Jim Crow* (Durham, N.C.: Duke University Press, 2004); and Sasha Torres, *Black, White, and in Color: Television and Black Civil Rights* (Princeton, N.J.: Princeton University Press, 2003).

11. For a general account of Greaves's life and career, see Noelle Griffis, "'This Film Is a Rebellion!' Filmmaker, Actor, *Black Journal* Producer, and Political Activist (1924–2014)," *Black Camera* 6, no. 2 (Spring 2015): 7–16; Adam Knee and Charles Musser, "William Greaves, Documentary Filmmaking, and the African-American Experience," *Film Quarterly* 45, no. 3 (Spring 1992): 13–25 (reprinted as chap. 1 in this volume); Kay Eastman and Brenna Sanchez, "Greaves, William 1926–2014," in *Contemporary Black Biography*, vol. 123, ed. Margaret Mazurkiewicz (Farmington Hills, Mich.: Gale, 2015), 66–69; and Steven Otfinoski, "Greaves, William," in *African Americans in the Visual Arts* (New York: Facts on File, 2011), 88–90.

12. Rick Prelinger, *The Field Guide to Sponsored Films* (San Francisco: National Film Preservation Foundation, 2006), vii.
13. On the United States Information Agency's development of its film production program in the 1960s, see Sonke Kunkel, *Empire of Pictures: Global Media and the 1960s Remaking of American Foreign Policy* (Oxford: Berghahn, 2016), 45–46. Letter from William Greaves to Hon. Joseph P. Addabbo, April 17, 1981, reprinted in *Hearings Before the Subcommittee on SBA and SBIC Authority, Minority Enterprise and General Small Business Problems*, Washington, D.C., May 21; June 4 and 10, 1981 (Washington, D.C.: Government Printing Office, 1981), 71.
14. See Lillian Jiménez, "Puerto Rican Cinema in New York: From the Margin to the Center," *Jump Cut*, no. 38 (June 1993): 60–66; and Noriega, *Shot in America*, 150–52.
15. *Jet* magazine claimed that Stanford was "the leading force in Greaves' firm winning the unusual contract to produce the film [*Voice of La Raza*]." "Ex-TV Producer, Anthony Quinn Team in Job Bias Film," *Jet*, June 10, 1971, 52. In the Virgin Islands, Stanford's adopted home to which she returned in 1971, the local newspaper gave her production credit for *Voice of La Raza* and other, unnamed films, including television spots. "Local Director's Film Deals with Prejudice," *Virgin Islands Daily News*, June 12, 1971.
16. U.S. Congress, House, *An Act to Amend the Small Business Act of 1953*, 15 U.S.C. 631 et seq.; 72 Stat. 384 et seq. Public Law 85–536, 384, 85th Congress, 1st session, July 8, 1958.
17. G. Cristina Mora, *Making Hispanics: How Activists, Bureaucrats and Media Constructed a New American* (Chicago: University of Chicago Press, 2014), 46.
18. These descriptions are drawn from an appendix attached to a 1988 hearing and William Greaves Productions' list of films. *The EEOC's Performance in Enforcing the Age Discrimination in Employment Act: Hearing Before the Special Committee on Aging*, United States Senate, 100th Congress, 2nd session, Washington, D.C., June 23 and 24, 1988 (Washington, D.C.: Government Printing Office, 1989), 510–11. *Voice of La Raza* cost $87,000 to produce. *Departments of State, Justice, and Commerce, the Judiciary and Related Agencies Appropriations for 1973 Part 4* (Washington, D.C.: Government Printing Office, 1972), 857.
19. For an overview of the historiography on the diverse manifestations of the movement, see Mario T. Garcia, ed., *The Chicano Movement: Perspectives from the Twenty-First Century* (New York: Routledge, 2014).
20. Dennis López, "Good-Bye Revolution—Hello Cultural Mystique: Quinto Sol Publications and Chicano Literary Nationalism," *MELUS* 35, no. 3 (Fall 2010): 198. See the primary sources collected in Darrel Enck-Wanzer, *The Young Lords: A Reader* (New York: New York University Press, 2010). On media representations in particular, see Lillian Jiménez, "Moving from the Margin to the Center: Puerto Rican Cinema in New York," in *The Ethnic Eye: Latino Media Arts*, ed. Chon A. Noriega and Ana M. López (Minneapolis: University of Minnesota Press, 1996), 22–37.
21. "Greaves Film Cops 2nd Festival Nod," *Afro-American*, September 25, 1971, 9.

22. Bill Nichols, "The Voice of Documentary," in *The Documentary Film Reader: History, Theory, Criticism*, ed. Jonathan Kahana (New York: Oxford University Press, 2016), 640.
23. Anthony Quinn Script Collection, California State University Northridge, Special Collections, box 41, folder 16. Among his papers are numerous reports and pamphlets regarding Chicano land rights claims and activism in New Mexico, the EEOC's hearing on discrimination in the film industry, and the Chicano movement in Los Angeles.
24. "Actor Quinn, Adler May Hoist Banner."
25. Rafael Pérez-Torres notes that for Latinos (Chicano/as in his analysis), "ethnic identity can be tied to linguistic skills." Rafael Pérez-Torres, "Chicano Ethnicity, Cultural Hybridity, and the Mestizo Voice," *American Literature* 70, no. 1 (March 1998): 155.
26. Mora, *Making Hispanics*, 49.
27. Maria San Filippo, "What a Long, Strange Trip It's Been: William Greaves' 'Symbiopsychotaxiplasm': Take One," *Film History* 13, no. 2 (January 2001): 217. On the relationship between psychodrama and Method acting in the 1950s and 1960s, see Shonni Enelow, *Method Acting and Its Discontents* (Evanston, Ill.: Northwestern University Press, 2015). She devotes the last chapter to *Symbiopsychotaxiplasm*.
28. *Symbiopsychotaxiplasm* has received a great deal of scholarly attention since its wide release in 2001 and the release of a Criterion Collection DVD in 2006. Insightful readings of the film's relationship to jazz can be found in Akiva Gottlieb, "'Just Another Word for Jazz': The Signifying Auteur in William Greaves's *Symbiopsychotaxiplasm: Take One*," *Black Camera* 5, no. 1 (October 2013): 164–83 (excerpted in chap. 23 of this volume); and Charles P. Linscott, "In a (Not So) Silent Way: Listening Past Black Visuality in *Symbiopsychotaxiplasm*," *Black Camera* 8, no. 1 (October 2016): 169–90.
29. William Greaves, "100 Madison Avenues Will Be of No Help," *New York Times*, August 9, 1970 (reprinted in chap. 13 of this volume).
30. Randy Ontiveros, "No Golden Age: Television News and the Chicano Civil Rights Movement," *American Quarterly* 62, no. 4 (December 2010): 908.
31. Ángel G. Flores-Rodríguez describes the way that mainstream media portrayed the Young Lords in Chicago as "an undisciplined street gang," in "On National Turf: The Rise of the Young Lords Organization and Its Struggle for the Nation in Chicago," *Op. Cit.*, no. 20 (2011–2012): 136.
32. Francisco X. Camplis, "Towards a Raza Cinema," in *Chicanos and Film: Representation and Resistance*, ed. Chon Noriega (Minneapolis: University of Minnesota Press, 1992), 297.

18
Afterthoughts on the Black American Film Festival

WILLIAM GREAVES

When told that they had been invited to participate in the 1989 12th Annual International Film Festival in New Delhi—under the banner of Black American Cinema—Cicely Tyson, Ruby Dee, Ivan Dixon, Michelle Parkerson, and Donald Bogle responded instantly, and with great enthusiasm. However, for all of us who participated in the festival and in the subsequent tour with our films to three other major Indian cities, this was not an exercise in frivolity. I, as the leader of the delegation, along with its other members felt we had embarked on a mission, of sorts. We saw the festival as an opportunity provided by the Government of India's Directorate of Film Festivals of the Ministry of Information and Broadcasting (in collaboration with the Indo-U.S. Subcommission on Education and Culture and USIA) to share the Black American experience in film with the Indian and foreign film community, but especially with the people of India. It was the first time that such a large number of Black American films had been shown in India.

The warm response given the Black American Cinema section of the festival by audiences and the press wherever the films were shown was most gratifying, and confirmed our belief that our presence had indeed served a purpose. After the New Delhi screenings, we went on to Calcutta, Bombay, and Trivandrum, where we were sponsored by the Nandan Film Center, the National Film Development Corporation, and the Kerala State Film Societies and Kerala State Film Development Corporation, respectively.

America, much like India, is a pluralistic society. African-Americans, Hispanics, Asians, and other "Third World" peoples—as well as groups with European ancestry such as Jews, Italians, and Poles—are considered "minorities" in the United States. The largest of these groups is the African-American, which numbers over 30

FIGURE 18.1 William Greaves (*second from right*), Ruby Dee (*far right*), Ivan Dixon (*second from left*), and others in India for the 12th Annual International Film Festival in New Delhi in 1989. Photographer unknown. Courtesy Louise Greaves.

million people and makes up approximately 13 percent of the total American population. These numbers are significant in and of themselves, but they become very meaningful when translated into marketing terms. The purchasing power of Black Americans is well over 200 billion dollars (the ninth largest consumer market in the world!), while the combined purchasing power of America's Black and Hispanic communities is in excess of 300 billion dollars a year. What do these facts and figures have to do with making movies? Well, a great deal, I feel.

Certainly from our perspective, as film producers and directors who happen to be members of America's largest minority group, this market is potentially a most important one. It could also become a market for films produced in India. At the same time, India is a potential market for Afro-American films. A key to the successful exploitation of these markets is the video cassette. This new technology has broken up the old patterns of theatrical distribution and has opened up, and is continuing to open up, an almost unlimited number of consumer "outlets" through which a movie can be distributed. Today there are roughly 60 million video cassette players in the United States (as opposed to 2 million in 1981!), and the American video market now accounts for over 5 billion dollars of yearly revenues to the film industry, a figure that exceeds Hollywood's worldwide grosses for the release of films to movie theaters. Indian, as well as African-American,

FIGURE 18.2 Greaves and American delegation in India meeting Mother Teresa during the 12th Annual International Film Festival in New Delhi in 1989. Photographer unknown. Courtesy Louise Greaves.

producers and distributors might do well to keep in mind that at least 10 percent of this American video market is in Black American homes.

One doesn't have to be a financial genius to calculate that this "Black" market for video cassettes is yielding roughly half a billion dollars in revenues to producers and distributors. Indeed, this estimate is a conservative one, because market surveys indicate that Afro-American consumption of Hollywood film products is greater in proportion to our numbers than it is in the American population generally.

Because of these developments, the independent producer can now look to the video cassette market as a source of revenue and financing. And, as a result, the future is beginning to look more promising for the Black independent film producer, assuming that the serious problem of video and cable piracy is finally resolved—a problem that governments worldwide will have to deal with if the theatrical motion picture industry itself is to survive. Additionally, expanding overseas theater and ancillary markets now accounts for over 50 percent of revenues for American films. It goes without saying that film producers and directors of the "parallel cinema" in India can also now achieve easier access to the hitherto almost impenetrable American marketplace. Transcending the economic advantages to both Indian filmmakers (especially those of the parallel cinema) and American filmmakers (especially Black independents), there is another dimension to such a cultural exchange: the need for a product which specifically caters to the real hunger for entertainment and information films not usually found in the traditional Hollywood product: i.e., commercial cinema.

Not that all Hollywood films are lacking in substance, special interest, and artistic merit, but the overwhelming majority of the movies produced by Hollywood and other commercial movie centers throughout the world follow conventional formulae in terms of style and subject matter—those that "work" at the box office. Other kinds of films would sell, too, if given the chance. This fact is now being proved by the proliferation of specialty theatrical movies and special interest videos in the American marketplace, some of which have gone on to earn considerable revenues. Indeed, America's independent producers, particularly those of its many minority groups, are increasingly paying more attention to the growing potential of America's expanding video cassette marketplace, to other developing ancillary markets, and to the growing potential of the international marketplace.

It is in the context of the foregoing that the special interest market (especially the video market) in America should take on a new meaning for Indian producers and distributors and that, conversely, an Indian market for Black American film should be, and will increasingly become, of interest to Black American filmmakers.

It should also be noted that Black American producers and directors are not only producers and directors of "Black" movies. A growing number, including Ivan Dixon and myself, work on mainstream productions as well as on productions dealing with the African-American experience. Many, like myself, are interested in making films beyond the borders of America: in Africa, India, China, Europe, and elsewhere. We are exploring the possibilities of joint ventures and co-production deals with foreign film producers.

With the help of video, cable, and satellite technology, the world of cinema is expanding. Ancillary markets, like home video and cable television, and international co-production deals, are making possible the production of special interest movies. Too often, in the mad, mad rush to recover an investment and turn a profit, the uniqueness, richness, and variety of world cultures have been pushed aside in favor of a homogenized and imitative product. Hopefully, new technologies and trends will permit independent filmmakers to exploit the artistic, as well as the financial, potential to be found in their own cultural identities.

NOTE

Reprinted from *Black American Literature Forum* (now *African American Review*) 25, no. 2 (Summer 1991): 433–36.

19
Ida B. Wells: A Passion for Justice

Personal Production Notes

MICHELLE DUSTER

Editor's Note: Duster is the great-granddaughter of journalist Ida B. Wells and worked as a production assistant on *Ida B. Wells: A Passion for Justice* (1989), which is available on YouTube. In an email to the editors on May 7, 2020, Louise Greaves wrote: "A 2020 Pulitzer Prize Special Citation was awarded to Ida B. Wells posthumously for her outstanding and courageous reporting on the horrific and vicious violence against African Americans during the era of lynching. I doubt this would have happened without Bill's film. She was barely known when the film came out back in 1989. It's our most popular film! It has become standard for Journalism, Women's Studies, and African American History Studies."

I was told that my grandmother, Alfreda Barnett Duster, spent decades editing her mother Ida B. Wells's autobiography, which had been left incomplete when Wells died in 1931. Then, during the 1960s, it took great effort to find a publisher willing to take on a book about a woman who was considered "radical," "militant," and "controversial" during her time, but in 1970 the University of Chicago Press published *Crusade for Justice: The Autobiography of Ida B. Wells* as part of the Negro American Biographies and Autobiographies Series, edited by John Hope Franklin.

In the 1980s William Greaves met my cousin Ben Duster IV, who told him about our family connection to Ida B. Wells and gave him a copy of the autobiography. The story of my great-grandmother's life was very much under-told and under-appreciated at that time, and Greaves decided to create a documentary film based on the book. In 1988, my father's generation worked closely with Greaves, providing information to him for the film. My uncle, Troy Duster, was interviewed and included in what became *Ida B. Wells: A Passion for Justice*. At the time, I was a graduate student at Columbia College Chicago film school, and Greaves asked me to work with the production team when he filmed in Chicago. He then asked me to work on the production in Memphis and arranged for me to have a place to stay.

This was my first experience in that part of the South. I had grown up in Chicago, surrounded by people who had migrated from the South to escape oppression and take advantage of new opportunities, so I was nervous to spend time in Memphis. Once there, I went with the film crew to various places that were connected to my great-grandmother's life, including Beale Street Baptist Church where she published her newspaper. The location that had the most profound effect on me was the field where her friends Thomas Moss, Calvin McDowell, and William Henry Stewart were killed. The fact that nothing had been built on that land after almost a century made me feel that somehow the space was haunted. It was very emotional for me to imagine the trauma those men experienced. It seemed that I could feel their spirits, as well as the spirits of thousands of other victims of horrible violence and domestic terrorism.

FIGURE 19.1 William Greaves standing next to the field where Ida B. Wells's friends—Thomas Moss, Calvin McDowell, and William Henry Stewart—were lynched. Photograph by Michelle Duster. Courtesy Michelle Duster.

Working with Bill gave me the opportunity to ask questions, explore issues, and expand my skills and knowledge about the filmmaking process. I was the only female on the four-person crew, and he treated me the same as he did everyone else, which made me feel appreciated and encouraged. While in Memphis, working as the assistant to the sound technician, I checked the equipment, labeled reels, and kept logs. I also had the opportunity to meet and interact with several of the scholars who were interviewed for the film, from whom I learned detailed information about my great-grandmother. One of the scholars, John DeMott, also provided great insight and encouragement as I wrestled to define my own identity in the midst of chronicling the larger-than-life legacy of Ida. I kept in touch with DeMott for more than twenty years after working on the film.

A year after the Memphis shoot, Greaves asked me to work with him in New York on the post-production of the film. He was again very helpful and found a place for me to stay during that summer. I had only been to the city once before, and he laughed at how I did not know how to hail a cab. I quickly learned how to navigate the subway system.

This phase of the work gave me the opportunity to meet Toni Morrison, who read excerpts of Ida's book for the film. I also learned how to work with photo archives as I searched for images that were needed, worked closely with Depu Mehta, who was editing the film [the credits list Mehta as an assistant editor and the film's production manager; Gary Winter as editor, and Nina Schulman as fine-cut editor], and traveled all over the city to drop off and pick up materials.

Watching Bill make decisions about what to keep in—or not—during the editing process was fascinating. It was a great learning experience to see, from the inside, how challenging it was to create a piece like this. The subject matter was expansive and difficult—as in violent: there were a lot of discussions about how many images of lynchings should be shown and how graphic they should be. And even though it was Bill's film, he still had to negotiate the expectations of funders and broadcast outlets. He didn't express his feelings directly to me, but I could see that some of these decisions were quite stressful for him.

Yet, it was inspiring to observe his level of focus and his determination to complete the film in the way that he felt was comprehensive and respectful. From working with and observing Bill, I learned how to treat people, and the material I'm working on, with respect. I also learned how to stay focused on a long-term goal and not compromise my own vision.

Once the film was complete in 1989, our family hosted a screening for Bill at the DuSable Museum of African American History in Chicago. It was such a proud moment for our family to see our ancestor's life depicted in a sweeping

FIGURE 19.2 Greaves with Toni Morrison during the shooting of *Ida B. Wells: A Passion for Justice* (1989). Photographer unknown. Courtesy Louise Greaves.

and deeply informative film. *Ida B. Wells: A Passion for Justice* helped the story of my great-grandmother become more well-known. The film is considered a classic and has helped educate and inspire people for the last thirty years.

Working with Bill opened up a world for me. Not only did I get a chance to learn from someone I consider a master filmmaker, but he also provided

FIGURE 19.3 Greaves and Michelle Duster at a screening of *Ida B. Wells: A Passion for Justice* (1989). Duster, the great-granddaughter of Wells, was a production assistant on the film. Photograph by Donald L. Duster. Courtesy Michelle Duster.

opportunities for me to meet other people who impacted me. For example, his office was next door to the Black Filmmaker Foundation, where I met both Warrington Hudlin, the founder, and his brother Reggie, as well as Rodney Stringfellow and George Sosa, who were history-makers themselves. I was so deeply affected by the experience that I decided to move to New York the following year.

Again, Bill was very encouraging and helpful. He provided introductions to several filmmakers who gave advice and encouragement. He recommended me for a job at the Schomburg Center for Research in Black Culture. Ultimately, I spent ten years working in New York City, gaining experience in various forms of communications and making life-long contacts.

Bill was not only an amazing filmmaker, he was an amazing man, and very generous in sharing his resources and knowledge. He was encouraging, he was honest, and my life would not be what it is without having had the experience of working with him.

Dossier on the *Symbiopsychotaxiplasm* Films

This dossier includes a variety of writings, by Greaves and others, beginning with what appears to be Greaves's initial sense of what the *Symbiopsychotaxiplasm* project would be. We have included this and other unpublished writings in which Greaves comments on the project in the wake of its rediscovery and subsequently as a new project, what became *Symbiopsychotaxiplasm: Take 2½*, began to evolve. Greaves's writings are supplemented by an interview with Dara Meyers-Kingsley, who found *Take One* in a closet and made it available to the public for the first time, and by essays by a broad range of scholars, which we hope will be useful for those who are interested in exploring and writing about the *Symbio* films, and for teachers and/or curators who might want to share the films with new audiences.

So far as we are able to determine, there are two distinct versions of *Symbiopsychotaxiplasm: Take One*: a first version, completed in 1971, and a second one, at one point called "Symbiopsychotaxiplasm: Take Two," for which Greaves expanded on the original version, once it had been rediscovered, by adding in bits of the other "Takes" at the beginning and end of the film, so that audiences could get a clearer sense of the original, multifilm project. The first person seen in this expanded version, the first "Alice," is Louise Archambault Greaves—a subtle tribute perhaps to his lifelong partner.

The expanded version of *Symbiopsychotaxiplasm: Take One* had its theatrical premiere in 2005. The Criterion edition of the *Symbiopsychotaxiplasm* films includes this second, expanded version of *Take One* and *Symbiopsychotaxiplasm: Take 2½*.

20

Proposal: *Theatrical Short Subject*

WILLIAM GREAVES

Editor's note: Greaves sent himself this proposal for a theatrical short, by registered mail, on March 9, 1967. It seems to have been delivered to him on March 10. The proposal is presented as it was sent (with two spelling corrections).

PROPOSAL
THEATRICAL SHORT SUBJECT
["by William Greaves" handwritten]

BASIC CONCEPT

There is a tremendous unstated need on the part of audiences for a new cinematic language; one in which a more total statement of reality can be made. A language which, on the one hand, brings the viewer more intimately into the inner mental operations of the creative cinema artist; while, at the same time, illuminates the inner operations of the human psyche as it struggles with the basic problems of social existence. A language whose intimacy catapults the viewer into a state of consciousness that broadens his perceptions and perspectives of social issues which are fiercely rocking the boat of what could become a Great Society. A language whose essence of sheer theatricality is created out of the fresh and innovative use of camera, director, actor and script.

It is this sort of cinema language which I would like to apply to this theatrical short, as opposed to the more conventional documentary or travelog approach currently in use. My film would be simultaneously cinema verité, documentary, avant-garde, dramatic. Let me explain.

The documentary aspect of my short shows how a film crew, actors and a director go about the business of shooting a film on location, of penetrating human character, of applying the laws of esthetics to the motion picture image and sound.

The dramatic aspect of the film will be found not only in the themes of marital strife, homosexuality and social responsibility which form the basis of the dramatic story being filmed, but also there will be drama in the struggle which takes place on the part of the actors, the director and crew to heighten the reality and dramatic intensity of their work.

The cinema verité aspect guarantees a spontaneity in the shooting, with its candid camera grasp of the before-the-lens, behind-the-lens drama. Audience response to this kind of film making is highly simpatico.

The avant-garde aspect... which will include not only the synthesis of documentary, dramatic and cinema verité, but also extensive use of improvisation technique in the work of the actors and director, extensive use by the director/cameraman and cameraman of the close-up and the extreme close-up, the several levels of reality which will simultaneously and theatrically bombard the viewer (the physical shooting of a film, the dramatic story, the actor's technical and creative problems in characterization, the film maker's struggle for a new, more effective cinema language), a Negro director whose unique presence gives an added social dimension to the film as he and his crew spontaneously break into the dramatic action, as they pursue their work (the director digging, probing a la Actors Studio method to get top performances from his actors), and finally the whole undertaking should have the flavor of a "happening," cinema-style.

THE STORY—"TAKE 1, TAKE 2...."

An avant-garde film crew arrives on a location in Central Park with two actors who play the roles of man and wife. They are to shoot a screen test of the two performers. They begin to film the crisis-climax scene of the feature film to be produced. The actors, director/cameraman, cameraman become unhappy with the limitations of the script; they feel it does not express the true nature of the characters' relationship to each other. They decide to improvise the basic situation which begins with a pursuit of the wife in Central Park by the husband. He is unable to get her to talk to him. Eventually, we learn that she has discovered that, despite their marriage, her husband has not given up his homosexual escapades... just this Sunday morning he has gone so far as to flirt with a young man in church. To her, it is painfully clear that he is not a man, and, despite his protestations that his homosexuality is a thing of the past, he is very much involved with it. She upbraids him for having shirked the responsibilities of a husband, father and citizen of a troubled society. He avoids having children, runs away from any kind of community involvement. To her mind, he lacks guts and courage. She is hurt, enraged and disgusted with him, and, as far as she is concerned, their marriage is all over. The husband tries to elicit compassion and understanding from his wife. He tries to get her to see how hard he is trying to make the marriage work; that he did not feel they were ready for children; that he cannot be crucified because he has not changed overnight; that he is trying—trying to change; that he needs her help, her empathy. He realizes that her inability to empathize—to feel for him in his struggle with his problem—is part of a larger problem that she, herself, has had in their marriage, which is the inability to give of herself—to feel anything when they make love and in the other ways in which they relate to each other—that in fact, she is sitting on top of her feelings; that she is afraid to have feelings, particularly about sex; that she is cold and frigid and does not help him to elicit his manhood. He goes on to confront her with her fears of becoming emotionally involved. He observes that she doesn't mind being involved in civic affairs and other activities outside of their home, but not with him. He muses that perhaps that is the reason that she married him in the first place, knowing about his homosexuality—knowing that in these circumstances she would never be asked to be a woman. He then goes on to accuse her of being homosexual herself—latent, but homosexual nevertheless. At least he has had the courage to admit his homosexuality, to try to deal with it. Where is her courage, he asks? He mentions all the incriminating evidence that suggests latent homosexuality in his wife—her competitiveness, her assumption of male roles in their everyday life, her tenderness toward her girlfriends and so forth. His confrontation of his wife with these and other observations are traumatic for her. She screams, she slaps him and begins to cry, and what ensues is a poignant scene in which she admits her inability to give of herself, her fear of her own emotions and where they might lead her. She asks his help and he asks her for her help and understanding. They leave the park—two weak people who are getting stronger.

FINAL THOUGHT

The entire story is foolproof from the point of theatricality in that, should the actors fail in their performances, the director and actors' struggle for high-quality performances will become the real drama... and there is always the backup of the story itself. If the actors succeed in their work, then obviously the director and crew aspect will recede into the background.

I see excellent close-up work with the actors. I see actors talking to the lens of the camera of the director/cameraman. I hear church bells in Central Park on a Sunday morning. I see people stopping to watch the shooting of the film. I see a great theatrical short.

21

Symbiopsychotaxiplasm: Take One Rediscovered

A Conversation with Dara Meyers-Kingsley

SCOTT MACDONALD

SCOTT MACDONALD: Richard Brody has called you "a secret hero of the history of cinema" [see chapter 28]. You're the one who rescued *Symbiopsychotaxiplasm: Take One* from obscurity.

DARA MEYERS-KINGSLEY: I'm certainly very pleased to be recognized for rediscovering Bill's film. I like being "a heroine of cinema" and being recognized for breaking open the canon, making a space for this film!

I was happy to give the film and the filmmaker a new life after it was shown in 1991 at the Brooklyn Museum. As you know, the film went on to play in many festivals, and people remarked how fresh the film seemed to them, more than twenty years after it was made.

I loved how the film was part cinéma-vérité film and part dramatic feature. And it was a film about making movies! A film within a film or play within a play; this kind of "meta"-structure has always been an intellectual interest of mine. The film seemed ripe for reassessment.

SM: Many of us have found our way into Bill's extensive filmmaking career through *Symbio*. How did you come to know his films?

DMK: I'd been showing African-American film and video at the museum prior to the retrospective of Bill's films in 1991. I was essentially the first full-time curator of film at the Brooklyn Museum, where we showed movies in a long, flat-floored, rectangular space that had a stage.

At first the museum wanted me to do screenings that were linked to the current art exhibitions on view, so I curated shows of Postwar Italian Cinema, Cleopatra's Egypt, and German Expressionist Film. But I was able to prove that I could bring in audiences *separately* for film by doing stand-alone film exhibitions the way MoMA does. I was working in a museum after all, and I firmly believed that film was art and should be exhibited as such on its own terms.

We filled a niche, too, and it worked. Many small repertory theaters in Manhattan had closed, but Brooklyn was a place of opportunity. We were bringing ten thousand people a year to the museum for film, and then the museum created the beautiful Cantor Auditorium, designed by Arata Isozaki and James Stewart Polshek, as part of its master plan.

Early on (in 1987), I did a three-month-long show called "Black American Cinema: Images of a Culture," which included films by Melvin Van Peebles and Julie Dash, and Oscar Micheaux, Stanley Nelson, Gordon Parks, and Bill—and guest speakers Bill, Gordon Parks, Amiri Baraka, Clyde Taylor, Valerie Smith, Tony Gittens, Pearl Bowser, Clayton Riley, and Stanley Nelson.

I also did a show that highlighted the work of women makers (including Julie Dash, Jacqueline Shearer, and Camille Billops) and one that focused exclusively on video, where I showed the work of Howardena Pindell, Marlon Riggs, and Philip Mallory Jones, among others.

These shows were *not* scheduled for Black History Month because I didn't believe in limiting the experience of art to Black History Month or Women's History Month or Native American History Month . . .

SM: I totally agree—it's patronizing and encourages a kind of cinematic segregation. Accomplished African-American films should be shown year-round.

DMK: I guess I discovered Bill and his films in the late eighties as I dove into the work; then I met Bill and his wife Louise.

SM: In his recent review of *Symbiopsychotaxiplasm: Take One*, Brody says that Louise Greaves told him you had looked at Greaves's work and saw that there was one film you hadn't seen, but that Bill said, "You don't need to bother with that one." Is that accurate?

DMK: I'm a curator who enjoys working closely with the artists. I try to get to know the artist's entire body of work so that I can make the most cogent decisions, but also the most creative exhibitions. That's the way I approached Bill's retrospective. I wanted to see everything, including that film stored away in a box in the closet.

When I did finally screen *Symbio*, I knew immediately that we had to show the film and that it had to lead off the retrospective. I thought *Symbio* was Bill's greatest work of cinematic art. A masterpiece. And I'm proud that so many others have confirmed this.

So we opened the Cantor Auditorium with *Symbio* and brought Bill's film back to life. The series included many films and, as in my earlier series, several speakers: Amiri Baraka, Donald Bogle, St. Clair Bourne, Paula Giddings, Manthia Diawara, Michele Wallace, and William Seraile.

SM: Did Bill really say, "There's one other film, but *you don't need to bother with it*"?

DMK: Exactly. He pooh-poohed it. He seemed embarrassed.

Of course, *Symbio* was unlike anything else Bill had made. I think he thought of himself as a different kind of filmmaker, a different type of storyteller, perhaps as a more traditional documentarian, a historical storyteller—and that his experimentation, boundary pushing, and risk-taking needed to play its role in his more controlled films.

Once *Symbio* started to take off, Bill made me a press packet, which I went back and looked at it the other day. I saw that Jim Hoberman reviewed the film after we showed it (I studied with Jim in graduate school at NYU); it was great to see how many people wrote about it.

FIGURE 21.1 William and Louise Greaves celebrating what the IFC Center ad announces is the first-ever New York theatrical engagement of *Symbiopsychotaxiplasm: Take One* (October 26 through November 1, 2005), presented by Steven Soderbergh, at the IFC Center. Courtesy Louise Greaves.

At the Brooklyn Museum, I'd curated by borrowing material from distributors and the artists: the museum didn't, and still doesn't, have a collection of films and videos. In 1993 I went to the Warhol Foundation, where I was the director of the film and video collections and had a huge collection to work with. Initially I was trained as an art historian, then as a film historian, and later I combined the two, curating installations and other time-based, performative and experiential work. Since I started curating in the late 1980s, the creation, presentation, and reception of the moving image has expanded way beyond traditional theaters and screening rooms to include works that are made for galleries and nontraditional art spaces, as well as forms of experimentation that blur the lines between film/video/art. Artists constantly surprise us.

22

The Country in the City

Central Park as Metaphor in Jonas Mekas's Walden *and William Greaves's* Symbiopsychotaxiplasm: Take One

SCOTT MACDONALD

*E**ditor's Note:* This essay was written before the expanded version of *Symbiopsychotaxiplasm: Take One* was made available in 2005.

On a map or from the air, nothing defines New York City more clearly than the rectilinearity of Central Park at the heart of the curvilinear island of Manhattan. And nothing encodes the paradox of the thinking that created Frederick Law Olmsted's first great park—and simultaneously distinguishes it from many of the parks inspired by Central Park—than the visually perfect geometry of its outline. The park simultaneously confirms the grid structure of the streets of Manhattan and dramatically interrupts the structure: streets that run vertically uptown and downtown or horizontally across town must, when they reach the horizontal and vertical boundaries of the park, leave their verticality and horizontality behind to traverse the park before rejoining the grid of streets and avenues at the far boundaries of the park's expanse. If the Cartesian clarity of midtown Manhattan has come to represent the efficiency of American capitalism that was making the United States a major industrial power during the years when the Greensward Plan was designed and Central Park constructed, the park represented (and continues to represent) a countersensibility: as Olmsted and Calvert Vaux predicted,

> the time will come when New York will be built up, when all the grading and filling will be done and when the picturesquely-varied, rocky formations of

the Island will have been converted into foundations for rows of monotonous straight streets, and piles of erect, angular buildings. There will be no suggestion left of its present varied surface, with the single exception of the few acres contained in the Park. Then the priceless value of the present picturesque outlines of the ground will be more distinctly perceived, and its adaptability for its purpose more fully recognized.[1]

Of course, this countersensibility has as its ultimate benefit the refreshment of those who use the park and, at least implicitly, their return to their workaday worlds in better frames of mind for productive labor and effective citizenship in a capitalist republic. Indeed, the very complexity of the Olmsted/Vaux design for Central Park was itself a product of the interest in efficiency that is encoded within the graphic design of the surrounding city: the articulation of the park's considerable acreage in a wide variety of mini-terrains, each with particular kinds of experiences to offer, was a way of insuring not only the maximum options for individuals interested in using the park, but the longevity of the park's ability to function as a relief from the commercial energies of the city. Over time, any individual could use the park in many different ways—and in effect, have many different re-energizing experiences.

The overall shape of the park, seen from a distance, is also suggestive of the cinematic image, especially of the various wide-screen images that became popular as television began to threaten the economic viability of the motion picture industry. Obviously, the length-to-width ratio of the park (approximately 5 to 1) is of a different order from even the widest of wide-screen cinema aspect ratios (Cinerama's ratio is 2.77 to 1; Cinema Scope, 2.5 to 1), but this discrepancy seems less an issue if we remember that the panoramic views offered by wide-screen cinema are contemporary versions of the full-fledged panoramas that were so popular in this country and in Europe during the years when the park was under construction (Paul Philippoteaux's 1884 panorama of Pickett's Charge in Gettysburg, for example, is 356 feet in circumference and 26 feet high). And it is also less an issue once we remember that Central Park and modern cinema have more in common than the graphic rectangularity of their visible shape, most obviously a commitment to a fundamentally narrative form of visual experience that is meant to provide at least the momentary illusion of "escape" from the demands of the workplace. In Olmsted's view the park offered "a series of landscape passages located and designed in strict sequence," so that the visitor might be led by what "meets the eye, and by the continued discovery of fresh objects."[2] If the Ramble—the series of woodsy paths laid out between Belvedere Castle to the north and The Lake to the south—was the first sequentially designed section of Central Park to be constructed and, as a result, of particular importance in Olmsted's thinking, the entirety of the park, in one sense or another, reflects this commitment to sequential visual experience.

Recently, much has been made of the way in which Olmsted's class-inspired elitism plays itself out in his presumption that by leading those less advantaged than himself along predesigned paths, he could improve their lives, but much the same pattern drives the modern film industry: movie directors access capital as a means of producing visual sequences that, at least in theory, refresh those individuals who choose to go where the directors take them. Granted, in the instance of Central Park, observers provide their own literal momentum, but in both instances, the sequential visual narrations are chosen by spectators who decide to put at least a portion of their leisure time under the direction of others.

In addition to these very general graphic and narrative parallels between Central Park and modern motion pictures, there is an interesting historical relationship worth exploring. In *The Park and the People*, Elizabeth Blackmar and Roy Rosenzweig are at pains to balance several generations of Olmsted worship with a detailed history of Central Park as a social space, as an arena where the interests of various classes and power groups within classes have collided.[3] As the authors make clear, before Olmsted and Vaux could demonstrate their genius by constructing the park described in Greensward Plan, the interests of those who made their homes on the land bounded by what is now 59th Street and 110th Street, Fifth Avenue and Central Park West had first to be ignored and then trampled. That 90 percent of these 1,600 people were immigrants (primarily Irish or German) and African Americans, and that many of these people resided in what was called Seneca Village, one of the most economically successful, largely African-American communities in New York State (in 1855 African Americans living in Seneca Village had a rate of home ownership five times greater than New Yorkers in general and thirty-nine times greater than other African-American New Yorkers), reveals that whatever interests in beauty and healthy living for the less privileged classes underlay the Olmsted/Vaux design, and whatever the aesthetic distinctions of this design and of the finished park, the sociopolitical history that made the building of Central Park possible was merely one more instance of the racism and religious intolerance so evident in American society then and now. Churches displaced by the park included two African-American Methodist churches—AME Zion and African Union—one racially integrated Episcopal church, and Mount St. Vincent Convent, established by the Sisters of Charity in 1847.[4]

Almost exactly a century after the construction of Central Park, anti–Vietnam War demonstrators gathered in Central Park Mall for a rally that was followed by a march down Fifth Avenue. This March 26, 1966, event was only the second oppositional political event ever held in the park (the first was a women's suffrage meeting in 1914); and it was to be the first of many such gatherings that characterized the 1960s and 1970s. Of course, the same period saw a flowering of oppositional cinematic activity, including the completion of the two most distinguished independent films to have used Central Park as a primary location: Jonas Mekas's *Walden* (shot from 1964 to 1968 and completed in 1968) and William Greaves's *Symbiopsychotaxiplasm: Take One* (shot in 1968, completed in the earliest version in 1971, and revised in 1995). That Mekas was a Lithuanian immigrant and Greaves an African-American native of Manhattan makes the fact of these two films a poignant historical note, especially since both film artists use the making of these films as demonstrations of political viewpoints critical of an "upper-class" Hollywood film industry that has been, for most of its history, as oblivious to the interests of immigrant groups and African America as were those who wiped out Seneca Village to make way for what Vaux called the "big art work of the Republic."

WALDEN

Jonas Mekas began his career as a filmmaker almost immediately upon his arrival in the United States—his *Lost Lost Lost* (1976) begins with the intertitle, "A WEEK AFTER WE LANDED IN AMERICA (BROOKLYN) WE BORROWED MONEY & BOUGHT OUR FIRST BOLEX"—almost as if his arrival necessitated a transformation, if not of his artistic consciousness, at least of the means with which he would express it: by the time he left Lithuania, Mekas had established himself as a significant poet with a defiantly personal sensibility, deeply hostile to the interests of major conglomerate nation states like Communist Russia and Nazi Germany.[5] Once he and his brother Adolfas had purchased their Bolex, Mekas transformed the diaristic tendency of his written verse into a diaristic cinema with few predecessors either in this country or abroad. From late 1949 on, Mekas chronicled first the New York City community of Lithuanians-in-exile and his own personal explorations of the city, and subsequently the development of what was to become the New York art scene of the 1960s and, for Mekas himself, a new, artistic "homeland." By the early 1960s he was completing films, though it was not until 1969 that his first major diary film—known at first as *Diaries, Notes and Sketches Also Known As Walden*, and more recently simply as *Walden*—was finished.

Mekas's *Walden* is a 177-minute film, each section of which includes two types of visuals—his generally, often gesturally, handheld chronicling of the events he sees; and the frequent intertitles that introduce imagery we're about to see or have just seen—and three types of sound: environmental sounds taped by Mekas (the sound of subways is a motif), narration by Mekas, and music. The particular quality of these various sources of information and to a certain extent their organization are implied by the film's opening intertitle, "DEDICATED TO LUMIERE," which precedes even the title of the film. For Mekas, and for some other filmmakers emerging from the New York underground during the 1960s, the Lumière Brothers' earliest films were an inspiration. Ironically, the inspiration they provided was less a function of the brothers' original, commercial concerns (the Lumières were camera manufacturers, and their one-shot films were a function of their interest in marketing the Cinématographe and their Cinématographe presentations) than of what was for a time a widespread idealization of the comparative simplicity and directness of the earliest films. For 1960s filmmakers interested in providing a critique of commercial culture and commercial media—and especially of the visual/auditory overload increasingly characteristic of television and of a desperate film industry trying to compete with the new mass medium—the Lumières' single-shot, extended views of what seemed to be the everyday realities of 1895–1896 offered a useful alternative, just as Thoreau's decision to live at Walden Pond a century earlier was an alternative to what he saw as the fast-paced life of Concord and Boston.[6]

Mekas's defiance of contemporary film standards is obvious in his consistent use of intertitles, which had been an essential dimension of Hollywood films until the advent of sound-on-film, at which point they quickly became at most, a visual vestige of a bygone era. In other words, like the informality of Mekas's hand-held imagery, his intertitles (presented in a typewriter typeface that provides a handcrafted feel) declare Mekas's alliance with the cinematic past, with his own past as a poet, and with the literary past represented by Thoreau's *Walden: or, Life in the Woods*, which Mekas read in German translation in the mid-1940s while living in a German prisoner-of-war camp, and again, in English, in 1961.[7]

While Thoreau's *Walden* provides the title for Mekas's film and its central metaphor (the intertitle, "WALDEN," is juxtaposed with images of Central Park lakes three times), Mekas's relationship to Thoreau, as evidenced in the film, is complex and even paradoxical. One obvious similarity between the film and the book is evident in the particular ways in which the authors draw attention to their authorship. Thoreau's narrative of his personal experiences at Walden Pond is from the outset defiantly personal. Indeed, in the second paragraph of "Economy," Thoreau confronts the issue of his use of the first person:

> In most books, the I, or first person, is omitted; in this it will be retained; that, in respect to egotism, is the main difference. We commonly do not remember that it is, after all, always the first person that is speaking. I should not talk so much about myself if there were anybody else whom I knew as well. Unfortunately, I am confined to this theme by the narrowness of my experience. Moreover, I, on my side, require of every writer, first or last, a simple and sincere account of his own life, and not merely what he has heard of other men's lives; some such account as he would send to his kindred from a distant land; for if he has lived sincerely, it must have been a distant land to me.[8]

Of course, Thoreau not only writes in the first person, his narrative is about his largely solitary life in the woods, a life so solitary—at least as it is depicted in *Walden*—that while he is "naturally no hermit," most of those with whom he communes on the most regular basis during his two years at Walden Pond are "brute neighbors."

Mekas's film is as fully first person as Thoreau's written narrative, a choice that for Mekas was at least as defiant of contemporary standards and expectations as was Thoreau's use of "I." The first visual image in Mekas's *Walden* is the filmmaker waking up, and from the beginning Mekas's visual imagery is framed as a first-person activity. In the opening minute of the film we see Mekas playing an accordion-like instrument and read the intertitle, "I CUT MY HAIR, TO RAISE MONEY, HAVING TEAS WITH RICH LADIES" (followed by images of Mekas having his hair cut).

Mekas's determination to make and release what would come to be known as a "diary film" defied the Hollywood traditions of suppressing both directorial identity and the process of producing the film we're seeing (of course, Mekas was not alone in this particular defiance; even as he was shooting the footage that would later become *Walden*, Fellini's *8½* was a hit on the arthouse circuit). Moreover, his decision to make a longer-than-feature-length film as a solo enterprise defied the corporate tradition of American cinema (and of popular European cinema as well). Further, Mekas's assumption that individual viewers should decide how much of the film they should experience during a particular screening (early on, *Walden* could be rented as individual 16mm reels) ignored the tradition that films were consumed in their entirety in a public forum controlled by distributors and exhibitors, in favor of a kind of access more like readers have to literary texts.

Of course, it is the centrality of the idea of Nature in both the literary and the cinematic versions of *Walden*—not the two works' defiantly personal stances—that accounts for Mekas's decision to use Thoreau's work as the central, guiding metaphor of his film. And it is the idea of Nature that suggests the most fundamental distinction between the visions of the two works. The fact that Thoreau's *Walden* was part of a particular American cultural moment when writers and painters were realizing the degree to which industrialization was threatening America's distinctive access to "wilderness" and to the connection with God available through the "Book of Nature" made it of particular relevance for Mekas, whose personal history had threatened a comparable loss. Mekas had spent most of his life in rural Lithuania, but after he had fled his homeland and once the partition of Europe at the end of the war had put Lithuania into Communist hands, Mekas found himself exiled both from Lithuania and from the immersion in nature that he had experienced there as a child and adolescent. Not surprisingly, this loss of access to homeland created a considerable nostalgia that is often a central issue in Mekas's diary films: *Lost Lost Lost*, for example, chronicles Mekas's gradual personal evolution from nostalgic Lithuanian-in-exile to American artist.

Thoreau's decision to leave Concord and live at Walden Pond for two-plus years in the hope that the privacy and serenity offered by the pond would allow him to plumb the depths of his soul was an attempt to defend his psychic health from what he saw as the increasingly pervasive tendency in modem man to have "no time to be anything but a machine,"[9] a human machine at the mercy of the larger machine of industrialization. As is suggested in Mekas's introduction of Central Park-as-Walden (and as is consistently confirmed during the remainder of the film), for Mekas the "natural" environment of the park is a way of making contact with his rural origins and the source of his identity, both of which he has been separated from by the industrial machines of modem Germany, the Soviet Union, and the other major nation-states whose decisions have determined Lithuania's modern history.

While both men see Nature as a refuge from the machine of industrialized society, however, the century that separates them causes their depictions of nature to seem at first like inversions of each other. In 1845 Thoreau needed to go no farther than a couple of miles outside of Concord to achieve the feeling of solitude. The location of Central Park on what was then the outskirts of New York City was a result of a combination of economic practicality (the less densely inhabited land was less expensive for the city to acquire) and of the same urge that took Thoreau to Walden Pond, the urge to leave the city behind. But judging from the imaging of the park in photography and cinema, the modern eye is less astonished by the park itself than by the spectacle of nature walled in by skyscrapers in virtually all directions; that is, by the "seam" between park and city. For Mekas, the beauty of Central Park was no longer a function of its being outside the city; the park's location so dramatically inside the city provided him with his most essential insight into Nature:

> In general, I would say that I feel there will always be Walden for those who really want it. Each of us lives on a small island, in a very small circle of reality, which is our own reality. I made up a joke about a Zen monk standing in Times Square with people asking, "So what do you think about New York—the noise, the traffic?" The monk says, "What noise? What traffic?" You *can* cut it all out. No, it's not that we can have all this today, but tomorrow it will be gone. It *is* threatened, but in the end it's up to us to keep those little bits of paradise alive and defend them and see that they survive and grow.[10]

The motif of Mekas's use of the various Central Park lakes in conjunction with his intertitle "WALDEN" is essentially a paradox: on one hand, Mekas recognizes that those hardly isolated bodies of water and the crowds of walkers, ice skaters, rowers who frequent them are virtually the opposite of the Thoreau of *Walden*, alone, gazing deep into the unruffled waters of Walden Pond at the dazzling pickerel and his soul. Indeed, on this level, Mekas's references to *Walden* might seem a form of humorous irony. On the other hand, however, this seeming irony unites the author and the filmmaker as fully as it distinguishes them.

While, in the popular imagination, Walden Pond's isolation and Thoreau's solitude there seem at the heart of *Walden*, in fact Thoreau was not a chronicler of "wilderness": even the pond's isolation was compromised, though not in a way he resents, by the train tracks that run past the pond across from his cabin. In fact, one of Thoreau's most elaborate descriptions in *Walden*—a description located strategically in "Spring," the penultimate chapter of his chronicle—focuses on the thawing of sand and clay on the sides of a deep cut "on the railroad through which I passed on my way to the village, a phenomenon not very common on so large a scale, though the number of freshly exposed banks of the right material must have been greatly multiplied since railroads were invented."[11]

SYMBIOPSYCHOTAXIPLASM: TAKE ONE

Central Park allows Mekas to pursue his solitary way within a "natural" environment—the quintessential "American" individualist. Indeed, even when

Mekas is with someone, as when he films Stan Brakhage crossing the park, Mekas remains a detached observer. On the other hand, for William Greaves, filmmaking was a fundamentally social activity, and he chose Central Park as the location for what became *Symbiopsychotaxiplasm: Take One* not only because it is a social space but because of the kind of social space it is. While Mekas wanders through the park, recording what interests or touches him, Greaves uses it as a background and a resource for a cinematic engagement of the ways in which creative individuals relate to one another when they find themselves outside the institutional structures within which their creativity is usually exploited. Indeed, for Greaves himself, the opportunity to participate in the project that generated *Symbiopsychotaxiplasm: Take One* came as an interruption of a busy career of producing sponsored documentary projects for such institutions as the United Nations and the United States Information Agency, and for his own William Greaves Productions, Inc.

Greaves wrote a brief script for an argument between a man and a woman, reminiscent of Edward Albee's *Who's Afraid of Virginia Woolf*: the woman complains bitterly about the abortions her partner has pressured her into having and charges him with being a homosexual; the man denies he is gay, claiming the time just isn't right for them to have children. The script for this argument was

FIGURE 22.1 William Greaves, cast, and crew in Central Park during the shooting of *Symbiopsychotaxiplasm: Take One* (filmed 1968, first edited version, 1971). Photographer unknown. Courtesy Louise Greaves.

used as if it were a screen test for pairs of actors who were asked to perform the scene in a variety of ways. Don Fellows and Patricia Ree Gilbert, the leads in *Symbiopsychotaxiplasm: Take One*, played the scene as conventional melodrama; another pair was asked to perform it as a musical.... In addition to filming the various versions of the argument, the crew was directed to film themselves filming the actors: that is, Greaves conceived the various performances of the scene as a catalyst for the interaction of crew, performers, and director that was the real focus of the project. And finally, Greaves also directed the crew to film their Central Park surround, whenever the activities of those observing the shoot seemed particularly interesting or energetic.

Originally, Greaves's plan was to use the considerable footage recorded of the performances, the production process, and its Central Park context for a series of five films: *Symbiopsychotaxiplasm: Take One, Take Two, Take Three, Take Four,* and *Take Five,* each of which would center on different performers. But the decision to run several cameras at once—necessary since the process of a cameraperson filming the performance could only be filmed by another camera—quickly used up Greaves's financial resources. The result was that sufficient material for all the projected "takes" was recorded, but only *Take One* was completed—and it not until 1971.

The intellectual sources for the *Symbiopsychotaxiplasm* project were several. Perhaps the most crucial of these is the source of the film's title, which is a take-off on "symbiotaxiplasm," philosopher/social scientist Arthur Bentley's term (in his *Inquiry Into Inquiries*) for any particular social organism within which human beings interact with one another and their environment.[12] Greaves added "psycho" to Bentley's term, "to focus more acutely on the role that psychology and creativity play when a group of people come together and function as a creative entity charged with the responsibility of making a film."[13]

Bentley's exploration of the various approaches to investigation in the social sciences is analogous to Greaves's project, on the level of both the actors performing the screen test (which is always an inquiry into the abilities of the actors who perform it) and the crew recording the action of screen test and surround. Indeed, Greaves planned from the beginning to "act" the role of incompetent or confused or at least passive film director in order to catalyze rebellion in both cast and crew and energize a multilayered inquiry into the cinematic process.

And while the rebellion he hoped for did not develop in precisely the way Greaves envisioned, it did finally occur: at one point, Gilbert becomes furious that she can't perform the scene the way she thinks Greaves wants her to and storms off, with Greaves following, but instead of recording their subsequent discussion, the crew, alienated from Greaves's process, remains behind. They also demonstrate their alienation by meeting together without Greaves's knowledge to discuss what seems to many of them the fiasco of the project. They filmed their discussion and gave the material to Greaves at the end of the shooting.

Greaves's decision to use Central Park as the location for his project has both general and particular relevance to the issues the film raises. Most obviously, Greaves, like Mekas, saw the park as a space that allows people to leave—for a limited time—the rigidity of their workaday schedules and enter a more "creative" environment, an understanding of the park that is relevant on all three levels of *Symbiopsychotaxiplasm: Take One*. For Alice and Freddy, the arguing couple, the expanses of Central Park provide both the psychic space and the comparative privacy to express their frustrations. The level of Alice's frustration and Freddy's surprise at her confronting him suggest that they have lived together while repressing their problems for some time, and this particular walk in the park is a result of Alice's desire to leave the puzzling "wonderland" of repression and make sense of her life. That her central bitterness centers on the abortions she's had, on her desire for a family, and on her "unnatural" sex with Freddy is nicely reflected in the park's embodiment of a traditional idea of Nature.

The park is equally relevant for the production process Greaves instigated. While the filming was done by men and women who had had considerable experience working on more conventional films, the very point of Greaves's method was to force actors and crew into unfamiliar ways of working, in the hope of freeing them to be more openly creative than conventional film production allowed. The comparatively open spaces of Central Park are analogous to the creative space Greaves offered cast and crew, though ironically—like Freddy, who claims over and over not to know what Alice is talking about—they have come to be so at ease with their more usual (controlled, repressed) ways of working that they cannot make sense of what Greaves is doing. And even on the level of the park surround, those visiting the park who come across the production are rewarded with the spectacle of creative activity within a space originally created, at least in part, for their aesthetic pleasure.

The analogy of Greaves's film and Central Park goes deeper than the general idea that, as a created, artistic space, the park is an appropriate environment for creative activity. For one thing, the economic background of the *Symbiopsychotaxiplasm* project recalls the economic history of the park. The economic realities of commercial film production would never have allowed Greaves to conceive a feature-length experimental film—much less a set of five features. Greaves's experiment was possible only because of the trickle-down effect of

Greaves's funding "angels'" financial success, combined with the angels' respect for the creative process in general and Greaves as a creative person.[14]

Further, just as Central Park was designed and built for a comparatively wealthy sector of the New York City population, and during its earliest years was used primarily, or at least most visibly, by the rich, *Symbiopsychotaxiplasm* not only was funded by independent wealth and shaped by the support of Greaves's patrons (whose generosity made possible the extensive shooting, and the shooting of the shooting) but for a long time was available only to those with considerable cultural resources: even once it had been rediscovered, *Symbiopsychotaxiplasm: Take One* was seen primarily at film festivals, in colleges and universities, and in art museums; that is, by people with sufficient leisure to pursue an interest in experimental cinema. To put this another way, just as Central Park provides only the illusion of escape from the realities of New York City—"illusion" because it is surrounded by and, in the long run, serves the capitalist energies of businesses and business people—*Symbiopsychotaxiplasm: Take One* was a brief cinematic "fling" made possible presumably by business successes, which was followed by Greaves's quick return to a more conventionally productive (and economically viable) filmic life in the city surrounding the park.

Having said all this, however, I must make a substantial qualification. Even if one were to decide that Central Park was a result of nothing more noble than a combination of the financial interests of those who stood to gain from its construction and the self-serving, class-inspired, paternalistic romantic egos of Olmsted and Vaux, in the long term, the democratic idealism that Olmsted and Vaux claimed as the basis of the Greensward Plan has, in fact, become a reality. Central Park *is* used by a huge, diverse population in a wide variety of ways, only a few of which can be said to be the property of the rich. This contemporary democracy of the park is clearly demonstrated by *Take One*. In fact, the only "character" in the film who might be said to represent the rich is a woman who rides past the production on horseback early in the film.

And if the characters in the film's melodramatic story and those men and women doing the filming are middle-class professionals, the people who are watching the production seem to be more broadly representative economically. In general, Greaves is at pains to create a broad representation of park-goers. In the opening credits, for example, the names of those who worked on *Symbiopsychotaxiplasm: Take One* are superimposed over a montage of people using the park. This montage—which is so fully reminiscent of Edward Steichen's photo exhibit *The Family of Man* (New York: Museum of Modem Art, 1955) as to be virtually an homage—presents dozens of people, seemingly of many heritages and a wide variety of economic circumstances, as representatives of the cycle of life: there are parents and babies, parents with older children, still older young people playing soccer, young lovers....

Further, within the body of the film, Greaves and his crew interface with a number of bystanders, including a middle-aged, alcoholic, homeless man who "sleeps in the bushes." Though this homeless man represents the most economically disenfranchised class of New York City residents, the film gives him a substantial voice—indeed, he has the film's last words—and reveals him as an (at least accidentally) astute commentator on the production. Victor's entrance into the film is announced on the soundtrack as we hear him say, "What is this thing? What is this thing? Oh, it's a *movie*—so who's moving whom?" If this man (and others like him: he mentions that there are "many sleeping in the bushes") has been excluded from or has dropped out of the economically productive sector of society and is, as he explains, unrepresented politically, he has found at least a temporary refuge in the park, just as Greaves's film has provided the man with a momentary escape from his social invisibility by offering him at least one brief moment of democratic "representation."

A final dimension of the analogy between Central Park and *Take One* involves the issue of race. As mentioned earlier, at the outset the Central Park project displaced the particularly successful African-American community at Seneca Village. Whether this was part of a conscious plan or not, the comparative sacrifice of African Americans in the interest of goals devised by European Americans seems of a piece with the history of American racial politics (a history also evoked by the fact that this community was named *Seneca* Village). Regardless of the racial attitudes of those who planned and developed Central Park, however, the forces of history have encouraged the racial integration planners might have avoided. By the 1920s African-American migration from the South had transformed Harlem, which lies directly north of the park, into one of the largest and most visible African-American communities in the nation. And by the 1960s the northern migration of Hispanics had further transformed sectors of this community into "Spanish Harlem." These transformations of Central Park's surround have transformed the nature of the community using the park for recreation, and this transformation is visible in *Symbiopsychotaxiplasm: Take One*. For example, the young people observing the film with whom Greaves and the crew interact early in the film are primarily African-American and Hispanic.

The integration evident within the park is also visible on the production level of the film, not only in the fact that Greaves himself is African American, but in his mixed-race crew and cast. Two crew members (Clive Davidson and Phil

Parker) are Black, and one of the five pairs of actors who dramatize the argument is a mixed-race couple. The 1971 version of *Take One* ends with final credits superimposed over shots of an African-American woman (Audrey Henningham) and her European-American partner (Shannon Baker); the 1995 revision ends the same way, but shots of this mixed-race pair also introduce the film. There seems little ethnic friction between cast and crew. Indeed, Greaves claimed, "The people who worked on *Symbiopsychotaxiplasm* were Age of Aquarius people who were in many respects shorn of the racist encumbrances that many White Americans are burdened with"[15]—though when Don Fellows jokingly says to Greaves, "You wanted to say a few words for George Wallace," Patricia Ree Gilbert's laughter seems forced and embarrassed, revealing perhaps that for the cast and crew race was not entirely invisible. Nevertheless, given the realities of the era, the production process of *Take One* seems virtually utopic.

More suggestive than the fact of Greaves's decision to use a mixed-race cast and crew is the way in which Greaves conceptualized his role as director vis-à-vis race:

> Clearly, we were working in a context of the urban disorders of the Sixties and the rage of the African-American community against the tyranny and racism of the American body politic. There was that general social background, plus the more specific struggles: the civil rights marches, the whole Vietnam War problem, police repression and the growing dissent over it.
>
> The film was an attempt to look at the impulses, the inspirations of a group of creative people who, during the making of the film, were being pushed to the wall by the process I, as director, had instigated. The scene that I had written was fixed, and I was in charge. I was insisting that this scene would be done by the cast and crew, even though it was making them very unhappy. The questions were, "When will they revolt? When would they question the validity, the wisdom, of doing the scene in the first place?" In this sense, it was a metaphor of the politics of the time.[16]

If in the mid-nineteenth century even the most successful of African-American communities could not slow the development of the park, by 1968 an African-American director could not only take charge of a mixed-race production but could see himself as a representative of "the Establishment." No one could argue that racism had disappeared by the mid-1960s, even in Central Park; but by 1968 Greaves himself had lived through substantial changes insofar as his own access to the means of film production were concerned.

It is clear that within the *Symbiopsychotaxiplasm* project, Greaves *is* the establishment. If some members of the crew are willing to criticize his direction, the actors—at least Fellows and Gilbert—seem a bit in awe of Greaves's reputation as actor and teacher of actors (for years, at the Actors Studio in New York). Indeed, when Gilbert finally rebels—as Greaves hoped she would—it is not precisely against him but rather against his telling her that she is doing a good job: she seems angry at herself and her own "incompetence," not at Greaves's direction.

That Greaves functions as the Establishment in *Take One*, however, will not blind anyone to the fact that Greaves's access to directorial control in this instance is anything but representative of the era. Indeed, one could argue that in the 1950s and 1960s opportunities for African Americans to direct commercial films were at a nadir: the increasing inclusion of Black performers in some Hollywood films had cost the Black Underground cinema its audience, and it was not until the 1980s that some African Americans began to have anything like a regular opportunity to direct. At most, Greaves enacts a metaphor for the establishment: he *is* in charge of this particular production, but the project itself is as distant from the established, white-dominated business of cinema as Central Park is from Hollywood.

Symbiopsychotaxiplasm: Take One is rich with paradox. For one thing, it was precisely Greaves's distance from the commercial mainstream that allowed him the opportunity to experiment with the filmmaking process and film form and provided him with a mindset that saw improvisation—on location and later in the editing room—as a logical creative option, an option located by the film within the larger history of African-American creativity by Greaves's use of Miles Davis's *In a Silent Way* to accompany the credits and as a motif during the rest of the film. Further, even if Greaves's sense of himself as the Establishment is, in a larger sense, ironic, considering the general lack of opportunity for African Americans to direct, the visual motif of Greaves and his cast and crew moving through Central Park provides us with at least an image of film history moving in the direction of equal opportunity. There is poignancy in the fact that one of the few identifiable locations in the park, other than the bridge at the northwest corner of the Lake, is a monument located just to the west of the Sheep Meadow and to the north of Tavern on the Green, erected in honor of fifty-eight men of the New York National Guard's Seventh Regiment who were lost during the Civil War. The monument, which is one of several locations where Alice and Freddy argue, is a reminder (a conscious one, according to Greaves) of the centuries-long road toward societal freedom and equal access African Americans had had to travel before even the *metaphor* of cinematic power provided by *Symbiopsychotaxiplasm: Take One* could be possible.

It is difficult to imagine New York City without Central Park. Even if we see the park as merely a space in the service of capitalist goals, the fact that it continues to exist in a section of the city where land values are as high as anywhere in the nation is a testament to the fact that the idea of Nature has remained a crucial component of the American psyche, so crucial that anyone interested in transforming the park must confront considerable resistance on the part of New Yorkers from a variety of classes. If the park has evolved in directions that would surprise Olmsted and Vaux, it remains not only another instance of capitalist development but a space that a good many of us continue to find startlingly beautiful and an aid to both physical and spiritual health. Similarly, even if we see all forms of "experimental" or "personal" cinema as trickle-down results of the commercial film industry, the cinematic alternatives demonstrated by Mekas's *Walden* and Greaves's *Symbiopsychotaxiplasm: Take One* suggest that as long as the industry remains powerful, those willing to offer creative alternatives to it not only will continue to work but will evolve in stature.

Even if Mekas assumed that *Walden* would be of interest only "to some of his friends and a few strangers," and even if *Symbiopsychotaxiplasm: Take One* represents a momentary interruption within what can seem a more conventional documentary career, as time has passed, these two films have become increasingly interesting, at least for that substantial group of us who remain fascinated by the full spectrum of film history. Indeed, it is difficult to think of two commercial films of the late 1960s, early 1970s that look more impressive today than these alternative films do. Whatever the nature of their limitations, Central Park itself and the films by Mekas and Greaves for which the park has served as explicit location and implicit inspiration offer a set of visionary experiences that continue to enrich our sense of the past and the present.

NOTES

This is a revised version of an essay that appeared in *Journal of American Studies* 31, no. 3 (December 1997), then as chapter 7 in *The Garden in the Machine* (Berkeley: University of California Press, 2001).

1. Frederick Law Olmsted and Calvert Vaux, "Designers' Report as to Proposed Modifications in the Plan," dated May 31, 1858; reprinted in *Frederick Law Olmsted Landscape Architect, 1822–1903*, ed. Frederick Law Olmsted, Jr., and Theodora Kimball, vol. 2 (New York: Putnam, 1928), 239.
2. Olmsted to H. G. Stebbins, "Examination of the Design of the Park and Recent Changes Therein," February 1872; Olmsted, "Annual Report to Central Park Commissioners," 1868.

3. The implications of Olmsted's class affiliations are a central topic, for example, in Elizabeth Blackmar and Roy Rosenzweig, *The Park and the People: A History of Central Park* (Ithaca, N.Y.: Cornell University Press, 1992).
4. See Blackmar and Rosenzweig, chap. 3.
5. The best source of information on Mekas's life and career as a filmmaker is David E. James, ed., *To Free the Cinema* (Princeton, N.J.: Princeton University Press, 1992).
6. In Mekas's *Walden*, the apparent informality of the Lumières' *Arrival of the Express at La Ciotat* (1895), *Feeding the Baby* (1895), and *Boys Sailing Boats, Tuileries Garden, Paris* (1896) was emulated in images of friends, train trips, and events in Central Park.
7. Mekas, phone interview with the author, August 24, 1995.
8. Henry David Thoreau, *Walden*, ed. J. Lyndon Shanley (Princeton, N.J.: Princeton University Press, 1971), 3–4.
9. Thoreau, 6.
10. Mekas interview in Scott MacDonald, *A Critical Cinema 2* (Berkeley: University of California Press, 1992), 101.
11. Thoreau, *Walden*, 303.
12. See Arthur F. Bentley, *Inquiry Into Inquiries: Essays on Social Theory*, ed. Sidney Ratner (Boston: Beacon Press, 1954).
13. Greaves, in Scott MacDonald, "Sunday in the Park with Bill," *Independent* 15, no. 4 (May 1992): 26.
14. Even Mekas's comparatively low-budget, 16mm process was expensive enough that Mekas needed to wait until the 1970s and the institution of public grant support for film through such organizations as the NEA and New York State Council on the Arts (NYSCA) to make completed films from footage shot in the 1950s and 1960s. *Walden*, the first of the diaries to be edited, was possible only as the result of a small grant (approximately $2,000) from the Albright-Knox Gallery in Buffalo arranged by Gerald O'Grady, who had invited Mekas to present some of the diary work at an arts festival in 1968.

    In a private conversation with me, Greaves once mentioned that Patricia Ree Gilbert was the "angel" who financed *Symbiopsychotaxiplasm*, though Louise Greaves—in my interview with her in this book (chapter 3)—indicates that while Gilbert was a benefactor, Manny Melamed was the primary "angel." Apparently Greaves's benefactors contributed something like $35,000 to the project. Greaves approximated that the total cost of *Symbiopsychotaxiplasm: Take One* was somewhere between $100,000 and $150,000 (including the cost of the 1995 revision) and claimed (in an unpublished interview with the author, July 8, 1995) to have put $70,000 into the project.
15. Greaves, in "Sunday in the Park with Bill," 28.
16. Greaves, in "Sunday in the Park with Bill," 29.

23

"Just Another Word for Jazz": The Signifying Auteur in William Greaves's *Symbiopsychotaxiplasm: Take One* (Excerpt)

AKIVA GOTTLIEB

Editor's note: Included here are the final paragraphs of Akiva Gottlieb's substantive overview of William Greaves's career and extended focus on *Symbiopsychotaxiplasm: Take One*.

The most compelling "character" in *Symbiopsychotaxiplasm* is, perhaps necessarily, an accidental figure. Unlisted in the film's credits, he's an eloquent self-described drunk named Victor who wanders onto the set to deliver a series of poetic rants against the political order of late 1960s America, and especially Mayor John Lindsay's New York City. When told that the crew is filming a *movie*, he sensibly asks, "So who's moving whom?" (In this context, it's a line too perfect to be scripted.) The camera stays focused on Victor for an inordinate amount of time, and as it becomes clear that he's a dynamic figure of interest, the production manager, Bob Rosen, asks him to sign a release form. It's only at this point that Greaves and his crew discover that Victor is homeless and sleeps in the bushes at Sixty-Ninth Street. Greaves seems baffled by this revelation and turns to his colleagues. "Did anyone know this?" Did anyone know that people sleep in the park? Bob Rosen claims that he lives mere blocks away, and has never seen anyone sleep in the park. Collectively, they want to know why Victor puts up with these conditions. "How can I fight politics," he responds, "I'm just one man." As Victor eventually moves on, having collected a few dollars from members of the crew, it becomes clear that another unwitting intervention has been staged—an individual has stepped in and fundamentally reshaped the film's environment, emphasizing that no matter how enlightened and socially progressive the film crew might be, they are still alienated from another level of reality. The meaning of the Establishment has again been recalibrated. That Greaves the editor, sifting through miles of footage, decided to make this scene the film's penultimate conflict seems quite significant.

What is the crew's responsibility to this homeless man? Why will the crew revolt against the director but not against a social order that causes such a man to sleep in the bushes? If the members of the crew consider their director frivolous (and perhaps morally reprehensible) for shooting a series of seemingly worthless screen tests during one of the most politically and racially charged seasons in American history, then are they not doubly culpable for assisting him in this folly? And what about the passive spectator? Can an audience be judged for judging the crew's indifference to this man's struggle? By casting himself as a self-aware banal figure—"Don't take me seriously!" Greaves says at one point, speaking directly to the camera—he is trying to arouse a sense of productive frustration, challenging both the crew and audience to consider assuming new kinds of social responsibility. The film features several occurrences of a camera being aimed back at the viewer, calling attention to the dialogics of the gaze, continually hinting at an imminent breaking of the fourth wall in which we will be called to account as well.

A BLAST FROM THE PAST

One major challenge to any historical classification of *Symbiopsychotaxiplasm: Take One* is distinguishing elements of parody from the apparent earnestness of the endeavor. Whether intentionally or not, Greaves's film works not only as an experimental documentary but as an ironic or parodic fiction about documentary filmmaking (and protest art) at an explosive historical moment, one that relied on nonfiction motion pictures in the form of news reporting. One can point to the burgeoning cinéma-vérité movement as the initial impetus for this exploration of controlled and uncontrolled "reality," but the period immediately anticipating and following *Symbiopsychotaxiplasm* also saw a movement of clearly fictionalized "documentaries" that played much more openly with evolving conceptions of cinematic realism and documentary aesthetics, challenging Jean-Luc Godard's formulation that "the cinema is truth 24 frames per second."

Jim McBride's film *David Holzman's Diary* (1967), to cite one prominent example, presents itself as a cinéma-vérité "found document," in which a young Godard-obsessed film student (played by L. M. Kit Carson) confesses his daily relationship struggles to a camera in his bedroom, eventually complaining that the camera does not reciprocate his emotional fervor. As David Kehr notes: "Where most independent productions are founded on self-righteous claims of truth and honesty, McBride's film wittily observes that Hollywood has no corner on illusionism. Even the black-and-white, hand-held camera still lies at 24 frames per second"[1] The film, which credits writer/director Jim McBride and cinematographer Michael Wadleigh—who would go on to direct the *Woodstock* (1970) documentary—does not hide its status as a work of fiction, and clearly derides the pieties of the direct cinema movement. A *New York Times* review from 1973 (when it was screened at the Whitney Museum), bearing the subhead "'David Holzman's Diary' Spoofs Cinema Verite,"[2] betrays an understanding of the film's obvious conceit. Other contemporaneous projects, like Haskell Wexler's *Medium Cool* (1969) and Norman Mailer's *Maidstone* (1970), used cinéma-vérité techniques to explore developments in American counterculture, but neither film is referred to as a documentary.

Despite the intricacies of the film's construction, nobody involved in *Symbiopsychotaxiplasm: Take One* has ever publicly challenged its status as an unscripted, unstaged documentary, in which spontaneous behavior dictated the outcome of the plot. Yet, as of February 2011, at least one participant in the *Symbiopsychotaxiplasm* experiment, the aforementioned Bob Rosen, is still concerned with asserting its veracity, protesting against the idea that he had been "played." In a long but fascinating comment left on a website hosting an interview with Greaves and Soderbergh, a still-passionate Rosen challenges a Wikipedia article's statement that Greaves's supposedly foolish on-set activity led (in)directly to the crew's rebellion and the eventual incorporation of their footage. In other words, Rosen contends that Greaves had nothing to do with the crew's collective decision to film its revolt:

> The crucial thing, as I have tried to point out elsewhere, is that Bill had no way of knowing what we (the crew) would do, if anything. The article glibly slides over this crucial issue: "This footage, of course, ends up in the final cut of the film...." What does the Wikipedia writer mean by "this" footage? THIS FOOTAGE was NOT "because of the constant filming on the set." It was

because of the filming WE did OFF the set, in the REAL world, behind Bill's back, without his knowledge. What does he mean by "of course"? He means that ONCE we gave Bill the footage, Bill of course saw what we had done, and made the most of it. As I said to Bill when he stepped out of the elevator on the penthouse floor at Amram's and I handed him those 4 rolls: "Bill, you're going to need this." Meaning: "You won't have a film without this footage."

Now, in this Wiki article, Bill is presented like he was God, that he somehow knew all along that it was only a matter of time before one of us got this "bright idea" to take the film away from him, out of his control, and film behind his back. Is it possible? Sure. Do I know for sure that Bill didn't have this plan in his mind BEFORE we did anything? No, BUT I am almost certain that he did NOT. How do I know? Because this is the way CREATION happens. ALL creation, even God does it that way.

It's called "evolution." There is no one directing it. No god-like auteur on the set "playing the fool" in order to get other people to complete His idea. I'm not saying Bill WAS a fool. I am just saying he wasn't a god. The "playing the fool" bit is Bill's retrospective revision (or the writer's revision), his attempt after the fact of creation to construct some fake narrative that restores the illusion that Bill knew what he was doing all the time.[3]

Rosen is trying to set the record straight, but in a more important sense, he is also attempting to maintain a sense of authorship, feeling that Greaves, "no godlike auteur," has unfairly been credited with more than he deserves. "Bill, you're going to need this," Rosen apparently says—thus creating what could have been the most dramatic scene of the film, had Rosen thought to bring along a camera and microphone—and the word *need* implies that the apparent ringmaster would have no film without Rosen's intervention. Rosen, of course, is the same figure that in 1968 turns to the camera to remind viewers: "The director does not know that we're photographing this scene." His invocation of "the REAL world," in reference to the crew's backroom meeting, is another fascinating category mistake, since the end of *Symbiopsychotaxiplasm* seems to critique the self-satisfied nature of the crew's revolt, as contrasted with the political struggle of Victor, the homeless man. Surely to Greaves's amusement, the game set up by the contradictions of *Symbiopsychotaxiplasm* is still being played.

By the time Greaves's film was released in 2005, the false documentary, in which fictitious events are presented using the tropes of documentary form, had developed into a subgenre, and the concept of direct cinema had come to seem outmoded and naïve. A taxonomy of these films might distinguish between wry, self-aware, "mocumentaries" like *This Is Spinal Tap* (1984), and faux-documentaries like *The Blair Witch Project* (1999), which dispense with recognizable performers and depend at least somewhat on the spectator's credulity in believing that she is watching "real" footage. Audiences had become used to seeing these postmodern documentary hybrid films, and *Symbiopsychotaxiplasm* might now be seen to represent nostalgia for "the real"—especially as seen through the mist of the 1960s—since the film's experimental frisson emerges from the belief in a "reality" that can be fractured, and a narrative center that can shift.

In a day-of-release review in the *New York Sun*, Nathan Lee called the film "a blast from the past that's as fresh as tomorrow," though he also emphasized the datedness of the film's concerns: "[It's] flower-power Pirandello, a High 60s groove on, like 'supra levels of reality,' man."[4] In a *New York Times* rave, Manohla Dargis admitted that the film feels "very of its experimental moment."[5] Due to the time lapse between *Symbiopsychotaxiplasm: Take One*'s moment of production and the moment it met the public, the film seems destined to remain an avant-garde hippie time capsule, not an early landmark of black experimental cinema. But one knows better than to say anything conclusive about a film whose shape continually morphs according to perspective.

NOTES

The full essay from which this chapter is excerpted appeared in *Black Camera* 5, no. 1 (2013): 165–83.

1. David Kehr, "David Holzman's Diary," *Chicago Reader*, http://www.chicagoreader.com/chicago/david-holzmans-diary/Film?oid=1061408, accessed June 8, 2011.
2. Nora Sayre, "Screen: 'David Holzman's Diary' Spoofs Cinema Verite," *New York Times*, December 7, 1973.
3. "William Greaves and Steven Soderbergh on 'Symbiopsychotaxiplasm,'" *Fast, Cheap Movie Thoughts* blog, May 6, 2010. When I wrote Bob Rosen on April 26, 2011, to confirm his authorship of the comment, he sent the following response: "Thanks for your inquiry. But what exactly does it mean to 'confirm' that it's indeed 'me'? Sure, it's me. But how can you be sure? Because I say so? Maybe 'Bob Rosen' doesn't exist at all, just some guy with an email address with the name 'bob' in it, just a fan of the film, as you apparently are, who has found a clever way to participate in the film's afterlife on this guy's blog. Or maybe 'Bob Rosen' is just another one of Bill's Actors Studio buddies who agreed to play the role of 'Production Manager' in the film, and is still playing it. And Bill will laugh when I send him a copy of this email. Isn't that precisely the whole point?"
4. Nathan Lee, "High '60s Groove," *New York Sun*, October 26, 2005.
5. Manohla Dargis, "Film Within a Film in 60's Time Capsule? Groovy," *New York Times*, October 26, 2005.

24
Symbiopsychotaxiplasm: Take 2

Produced and Directed by Steve Buscemi and William Greaves; the Concept by William Greaves

WILLIAM GREAVES

*E*ditor's note: This is an uncorrected draft of the plan for what would become *Symbiopsychotaxiplasm: Take 2½*, dated May 5, 1999. We have echoed the format of this draft, with a few very minor adjustments.

The basic framework of the production.

The time is 1968.

The first part of **Symbiopsychotaxiplasm: Take 2** will start with the end of the already-produced **Take One** (see attached video) which includes the confrontation on the grass between the crew and Bill, the homeless man named "Victor," and the arrival of Shannon and Audrey Henningham, the two interracial actors who portray the new husband and wife, Freddy and Alice. They repeat the same screen test sequences as seen in the original production of **Take One**, except that we will have two new elements in this first part of **Take 2**. They are: new scenes of crew dissent and criticism of Bill's direction and work on the screen test, and the appearance of Marcia Karp, a professional psychodramatist on the scene. She is involved to help Bill probe into the off-camera real life experiences of Shannon Baker and Audrey Henningham as they try to bring the characters Alice and Freddy to life.

In all other respects, the style and format of **Take 2**'s first part, filmed in 1968, is quite similar to the treatment developed in **Symbiopsychotaxiplasm: Take One**. In other words, we will see the same multi-camera crew filming, cinema vérité style, all of the happenings that transpire in the film within a film, within a film that characterized **Take One**.

Now we flash forward three decades to 1999!!! It is late autumn, early Fall and the leaves are yellow and brown and falling. We find ourselves in the midst of the filming of what can be called the sequel to **Take 2**. This *second part* of **Take 2** surprisingly reveals the same cast and key crew as its 1968 counterpart! However, everyone is 30 years older!!!

From the written dialogue spoken by the 2 actors in the scene, we learn that the characters, Freddy and Alice, have divorced long ago and gone their separate ways. She, to mother his child and place her up for adoption. He, to find his daughter after all these years of separation, has requested the urgent meeting with her in the park (on the same foot bridge that Pat Gilbert and Don Fellows played their scenes in **Symbiopsychotaxiplasm: Take One**). The scripted dialogue reveals that Freddy has exhausted himself in his fruitless attempts to track down and find their daughter. Freddy is angry with Alice for giving away "their child" who is now 30 years of age. She is resentful that he never asked about "his Black child" until a few days ago. However, they conceal their mutual rage with the forced pleasantries of meeting for the first time in 30 years.

Steve, the new director on the sequel section of **Take 2**, will encourage the actors to improvise the basic situation which follows a skeletal script. He will also attempt, with Bill who is now writer-cameraman on the shoot, to develop a feature film out of their improvisations.

To assist in the creative process of finding the right motivations and basic circumstances that could contribute to the dramatic and psychological intensity of the film, psychodramatist Marcia is encouraged by Steve and Bill to rummage into the personal lives of the actors to find related events in their own lives that will fuel the dramatic intensity of a possible feature film. These related events will be re-enacted in psychodramas (i.e. in real life improvisations from the actors' own personal lives). Marcia gets the idea of using a female crew member who has some experience in acting, to "stand in" during the psychodrama as the long lost daughter who has been searching for her parents. This development results in a curious family reunion.

These supporting events will be discussed by Steve, Bill as the writer, and the actors as possible fictional material for the feature that Buscemi and Greaves plan to co-produce. Issues such as interracial marriage in the '60's, the invasion of the privacy of the actors result into heated discussions and criticism, as the line between art, creativity, and psychological vulnerability becomes blurred. Even the crew gets involved, and issues of the media's role in the invasion of privacy touch off more heated debates.

Pat Gilbert and Don Fellows, the two actors who appeared in **Take One** (now 30 years older), will also be on hand to critique what is being attempted. Throughout, Steve and Bill and the crew will film those serendipitous events that will inevitably swirl around, and pop into, the symbiotaxiplasm of a movie crew filming on location in Central Park.

While all this is going on, as the multi-camera and sound crew films the entire creative process, in a crew room, off the set, they critique it. They will specifically criticize Steve the new director, Bill the writer, the actors, and the skeletal script Bill has devised for the actors to play and then improvise on. The over arching question persists with all concerned: "Why on earth are Steve and Bill making this film which isn't a film?"

The ending of the film is not known at this point, except that we do know that there will be a **Symbiopsychotaxiplasm: Take 3** coming down the pike next year or maybe as late as three decades from now!!! One thing is certain and that is this, that drama and aesthetics in **Symbiopsychotaxiplasm: Take 3** will, like its predecessors **Take One** and **Take 2**, obey the "laws" of chaos theory, the Heisenberg Principle of Uncertainty, the second law of thermodynamics, the Stanislavsky System, the Method of Lee Strasburg and the cosmic consciousness of Sri Aurobindo. It will also reflect the thinking of the eminent social science philosopher Arthur Bentley who in his book, *Inquiry Into Inquiries*, develops the concept of the "symbiotaxiplasm" which denotes all those objects and events that surround and influence human beings and conversely, the human being's impact on his/her physical, natural (?), social, political and cultural environment.

25
Some Concepts and Logistics in Shooting the Two Excerpts of Take 2½

WILLIAM GREAVES

Editor's Note: This unpublished essay, dated October 21, 2003, is presented as closely as possible to its original format.

What we have here is a short documentary film on the creative process, specifically, as it applies to the art of acting and directing for film and television. Our documentary film about a film being made involves the shooting of a short episode, which could be used by the actors as a sample reel of their talent or a demo reel of the director's skill and even a selling sample reel to raise the funds for a feature film the director has in mind. Paradoxically, it's also an extension in time of what's been happening to the characters in that original screen test on which the documentary *Symbiopsychotaxiplasm: Take One* was made in 1968. Thus, we now see the two characters, Alice and Freddy, in their lives, 35 years later. If one of these episodes that we are filming is a "smoker" it may be a perfect sample for the director to use for raising the cash for the feature he plans to pitch to his prospective backer.

The entire acting sequence is filmed on each of 12 different locations!

When Bill's friend, Steve Buscemi, arrives, he will consult and coach William Greaves as the latter directs the sequence in its entirety in each location. Therefore, the following shooting procedure will be pursued:

1. Greaves will shoot a complete run-through of the 15-minute sequence at twelve different locations. In other words, there will be 12 major takes of the sequence.

2. After he films each sequence, Marcia, the psychodramatist, and Buscemi are going to advise Bill on ways he can improve the shooting as well as tune up the actors' instruments and thus enhance the impact of the sequence. In other words, when the psychodramatist takes over, she probes the actors for emotional, psychological connections of the characters with the actors' personal life and indicates how the actors can draw on these personal life experiences in playing the scene. In some of the run-throughs Bill will use different interpretations by the actors on their characterizations which Buscemi will comment and advise on.
3. As the psychodramatist, Buscemi and Bill work on enhancing the creative work of Bill and the actors, we find out that Bill's hidden task is to determine which run-through, of the sequence, is most appropriate to convince a potential backer to put up funds for a feature film.
4. However, since the entire 15-minute sequence can be split up and divided by the editor into cinematic fragments, from the 12 locations, our creative problem then is to find out, in the editing room phase of the project, which is the best approach; the sequence in *one* location *or* the sequence spread out over the multiple locations.
5. If there is time, for extra dramatic impact, we might possibly try one of the scenes from Bill's original script at the end with consulting input by the psychodramatist and/or Buscemi.
6. True creativity is a never-ending process—that's what the creative process in this project is all about.

26

The Symbiopsychotaxiplasm Effect on Filmmaking Dynamics

An Editor's Examination of the Power of Corruption on Expectations in Filmmaking

WILLIAM GREAVES

Editor's Note: This brief discussion is not dated and no author is indicated, but it seems to have been written by Greaves at some point during the lead-up to the production of *Symbiopsychotaxiplasm: Take 2½*. It is presented, as closely as possible, in its original format, with a few minor corrections.

Two strong forces in film production are: the massive act of faith that a director crew and actors commit; and the unspoken: 'find a solution' cooperative spirit that is subjugated to the material and the director's vision.

Take One explored the corruption of this dynamic by showing a director who subtly undermines the crew's view of the material and his vision and pushes the faith of the crew and cast into doubt. This amplifies the frustration and the warped perception of reality shared by all of the participants, including the audience. (Highlighted to a large extent by the introduction of Victor the homeless man as a reminder of the actual importance of on-set issues vs. "real world" problems, war, starvation, etc.)

Take Two has the potential to take this same paradigm along another path. Where *Take One* examined the destabilization that would occur if the director worked as an unstable factor; *Take Two* has the potential to examine two significant elements of filmmaking: what happens when an actor acts counter to the cooperative spirit and the material, and how an audience is a reactive part of the film's environment.

Actors that break with the director's vision or material are often "read" as bad performances or poor acting (leaving the audience to feel bored, or disconnected or hostile towards the material). But this introduces a fascinating issue—if an actor subverts a film for ulterior motives (wants to meet another actor, travel to an exotic location, have people admire them, etc.) how does this affect the outcome, the post production, the style of direction, the crew belief or the other actors?

The use of psychodrama has the potential to reveal an actor's alternate agenda and could potentially expose parts of the actor's personality and motivation they had hoped to keep hidden, leading to anger and resentment to everyone related to a film. This anger is the central conflict: a single person's agenda vs. the entire establishment of crew, director, other actors and expectations of "how a film should be made."

In fact—perhaps essential to this "how a film should be made" attitude—there comes the question: "Why is it that films are made the way they are?"

It is a mistake to think the creative force of film stops with production. Very nearly all of the film's symbiotaxiplasm is fabricated during post-production, which takes into account environments that have little conscious influence on a production. Principally: audience reaction (to assembled sequences), which is impossible to gauge during production, but is paramount during post.

In this regard, *The Symbio Cinematic Environment*, which focuses on the performance aspect of the actors and their interactions with a psychodramatist as a tool to increase creative energy, and talks about an audience's reaction to this catalyst, misses perhaps the most important element: the process a director and editor go through to construct "reality."

In the end the post process has a vastly more influential effect on the stated Heisenberg Principle and Thermodynamic Laws, to the audience's view.

Audiences will be stirred not by the heightened performances of the actors, or the passion of the reactions from the psychodramatist, but by the post production juxtaposition of those elements, encouraging them to question "what films are made of." If we look to break new ground with this film, it will not be enough to look at reflexive cinema as a *production* experience (this has been well covered starting in the 50s with cinéma vérité, through recent work by Lars Von Trier and even Michael Moore), better to include the audience in the discussion, and alternatives in the process of post to let them see how they are being manipulated *after* the cameras finish shooting.

27

The Symbio Cinematic Environment

An Aesthetic Yet Scientific Theory for the Film

WILLIAM GREAVES

Editor's Note: Handwritten on this document are the date, June 8, 2004, and "Submitted by Wm Greaves"; it is presented in its original format with minor corrections.

The Heisenberg Principle of Uncertainty states that "we'll never know what the true nature of existence is because when the electron microscope scans an atom it destroys it." Analogically speaking when the microscopic lens of the motion picture camera looks at the mind and soul of the actor, the actor, aware that he is being invaded by the camera, loses his spontaneous energy, vitality and emotional truth. In short, the vital energy of the performance is lost. Thus, we, the audience lose our understanding and empathy with his/her character and the drama. This triggers a rise in the degree of frustration in both the crew and director. They realize that they must rescue the film from dying. Expressing their frustration behind the camera and off the set, they are thus energetically motivated or inspired to increase the level of dramatic life and truth of the movie. The audience, in turn, witnesses an explosion of creative energy behind the camera on the part of the crew. The director, and finally the editors, all calculate how, using the shot and sequence selection process, to enhance and increase the dramatic quality of the movie. This behind the camera enhancement through selection activity also spills out among the camera crew and director who find themselves focusing on the social non-film professional environment of everyday life that swirls around the camera crew on the park's shooting locations.

Fearing he may be losing the dramatic impact of his movie on an increasingly bored audience, the director increases the creative quality of his work with the actors with the assistance of a psychodramatist who is able to penetrate the depths of the actors' emotional subconscious life and stir up a powerful emotions that bring the actors' performances to a level of enhanced energy and psychic life that exceeds the viewer's and even the director's wildest expectation. This surge of creative energy boils over and arouses the movie's audience, and as a consequence, builds and may result in a powerful motion picture with extraordinary emotional impact on the once bored audience, who in their arousal, confirm the validity of the Second Law of Thermodynamics which states that energy transforms inertial systems until it dissipates into an entropic climax and the bored or aroused audience goes home.

28

The Daring, Original, *and* Overlooked

Symbiopsychotaxiplasm: Take One

RICHARD BRODY

What if they made a revolution and nobody saw it? That's what happened in 1968, when William Greaves filmed one of the most daring and original movies of the time, *Symbiopsychotaxiplasm: Take One*. He completed it in 1971, but it wasn't shown publicly until 1991, when it became a new entry in the history books but wasn't the rewriting of them that it should've been.

Greaves, who was then working as a documentary filmmaker and television producer (notably of public television's *Black Journal*, where he was also an on-camera host), made a film about a couple in a state of sexual and romantic crisis. It's also a film about the attempt to make that film, and its frame-breaking, frame-multiplying reflexivity lends the small-scale action a vast, world-embracing scope. It's anything but a cramped theoretical exercise; fueled by the power of Greaves's vision and the energy of his character, it's an intimate film that feels bigger than life.

Its originality lies partly in its mode of production—which is itself one of the movie's central subjects. It's one of the greatest movies about filmmaking ever made, and one that would have spoken to young independent filmmakers of the time. It's a vision of filmmaking that didn't get seen when it could've made a decisive difference for a new generation.

Symbiopsychotaxiplasm: Take One is now readily available (there is a Criterion edition). It will be screened this Saturday at "Tell It Like It Is: Black Independents in New York, 1968 to 1986," which runs February 6th through 19th at Film Society of Lincoln Center. And it was screened and discussed on Monday evening at the Brooklyn Historical Society. I had the privilege of taking part in

FIGURE 28.1 *From left*: Louise Archambault Greaves, Su Friedrich, Liani Greaves, and David Greaves. Louise Greaves: "That photo was taken at a screening of *Take One* at the Brooklyn Historical Society not very long after Bill passed away. Steve Buscemi introduced the film; Su moderated the panel discussion that followed, with Richard Brody and Shola Lynch. It was the night of a *huge* winter storm—and the screening room was packed. The beautiful young woman standing next to David is Liani Greaves (his daughter/my granddaughter)." Photographer unknown. Courtesy Louise Greaves.

the discussion with the filmmakers Shola Lynch and Su Friedrich, following an introduction by Steve Buscemi, who saw the film at Sundance in 1992 and had a hand in making its sequel (which was released in 2005). A special and unexpected delight was the presence of Greaves's widow, Louise Greaves, and his son, David Greaves (who co-edited the film with him), who took part, from their seats among the audience, in the discussion.

Here's the story that Louise Greaves told. (Greaves himself tells a version of it in his 1994 interview with Scott MacDonald in *A Critical Cinema 3* [Berkeley: University of California Press, 1998].) After completing the film in 1971, William Greaves believed that he had made a masterpiece, and that the only place to première it was the Cannes Film Festival. So he carried the print to France himself, where it was screened for programmers. The projectionist made the mistake of showing the reels out of order—though, as Louise added, the film would likely have been hard for them to grasp even in its proper order. The film was turned down. Greaves came home, figured he had made a mistake, and put the film in his closet.

Flash ahead, Louise Greaves said, to the early 1990s. The Brooklyn Museum was organizing a complete retrospective of Greaves's films. The curator, having seen all of Greaves's films that had been released, asked whether there was anything else. He explained that there was an undistributed film that she needn't bother with, but she told him that she didn't mind, it was her job to see everything. Upon reviewing it, she declared that this film, *Symbiopsychotaxiplasm: Take One*, was the one for the opening night of the retrospective. Louise Greaves didn't name this inspired and inspiring curator [Dara Meyers-Kingsley; see chapter 21], who is a secret hero of the history of cinema.

The ingenuity of William Greaves's film is his singular ability to turn the story of its production into a central and natural element of the film. Greaves wrote a text—a brief scene, about ten or fifteen minutes long, that's a fight between a man and woman, Freddie and Alice. She angrily flings two grievances at him: he has forced her to have an abortion each time she's become pregnant, and she says that his unwillingness to commit to their life as a family is because he's a closeted homosexual (she repeatedly calls him a "faggot"). Filming in Central Park, Greaves gets several pairs of actors to play the scene, as if doing screen tests, until settling on one pair, Don Fellows and Patricia Ree Gilbert, who are white, seemingly in their mid-to-late thirties, middle class in their style and tone. They play like cut-rate versions of Jack Lemmon and Shelley Winters.

There are three cameras on the action. One is filming the actors as they perform, and one is filming Greaves working with the actors and whatever else seems to be of interest in the surrounding environment. Then Greaves himself has a camera, and he films whatever captures his fancy. His explanation to the cast and crew of these rules of the game is itself in the film. Much of the action is what takes place when the actors aren't doing their scene—it's a documentary about the crew on location. The actors are playing their roles and themselves as actors; Greaves, the camera operators, sound recordists, and other members of the crew are playing themselves. The situations that come up in the course of the shoot—such as a police officer trotting up on horseback and asking to see the crew's permit, or a crowd of teenagers gathering to watch the shoot—are integrated into the action.

At times, Greaves shows the simultaneous footage of two or three cameras at the same time, not exactly through split screens but by means of a black matte, as if in a photo album, that gives the multiple screens multiple windows. The film also includes three remarkable interludes–called X-1, X-2, and X-3—that are lengthy scenes that the crew shot of themselves in the production office, in Greaves's absence and without his knowledge. There, members of the crew debate the merits of the film, scrutinize and interpret Greaves's methods and motives, criticize his abilities, intuit his ideas. The result isn't quite a mutiny or a revolt—they continue to work on the film with undiminished engagement—but it is a boldly independent act to use his equipment and resources to make a film of their own within the film, which they then offer Greaves as part of the film.

The scenes shot by the crew were a part of their calculated surprise—they say, on camera, that Greaves didn't know that they were doing it, and in the scenes they address him directly, into the camera, and wonder whether he'll care to include these discussions in the film. Greaves voted, so to speak, with his editing table: they're in the film and they're crucial parts of it.

At the Brooklyn Historical Society on Monday, Shola Lynch wondered onstage how Greaves reacted when he saw this footage for the first time, and asked David Greaves about it. The answer is that Greaves told his son of his great regret that he wasn't filming himself in his editing room to capture his own reaction to seeing it. Greaves had been told that a surprise was in store for him, but the surprise that he got far exceeded his expectations.

The essence of great direction is great production. Original filmmakers are, above all, ones who reconsider and reinvent the process of filmmaking to make it fit with their own needs, desires, impulses, ideas. In the studio system, directors had to fight to take control of the process—they often had to become producers as well. Independent filmmaking is an open field; directors are usually, of necessity, their own producers, or working in close sympathy with producers who share their vision—which is why it's all the more surprising when independent filmmakers don't give the impression of rethinking the filmmaking process but merely impressing their subjects and styles on ready-made structures.

The matter is all the more urgent in modern cinema, where the veil of fiction—the opaque wall of narrative—is lifted to reveal the ostensible wizard behind the curtain. Pushed to its greatest extreme, the newfound method of production would be integrated into the film itself, would even be its very subject. Greaves realized that ideal, concretely and passionately and personally in *Symbiopsychotaxiplasm: Take One*, but his modernism is no arid abstraction. He doesn't eliminate characters but multiplies them, turning even the crew—including himself—and even passersby into characters. He doesn't suppress stories, he proliferates them, giving relationships among the cast and crew and passersby a weight to equal that of the scripted action.

At the center of the action is Greaves, who had been an actor (he studied at the Actors Studio). Here, he evokes a classical comic cinema, that of the director as antic performer, starting with Max Linder and Charlie Chaplin, Erich von Stroheim and Orson Welles, Jacques Tati and Jerry Lewis—and the trope is apparent to his crew, who, in one of their production-office discussions, cite his theatrical nature and his efforts to explore his own multiple masks and identities.

Yet the movie is no mere self-exploration or self-reflection but a vision of the times, a crucial work of late-sixties politics in action. First of all, the collective organization that Greaves generates, through his plans and his personality, his ideas and his instincts, is a sort of artistic utopia. It's a notion of nonauthoritarian leadership that is nonetheless oriented by a charismatic leader, a structure that offers rules and makes room for its participants to bend them, in which uncertainty is a given, self-questioning is central, and open-mindedness, spontaneity, flexibility, and curiosity are prime values.

Greaves tells the crew that everything in the movie is meant to connect to the idea of sexuality. At the time of the shoot, abortion was illegal in New York State (it wasn't legalized until 1970—New York was one of the first states to do so) and so was homosexuality (the state's sodomy laws weren't struck down until 1980). The couple's sexual troubles are power troubles, the emotional extractions or physical threats by which Freddie gets Alice to have illegal abortions (which, as she says, put her health at great risk).

One technician looks beyond the anti-homosexual prejudice to see the gender stereotypes that the couple is perpetuating—that Alice is attempting to puncture Freddie's power and also to diminish him by challenging his ability to satisfy her. The speaker also translates Greaves's rather euphemistic middle-class, nearly middle-aged dialog into blonde and raw sexual terms; he wants to hear Alice and Freddie talk frankly about performance, about pleasure and satisfaction, about their sex organs, about orgasm and endurance, to strip the gender battle to its primal sexual essence, to de-socialize it and get to the elements that aren't a part of polite society.

What of poverty, what of prejudice? Greaves is a magician; he pulls a rabbit out of a hat, but, being a real magician rather than a fake one, he doesn't plant the rabbit there but finds it there by chance. The movie's climactic scene stars Victor, a homeless man living in Central Park, whom the crew randomly encounters. Victor is an artist and a displaced person, a crude man of casual hatred and a flamboyant man of exaggerated refinements, a bohemian who places himself twenty years ahead of his time and a vestige of an era that was kinder to the bohemian. Rising rents forced him out of his home onto the streets. Yet he's no street angel; he's an angry man filled with free-flowing contempt, a frustrated creator fueled with an urge for destruction. Victor is a living vision straight from the works of Céline, a force of unresolved and worsening class conflict, a raving poet of the psychic underworld, a roving madman and a stunted genius and a frustrated bore. Victor is, in a way, the counterpart to Greaves himself, the man without a structure, the energetic person left to his own devices; his rage is the alternative to efforts to construct a better organized, more supple societal order.

What difference would it have made had Greaves's film come out in a timely way—had it been screened at Cannes, and appeared here in the early 1970s? For starters, it would have exalted the very notion of an independent filmmaker as a process-oriented filmmaker, of a political filmmaker as personal filmmaker—and of a black filmmaker as a sophisticated aesthete and a master of complexity, as an intellectual artist of the first rank.

Greaves was up there with John Cassavetes and Shirley Clarke in the blend of sophisticated modernism and emotional fury, of self-implication and formal innovation, of self-revelation and revelation of the heart of the times. Greaves is even more extreme in his formal explorations; the only work of the era that's comparable is Orson Welles's *F for Fake*, from 1974. Greaves was the founder of a movement that didn't happen, the center of a collective that didn't coalesce, the father of a generation that—well, I was tempted to say that it wasn't born, but he is at least the symbolic patriarch of dispersed acolytes. One such acolyte is Kathleen Collins, who was a production assistant on *Symbiopsychotaxiplasm: Take One*. Her nearly lost, unreleased film *Losing Ground* [1982] opens the Lincoln Center series on Friday.

NOTE

Reprinted from the *New Yorker*, February 5, 2015.

29
Still No Answers

AMY TAUBIN

The tumultuous New York film and theater world of the late 1960s oscillated between two opposing ideas: the auteur and the collective. The American version of *Cahiers du cinéma*'s auteur theory inflated the idea of the director as "auteur" into that of an individual artist whose stardom could eclipse that of any mere actor and whose power was greater than the Hollywood studio system. On the other hand, the sixties counterculture at large, and in particular its political wing—the overlapping civil rights movement and the New Left, which was primarily an anti–Vietnam War movement—idealized the collective, the commune, and the group, notwithstanding the fact that its image was built around its leaders and stars. In this crazy, mixed up moment, the films of the radical documentary collective New York Newsreel (soon to become Third World Newsreel) showed at the Filmmakers Cinematheque side-by-side with the works of such avant-garde filmmakers as Andy Warhol and Stan Brakhage, the cinéma-vérité films of Richard Leacock, D. A. Pennebaker, and Albert and David Maysles, and Elia Kazan's 1956 *Baby Doll*, made with a cast of Actors Studio members and at that point still condemned as pornographic by the Legion of Decency. Early in 1968, Leacock and Pennebaker's company acquired Jean-Luc Godard's *La Chinoise* [1967] and brought the celebrated French new wave director to the United States to tour with the film. Godard returned to Paris just in time to take to the streets in May of 1968, but he returned to the United States in the fall of that year—his identity now split between JLG the auteur and JLG a member of the Dziga Vertov Film Group—to collaborate with Leacock and Pennebaker on *One American Movie (One AM)*, a project he abandoned in postproduction. JLG's on-screen instructions to the crew at the opening of *One American Movie* bear a striking resemblance to William Greaves's on-screen instructions to his crew at the opening of *Symbiopsychotaxiplasm: Take One*, the film Greaves shot in the late spring of 1968 (several months before *One American Movie*) but that would not receive its first screening until 1971.

Greaves's film was certainly of its moment, and the director was perhaps uniquely situated to appreciate the various currents that informed it. He had a connection to all the worlds mentioned above, and a foot in several others as well, yet he remained something of an outsider to these groups, apart from any overriding political identification, except for his abiding, and at times quite practical, concern with civil rights, a cause he quietly and effectively championed throughout his career, often in groundbreaking ways. At the time he shot *Symbiopsychotaxiplasm: Take One*, he had just been appointed executive producer of National Educational Television's public-affairs series *Black Journal*, then the only national television series dealing with African-American life. (Greaves became executive producer after the staff staged a walkout to protest white control of the show.) He also had his own documentary film production company and was a member of the Actors Studio, where he participated as a director, actor, and teacher.

[Here Taubin reviews general information about Greaves's early career.]

What was immediately striking about *Symbiopsychotaxiplasm: Take One* was that it did not directly engage race or racism, although the fact that Greaves is both the film's director-writer-producer and its on-screen protagonist—the focus of almost every scene—guaranteed that the viewer, regardless of race, had to confront whatever racial stereotypes she or he held. Quite simply, in 1968, there were at best a handful of African-American directors working in television and no African-Americans directing feature films. For an African-American director to make a feature film, let alone one as experimental as a film by Warhol or Godard, could not have been imagined if Greaves hadn't gone out and done it.

Symbiopsychotaxiplasm: Take One uses a single situation as the basis for a theme-and-variation structure that interrogates every aspect of the filmmaking process as well as the categories of fiction and documentary. The film is posed as a screen test, not for a film that is yet to be made but as an end in itself. In Central Park, on a beautiful summer day, a film crew is assembled to record two actors playing a scene that has the ring of a hack imitation of Edward Albee's *Who's Afraid of Virginia Woolf?* or one of Tennessee Williams's vitriolic marital battles. This scene is an irritant (at one point, the soundman attacks Greaves for making him listen to something so ugly through his headphones over and over, for days), like the grain of sand in the oyster.

On-screen the director (Greaves) outlines the responsibilities of the crew. The film is being shot by three 16mm cameras, each equipped with a zoom lens and a magazine that holds eleven minutes of film, and all three synced, in the clumsy technology of the day, to reel-to-reel sound recorders. One cameraman, Greaves instructs, is to focus solely on the actors playing the scene; another cameraman is to film the crew that is shooting the scene; and the third is to include the actors and the crew, as well as onlookers and anything interesting that's happening in the park. (Sometimes Greaves himself wields a fourth camera.) Since the theme of the film is sexuality, Greaves explains, the third cameraman should try to capture anything that relates to it: "Look, there's that woman with the tits," he says, and as the camera whirls to show us a woman on horseback, he continues, "Get her, get her, they're bouncing." "Greaves, you're a dirty old man," jokes one of the crew members, and Greaves, once again in the center of the shot, responds with no trace of embarrassment, "Don't take me seriously."

Indeed. Well, how exactly are we meant to view a director who is behaving, in the lingo of the day, like a sexist pig? That is the question the film raises right from the start. Who is this director? Is he the "real" William Greaves, or is he a fictional construct, or partly both, or are they one and the same? Is he, in addition to being outrageously sexist, as incompetent a director as his sometimes confusing instructions suggest, or is he playing at being sexist and incompetent in order to provoke the crew? And what about that bit of badly written psychodrama? Given that in May of 1968 the war was raging in Vietnam, students were occupying university buildings, the French left had almost staged a successful takeover of the government, and a string of assassinations had begun, this drama would be absurdly reactionary if it were taken at face value. Is the crew's eventual antagonism, then, part of his master plan to dramatize the other major, though not explicitly stated, theme of the film: power, in particular the power struggle between the leader and the group?

The scene that Greaves has written to test the actors' chops also limns, however crudely, another familiar power struggle. A woman named Alice is in a rage at her husband, Freddy. She attacks him for being a "faggot" and forcing her "to have one abortion after the other." The scene is written to call attention to its stagey quality. At one point, the husband even tells the wife to "stop acting," which is as hilarious a double entendre as is Greaves's "Don't take me seriously." But Greaves seems determined to find what is referred to, in Actors Studio terminology, as the inner reality of the scene and the characters and, to that end, stages it again and again, interrupting it to give directions to the actors, who become increasingly bewildered and frustrated. "I don't know whether to play a bisexual... a butch fag, or a faggy fag," says the actor playing Freddy, before concluding, "I'd like to play him as a closet fag, so I'll just play it straight." As he continues, a loud bleep censors what is rapidly turning into an exposé of homophobia. One of the most interesting aspects of the film's focus on sexuality is that, at this point in 1968, the political discourses around feminism and homosexuality were only beginning to be articulated. One wonders, first, if Greaves has written this supposedly spontaneous riff spoken by the actor playing Freddy, and if so, does he mean it as a provocation? Or is the actor playing Freddy speaking as himself and unaware of what today seems blatantly homophobic? Similarly, some of the crew members trash Alice for doing what women are programmed to do, "cut off a man's balls," a thesis with which none of the female crewmembers take issue. If this film is about sexuality, as Greaves claims, is it possible that he was attuned to what at that moment was a largely inchoate feminist and gay consciousness that would soon challenge the male heterosexual privilege that every man involved in the film seems to take for granted?

Built on such an unstable social/political/psychological ground, *Symbiopsychotaxiplasm: Take One* invites endless speculation both from the audience and from everyone on the screen. Increasingly restive, the crew decide to film themselves criticizing Greaves and his film, wondering all the while if the director has manipulated them into becoming his antagonist. They give him the footage

FIGURE 29.1 Actors Audrey Henningham and Shannon Baker during the shooting of *Symbiopsychotaxiplasm: Take One* in 1968. Courtesy Louise Greaves.

FIGURE 29.2 Actors Audrey Henningham and Shannon Baker in *Symbiopsychotaxiplasm: Take 2½* (2005). Courtesy Louise Greaves.

they've shot of themselves, and, whether or not he instigated their acting out for the camera, it makes its way into the finished film. To add to the confusion, Patricia Ree Gilbert and Don Fellows, the actors who play Alice and Freddy, are sometimes replaced by other actors, among them the then unknown Susan Anspach, who carries a parasol and sings Alice's lines as if she were Catherine Deneuve in *The Umbrellas of Cherbourg*.

If the production process sounds like a recipe for chaos, *Symbiopsychotaxiplasm: Take One* is anything but. Thanks to Greaves's lively, innovative editing (involving some of the most surprising contrapuntal double and triple splitscreen images in the history of movies), the film has the polyrhythmic elegance of its Miles Davis score. More than mere background music, the score is the abstract model for the film's improvisations on a theme and also an expressive element in its own right.

Greaves shot about 130,000 feet of 16mm film (roughly fifty-five hours) for the *Symbiopsychotaxiplasm* project, which he originally conceived as a series of five movies. *Take One*, in fact, ends with a close-up of Audrey Henningham, briefly seen in the role of Alice, and the words: "Coming soon: *Symbiopsychotaxiplasm: Take Two*." But with no distributor adventurous enough to give *Take One* a theatrical release (for three decades, it received only occasional museum and festival screenings), it was impossible for Greaves to follow through with his plan. Nevertheless, he held on to the original footage, which, being 16mm color reversal (the workhorse stock for avant-garde and documentary filmmakers in the sixties), didn't decay. In 1992, Steve Buscemi saw a screening of *Take One* at Sundance, and ten years later he and Steven Soderbergh (who has manifested in his own narrative experiments something of Greaves's teasing humor and desire to expose the ghosts in the machine) offered to help produce at least one sequel.

Symbiopsychotaxiplasm: Take 2½ combines material shot in 1968, and originally planned for *Take Two*, with an update shot thirty-five years later. Actors Audrey Henningham and Shannon Baker, who play the interracial couple in one of the "screen tests" at the end of *Take One*, are reunited as themselves and as their characters, Alice and Freddy. In the fiction, Alice, who has had a successful career as a singer in Europe, returns to New York in response to a desperate phone call from Freddy, who is dying of AIDS and wants Alice to adopt a teenage girl he has been fostering. He rationalizes his request as his way of giving Alice what she once wanted—a child. But Alice sees the request as Freddy being presumptuous and imposing his needs on her, as he always did. That a happy ending can be wrested from what at first seems like an impasse is a credit to both the actors and Greaves's direction. And, indeed, the consonance of fictional and documentary reunion and resolution in the film makes it in some ways resonate more forcefully—and poignantly—than *Take One*. If *Take 2½* lacks the minimalist audacity of Greaves's original conception (imagine seeing the clunky Alice and Freddy dialogue repeated over five films), it has a bitter sweetness that testifies to how much has been lost and found by everyone on the screen—and us as well.

NOTE

Reprinted from the booklet accompanying the Criterion DVD release of *Symbiopsychotaxiplasm: Take One* and *Symbiopsychotaxiplasm: Take 2½* in 2006.

30

"We're Not Raping Bill"

Race and Gender Politics in Symbiopsychotaxiplasm: Take One *and* Take 2½

JOAN HAWKINS

In *Camera Lucida*, Roland Barthes develops two ideas regarding photography: the *studium*, which denotes the cultural, political, and semiotic interpretation of a photograph, and the *punctum*, the seemingly unintended but wounding and personally touching detail that establishes a direct relationship between the photographed subject and the viewer. The punctum simultaneously takes the viewer out of the photograph, distracts the viewer from the photograph's preferred reading ("disturbs the studium," Barthes says), and *binds* the viewer more directly to the subject matter. It frequently reveals itself after the fact, when one is no longer looking at the photograph. It's a nag, "a sting, a speck, cut, little hole,—and also a cast of the dice." It is "that accident which pricks me (but also bruises me, is poignant to me)."[1] It is linked to the essential meaning that one ultimately attaches to the photo; it reveals the photo's essence and significance to the viewer.

I begin with this discussion of Barthes as a means of explaining this essay, which takes as its point of departure some seemingly random lines in *Symbiopsychotaxiplasm: Take One*. I realize that using Barthes in this way is in some ways antithetical to the theorist's work. He does explicitly state that, for him, the punctum is something the viewer brings to a photo, and for that reason, he says, it does not exist in cinema. The temporal dimension of film, he says, is such that the movie moves too quickly for the viewer to become fixated on a specific detail. And, for Barthes, the punctum is always visual. Nonetheless, his formulation of the punctum comes closest to the binding quality of the seemingly extraneous lines in *Symbiopsychotaxiplasm* that have nagged me since I first saw the film almost twenty years ago, and which seem to me to reveal something essential about the work.[2]

As has been noted throughout this volume, *Symbiopsychotaxiplasm: Take One* chronicles the making of an experimental film. Director William Greaves repeatedly films the same scene—a couple breaking up—while a second crew films the filming of that scene. As the shoot continues, the crew begin to wonder what exactly the film is about and whether Greaves knows what he's doing. "He's into blocking," the cinematographer notes, "but he doesn't direct." Finally, the disgruntled crew begin to meet, filming their own critique of the film and the production process. That footage—the crew's documentary of their own discontent—is intercut with the footage Greaves himself has organized (both the ostensible movie—the scene between Freddie and Alice—and Greaves's documentary of the making of that film); the result is *Symbiopsychotaxiplasm: Take One* (shot in 1968, first edited version, 1971).³

The crew's footage is striking on several counts, but one thing that has always arrested me—taken me out of the film—has been the language the crew use to describe what they're doing. "We're not trying to take the film away from the director," the cinematographer says. That seems reasonable enough. But then Bob Rosen, the production manager, adds, "It's not like we got together to rape Bill Greaves." This is followed by no fewer than three protestations that "we're not raping Bill."

The notion of critique as rape, the rape of a Black filmmaker, sits uneasily here alongside the references to sexual violence that take place within the scene that Greaves himself repeatedly rehearses. In this essay I explore the racial and sexual violence, racial and sexual politics that characterize this film, which are heightened by the experimental editing and scene composition that mark the *Symbiopsychotaxiplasm* films. It is perhaps only within the confines of an experimental film that the full contradictions of 1960s racial and sexual politics can be explored; certainly, the experimental nature of *Symbiopsychotaxiplasm* makes such an exploration a key point of both *Take One* and *Take 2½*.

The essay is organized rather like the films themselves—not as one linear argument but more as a series of linked, intersecting discussions. As Greaves demonstrates with his films, there is no linear way (ruled, as that is, by cause-and-effect logic) to get at the contradictions that structured—and still structure—post–World War II American culture. The nonlinear approach enables me to consider the frequently competing aspects of a pair of films that ultimately raise more questions than they answer. That is their genius, but it is also what thwarts a conventional critical argument. Intersecting discussions will also allow me to write myself into the critical process. As I noted at the beginning of this piece, the essay grows out of "a sting," "an accident," "a wounding"—a punctum—that makes it difficult for me to uniformly mobilize a traditional critical voice.

SYMBIO(PSYCHO)TAXIPLASM

As Scott MacDonald notes, the title of the film *Symbiopsychotaxiplasm* throws the viewer off immediately—puts her on alert, tells her there is something she doesn't know.[4] It's a compound noun, invented by Greaves, and constructed from competing disciplines. "Symbiotaxiplasm" comes from the work of Arthur Bentley, an American political scientist and philosopher who also worked in the fields of epistemology, logic, and linguistics. The term refers to any social unit of people and everything they touch and everything they're involved with. This film includes the cast and crew as the social unit of people, as well as the filmmaking process, the crew's revolt, and Central Park—which throws up its own set of characters: a cop asking about permits, happy couples on the lawn, a homeless man.

Into this sociological stew, Greaves inserts "psycho"—a reference to psychodrama and, by extension, to method acting. Psychodrama was developed by Jacob L. Moreno and is an action method frequently used as a means of therapy. Under the direction of a licensed therapist (called the "director"), a psychodrama group helps an individual reenact real-life past situations or inner mental processes. The point is to evaluate behavior and to achieve a sort of breakthrough, as an individual reenacts traumatic episodes with someone *playing the role of* the person who actually influenced her—her mother, say. It's a therapy method that borrows heavily from theater and grew up roughly in tandem with the Stanislavsky Method of drama, a formal process in which an actor builds a character from the inside out, drawing on his or her own life experience to find the emotional intensity the role demands. Greaves himself had trained in this method at the Actors Studio with Lee Strasberg. Some of his nondirection in *Symbio* ("he knows how to block, but he doesn't direct") reads like Strasberg's— and later John Cassavetes's—injunction that the actor has to find his or her own way into the character being portrayed. The director's job is to create the social unit that will enable the actor's inner work and make it productive, and to give shape to the larger context of the play or film.

"Psycho," of course, also means "mad," "crazy." And to some extent *Symbiopsychotaxiplasm* is a lunatic experiment. For *Take One*, Greaves told the cast and crew that he was making a sort of documentary, filming the filming of a scene. But he deliberately created a scene that was itself problematic—"sordid," soundperson Jonathan Gordon calls it, with poorly written dialogue. He rehearses several couples saying the same lines, but it's unclear to what effect. Is he trying to cast the film? Or is he trying to make a meta-film about the way in which a film is constructed, is cast, is dependent on all the moving parts; what Robert

Stam calls "a rewriting of the history of filmic reflexivity"?[5] His intentions are unclear. Worse still, he doesn't seem to know how much film he's wasting, or how much there even is. At one point, Bob Rosen explains to him that "all the magazines should have a piece of tape on them" and that these pieces of tape should be numbered.

The lack of inventory control allows the crew to steal film for their own documentary, and perhaps finally drives them to do so. As Gordon notes in his comments, the nondirection of the film is "interesting." It has "enabled us to sit here and talk like this, has compelled us, even, to be interested in this way." So there's a way in which the crew acknowledges there may be a point to Greaves's nondirection, that the nondirection may in fact be a sign of singular competence in an experimental milieu. But the waste of money and film is more difficult to rationalize in any 1960s filmmaking context, and it is that which raises true anxiety about the director's ability. Nondirection is one thing; money is another.

At the time Greaves shot *Symbiopsychotaxiplasm: Take One*, he was also the executive producer of *Black Journal*, an American public affairs television program that was first broadcast on NET in 1968. He knew about production costs and budgets, just as—as a former actor—he knew about good dialogue. What he wanted to do with this cinematic dumbshow of incompetence, he said, was to create a social situation in which a certain rebellion would be fomented. He wanted to see "when a revolt against authority take[s] place."[6]

I said earlier that this was a mad experiment. Certainly it was an expensive one. There was no guarantee that the crew would rebel in the way that Greaves anticipated. We don't see the actors rebel as Greaves hoped they would. But the director's desire to see at what precise moment "rebellion against authority take[s] place" is part and parcel of the larger social context in which the film unfolds. That is, the symbiotaxiplasm of the filmic process is not only the cast and crew making a movie in Central Park. It is the cast and crew making that film within the larger national context. As Akiva Gottlieb notes, *Symbiopsychotaxiplasm: Take One* "both documents and formally enacts the major political and identity struggles of 1960s America."[7] And it does so, in part, by foregrounding a certain racial impasse.

We frequently discuss the importance of the 1960s Civil Rights Movement, but that discussion tends to bracket off racial politics, to deny the degree to which racial activism was also part of the 1960s student movement. Initially beginning over issues of free speech, the student movement of the sixties is generally remembered as an antiwar movement, and I don't mean to deny the importance of the Vietnam War and the draft in fomenting resistance. But during 1968 the radical impulse extended to the academy and to the arts as well.

Across the country, students went on strike, demanding what was then called a "relevant" education. By "relevant," they did not mean job skills and training. They meant an education that was less white, less patriarchal; an education that reflected the world in which they actually lived.

The longest student-faculty strike took place at San Francisco State College. From November 6, 1968, to March 21, 1969, business as usual on campus effectively stopped, as faculty and students marched and demonstrated for a more inclusive curriculum. The Third World Liberation Front and the Black Student Union set the agenda, protesting the lack of diversity on campus and the Eurocentrism of course content. "Education from kindergarten to college failed to focus on subject matter that was germane to the life experiences of people in the minority community," John Bunzel writes.[8] Even worse, the education system replicated the racial power imbalance of society as a whole. And so, across the country, students and faculty agitated for academic change. When the strike finally ended, San Francisco State became one of many colleges with a nascent Black Studies Department. Similarly, at Columbia University, protests erupted during the spring of 1968 when students discovered the links between the university and the institutional apparatus supporting the Vietnam War. But the instigating cause of the demonstrations was student concern over a segregated gymnasium scheduled to be constructed in nearby Morningside Park. The protests resulted in the now famous weeklong student occupation of several university buildings at Columbia. Once again, it was the Black Student Union that led the way.

"When does revolt against authority take place?" Greaves asked. In the 1960s it frequently took place at the moment when the connection between racial inequality and American hegemony was unmasked, the point at which the fundamental and foundational nature of U.S. racism was revealed. And it took place at that precise moment for white privileged students as well as for African Americans.

Against this backdrop, then, the ultimate rebellion of the *Symbiopsychotaxiplasm* crew—a rebellion Greaves both desired and instigated—takes on a racial cast. Bob Rosen, who worries about the implications of questioning a Black director's qualifications, directly states this. That is why he repeatedly says that they're not trying to take the film away from Bill, they're not trying "to rape Bill Greaves" with their secret meetings. Which means that some of them must worry that this could indeed seem like a rape. In fact, the woman recording sound in the "X" sections of the film directly challenges Rosen on this point.[9] Refusing the idea that these sessions are a form of collaboration (Rosen thinks they might be included in the final film), she says, "You're taking away a director's film from the director." In the background someone asks, "Is that rape?"

As the film itself makes clear, there is almost nothing the crew can do in this context that does not in some way "rape" Bill, violate him. Certainly there is nothing they can do that is not racist or, more precisely, that does not inadvertently participate in the racist structures of society. That is, the genius of the experiment is in the way it lays bare the fundamental *institutional* racism that comes into play whenever an authority figure is Black. To challenge the person's credentials, his ability, has definite politico-racial implications. But so does refusing to do so, as though one can't afford to accord the respect of honest critique to a director who happens to be Black. Once race comes into play, no crew member can behave in a racially neutral way. This has nothing to do with the individual views, impulses, and beliefs of Rosen or any of the crew members. But it has everything to do with the larger sociopolitical situation in which the social unit finds itself. In this sense, *Symbio*'s sociological experiment does in fact become psychodrama, as the larger national trauma is explored in a controlled environment, by actors who played no role in the creation of the originary racial wound.

"WE'RE NOT RAPING BILL"

Thematically, both the crew's footage and the fiction Greaves is rehearsing deal with secrets: revealing them and dragging them out into the light. Visually this is reinforced through a dialectical interior/exterior structure. "Over the Cliff," the film Greaves is making, is shot in a brightly lit open space, Central Park. The frame is not cluttered, and even in the frequent close-up scenes of the couple, Freddie and Alice, there is the strong intimation of off-screen, open space all around the actors and crew. The crew's film, "X," on the other hand, is shot in a poorly lit room, where people and equipment are crowded. The frame is packed, and there's an ongoing visual joke as crew members try to untangle themselves from chords without stepping on the person next to them.

It's important to note here that viewers have no idea *where* the crew is. As Scott MacDonald pointed out to me, they must have agreed to find a secret room where they could express their desire to try to "penetrate" Greaves's thinking, to find their way into the meaning of the open process he's instigated. Of course, the meeting doesn't fulfill this desire. Ultimately, near the end of the film, they give it up and directly confront the director, out in open—sitting on

FIGURE 30.1 Meeting of the crew to discuss Greaves's direction during the shooting of *Symbiopsychotaxiplasm: Take One*. Photographer unknown. Courtesy Louise Greaves.

the grass in Central Park. It is something they could have ostensibly done at the very beginning, in which instance the anxiety about "raping Bill"—about taking the film away from him—would never have had currency.

If, despite its creators' intentions, "X" enacts a certain problematic racial politics, it also vocalizes a problematic gender-sexual regime. Throughout their film the crew criticize Greaves for the horrible dialogue he's written. It's here that they come closest to performing the function of what Bob Rosen calls "the chorus," the singers within a Greek play who judge and analyze the unfolding meaning of the historico-mythical story being enacted. Like much Greek tragedy, the scene Greaves has written is a family story full of sexual secrets, a history that has broad social implications.

In the recurring drama, Alice rages against her husband, Freddie, whom she accuses of looking at another man and, more pointedly, of being a "faggot." As the scene goes on, she says he's never wanted children, that he's forced her to have one abortion after another. She also says that every time she's had sex with him, it's felt like rape. This dialogue is written, Amy Taubin notes, "to call attention to its stagy quality. At one point the husband even tells the wife to 'stop acting.'"[10] In that sense—the theatrical sense—the scene reads more like psychodrama (people playing a role) than like naturalistic dialogue. In *Symbiopsychotaxiplasm: Take 2½*, the connection is made explicit as a trained psychotherapist joins the cast and crew onscreen and stages a formal psychodrama session with the actors.

But even as psychodrama, the dialogue is, as MacDonald points out, "almost inconceivable at that time," when both abortion and homosexuality would have to remain secret (not openly disputed in Central Park).[11] And so it reads here as the same kind of provocation that Greaves staged through his apparent lack of direction. As Jonathan Gordon noted earlier, it "enabled us to sit here and talk like this, has compelled us, even, to be interested in this way" in a topic that had a great deal of 1968 currency: the critique of institutionalized heteronormative bourgeois marriage.

Certainly, the cast's discussion of the scene participates in the kind of heterosexual male critique of institutionalized marriage that characterized much artculture of the 1960s. I'm thinking here of plays by Arthur Miller and Edward Albee; novels by John Updike, Henry Miller, Vladimir Nabokov, Jack Kerouac, and Norman Mailer; films by John Cassavetes and Mike Nichols. "Now I look at it this way," Gordon says during one of the crew conversations, "I see every American man, at some time in his life, saying these lines to every American woman. Every American woman says to every American man, 'Where are we?' and 'Nothing changes.' 'Nothing is revealed.'" Women are programmed, the crew says, "to cut off a man's balls." In an exchange with the crew, Bob Rosen makes the connection to Albee—and this larger marriage-critique culture—explicit, in order to complain about Greaves's writing.

> ROSEN: It's not like Edward Albee. I mean Edward Albee writes, you know, *Who's Afraid of Virginia Woolf?* And George and Martha are super dramatic people—given lines that are brilliant lines, fantastically brilliant.

GORDON: This is not good writing.
ROSEN: This is bad writing...
WOMAN CREW MEMBER: Human life isn't necessarily well written...
ROSEN: But that's the whole point.
GORDON: That's the whole point.

There's more than a little essentialism in this attempt to recuperate Greaves's poorly written, but highly stagy, scene as an honest bit of naturalism ("human life isn't necessarily well written"). It's interesting that the crew focus so quickly on Alice's charge that Freddie is a "faggot" and criticize *her*, that they readily read her charge as hyperbolic metaphor—a way of accusing Freddie of being "ineffectual," of emasculating him, of "cutting off his balls." At no time does anyone entertain the idea that Freddie might in fact be gay, or at least bisexual; that he might be struggling with his sexuality within the rigid confines of a closed heterosexual relationship. This gap persists, despite the couple's allusion to something that happened before their marriage and despite Freddie's dark mutterings about therapy and "treatment."

Feminist reproductive issues are similarly ignored. It is Alice who does much of the talking in the scene, but the cast doesn't take up the larger context of her complaint. Her *main* complaint is not that Freddie looks at men or even that he's a lousy lover, but that he calls the reproductive shots. He determines whether they will have children; he forces her to get abortions—"killing my babies one after the other." In the sexual economy of this relationship, Alice exercises the only power she has: to wound him ("cut off his balls") and to leave. The reason I believe this is that even while she is accusing him (and "accusing" is the operative word) of being gay, she is simultaneously suggesting they have a baby ("all right, then, let's have a baby," she says, when he tells her he wants children too).

As for Alice's charge that Freddie is gay, it opens a directional thread that—to the modern ear—is jarring. "I don't know whether to play a bisexual," the actor playing Freddie complains, "a butch fag, or a faggy fag. I'd like to play him as a closet fag, so I'll just play it straight." As Taubin writes, this rapidly turns "into an exposé of homophobia. One of the most interesting aspects of the film's focus on sexuality is that, at this point in 1968, the political discourses around feminism and homosexuality were only beginning to be articulated. One wonders, first, if Greaves has written this supposedly spontaneous riff spoken by the actor playing Freddie, and if so, does he mean it as a provocation? Or is the actor playing Freddie speaking as himself and unaware of what today seems blatantly homophobic?"[12] This confusion over what people actually believe extends to the crew as well. Jonathan Gordon is clearly struggling as he lapses into an uncharacteristically inarticulate moment. "See that's the whole thing. 'Faggot' is not a homosexual. 'Faggot' is a certain kind of mentality. And Freddy happens to be a 'faggot'; but not because he may or may not be homosexual. Because a 'faggot'—he doesn't know what he wants and he's like a 'faggot.'"

"If this film is about sexuality, as Greaves claims," Taubin writes, "is it possible that he was attuned to what at the moment was a largely inchoate feminist and gay consciousness that would soon challenge the male heterosexual privilege that every man involved in the film takes for granted?"[13] There is no way of answering this question, of course. What does seem clear, though, is that Greaves is mining gender politics and racial politics, and possibly suggesting a connection between them. This becomes clearer in *Symbiopsychotaxiplasm: Take 2½*.

For much of *Symbio: Take One*, Patricia Ree Gilbert and Don Fellows, both white, play Alice and Freddie. But they are sometimes replaced by other actors. The then unknown Susan Anspach, for example, plays Alice in one scene, singing Alice's lines as though she were Catherine Deneuve in *The Umbrellas of Cherbourg* (Jacques Demy, 1964). But at the end of the film, Audrey Henningham, who is African American, and Shannon Baker, who is white, play the scene as an interracial couple.

They are reunited in *Symbiopsychotaxiplasm: Take 2½*, both as themselves and as their characters Freddie and Alice. In the fictional story, Alice has a successful singing career in Europe. She has returned to New York in response to a desperate call from Freddie, who is dying of AIDS (once again raising the question of his sexuality—or perhaps answering it). They reunite in Central Park, the place where they seemingly broke up. Once there, Freddie explains that he wants Alice to take care of a young African-American girl—Jamilla—whom he has been fostering. He rationalizes this, saying it's a way of giving Alice the child she once wanted. But Alice sees it as his way of imposing his needs on her, the way he always did. She is hurt that he brought her to New York not to reunite with her but to make her responsible, yet again, for the choices he's made in his life.

Symbiopsychotaxiplasm: Take 2½ focuses on the two characters and the actors playing them, rather than on the crew. And here Greaves does get the rebellious response from the actors he said he'd hoped for in the first film. *Take 2½* incorporates onscreen psychodrama. Psychotherapist Marcia Karp digs into Henningham's and Baker's psyches, in order to help them more effectively create their characters. But things escalate quickly. "It was so powerful, it scared the shit out of me," Greaves later claimed, and Henningham does rebel, at one point walking away from Karp and Freddie/Baker, refusing to continue. The emphasis here is on the roles we play in life: professional and personal, past and present. It is—as Greaves said—a remarkably powerful "performance" as characters and actors blur. Henningham and Baker rage against each other, and it is not always clear when they are speaking, as actors, about their professional working relationship, and when they are speaking, in character, as Alice and Freddie.

This would be strong stuff, no matter which actor-pair from *Take One* played it. But the fact that it is an interracial couple has the effect of merging the racial and sexual politics of the first film and mapping them onto a domestic story. Given the racial history of this country, it is impossible not to read Baker's request in starkly political terms. He is asking a Black woman, to whom he denied her own children, to take care of his, thus effectively casting her in a Mammy role. The fact that he seems oblivious to this, seems to think he is doing her a favor, is just indicative of how racially myopic he is. At the end, Alice does agree to meet Jamilla (who conveniently happens to be in the park), and it is unclear whether Greaves means for us to see this as some kind of salvific and healing act, or if it is another case of human life not being particularly well-written.

There is a final secret that is quite literally dragged into the light near the end of *Symbiopsychotaxiplasm: Take One*. I am speaking of the extended scene with Victor, the alcoholic homeless artist. He lives, he says, under a bush, and as he signs the release form, he gives his address as "69th St. in the Park." He was evicted, he said, because he owed two weeks rent; all his brushes and paintings are still at the hotel where he had been living. Both Greaves and Rosen are surprised that he's *sleeping* in the park. "Are there many people who sleep in the park?" Greaves asks. When Victor tells him there are, the director turns to Rosen and asks, "Did you know?"

Victor is an interesting figure for many reasons. Scruffily handsome and articulate, he tells Greaves he went to Columbia for four years. Greaves's manner noticeably changes as Victor ticks off the things he's studied. He appears here as a stunning indictment of a bankrupt capitalist system. What the hippies are doing, he tells Greaves, he was doing twenty years ago. He gives a trenchant critique of John Lindsay, then mayor of New York. Victor had heard him speak the previous day and says, "I thought I was at Versailles, baby." It is Victor who asks the most pertinent question about the project and who makes the most pointed political comment in the film. "When you have to live on someone else's back," he says, "it's a penis of a dollar." When told that Greaves is making a movie, he asks the question that has been haunting the crew all along. "Oh, it's a *movie*," he says. "So who's moving whom?"

NOTES

Special thanks to Scott MacDonald for his help and encouragement.

1. Roland Barthes, *Camera Lucida*, trans. Richard Howard (New York: Noonday Press, 1980), 27.
2. It works better for me than Kristin Thompson's elaboration of stylistic excess, for example, which she describes as "nondiegetic moments" that "are constantly present, a whole 'film' existing in some sense alongside the narrative film we tend to think of ourselves as watching." Kristin Thompson, "The Concept of Cinematic Excess," in *Narrative, Apparatus, Ideology: A Film Theory Reader*, ed. Philip Rosen (New York: Columbia University Press, 1986), 132–33.
3. This is further complicated by the fact that the film we currently see under the title *Symbiopsychotaxiplasm: Take One* includes footage that was not in the original film. The opening shot of the film, for example, is a high-angle shot that would be impossible to get with the equipment we see on camera, and it was inserted later.
4. Debra McClutchy, *Discovering William Greaves*, documentary accompanying *Symbiopsychotaxiplasm: Two Takes by William Greaves* (Irvington, N.Y.: Criterion Collection, 2006).
5. Robert Stam, *Reflexivity in Film and Literature: From Don Quixote to Jean-Luc Godard* (New York: Columbia University Press, 1992), xviii.
6. McClutchy, *Discovering William Greaves*.
7. Akiva Gottlieb, "'Just Another Word for Jazz': The Signifying Auteur in *Symbiopsychotaxoplasm: Take One*," *Black Camera* 5, no. 1 (Fall 2013): 164 (excerpt reprinted in chap. 23 of this volume).
8. John H. Bunzel, "Black Studies at San Francisco State," *Public Interest* 13 (1968): 22–38, available at *National Affairs*, no. 45 (Fall 2020), https://www.nationalaffairs.com/public_interest/detail/black-studies-at-san-francisco-state.
9. At one point we see a clapper board for the crew's film that says "X/Roll one," so I use "X" as the crew's film title throughout this essay.
10. Amy Taubin, "Still No Answers," booklet accompanying *Symbiopsychotaxiplasm: Two Takes by William Greaves* (Irvington, N.Y.: Criterion Collection, 2006), n.p. (reprinted in chap. 29 of this volume).
11. McClutchy, *Discovering William Greaves*.
12. Taubin, "Still No Answers."
13. Taubin, "Still No Answers."

31
Symbiopsychotaxiplasticity

Some Takes on William Greaves

FRANKLIN CASON, JR., AND TSITSI JAJI

When the Brooklyn Museum screened *Symbiopsychotaxiplasm: Take One* as the opening film in a 1991 retrospective of William Greaves's work, it was hailed as a major discovery, revealing a new side of the rich artistic practice of a filmmaker, actor, musician, and teacher hitherto recognized primarily for his documentaries. Twenty years earlier, he had taken a print of *Symbiopsychotaxiplasm: Take One*, a film composed of footage shot in the summer of 1968 and edited over the next three years, to Cannes. However, the reels were projected out of order at a prescreening, and a work that relied on what Greaves called "intelligible chaos" instead baffled the few who saw it.[1] The film failed to find a distributor and instead languished in Greaves's storage. When *Take One* finally came to light in 1991 (we refer throughout the essay to *Symbiopsychotaxiplasm: Take One* and *Symbiopsychotaxiplasm: Take 2½* as *Take One* and *Take 2½*), responses reflected nostalgia for the experimentalism and political defiance of the sixties, as well as the excitement of viewing a manifestly multicultural crew and cast working under an African-American director on Ektochrome film.

The following year the film screened at Sundance, garnering fervent champions in Steve Buscemi and later Steven Soderbergh. With their backing, Greaves was able to revisit his original vision for the project, a series of five films, or "takes," each focusing on a specific aspect of the original film. In 2005, *Take 2½* was released. A complex composition in triptych form, *Take 2½* consists of, first, the 1968 footage he edited into "Take Two," which begins the film; a documentary of a question-and-answer session that followed the screening of *Take One* (which ends with an advertisement "Coming Soon: *Symbiopsychotaxiplasm: Take Two*" featuring the actors who are in fact used in "Take Two"); and a third

FIGURE 31.1   William Greaves, cast, and crew in Central Park during shooting of *Symbiopsychotaxiplasm: Take 2½* (2005). Courtesy Louise Greaves.

section of contemporary footage that explores what the characters Freddie and Alice (and the actors) have been up to in the thirty years since the first film. However, where *Take One* was hailed as an *avant-la-lettre* exemplar of self-reflexive cinema, *Take 2½* found more mixed reactions. As Maria San Filippo writes, "*Take 2½* is neither as hip nor as iconoclastic as *Take One*, and its lack of vitality seems as much a sign of the times as of Greaves's and his collaborators' ages."[2]

We begin with a conceptual framework for considering the two films as documents whose differences are as important as their individual content as single works, drawing on David Scott's work on historiography, futurity, and form as a model for reading Greaves's 1968 and 2005 *Takes* comparatively. We then present a brief overview of the two films and their diverging receptions, seizing on what is most tantalizing for theorizing their production: the fact that Greaves outlined his own theory of production for the 1968 shoot. His claims for his films as political interventions open onto a discussion of classic self-reflexive cinema and apparatus theory. We are interested in theorizing *Take 2½* as the mature work of a major artist. Considering *Take One* and *Take 2½* in *dialogue* with each other opens new theoretical ground with regard to the

FIGURE 31.2 Greaves and Steve Buscemi during shooting of *Symbiopsychotaxiplasm: Take 2½* (2005). Photographer unknown. Courtesy Louise Greaves.

politics of the apparatus and the director-actor-crew relationship, as well as Greaves's sophisticated meditation on the relationship between improvisation and reproducibility.

TAKE ONE: ON REVISION

In *Conscripts of Modernity*, David Scott proposes that *The Black Jacobins*, a history of the Haitian revolution published by C. L. R. James in 1938, and revised in 1963, offers a useful model for how conditions in the present shape the way the past is represented and to what future ends it is imagined.[3] Scott shows that, like Greaves, James seeks to account for tensions between individual and collective action. A brief overview of Scott's project is helpful if we are to see these parallels. Scott suggests that James in 1938 was an anticolonial nationalist writing *The Black Jacobins* as an account of Haiti's revolutionary potential that spoke to struggles in the late thirties and projected a particular postcolonial future, but that history was understood differently in the postindependence moment of James's 1963 revision. His central insight is to show that "the way one defines an alternative *depends* on the way one has conceived the problem."[4] Furthermore, Scott is interested in two modes of emplotment in evidence in James's work: romance and tragedy. Romance, which stresses the heroic individual's revolutionary overcoming and looks to a future redemption, seems to be the dominant literary mode in James's 1938 rendering, but in the 1963 revision, he adds six paragraphs that shift the dominant mode to tragedy, a form that "offers an agonic confrontation [with] no necessary promise of rescue or reconciliation."[5] The essential modern tragic conflict, Scott maintains, is one between an individual's commitment to freedom and her social responsibility.

What do Scott's insights have to offer for a reading of Greaves's *Take One* and *Take 2½*? We contend that reading the *Symbiopsychotaxiplasm* films as part of a tripartite structure—with footage from 1968, 1991, and 2002—is essential to grasping Greaves's reflection on revolutionary history. This tripartite form confronts the viewer with the gap between the utopian and experimental revolutionary spirit of the original shoot and the more ambiguous, postrevolutionary angst of the post-9/11 moment in the United States. If we recall that Greaves's long and deep commitment to racial solidarity marks not only his aesthetics but his politics as revolutionary, the *Symbiopsychotaxiplasm* films need not be viewed as isolated idiosyncratic pieces in his oeuvre, but rather should be viewed within a continuum of engaged work that includes *The First World Festival of Negro Arts* (1966), *The Fighter* (1971), and *Nationtime—Gary* (1973), as well as more recent documentaries on Ida B. Wells (1989) and Ralph Bunche (2001). Greaves himself considered the film on the 1966 festival to be one of his most experimental, as it combined a poetic script (including his reading of Langston Hughes's "The Negro Speaks of Rivers") with realist documentary footage.

TAKE TWO: RECEPTIONS OF THE *SYMBIOPSYCHOTAXIPLASM*S

"A film about its own 'making-of' documentary," *Take One* lends itself well to the challenge of theorizing production.[6] If at its roots *theory* is "a looking at, viewing, contemplation, speculation" (OED), *Symbiopsychotaxiplasm* indeed trains its audience to theorize the process of film production. In the summer of 1968, Greaves gathered five pairs of actors to perform a "screen test" dialogue in which the woman in each pair accused the man of having affairs with other men and of pressuring her into having multiple abortions she did not want. Greaves told the film's crew that their task was not to simply capture the actors' performances, but rather to film the film being filmed, and to this end he assigned three cameras for each shot. The crew included four cameramen: the first camera was operated by the primary crew and trained on the actors; a second camera filmed Greaves and his crew at work filming the actors; a third camera focused on the wider surroundings, gathering footage of passersby and onlookers. In Greaves's instructions, the third cameraman was "in charge of filming this film being filmed," and Greaves himself would occasionally use a fourth camera to capture additional miscellaneous footage.

Over the course of the shoot, the crew's patience was strained by their work's repetitiveness. The directorial ruse left the crew feeling lost; Phil Parker concluded that Greaves did not know how to direct. Given that he had already made the pathbreaking documentaries *Emergency Ward* (1958) and *Still a Brother: Inside the Negro Middle Class* (1968), in addition to his distinguished career as a stage and screen actor and acting teacher, the crew's frustrations actually testify to the ingenuity of Greaves's experiment rather than to any ineptitude on his part. As his production notes state, his task was to "refuse to give a total explanation of the film!... Give only as much of an explanation as will satisfy the performers and film crew. To give more will kill the truth and spontaneity of everyone. Rumors of unrest and revolution in the crew should develop, should lead to encounters with the director."[7]

Greaves hoped to goad the crew and cast into a rebellion that would lead to confrontation and improvisation. While he has often noted that he looked for even more conflict than what emerged, he edited into the film a discussion with the crew and cast during production where he stressed, "The important thing is that we surface from this production experience with something that is entirely exciting and creative as a result of our collective efforts, as a result of Marsha's efforts, as a result of Audrey, and Sy Mottel; you, Jonathan, you, Bob, Roland Mitchell, Nicky, Frank Baker, Barbara Linden.... It's important that as a result of the totality of all of these efforts, we arrive at a creative cinema experience."

We are particularly interested in the clues Greaves leaves as to his role as instigator. For example, the dates on the slates for the scenes in which Audrey Henningham and Shannon Baker act out the script show that they were recorded on 8/3. This is the couple who are present on the lawn when the crew discuss the script's weaknesses with Greaves. It is only three days later, on 8/6 that the crew sequester themselves to discuss the production process, in what they decide to call a coup. Maria San Filippo elegantly sums up the film's effect, noting how the crew's rebellion calls "attention to the artifice and operations of cinema by insistently posing the question of how much of what we're watching is real. The single most successful technique used to this effect is that of Rosen's employment of direct address in assuring the spectator, 'The director does not know that we're photographing this scene.'"[8] Greaves has, indeed, confirmed that the crew's actions took place without his knowledge, but as San Filippo insists, this claim's truth or untruth is unknowable. Even Rosen himself adds a caveat that plays with our faith in his words, reminding both the crew and the viewer that "For all anybody knows, Bill is standing right outside the door, and he's directing this whole scene.... Nobody out there [in the viewing audience] knows whether we're for real."

As we have noted, reactions to *Symbiopsychotaxiplasm: Take 2½*, shown at Sundance in January 2005, were decidedly more mixed. Critics focused on the script's plot, which Audrey Henningham and Shannon Baker rehearse and act on camera, rather than on the production process itself, suggesting that those aspects of experimental praxis so visible and arresting in *Take One* are less legible in *Take 2½*. As Manohla Dargis wrote in a review later in 2005, "*Take 2½* is oddly moving because the film reveals not only how time has affected everyone in the intervening years but also how very straight filmmaking in this country has become."[9] What if Dargis is premature in her lamenting how "straight" filmmaking in this country has become? Are there ways to look backwards at a process defined by openness, uncertainty, and indeterminacy that do not ultimately reinforce narratives of increasingly stable, conservative, and limited possibilities for the making of art? Signs of revolt in *Take 2½* become clearer as we attend to its production.

We have already noted *Take 2½*'s tripartite structure, beginning with "Take Two": footage from the 1968 shooting edited into a new segment focused on Audrey Henningham and Shannon Baker's use of psychodrama in working through the screen test script, followed by a talkback at a screening of *Take One*; followed by digital video footage shot in 2003 featuring the same actors and a partially new crew. The shift in historical perspective and methodology is foregrounded. Not only do we see the actors, Greaves, and crewmembers aging over this gap, but the shift in medium from 16mm film to digital video offers two very distinct phenomenological experiences. In the latter, the camera creates a telenovela-like effect, which is heightened by the comparatively brief time onscreen for the crew (in comparison to the 1968 footage) and the correspondingly extended focus on the two actors and Greaves's relationship to them as director and acting coach. Indeed, *Take 2½* shows him directing the acting far more than directing the shoot.

TAKE THREE: TAKE 1.0

Part of the initial interest in *Take One*'s release was the debate over what Greaves had in mind before shooting, and what transpired during the shoot versus the editing. The common refrain that the film didn't really become "one" until the crew filmed its rebellion (despite the fact that the crew actually began debating the process on screen before the shooting was over) raises questions: Did Greaves know what he was doing during the shooting process? And if he did not want the cast and crew to be provoked into some kind of response (up to and including the crew's outright uprising), what in fact was the "plan" or "concept"? In his synopsis, he writes: "The film is *rebellion*! Rebellion against traditional cinema form. The hippies on the crew are for love and rebellion, in contradistinction to the screen test characters, Alice and Freddy, who are suburbanites, caught in a life of conformity."[10]

The dialogue written by Greaves seems consciously designed to instigate a reaction from the actors. On the one hand, he considers it an intentionally limited script, which can be lifted to artistic heights through the actors' craft, but on the other hand, its triteness and disturbing content (particularly in its most homophobic moments) push the actors to the edge. As he has put it, "The script the actors enact is, on the one hand, somewhat banal; but on the other, it is transformed into something truly important and rewarding when the actors become inspired.... In the classes where I train actors, I have the actors regularly perform what I call 'neutral' dialogue with changing sets of motivations. The text of the screen test is partly based on this acting exercise."[11]

As it turned out during the shoot, it was not the cast who had trouble with Greaves's demands so much as the crew. This has been attributed to the actors' professionalism and the effect that gaining a reputation for confronting a director might have on an actor's chances of being cast in future productions in a fiercely competitive environment such as New York. From the crew's own account in their "rebellion" document, they had little idea what Greaves had in mind. At one point during the 8/3 shooting, the crew, cast, and Greaves gather on the lawn, in a moment that may be seen as documenting the beginning of the crew's "rebellion." After Rosen and Gordon challenge Greaves on the path he's taking, he seems to be revealing the rules to the game he set up in the initial "synopsis." He addresses the crew and cast on-camera:

> This sort of palace revolt . . . is not dissimilar to the sort of revolution that's taking place in America today, in the sense that I represent the establishment, and I've been trying to get you to do certain things which you've become in a certain sense disenchanted with. You know? Now, your problem is to come up with creative suggestions, which will make this into a better production than we now have.

When Rosen interrupts to say, "I don't understand at all," Greaves responds, "It doesn't matter whether or not you understand it. The important thing is that we surface from this production experience with something that is entirely exciting and creative as a result of our collective efforts."

When the film was presented at the Brooklyn Museum retrospective, Greaves's program notes again addressed the film's provocative nature: "*Take One* is also about revolution. It expresses the mood of the 1960s in America with respect to Vietnam, civil rights, suffocating morality, and traditional life-styles. The film mimics this revolt. In this case, the director is the authority under assault."[12]

But if Greaves was interested in a project that would involve conflict, how could this not be considered an attempt to "provoke" some kind of response? As he recalls, "We were dealing with some of the basic points of drama, which is conflict and development, progression, a rising conflict into some kind of crisis, climax and some resolution. It may not happen as we would like it, but some variant of that theme will occur. The problem for the filmmaker is to find what the variant is and how to put it together in the editing room with the materials you have."[13]

For Greaves, the postproduction phase was as essential to his creative process and his role as director, as any other element. In his words, "The final equilibrium of *Take One* is achieved in the editing room, but in achieving it, a new disequilibrium—or struggle—is pursued between the film and its audiences."[14] Take, for example, the extensive use of the triptychs. Throughout both *Take One* and *Take 2½*, Greaves composes screen views that show not just two (a relatively familiar conceit) but three images. He also uses triptychs to convey to the viewing audience the experience of simultaneity on the shoot with multiple cameras trained on different parts of the production process. But these are not just multicamera shots, but often complex multiscenes, juxtaposing multiple couples, different days, functioning as a way to transition between days, scenes, or couples nonchronologically.

Production manager Bob Rosen has written several rebuttals to Greaves's descriptions of *Symbiopsychotaxiplasm*. Because his criticism and Greaves's response hinge on very specific statements, it is worth quoting from their exchange at length:

> What amazed me was to hear Bill talking about what had happened during the shooting as something he'd somehow had in mind from the start.... If we (the crew) hadn't gone off and filmed ourselves—quite unbeknownst to the director until after the final wrap—there'd hardly have been any film to put together at all. It's to Bill's credit that, once in the editing room, he certainly made the most of the footage, but to claim after all these years that he had deliberately adopted a "flawed, vulnerable persona" in order to provoke the crew and the cast to rebel on camera....[15]

As arch as these comments may seem, rather than criticizing Greaves as a haphazard director, Rosen commends the director for taking creative risks, linking the film's embrace of chance with the spirit of the time:

> What if it was made by a flawed, vulnerable director, who was struggling to do something new and different without perhaps knowing what he was doing? Bill had a lot of courage to undertake the project in the first place. I only wish he had the courage now not to claim he had just been pretending. It's precisely this quality of openness and vulnerability that made the film so funny—and so touching.

Rosen's reactions raise several interesting questions. Part of the confusion arises from the "synopsis," which only some of the crew had seen when the shoot commenced. Maria Zeheri speaks about it in defense of Greaves's process, Phil Parker claims he has seen it but not understood it, and Rosen claims not only to have seen it but to have spoken with Greaves about it; however, he has found that this didn't make things any clearer.

Scott MacDonald's interview with Greaves seemed to spark Rosen's objections. MacDonald has noted that Greaves began with the intention to adopt the persona of a director who is "not entirely clear about where the process he has set in motion is going" and expected that this persona would confuse and frustrate the crew, leading, eventually, to some sort of a rebellion. According to MacDonald, Greaves saw the *Symbiopsychotaxiplasm* project as "a metaphor for the sociopolitical experience of the sixties, a paean to rebellion against oppression—in this case, the oppression of the conventional, hierarchical power structure of director/actor/crew that had developed during the history of commercial cinema."[16] Greaves did not foresee how slowly this rebellion would simmer, nor that it would come from the crew not the cast, but nevertheless, he eventually did foment a mini-putsch.

Rosen writes about the project as if it were the document of an event rather than a constructed object. He suggests there is a bit of deceit in Greaves's contemporary explanation of the production. Both of them speak to the importance of the process, but Greaves seems to identify the process as continually evolving, making what he knew and when he knew it less relevant. Rosen seems to prefer this to the idea that Greaves was "pretending," that, in other words, he had certain pretenses about what he was doing (playing with certain conventions, pushing buttons, etc.). Ironically, neither premise demands either that Greaves worked consistently "without knowing what he was really doing" (until he saw the footage shot by the crew) or that he worked from a consistently detailed plan, which could not be changed by the situation as it presented itself at different points along the production, for example, between the preproduction concept notes and the postproduction editing process.

Greaves's published response to Rosen seems at pains to correct this preconception or confusion that surrounds the film. Having directed what was already by 1968, a substantial body of acclaimed work, he declares, "I was consciously violating many of the basic conventions of filmmaking. These violations in scripting, shooting strategy, and directing of the two actors were often new and disturbing to the crew. They provoked discussion behind my back and, eventually, the crew's open rebellion." He does, however, confirm that he did not consciously construct "a vulnerable persona to provoke the crew's on-camera revolt":

> Rather than "pretending" vulnerability, I was consciously allowing myself to be vulnerable in order to increase my credibility as a person on the screen. For a director to allow him—or herself—to be vulnerable on camera in this competitive world of filmmaking takes some courage.... This vulnerability did not end on the shooting location, but carried over into my work as the film's editor. Needless to say, the crew's revolt was critical to the film. It contributed mightily to the dramatic tension and humor.[17]

However, he stresses that the actors' performances are also key, and pointedly suggests that it might take more than the crew's footage to make an interesting film. "Without [the actors'] outstanding artistry and craft, this film would have fallen apart." In fact, these multiple layers activated by the film process seem to be a microcosmic example of Bentley's notion of a symbiotaxiplasm at work.

Greaves gives relatively little indication of how American social scientist and philosopher Arthur Bentley shapes his concept for the film. Bentley's term "symbiotaxiplasm" and the context in which it was first articulated offer what was already a curiously anachronistic theoretical archive in 1968. Bentley, a contemporary of John Dewey, shared the interests in pragmatism, classification of knowledge, and social institutions of his better-known colleague. He proposes the term "symbiotaxiplasm" in the opening essay of *Inquiry Into Inquiries*, "Knowledge and Society." As he defines it, a symbiotaxiplasm "would be the mass of men (or, alternatively, any associated animals) and assimilated things which forms the society, regarded as matter. Symbiotaxis would be the social process or function, regarded as such … [further] tentative terms are homoplasm for the human constituents of a symbiotaxium, and heteroplasm for the non-human constituents."[18] Two things to note here: First, a symbiotaxiplasm implies an approach that embraces *all* elements of a given situation: the environment, humans, nonhumans, and, the conditions of possibility, and the hidden ideological apparatuses that enable and frame it. Second, there is a clear interest in attending to precisely the relationship between the human and the nonhuman, and this nonhuman may well be the technologies not only of self, but of prosthetic extension which allow an observer or participant-observer to examine the symbiotaxis in its totality.

The parallels with film apparatus theory are remarkable, and indicate that, far from espousing a set of barely credible tenets, Greaves brings a sophisticated and clearly defined philosophy to the film process. As he admits during the question-and-answer segment in *Take 2½*, "there are a number of other very esoteric concerns that I had in making the film," including the Heisenberg Principle of Uncertainty, Stanislavski's approach to acting, chaos theory, and elements of his guru Aurobindo's mysticism. Adding the term "psycho," which "designates the mental mechanisms that are involved in the creative process as the individual moves through any given environment," sets up other clear parallels with apparatus theory and its roots. Here we want to lay out some of the key elements in apparatus theory that will facilitate a comparative reading of *Take One* with *Take 2½*.

TAKE FOUR: ON THE APPARATUS AND SELF-REFLEXIVITY

As a pioneering self-reflexive film about filmmaking, *Take One* has sometimes been reduced to the politicized practices of the 1960s and 1970s, particularly those found in Bertolt Brecht's avant-garde theater and the films of Jean-Luc Godard. Godard was inspired by Brecht's notion that passive audiences needed to be distanced from the illusions on stage. At the root of political approaches to cinematic self-reflexivity is the desire to distance the viewer from the pleasure usually expected when watching films. The uncritical pleasure promoted by mainstream narrative cinema is seen as an ideological tool used to manipulate film viewers.

Cinematic self-reflexive practices expose the social use, or ideology, "inherent" in cinematic technology itself. This became an important element of the "Apparatus" theories that proliferated in 1970s film theory. But technological and mechanical analogies have always been used to explain cinematic experience. Crucial to Greaves's project is his own theoretical approach to film technology, which predates and prefigures later developments in apparatus theory, particularly in the psychoanalytically rooted writings of Jean-Louis Baudry. This confluence of ideas includes highlighting the important effect of identification between different subject or spectator positions in relation to the cinematic apparatus. Greaves notes in his synopsis, "The strength, along with the excitement and challenge of this project, is its *basic conflict*, which is that of identification . . . identification of the actor with the part, the characters with each other, the actors with the director, the crew with the script, with the actors, with the director etc."[19]

Greaves is less committed to Marxist and psychoanalytic analysis than most classic apparatus theorists. Still, he ponders in the synopsis: "What is the psychoanalytical significance of this piece? Is it a dream that has the façade of truth or truth with the façade of a dream? Is it chaos masquerading as order or order simulating chaos? The piece, i.e., this film, must be susceptible to analysis, and yet it must be as unfathomable as the cosmos."[20] His ideas for this film share some of apparatus theory's basic interest in political, psychological critique—the "psycho" in *Symbiopsychotaxiplasm* and the "revolution" talk parallels Brechtian takes on illusion, realism, self-reflexivity, and breaking with the medium's conventional forms.

Baudry and Greaves both reinvoke Freud's use of photography and the microscope as analogical models. Recalling that in *The Interpretation of Dreams*, Freud attempts "to integrate dream elaboration and its particular 'economy' with the psyche as a whole," Baudry reminds that Freud assigns an optical model to this integral psyche: "Let us simply imagine the instrument which serves in psychic productions as a sort of complicated microscope or camera."[21] At issue here is the privileged position of visual technologies at the intersections where science and ideology are produced. Baudry asks, "Does the technical nature of optical instruments, directly attached to scientific practice, serve to conceal not only their use in ideological products but also the ideological effects which they may themselves provoke? Their scientific base would assure them a sort of neutrality and help to their being questioned."[22]

Greaves also speaks of the camera as analogous to a microscope. Noting that the psyche, the human soul, is notoriously difficult to record, he has stated, "Of course, as the camera investigates that part of the cosmos, the individual psyches being observed recoil." Greaves is interested in how behavior is then suddenly structured in ways it would never have been without the camera's intrusion, which he views as "a psychological version of the Heisenberg Principle." He uses the language of scientific research, characterizing the film as "an environment in which movie cameras were set up to catch the process of human response."[23] In *Symbiopsychotaxiplasm*, he sets out to observe the human subjects involved in a film in their natural habitat.

Greaves was far less negative than Baudry about the overall viewing situation apparatus theory examines. His approach is closer to those who tried to open up the rigid, teleological quality of early apparatus work. Constance Penley, instead of seeing inherent ideological effects embedded in the technology itself (lenses, cameras, projectors, the technological ability to construct "realistic" images, etc.), finds "that rather than fulfilling a role of giving cinematic *pleasure* or *satisfaction* ... this kind of filmmaking [self-reflexive/avant-garde] represents an extreme form of cinema's capacity for serving a *defensive* function for the spectator/subject."[24] But even this "defensive" position, which posits an ideological activism to a particular film practice, has also been criticized for assumptions it makes about "the spectator/subject."

One of the most articulate critics of apparatus theory, Judith Mayne, has noted that a major limitation is its tendency to assume that specific textual approaches have the automatic effect of reassigning dominant subject/object relationships as well as subject positions. However, this is by no means a given. A particular textual strategy may not produce anything at all in the viewer, or it may produce an unforeseen effect or identification. Thus, Mayne argues, "there is no such thing as an inherently radical technique, and there is no such thing as an inherently conservative one." This argument may well unsettle those film scholars who are invested in early versions of apparatus theory, but this is precisely why she calls for revisions of such ideological assumptions.[25] And Greaves's work offers a perfect point of entry into this debate.

Among the most extreme examples of this approach to film theory and practice are Jean-Luc Godard's late 1960s films. During this period, it was common for Godard to formulate slogans like, "In a movie, there is not pure technique, there is nothing like a neutral camera or zoom. There is just social use of the zoom. The social use of the camera."²⁶ The politics of self-reflexive cinema was at the time itself a reflection of overall distrust and cynicism about political art, or as Godard famously stated, "The problem is not to make *political* films but to make films *politically*."²⁷ *Symbiopsychotaxiplasm* has often been compared to Godard's more experimental work, and Greaves himself has noted the connection.²⁸

TAKE FIVE: 1 PLUS ONE = 2½ AND OTHER JAZZ EQUATIONS

If *Take One* appears optimistic, even utopian, looking to future horizons, *Take 2½* strikes a different chord. This tripartite film's third section is a new scenario that traces the characters, Alice and Freddie, meeting in New York after decades apart. Not only does the contrast between how these actors looked in 1968 and their present-day embodiment shock us into an awareness of the passage of time, but so too does the footage of Greaves himself—much thinner and more avuncular—and other original crew members, including Jonathan Gordon and Terry Filgate. The Central Park setting has changed too. As film critic Jonathan Romney notes, "Together, the *Symbiopsychotaxiplasms* offer a complex, time-seasoned contemplation on memory, repetition, aging, and changes in New York culture and in attitudes to cinema (in 1968, Greaves's filming drew fascinated crowds; today, no one looks twice at a DV shoot in the Park)."²⁹

By presenting the 1968 footage in a new "Take Two" nested within the complete film *Take 2½*, Greaves insists on this passage of time, foregrounding for us the historical and personal events that shape it. For those crew members who joined him to work for the first time on the 2003 shoot, the primary question was, "What is Bill going to do in this picture to get that kind of conflict . . . and is conflict necessary?" While there was no obvious conflict inherent to the shoot itself, there was a sense that the group was reaching for something, something that had perhaps irretrievably passed on. As one crew member states on-screen in *Take 2½*, "This is almost more a history lesson than anything. . . . The relationship of the crew to the director has changed, just as a natural evolution in film history. . . . We can't create that conflict." For crew and viewer alike, the film also poses a logical puzzle. Much of the pleasure of making (as well as viewing) *Take One* comes out of the uncertainties cultivated by the shifting viewpoints, Greaves's instabilities and vulnerabilities as a director, and the efforts of the other members to decipher his plans. The game that we, as an audience, play is one of shifting identifications. We are never sure whom to identify with, and why.

How does identification play out in "Take Two" and *Take 2½*? Is it different after we know the game being played? Do *Take One* and "Two" trick us into thinking we know the game played in *Take 2 ½*? *Take 2½* seems to be an attempt to see just how crucial the initial "rebellion" is to subsequent "Takes." The test of *Take 2½*'s effectiveness lies in seeing if a film could be made without the power of the crew's footage.

Perhaps, however, Greaves has another ruse here. Despite our expectations (raised in "Take Two") that the balance of interest and action rests with the crew, he pays far more attention to the actors in *Take 2½*. This focus is prefigured in "Take Two" with intriguing (even baffling) footage of Henningham and Baker rehearsing a scene with the aid of a psychodrama coach, Marcia Karp. At Greaves's suggestion, she works with Baker to help him uncover the emotional colorings in his portrayal of Freddie, and Baker is able to find what he is reaching for, telling Greaves, "She hit on the thing that I was working on ... it was like an arrow." Greaves has edited "Take Two" to focus on his work with the actors, and we are reminded clearly that his career as a teacher in the Actors Studio was well established at this point. He encourages the actors:

> Having explored this whole thing in depth through the agency of pyschodrama it would be very interesting to return to the scene (I was talking to Marcia about it) ... and see what new qualitative values have been added to your characterizations as a result of the removal of certain blocks and the increase of certain bases of empathy you have for each other and ah, I was wondering whether or not the conflict of the two characters would be ah more interestingly illuminated.

This is followed immediately by a close-up of Greaves, Karp, Baker, and Henningham, then a cut to a double screen, shifting attention away from the art of acting to the art of film-production and editing. Underscoring his point, Greaves announces: "Take 2, take 2, take 2 of take 2."

Early in the shooting of the latter-day footage of *Take 2½*, returning crew member Jonathan Gordon takes a moment to ask Greaves on camera, "What exactly are you trying to do with the second thing? Surely what we're doing at the festival is not enough to make a film. It's a part of a larger vision that you have. What is that?" Greaves answers with a chuckle, "I don't know," and Gordon jokes, "I think we need Bob Rosen here." Although Greaves seems willing to entertain Gordon's question, which he calls "explosive," before he can proffer a fuller answer, the production manager urges that they move on and the question goes unanswered.

Later, one crew member asks about whether *Take 2½* makes any equivalent statement to the anti-Vietnam stance implicit in *Take One*. While Greaves answers wryly that everyone wants to be a director, and George W. Bush seems to want to be director of the whole world, he does not engage deeply with the question. We would suggest that Greaves is evasive precisely because his vision here is trained on intimate rather than monumental horizons. In the words of Victor, the homeless alcoholic who wanders onto the shoot at the end of *Take One*, a post-9/11 Greaves knows "I can't fight politicians. I can't fight money 'cause I don't have money . . . it's called controlled press and I'm well aware of it." While critics such as Romney and San Filippo lament that "the vivid candy pastels of the 1968 16mm footage are replaced by a glassier, more literal DV image,"[30] the digital cameras in the hands of Greaves and his crew effectively evoke televisual viewing in the age of the 24-hour news cycle. However, the stories these cameras capture are ones likely to escape the notice of "controlled press," stories that touch on the ways race, class, gender, and sexuality, and their intersectionalities are lived by the very subjects Greaves has consciously followed throughout his career.

Greaves chose to shoot *Take 2½* during the New York City Marathon. Consequently, the street noise and restrictions on movement impinge as signs of urban public life on Freddie's and Alice's private histories. The literal foot-fall on New York streets emphasizes the film's locality. By 2003 New York had become a hyper-policed space, as we see when the park ranger extends his range of surveillance via walkie-talkie technology. He eventually informs them that the area is off limits due to the marathon, in striking contrast with the encounter with a bemused but permissive policeman in *Take One*.

In *Take 2½*, on-screen policing recalls the Rockefeller drug laws that complicate Freddie's life as a drug-user, foster parent, and HIV-positive man. Greaves also writes into the scenario a marked class disparity between Freddie and Alice. Alice is wealthy enough to fly to New York upon Freddie's request, and to send him to a spa in Europe as therapy, while Freddie's foster-parenting brings him in constant touch with poor families whose children are at greatest risk of entering the system. The liberal politics that Gordon and Buscemi seek when they ask Greaves what has happened to the explicitly antiwar message of *Take One* obscure this film's *real* politics, which are centered on the AIDS epidemic, drug laws, post-9/11 police vigilance, and race/class dynamics.

Commentators on *Take One* have noted that race goes remarkably unremarked in the film, given that such a multiracial, international cast led by an African-American director of Caribbean heritage was anything but business-as-usual in 1968. The irony is that this is still a rarity. However, one of the few references to black culture that Greaves does make in *Take One* is the use of jazz as a metaphor in the film: "We simply don't know where we will land with this creative undertaking. It is a study of the *creative process* in action. Also, the film is *Jazz*! It is improvisation. It is an exploration into the future of cinema art."[31] This statement should not imply that jazz is a music that is intuited, lacking plan, process, or preparation, created on the spot, for this would disregard the rigorous training, aural fluency, and instrumental virtuosity necessary. Greaves's theory of jazz as presented here is that it is fundamentally a future-oriented exploration, anchored not so much in the here-and-now as in the still-to-come. In his elaborations on jazz's significance, he has stated, "*Take One* was also heavily influenced by jazz, which, to me as a Black man, is an attempt on the part of an enchained human spirit to break free from the prison bars of mechanical tempo and to liberate itself. Analogically, traditional dramatic structure was for me a conventional prison from which I sought to escape with the free style of the film."[32] These statements are, of course, broad and gain far more weight when we pay attention to the specific choices of recorded jazz Greaves selects to accompany his film. Here, *Take One* and *Take 2½* could hardly be more different.

By the time *Take One* was edited in 1971, Miles Davis's innovative and controversial album *In a Silent Way* (released in 1969) had made it to the Billboard Top LPs list. Innovations included John McGlaughlin on electric guitar and a quasi-compositional role for the producer, Ted Maceo. Using this album for the soundtrack (along with recordings of one of the record's sidemen, Joe Zawinul) figured jazz not simply as an inspired yet essentially spontaneous outpouring but as an object produced out of contemplation, listening, and minutely timed editing. Greaves drew a parallel between the hours of raw footage shot in 1968 and the unreleased sessions of Miles Davis and band,[33] and the edited text of *Take One* and the edited album *In a Silent Way*.

Take 2½'s soundtrack, in contrast, features bassist Ron Carter's album, "The Golden Striker." Without a drummer, the album has been reviewed as "chamber jazz of a high order."[34] In the time since *Take One*, jazz has migrated to the popular equivalent of chamber music to be heard in domestic spaces, underscoring Greaves's interest in the intimate and familial dynamics that Freddie and Alice struggle over.

The scenario in *Take 2½* centers on Freddie's efforts to convince Alice to take his foster-daughter, Jamilla, under her wing. As Henningham and Baker rehearse the script, their performances are slowly infused with elements of their past and present. With Karp back as psychodramatist, the two actors draw on the Actors Studio method in their on-screen preparations. Freddie's efforts to convince Alice to become a mother figure for Jamilla reignites pain from the early moment of "Take Two" (shot in 1968) when envisioning a shared future was so unsuccessful.

Here David Scott's claims about how the imagined futures of a particular present inform the ways the past is played back are useful. As Scott stresses, a past narrated as romance centers strictly on the heroic individual. In *Take One*, Greaves himself plays that role: the lone director, wrapped in thought wandering across the ridges of Central Park. Other heroic figures include Alice, Freddie, Gordon, and Rosen. *Take 2½*, however, reflects many elements of tragedy. When Freddie invites Alice back to New York, he withholds the question of

FIGURE 31.3 William and Louise Archambault Greaves at the Tribeca Film Festival in 2005, with premiere of *Symbiopsychotaxiplasm Take 2½*. Photographer unknown. Courtesy Louise Greaves.

Jamilla (and therefore of a kind of shared future). Thus his encounters with Alice are real-time struggles over the meaning of their relationship, death, and selfhood, with no guarantee in the script that their discussions will lead to a resolved future. The dialogue grows out of a prepared text but is improvised as the shoot unfolds. This uncertainty is a hallmark of the tragic mode of history, as Scott identifies it.

For Scott, the modern tragic conflict is one between an individual character's commitment to freedom and the character's social responsibility. In *Take 2½*, such conflict drives each character and the relationships among the members of the crew closest to Greaves. Freddie and Alice eventually envisage a future where, through Jamilla, they remain emotionally connected, and Alice can taste the joys and sorrows of motherhood—yet this utopian vision is enabled by the revision of history effected in the tripartite structure of *Take 2½*.

The openness to risk which Greaves spoke so much of in *Take One* may in fact only become available with age and a perspective on life that includes the inevitability of death. This ability to rest with the one shared harmatia, or "tragic flaw," of humankind is figured visually throughout *Take 2½*: rather than correcting splotchy lighting and other flawed visual artifacts, or editing out moments where the crew is bored and impatient but not particularly interesting, Greaves accepts without judging these contingencies and elements of the collective life and environment, the symbiotaxiplasm, of his shoot and yet remains open to the future, ready to record it and revisit it, ready to do the work that Scott highlights, constantly reexamining utopian visions of the future that informed accounts of the past in order to more adequately address his own time. In so doing, Greaves maintains a symbiopsychotaxiplasticity that may be a model for political comportment in our age of perpetually accelerating change.

NOTES

Reprinted, with minor revisions, from *Cultural Studies* 28, no. 4 (March 2014): 574–93.

1. Scott MacDonald, "William Greaves," in *A Critical Cinema 3: Interviews with Independent Filmmakers* (Berkeley: University of California Press, 1998), 41–63.
2. Maria San Filippo, "Lost and Found: *Symbiopsychotaxiplasm: Take One* and *Take 2½*," *Cineaste* 31, no. 2 (2006): 48–49.
3. David Scott, *Conscripts of Modernity: The Tragedy of Colonial Enlightenment* (Durham, N.C.: Duke University Press, 2004).

4. Scott, 5–6.
5. Scott, 135.
6. Jonathan Romney, "Sign of the Times: William Greaves's Symbiopsychotaxiplasms," *Modern Painters* (December 2005/January 2006): 44–47.
7. Scott MacDonald, *Screen Writings* (Berkeley: University of California Press, 1995), 33.
8. San Filippo, "Lost and Found," 48–50.
9. Manohla Darghis, "Film Within a Film in 60's Time Capsule? Groovy," *New York Times*, October 26, 2005, http://movies.nytimes.com/2005/10/26/movies/26symb.html.
10. MacDonald, *Screen Writings*, 34.
11. MacDonald, 48.
12. MacDonald, 48.
13. Adam Knee and Charles Musser, "William Greaves, Documentary Filmmaking, and the African-American Experience," *Film Quarterly* 45, no. 3 (Spring 1992): 13–25 (reprinted in chap. 1 of this volume).
14. MacDonald, *Screen Writings*, 47.
15. Robert Rosen, "Letter to the Editor (Robert Rosen) and Response (William Greaves)," *Independent* 15, no. 6 (July 1992).
16. MacDonald, *Screen Writings*, 32.
17. Rosen, "Letter to the Editor," 2.
18. Arthur Bentley, *Inquiry Into Inquiries*, ed. Sidney Ratner (Boston: Beacon Press, 1954), 13.
19. MacDonald, *Screen Writings*, 34.
20. MacDonald, 34.
21. Sigmund Freud, *The Interpretation of Dreams*, trans. A. Brill (New York: Macmillan, 1913), 425.
22. Jean-Louis Baudry, "Ideological Effects of the Basic Cinematographic Apparatus," *Film Quarterly* 28, no. 2 (1974–1975): 39–47.
23. MacDonald, *A Critical Cinema*, 56.
24. Constance Penley, *The Future of an Illusion: Film, Feminism and Psychoanalysis* (Minneapolis: University of Minnesota Press, 1989), 17.
25. Judith Mayne, "Paradoxes of Spectatorship," in *Critical Visions in Film Theory*, ed. Tim Corrigan, Patricia White, and Meta Mazaj (New York: Bedford/St. Martins, 2010), 102.
26. Kent E. Carroll, "Film and Revolution: Interview with the Dziga-Vertov Group," in *Focus on Godard*, ed. Royal S. Brown (Englewood Cliffs, N.J.: Prentice Hall, 1972), 58.
27. Colin MacCabe, *Godard: Images, Sound, Politics* (Bloomington: University of Indiana Press, 1980), 19.
28. Lillian Jimenez, "Profile: William Greaves," *Independent* 3, no. 10 (October 1980): 8–11. Late in 1968 Godard traveled to the United States to collaborate with documentary filmmakers D. A. Pennebaker and Richard Leacock. Godard envisioned *1AM* as a film about the politics of the day, as well as about filmmaking. Both *1PM* and *Take One* combine "cinéma-vérité-like" footage documenting the location shooting, and "staged" scenes with actors (primarily Rip Torn in *1PM*), and include

"dialogue" (for example, the "interview" in *1PM* with a woman who works on Wall Street; Godard is seen asking her questions from a distance and giving her dialogue to speak via a wireless earphone).

Both films also had almost mythological production histories. *Symbiopsychotaxiplasm* disappeared from distribution shortly after it was made, while Godard abandoned *1AM*, leaving Pennebaker to complete his own version, *1PM*, a behind-the-scenes film about making *1AM*. Similarly, at one point in the 1968 footage used in *Take 2½*, during the crew's rebellion footage, Bob Rosen claims that their act of rebellion was unprecedented. While Rosen is probably correct, it is difficult not to see Pennebaker's film as an example of a production's crew member literally "taking the film away" from the director (in this case with the director's consent) and making his own version, the scenario Greaves's crew went to great lengths to avoid. Both films were commentaries on the state of politics in 1968 (Greaves's more subtly so, perhaps). Godard was convinced he was going to document the inevitable revolution in the United States. His failure to grasp U.S. politics was one of the reasons the film was abandoned. No revolution was to come to the United States, nor was it to materialize in France after he returned. The political nostalgia one feels in *1PM*, released four years after the original footage was shot, seems more cynical than the less overtly negative subtext of *Symbiopsychotaxiplasm*. The strange sense that some form of "rebellion" might have *actually* been achieved in the film is comparatively optimistic.

29. Romney, "Signs of the Times," 46.
30. Romney, 46.
31. MacDonald, *Screen Writings*, 34.
32. MacDonald, 34.
33. The unreleased sessions are now available in the boxed set "The Complete in a Silent Way Sessions" (Columbia/Legacy, 2001).
34. Thomas Conrad, "Ron Carter: The Golden Striker," *Jazz Times*, April 25, 2019, https://jazztimes.com/archives/ron-carter-the-golden-striker/.

End of the Dossier on the *Symbiopsychotaxiplasm* Films

32

A Guy Who Could Think Around the Corner

Ralph Bunche: An American Odyssey

PATRICIA R. ZIMMERMANN

The title of this essay draws from an observation from Judge William Bryant, a former student of Ralph Bunche at Howard University and an interview subject in William Greaves's monumental *Ralph Bunche: An American Odyssey* (2001). Describing Bunche's intellectual adroitness as an academic and a diplomat, Bryant observes: "I always thought of Bunche as being a guy who could think around the corner so to speak.... He can think as far as most people can think and then he can see around the corner."

Ralph Bunche (1903–1971) was an intellectual, writer, and diplomat for the United Nations and the first African American to win the Nobel Peace Prize, for brokering an armistice between Israel, Transjordan, Egypt, Syria, and Lebanon in 1950. He served the United Nations for two decades, working on peacekeeping, decolonization, human rights, and civil rights. He also was chief drafter of the UN Charter (1945), which dealt with trusteeship and decolonization.[1]

It is important to situate the Greaves film and the surrounding media materials generated to support it, as it moved into festival, museum, and educational sectors, within the context of the fiftieth anniversary of the awarding of the Nobel Peace Prize to a person of color. *Ralph Bunche: An American Odyssey* is the first feature-length film chronicling the life and impact of Ralph Bunche. But the project's monumentality extends beyond Bunche, as it constitutes a racialization of the history of the twentieth century, and in particular the relationship between U.S. race relations and international human rights—beginning with Bunche's birth in 1903 and ending with the release of the film in 2002.

Ralph Bunche: An American Odyssey operates as an epic, transnational mode of documentary that combines the linear forward drive of twentieth-century political and racial histories with more spatialized structures of African-American intellectual thought and world politics in conflict zones. The word "odyssey" in the title is apt, alluding to mythical storytelling structures based on journeys and suggesting a movement and exploration across different locations in a quest for knowledge. Part of the political and analytical power of the film resides in its insistence on global interconnections between the concepts of human rights, civil rights, political theory, and pragmatic politics, a dialectical structure connecting the micro-political elements of a particular country or place to a macro-political concept of international human rights and interconnections.

It is also important to situate the epic sweep of *Ralph Bunche* within the historical context of other epic documentary projects that engage a global perspective and look for linkages across nations through a conceptual lens organized into sections. These films include Fernando Solanas and Octavio Gettino's *Hour of the Furnaces* (1968), Peter Watkins's *The Journey* (1984–1987), Michael Glawogger's Global Trilogy (*Megacities*, 1998; *Workingman's Death*, 2005; *Whore's Glory*, 2012), and collaborative new-media projects such as Liz Miller's *The Shoreline* (2016), which looks at activist initiatives to create positive ecological change in the face of global warming in India, Norway, Canada, New Zealand, Bangladesh, Chile, and the United States, through short videos and an atlas chronicling sea-level rise.

On the surface, *Ralph Bunche* looks like an aesthetically conservative expository public television documentary employing interviews with experts and supporting their contentions with illustrations from archival footage to document the life of a black intellectual, diplomat, and civil rights activist. If we, too, "look around the corner," however, the project is much more complex, an intervention into thinking intellectually, politically, and critically about race in America and its intertwined relationships with the world.

Ralph Bunche revolves around an absence: it features no original interviews with Bunche, who died in 1971, thirty years before the film was completed. Rather than a liability or a loss, however, this absence is generative: the film moves beyond Bunche as an individual and any need to center and structure his story as a melodrama charting conflicts between public and private spheres. Instead, it concentrates on key historical moments in the twentieth century when race, decolonization, and international human rights issues were entangled, and Bunche contributed analysis and policy. The film flips the traditional tropes of biography that privilege the personal as it engages the political and emphasizes pathos. In *Ralph Bunche*, the political and the historical constitute primary structures on which Bunche had complicated agency. Rather than pathos, the film mobilizes ethos and logos, assembling a mosaic of African-American and Euro-American scholars of Bunche, various politicians and diplomats, and actors reading from Bunche's writings to unpack the racial issues within international relations. Although the film does function as a reclamation of the importance of Bunche for American and international history, when we look around the corner at Greaves's entire extended project of feature film, short films, study guides, website, and supplemental material, we see that this magnum opus is actually a project to understand Bunche within the racialized history of the twentieth century.

Greaves produced, directed, and wrote many films across his vast career, including sponsored films, television shows, and documentaries. He produced short films for the United States Information Agency and the United Nations. And he made several film biographies of prominent figures in African-American history. These films, which share a strategy of restoring major black intellectuals and artists to American history, include *Booker T. Washington: The Life and Legacy* (1982), *Frederick Douglass: An American Life* (1985), and *Ida B. Wells: A Passion for Justice* (1989). He also made films on Spencer Williams, the early black filmmaker, and Jackie Robinson, the athlete and activist. His Ralph Bunche epic project can be situated as a culmination of many decades of a filmmaking career, seeking to reclaim significant black intellectuals, artists, and political activists as crucial agents in American and world history.

Ralph Bunche: An American Odyssey was based on the Brian Urquhart biography of the same name. Urquhart was Bunche's coworker and protégé at the United Nations, as well as former undersecretary general there. He was a close friend and biographer of Bunche. The film took more than ten years of researching and assembling archival material from manuscripts, photos, newsreels, and scholarly writings. The original cut was seventeen hours long, though it was eventually edited down to a two-hour version for broadcast on Public Television.[2] It was sponsored by the Schomburg Center for Research in Black Culture in New York City, with major funding by the Ford Foundation, the National Endowment for the Humanities, the Corporation for Public Broadcasting, Camille O. Cosby and William H. Cosby, Jr., the John D. and Catherine T. MacArthur Foundation, and the National Black Programming Consortium.[3] To compile the film, Greaves assembled over 400,000 feet of film and 3,000

FIGURE 32.1 William Greaves, Bobby Shephard, and Louise Greaves during the shooting of *Ralph Bunche: An American Odyssey* (2001). Photographer unknown. Courtesy Louise Greaves.

individual photos. This material was subsequently donated to the Schomburg Center. Additionally, Greaves determined that the copyright and all profits earned from the film would go to the Schomburg.[4]

This essay analyzes Greaves's magnum opus, *Ralph Bunche: An American Odyssey*, as an ambitious attempt to create a polyvocal historiography linking the American civil rights movement with decolonization in Africa by pivoting on the through-line of Bunche's biography. Although on the surface the two-hour PBS film may read as a straight-line, linear biographical chronology of Bunche, this reading belies a more complex historiographic structure that works to recover the history of African Americans and racism in the United States, and of colonization and decolonization, through a deep dive that not only creates context but complicates the genre of biography. As one scholar interviewed in the film notes, Bunche could "discuss, probe, look for words and concepts that could be put together"—a conceptual model of probing and putting together that also operates as Greaves's Bunche project design.

The Bunche project includes the two-hour film for PBS broadcast, a seven-and-a-half-hour set of twelve modules, ranging from fifteen to twenty-five minutes, that explore the same issues in greater depth, produced for use in schools and universities; and an elaborate teacher's study guide that includes glossaries of terms, biographies, and questions to be engaged before, during, and after screenings. As a massive project with many media components, *Ralph Bunche* anticipates transmedia projects that move through many different iterations, formats, and audiences to customize and adapt ideas for different contexts ranging from broadcast, to schools, to film festivals, to online environments.

The significance of *Ralph Bunche* was not immediately apparent in the few, mixed reviews the film received when it was released. Dennis Harvey, writing in *Variety*, notes, "Important but underappreciated figure's saga is engrossing, though rather dry treatment here will limit pic's own 'odyssey' to repeat PBS airings." The review recounts the trajectory of Bunche from professor and intellectual in the 1930s to diplomat in the post–World War II period for the United Nations and subsequent investigation by Joseph McCarthy for being a "concealed Communist" in the 1930s as part of the Negro Congress. It notes, rather negatively: "Package is solidly pro if unimaginative, hewing very much to the standard pubcaster style.... Sidney Poitier's narration is also notably stiff at times."[5] Writing in the *Christian Science Monitor*, David Sterritt offered a different position on the film. He asks at the opening of his review, "Who was Ralph Bunche and why should Americans care about his life?," and calls the film an "engrossing documentary." Sterritt's review features many quotes from Greaves recounting his production odyssey in making the film, where he approached two hundred foundations, three hundred to four hundred corporations, and a hundred black businesses.[6]

THE FEATURE FILM

The phrase "to think around the corner" can be leveraged as a theoretical model to situate William Greaves as a major African-American documentary filmmaker who made many historical films. *Ralph Bunche: An American Odyssey* refuses the straight line and instead moves around the corner of major historical events to interweave three separate strands: a reclamation of the life of Ralph Bunche, the history of race in America, and colonization/decolonization in

Africa. The film constitutes the first film on Ralph Bunche, who, in addition to his other accomplishments, wrote, as one black historian in the film contends, some of the most important essays on race in America, on par with W. E. B. Du Bois.

The film moves from Bunche's early life in Detroit, to his college years at UCLA, to his life as graduate student at Harvard, his time as a professor at Howard University, his work with the Office of Strategic Services (OSS) during World War II as an analyst of Africa, his work with the United Nations in its founding stages, his brokering of an armistice in the Middle East, his work on decolonization in the Congo, and his involvement in the U.S. Civil Rights Movement.

This film is narrated by Sidney Poitier, who Bunche had known for decades, and features forty different scholars, colleagues, and Bunche family members. However, the film does not engage much with Bunche's personal life beyond describing his marriage and interviewing one of his children; it is decidedly not about Bunche as a private person but about Bunche as a public figure, an intellectual, and a diplomat. The interviewees narrate not only the progression of Bunche's public life but also, and perhaps most significant, the complexities of his intellectual ideas and his diplomatic strategies.

As a result of these interviews, combined with actors reading from Bunche's published writing, the film transcends what could be the reductive linear bio-pic to provide deep dives into historical and political context, combined with salient theorization of race and decolonization. It provides an operatic sweep of the twentieth century through the figure of Bunche, a *longue durée* investigation that demonstrates that race, civil rights, internationalism, and decolonization are irrefutably entwined.

The film opens with a provocation to move around three different corners of Bunche's life: international relations with Nikita Khrushchev and the Soviets; American politics during the McCarthy era; and militant Black Power movements in the United States. The first clip shows archival footage of Khrushchev, and the voice-over asks if Bunche was simply a tool of the West. The second shows the McCarthy Hearings in the United States and asks if Bunche was a secret agent for the Soviets. The third shows images from the 1960s and explains in voice-over that some militant African Americans saw him as an international Uncle Tom, the "ultimate model Negro." After these three sequences, the narration states that Bunche "remains an enigma in American and world history."

The film is organized on multiple vectors: a linear progression through the twentieth century, race and civil rights in the United States, and global politics related to conflict zones. Within these vectors, it enacts various dialectical juxtapositions. For example, early on, it chronicles how Bunche played a key role in resisting the Nazi invasion of North Africa during World War II, by providing research and analysis. Working for the OSS, each week Bunche prepared a situation report; these reports took the form of manuals on life in Africa, describing indigenous cultures, institutions, and colonial administrations. A clip from the U.S. propaganda film *The Negro Soldier* (1944), inserted as a voice-over, explains that Bunche proposed that the Office of War Information produce documentaries on the contributions of black Americans to the war effort. Ironically, as the voice-over elaborates, although Bunche was promoted to the head of the African Section of the OSS, many resented bringing in an American Negro. Next, Jonathan Holloway, a Bunche scholar, assesses Bunche's departure from academia to become "a full-time agitator." He observes, "He's gone, he's on the inside." Later the narration indicates that "not all in the black community agree with Bunche." David Levering Lewis, a historian, explains that as Bunche entered government service, radicals felt he had betrayed his intellectual principles and been co-opted into the establishment.

The center of the film focuses on the problem of Palestine and Israel, moving between Bunche's conceptual analysis, the on-the-ground contentious politics, and global mediation efforts that led to Bunche receiving the Nobel Peace Prize in 1950. This section of the film elaborates the intricacies of diplomacy and brokering an armistice. Over shots of Palestine, an actor reads from a report Bunche wrote, where he observed, "the problem can't be solved on the bases of abstract justice. Both Arabs and Jews are here and intend to stay." Next, Abba Eban notes in an interview that he worried that Bunche would side with the Arabs. Brian Urquhart explains, "Bunche believed that the special committee on Palestine should talk to everybody." The next interview follows this strategy of dialectic. M. T. Medhi asserts that the question of Israel and Palestine is "not a religious problem but of foreigners coming to occupy Palestine." Bunche drafts the majority report on partition, and by November 1947 the UN General Assembly votes on the partition into two states, one with Arabs and Muslims and the other for Jews, but with an economic union. In May 1948 the British leave, and a full-scale war ensues, with forces from Egypt, Jordan, and Syria involved. This sequence includes images of the flight of Palestinians. This critical section illustrates a key editing strategy of the film where a dialectical montage of ideas and positions elaborates conflicts and problematizes the linear drive of history.

Bunche and Bernadotte, the Swedish UN mediator on the conflict, return and want Jerusalem included within the Arab sector, a position with which the Israelis disagree. A newsreel chronicles the Bernadotte assassination. Bunche must take the helm. In a letter read by an actor, Bunche notes, "Now I am stuck ... as acting mediator." Scenes of Bunche at the UN Security Council follow. At a retreat with all sides in Rhodes, he advocates for an armistice, brokering discussions between Egyptians and Israelis. A voice-over reads from one of Bunche's letters: "This is killing work." The scene deglamorizes the negotiation process of the Rhodes Armistice talks in 1949 through a strategy of juxtaposing different ideological positions, conflicts, and national identities. The voice-over contends that Arabs felt Bunche was not sympathetic to Arab people. In an interview, Medhi declares that Bunche's mandate "was to bring peace to Palestine, not to bring justice to the Palestinians." This sequence on the Israel and Palestinian conflict illustrates a central strategy of the film, which is to enact a dialectical tactic of juxtapositions between the United States and the globe and between different ideological and conceptual viewpoints, a strategy of moving around the corners of history rather than in a straight line.

THE SHORT VIDEOS

Ralph Bunche: An American Odyssey predates and anticipates twenty-first-century documentary projects that migrate across the analog and digital and are embodied with different permutations and iterations that adapt to context and purpose.[7] These are works that move among festivals, broadcast, museums, educational venues, community settings, and different political/social/geographical contexts, shape-shifting in adaptive modes to different kinds of audiences, goals, limitations. Beyond the quest for large audiences in theaters or broadcast, these transmedia practices concentrate on micro-audiences, foregrounding engagement with a topic and dialogic encounters.

Beyond the feature-length film for national public television broadcast, Greaves produced a series of fourteen individual short video modules that elaborated periods of Bunche's life and national and international issues in more detail for secondary and postsecondary educational contexts, where a longer film would not be viable given the time constraints of class meeting times. The shortest film is twenty minutes; the longest, forty minutes. The lengths suggest that these pieces were designed to start conversations rather than to be passively consumed in a theater. It is important to note that in all the publicity materials, these shorts are identified as "modules" rather than short films; "module" suggests alignment with an educational organization of knowledge rather than a film festival entry. The word "module" also indicates that the shorts were not framed as auteurist texts but as components of a larger embodied classroom dialogue, as jumping-off points for engagement with history and ideas.

The fourteen modules follow the historical structure of both the Urquhart biography and the feature-length film. They are numbered one through twelve, with two pieces in two parts. The titles of the modules link to sections in the feature-length film, including "Early Years/Early Influence," "The Making of a Scholar/Activist," "Race, An American Dilemma," "Mr. U.N.," "The Peacemaker in Palestine," "International Troubleshooter," "Crisis in the Congo," and "The Man Behind the Myth." The modules deepen and expand sequences in the feature film, providing longer interviews with scholars, more archival footage, and a closer look at the nuances of each period.

The twelve pieces progress chronologically across Bunche's life but are not organized in any personal trajectory. Instead, echoing the film, their organization revolves around turning points and crisis points in American and international history, with each of the video modules dealing with a particular period as a discrete unit of history. This structure suggests an innovative documentary historiography based on postulating that events are comprised of actions and conflicts not just between governments, but also between organizations, constellations of agency, institutions, conflicting ideologies, negotiation, analysis, policy, written articulation, and intellectual models and debates.

TEACHER'S GUIDE

To position *Ralph Bunche: An American Odyssey* as simply an independently produced feature-length documentary winding its way through the festival and public television circuits is to ignore the vast transmedia enterprise established so that the project could engage educational sectors in racializing and internationalizing American history. In this way, the project, with all its components, looks around the corner of the feature-length biopic to move beyond broadcast and festival audiences to more specialized audiences. It is a shift from a documentary practice promoting an auteur-framed expository cinema to a community-located cinema of utility.

To this end, an elaborate teacher's guide was created as both supplement and expansion of the twelve short modules. The supplemental materials are organized around a wide range of complex political and historical issues, such as conflict resolution, peacekeeping, trusteeship and decolonization, international organizations, race relations and civil rights, independence in Africa, colonialism, and human rights. The guide deals with a wide range of countries, including Cyprus, Congo, Palestine, Ghana, and Togo, as well as the region of Southeast Asia.[8]

The front page of the guide features a quote from Ralph Bunche: "I have a deep-seated bias against hate and intolerance. I have a bias against war, and a bias for peace. I have a bias that leads me to believe in the essential goodness of my fellow man, which leads me to believe that no problem of human relations is ever insoluble."[9] Overall, the guide is divided into two parts: one is a general reference section containing a glossary, biographies, a bibliography, a timeline on key events in Bunche's life coordinated with events in U.S., African-American, and world history; the other is organized into twelve modules corresponding to the individual short videos.

The printed guide is designed in a modular format that can be adapted to various teaching situations and classes. It was developed in coordination with the National Council for Social Studies and the National Center for History in the Schools, specifically for high school and college curricula in peace and conflict resolution, the United Nations, international relations, African-American studies, civil rights, decolonization, sociology, and career planning.

Each module begins with a specific quote from Ralph Bunche, establishing him as a major African-American intellectual. The separate modules function on two levels: First, they provide historical elaboration of people, places, and events, expanding and deepening the context of the particular film module. Second, they frame and organize the spectatorial engagement with the films by using sets of questions entitled "While You Watch" and "After You Watch," and postviewing discussion questions, activities, and research project suggestions and worksheets. These structures suggest a strategy of mobilizing active intellectual engagement rather than passive viewing, by framing film watching not as simple consumption of information but as a dialectical engagement between student and film that requires questioning, probing, and digging deeper for implications and historical evidence and analysis.

For example, module 3 is entitled "A Black Scholar Investigates Colonialism." The Bunche quote on the module is, "The pattern of racial persecution and exploitation is universal." The module covers Bunche's two-year period in Africa and the Far East between 1936 and 1938, where he studied the impact of colonialism on indigenous peoples. The module looks at his writing of *A World View of Race* (1936), which linked the rise of fascism to racism; as well as his experiences in South Africa, his travels in East Africa, the strain on his marriage, and encounters with poverty in China. Historical background about the worldwide Great Depression and the rise of fascism frames the module, which also outlines terms to know such as "colonialism," "imperialism," "Pan-Africanism," and "lynching"; people to know (Benito Mussolini, Paul Robeson, Jomo Kenyatta); and places referenced, such as Northwestern University, the London School of Economics, Belgian Congo, Uganda, Malaysia, Indonesia, and Singapore.

The module includes guides for four areas of engaged watching, with sections of questions in categories such as "Before You Watch," "While You Watch," "After You Watch," and "Digging Deeper: Activities and Research Projects." These different categories of spectatorship underscore an interactive modality rather than a top-down intellectual system, echoing the dialectic structures of the feature film's editing. The questions in the "While You Watch" section are simple but open-ended, to spur students to think more widely and to make connections: "What was the focus of Ralph Bunche's research project in Africa and Asia?" "What was the effect of colonial powers' propaganda on the world and on colonized peoples?" "What observations does Bunche make about the people he meets in South Africa?"

The almost three-hundred-page "Teacher's Guide and Source Materials That Accompany *Ralph Bunche: An American Odyssey*" considers a film not as a fixed object but as an opening to explore around the corners to open up knowledge, engagement, exploration, and debate. The Teacher's Guide moves the film from a position of fixity to a position of interaction and exploration of the multiple corners that comprise the multiplicity of ideas, nations, people, and locations in the film. The guide suggests that the life span of a documentary needs to be considered beyond high-profile and glamorous festival and broadcast circuits to encompass the documentary's educational usage. However, it is precisely in the migration of the film across multiple sectors that Greaves's transmedia orientation and approach can be discerned as a way to interact with and mobilize different sectors of film spectatorship.

THE WEBSITE

Like most independent feature-length documentaries produced in the past twenty-five years, *Ralph Bunche: An American Odyssey* has a website that provides additional background information. Throughout the website, the film is referred to as directed by William Greaves, narrated by Sidney Poitier, and based on the biography by Brian Urquhart. However, the website does more than function as an online publicity brochure. Instead, it extends the reach of the project beyond festivals, museums, and broadcast venues into educational and community sectors where the film functions as a stimulator for discussion that racializes American history. The website further recalibrates the feature film as a dialogue about race, decolonization, and human rights in which the United States and the world are linked. It website shifts from a publicity function to an archival and dialogic function, providing additional information and resources in sections called "About the Movie," "Educational Resources," "Purchasing Info," "The Making of the Movie," "About the Educational Modules," "Site Credits," "Join Our Mailing List," and "The William Greaves Video Collection."

The "Making of the Movie" section features an extensive interview with Greaves by film critic and scholar David Sterritt.[10] The interview eschews a focus on Greaves as a filmmaking auteur promoting his most recent film and instead probes Greaves's own conceptual and intellectual strategies in approaching a subject as vast and complex as Ralph Bunche. Sterritt points out that a film of such scope with so much factual material could easily have become "noncompelling and non-dramatic," then continues to dive into how Greaves worked through and figured out a strategy to combine a variety of materials covering an entire life within a history of the twentieth century, through the lens of race and decolonization. Throughout the interview, Greaves elaborates the dialectics between the personal in the figure of Bunche and the political in terms of world events, between the United States and the world, and between civil rights and decolonization. Thus the interview sidesteps the usual auteurism of filmmaker interviews and instead focuses on the historiographic process Greaves engaged in order to assemble a film out of myriad materials. Greaves admits he knew who Bunche was but did not know that much about him. He wondered, "How could a black man, in pre–civil rights America, attain this level of prominence? And then somehow be forgotten. He was a mystery."

In the Sterritt interview, Greaves points out that the team knew "the viewer had to become involved viscerally as well as intellectually ... the problem was compounded by the fact that we were doing a film about a scholar, a diplomat who thinks and speaks in abstract terms—and film, needless to say, is a visual medium." Greaves explains that the larger issues with which Bunche was engaged motivated the research on the "whole anti-colonialist, anti-imperialist, anti-fascist thrust of his life." Greaves reveals that he envisioned the film as a motivator for young people to engage a story of a talented, gifted individual who understood how to give back to society. But he also explains that the film travels through what he terms "a huge historical canvas" of the twentieth century that is relevant for the twenty-first century.

The "About the Movie" section of the website describes the film as combining the personal story of Bunche and the larger national and international domains he interacted with: "Against a backdrop of U.S. and world history that Bunche had a hand in shaping, the film tells the compelling personal story of the legendary African-American scholar turned statesman and the contributions he made to international diplomacy, decolonization of the world, peacekeeping, and human rights in pre–civil rights America."[11] Throughout, the website toggles between the United States and the world, rather than the personal and the political. The website positions *Ralph Bunche* as a film not simply about a person or a biography but about ideas. The page also features testimonials about the significance of the film from scholars, museum librarians, programmers, and reviewers such as Erik Barnouw, William Sloan, Henry Louis Gates, and Geoff Gilmore.

The "Educational Resources" section includes subsections: "High School Teacher's Guide," "Instructor's Notes," "Recommended Reading," "Online Resources," "Online Educational Materials," and "Other Videos by Greaves About the African American Experience." The section also includes a range of material for sale, which suggests Greaves's strategy of looking around the corner, as the materials available extend beyond the film. Material for sale includes the feature-length two-hour documentary, but also the teaching modules, a reprint of Bunche's important treatise *A World View of Race*, and video documentation of a conference at the Ralph Bunche Institute for International Studies of the City University of New York in 1986, entitled "Ralph Bunche: The Man and His Times."

The project's insistence on moving beyond the person and the personal to the intellectual and the political is underscored in two sections, "Recommended Reading" and "Online Resources." The former section is divided into four subsections: "About Ralph Bunche," "By Ralph Bunche," "About the United Nations," and "General References." "About Ralph Bunche" lists the books written by scholars featured in the film or advisors to the project, including Brian Urquhart, Charles P. Henry, Jonathan Holloway, Ben Keppel, and Benjamin Rivlin.[12] "By Ralph Bunche" lists his major writings from which both the feature-length documentary and shorter modules draw for historical analysis of policy making and also for readings by actors in voice-overs.

Although the feature-length film focuses primarily on Bunche's public efforts at diplomacy and actions in the world rather than his more nuanced work as a major African-American scholar and writer on race and decolonization, this section of the website documents his major contributions as a thinker. It lists his addresses, his PhD dissertation on Togoland and Dahomey (1934), booklets for various organizations, research memoranda, and essays. The writing spans the geographies of the United States, Africa, and the Middle East. Of particular note is Bunche's work for the Carnegie-Myrdal Study, *The Negro in America*, published in 1940, before the United States entered World War II. The memoranda written by Bunche include "A Brief and Tentative Analysis of Negro Leadership," "Conceptions and Ideologies of the Negro Problem," "Ideologies, Tactics and Achievements of Negro Betterment and Interracial Organizations," and "The Political Status of the Negro."[13]

The "Online Resources" section provides further evidence of Greaves's conceptual model that braids African-American intellectual work, U.S. civil rights, and international relations connected to human rights. The section features six subsections, which move from the person of Ralph Bunche to national and international issues: "About Ralph Bunche," "Conversations with Sir Brian Urquhart," "Civil Rights and Human Rights," "Decolonizations," "Peaceful Uses of Atomic Energy," "Peacemaking, Mediation, and Conflict Resolution."

These sections expand beneath and beyond the film by carving out the intellectual terrain Bunche occupied, how scholars have analyzed his ideas and impact since his death, and the complexities of the larger international political issues. Like the feature film, the website's conceptual underpinnings braid together Bunche the person, Bunche the intellectual, African-American intellectual thought, decolonization, international relations, and civil rights.

EXHIBITION OF THE FILM

A press release about the film for a screening with Greaves in person at Mount Holyoke College in 2004 notes that "this seminal documentary explores the meaning of Bunche's accomplishments and his contribution to global decolonization, conflict resolution, and human rights advancements."[14] The thirty-page preliminary public relations plan for *Ralph Bunche: An American Odyssey*, prepared by Michael Shepley, indicates that the epic nature of the film and its significance as the first one ever made on Bunche, who was not a known figure in American popular culture, required a carefully considered outreach strategy. The plan made clear that the film had a target audience of young people, but this population did not watch public television. As a result, the plan included a large section focusing on promotional campaigns to postsecondary and secondary institutions. It included targeting organizations outside of the film and television milieu, such as the Ralph J. Bunche International Affairs Center at Howard University, National Alliance of Black School Educators, African American Educators of Social Studies, U.S. Institute of Peace, United Nations Associations of America, National Association for Equal Opportunity in Higher Education, United Negro College Fund, and Association for the Study of Afro-American Life and History.

The public relations plan clearly identifies the film as an educational tool "to stimulate discussion and enhance understanding about Dr. Bunche's life and accomplishments among educators and students alike."[15] It would develop materials to target secondary schools, colleges, and organizations promoting peace and peaceful conflict resolution, including study guides, a website, conflict resolution training materials, and articles. A thousand videos, teacher's guides, and biographies were to be donated to inner city schools and to nonprofit organizations "working for peace, conflict resolution, economic and social justice, the improvement of race relations, and fostering academic excellence among disadvantaged youth."

The film was also positioned as a way to "introduce students to post–World War II twentieth-century history," especially on the United Nations and struggles for democracy and human rights. This two-pronged approach confirms that the film was positioned not simply as a feature-length film for festivals and broadcast but as a work that would be seen in political, diplomatic, and educational organizational sectors where the content and arguments it made might be more important than the form.

The plan hits the issue of Bunche's obscurity head-on, arguing that the publicity campaign would require a significant education component. It sees the dissemination of the film in two sectors: public television stations and organizations like the United Nations, and conferences and schools. Because of the complexity of the politics in the film and of Bunche's writing and life, the public relations plan devised a tactic to simplify by focusing on the life story. The elements included a short biographical portrait, a time line of key dates, excerpted comments from interviewees, a fact sheet on the film, and stories on Greaves and Urquhart. The plan called for three people to represent the film in interviews: Greaves as director, Sidney Poitier as narrator, and Urquhart as author.

The exhibition of *Ralph Bunche* evidences further examples of Greaves's strategy of moving among festivals, broadcast, and educational sectors. The two-hour version of the film was produced for public television, but the original idea was to create a multipart series composed of episodes, an idea that was not viewed as scalable given budgetary and programming constraints. To compensate, the film's exhibition strategy confirms the multipart strategy described here. Such a strategy is instructive for documentary studies, which often default to analysis of cinematic texts rather than the economic infrastructure in which works are made and circulate, which requires both archival and political economy analysis.

The film played in many important film festivals focusing on social issues in the United States, including the Houston International Film Festival (where it won the Gold Award for Documentary Feature), Human Rights Watch International Film Festival, Lake Placid Film Festival, National Black Theater Festival, Philadelphia International Film Festival, Sundance, and the USA International Film Festival.[16]

Beyond these festivals, the film garnered further exhibition. In the higher education sector, it played at Bard College, Bates Colleges, City University of New York, Colgate University, Morehouse College, Spelman College, Syracuse University, UCLA, University of Central Florida, University of Houston, University of Illinois, University of Maryland, University of Oklahoma, and Yale University, among many other colleges and universities. At the University of Illinois, the film was presented as a special event in 2001 called "The Making of *Ralph Bunche: An American Odyssey*," which featured Greaves in discussion about the processes involved in researching the film. This event was cosponsored by the Afro-American Studies and Research Program and Center for African Studies at the university, as well as the Departments of Education, Anthropology, Cinema Studies, English, History, Political Science, Sociology, Women and Gender Studies, and Theatre. The event featured two screenings of the film.[17]

In the art and nonprofit organizational sector, the film was screened at the Black Filmmakers Hall of Fame, Harvard Club, Library of Congress, Museum of Modern Art, National Council for the Social Studies, and Schomburg Center for Research in Black Culture.[18]

MORE THAN FOUR CORNERS

Ralph Bunche: An American Odyssey is a significant documentary film in the massive oeuvre of William Greaves. It anticipates twenty-first-century documentary practices that combine the digital, the analog, and embodied modular approaches that can be mobilized to create new communities and reorganized to adjust to different political and social specificities. It is an early example of a transmedia practice across different sectors of broadcast. The project is also part of the modern tradition of the global documentary, where connections between different locations and politics are rendered through reconceptualizations of the world.

As a film, a transmedia project, and an intellectual mission to think about the relationships between the United States and the globe through the lens of race, *Ralph Bunche: An American Odyssey* enacts a racialized and globalized epistemology of looking around the corners of ideas, politics, practices, and people to ask spectators to think differently. This is a project that pushes the spectator away from the straight lines of chronological history to experience what critical historiographers called a "crooked history," where the temporal and the spatial twist together. It proposes that ideas, politics, and places have more than four corners, and that it is urgent to look around and find all the corners available in order to enter into the dialectics of race, civil rights, human rights, conflict zones, and the globe.

NOTES

1. "Ralph Bunche: An American Odyssey Fact Sheet," public relations campaign.
2. Mel Watkins, "William Greaves, a Documentarian and Pioneering Journalist, Dies at 87," August 26, 2014, *Pan-African Biographies*, http://jenkinspanafricanbios.blogspot.com/2014/09/william-greaves-black-journal-host-and.html.
3. "Making the Movie," *Ralph Bunche: An American Odyssey*, PBS, https://www.pbs.org/ralphbunche/filmmaking_about3.html, accessed September 3, 2018.
4. Michael Shepley, "*Ralph Bunche: An American Odyssey* Preliminary Public Relations Plan," March 22, 2000, United Nations Archives, https://search.archives.un.org/uploads/r/united-nations-archives/4/0/a/40a30676ce558c51789714befada5cd04d669a464d1fcf79dee7a22c4502839a/S-1093-0078-05-00005.pdf.
5. Dennis Harvey, "Ralph Bunche: An American Odyssey," *Variety*, February 11, 2001, https://variety.com/2001/film/reviews/ralph-bunche-an-american-odyssey-1200466832/.
6. David Sterritt, "A Director Driven to Do a Little Good," *Christian Science Monitor*, February 2, 2001, https://www.csmonitor.com/2001/0202/p15s1.html.
7. For an overview of such documentary transmedia projects, see Patricia R. Zimmermann and Helen De Michiel, *Open Space New Media Documentary: A Toolkit for Theory and Practice* (London: Routledge, 2018); and Dale M. Hudson and Patricia R. Zimmermann, *Thinking Through Digital Media: Transnational Environments and Locative Places* (London: Palgrave Macmillan, 2015).

8. Shepley, "*Ralph Bunche*."
9. "Teacher's Guide and Resource Materials," *Ralph Bunche: The Odyssey Continues*, general reference section, 1.
10. "The Making of the Movie," *Ralph Bunche: An American Odyssey*, http://ralphbunche.com/filmmaking.html, accessed January 2, 2019.
11. "About the Movie," *Ralph Bunche: An American Odyssey*, http://ralphbunche.com/about.html, accessed January 2, 2019.
12. Brian Urquhart, *Ralph Bunche: An American Odyssey* (New York: Norton, 1993); Robert R. Edgar, ed., *Ralph Bunche: An African American in South Africa* (Athens: Ohio University Press, 1992); Charles P. Henry, *Ralph Bunche: Selected Speeches and Writings* (Ann Arbor: University of Michigan Press, 1995); Jonathan Holloway, *Confronting the Veil: Abram Harris Jr., E. Franklin Frazier, and Ralph Bunche, 1919–1941* (Chapel Hill: University of North Carolina Press, 2002); Ben Keppel, *The Work of Democracy: Ralph Bunche, Lorraine Hansberry and Kenneth Clark* (Cambridge, Mass.: Harvard University Press, 1995); Benjamin Rivlin, ed., *Ralph Bunche: The Man and His Times* (New York: Holmes & Meyer, 1990).
13. Gunnar Myrdal, *An American Dilemna: The Negro Problem and Modern Democracy* (New York: Harper and Brothers, 1944).
14. "William Greaves to Speak on Life and Legacy of Statesman Ralph Bunche," press release, Mount Holyoke College, February 2, 2004, https://www.mtholyoke.edu/media/william-greaves-speak-life-and-legacy-statesman-ralph-bunche.
15. Shepley, "*Ralph Bunche*."
16. "Making the Movie."
17. "The Making of *Ralph Bunche An American Odyssey*," announcement, University of Illinois, https://cas.illinois.edu/index.php/node/1326, accessed November 11, 2018.
18. "Making the Movie."

33
Revealing Greaves

Unhiding His Archive

SHOLA LYNCH

Q: What do these outstanding people have in common? Lou Adler, Harry Belafonte, Bill Cosby, Ruby Dee, Ricardo Montalbán, Rita Moreno, Gil Noble, Brock Peters, Sidney Poitier, Anthony Quinn.

A: All have narrated films which champion the cause of social progress in America . . . films, which have been directed and produced by the Emmy Award winning filmmaker William Greaves, winner of over 60 international film festival awards.
—William Greaves Productions promotional pamphlet, circa 1988

The William Greaves collection had been acquired by the Schomburg Center for Research in Black Culture at the New York Public Library, or so the rumor went among researchers. But few had actually accessed the material held by the Moving Image & Recorded Sound Division. As the newly minted curator of the division, as well as a filmmaker, I was enormously excited by the prospect of a collection reflecting a founding father of independent filmmaking's entire career trajectory. I wondered what clues the collection could reveal about Greaves's dedication to his craft through a decades-long career that involved more than two hundred documentaries and several narrative films. Beyond the finished works, the collection might hold the documentary interviews, outtakes as well as archival footage, and photos focused on subjects that explored Black perspectives largely unrecognized by the broader media, as well as his feature films. In its entirety, the accumulation had the potential to be a treasure trove for scholars and students of history, culture, and film. At least this was the hypothesis.

Greaves certainly had a "right time, right place" career that lent itself to this assumption. He reflected in a 2001 oral history interview conducted at the Schomburg Center that by the accident of his birth in 1926, he'd been "drenched in the afterglow of the Harlem Renaissance." He grew up in the shadow of Harlem's heyday and down the street from the Harlem branch of the New York Public Library on 135th Street, which became the nexus of Black thought after purchasing Arturo Schomburg's ten-thousand-item collection. The library pulled him intellectually and became a refuge for the Stuyvesant High School student. It also housed the American Negro Theatre, which fanned an interest in acting. After attending the City of College of New York to study engineering, Greaves appeared in the all-Black cast films *Sepia Cinderella* (1947), *Miracle in Harlem* (1948), and *Souls of Sin* (1949).

Later, frustrated by roles that limited and often stereotyped Black characters, Greaves gravitated from in front of the camera to behind it, into filmmaking, and began to study the craft at the City University's film institute. With few film-job prospects and no opportunity for serious training in the United States available to Blacks, Greaves moved to Canada and landed a job with the National Film Board. He honed his nonfiction storytelling, making films, though none of them, as he recalled, "dealt with the Black experience." After eleven years he became restless and wanted to engage more fully with the fight for civil rights through his film work. He secured a job with the United Nations and returned to the United States.

In 1968, after the assassination of Martin Luther King, Jr., and a summer of riots, broadcasters looked to integrate their staff with Black journalists and producers. Greaves, uniquely qualified as a seasoned filmmaker, took the mantle for a new news show called *Black Journal* that would be produced by Black makers and solely focused on unmuting and illuminating the views of Black America in the media. With a fierce independence, and by reconnecting with the intellect and perspective cultivated in the post-Renaissance afterglow of his childhood, Greaves had come full circle and would continue to be propelled by it through a long and productive career.

With all this in mind in 2013, when I arrived at the Schomburg Center and eagerly asked the Moving Image & Recorded Sound Division staff about the collection, I was surprised at the response. No one knew the collection's whereabouts or even what it contained.

The division's founding curator had retired in 2009, after nearly forty years on the job and having acquired roughly five thousand square feet of audio and moving-image material. Many collections had been taken in by the Schomburg and shipped to storage on the principle that they were safe with the library and would be processed one day soon. This story is similar for archives and libraries across the country. All best intentions aside, without the necessary financial backing, "one day soon" turns into decades. The Schomburg staff had done its best to provide public access to the 10 percent of the division's holdings that had been processed and cataloged. But without even a collection list, the entirety of the collection was essentially hidden. Would unearthing potential discoveries, like the Greaves collection, be enough of an incentive to take responsibility for a massive undertaking?

The Schomburg Center is named after the collection's founding curator, Arturo Alfonso Schomburg. A curious boy of African, German, and Puerto Rican heritage, he grew up in Puerto Rico. As the story goes, one day during a world history lesson in elementary school he asked about Black history. His teacher informed him that it didn't exist, that Black people had not made any contributions to world culture or history. While the answer didn't register as accurate, Schomburg had no evidence to the contrary. Later, when he finished school and immigrated to Harlem, well before the Renaissance, he searched out and discovered histories, novels, poetry, photographs, and art works by and about Black people. Funded by his mail clerk's salary, he amassed approximately ten thousand items over more than twenty years. In his essay "The Negro Digs Up His Past" (1925), Schomburg described the items in his collection as "vindicating evidences," perhaps in response to his grade school teacher. "When we consider the facts," he continued, "certain chapters of American history will have to be reopened" in order to "make history yield for him [the Negro] the same values that the treasured past of any people affords." Schomburg's project blossomed, and his collection flourished into a center with five divisions that are the stewards and access points for nearly eleven million vindicating pieces of evidence.

My learning the details of Schomburg's mission made the problem of managing the Moving Image & Recorded Sound Division seem more like an opportunity. Stored and almost forgotten, five thousand square feet of Black history's gestures had been bound and voices silenced, including those of William Greaves. My mission became to liberate and vindicate this evidence.

One of my first tasks became organizing the division's papers and files. Among them, I discovered many key documents, including the deed for "The William Greaves Film Collection." Signed by Greaves on December 1, 1988, the agreement detailed the sale of "approximately three million feet of motion picture and sound recordings representing original negatives, work prints, raw footage, original ¼-inch audio tape recordings and production sound tracks from the works of the Seller." The deed confirmed that we had a sizable collection but did not include a complete film list or an inventory or even a box count of what had been acquired.

There could only be three possible locations: on-site at the Schomburg, off-site at a New York Public Library storage location, or in an independent off-site storage facility. Given the collection's size, the staff and I ruled out on-site. Since the NYPL's off-site storage required inventories and item-level barcodes, it also seemed unlikely. We discovered about twenty boxes identified as Greaves material but clearly not the entire collection. The off-site storage location turned out to hold nearly three thousand of the division's entire five thousand square feet of holdings, or 1,791 boxes of collection material. The Greaves collection had to be among them.

The division's senior librarian shared the manifest managed by the storage company. The unwieldy document caused immediate panic. More than 150 pages long, the spreadsheet included no collection names for more than eleven hundred entries and partial information for the remaining boxed collections. It all seemed indecipherable. I dedicated time every day to poring over the pages, trying to unravel its mysteries.

While the catalog didn't offer any clues about the Greaves collection, it had a few items that provided some background on Greaves. Nine of his films could be accessed, including *From These Roots* (1974), which he coproduced with the Schomburg Center, using its archives to tell the story of the Harlem Renaissance and the voices of resistance associated with the "New Negro" movement. In the 2001 video oral history interview, Greaves recounted the Schomburg Library's importance to his work and intellectual development. He remembered seeing Arturo Schomburg, although he never spoke to him directly. Ms. Handy, Greaves's grade school teacher, brought her famous blues-man brother, W. C. Handy, into class one day to perform for students. Greaves watched the pioneering independent filmmaker Oscar Micheaux carrying film cans, which he thought were suitcases, down the street to the bar and grill near Greaves's apartment building. Micheaux occasionally screened his films at the bar, and little William would be among the neighborhood kids who would pull themselves up to the window to watch the images moving on the wall. Greaves would see the poet Langston Hughes walking the streets. He took an African history class taught by the playwright Lorraine Hansberry's uncle, Leo, and sat with the historian John Henrik Clarke, the Schomburg librarian Jean Blackwell Hutson, and the journalist J. A. Rodgers. For Greaves, history was not an abstract concept. Black history lived and breathed through the people he encountered.

Finally one day, while I was examining the storage manifest and identifying collections, the letters "WG" jumped out of the document, not in the Major Description column of collection names but in the Reference, Box Number, and Notes columns. Now it seemed so obvious. His initials, "WG"! More than four hundred boxes had been acquired in 1988 and were sent to storage ten years later. There they had remained, forgotten but not lost.

The next step was to secure the funding to process and restore the collection. Raising the funds to untangle this problem required buy-ins from the Schomburg's director and the director of the Research Libraries and the president of the New York Public Library. It required a strategic plan and additional staff to implement it. After a few hurdles and many, many meetings, the division had the green light to work with the development department to submit grants and pitch donors.

On August 25, 2014, in the middle of these efforts, William Greaves passed. A dime had not yet been raised. He didn't know that the push to unhide *his* collection led in great part to raising enough funding to inventory the entire Moving Image & Recorded Sound Division's holdings. After numerous rejections from funders, an anonymous donor came through with a two-year grant that later would be renewed for a total of hundreds of thousands of dollars. The goal of inventorying the division's holdings, as a major step toward access, would become a reality. Through this process, and at long last, an item-level list exists for the entire William Greaves Film Collection.

The 150-page inventory listing details 12,161 film, audio, and video items related to completed works, rough cuts, outtakes, interviews, vérité and archival footage, as well as press, panels, photos, music, and trailers for dozens of film projects. Inventoried in no particular order, based on a library-wise "more product, less process" approach to archival processing, the list's pages, numbers, and formats tell a story.

Of the 5,216 film elements, the vast majority are 16mm. The audio count is 3,975, and video is 2,969. The formats reflect the technological changes that distributors demanded over the decades. By the output archived, one thing is clear: Greaves worked continuously. He made films, television programs, and public service announcements. He had independent projects, and he worked with networks, distributors, and corporations. He interviewed or worked with an astonishing range of people significant to Black history and culture, from Langston Hughes and Duke Ellington to Maya Angelou, Muhammad Ali, and Amiri Baraka. He also grappled with subjects ranging from art and entertainment to race, politics, and economics.

The collection reflects his arc from acting to filmmaking. It includes film prints from his acting days with *Miracle in Harlem* (1948) and *Lost Boundaries* (1949). From his time honing his craft working with the Canadian government, there is *Emergency Ward* (1959), his best-known work from this period and among the earliest films he directed. While Greaves's Canadian films are not well represented in the collection, there are a few more-intimate items like an audio reel titled, "Canadian Drama Studio 1950's—Bill Teaching," and one labeled "West Indies Cruise S.S. Mauritania, Jan. 21–Feb. 8, 1950." There are also several intriguing undated films that could be home movies; they're marked "Personal—Greaves."

When Greaves returned to the United States in the early 1960s, he started his own production company. In the Schomburg oral history he explained that the basic motivating principle that led him behind the camera was "to produce films that in one way or another paid either homage to the African-American experience or to Africa and that variously attack the outrageous vilification campaign that had been launched against Black people ever since the end of slavery because they needed to find some sort of philosophical basis for oppressing us." In the context of the Civil Rights and Black Power movements, his goal to direct, produce, and write "films that would balance the scale" flourished from this point until the end of his career and represents the bulk of the Schomburg collection.

When one scrolls through the inventory, compiled in no particular order, the abbreviated titles and project names, transcribed from the original objects, pop off the page and read like an extended poem reflecting the balance to history Greaves sought to create:

Black Power: Myth or Reality
From These Roots
Ida B Wells Narration—Toni Morrison
Greaves Birthday Party
Director St. Clair Bourne
Black Journal: Malcolm X Producer/Director Madeline Anderson
Ethiopia
Goa India
First World Festival
Who's Standard English?
Emergency Ward
Voice of La Raza
Frederick Douglass

Personal—Greaves
Symbiopsychotaxiplasm—Take 2
That Job Interview
Marijuana Affair
Langston Hughes (12/13/1966)—Interview
In the Company of Men
Lost Boundaries
Where Dreams Come True
Space for Women
To Free Their Minds
John Henry Clark Interview—for African Art
Making Fair Housing Work
Percy Sutton
June Christmas
Tribute to Robeson (Carnegie Hall)
Black Convention (3/10–12, 1972)
Thrilla in Manila
Malcolm & Rap
On Liberty
Hypertension
From These Roots—French Version
Anthony Quinn in Search for Pancho Villa
Ralph Bunche Interviews
Vincent Brown
Amiri Baraka
Just Doin' It
That's Black Entertainment

While the collection is only inventoried and partially processed, it is one giant step closer to access and a fuller understanding of Greaves's work and its impact. Through his "vindicating evidences," a narrative of Greaves as a Harlem boy profoundly shaped by the spirit of the Renaissance, becoming a new Negro, and creating works that span contemporary Black history emerges. Greaves is looking to find and refine his voice with a sense of responsibility and in service of his mission. In his Schomburg oral history, he explains, "When one makes a good film, whether dramatic or documentary, one is performing a major surgery on the psyches of the audience." In his skilled hands, his films reshape our understanding of ourselves. Through the odyssey of unhiding his archive, our hope is to fully reveal William Greaves, the man and the maker.

Filmography

RESEARCHED AND ASSEMBLED BY AURORE SPIERS

This filmography lists the films and television programs that William Greaves worked on and appeared in between the mid-1940s and 2008. Our starting point was Scott MacDonald's *A Critical Cinema 3: Interviews with Independent Filmmakers* (1998), where MacDonald lists fifty-six titles produced, directed, and/or written by Greaves between 1958 and 1990. In this filmography, we have added thirty-eight new titles, including the "race films" Greaves acted in during the 1940s and the documentaries he made for the National Film Board of Canada (NFB) between 1952 and 1960. Information was compiled from direct viewing of credits whenever copies were available. We are also grateful to Louise Archambault Greaves and David Greaves, who provided and verified the credits for many titles. Thanks to them, this filmography reflects the scope of Greaves's career and is the most comprehensive to date. Although it remains incomplete, especially since Greaves was not always credited for his work, and should be considered a work in progress, our hope is that this filmography will serve as a useful resource.

We have not listed individual episodes of *Black Journal*. Information about how to access episodes is available at the California Newsreel site, http://newsreel.org/video/BLACK-JOURNAL.

Titles are listed chronologically, and titles from the same year are listed alphabetically. The information for each title includes: Greaves's credit, director credit if available and other than Greaves, producer credit, date, original production format if known, runtime, and technical specifications. Because the titles we viewed were available only on VHS and DVD and online, the information regarding original production format is often tentative. An asterisk [*] precedes the titles for which we were unable to verify Greaves's involvement. Titles that we could not locate are followed by a dagger [†].

Availability is not listed, but readers may refer to WorldCat (https://www.worldcat.org/) as well as individual library and archive catalogs for many titles listed in this filmography. Today Greaves's most widely available films are *Symbiopsychotaxiplasm: Take One* (1968) and *Symbiopsychotaxiplasm: Take 2½* (2005), which were released in a special two-disc edition by the Criterion Collection in 2006. Greaves's "race films" are available online and/or on DVD, except for *The Fight Never Ends* (1948). Almost all the titles produced by the NFB are available in their collections, and some are available for streaming on their website at https://www.nfb.ca/. Many of the later documentaries produced by Greaves are available at universities and public libraries across the United States. Others may be found on the American Archive of Public Broadcasting (https://americanarchive.org/), Internet Archive (https://archive.org/), and YouTube (https://www.youtube.com/).

We thank Nicole Morse for contributions to the early drafts of this filmography. We would also like to thank the archivists and librarians we have contacted and worked with over the years, especially Nancy Spiegel from the University of Chicago Library, Ana Appleyard from the National Film Board of Canada, and the Time-Based Media Conservation Team at the Smithsonian National Museum of African American History and Culture. Our deepest gratitude goes to Louise Archambault Greaves, whose unwavering support carried us through.

*We Hold These Truths (actor). [No other information available.]†

The Colored Harvest: "America's Number One Mission Responsibility" (actor; The Josephite Fathers). ca. 1946–1952. 21 minutes; black and white; sound.

*Sepia Cinderella (actor; dir. Arthur H. Leonard). 1947. 35mm; 70 minutes; black and white; sound.

The Fight Never Ends (actor; dir. Joseph Lerner; William D. Alexander). 1948. 35mm; 64 minutes; black and white; sound.†

Miracle in Harlem (actor; dir. Jack Kemp; Jack Goldberg). 1948. 35mm; 71 minutes; black and white; sound.

Lost Boundaries (actor; dir. Alfred L. Werker; Louis de Rochemont). 1949. 35mm; 99 minutes; black and white; sound.

Souls of Sin (songwriter ["Disappointment Blues" and "Lonesome Blues"], actor; dir. Powell Lindsay). 1949. 35mm; 64 minutes; black and white; sound.

*The Settler (narrator; dir. Bernard Devlin, Raymond Garceau; National Film Board of Canada). 1952. 16 minutes; black and white; sound.

Eye Witness No. 51 (editor; National Film Board of Canada). 1953. 11 minutes; black and white; sound.

Canadian Venture (editor; dir. Caryl Doncaster; National Film Board of Canada, Tom Daly). 1956. 22 minutes; black and white; sound.

Forest Fire Suppression (editor; dir. Lawrence Cherry; National Film Board of Canada). 1956. 22 minutes; black and white; sound.

Looking Beyond: Story of a Film Council (editor; dir. Stanley Jackson; National Film Board of Canada). 1957. 19 minutes; black and white; sound.

Profile of a Problem Drinker (aka *David: Profile of a Problem Drinker*) (editor; dir. Stanley Jackson; National Film Board of Canada). 1957. 29 minutes; black and white; sound.

Putting It Straight: A Story of Crooked Teeth (director, editor; National Film Board of Canada, Tom Daly). 1957. 13 minutes; color; sound.

Blood and Fire (editor; dir. Terence Macartney-Filgate; National Film Board of Canada, Roman Kroitor, Wolf Koenig). 1958. 29 minutes; black and white; sound.

The Face of the High Arctic (editor; dir. Dalton Muir; National Film Board of Canada, Hugh O'Connor). 1958. 12 minutes; color; sound.

High Arctic: Life on the Land (editor; dir. Dalton Muir; National Film Board of Canada, Hugh O'Connor). 1958. 21 minutes; color; sound.

Islands of the Frozen Sea (editor; dir. Dalton Muir, Hugh O'Connor, Strowan Robertson; National Film Board of Canada, David Bairstow). 1958. 29 minutes; black and white; sound.

Smoke and Weather (director, writer, editor; National Film Board of Canada, Tom Daly). 1958. 16mm; 22 minutes; color; sound.

Stigma (editor; dir. Stanley Jackson; National Film Board of Canada, Tom Daly). 1958. 20 minutes; black and white; sound.

Trans-Canada Summer (editor, sound effects; dir. Ronald Dick, Jack Olsen, Jean Palardy; National Film Board of Canada, Tom Daly). 1958. 56 minutes; color; sound.

Emergency Ward (director, editor; National Film Board of Canada, Roman Kroitor, Wolf Koenig). 1959. 16mm; 29 minutes; black and white; sound.

Four Religions (director [4th segment on "Christianity"], editor; National Film Board of Canada, James Beveridge). 1960. 16mm; 59 minutes; black and white; sound.

Leadership Discipline: You Have Control (editor; dir. Donald Wilder; National Film Board of Canada). 1960. 16mm; 26 minutes; black and white; sound.

Cleared for Takeoff (producer, director; United Nations Television). 1963. 16mm; 28 minutes; black and white; sound.

Roads in the Sky (producer, director, editor; The Public Information Office, International Civil Aviation Organization). 1963. 16mm; 28 minutes; color; sound.

The First World Festival of Negro Arts (director, writer, cocinematographer with Georges Bracher, narrator; William Greaves Productions, Inc., for Motion Picture and Television Service of the United States Information Agency). 1966. 16mm; 40 minutes; black and white; sound.

Wealth of a Nation (producer, director, writer, editor, narrator; William Greaves Productions, Inc., for Motion Picture and Television Service of the United States Information Agency). 1966. 35mm; 21 minutes; black and white; sound.

Beauty and Fashions of the Women of Senegal (producer, director, writer, editor; William Greaves Productions, Inc., for Motion Picture and Television Service of the United States Information Agency). 1967. 16mm; 15 minutes; color; sound.†

Still a Brother: Inside the Negro Middle Class (coproducer with William B. Branch, director, editor, cinematographer; William Greaves Productions, Inc.). 1968. 16mm; 90 minutes; black and white; sound.

Black Journal (executive producer, episodes 3–24, cohost with Lou House [aka Wali Sadiq], episodes 1–24; dir. Stan Lathan; National Education Television [NET]). 1968–1970. Broadcast television; series of twenty-four 60-minute programs; color; sound.

In the Company of Men (Presented by Newsweek Magazine) (producer, director, cowriter with Jack Godler, editor; William Greaves Productions, Inc.). 1969. 16mm; 53 minutes; black and white; sound.

Choice of Destinies (producer, director, writer, editor; William Greaves Productions, Inc., WNBC New York). 1970. Broadcast television; 60 minutes; color; sound.†

The Job Interview (producer, director, writer, editor; William Greaves Productions, Inc., for United States Department of Labor). 1970. 16mm; 20 minutes; color; sound.†

On Liberty (director of one episode of a dramatic series; WGBH Boston). 1970. Broadcast television; 60 minutes; color; sound.†

Symbiopsychotaxiplasm: Take One (coproducer with Manuel Melamed, director, writer, editor, actor; William Greaves Productions, Inc.). Shot 1968; first edited version, 1971. 16mm; 70 minutes [revised to 74½ minutes, 1994]; color; sound.

The Fight of the Champions (producer, director, cinematographer, editor; William Greaves Productions, Inc., for Perenchio-Cook). 1971. Produced

immediately after first Ali/Frazier fight. 8mm (for home viewing); 20 minutes; color; sound.†
*To Free Their Minds (director, writer, narrator; William Greaves Productions, Inc., for Dillard University). 1971. 16mm; 34 minutes; color; sound.
The Fighters (producer, director, editor; William Greaves Productions, Inc., GUTS). 1972. 16mm; 93 minutes; color; sound [see Ali, the Fighter (1975) and The Fight (1991 premiere)].
On Merit (producer, director, writer, editor; William Greaves Productions, Inc., for United States Civil Service Commission). 1972. 16mm; 23 minutes; color; sound.
Struggle for Los Trabajos (producer, director, cinematographer, editor, writer; William Greaves Productions, Inc.). 1972. 16mm; 33 minutes; color; sound.
The Voice of La Raza (producer, director, cowriter with José García Torres, coeditor with John Dandre, cocinematographer with José García Torres; William Greaves Productions, Inc., for the Equal Employment Opportunity Commission). 1972. 16mm; 39 minutes; color; sound.
Childhood Schizophrenia (producer, director, writer, editor; William Greaves Productions, Inc., for Ittleson Foundation). 1973? 16mm; 20 minutes; black and white; sound.†
A Matter of Choice (producer, director, writer, editor; William Greaves Productions, Inc., for U.S. Department of Health, Education, and Welfare). 1973. 16mm; 30 minutes; color; sound.†
Nationtime—Gary (producer, director, cocinematographer with David Greaves, coeditor with David Greaves; William Greaves Production, Inc.). 1973. 16mm; 58 minutes; color; sound.
Power Versus the People: A Look at Job Discrimination in Houston (producer, director, editor; William Greaves Productions, Inc., for Equal Employment Opportunity Commission). 1973. 16mm; 37 minutes; color; sound.
Someone Who Cares (producer, director, writer, editor; William Greaves Productions, Inc., for United States Department of Labor—Job Corps). 1973. 16mm; 30 minutes; color; sound.†
EEOC Story: A Look at the Work of the Equal Employment Opportunity Commission (producer, director, writer, cinematographer; William Greaves Productions, Inc., for Equal Employment Opportunity Commission). 1974. 16mm; 35 minutes; color; sound.
Every Nigger Is a Star (cinematographer; producer, Lucien Chen; director, star, Calvin Lockhart). 1974. 16mm?; ? minutes; color; sound (film opened in Nassau, Bahamas, and Kingston, Jamaica, but was never in general release.)†

From These Roots: A Review of the Harlem Renaissance (producer, director, writer, coeditor with David Greaves; William Greaves Productions, Inc.). 1974. 16mm; 30 minutes; black and white; sound.

Whose Standard English? (cinematographer, editor; William Greaves Production, Inc., for Dillard University). 1974. 16mm; 16 minutes; color; sound.

You've Got a Number (producer, director; Williams Greaves Productions, Inc., for Social Security Administration). 1974. 16mm; black and white; sound.

Ali, the Fighter (2nd version of Ali/Frazier fight; producer, director, editor; William Greaves Productions, Inc., GUTS). 1975. 16mm; 87 minutes; color; sound [see *The Fighters* (1972) and *The Fight* (premiere 1991)].

A Nation of Visitors (producer, director, writer, editor; William Greaves Productions, Inc., for United States Information Agency). 1975. 16mm; 20 minutes; color; sound.†

Opportunities in Criminal Justice (producer, director, writer; William Greaves Productions, Inc., for National Urban League). 1975. 16mm; 35 minutes; color; sound.†

The Hard Way (producer, director, writer, editor; William Greaves Productions, Inc., for U.S. Department of Health, Education, and Welfare). 1976. 16mm; 25 minutes; color; sound.†

Just Doin' It: A Tale of Two Barbershops (producer, director, cowriter with Lou Potter, coeditor and cocinematographer with David Greaves; William Greaves Productions, Inc.). 1976. 16mm; 28 minutes; color; sound.

The Marijuana Affair (producer, director, editor, cowriter with Woody Robinson; William Greaves Productions, Inc., Lucien Chen, Film Productions Jamaica, Ltd.). 1976. 35mm; 90 minutes; color; sound.

In Search of Pancho Villa (producer, director, writer, editor; William Greaves Productions, Inc., Anthony Quinn). 1978. 16mm; 15 minutes; color; sound.

Where Dreams Come True (producer, director, writer, coeditor with Roger Wyatt; William Greaves Productions, Inc., for National Aeronautics and Space Administration. 1979. 16mm; 29 minutes; color; sound.

Your Housing Rights (producer, director, writer, editor; William Greaves Productions, Inc., for United States Housing and Urban Development). 1979. 16mm; 25 minutes; color; sound.†

*Gettin' to Know Me (director [episode 6 "A New Home" and episode 7 "Watusi's Wall of Respect"]; International Instructional Television Cooperative, Inc., MultiCultural Children's Television). 1980. 16mm; 30-minute episodes; color; sound.

Bustin' Loose (executive producer; dir. Oz Scott; Michael S. Glick). 1981. 35mm; 94 minutes; color; sound.

A Piece of the Pie (producer, director, writer, editor; William Greaves Productions, Inc., Exxon). 1981. 16mm; 30 minutes; color; sound.†

Space for Women (producer, director, writer; William Greaves Productions, Inc., for National Aeronautics and Space Administration). 1981. 16mm; 32 minutes; color; sound.

Booker T. Washington: The Life and the Legacy (coproducer with Billy Jackson, director; William Greaves Productions, Inc., for National Park Service). 1983. 16mm; 29 minutes; color; sound.

No Time for Privacy (producer, director; William Greaves Productions, Inc., for American Cancer Society). 1983. 16mm; 25 minutes; color; sound.

A Plan for All Seasons (producer, director, writer, editor; William Greaves Productions, Inc., for Social Security Administration). 1983. 16mm; 40 minutes; color; sound.

*Space for Security (producer, director, writer; William Greaves Productions, Inc., for National Aeronautics and Space Administration). 1983. 16mm; 30 minutes; color; sound.†

Fighter for Freedom: The Frederick Douglass Story (producer, director, cowriter with Lou Potter; William Greaves Productions, Inc., for National Park Service). 1985. 16mm; 19 minutes; color; sound [short, children's version of *Frederick Douglass: An American Life* (1985)].

Frederick Douglass: An American Life (coproducer with Dwight Williams and Louise Archambault, director, coeditor with Alonzo Speight, cowriter with Lou Potter; William Greaves Productions, Inc., for National Park Service). 1985. 16mm; 33 minutes; color; sound [included in the exhibit at the Frederick Douglass National Historic Site in Washington, D.C.].

Beyond the Forest (producer, director, writer, editor, narrator; William Greaves Productions, Inc., for Indian Red Cross). 1986. 16mm; 53 minutes; color; sound.

Black Power in America: Myth . . . or Reality? (coproducer with Louise Archambault, director, cowriter with Lou Potter, editor, narrator, interviewer, cinematographer; William Greaves Productions, Inc.). 1986. 16mm; 58 minutes; color; sound.

Golden Goa (producer, director, writer, editor, narrator; William Greaves Productions, Inc., for Government of India). 1986. 16mm; 45 minutes; color; sound.

On the Wings of Adversity (producer, director, writer, editor; William Greaves Productions, Inc., for National Center for Neighborhood Enterprises). 1986. Video; 30 minutes; color; sound.

Take the Time (producer, director, writer, editor; William Greaves Productions, Inc., for American Cancer Society). 1987. 16mm; 18 minutes; color; sound.

The Best of Black Journal (cohost with Lou House [aka Wali Sadiq], executive producer; dir. Robert Wagoner ["Culture in the South"], St. Clair Bourne ["Black Dance"], Kent Garrett ["Modern and African Art"], Horace Jenkins ["Black Beauties and Hairstyles"], Madeleine Anderson ["Malcolm X"]; National Education Television [NET]). 1988. 56 minutes, five program segments from NET's *Black Journal* (1968–1970); color; sound.

The Deep North (producer, director, editor; William Greaves Productions, Inc., WCBS, New York City). 1988. 16mm; 52 minutes; color; sound.

Ida B. Wells: A Passion for Justice (coproducer with Louise Archambault, director, writer; William Greaves Productions, Inc.). 1989. 16mm; 55 minutes; color; sound.

That's Black Entertainment (host, codirector with G. William Jones; Skyline Entertainment). 1989. Video; 58 minutes; color and black and white; sound.

Memories of the Group Theater (producer, director; William Greaves Productions, Inc., for the Actors Studio, New York). ca. 1990. 8 minutes; black and white; sound.

"Resurrections: Paul Robeson." (Pilot for a Black Entertainment Television series, not produced). 1990.

A Tribute to Jackie Robinson (producer, director; William Greaves Productions, Inc., for Jackie Robinson Foundation). 1990. Video; 18 minutes; color; sound.†

The Fight (producer, director, editor; William Greaves Productions, Inc., GUTS). 1991 (premiere at Brooklyn Museum). 16mm; 126 minutes; color; sound [see *The Fighter* (1972) and *Ali, the Fighter* (1975)].

Spencer Williams: Remembrances of an Early Black Film Pioneer (narrator; dir. Walid Khaldi; Walid Khaldi). 1995. Video; 57 minutes; color and black and white; sound.

Cinéma Vérité: Defining the Moment (interviewee; dir. Peter Wintonick; National Film Board of Canada, Eric Michel, Adam Symansky). 1999. 35mm; 193 minutes; color and black and white; sound.

Paul Robeson: Here I Stand (interviewee; dir. St. Clair Bourne). 1999. Television: American Masters Series.

Ralph Bunche: An American Odyssey (executive producer, director, cowriter with Leslie E. Lee, supervising editor; William Greaves Productions, Inc., Louise Archambault). 2001. 35mm; 117 minutes; color and black and white; sound.

Television in America: An Autobiography (episode 8 "William Greaves": interview recorded December 16, 2002; Independent Production Fund). 2002. Episode of television series; 57 minutes; color and black and white; sound.

Ralph Bunche: The Odyssey Continues (director, executive producer, supervising editor; William Greaves Productions, Inc., Louise Archambault). 2003. Digital (twelve video modules of differing lengths); 448 mins; color and black and white; sound.

Symbiopsychotaxiplasm: Take 2½ (coproducer with Louise Archambault, director, supervising editor). 2005. Digital; 99 minutes; color; sound.

Discovering William Greaves (interviewee; two-disk set produced by Debra McClutchy, Criterion Collection). 2006. Digital; 61 minutes; color; sound.

Our Paul: Remembering Paul Robeson (interviewee; Criterion Collection). 2007. Digital; 19 minutes; color; sound.

Blacklist: Recovering the Life of Canada Lee (interviewee; dir. Kenny Kilfara, Tim Nackashi; Kenny Kilfara, Tim Nackashi, Jonathan Skurnik). 2008. Format unknown; ? minutes; color; sound.

Bibliography

RESEARCHED AND ASSEMBLED BY AURORE SPIERS

This bibliography lists the major writings about and by William Greaves published in books, journals, newspapers, and popular magazines during his lifetime and after his death in 2014. Access to pdfs of many of these writings is available at the Greaves website, www.williamgreaves.com.

The bibliography focuses primarily on the United States, where Greaves has received the most critical attention. We have included several reviews of Greaves's films, but more may be found by searching for individual film titles in national and local newspapers contemporary with those films' releases. Essays, articles, and interviews published for the first time in this volume are not listed.

BOOKS AND JOURNALS

Alexander, George. "William Greaves." In *Why We Make Movies: Black Filmmakers Talk About the Magic of Cinema*, 28–45. New York: Harlem Moon, 2003.

Bahn-Coblans, Sonja, and Arno Heller. *William Greaves:* Just Doin' It *(1976): An Analysis*; Studien zum amerikanischen Dokumentarfilm, Bd. 7. Göttingen: WVT Wissenschaftlicher Verlag Trier, 1997.

"The BFC/A Announces the New William Greaves Collection." *Black Camera* 18, no. 2 (Fall/Winter 2003): 7–11.

Bourne, St. Clair. "Breaking Through at *Black Journal*." *Black Renaissance Noire* 4, no. 2/3 (Summer/Fall 2002): 83–90.

———. "Career Achievement Award: An Independent for All Seasons: William Greaves." International Documentary Association (January 2005). http://www.documentary.org/magazine/career-achievement-award-independent-all-seasons-william-greaves.

Boyd, Melba Joyce. "Canon Configuration for Ida B. Wells-Barnett." *Black Scholar* 24, no. 1 (Winter 1994): 8–13.

Cason, Franklin, Jr., and Tsitsi Jaji. "Symbiopsychotaxiplasticity: Some Takes on William Greaves." *Cultural Studies* 28, no. 4 (March 2014): 574–93. Reprinted as chapter 31 in this volume.

Colvin, J. Brandon. "Explaining Varda's *Lions Love*: A European Director Responds to an American Cultural Marketplace." *Studies in French Cinema* 16, no. 1 (2016): 19–31.

Cowans, Jon. "Black-White Couples and Internal Decolonization." In *Empire Films and the Crisis of Colonialism, 1946–1959*, 289–333. Baltimore: Johns Hopkins University Press, 2015.

Eastman, Kay, and Brenna Sanchez. "Greaves, Willam 1926–2014." In *Contemporary Black Biography* 123, ed. Margaret Mazurkiewicz, 66–69. Farmington Hills, Mich.: Gale, 2015.

Ellis, Jack C., and Betsy A. McLane. *A New History of Documentary Film*, 271–73. New York: Continuum, 2005.

Enelow, Shonni. *Method Acting and Its Discontents: On American Psycho-Drama*, 103–22. Evanston, Ill.: Northwestern University Press, 2015.

Euvrard, Janine. "William Greaves." In *Le Cinéma noir américain*, ed. Mark Reid et al., 151–54. Paris: CinemAction/Cerf, 1988.

Geiger, Jeffrey. "'Uncontrolled' Situations: Direct Cinema." In *American Documentary Film: Projecting the Nation*, 154–85. Edinburgh: Edinburgh University Press, 2011.

Gottlieb, Akiva. "'Just Another Word for Jazz': The Signifying Auteur in William Greaves's *Symbiopsychotaxiplasm: Take One*." *Black Camera* 5, no. 1 (Fall 2013): 164–83. Excerpt reprinted as chapter 23 in this volume.

Griffis, Noelle. "'This Film Is a Rebellion!': Filmmaker, Actor, *Black Journal* Producer, and Political Activist William Greaves (1926–2014)." *Black Camera* 6, no. 2 (Spring 2015): 7–16.

Heitner, Devorah. *Black Power TV*. Durham, N.C.: Duke University Press, 2013.

——. "'Regular Television Put to Shame by Negro Production': Picturing a Black World on *Black Journal*." In *Watching While Black: Centering the Television of Black Audiences*, ed. Beretta E. Smith-Shomade, 77–88. New Brunswick, N.J.: Rutgers University Press, 2012.

Holloway, Jonathan Scott. "The Black Body as Archive of Memory." In *Jim Crow Wisdom: Memory and Identity in Black America Since 1940*, 67–101. Chapel Hill, N.C.: University of North Carolina Press, 2013.

Jaji, Tsitsi. "Negritude Musicology: Poetry, Performance, and Statecraft in Senegal." In *Africa in Stereo: Modernism, Music, and Pan-African Solidarity*, 66–110. Oxford: Oxford University Press, 2014.

James, Erica Moiah. "*Every Nigger Is a Star*: Reimagining Blackness from Post–Civil Rights America to the Postindependence Caribbean." *Black Camera* 8, no. 1 (Fall 2016): 55–83.

Knee, Adam. "*Symbiopsychotaxiplasm: Take One*: Film History Revised." *Sightlines* 25, no. 4 (Fall 1992): 10–12.

Knee, Adam, and Charles Musser. "William Greaves, Documentary Film-Making, and the African-American Experience." *Film Quarterly* 45, no. 3 (Spring 1992): 13–25. Reprinted as chapter 1 in this volume.

Linscott, Charles "Chip" P. "In a (Not So) Silent Way: Listening Past Black Visuality in *Symbiopsychotaxiplasm*." *Black Camera* 8, no. 1 (Fall 2016): 169–90.

MacDonald, Scott. "The Country in the City." In *The Garden in the Machine: A Field Guide to Independent Films About Place*, 223–46. Berkeley: University of California Press, 2001. Revised version included as chapter 22 in this volume.

——. "Desegregating Film History." In *Adventures of Perception: Cinema as Exploration (Essays/Interviews)*, 23–34. Berkeley: University of California Press, 2009.

——. "Film Production as Ethnic Utopia." In *Adventures of Perception: Cinema as Exploration (Essays/Interviews)*, 43–51. Berkeley: University of California Press, 2009.

——. "William Greaves." Interview in *A Critical Cinema 3: Interviews with Independent Filmmakers*, 41–63. Berkeley: University of California Press, 1998.

——, ed. "William Greaves." In *Screen Writings: Scripts and Texts by Independent Filmmakers*, 31–48. Berkeley: University of California Press, 1995. Includes "*Symbiopsychotaxiplasm: Take One*: Director's Early Notes Prior to and During Production in the Spring of 1968," transcript of an excerpt from *Symbiopsychotaxiplasm: Take One*, and "Program Notes for *Symbiopsychotaxiplasm: Take One*."

Martin, Michael T. "Madeline Anderson in Conversation: Pioneering an African American Documentary Tradition." *Black Camera* 5, no. 1 (Fall 2013). Comments on *Black Journal* and Greaves, 82–86.

McClain, P. "*Ralph Bunche: An American Odyssey*, Produced by William Greaves; *Citizen King*, Produced by Orlando Bagwell and W. Noland Walker." *Political Communication* 24, no. 4 (2007): 489–91.

McMurry, Linda O. "*Ida B. Wells: A Passion for Justice* by William Greaves and Louise Archambault." *Journal of American History* 79, no. 3 (1992): 1275–76.

Murphy, David. "Dakar 66: Chronicles of a Pan-African Festival." *African Arts* 50, no. 1 (Spring 2017): 80–82.

———. *The First World Festival of Negro Arts, Dakar 1966*. Liverpool: Liverpool University Press, 2016, 1–42, 121–23.

Murphy, J. J. "Human Life Isn't Necessarily Well-Written: William Greaves's *Symbiopsychotaxiplasm: Take One* and *Take 2½*." In *Rewriting Indie Cinema: Improvisation, Psychodrama, and the Screenplay*, chap. 5. New York: Columbia University Press, 2019.

Murray, James P. "William Greaves: Documentaries Are Not Dead." *Black Creation* 4, no. 1 (Fall 1972): 10–11.

Otfinoski, Steven. "Greaves, William." In *African Americans in the Visual Arts*, 88–90. New York: Facts on File, 2011.

"The Political Documentary in America Today [Comments by Michael Renov, David Walsh, Paula Rabinowitz, Thom Andersen, Philippe Diaz, Debra Zimmerman, Karen Cooper, William Greaves, Clinton McClung, and Jon Miller]." *Cineaste* 30, no. 3 (Summer 2005): 29–36.

Reid, Mark A. "Male-Directed New Black Independent Cinema." In *Redefining Black Film*, 125–36. Berkeley: University of California Press, 1993.

San Filippo, Maria. "What a Long, Strange Trip It's Been: William Greaves' 'Symbiopsychotaxiplasm: Take One.'" *Film History* 13, no. 2 (2001): 216–25.

Wofford, Tobias. "Diasporic Returns in the Jet Age: The First World Festival of Negro Arts and the Promise of Air Travel." *Interventions* 20, no. 7 (2018): 2–3.

———. "Jets and Modernity in William Greaves's *First World Festival of Negro Arts*." *Interventions* 20, no. 7 (2018): 7–13.

Young, Vershawn Ashanti. "Introduction: Performing Citizenship." In *From Bourgeois to Boojie: Black Middle-Class Performances*, 1–38. Detroit: Wayne State University Press, 2011.

Zimmermann, Patricia R., and Scott MacDonald. "1991 William Greaves—on *Symbiopsychotaxiplasm: Take One* (1971)." In *The Flaherty: Decades in the Cause of Independent Cinema*, 226–30. Bloomington: Indiana University Press, 2017. Edited discussion of the film at the Robert Flaherty Film Seminar.

NEWSPAPERS, POPULAR MAGAZINES, SYMPOSIUM BROCHURES, AND DVD FEATURES

Atkinson, Michael. "'Symbiopsychotaxiplasm: Take One.'" *Village Voice*, October 18, 2005. http://www.villagevoice.com/film/symbiopsychotaxiplasm-take-one-6401521.

A. W. "Movie Review: The Screen [*Miracle in Harlem*]." *New York Times*, October 24, 1949.

Backström, Fia, and Martine Syms. "William Greaves: Psychodrama, Interruption, and Circulation." Brochure for symposium held at Princeton University, February 21, 2020. Includes writings by Backström and Syms, Jared Sexton, Aria Dean, and Devorah Heitner.

Baltimore Afro-American. "Calvin Lockhart in New Jamaican Film," January 28, 1975.

Black Film Center/Archive. "The BFC/A Announces the New William Greaves Collection." *Black Camera* 18, no. 2 (Fall/Winter 2003): 7, 11.

"Black Filmmaker Gets Atlanta Festival Award." *Milwaukee Star*, July 17, 1971.

Bourne, St. Clair. "*Black Journal*: A Personal Look Backward." Independent Documentary Association, April 1, 1989. https://www.documentary.org/feature/black-journal-personal-look-backward. Reprinted as chapter 14 in this volume.

Boyd, Melba Joyce. "Reviewed Works: *Ida B. Wells: A Passion for Justice* by William Greaves; *Ida B. Wells-Barnett: An Exploratory Study of an American Black Woman, 1893–1930* by Mildred I. Thompson; *The Selected Works of Ida B. Wells* by Trudier Harris and Ida B. Wells." *NWSA Journal* 6, no. 1 (Spring 1994): 133–37.

Brody, Richard. "The Daring, Original, *and* Overlooked: *Symbiopsychotaxiplasm: Take One*." *New Yorker*, February 5, 2015. Reprinted as chapter 28 in this volume.

———. "The Muhammad Ali Documentary That Gets to the Existential Heart of Boxing." *New Yorker*, June 13, 2016. https://www.newyorker.com/culture/richard-brody/the-muhammad-ali-documentary-that-gets-to-the-existential-heart-of-boxing.

Bui, Camille. "Symbiopsychotaxiplasm: Take One." *Cahiers du Cinéma* 738 (November 2017): 19.

Campbell, Howard. "Dudley, the Actor: Former Statesman Remembered for Role in Marijuana Affair." *Jamaica Observer*, January 25, 2012. http://www.jamaicaobserver.com/entertainment/DUDLEY-THE-ACTOR_10630715.

Canby, Vincent. "The Screen: Ali-Frazier Bout Is Star of 'The Fighters.'" *New York Times*, January 5, 1974.

Clark, Ramsey. "Journal Gets NATRA Award." *Milwaukee Star*, September 13, 1969.

Chicago Metro News. "From These Roots," September 27, 1975.

Collins, Glenn. "Celebrating the Memory and Art of Paul Robeson." *New York Times*, October 30, 1988.

Crowther, Bosley. "'Lost Boundaries', Racial Study with Mel Ferrer in Lead, New Feature at Astor." *New York Times*, July 1, 1949.

Dallos, Robert E. "11 Negro Staff Members Quit N.E.T. 'Black Journal' Program." *New York Times*, August 21, 1968.

———. "Negro Middle Class 'Revolution' Subject of Negro-Made TV Show." *New York Times*, April 26, 1968.

Di Chiara, Jacqueline. "The Story of Ralph Bunche Through William Greaves." *AIM: America's Intercultural Magazine* 31, no. 2 (2004): 46–48.

Euvrard, J. "William Greaves: 'Les Etats-Unis, c'était presque l'Afrique du Sud. Les choses ont beaucoupé changé.'" *CinémAction* 46 (January 1988): 46.

Gaspard, John. "William Greaves and Steven Soderbergh on *Symbiopsychotaxiplasm*." *Fast, Cheap Movie Thoughts*, May 6, 2010. http://fastcheapmoviethoughts.blogspot.com/2010/05/william-greaves-and-steven-soderbergh.html, no longer accessible.

Goodman, Walter. "Profile of an Early Traveler on the Road to Civil Rights." *New York Times*, December 19, 1989.

Gould, Jack. "TV Review: N.E.T. Program Views Negro Middle Class." *New York Times*, April 30, 1968.

Greater Milwaukee Star. "It Ain't Easy. Black Film Directors Face Near Impossible Task," August 29, 1970.

Harris, Brandon. "The Essential Black Independents." Fandor.com, August 12, 2014. https://www.fandor.com/keyframe/the-essential-black-independents?utm_medium=spotlight_articles&utm_source=fandor.

Harvey, Dennis. "Sundance Reviews [*Ralph Bunche: An American Odyssey*]." *Daily Variety* 270, no. 51 (February 12, 2001): 12, 19.

Hatch, James. "William Greaves: Filmmaker." *Artist and Influence* 9 (1990): 54–81.

Hubert, Craig. "The Revolution Was Televised: On the Legacy of *Black Journal*." *BlouinArtInfo*, February 11, 2015, 1–5.

Hudson, David. "William Greaves, 1926–2014." Fandor.com, August 27, 2014. https://www.fandor.com/keyframe/daily-william-greaves-1926-2014?utm_medium=spotlight_articles&utm_source=fandor.

Indianapolis Recorder. "'The Marijuana Affair' Now Ready for Release," October 4, 1975.
Italie, Hillel. "Prolific Producer of a Variety of Films." *Washington Post,* August 28, 2014.
Jimenez, Lillian. "Profile: William Greaves." *Independent* 3, no. 10 (October 1980): 8–11.
Koresky, Michael. "Man with a Plan: William Greaves in *Symbiopsychotaxiplasm Take One.*" Criterion .com, February 5, 2014. https://www.criterion.com/current/posts/3001-man-with-a-plan-william-greaves-in-symbiopsychotaxiplasm-take-one.
Lee, Nathan. "High 60s Groove." *New York Sun,* October 26, 2005. http://www.nysun.com/arts/high-60s-groove/22062.
Lee, Rohama. "The Whirlwind World of William Greaves." *American Cinematographer* 66, no. 8 (1985): 68–72.
Martin, Marcel. "Portraits de cinéastes: la carrière exemplaire de William Greaves." *Image et Son* 363 (July–August 1981): 89–91.
McClutchy, Debra. *Discovering William Greaves.* DVD, Disc 1, *Symbiopsychotaxiplasm: Two Takes by William Greaves.* Irvington, N.Y.: Criterion Collection, 2006.
Milwaukee Star. "New Bill Greaves Film," July 13, 1972.
Murray, Noel. "William Greaves (1926–2014): Experimental Filmmaker and Documentarian." *Dissolve,* August 27, 2014. http://thedissolve.com/news/3079-william-greaves-1926-2014-experimental-filmmaker-a/.
New York Times. "Still a Brother," April 28, 1968.
Nichols, Lewis. "The Play: Uptown Jason." *New York Times,* March 10, 1945.
Plain Dealer (Cleveland). "Cinderella Dream Story Comes True for Philadelphia Girl," February 14, 1947.
———. "Composer of 'African Lullaby,'" September 25, 1953.
Reggae Films UK. "The Marijuana Affair (1975)—Coming Soon...," October 13, 2008. http://reggaefilms.blogspot.com/2008/10/marijuana-affair-1975-coming-soon.html.
Romney, Jonathan. "Sign of the Times: William Greaves's Symbiopsychotaxiplasms." *Modern Painters* (December 2005/January 2006): 44–47.
San Filippo, Maria. "Symbiopsychotaxiplasm: Take One and Take 2½." *Cineaste* 31, no. 2 (Spring 2006): 48–49.
———. "What a Long, Strange Trip It's Been: William Greaves' *Symbiopsychotaxiplasm Take One.*" *Senses of Cinema* (February 2001). http://sensesofcinema.com/2001/overlooked-underrated/symbio/.
Scott, A. O. "Peeling Back the Layers of Black Indie Film." *New York Times,* February 6, 2015, C1, C18.
Taubin, Amy. "Still No Answers." In booklet accompanying Criterion DVD release of *Symbiopsychotaxiplasm: Take One* and *Symbiopsychotaxiplasm: Take 2½* in 2006. Reprinted as chapter 29 in this volume.
Topeka Post-Review. "Film Makers Tell How They Broke Racial Barrier," November 24, 1970.
Toronto Star. "Filmmaker Spent Time at NFB," August 28, 2014.
Warren, Freda. "Ralph Bunche Reconsidered: An Interview with William Greaves." *Cineaste* 2 (2001): 35–37.
Watkins, Mel. "William Greaves, a Documentarian and Pioneering Journalist, Dies at 87." *New York Times,* August 27, 2014.
Weekend All Things Considered. "Profile: Story of 'Symbiopsychotaxiplasm, Take One,' a Legendary Underground Film Made in 1968, as Its Sequel Is to Be Screened at This Year's Sundance Film Festival," January 23, 2005. http://go.galegroup.com.proxy.uchicago.edu/ps/i.do?p=LitRC&sw=w&u=chic_rbw&v=2.1&it=r&id=GALE|A161908669&asid=31d62db930f5b9b9501769c336cbe596.
"William Greaves Receives 2012 Paul Robeson Award." *Equity News* 97, no. 8 (October/November 2012): 5.
"William Greaves/*Symbiopsychotaxiplasm: Take One* (1968)/August 8, 1991." *Wide Angle* 13, nos. 1–4 (1995): 128–34.

BY WILLIAM GREAVES

Greaves, William. "*Black Journal*: A Few Notes from the Executive Producer." *Television Quarterly* 8, no. 4 (Fall 1969): 66–72. Reprinted as chapter 12 in this volume.

———. "Discussion of *Symbiopsychotaxiplasm: Take One*," Robert Flaherty Film Seminar, 1991. In *The Flaherty: Decades in the Cause of Independent Cinema*, ed. Scott MacDonald and Patricia R. Zimmermann, 226–30. Bloomington: Indiana University Press, 2017.

———. "The First World Festival of Negro Arts: An Afro-American View." *The Crisis* 73, no. 6 (June–July 1966): 309–14, 332. Reprinted as chapter 7 in this volume.

———. "Log: *In the Company of Men*." *Film Library Quarterly* 3, no. 1 (Winter 1969–70): 29–34.

———. "100 Madison Avenues Will Be of No Help." *New York Times*, August 9, 1970. Reprinted as chapter 13 in this volume.

———. "*Symbiopsychotaxiplasm: Take One*: Director's Early Notes Prior to and During Production in the Spring of 1968." In *Screen Writings: Scripts and Texts by Independent Filmmakers*, ed. Scott MacDonald, 31–48. Berkeley: University of California Press, 1995. Transcript of excerpt from *Symbiopsychotaxiplasm: Take One* and "Program Notes for *Symbiopsychotaxiplasm: Take One*."

———. "Two Fighters on Film." *African American Review* 50, no. 4 (Winter 2017): 587–89.

Contributors

ST. CLAIR BOURNE (1943–2007) was a filmmaker whose filmmaking career began at *Black Journal*, during William Greaves's executive directorship; his films include *Malcolm X Liberation University: Black Journal* (1969); *Let the Church Say Amen!* (1974); *In Motion: Amiri Baraka* (1983); *Langston Hughes: The Dream Keeper* (1986, 1988); *Making* Do the Right Thing (1989); *Paul Robeson: Here I Stand* (1999); *John Henrik Clarke: A Great and Mighty Walk* (1996); and *Half Past Autumn* (2000).

RICHARD BRODY has written film reviews for the *New Yorker* since 1999 and has been the movie-listings editor at the magazine since 2005. In 2009 he published *Everything Is Cinema: The Working Life of Jean-Luc Godard* (Henry Holt). In December 2014 he was made a Chevalier Knight in the Ordre des Arts et des Lettres for his contributions in popularizing French cinema in America.

FRANKLIN CASON, JR., was visiting professor at the Franklin Humanities Institute at Duke University (2019–2020) and is an assistant professor in the Department of English at North Carolina State University. He earned an M.F.A. degree from the School of the Art Institute of Chicago and a PhD degree from the University of Florida. His research explores aesthetics and pragmatism in African-American cinema.

MICHELLE DUSTER teaches at Columbia College Chicago. She cowrote/edited (with Bernard C. Turner) the children's history book *Tate and His Historic Dream* (Highlights of Chicago Press, 2014), edited *Ida in Her Own Words: The Timeless Writings of Ida B. Wells* (Benjamin Williams, 2008), wrote/edited *Ida from Abroad* (Benjamin Williams, 2010), and was a co-editor of *Michelle Obama's Impact on African American Women and Girls* (Palgrave Macmillan, 2018).

AKIVA GOTTLIEB is a freelance writer who has contributed articles and reviews to the *Nation, Los Angeles Review of Books, Variety, Los Angeles Times, Audible Range, Slant,* and many other publications. He was a managing editor of *Documentary* magazine from 2016 to 2018.

JOAN HAWKINS is associate professor of cinema and media studies at Indiana University-Bloomington. She has written extensively on horror and experimental film. Her books include *Cutting Edge: Art Horror and the Horrific Avant-garde* (University of Minnesota Press, 2000); *Downtown Film and TV Culture 1975–2001* (Intellect/Chicago, 2015); and *William S. Burroughs Cutting Up the Century,* co-edited with Alex Wermer-Colan (Indiana University Press, 2019). With Charles Cannon and Christopher Dumas, she is currently editing a two-volume anthology on 1968.

TSITSI JAJI is associate professor of English and African & African American studies at Duke University. She earned a PhD degree in comparative literature from Cornell University. She is the author of *Africa in Stereo: Music, Modernism, and Pan-African Solidarity* (Oxford University Press, 2014), which features Greaves's film *The First World Festival of Negro Arts,* and has published two poetry collections, *Beating the Graves* (2017) and *Mother Tongues* (2019).

ALEXANDER JOHNSTON is assistant professor of film at Seattle University. He does research and creative work examining the politics and aesthetics of documentary and new media practices. His scholarship has been published in the *Journal of Sport and Social Issues* and *INCITE Journal of Experimental Media.* His films and GIF cycles, including *NOW! AGAIN!* (2014), *Ra*ist President* (2016), and *Evidence of the Evidence* (2017), have screened at the Berlinale, IndieLisboa, the Walker Art Center, and San Francisco's Other Cinema.

KATHERINE KINNEY, associate professor at the University of California, Riverside, teaches twentieth-century American literature and film. The author of *Friendly Fire: American Images of the Vietnam War* (Oxford University Press, 2000), she is currently writing a book on film acting in 1960s film. She has articles forthcoming on Black actors and direct address in the *Journal of Cinema and Media Studies* and on Beat film for an MLA volume on teaching Beat

Generation literature. Other recent articles include "The Haunting of Don Draper," *Pacific Coast Philology* (2014), and "The Resonance of Brando's Voice," *Postmodern Culture* (2014).

ADAM KNEE is dean of the Faculty of Fine Arts, Media & Creative Industries at Singapore's Lasalle College of the Arts. Prior to this, he held appointments at the University of Nottingham Ningbo China (where he was head of the School of International Communications and professor of film and media studies), Nanyang Technological University (Singapore), and Ohio University (United States). He has published widely on topics pertaining to U.S. and Asian popular cinemas.

SHOLA LYNCH oversees the collections of motion pictures, video recordings, music, and spoken-arts recordings at the Schomburg Center for Research in Black Culture. Her films include the feature documentary *Free Angela and All Political Prisoners* (2013) and the Peabody Award–winning *Chisholm '72—Unbought & Unbossed* (2004). Lynch earned an M.A. degree in American history and public history management from the University of California, Riverside, and an M.A. in journalism from Columbia University. In her youth she was an Olympic-caliber athlete. At the age of two she began acting on the children's series *Sesame Street* and did so until she was six.

SCOTT MACDONALD has published eighteen books on independent cinema; most recently *Avant-Doc, Intersections of Documentary and Avant-Garde Cinema* (Oxford, 2014); *Binghamton Babylon: Voices from the Cinema Department, 1967–1977 (a nonfiction novel)* (SUNY Press, 2015); *The Flaherty: Decades in the Cause of Independent Cinema*, with Patricia R. Zimmermann (Indiana University Press, 2017); and *The Sublimity of Document: Cinema as Diorama (Avant-Doc 2)* (Oxford University Press, 2019). He teaches at Hamilton College and directs the F.I.L.M. Series.

DARA MEYERS-KINGSLEY was the first film and video curator for the Brooklyn Museum, starting her job there in 1988 and staying until 1993, when she became director of the Film and Video Collections at the Andy Warhol Foundation. She is currently director of the Office of the Arts and of the Muse Scholar Program at Hunter College, CUNY. She has curated exhibitions at the Museum of Contemporary Art, Los Angeles (MOCA), the Museum of Contemporary Art in Chicago, the Andy Warhol Museum, the Center for Jewish History, and other art venues.

CELESTE DAY MOORE is assistant professor of history at Hamilton College. She received her PhD degree from the University of Chicago. She has been a fellow at the Institut d'Études Politiques in Paris and the Carter G. Woodson Institute for African-American and African Studies at the University of Virginia. She is author of *Soundscapes of Liberation: African-American Music in Postwar France* (Duke University Press, 2021).

J. J. MURPHY is an accomplished filmmaker (*Sky Blue Water Light Sign*, 1972; *Print Generation*, 1974; *Horicon*, 1994) and author of *Me and You and* Memento *and* Fargo*: How Independent Screenplays Work* (Continuum, 2007); *The Black Hole of the Camera: The Films of Andy Warhol* (University of California Press, 2012); and *Rewriting Indy Cinema: Improvisation, Psychodrama, and the Screenplay* (Columbia University Press, 2019). Murphy retired as Hamel Family Distinguished Chair in Communication Arts at the University of Wisconsin-Madison in 2019.

CHARLES MUSSER is professor of American studies, film & media studies and theater studies at Yale University and a leading scholar of early cinema. His *Before the Nickelodeon: Edwin S. Porter and the Edison Manufacturing Company* (University of California Press, 1991) is a classic in the field. With Pearl Bowser and Jane Gaines, he co-edited *Oscar Micheaux and His Circle: African American Filmmaking and Race Cinema of the Silent Era* (Indiana University Press, 2001). With Jacqueline Najuma Stewart, he curated *Pioneers of African-American Cinema* (2016), a five-DVD box set for Kino Lorber.

LAURA ISABEL SERNA is associate professor in the Critical Studies Department in the Division of Cinema and Media Studies at the University of Southern California. She has published essays on a range of topics in Mexican film culture during the silent era and is the author of *Making Cinelandia: American Films and Mexican Film Culture* (Duke University Press, 2014). Her edited collections include *Silent Cinema and the Politics of Space* (2014) and *Land of Necessity: Consumer Culture in the U.S.-Mexico Borderlands* (2010).

AURORE SPIERS is a PhD degree candidate in the Department of Cinema and Media Studies at the University of Chicago. Since 2015 she has been an editorial contributor to the Women Film Pioneers Project, edited by Monica Dall'Asta, Jane Gaines, and Radha Vatsal and published by the Columbia University Libraries online.

CONTRIBUTORS

JACQUELINE NAJUMA STEWART is professor in the Department of Cinema and Media Studies at the University of Chicago and chief artistic and programming officer at the Academy Museum of Motion Pictures. She is author of *Migrating to the Movies* (University of California Press, 2005) and co-editor of *L.A. Rebellion: Creating a New Black Cinema* (University of California Press, 2015). With Charles Musser, she curated the DVD collection *Pioneers of African-American Cinema* (2016) for Kino Lorber. She is the host of *Silent Sunday Nights* on Turner Classic Movies.

AMY TAUBIN is a contributing editor for *Sight & Sound* and *Film Comment*. A long-time critic, she has written for the *Village Voice*, *Millennium Film Journal*, *Artforum*, and other journals—often on independent cinema and video. Her *Taxi Driver* (2000) is part of the BFI Classics series. From 1983 to 1988 she was curator of video at The Kitchen in New York City. She has appeared in several films, including Michael Snow's *Wavelength* (1967) and Yvonne Rainer's *Journeys from Berlin/1971* (1980).

JOSEPH UNDERWOOD is assistant professor of art history at Kent State University and an active curator. With Tameka Ellington, he curated "TEXTURES: The History and Art of Black Hair," for Kent State University Museum, September 2020–May 2021; "The View from Here: Contemporary Perspectives from Senegal," which premiered at the 2018 Dakar Biennale and toured other venues; as well as other shows. He has written frequently for *African Arts*.

PATRICIA R. ZIMMERMANN is professor of screen studies in the Roy H. Park School of Communications at Ithaca College and codirector of the Finger Lakes Environmental Film Festival (FLEFF). She is author of *Reel Families: A Social History of Amateur Film* (Indiana University Press, 1995); *States of Emergency: Documentaries, Wars, Democracies* (University of Minnesota Press, 2000); *Thinking Through Digital Media: Transnational Environments and Locative Places* (Palgrave, 2015, with Dale Hudson); *Open Spaces: Openings, Closings, and Thresholds of Independent Public Media* (St. Andrews Press, 2016); and, with Scott MacDonald, *The Flaherty: Decades in the Cause of Independent Cinema* (Indiana University Press, 2017).

Index

abortion: as metaphor for Vietnam War, 57; in *Symbiopsychotaxiplasm: Take One*, 56, 327, 329, 352, 354, 358, 369–71
Academy of Motion Picture Arts and Sciences, xxx
acting: L. Greaves and, 96–97, 127; W. Greaves on, 114–15, 129–33; W. Greaves's acting workshops and, 44–46, 96, *97*, 114–15, 126–28, *126*; W. Greaves's early film roles and, xvii, 2–3, 31–39, *38*, 122–23, 414, 418; W. Greaves's relationship with Actors Studio and, xvii, 3, 120–21, *121–22*, 123–24, 128–33; W. Greaves's theater roles and, 2–3, 26–31, *27*, *30*, 39–40, 115–22, *116*, *118*, 274
Actor Prepares, An (Stanislavsky), 190. See also Stanislavsky Method
Actors Studio: *Baby Doll* (Elia Kazan, 1956) and, 356; Black actors in, 120; Greaves and, xvii, 3, 35–36, 40, 120–21, *121–22*, 123–24, 128–33, 357, 364; history and teachers at, 123–24; *Lamp Unto My Feet* and, 120–21, *121–22*; Method acting and, 96, 364; psychodrama and, 292
Adair, Peter: *Word Is Out: Stories of Some of Our Lives* (1977), 266
Adam Smith's Money World (television program, 1984–1997), 8
Adler, Lou, 285
Advocates, The (television program), 266
African Academy of Arts and Research, 25–26, 274
African dance, xvii, 2, 25–26, 115, 143–44, 274
"African Lullaby" (Greaves), *xxviii*
Africans, The (television series, 1986), 266

Agui Carter, Maria, 63
Ailey, Alvin, 143–44, 148, 154
Albee, Edward, 327, 357, 369–70
Albuquerque Journal (newspaper), 285
Alcindor, Lewis, Jr. (later Kareem Abdul Jabbar), 178
Aldridge, Cathy, 171, 175
Alexander, George, 19, 81–82, 91, 92–94
Alexander, Ron, 42
Alexander, William, xxii, 15, 31–32, 35, 39, 101
Ali, Muhammad, xx, 417. See also *Fight of the Century* (1971)
Ali, the Fighter (William Greaves, 1975), 12, 67–68, 208
Ali, the Man (Rick Baxter, 1975), 208
Alinsky, Saul, 48
All My Babies: A Midwife's Own Story (George Stoney, 1953), xix, 44
Allen, Richard, 177
Alvarez, Santiago, 260
Alvin Ailey Company, 143–44, 148, 154
American Civil Liberties Union (ACLU), 259–60
American National Theatre and Academy (ANTA), 119
American Negro Theatre (ANT): Greaves and, 2–3, 26–29, 115–19, *116*, 120, 274; Hughes and, 50; Poitier and, 117–18; Schomburg Center for Research in Black Culture and, 414
American Society of African Culture (AMSAC), 152, 156, 282n14
Amsterdam News (newspaper), 128, 171, 175

Anchor Bay, 208
Anderson, Lindsay: *Every Day Except Christmas* (1957), 4–5
Anderson, Madeline, xxii, 1–2, 8, 53, 54, 253
Anderson, Marian, 158
Anderson, Maxwell, 121
Angelou, Maya, 417
Anna Lucasta (Yordan), 28
Annan, Kofi, 91
Anspach, Susan, 58, 131–32, 360, 371
Anti-Defamation League, 200
apparatus theories, 385–87
Applebaum, Lou, 39, 41–42
Archer, Osceola, 117
Arrival of the Express at La Ciotat (Lumière Bros, 1895), 335n6
Artis, William, 24
Ashes and Embers (Haile Gerima, 1982), 83
Ashur, Geri, 264
Asian American communities, 265
Aurobindo, Sri, xviii, 95, 101, 102, 158, 343, 384
auteur theory, 356
avant-garde cinema, 10–11
Avildsen, John G.: *Rocky* (1976), 68

Baby Doll (Elia Kazan, 1956), 356
Back to Bataan (Edward Dmytryk, 1945), 37
Bahn-Coblans, Sonja, 19, 68–77
Bailey, Mildred, 26
Baird, Bill, 26
Baker, Josephine, 154
Baker, Shannon: in *Symbiopsychotaxiplasm: Take One*, 332, *359*, 371; in *Symbiopsychotaxiplasm: Take 2½*, 66–67, 203, *360*, 361, 371–72, 378, 379, 388, 391
Baldwin, James, 46, 158
Bank, Mirra: *Yudie* (1974), 265–66
Baraka, Amiri, xxvii, 12, 53, 316, 317, 417
Barnouw, Erik, xix, 407
Barthes, Roland, 362
Barton, Peter: *Janie's Janie* (1971), 264
Batten, Tony, 230, 244
Baudry, Jean-Louis, 385–86
Baxter, Rick: *Ali, the Man* (1975), 208
Bearden, Romare, 152
Bedford Stuyvesant Restoration Corporation, 249–50
Belafonte, Harry, xxix, 41, 46, 80, 86, 117, 178
Belgrad, Daniel, 135n39

Benequist, Larry, 39
Bentley, Arthur, 55, 102, 328, 364, 384
Bernadotte, Folke, 402
Bèye, Ben Diogaye, 153
Billops, Camille, 316
Birth of a Nation, The (D. W. Griffith, 1915), 82
"Black American Cinema: Images of a Culture" (Brooklyn Museum, 1987), 316
Black American Literature Forum (journal), 215–16
Black Entertainment Television, xxviii–xxix
Black Filmmaker Foundation, 307
Black independent filmmaking: Greaves on, xxii–xxiii, 78–87, 93–95, 249; International Film Festival of India (New Delhi, 1989) and, 299–302, *300–301*; market for, 299–302. *See also* Micheaux, Oscar; race movies
Black Jacobins, The (James), 376–77
Black Journal (television program): audience reactions to, 228–30, 240–42; Bourne and, 53, 54, 239, 239–45, 252, 254, 276, 280, 280–81n1; Brown and, 261; on education, 259–60; Emmy Awards and, 9, 256, *257*; *The Fight* and, 218; funding and costs of, 53, 231–32, 244, 258, 261; Greaves as cohost of, xviii, 2, 8, 53, 240, 252–53, 255, 287; Greaves as executive producer of, xviii, 2, 8–10, 53–54, 188, 208–9, 242, 244, *247*, 254–57, *257*, 261–62, 271–73, *272*, 276–80, 287, 357, 365, 414; Greaves on, 226–32, 233–38; Newsreel and, 258–61; origins of, 8–9, 240–42, 253–54; palace revolt at, 8, 53, 254–56; Pan-Africanism and, xx, 272–73, 276–80; purpose and relevance of, 16, 52–54, 226–28, 229, 239–45, 252, 256–58, 271–72, 276–80; reviews of, 230–31, 253–54; training program and, xxii, 230, 242–43, 278–80; Van Peebles and, 275
"*Black Journal*: A Few Notes from the Executive Producer" (Greaves), 226–32
"*Black Journal*: A Personal Look Backward" (Bourne), 239–45
Black masculinity, 173–74
Black Orpheus (Marcel Camus, 1959), 157
Black Panthers, 253, 256–57, 258, 279
Black Panthers (Newsreel, 1968/69), *247*, 259
Black Perspective on the News (television program), 244
Black Power, 257–58
Black Power (Carmichael and Hamilton), 9, 256

Black Power in America: Myth or Reality (William Greaves, 1986), 15, 113
Black Power movements, 400
Black Student Union, 366
Black Underground cinema, 333
Black women: beauty standards and, 178–79; *Black Journal* and, 253; civil rights movement and, 173–74; education and, 176–77; in *Ida B. Wells*, 163–64; in LA Rebellion films, 172; as ladies, 169–72; in *Still a Brother*, 161–79, 180–81, 182–83; in *Symbiopsychotaxiplasm: Take 2½*, 163–64, 372; in white-collar jobs, 167–68; as wives, 166–67; women's studies and, 176
Blackmar, Elizabeth, 321
Blacks in American Film and Television (Bogle), 39
Blair Witch Project, The (Daniel Myrick and Eduardo Sánchez, 1999), 339–40
Blais, Roger: *The Magic Mineral* (1959), 43
Blake, Eubie, xx
Blake, Jody, 152
Bless Their Little Hearts (Billy Woodberry, 1984), 172
Blood and Fire (Terence Macartney-Filgate, 1958), 43
Bloody Sunday (1965), 173
Bogle, Donald, 39, 88, *88*, 299, 317
Boissier-Palun, Léon, *150*
Bolex, 322
Bond, Julian, 175
Bonner, Edwin, 30, 119
Bontemps, Arna, 108
Booker T. Washington: The Life and Legacy (William Greaves, 1982), xxviii–xxix, 14, 397
Boomerang (Elia Kazan, 1947), 38
Boone, Richard, 35
Boscana, Lucy, 263
Boston Globe (newspaper), 252
Bourne, St. Clair: *Black Journal* and, xxii, 8, 53, 54, 230, 239–45, 252, 254, 276, 280, 280–81n1; Brooklyn Museum retrospective and, 317; career of, 266; on "frontism," 257; Greaves and, 1–2, 19, 77–81, 183; *Let the Church Say Amen!* (1973), 266
Bowser, Pearl, xxix–xxx, 316
Boynton, Amelia, 173
Boys Sailing Boats, Tuileries Garden, Paris (Lumière Bros, 1896), 335n6
Bracher, M. Georges, 152, 153, 156

Bracher, Maya, 153
Brakhage, Stan, 326–27, 356
Branch, William B.: *Black Journal* and, 254; *Still a Brother* and, 6, 8, 51, 161, *162*, 163, 164, 165, 182, 254, 255
Brando, Marlon, 3, 35, 120
Brecht, Bertolt, 384–85
Brian's Song (Buzz Kulik, 1971), 223–24n16
Briggs-Hall, Austin, 28, 274
Bright, Hazel, 54
Brody, Richard, 215, 219, 315, 316
Brooke, Edward W., 248
Brooklyn Museum (New York City), 1, 208, 315–18, 352, 374, 381
Brooks, James, 82
Brown, Clarence: *Intruder in the Dust* (1949), 38
Brown, H. Rap, 174
Brown, LaShanda Q., 18
Brown, Tony, 244–45, *257*, 261
Brown v. the Board of Education (1954), 37
Browne, Roscoe Lee, 120
Browne, Sadie, 28
Bryant, William, 395
Bunche, Ralph, 28, 29, 52, 89–90, 395, 397. See also *Ralph Bunche: An American Odyssey* (William Greaves, 2001)
Bunzel, John, 366
Burnett, Charles, xxii–xxiii; *To Sleep with Anger* (1990), 83
Burroughs, Margaret, 177–78
Burton, Phil, 230
Buscemi, Steve, xxi, 350–51, 361, 374, *376*
Bush, George W., 389
Bush Mama (Haile Gerima, 1975), 172
Bustin' Loose (Oz Scott, 1981), xx, 2, 15, 81–82, 83, 90
Butts, Hugh F., 201–2

Cahiers du cinéma (film magazine), 356
Cambridge, Godfrey, 271
Camera Lucida (Barthes), 362
Campbell, Leslie R. "Les," 260–61
Camplis, Francisco X., 295
Camus, Marcel: *Black Orpheus* (1959), 157
Canada, xviii. See also National Film Board of Canada
Cane River (Horace B. Jenkins, 1982), 266
Canegata, Carl, 48
Cannes Film Festival, 55, 351, 374
Carmichael, Stokely, 9, 52, 256, 258, 259

Carnegie Endowment, 53
carreta, La (Marqués), 263
Carson, L. M. Kit, 338
Carter, Ron, 390
Cassavetes, John, 355, 364, 369
Castaldi, Peter, 19, 81, 82–87
Catabalis, William, 49
CBS News (television program), 266
Central Intelligence Agency (CIA), 152, 156
Central Park (New York City): design and significance of, 319–22, 330, 334; race and racial politics and, 321, 331; in *Symbiopsychotaxiplasm: Take One*, 57–58, 322, 327–34, 367–68; in *Symbiopsychotaxiplasm: Take 2½*, 387; in *Walden*, 322–27, 329, 334
Chaplin, Charlie, 353–54
Chartwell Artists, 208, 222
Chase-Riboud, Barbara, 155–56
Chavis, Benjamin F., Jr., 202
Chicago Defender (newspaper), 253, 277
China, 87–89, 88–89, 93
Chinoise, La (Jean-Luc Godard, 1967), 356
Choy, Christine, 264–65; *Mississippi Triangle* (with Worth Long and Allan Siegel, 1983), 265; *From Spikes to Spindles* (1975), 265; *Teach Our Children* (1972), 265; *Who Killed Vincent Chin?* (with Renee Tajima, 1989), 265
Chris and Bernie (Deborah Shaffer and Bonnie Friedman, 1974), 265–66
Christian Science Monitor (magazine), 26, 399
Christmas, June Jackson, 15
Christophe, Henri, 108. See also *Henri Christophe* (Hammerman)
Chronique d'un été—Paris 1960 (Jean Rouch, 1961), xix
Churchill, Jack, 64
Churchill, Savannah, 119
CIA (Central Intelligence Agency), 152, 156
cinéma-vérité documentary: *Black Journal* and, 260; *Cleared for Takeoff* and, 47; *In the Company of Men* and, 189; *The Fight* and, 212; Godard and, 393–94n28; Greaves and, xix, 5, 10–11, 131, 347; *Just Doin' It* and, 68–77; National Film Board of Canada and, xviii, 43–44; spoofs of, 337–38; *Still a Brother* and, 163, 255; *Symbiopsychotaxiplasm: Take One* and, 114, 311–12; *Voice of La Raza* and, 285
City of Gold (Colin Low and Wolf Koenig, 1958), 44

Civil Rights Act (1957), 286
Civil Rights Act (1964), 286
civil rights movement: *Black Journal* and, 239; Black women and, 173–74; Greaves and, xviii, 5, 46; *Ralph Bunche* and, 398–401; *Still a Brother* and, 173–74; student movement of the 1960s and, 365. See also Kerner Commission (National Advisory Commission on Civil Disorders); King, Martin Luther, Jr.
Civil Service Commission, 13
Civil War, The (Ken Burns, 1990), 67
Clarke, John Henrik, 28, 274–75, 278, 416
Clarke, Richard, 168
Clarke, Shirley, 5, 48, 355
Cleared for Takeoff (William Greaves, 1963), 5, 47, 51
Cleaver, Eldridge, 259, 279
Clurman, Harold, 35
Colin, Charles, 30–31
Collins, Kathleen, xxii, xxix; *Losing Ground* (1982), 355
colonialism, 77, 404–5
Color Us Black! (Dick McCutcheon, 1968), 252
Columbia Revolt (Newsreel, 1968), 247, 259
Columbia University, 176–77, 366
Columbus, John, 63, 65–66
Combahee River Collective, 166, 177
Comeno, El (newspaper), 252
Commission on Civil Rights, 286–87
Community Control (1968), 247, 260–61
Congress of Racial Equality (CORE), 52, 174
Conscripts of Modernity (Scott), 376–77
Cook, Mercer, 157, 160n15
Cooke, Alistair, 5, 47–48
Cooke, Jack Kent, 209–10, 213–14
Coppola, Francis Ford: *The Godfather* (1972), 36
CORE (Congress of Racial Equality), 52, 174
Corporation for Public Broadcasting, 90, 397
Cosby, Camille O., 90, 397
Cosby, William H., Jr., 90, 397
Coskun, Çiçek, 223–24n16
Countee, Samuel, 40–41
Cowley, Richard and Margaret, 193–94
Crawford, Cheryl, 35
Crichlow, Ernest, 24
Crimmins, Denny, 188
Crisis, The (journal), 157–59
Crowe, Larry, 19, 20–21, 54, 68, 95

Crusade for Justice: The Autobiography of Ida B. Wells (Wells), 303–4
Cry the Beloved Country (Paton), 121
Cullen, Mrs. Countee (Ida Cullen Cooper), 109

Dafora, Asadata, 25–26, 115, 274
Dakar, Senegal. *See* First World Festival of Negro Arts (Dakar, Senegal, 1966)
Dallos, Robert E., 255
Daly, Tom, 42, 43, 101
Damas, Léon-Gontran, 158
Daniels, Jonathan, 397
Darby, Charles, 195–96, 203
Dargis, Manohla, 340, 379
Dash, Julie, xxii–xxiii, xxix, 316; *Daughters of the Dust* (1991), 172
Daughters of the Dust (Julie Dash, 1991), 172
David Holzman's Diary (Jim McBride, 1967), 338
David Wolper Productions, 247
Davidson, Clive, 331–32
Davis, Miles, 30–31, 64, 333, 360, 390
Davis, Ossie, xx, 162, 163, 182
Davis, Sammy, Jr., 178
Dawn, Marpessa, 157
de Jesús, Carlos: *The Devil Is a Condition* (1972), 264; *The Picnic* (1976), 265
De Paur Chorus, 143
DeCarava, Roy, 82
decolonization, 47–48, 398–401
Dee, Ruby, 30, 88, *88*, 119, 288, 299, *300*
Deep Are the Roots (d'Usseau and Gow), 117
Deep North, The (William Greaves, 1988), 11, 187, 200–204
Defenders, The (television series, 1961–1964), 192
Deluca, Maria, 61
DeMott, John, 305
Demy, Jacques: *The Umbrellas of Cherbourg* (1964), 360, 371
Deneuve, Catherine, 360, 371
Dennis, Joseph A., 249–50
Desgraves, Cleante, 25
Desgraves, Mark, 24, 25, 274
Dessalines, Jean-Jacques, 116–17
Devil Is a Condition, The (Carlos de Jesús, 1972), 264
Dewey, John, 384
Diamond, Johnny, 131–32
Diawara, Manthia, 317

Diggs, Charles, xxvii
direct cinema, xix, xx, 339
Dixon, Don, 51
Dixon, Ivan, 88, 299, *300*, 302
Dixon, Mr. (teacher), 23
Dmytryk, Edward: *Back to Bataan* (1945), 37
docudrama, 212–22
Dodson, Owen, 26, 117. *See also Garden of Time* (Dodson)
domestic violence, 167
Douglas, Aaron, 108
Douglas, Emory, 279
Douglass, Frederick, 21, 177
Down These Mean Streets (Thomas), 263
Drake, St. Clair, 166–67, 169, 175, 182
Drew, Charles, 177
Du Bois, W. E. B., 14, 21, 27, 117, 177, 400
Duncan, Todd, 30, 177
Dunham, Katherine, 6, 154
Durham, Yancey ("Yank"), 214
DuSable Museum of African American History (Chicago), 177
d'Usseau, Arnaud, 117
Duster, Alfreda Barnett, 303
Duster, Ben IV, 303–4
Duster, Michelle, *307*
Duster, Troy, 304
DuVernay, Ava, xxii–xxiii
Dziga Vertov Film Group, 356

Eban, Abba, 401
Ebony (magazine), 178
education, 259–60
EEOC. *See* Equal Employment Opportunity Commission (EEOC)
EEOC Story (William Greaves, 1972), 288
8½ (Federico Fellini, 1963), 324
Elisofon, Eliot, 153
Ellington, Duke, 6, 50, 143, 148, 154, 157, 417
Emergency Ward (William Greaves, 1959), xix, 4–5, 43–44, 48, 131, 378, 418
Emmy Awards, 9, 256, *257*
Enwonwu, Ben, 154
Equal Employment Opportunity Commission (EEOC), 13, 107–8, 285–88. *See also Voice of La Raza* (1972)
Etoile, Marian, 249
Everson, Kevin Jerome, xxiii

Every Day Except Christmas (Lindsay Anderson, 1957), 4–5
Experimental Studio Group, 127

F for Fake (Orson Welles, 1974), 355
Faith, Percy, 31
Family of Man, The (Steichen), 330–31
Farmer, James, 52
Featherstone, Ralph, 172, 174
Feeding the Baby (Lumière Bros, 1895), 335n6
Fellini, Federico: *8½* (1963), 324
Fellows, Don: in *Symbiopsychotaxiplasm: Take One*, 58, 60, *60*, 328, 332–33, 352, 360, 371
Ferguson, Andy, 278–79
Ferguson, Herman B., 260–61
Ferrer, José, 3, 16n4, 39–40, 122–23
Festival Mondial des Arts Nègres (FESMAN). *See* First World Festival of Negro Arts (Dakar, Senegal, 1966)
Fetchit, Stepin, 32–34
Feury, Peggy (Margaret), 35, 46, 127–28
Fight, The (William Greaves, unreleased): *Black Journal* and, 218; as docudrama, 211–22; shooting and production of, 206–11, 266; *Symbiopsychotaxiplasm: Take One* and, 208–9, 210, 220–21
Fight Never Ends, The (Joseph Lerner, 1948), xvii, 32
Fight of the Century (1971): Greaves's documentary on, 111–12, 206–9, *211*. *See also Fight, The* (William Greaves, unreleased); production and promotion of, *207*, 209–10
Fighter, The (William Greaves, 1971), 377
Fighters, The (William Greaves, 1972), 208, 211–20
Filgate, Terry. *See* Macartney-Filgate, Terence
Film Jamaica Productions, xxix
Film Library Quarterly (journal), 188
FilmWatch initiative, xxx
Finian's Rainbow (musical), 3, 29, 119, 120
First World Festival of Negro Arts (Dakar, Senegal, 1966), 5–6, 49, 139–47, *140*, 149–59, *150–51*
First World Festival of Negro Arts, The (William Greaves, 1966): experimentation and, 67; D. Greaves and, 107; Hughes in, 5–6, 50, *50*, 276, 377; shooting and production of, 49, 149, 153; significance of, 5–6, 82, 148–49, 153–57, 159, 287; *Symbiopsychotaxiplasm* project and, 377
Flores-Rodríguez, Ángel G., 298n31
Fodéba, Kéita, 158
Fonda, Jane, xxvii

Fontanez, Angela, 54
Ford Foundation, 53, 90, 248, 249, 260–61, 397. *See also* National Educational Television (NET)
Franklin, John Hope, 303
Frazier, E. Franklin, 180
Frazier, Joe, xx. *See also* Fight of the Century (1971)
Frederick Douglass: An American Life (William Greaves, 1985), xxviii–xxix, 14, 397
Free Cinema, 4–5
Freeman, Al, Jr., 120
Freight (White), 29, 120
French, La Verne, *30*
French, Robin, 111–12, 209
French New Wave, 10–11
Fresh Seeds in the Big Apple (Third World Newsreel, 1975), 265
Freud, Sigmund, 190, 385–86
Friedman, Bonnie: *Chris and Bernie* (with Deborah Shaffer, 1974), 265–66
Friedrich, Su, *104*, 350–51, *351*
From Spikes to Spindles (Christine Choy, 1975), 265
From These Roots (William Greaves, 1974): Harlem Renaissance and, xx, 2, 13–14, 44; reception of, xxvii, 82, 94, 266; Schomburg Center for Research in Black Culture and, 416; shooting and production of, 108–10; still photographs in, 13–14, 67
Fruchter, Norman, 259, 269n52
Fuller, Hoyt, 152

Gaddis, William, 54
Gaines, Jane, xxix–xxx
Gallagher, Steve, 63–64, 66
Garcia, Antonina, 193
García Torres, José, 262–64, 285, 287
Garden of Time (Dodson), 3, 26, *27*, 28–29, 115–16, *116*, 274
Garfield, David, 120, 123–24
Garner, Peggy Ann, 35
Garrett, Kent: *Black Journal* and, 8, 53, 54, 230, 252, 254, 278–79; career of, 79, 266; Greaves and, 1–2
Gary, Ja'Tovia, xxiii
Gascon, Jean, 135–36n40
Gates, Henry Louis, 407
Gentleman's Agreement (Elia Kazan, 1947), 37
Gerber, Ellen, 46

INDEX

Gerima, Haile, xxii; *Ashes and Embers* (1982), 83; *Bush Mama* (1975), 172
Germany, 93
Getino, Octavio: *La hora de los hornos* (with Fernando Solanas, 1968), 260, 396
Giddings, Paula, 317
Gilbert, Patricia Ree: funding of *Symbiopsychotaxiplasm: Take One* and, 100, 335n14; in *Symbiopsychotaxiplasm: Take One*, 58, 59–60, *60*, 328, 332–33, 352, 360, 371
Gilmore, Geoff, 407
Giovanni, Nikki, 269n42
Gittens, Tony, 316
Glawogger, Michael: *Megacities* (1998), 396; *Whore's Glory* (2012), 396; *Workingman's Death* (2005), 396
Glory (Edward Zwick, 1989), 83
Glover, Guy, 42
Godard, Jean-Luc, 62, 337–38, 356–57, 384–85, 386–87; *La Chinoise* (1967), 356
Godfather, The (Francis Ford Coppola, 1972), 36
Godler, Jack, 199
Goldberg brothers, 32
Gonzales, Rudolfo "Corky," 291
Gordon, Jonathan, 131–32, 364, 369, 370–71, 380–81, 387, 388–89
Gottlieb, Akiva, 222, 223n7, 365
Gould, Jack, 230–31
Gow, James, 117
Graham, Katharine, 249
Grant, Bev, 264
Greaves, David: L. Greaves and, 99; interview with, 107–13; *Just Doin' It* and, 70; photographs of, *351*; *Symbiopsychotaxiplasm* project and, 350–51, 353
Greaves, Garfield Gilbert Hannibal, 20–22, 36, 273–74
Greaves, Liani, *351*
Greaves, Louise Archambault: as actress, 96–97, 127; Brody and, 316; family and background of, 96–97; on *The Fight*, 212, 213, 217; on First World Festival of Negro Arts, 160n12; Greaves and, xviii, 96–106, *103*; Greaves on, 95; on *Ida B. Wells*, 303; interview with, 96–106; photographs of, *103–4, 317, 351, 391, 398*; as producer, xx, 99–100; *Symbiopsychotaxiplasm* project and, 309, 350–52
Greaves, Maiya, 99
Greaves, Taiyi, 99

Greaves, William: overview of career and legacy of, xvii–xxiii, xxvii–xxix, 1–16, 414; as dancer, xvii, 2, 25–26, 115, 274; as documentary filmmaker, xvii–xxiii, 4–16; family, childhood and youth of, 2, 20–26, *23*, 102–3, 273–75, 414; global perspective on, 87–95, 101–2; Hollywood and, 77–84; illness and death of, 103–6; interviews with, 17–19; as songwriter, xvii, xxvii, *xxviii*, 30–31; training as filmmaker and, 4, 40–41, 123. *See also* acting; *and specific films*
Gregory, Dick, xxvii, 80, 86, 174
Grey Advertising, 252
Grierson, John, 4–5, 15, 41, 42–43, 101
Grierson on Documentary (Grierson), 41
Griffith, D. W.: *The Birth of a Nation* (1915), 82
Griffith, Michael, 201
Group Theater, 35
Growing Up Female (Julia Reichert and Jim Klein, 1972), 265–66
Guilbeault, Luce, 45
Guyse, Sheila, *30*, 120

Haitian Revolution, 24, 274
Haizlip, Ellis, 248
Hall, Stuart, 217
Hamilton, Charles, 9, 15, 256, 258
Hamlet (Shakespeare), 117
Hammerman, Dan. *See Henri Christophe* (Hammerman)
Handy, W. C., 416
Hansberry, Lorraine, 28, 416
Hansberry, William Leo, 9, 28, 85–86, 101, 158, 274–75, 278, 416
Hare, A. Paul, 193–94
Hare, June Rabson, 193–94
Hare, Nathan, 175
Harlem Renaissance, xxvii, 21, 273–74, 414. *See also From These Roots* (William Greaves, 1974)
Harlem Renaissance, The (Huggins), 13
Harlem Riot (1943), 193
Harris, Doug, 111
Harris, Julie, 35
Hart, Mable, *30*
Harvey, Dennis, 399
Hatch, James, 18, 22–25, 26–31, 42, 54, 87–89, 134n23
Hatcher, Richard, xxvii, 15, 80, 86, 111

Hathaway, Henry: *The House on 92nd Street* (1945), 38
Hayes, Isaac, 80
Haynes, George Edmund, 28, 274–75
Healy-Ray, Ken, 42
Heath, Gordon, 26, 85, 115, 117
Hecht, Ben, 3. See also *Twentieth Century* (Hecht and McArthur)
Heisenberg Principle of Uncertainty, 61–62, 198–99, 343, 347, 348, 384, 386
Heisler, Stuart: *The Negro Soldier* (1944), 401
Heller, Arno, 19, 68–77
Henningham, Audrey: in *Symbiopsychotaxiplasm: Take One*, 332, *359*, 371; in *Symbiopsychotaxiplasm: Take 2½*, 66–67, 203, *360*, 361, 371–72, 378, 379, 388, 391
Henri Christophe (Hammerman), 3, 28, 29, 116–17, 118–19, 274
Henry, Charles P., 407
Herald Pictures, 32
Herskowitz, Richard, 61–62
Heyerdahl, Thor, 233
Hibler, Al, 31
Hightower, Donna, 31
Hill, Abram, 28, 29, 116, 117, 119
Hill, Joe Newton, 29
Hispanic, use of term, 288
Hispanic communities, 262–65. See also *Realidades* (television program); *Voice of La Raza* (1972)
Hoberman, Jim, 317
Hobson, Charles, 8, 53, 249–50, 252, 253, 255–56, 266
Hobson, Sheila Smith, 8, 168, 253, 254, 255–56, 258
Hoffman, Dustin, 192
Holloway, Jonathan, 401, 407
Hollywood Foreign Press Association, xxvii
homophobia, 358–59, 370–71
homosexuality: gay filmmakers and, 266; in *Symbiopsychotaxiplasm: Take One*, 56–57, 327, 329, 352, 354, 358–59, 369–71
Hooks, Robert, 255–56
hora de los hornos, La (Octavio Getino and Fernando Solanas, 1968), 260, 396
Hospital (Frederick Wiseman, 1968), 4–5
House, Lou (later Wali Sadiq), 9, 53, 240, 252–53, 256, 272, *272*
House on 92nd Street, The (Henry Hathaway, 1945), 38
Howard University, 176–77, 252

Hudlin, Reggie, 307
Hudlin, Warrington, 307
Huggins, Nathan, 13
Hughes, Langston: Dodson and, 29; in *The First World Festival of Negro Arts*, 6, 50, *50*, 276, 377; First World Festival of Negro Arts and, 143, 154, 156; Greaves and, 82, 156, 416, 417; Johnson and, 177; Nugent and, 109
Humphrey, Hal, 254
Hutson, Jean Blackwell, 28, 274–75, 278, 416
Hylton, Richard, *38*

I Remember Harlem (William Miles, 1981), 14, 265
Ida B. Wells: A Passion for Justice (William Greaves, 1989), xxviii–xxix, 1, 14, 67, 87, 163–64, 303–7, *306–7*, 377, 397
Imagenes Latinas (television program), 264
Impromptu Theatre, 191
In a Silent Way (Davis), 333, 390
In the Company of Men (William Greaves, 1969), xix, 11, 187–89, 192, 194–200, 202–4, 266, 292
In the Event Anyone Disappears (Third World Newsreel, 1974), 265
India, 47–48, 101–2. See also International Film Festival of India (New Delhi, 1989)
Inquiry Into Inquiries (Bentley), 55, 328, 384
Inside Bedford-Stuyvesant (television program), 16, 247, 249–51, 252, 257, 258–59
institutional racism, 367
Interface (PBS program), 243–44
International Civil Aviation Organization (ICAO), 5, 46
International Film Festival of India (New Delhi, 1989), 87–88, 102, 299–302, *300–301*
Interpretation of Dreams, The (Freud), 385–86
interracial couples, 179–80
intertitles, 322, 323, 324, 326
Intruder in the Dust (Clarence Brown, 1949), 38
Islin, Jay, 263
Isozaki, Arata, 316
Israel, 401–2
Ivie, Ardie, 244

Jackson, Ann, 35
Jackson, J. Denis, 178, 196–97
Jackson, Jesse, xxvii, 12, 80, 86, 111
Jacobs, Jim, 216
Jacobs, Louis, 40
Jafa, Arthur, xxiii

INDEX

Jaji, Tsitsi, 153
James, C. L. R., 376–77
Janie's Janie (Peter Barton, 1971), 264
jazz: in *The First World Festival of Negro Arts*, 154; Greaves on, 238; Hobson and, 250; as metaphor in *Symbiopsychotaxiplasm: Take One*, 64, 390; as soundtrack in *Symbiopsychotaxiplasm: Take One*, 64, 333, 360, 390. *See also* Davis, Miles
Jenkins, Horace B.: *Black Journal* and, 8, 53, 252, 254, 259–60; *Cane River* (1982), 266; career of, 266, 279–80; *Nationtime—Gary* and, 54
Jennings, Peter, 54
Jet (magazine), 177, 287–88
Jimenez, Vicente, 290–91
Joe's Bed-Stuy Barbershop: We Cut Heads (Spike Lee, 1982), 16n9
John D. and Catherine T. MacArthur Foundation, 90, 397
John Golden Auditions, 118–19
John Loves Mary (Krasna), 30, 119
Johnson, Bob, 177
Johnson, Buddy, 31
Johnson, George and Joan, 178
Johnson, John H., 169–70, 178–79
Johnson administration, 288. *See also* Kerner Commission (National Advisory Commission on Civil Disorders)
Jones, Marlene, 166–67, *167*
Jones, Philip Mallory, 316
Jordan, Millicent F., 175–76, 177–78
Journey, The (Peter Watkins, 1984–1987), 396
Joyce at 34 (Claudia Weill, 1974), 265–66
Judge, Al, 197
Julian, Percy, 175
Just Doin' It (William Greaves, 1976), 15, 68–77

Karenga, Maulana, 174
Karp, Marcia, 187, 203, 371–72, 388, 391
Kazan, Elia, *xxix*, 35, 44, 117, 123; *Baby Doll* (1956), 356; *Boomerang* (1947), 38; *Gentleman's Agreement* (1947), 37; *Pinky* (1949), 37; *Viva Zapata* (1952), 41
Kehr, David, 338
Kellermann, Peter Felix, 193
Kelley, Robin D. G., 273
Kemp, Jack: *Miracle in Harlem* (1948), xvii, 2, 31, 32–34, *33*, 414, 418
Ken Burns: *The Civil War* (1990), 67
Kennedy, Arthur, 35

Kennedy, Robert, 249
Kennedy administration, 5
Keppel, Ben, 407
Kerner, Otto, Jr., 248
Kerner Commission (National Advisory Commission on Civil Disorders): overview of, 248; *Black Journal* and, xviii, 8, 240, 276; findings and recommendations of, 52–53, 163, 201, 248–49, 257, 271; Latinos and, 262
Kerouac, Jack, 369
Kgositsile, Keorapetse, 154
Khrushchev, Nikita, 400
Killer's Kiss (Stanley Kubrick, 1955), 41
King, Coretta Scott, xxvii, 8, 12, 86, 241, 253
King, Martin Luther, Jr.: assassination of, 8, 165; in Chicago, 200; Greaves on, 52; in *Still a Brother*, 174; in *Wealth of a Nation*, 5, 48–49
King, Rick: *Off the Wall* (1976), 10–11
Kitt, Eartha, 31
Klavun, Walter, 192, 195–98
Klein, Jim: *Growing Up Female* (with Julia Reichert, 1972), 265–66
Klotman, Phyllis, xxii
Knapp, Jack, 40
Knee, Adam, 218
Knight, Arthur, 40
Koenig, Wolf, 42; *City of Gold* (with Colin Low, 1958), 44; *Lonely Boy* (with Roman Kroitor, 1962), 43, 61
Kopple, Barbara, 15
Krasna, Norman, 30, 119
Kroiter, Roman, 42, 44; *Lonely Boy* (with Wolf Koenig, 1962), 4–5, 43; *Universe* (with Colin Low, 1960), 43
Kubrick, Stanley: *Killer's Kiss* (1955), 41
Kulik, Buzz: *Brian's Song* (1971), 223–24n16

L.A. Rebellion film movement, xxii, 172
labor discrimination, 286–88, 289–95
Lamp Unto My Feet (CBS series), 120–21, *121–22*
Lancaster, Burt, 210
Lascelles, George H. H., *150*
Lathan, Stan, 54, 79, 230
Laura (Otto Preminger, 1944), 26
Leacock, Richard, 356, 393–94n28
leadership, 354
Lee, Canada, 48, 85
Lee, Nathan, 340
Lee, Rohama, 40

Lee, Spike, xxii–xxiii, xxix, 82–83; *Joe's Bed-Stuy Barbershop: We Cut Heads* (1982), 16n9
Legion of Decency, 356
Lemmon, Jack, 352
Lennard, Jean, 40
Leonard, Arthur H.: *Sepia Cinderella* (1947), 414
Lepsius, Karl Richard, 77
Lerner, Joseph, 32; *The Fight Never Ends* (1948), xvii, 32
Let the Church Say Amen! (St. Clair Bourne, 1973), 266
Lewis, David Levering, 401
Lewis, Jerry, 353–54
Lewis, Richard, 123
Lewis, Robert, 35
Liben, Laura, 264
Like It Is (television program), 16, 247, 249, 255–56
Linder, Max, 353–54
Lindsay, John V., 248, 372
Lindsay, Powell: *Souls of Sin* (1949), xvii, 31–32, 34–35, *34*, 121, 414
Lipton, Lawrence, 48
Locke, Alain, 29
Logan, Ella, 29
Logan, Joshua, 123
Lonely Boy (Wolf Koenig and Roman Kroitor, 1962), 4–5, 43, 61
Long, Worth: *Mississippi Triangle* (with Christine Choy and Allan Siegel, 1983), 265
Lorre, Peter, 190
Los Angeles Times (newspaper), 254
Losing Ground (Kathleen Collins, 1982), 355
Lost Boundaries (Alfred L. Werker, 1949): Applebaum and, 42; Greaves and, xvii, 2–3, 32, 37–39, *38*, 85, 121–22, 127, 418; screenings of, 114
Lost in the Stars (musical), 30, *30*, 32, 89, 120, 121–22
Lost Lost Lost (Jonas Mekas, 1976), 322, 325
Louis, Joe, 32
Loving v. Virginia (1967), 179
Low, Colin, 42; *City of Gold* (with Wolf Koenig, 1958), 44; *Universe* (with Roman Kroiter, 1960), 43
Lowry, Jim, 249–50, 251
Lucas, Leroy, 278–79
Lumière Brothers, 323
Luthuli, Albert, 158
Lynch, Shola, 350–51, 353
lynchings, 180, 304, *304*

MacArthur Foundation, 90, 397
Macartney-Filgate, Terence, 42, 61, 387; *Blood and Fire* (1958), 43
MacDonald, Jimmie, 54, *257*
MacDonald, Scott: on *The Fight*, 211–12; interview with Greaves and, 31–36, 36–39, 54–55, 56–60, 64–65, 66–68, 90–92, 382–83; on *Symbiopsychotaxiplasm: Take One*, 364, 367, 369
Maceo, Ted, 390
Machover, Robert, 269n52
Magic Mineral, The (Roger Blais, 1959), 43
Maguire, Dorothy, 35
Maidstone (Norman Mailer, 1970), 338
Mailer, Norman, 369; *Maidstone* (1970), 338
Makavejev, Dusan, 62
Malden, Karl, 82
Mambéty, Djibril Diop, 153
Mamoulian, Rouben, 30, *30*
Mankiewicz, Joseph L.: *No Way Out* (1950), 16n2, 37, 121
Mann, Daniel, 35, 40, 123
March, Liska, 82
March of Time (short film series), 38
Marcorelles, Louis, 55
Marijuana Affair, The (William Greaves, 1976), xxix, 15, 79
Marineau, René, 189, 191, 193
Mariposa Film Group, 266
Marqués, René, 263–64
marriage, 166–67
Massachusetts 54th, The (Jacqueline Shearer, 1991), 14
Materre, Michelle, 61
Mayfield, Julian, *30*, 117–18, 121
Mayne, Judith, 386
Maysles, Albert and David, xix, 356
Mbadiwe, Kingsley, 282n14
MCA New Ventures, 81–82
McArthur, Charles, 3. See also *Twentieth Century* (Hecht and McArthur)
McBride, Jim: *David Holzman's Diary* (1967), 338
McCall, H. Carl, xxvii
McCarthy, Joseph, 41, 399
McCarthy, Kevin, 46, 127–28
McCarthy Hearings, 400
McClendon, Rose, 108–9
McCutcheon, Dick: *Color Us Black!* (1968), 252
McDonald, Fergus, 42

McDowell, Calvin, 304, *304*
McGlaughlin, John, 390
McKay, Claude, 108, 110
McLaren, Norman, 42; *Neighbors* (1952), 43
McLean, Grant, 46
McLucas, Leroy, 54
Medhi, M. T., 401
Medium Cool (Haskell Wexler, 1969), 10–11, 338
Megacities (Michael Glawogger, 1998), 396
Mehta, Depu, 305
Mekas, Adolfas, 322
Mekas, Jonas, 322–27, 329; *Lost Lost Lost* (1976), 322, 325; *Walden* (1968), 322–27, 329, 334
Melamed, Manny, 100–101, 335n14
Men of Bronze (William Miles, 1976), 265
Menon, Krishna, 89
Mercure, Monique, 45
Method acting: Greaves and, 44, 96, 124–26; *Lost Boundaries* and, 114. *See also* Actors Studio; psychodrama; Stanislavsky Method
Metromedia, 249
Meyers, Sidney: *The Quiet One* (1948), xix
Meyers-Kingsley, Dara, 315–18, 352
Micheaux, Oscar: Brooklyn Museum and, 316; Greaves and, xxiii, xxix–xxx, 15, 21–22, 32, 273, 416; significance of, xxii, 37
Miles, William: *I Remember Harlem* (1981), 14, 265; *Men of Bronze* (1976), 265
Miller, Arthur, 192, 369
Miller, Henry, 369
Miller, Liz: *The Shoreline* (2016), 396
Minority Enterprise Small Business Investment Company (MESBIC), 78
minority programming, 243–44
Miracle in Harlem (Jack Kemp, 1948), xvii, 2, 31, 32–34, *33*, 414, 418
Mississippi Triangle (Christine Choy, Worth Long, Allan Siegel, 1983), 265
Monod, Theodore, 153
Montague, Lee, 49
Moore, Michael, 347
Moore, Richard B., 28, 108, 175, 177, 274–75
Mora, Cristina, 288
Moreno, Jacob L., 101, 187, 189–94, 199, 238, 364. *See also* psychodrama
Moreno, Rita, 288, 293
Moreno, Zerka, 200–201, 202
Moreno Institute, 200. *See also* psychodrama

Morgan, Robin. *See Sisterhood Is Powerful* (Morgan)
Morris, Errol, 15
Morris, Horace, 181–82, 255
Morrison, Toni, 14, 305, *306*
Moss, Thomas, 304, *304*
Mother Teresa, *301*
Movshon, George, 47–48
Moynihan Report (1965), 166
Muir, Phyllis Emily, 21, 274
Mulford, Marilyn, 264
Mulholland, Donald, 42
Murray, Madalyn E., 5, 48
Musser, Charles, xxix–xxx, 218
Myrick, Daniel: *The Blair Witch Project* (with Eduardo Sánchez, 1999), 339–40

NAACP (National Association for the Advancement of Colored People), 32, 248
Nabokov, Vladimir, 369
Naremore, James, 128
NASA (National Aeronautics and Space Administration), 13
Nation (magazine), 26
National Advisory Commission on Civil Disorders. *See* Kerner Commission (National Advisory Commission on Civil Disorders)
National Association for the Advancement of Colored People (NAACP), 32, 248
National Association of Black Media Producers, 54, 261
National Black Political Convention (Gary, Indiana, 1972), xxvii. *See also Nationtime—Gary* (William Greaves, 1973)
National Black Programming Consortium, 90, 397
National Center for History in the Schools, 404
National Council for Social Studies, 404
National Education Association (NEA), 335n14
National Educational Television (NET), 51–52, 162, 165, 248. *See also Black Journal* (television program); *Still a Brother: Inside the Negro Middle Class* (William Greaves, 1968)
National Endowment for the Arts (NEA), 247–48
National Endowment for the Humanities, 90, 397
National Film Board of Canada: Applebaum and, 39; Greaves and, xviii, xxvii, 4–5, 41–46, 61, 123, 124, 209, 414
National Park Service, 14
National Urban League, 119, 181

Nationtime—Gary (William Greaves, 1973), xix, xxvii, 12–13, 54, 80, 86, 110–11, 377
Nazi Germany, 401
NBC White Paper (television program), 247
"Negro Digs Up His Past, The" (Schomburg), 415
Negro Family, The (Moynihan Report, 1965), 166
Negro in America, The (Bunche), 408
Negro Soldier, The (Stuart Heisler, 1944), 401
"Negro Speaks of Rivers, The" (Hughes), 50, 154, 276, 377
Nehru, Jawaharlal, 89
Neighbors (Normal McLaren, 1952), 43
Nelson, Stanley, xxix, 316
New Day Films, 16
New York City: documentary filmmaking in, 246–47, 249–51, 258–66. See also *Black Journal* (television program); Brooklyn Museum (New York City); Central Park (New York City)
New York City Marathon, 389
New York Newsreel (later Third World Newsreel), 356
New York Public Library. *See* Schomburg Center for Research in Black Culture (New York Public Library)
New York State Council on the Arts (NYSCA), 265, 335n14
New York Sun (newspaper), 340
New York Times (newspaper): on *Black Journal*, 230–31; on *David Holzman's Diary*, 338; on *The Fighters*, 222–23n2; on *Garden of Time*, 26; Greaves's op-ed in, 194–95, 261–62, 292; on *Realidades*, 264; on *Symbiopsychotaxiplasm: Take 2½*, 340
Newman, Paul, 82
Newsreel, 16, 247, 258–61, 264–65
newsreels, 32
Newsweek (magazine), 187–88, 194, 292
Newton, Huey, 240–41, 259
Nichols, Bill, 264–65, 289
Nichols, Mike, 369
Nielson, Leslie, 122
Night Mail (Harry Watt and Basil Wright, 1936), 4
Nixon administration, 258, 261, 288
No Way Out (Joseph L. Mankiewicz, 1950), 16n2, 37, 121
Noble, Gil, 14, 255–56
Nolte, John, 189, 203
Nugent, Bruce, 108–9

Odd Man Out (Carol Reed, 1947), 42
O'Farrell, Leo, 249
Off the Wall (Rick King, 1976), 10–11
Offley, Hilda, 32
O'Grady, Gerald, 335n14
Ojike, Mbonu, 282n14
Okeke, Uche, 157
Olmsted, Frederick Law, 319–22, 330, 334
On Merit (William Greaves, 1972), 13
On Strivers Row (Hill), 27
One American Movie (One AM) project, 356–57, 393–94n28
One P.M. (D. A. Pennebaker, 1972), 393–94n28
"100 Madison Avenues Will Be of No Help" (Greaves), 233–38
O'Neal, Frederick, 29, 117
Ontiveros, Randy, 294
Orizu, A. A. Nwafor, 282n14
Oscar Micheaux and His Circle (Bowser et al.), xxix–xxx
O'Shaughnessy, John, 29
Ottawa Civil Service Recreational Association (RA), 127
Ottawa Film Society, 114
Our Time Press (newspaper), 113

Palestine, 401–2
Palewski, Stephanie, 264
Pan-Africanism, xx, 155, 272–80
panoramas, 320
Park and the People, The (Blackmar and Rosenzweig), 321
Parker, Phil, 331–32, 378, 382
Parkerson, Michelle, 88, 299
Parks, Gordon, 316; *World of Piri Thomas, The* (1968), 262–63
Paton, Alan, 121
Paz, Octavio, 291
Penley, Constance, 386
Pennebaker, D. A., 43, 356; *One P.M.* (1972), 393–94n28
Perenchio, Jerry, 111–12, 208, 209–10, 212–14, 215, 222
Pérez-Torres, Rafael, 298n25
Perlmutter, Alvin H., 8, 53, 240, 252, 263
Peters, Brock, xx, 23, 134n14, 134n21
Peterson, Louis, Jr., 35, 119
Philippoteaux, Paul, 320
photography, 362, 385–86

Picnic, The (Carlos De Jesus, 1976), 265
Pindell, Howardena, 316
Pinky (Elia Kazan, 1949), 37
Pinn, Peggy, 230, 253
POEM/1965 (Greaves), 137–38
Poitier, Sidney: acting career of, 37; Actors Studio and, 120; American Negro Theatre and, 117–18; beauty standards and, 178; civil rights movement and, 46; in *Freight*, 29; Greaves and, xxix, 2, 41, 121; in *Nationtime—Gary*, 80, 86; *Ralph Bunche* and, 399, 400, 405–6
Polaroid, 261
Pollard, Fritz, 32
Polshek, James Stewart, 316
Porter, James, 154
Potter, Lou, 240, 241, 252, 254, 277
Power Versus the People (William Greaves, 1973), 288
pragmatism, 384
Prelinger, Rick, 287
Preminger, Otto: *Laura* (1944), 26
Pressman, David, 35, 123
Primus, Pearl, xvii, 26, 115, 117, 274
Prince, Van, *30*
Pryor, Richard, xx, 2, 83
Prysok, Arthur, 31
psychoanalytic analysis, 385–86
psychodrama: concept and origins of, 189–92; in *In the Company of Men*, 11, 187–89, 192, 194–200, 202–4, 292; in *The Deep North*, 11, 187, 200–204; sociodrama and, 192–94; *Symbiopsychotaxiplasm: Take One*, 10–12, 58, 187, 198, 292, 347, 364; in *Symbiopsychotaxiplasm: Take 2½*, 187, 203, 347, 369, 371–72, 379–80, 388, 391; in *Voice of La Raza*, 292–94
Public Broadcasting Service (PBS), 248, 265–66
Pueblo se levanta, El (Newsreel, 1971), 259
Puerto Rican Educational and Action Media Council, 263
Puerto Rican Traveling Theatre, 263
Puerto Rican communities, 262–65
punctum, 362
Putting It Straight (William Greaves, 1957), 43

Quiet One, The (Sidney Meyers, 1948), xix
Quinn, Anthony: Actors Studio and, 35; in *Voice of La Raza*, 108, 285, 288, 289–90, 291, 293

race, racial politics, and racism: Central Park and, 321, 331; *In the Company of Men* and, 194–200, 202–4; *The Deep North* and, 200–204; *The Fight* and, 218–19; Greaves on, 52–53, 93, 124, 194–95, 233–38, 262; labor discrimination and, 286–88, 289–95; *Ralph Bunche* and, 398–401; sociodrama and, 193–94; *Still a Brother* and, 294; *Symbiopsychotaxiplasm: Take One* and, 331–33; *Voice of La Raza* and, 286, 289–95. *See also* civil rights movement
race movies, xvii, xxii, xxvii, 21–22, 31–35, 36–39. *See also* Micheaux, Oscar; *specific movies*
radio, 250
Raging Bull (Martin Scorsese, 1980), 68
Ralph Bunche: An American Odyssey (Urquhart), 91, 397, 403, 405–6
Ralph Bunche: An American Odyssey (William Greaves, 2001): as epic documentary, 395–97, 408–9; funding of, 90, 397; media components and supplemental materials of, xx, 90, 399, 402–7; as polyvocal historiography, 398–402; public relations plan for, 408–9; reviews of, 399; screenings of, 91, 94, 408–10; shooting and production of, 102, 397–98, *398*; significance of, 89–92, 95, 102, 410–11; *Symbiopsychotaxiplasm* films and, 377
Randolph, A. Phillip, 174
Randolph, Johnny, 46
Ratcliff, Anthony, 152
Ray, Satyajit, *xxix*
raza, la, use of term, 288. *See also Voice of La Raza* (1972)
Realidades (television program), 263–64, 287, 295n3
Redford, Robert, 82
Reed, Carol: *Odd Man Out* (1947), 42
Reichert, Julia: *Growing Up Female* (with Jim Klein, 1972), 265–66
Reiner, Rob: *This Is Spinal Tap* (1984), 339–40
"Resurrections: Paul Robeson" (William Greaves, 1990), xxviii–xxix
Richter, Hans, 40
Riggs, Marlon, 316
Riley, Clayton, 316
Ritt, Martin, 40, 123
Rivlin, Benjamin, 407
Roads in the Sky (William Greaves, 1963), 46
Robeson, Paul, 32, 82, 85
Robeson, Susan, 265
Robinson, Sugar Ray, 216

Robles, Tom, 290, 291–92
Rochemont, Louis de, 2, 4
Rocky (John G. Avildsen, 1976), 68
Rodgers, J. A., 416
Roemer, Michael, 39
Rogers, J. A., 28, 274–75
Roker, Roxie, 249–50
Romney, Jonathan, 387, 389
Roosevelt, Eleanor, 89, 91
Roots (miniseries, 1977), 223–24n16
Rosen, Bob: in *Symbiopsychotaxiplasm: Take One*, 62, 131–32, 336–37, 363, 365, 366–67, 368–70, 372, 379, 380–81; on *Symbiopsychotaxiplasm: Take One*, 64, 338–39, 382, 382–83, 393–94n28
Rosenbaum, Max, 39
Rosenthal, Alan, 62
Rosenzweig, Roy, 321
Rosette, Belle, 25
Rouch, Jean, 44; *Chronique d'un été—Paris 1960* (1961), xix
Ruins of Empires (Volney), 145–46
Russell, McKinney, 48
Rustin, Bayard, 175, 178
Ryder, Alfred, 46

Sabourin, Marcel, 45
Sadiq, Wali (born Lou House), 8, 9, 53, 240, 252–53, 256, 272, *272*
San Filippo, Maria, 375, 379, 389
San Francisco State College, 366
Sánchez, Eduardo: *The Blair Witch Project* (with Daniel Myrick, 1999), 339–40
Sanchez, Jamie, 263
Sands, Diana, 120
Sarrazin, Michael, 45, 127
Savage, Augusta, 23–24
Scheuer, Steven, 119
Schomburg, Arturo Alfonso, 278, 414, 415, 416
Schomburg Center for Research in Black Culture (New York Public Library), 278, 397–98, 413–19
Schulman, Nina, 305
Schuyler, George, 109
Scorsese, Martin: *Raging Bull* (1980), 68
Scott, David, 375, 376–77, 391–92
Scott, Oz: *Bustin' Loose* (1981), xx, 2, 15, 81–82, 83, 90
Seale, Bobby, 259
Seifert, Charles C., 274
Selassie, Haile, 155
self-reflexivity, 62, 206, 384–87

Selma to Montgomery marches (1965), 173, 201
Seltzer, Leo, 40
Sembène, Ousmane, 153
Seneca Village, 321, 331
Senghor, Colette, *150*
Senghor, Leopold, 142, *150–51*, 155, 156, 157
Sepia Cinderella (Arthur H. Leonard, 1947), 414
Seraile, William, 317
Sesame Street (television program), 266
sexism, 174, 358
sexuality: in *Still a Brother*, 179–81; in *Symbiopsychotaxiplasm: Take One*, 56–57, 327, 329, 352, 354, 358–59, 369–71
Shabazz, Betty, 86
Shaffer, Deborah: *Chris and Bernie* (with Bonnie Friedman, 1974), 265–66
Shakespeare, William, 117
Shanker, Albert, 9, 256–57, 259–61
Sharp, Albert, 29
Shearer, Jacqueline, 316; *The Massachusetts 54th* (1991), 14
Shephard, Bobby, *398*
Shepley, Michael, 408–9
Sherwood, Mr. (teacher), 23–24
Shoreline, The (Liz Miller, 2016), 396
Shubert, Lee, 119
Siegel, Allan: *Mississippi Triangle* (with Christine Choy and Worth Long, 1983), 265
Silvera, Frank, 35, 41, 120
Silverstein, Morton: interview with Greaves and, 18, 21–22, 25–26, 31, 36, 37, 39–53, 53, 54
Simmons, Norbert, 78
Siroka, Jaqueline Dubbs, 200
Siroka, Robert, 200, 201, 203
Sissle, Noble, 108
Sisterhood Is Powerful (Morgan), 253
16th Street Baptist Church bombing (Birmingham, Alabama, 1963), 156, 173
Sloan, William, 44, 48, 55, 407
Small Business Act (1954), 288
Smith, Cauleen, xxiii
Smith, Osborn, 54
Smith, Sheila (Sheila Smith Hobson), 8, 168, 253, 254, 255–56, 258
Smith, Valerie, 316
Smith, Vashti, *150*
Smoke and Weather (William Greaves, 1958), 43
sociodrama: concept of, 192–94; *In the Company of Men* as, 194–200, 202–4; *The Deep North*

as, 200–204; *Symbiopsychotaxiplasm: Take One* as, 198; *Voice of La Raza* as, 292–94
Soderbergh, Steven, xxi, 361, 374
Solanas, Fernando: *La hora de los hornos* (with Octavio Getino, 1968), 260, 396
Soleri, Paolo, 49
Sosa, George, 307
Soul! (television program), 247
Souls of Sin (Powell Lindsay, 1949), xvii, 31–32, 34–35, *34*, 121, 414
Soviet Union, 156–57
Soyinka, Wole, 154
St. Jacques, Raymond, 120
Stam, Robert, 364–65
Stanford, Olivia, 108, 287–88
Stanislavsky System, 44, 96, 190, 343, 364, 384. See also Method acting
Stanley, Kim, 35
Stapleton, Maureen, 35
Stegreiftheater, 189
Steichen, Edward, 330–31
Steiger, Rod, 35
Sternberg, Patricia, 193
Sterritt, David, 399, 406–7
Stevens, George, 48
Stevens, George Jr., 5
Stewart, William Henry, 304, *304*
Still a Brother: Inside the Negro Middle Class (William Greaves, 1968): Black women in, 161–79, 180–81, 182–83; Branch and, 6, 8, 51, 161, *162*, 163, 164, 182, 254, 255; cinéma-vérité documentary and, 163, 255; civil rights movement and, 173–74; as exploration of Black middle class, xx, 6–8, 51–52, 161–62, 209, 255; racial relations and, 294; reviews and reception of, 255; self-image and beauty standards in, 178–79; sexuality in, 179–81; shooting and production of, xx, *162*, 164–65, *164*, 255, 378; title of, 181–82
Stojanović, Lazar, 60–61, 62
Stoney, George, 44, *45*; *All My Babies: A Midwife's Own Story* (1953), xix, 44
Stott, William, 152–53
Strasberg, John, 46
Strasberg, Lee: Actors Studio and, 35–36, 96, 123, 364; criticisms of, 128; Greaves and, 35–36, 40, 44, 101, 124–26, 128–29, 343, 364
Streetcar Named Desire, A (Williams), 120
Stringfellow, Rodney, 307

Stroheim, Erich von, 353–54
Struggle for Los Trabajos (William Greaves, 1972), 288
student movement of the 1960s, 365–66
Students for a Democratic Society (SDS), 258–59
studium, 362
Styx, John, 46
Summer of '68 (Newsreel, 1968), 247
Sundance Film Festival, 351, 361, 374, 379
Sundance Lab, 82
Suntan Studios, 32
Swanson, Gloria, 3, 16n4, 39
"Sweet Flypaper of Life" (Hughes and DeCarava), 82
Sweeting, Earl, 278
symbio cinematic environment, 347, 348–49
Symbiopsychotaxiplasm project: proposal for theatrical short and, 311–14; versions of, 309
Symbiopsychotaxiplasm: Take One (William Greaves, 1968/1971): acting workshops and, 115, 131–32; Barthes on punctum and, 362; Brooklyn Museum retrospective and, 1, 315–18, 352, 374, 381; Cannes Film Festival and, 55, 351, 374; Central Park in, 57–58, 322, 327–34, 367–68; cinéma-vérité documentary and, 114; compared to *Take 2½*, 66–67, 375–77, 387–92; context of, 356–57, 365–66; elements of parody in, 61, 337–40; experimentation and, xx–xxi, 55–56, 61–65, 114; *The Fight* and, 208–9, 210, 220–21; filmmaking dynamics in, 346–47; final credits of, 332; funding and costs of, 54–55, 100–101, 329–30, 335n14, 365; D. Greaves and, 113; intellectual sources for, 55, 61–62, 102, 128–29, 328, 364, 384–87; interludes (scenes shot by crew) in, 59–60, 352–54, 359–60, 363, 366–70, *368*, 379; jazz as metaphor in, 64, 390; original plans for, 328; originality of, 350–51, 352–55; psychodrama in, 10–12, 58, 187, 198, 292, 347, 364; racial and sexual politics of, 331–33, 363, 365–71, 372, 390; reception and reviews of, 340, 374–75, 379, 380–81; screenings of, 18–19, 266, 317, 350–52, *351*, 360–61, 374, *391*; self-reflexivity in, 384–87; sexism and homophobia in, 358–59, 370; sexuality in, 56–57, 327, 329, 352, 354, 358–59, 369–71; shooting and production of, 327, 357–61, *359*, 363, 364–65, *368*, 380–84; as sociodrama, 198; soundtrack of, 64, 333, 360, 390; symbio cinematic environment and, 347, 348–49; as theory of film production, 377–78; triptychs in, 381–82; Victor in, 65–66, 331, 336–37, 354–55, 372, 389

Symbiopsychotaxiplasm: Take 2½ (William Greaves, 2005): Black women in, 163–64, 372; compared to *Take 1*, 66–67, 375–77, 387–92; experimentation and, xxi; filmmaking dynamics in, 346–47; intellectual sources for, 343; psychodrama in, 187, 203, 347, 369, 371–72, 379–80, 388, 391; racial and sexual politics of, 363, 369, 371–73; reception of, 375, 379–80, 389; shooting and production of, 344–45, *360*, 361, 374–75, *375*, *376*; soundtrack of, 390; symbio cinematic environment and, 347, 348–49; triptychs in, 381–82; uncorrected draft of the plan for, 341–43
Syms, Martine, xxiii

Tajima, Renee: *Who Killed Vincent Chin?* (with Christine Choy, 1989), 265
Tandy, Jessica, 120
Tanen, Ted, 152, 156
Tati, Jacques, 353–54
Taubin, Amy, 369, 370–71
Taylor, Clyde, 243, 316
Teach Our Children (Christine Choy, 1972), 265
Ted Bates Advertising, 252
television: Greaves on role of, 233–38; minority programming and, 16, 243–44, 246–48, 249–51, 262–65. See also *Black Journal* (television program); Kerner Commission (National Advisory Commission on Civil Disorders); National Educational Television (NET); *Realidades* (television program)
Television Quarterly (journal), 276
Teresa, Mother, *301*
Theatre of Spontaneity, The (Moreno), 190, 199
Thermodynamics Laws, 62, 343, 347, 349
30 Minutes (television program), 266
Third World Liberation Front, 366
Third World Newsreel, 16, 265
This Is Spinal Tap (Rob Reiner, 1984), 339–40
Thomas, Franklin A., 15, 249
Thomas, Piri, 263
Thomas, Vassal, 171
Thompson, Kristin, 374n2
Thoreau, Henry David, 323–27
Time-Life Broadcast, 247
Tirolien, Guy, 158
To Sleep with Anger (Charles Burnett, 1990), 83
Today (magazine), 49

Tony Brown's Journal (television program), 245
Toronto Star Weekly (newspaper), 128
Torres, Sasha, 225n34
Treviño, Jesus: *Yo Soy Chicano* (1972), 264
Tribute to Jackie Robinson, A (William Greaves, 1990), xxviii–xxix
Trumbo, Dalton, 37
Trump, Donald, 222
Tshaka, Jackie, 55
Twentieth Century (Hecht and McArthur), 3, 39–40, 122–23
Two Dollars and a Dream: The Story of Madam C. J. Walker (1987), 266
"Two Fighters on Film" (Greaves), 215–16
Tyson, Cicely, 88, *88*, 299

Umbrellas of Cherbourg, The (Jacques Demy, 1964), 360, 371
uncertainty principle, 347, 348
UNIA (Universal Negro Improvement Association), 21, 274
United Federation of Teachers, 259–61. See also Shanker, Albert
United Nations (UN): Bunche and, 28, 52, 89, 91, 395, 397, 401–2; Greaves and, xviii, 5, 46–48, 89, 209, 275, 397, 414; Urquhart and, 397
United States Information Agency (USIA): documentary filmmaking and, 156, 248; Greaves and, xviii, 5–6, 48–51, 152–53, 209, 275–76, 287, 397. See also *The First World Festival of Negro Arts* (William Greaves, 1966)
Universal Declaration of Human Rights (UDHR, 1948), 90
Universal Negro Improvement Association (UNIA), 21, 274
Universal Pictures, 77–78
Universe (Roman Kroiter and Colin Low, 1960), 43
Updike, John, 369
Urban League, 119, 181
Urquhart, Brian, 91, 397, 401, 403, 405–6, 407

Valdez, Luis, 291
Van Dyke, Willard, 48, 187
Van Peebles, Melvin, xxix, 4, 248, 275, 316
Variety (magazine), 241, 251, 399
Vaux, Calvert, 319–22, 330, 334
Vertov, Dziga, 62

Vietnam War: Ali and, 12; anti–Vietnam War movement and, 321–22, 356, 365, 366; *Black Journal* and, 53, 256, 278–79; Greaves and, 56, 62, 73, 389
Visiones (television program), 264
Viva Zapata (Elia Kazan, 1952), 41
Voice of La Raza (William Greaves, 1972), 107–8, 285–86, 288–95
"voice-of-god" narrators, xx
Volney, Constantin François de Chassebœuf, count of, 145–46, 235–36
Von Trier, Lars, 347

Wadleigh, Michael, 113, 338; *Woodstock* (1970), 113, 338
Wagoner, Bob, 230
Walden (Jonas Mekas, 1968), 322–27, 329, 334
Walden (Thoreau), 323–27
Walk Hard (Hill), 29
Wallace, George, 9, 256–57
Wallace, Michele, 317
Wallach, Eli, 3, 35
Ward, Richard, 120
Warhol, Andy, 356
Warhol Foundation, 318
Warren, Freda, 19, 89–90, 94–95
Washington, Booker T., 21
Watkins, Peter: *The Journey* (1984–1987), 396
Watt, Harry: *Night Mail* (with Basil Wright, 1936), 4
Wayne, David, 120
WBAI (radio station), 250
Wealth of a Nation (William Greaves, 1964), 5, 48–49, 137–38, 287
Weill, Claudia: *Joyce at 34* (1974), 265–66
Weill, Kurt, 121
Welles, Orson, 353–54; *F for Fake* (1974), 355
Wells, Ida B., 180, 303–4. See also *Ida B. Wells: A Passion for Justice* (William Greaves, 1989)
Werker, Alfred L. See *Lost Boundaries* (Alfred L. Werker, 1949)
Wetmore, Kevin, 133n5
Wexler, Haskell: *Medium Cool* (1969), 10–11, 338
Weymouth, Elizabeth Morris "Lally" Graham, 249
Wharton, Clifton, Jr., 15, 113
Where Dreams Come True (William Greaves, 1979), 13
Whipper, Leigh, 108

White, Charles, 155–56
White, Kenneth, 29, 120
white-collar jobs, 167–68
Who Killed Vincent Chin? (Christine Choy and Renee Tajima, 1989), 265
Whore's Glory (Michael Glawogger, 2012), 396
Who's Afraid of Virginia Woolf? (Albee), 327, 357, 369–70
Wilkins, Roy, 174, 248
William Greaves Film Collection (Schomburg Center for Research in Black Culture, New York Public Library), 413–19
William Greaves Productions, xviii, xxii, 10, 287, 357, 418
Williams, Daniel Hale, 177
Williams, Marion, 143
Williams, Spencer, xxii, xxix, 15, 37, 397
Williams, Tennessee, 120, 357
Willis, Edgar E., 223–24n16
Wilson, Reginald, 279
Winkler, Don, 40
Winter, Gary, 305
Winters, Shelley, 3, 352
Wiseman, Frederick, xix; *Hospital* (1968), 4–5
Wofford, Tobias, 154–55
Womack, Ytasha, xxiii
women. *See* Black women
women's studies, 176
Woodberry, Billy, xxii; *Bless Their Little Hearts* (1984), 172
Woodruff, Hale, 152
Woodstock (Michael Wadleigh, 1970), 113, 338
Word Is Out: Stories of Some of Our Lives (Peter Adair, 1977), 266
Workingman's Death (Michael Glawogger, 2005), 396
World of Piri Thomas, The (Gordon Parks, 1968), 262–63
World View of Race, A (Bunche), 404–5, 407
Wright, Basil: *Night Mail* (with Harry Watt, 1936), 4
Wright, Nathan, 175

X, Malcolm, 52, 53, 250

Yevtushenko, Yevgeny, 50, 156
Yo Soy Chicano (Jesus Treviño, 1972), 264
Yo soy Joaquín (Gonzales), 291

Yordan, Philip, 28
Young, Whitney M., 174
Young American, A (Bonner), 30, 119
Young Lords, 259, 294
Yudie (Mirra Bank, 1974), 265–66

Zanuck, Darryl, 37
Zawinul, Joe, 390
Zeheri, Maria, 382
Zimmermann, Patricia, 62–63
Zwick, Edward: *Glory* (1989), 83

GPSR Authorized Representative: Easy Access System Europe, Mustamäe tee
50, 10621 Tallinn, Estonia, gpsr.requests@easproject.com

www.ingramcontent.com/pod-product-compliance
Lightning Source LLC
Chambersburg PA
CBHW050934300426
44108CB00011BA/734